SO-BBS-122

The Human Species

AN INTRODUCTION TO BIOLOGICAL ANTHROPOLOGY

SECOND EDITION

John H. Relethford
State University of New York
College at Oneonta

Mayfield Publishing Company
Mountain View, California
London • Toronto

DONATED TO
THE COLLEGE OF STATEN ISLAND
LIBRARY

Copyright © 1994, 1990 by Mayfield Publishing Company
All rights reserved. No portion of this book may be reproduced in any form or by any
means without written permission of the publisher.

Library of Congress Cataloging-in-Publication Data
Relethford, John.
    The human species : an introduction to biological anthropology /
John H. Relethford. — 2nd ed.
        p.   cm.
    Includes bibliographical references and index.
    ISBN 1-55934-206-4
    1. Physical anthropology.   I. Title.
GN60.R39   1993
573—dc20   93-3659
                                                            CIP

Manufactured in the United States of America

10 9 8 7 6 5 4 3 2 1

Mayfield Publishing Company
1280 Villa Street
Mountain View, California 94041

Sponsoring editor, Janet M. Beatty; production editor, Lynn Rabin Bauer;
manuscript editor, Lauren Root; text designer, Al Burkhardt; cover designer, Steve
Naegele; cover photographs: *Australopithecus afarensis* reconstruction photograph by
D. Finnin/C. Chesek © American Museum of Natural History. Modern human
photograph by Roy Temple, Connecticut State University Media Center; art editor,
Susan Breitbard; illustrators, Barbara Barnett, Susan Breitbard, Joan Carol, Marilyn
Kreiger, Leonard Morgan, and Alan Noyes; color photo researcher, Melissa Kreischer;
manufacturing manager, Martha Branch. The text was set in 10/12 Galliard by
Thompson Type and printed on 50# Somerset Matte by Arcata Graphics.

Preface

This textbook is an introduction to the field of biological anthropology, the science concerned with human biological variation and evolution. In this text I approach the field using an organizational framework based on five questions about the human species.

Organization

The book is divided into five parts, each focusing on a specific question about the human species. Part 1 addresses the question, "What is evolution, and how does it operate?" Chapter 1 provides an introduction to the field of anthropology, followed by a discussion of the nature and history of evolutionary science. Chapter 2 treats human genetics from molecular and Mendelian perspectives to provide genetic background for looking at evolutionary theory. Chapter 3 provides an in-depth examination of microevolutionary forces—the mechanisms responsible for evolutionary change—and gives examples of microevolution in human populations. Chapter 4 moves on to the study of long-term evolutionary change: macroevolution.

With this evolutionary background in place, Part 2 deals with the question, "How do humans differ from one another, and why?" Human beings show a great deal of biological variation. Why? What does it mean? How can this variation be interpreted in terms of evolutionary theory? Chapter 5 provides case studies of human microevolution from across the world in many cultures. Chapter 6 contrasts the microevolutionary approach with the older, outdated, "racial" approach to human variation.

Part 3 deals with variation on a different scale. Instead of looking at similarities and differences among humans, this section of the text looks at similarities and differences between humans and other animals. Part 3 asks, "What are humans?" and "How are we related to other living creatures?" Three chapters examine human biology and behavior from this comparative perspective. Chapter 7 focuses on general trends in the biology and behavior of mammals. Chapter 8 deals with the primates—a specific group of mammals that includes monkeys, apes, and humans. Chapter 9 looks more closely at the similarities and differences between humans and apes, our closest living relatives.

Once we have examined the differences between humans and other animals, we can investigate how these differences evolved. Part 4 asks, "What are our origins?" and "How did we evolve?" Chapter 10 provides some background on the methods of analysis used in answering these questions and also reviews the evolutionary history of life up to the origin of the primates. Chapter 11 continues this discussion, looking at primate evolution through the origin of early apes. Chapter 12 looks at the evolution of the first hominids, our human ancestors—the small-brained, upright-walking *Australopithecus* and the larger-brained, tool-making *Homo habilis*. Chapter 13 focuses on the evolution of our genus over the past 1.5 million years and looks at the biology and behavior of *Homo erectus* and *Homo sapiens*.

Part 5 returns to living populations and asks the question, "How do human biology and culture interact?" The next four chapters explore how changes in cultural behavior affect biological variation, particularly in today's rapidly changing world. Chapter 14 examines human growth, especially biological, cultural, and environmental effects on growth patterns. Chapter 15 looks at biological and cultural adaptations to environmental stresses, such as climate, high altitude, and modernization. Chapter 16 provides a comparative approach to the study of human health and disease. Chapter 17 deals with the demography of human populations.

Not all instructors will necessarily use the same sequence of chapters. Some may prefer to move topics around. I have attempted to write each of the five parts in a way to make such changes possible. For example, an instructor who opts to cover all the material on human variation at the end of the course might use the sequence of Parts 1, 3, 4, 2, and 5. An instructor who chooses to cover human evolution at the end of the course could use the sequence of Parts 1, 2, 5, 3, and 4.

Features

Throughout the text, I have attempted to provide both new material relevant to the field and fresh treatments of traditional material. Key features of the text are as follows:

• *All areas of contemporary biological anthropology are covered.* Many traditional texts in this field cover the basics of evolution and genetics, primate studies, the fossil record for human evolution, and selected studies of human variation. This text provides a more balanced treatment of the field of biological anthropology, including chapters on subjects often largely neglected. This text has separate chapters on case studies in microevolution, human growth, human health and disease, and demography. No other introductory biological anthropology textbook has separate chapters on *all* of these areas, or includes the same diversity of case studies.

• *The relationship between biology and culture is a major focus.* The biocultural framework is introduced in the first chapter and integrated throughout the text. All of the chapters in Part 5 ("Human Biology and Culture") specifically address the biocultural approach in our modern world, providing many contemporary examples relevant to student interest.

• *Behavior is discussed in an evolutionary context.* I have not devoted separate chapters to primate behavior or the archaeology of early humans because I believe that such material must be covered along with biological evolution. Thus, in the chapters on evolutionary theory I include discussions of behavior genetics (Chapter 2), inbreeding (Chapter 3), and sociobiology (Chapter 4). The chapters on human variation and microevolution discuss migration, marriage patterns, and social structure (Chapter 5), as well as race and intelligence (Chapter 6). The chapters on mammals and primates (Chapters 7–9) integrate aspects of taxonomy, biology, and behavior that are often covered separately. The chapters on primate and human evolution (Chapters 10–13) all consider trends in behavioral evolution as part of the overall evolutionary process. Finally, a separate section focuses entirely on the relationship between biology and culture in today's world (Chapters 14–17).

• *The emphasis is on the human species.* Understanding ourselves requires consideration of our nonhuman primate relatives. Many texts, however, focus on nonhuman primates to the exclusion of the human species. Here, nonhuman primates are not treated in isolation, but rather in terms of what they can tell us about the human condition. I emphasize the biology and behavior of the human species throughout the text, which includes a detailed comparison with apes in Chapter 9.

• *Hypothesis testing is emphasized.* From the first chapter, where students are introduced to the scientific method, I emphasize *how* various hypotheses are tested. Rather than provide a dogmatic approach with all the "right" answers, this text examines evidence about human variation and evolution in the context of hypothesis testing. An example of this approach can be seen in the chapters on human evolution, where the data are discussed first and then followed by consideration of alternative models and explanations of evolutionary trends. The history of various controversies is also examined, so that students can see how new data can lead to changes in basic models.

• *There is a separate appendix on mathematical population genetics.* Some instructors cover population genetics with a minimum of mathematics, whereas others include a great deal of mathematics. Since it is difficult to write a chapter on microevolutionary forces that can be used in both contexts, I have moved most of the mathematical treatment to a separate appendix. The basic concepts of the evolutionary forces are covered in Chapter 3 more from an intuitive approach, while a detailed mathematical treatment is given in the appendix. In this way, instructors can tailor their reading assignments to fit their preferred method.

New to this Edition

Every chapter of this edition has been carefully revised in light of new findings in the field and comments received from users of the first edition. To make the text as useful and up-to-date as possible, I've made the following changes:

• The chapter on macroevolution has been moved earlier in the text so that it now follows the chapter on microevolution; this sequence provides a better continuity in the treatment of evolutionary principles.

• A new chapter (Chapter 15) pulls together previously separate material on human adaptation, adding more case studies and consideration of cultural adaptations. Topics include types of adaptation, climatic adaptation, high altitude adaptation, and the biological effects of modernization.

• A review of cell biology has been added to the end of Chapter 2 to help underprepared students better understand the basics of genetics. Recent developments in genetics, both molecular and quantitative, have been added to the body of Chapter 2.

• A new chapter on the fossil record (Chapter 10) is included. This chapter reviews methods of paleontological analysis and the fossil record of life on earth prior to primate origins *before* plunging into the primate fossil record.

• Chapter 5 has been extensively revised; it contrasts studies of gene flow and genetic drift with studies of natural selection.

• Information on gender differences has been added; e.g., Chapter 9 looks at gender differences in the brain and Chapter 13 explores male-female differences in division of labor.

• Chapter 6 includes new interpretations of the evolution of human skin color.

• Chapter 7 has a revised discussion of alternate methods of classification: phenetics, cladistics, and evolutionary taxonomy.

• Chapter 9 offers revised material on human/ape similarities and differences, especially language acquisition and tool manufacture.

• Chapter 11 includes new fossil discoveries on primate origins and evolution, including new controversies regarding anthropoid origins, and new data on Miocene ape evolution.

• Chapter 12 contains new ideas about interpretations of the behavior of early hominids and new models of the evolution of the human brain (e.g., the "radiator" theory).

• New interpretations of the mitochondrial DNA evidence for the origin of modern humans are presented in Chapter 13; this chapter also covers the assimilation model as an alternative to the multiregional and recent African origin models.

• New information on human growth patterns in the modern world, focusing on the impact of pollution on human growth and development are included in Chapter 14.

• Chapters 16 and 17 have been significantly updated, with new material on AIDS, studies of fertility, smallpox epidemics in Finland, and injury mortality rates in the U.S.

• A new appendix (Appendix 2) is included that provides a detailed taxonomy of living primates.

Study Helps

To make this text more accessible and interesting, I have included frequent examples and illustrations of basic ideas in the hope that students will gain familiarity with the fundamental concepts of biological anthropology. I have kept technical jargon to a minimum; yet every introductory text contains a number of specialized terms that students must learn. The first mention of these terms appears in **boldface** type, and accompanying short definitions appear in the text margins. A glossary is provided at the end of the book, often providing more detailed definitions.

Each chapter ends with a summary and a list of supplemental readings. The summaries put each chapter's material in more general terms and help students relate the content to other chapters. The supplemental readings are included for those who wish to look further into a given topic, either for clarification or to satisfy an awakened curiosity. A list of references appears at the end of the book, providing the complete reference for studies cited in the text.

Ancillaries

The *Instructor's Manual* includes a test bank of more than 700 questions, as well as chapter overviews and outlines, topics for class discussions, and sources for laboratory equipment.

A *Computerized Test Bank* is available free of charge to qualifying adopters. It is a powerful, easy-to-use test generation system that provides all test items on computer disk for IBM-compatible and Apple Macintosh computers. Instructors can select, add, or edit questions, randomize them, and print tests appropriate for their individual classes. The system also includes a convenient "gradebook" that enables the instructor to keep detailed performance records for individual students and for the entire class; maintain student averages; graph each student's progress; and set the desired grade distribution, maximum score, and weight for every test.

FREE COPY FREE COPY FREE COPY FREE COPY FREE COPY FREE COPY FREE COPY FREE COPY

Acknowledgments

My thanks go to the dedicated and hardworking people at Mayfield, both those I have dealt with personally and the others behind the scenes. I give special thanks to Jan Beatty, sponsoring editor, for continued encouragement and support. I am also extremely grateful to Lynn Rabin Bauer, production editor, for her dedication and patience. Pamela Trainer, permissions editor, and Lauren Root, copy editor, were also extremely helpful.

I also thank my colleagues who served as reviewers: Helen L. Ball, University of Massachusetts; Douglas E. Crews, Ohio State University; Janis Hutchinson, University of Houston; Lyle Konigsberg, University of Tennessee; Paul Sciulli, Ohio State University; Mark Stoneking, Pennsylvania State University; Alan Swedlund, University of Massachusetts; Jane Underwood, University of Arizona; and Dennis van Gerven, University of Colorado. Having been a reviewer myself, I appreciate the extensive time and effort these individuals have taken. Since textbooks, like evolution, develop from what existed before, I also thank those who served as reviewers on the first edition: Evelyn J. Bowers, Ball State University; Marc R. Feldesman, Portland State University; Francis E. Johnston, University of Pennsylvania; Michael Alan Park, Central Connecticut State University; Becky A. Sigmon, University of Toronto; David Glenn Smith, University of California at Davis; Wenda Trevathan, New Mexico State University; Milford H. Wolpoff, University of Michigan; and Stephen L. Zegura, University of Arizona.

My special thanks to other colleagues who have spent time discussing the first edition and offering ideas for revision: Kathryn Dettwyler, Texas A&M University; Lynnette Leidy, University of Massachusetts; Lorena Madrigal, University of South Florida; and Lawrence M. Schell, State University of New York at Albany.

With this second edition, I take the liberty of giving two dedications. The first is to the memory of my parents, Guy and Olive Relethford. The second is to my family: to my wife and best friend, Hollie Jaffe, and to my wonderful sons, David, Benjamin, and Zane. You make it all worthwhile.

Contents

FREE COPY FREE COPY FREE COPY FREE COPY FREE COPY FREE COPY FREE COPY FREE COPY FREE COPY

CHAPTER 15   Human Adaptation   433

CHAPTER 16   Human Health and Disease   455

FREE COPY   FREE COPY   FREE COPY   FREE COPY   FREE COPY   FREE COPY   FREE COPY   FREE COPY

CHAPTER 17   **The Demography of Human Populations**   487

EPILOGUE   **The Future of Our Species**   507

APPENDIX 1   **Mathematical Population Genetics**   509

APPENDIX 2   **Taxonomy of Living Primates**   519

Glossary   530

References   543

Index   556

FREE COPY FREE COPY FREE COPY FREE COPY FREE COPY FREE COPY FREE COPY FREE COPY

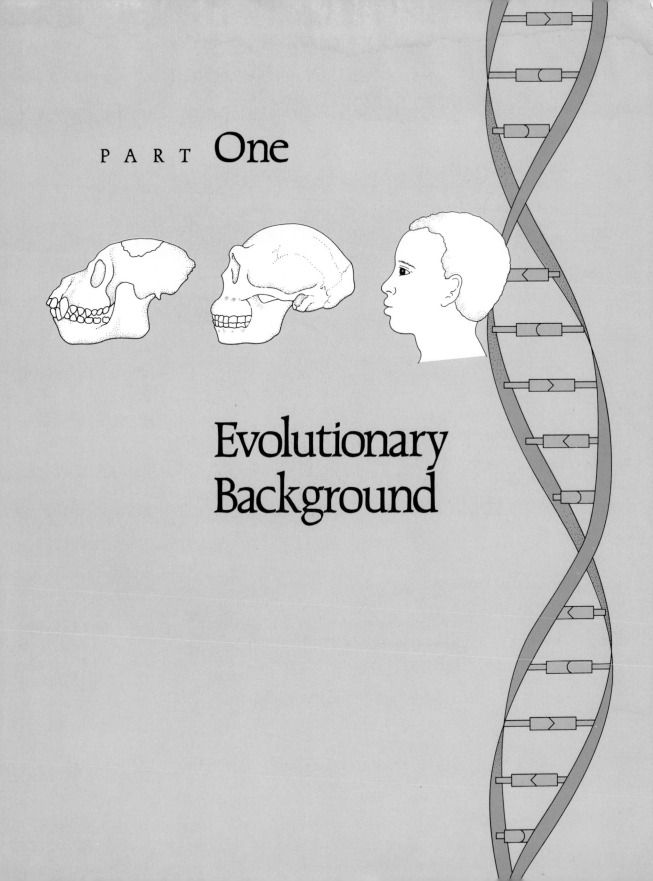

PART One

Evolutionary Background

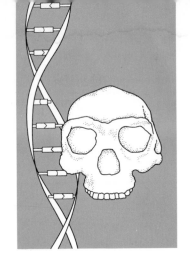

CHAPTER 1

The Study of Biological Anthropology

What is anthropology? To many people, it is the study of the exotic extremes of human nature. To others, it is the study of ancient ruins and lost civilizations. The study of anthropology seems strange to many, and the practitioners of this field, the anthropologists, seem even stranger. The stereotype of an anthropologist is a pith-helmeted, pipe-smoking eccentric tracking chimpanzees through the forest, digging up the bones of million-year-old ancestors, interviewing lost tribes about their sexual customs, and recording the words of the last speakers of a language. Another popular image presented in the media is Indiana Jones, the intrepid archaeologist of the film *Raiders of the Lost Ark*. Here is a man who is versed in the customs and languages of many societies past and present, feels at home anywhere in the world, and makes a living teaching, finding lost treasures, rescuing beautiful women in distress, and fighting Nazis (Figure 1.1).

Of course, Indiana Jones is a fictional character. Some real-life anthropologists are almost as well known, such as Jane Goodall, Margaret Mead, Donald Johanson, and the late Dian Fossey. These anthropologists have studied chimpanzees, Samoan culture, the fossils of human ancestors, and gorillas. Their research conjures up images of anthropology every bit as varied as the imaginary adventures of Indiana Jones. Anthropologists do study all these things, and more. The sheer diversity of topics investigated by anthropologists seems almost to defy any sort of logic. In one department of anthropology, for example, the research interests of the faculty range from studies of human population genetics to Caribbean music, from Iroquois history to goddess worship, and from the skeletal anatomy

anthropology The science that investigates human biological and cultural variation and evolution.

culture Behavior that is learned and socially transmitted.

of prehistoric Indians to mental health among the rural poor in the United States. The methods of data collection and analysis are almost as diverse. What pulls these different subjects together?

In one obvious sense, they all share an interest in the same subject— human beings. In fact, the traditional textbook definition of anthropology is the "study of humans." Though this definition is easy to remember, it is not terribly useful. After all, scientists in other fields, such as researchers in anatomy and biochemistry, also study humans. And there are many fields within the social sciences whose sole interest is humans. History, geography, political science, economics, sociology, and psychology are all devoted to the study of human beings, and no one would argue that these fields are merely branches of anthropology.

What Is Anthropology?

What, then, is a suitable definition of anthropology? **Anthropology** could be described as the science of human cultural and biological variation and evolution. The first part of this definition includes both human culture and biology. **Culture** is learned behavior. Culture includes social and economic systems, marriage customs, religion, philosophy, and all other behaviors that are acquired through the process of learning rather than being instinctual. The joint emphasis on culture and biology is an important feature of anthropology, and one that sets it apart from many other fields. A biochemist may be interested in specific aspects of human biology and consider the study of human cultural behaviors less important. To a sociologist, cultural behaviors and not human biology are the main focus of attention. Anthropology, however, is characterized by a concern with *both* culture and biology as vital in understanding the human condition.

Figure 1.1

Indiana Jones, the fictional archaeologist who serves as many people's model for an anthropologist.   (Eva Sereny, © Lucasfilm Ltd. [LFL] 1984. All Rights Reserved.)

Biology and Culture

To the anthropologist, humans must be understood in terms of learned behavior as well as biology. We rely extensively on learned behaviors in virtually all aspects of our life. Even the expression of our sexual drives must be understood in light of human cultural systems. Although the actual basis of our sex drive is biological, the ways in which we express it are shaped by behaviors we have learned. The very inventiveness of humans, with our vast technology, is testimony to the powerful effect of learning. On the other hand, however, we are not purely cultural creatures. We are also biological organisms. We need to eat and breathe, and we are affected by our external environment. In addition, our biology sets certain limits on our potential behaviors. For example, all human cultures have some type of social structure that provides for the care of children until they are old enough to fend for themselves. This is not simply kindness to children; our biological position as mammals requires such attentiveness to children for survival. In contrast with other animal species, whose infants need little or no care, human infants are physically incapable of taking care of themselves.

Anthropology is concerned not only with culture and biology, but also with their interaction. Just as humans are not solely cultural or solely biological, we are not simply the sum of these two, either. Humans are biocultural organisms, which means that our culture and biology influence each other. The **biocultural approach** to studying human beings is the main theme of this book, and you will examine many examples of biocultural interaction. For now, however, consider one—population growth (which will be covered in greater detail in Chapter 17). The growth of a population is in part dependent on how many people are born relative to how many die. If more people are born than die in a given period of time, then the population will grow. Obviously, population growth is in part caused by biological factors affecting the birth and death rates. A variety of cultural factors, such as economic system and marriage patterns, also affect population growth. In the United States today the birth rate has been dropping, in part because more and more people have postponed marriage and childbearing to further their educations and careers. Also, the availability of birth control allows people to determine how many children they will have.

Thus, a variety of cultural factors, including technological changes and ideological outlooks, affect the birth rate. Developments in medicine and medical care also change the death rate. Further, changes in biological factors can lead to cultural changes. For example, the slowing of the birth rate has led to a reduction in the number of college students during the past decade. This change will further affect aspects of our society such as college admissions standards, availability of federal funds for education, and competition for jobs among graduates.

The entire process of population growth and its biological and cultural implications is considerably more complicated than described here. The basic point, however, should be clear: by studying the process of population growth we can see how cultural factors affect biological factors and vice versa.

The biocultural perspective of anthropology points to one of the unique strengths of anthropology as a science: it is **holistic,** meaning that it takes into consideration all aspects of human existence. Population growth again provides an example. Where the sociologist may be concerned with effects of population growth on social structure and the psychologist may be concerned with effects of population growth on psychological stress, the anthropologist is interested potentially in all aspects of population growth. In a given study, this analysis may include the

biocultural approach
Studying humans in terms of the interaction between biology and culture in evolutionary adaptation.

holistic Integrating all aspects of existence in understanding human variation and evolution.

variation The differences that exist between individuals or populations.

comparative approach Comparing human populations to determine common and unique behaviors or biological traits.

evolution Change in populations of organisms from one generation to the next.

relationship among diet, fertility, religion, disease, social systems, nutrition, and political systems, to name but a few factors.

The biocultural nature of anthropology makes it a difficult subject to classify in college catalogs. By now you are aware that different academic departments are grouped under the arts, humanities, natural sciences, mathematics, and social sciences. Where does anthropology, with its interest in both human culture and biology, fit in? Is it a natural science or a social science? Most colleges and universities place departments of anthropology with the social sciences, primarily because of the historical fact that the majority of anthropologists have been concerned with cultural anthropology. Many schools, however, allow completion of a biological anthropology course to fulfill a natural science requirement. The artificial distinctions drawn between different branches of learning should not prevent you from seeing that anthropology has strong ties with both the natural and social sciences.

Variation

A major characteristic of anthropology is its concern with **variation.** In a general sense, variation refers to differences among individuals or populations. The anthropologist is interested in differences and similarities among human groups, in terms of both biology and culture. Anthropologists use the **comparative approach** to attempt to generalize about those aspects of human behavior and biology that are similar in all populations and those that are unique to specific environments and cultures. How do groups of people differ from one another? *Why* do they differ? These are questions about variation, and they apply equally to cultural and biological traits (Figure 1.2). For example, do all human cultures practice the same marriage customs? (They don't.) Are there discernible reasons that one group has a certain type of marriage system? An example of a biological trait that raises questions about variation is skin color. Can groups be characterized by a certain skin color, or does skin color vary within groups? Is there any pattern in the distribution of skin color that makes sense in terms of environmental differences?

Evolution

Evolution is change in living organisms over generations. Both cultural and biological evolution interest anthropologists. How and why do human culture and biology change? For example, anthropologists may be interested in the origin of marriage systems. When, how, and why did certain marriage systems evolve? For that matter, when did the custom of marriage first originate, and why? As for skin color, an anthropologist would be interested in what skin color the first humans may have had, and where, when, how, and why other skin colors may have evolved.

Figure 1.2

Biological variation in a group of children.   (© Peter Menzel/Stock Boston)

Adaptation

In addition to the concepts of variation and evolution, the anthropologist is interested in the process of **adaptation.** At the broadest level, adaptations are advantageous changes. Any aspect of biology or behavior that confers some advantage on an individual or population can be considered an adaptation. Cultural adaptations include technological devices such as clothing, shelter, and methods of food production. Such technologies can improve the well-being of humans. Cultural adaptations also

adaptation The process of successful interaction between a population and an environment.

include social systems and rules for behaviors. For example, the belief in certain societies that sexual relations with a woman must be avoided for some time after she gives birth can be adaptive in the sense that these behaviors influence the rate of population growth.

Cultural adaptations may vary in their effect on different members of a population. What is adaptive for some people may not be adaptive for others. For example, changes in certain tax laws may be advantageous for certain income groups and disadvantageous for others. Beliefs that reduce population growth can be adaptive in certain environments but nonadaptive in others.

Adaptations can also be biological. Some biological adaptations are physiological in nature and involve metabolic changes. For example, when you are too hot, you will sweat. Sweating is a short-term physiological response that removes excess heat through the process of evaporation. Within limits, it aids in maintaining a constant body temperature. Likewise, shivering is an adaptive response to cold. The act of shivering increases metabolic rate and provides more heat.

Biological adaptations can also be genetic in nature. Here, changes in genes over many generations produce variation in biological traits. The darker skin color of many humans native to regions near the equator is one example of a long-term genetic adaptation. The darker skin provides protection from the harmful effects of ultraviolet radiation (see Chapter 6 for more information on skin color and variation).

Anthropologists look at patterns of human variation and evolution in order to understand the nature of cultural and biological adaptations. In some cases, explanations are relatively clear, whereas in others we still seek explanations for the adaptive value of any given behavior or trait. In such a quest, we must always remember two important rules about adaptation. First, adaptations are often specific to a particular environment. What is adaptive in one environment may not be in another environment. Second, we must keep in mind that not all aspects of behavior or biology are adaptive. The forward-jutting human chin, for example, seems not to reflect any adaptive "value" or "function." Instead, it is caused by different rates of growth within the jaw.

The Subfields of Anthropology

In a general sense, anthropology is concerned with determining what humans are, how they evolved, and how they differ from one another. Where other disciplines focus on specific issues of humanity, anthropology is unique in dealing simultaneously with questions of origins, evolution, variation, and adaptation.

Even though anthropology has a wide scope that appears to encompass anything and everything pertaining to humans, the study of anthropology in the United States is often characterized by four separate subfields, each with a specific focus. These four subfields are cultural anthropology, anthropological archaeology, linguistic anthropology, and biological anthropology.

Cultural anthropology. **Cultural anthropology** deals primarily with variation in the cultures of populations in the present or recent past. Its subjects include social, political, economic, and ideological aspects of human cultures. Cultural anthropologists look at all aspects of behavior within a society. Even when they are interested in a specific aspect of a culture, such as marriage systems, they look at how these behaviors relate to all other aspects of culture. Marriage systems, for example, may have an effect on the system of inheritance and may also be closely related to religious views. Comparison of cultures is used to determine common and unique features among different cultures. Information from this subfield will be presented later in the book to aid in the interpretation of the relationship between human culture and biology.

Anthropological archaeology. Archaeology is the study of cultural behaviors in the historic and prehistoric past. **Anthropological archaeology** uses the methods of archaeology to infer the behaviors of past societies. The archaeologist deals with such remains of past societies as tools, shelters, remains of animals eaten for food, and other objects that have survived. These remains, termed *artifacts,* are used to reconstruct past behavior. To help fill in the gaps, the archaeologist makes use of the findings of cultural anthropologists who have studied similar societies. Archaeological findings are critical in understanding the behavior of early humans and their evolution. Some of these findings for the earliest humans are presented later in this text.

Linguistic anthropology. **Linguistic anthropology** is the study of language. Spoken language is a behavior that appears to be uniquely human. This subfield of anthropology deals with the analysis of languages usually in nonliterate societies and with general trends in the evolution of languages. A major question raised by linguistic anthropology concerns the extent to which language shapes culture. Is language necessary for the transmission of culture? Does a language provide information about the beliefs and practices of a human culture?

Biological anthropology must consider many of the findings of linguistic anthropology in the analysis of human variation and evolution. When comparing humans and apes, we must ask whether language is a unique human characteristic. If it is, then what biological and behavioral differences exist between apes and humans that lead to the fact that one species has language and the other lacks it? Linguistics is also important in considering human evolution. When did language begin? Why?

Biological anthropology. The subject of this book is the subfield of **biological anthropology,** which is concerned with the biological evolu-

cultural anthropology
Focuses on variations in cultural behaviors among human populations.

anthropological archaeology Focuses on cultural variation in prehistoric (and some historic) populations by analyzing the culture's remains.

linguistic anthropology Focuses on the nature of human language, the relationship of language to culture, and the languages of nonliterate peoples.

biological anthropology Focuses on the biological evolution of humans and human ancestors, the relationship of humans to other organisms, and patterns of biological variation within and among human populations. Also referred to as physical anthropology.

tion and variation of the human species, past and present. Biological anthropology is often referred to by another name—*physical anthropology*. The course you are currently enrolled in might be known by either name. Actually, the two names refer to the same field. Early in the twentieth century the field was first known as physical anthropology, reflecting its then primary interest in the *physical* variation of past and present humans and our primate relatives. Much of the research in the field focused on descriptive studies of physical variations with little theoretical background. Starting in the 1950s, physical anthropologists became more familiar with the rapidly growing fields of genetics and evolutionary science. As a result, the field of physical anthropology became more concerned with biological processes, particularly with genetics. After a while, many in the field began using the term *biological anthropology* to emphasize the new focus on biological processes. In most circles today, the two terms are used more or less interchangeably.

There are several traditionally defined areas within biological anthropology, such as primate studies, paleoanthropology, and human variation. Primate studies are concerned with defining humans in the natural world, specifically in terms of the primates (a group of mammals that includes prosimians, monkeys, apes, and humans). Primate studies look at the anatomy, behavior, and evolution of the primates as a standard of comparison with those aspects of humans. In this way, we can learn something about what it is to be human.

Paleoanthropology is the study of the fossil remains of human evolution. Researchers in this field are interested in determining who our ancestors were, and when, how, and why they evolved. Paleoanthropologists work closely with archaeologists to reconstruct the behaviors of our ancestors.

The study of human variation is concerned with how and why humans differ from each other in their biological makeup. This subfield considers the ways in which culture and biology interact in the modern world, including such topics as the genetics of populations, demography (the study of population size and composition), physical growth and development, and human health and disease. Several decades ago, human variation was the concern of only a few biological anthropologists. Today it is perhaps the largest research area within biological anthropology.

Figure 1.3 shows three biological anthropologists in the midst of their research. Barbara Smuts is an associate professor of anthropology and psychology at the University of Michigan. Much of her research has focused on the behavior of baboons, particularly the social relationships between mothers and daughters. She is currently involved in two new projects, one of which is a study of olive baboons in Africa that will examine social relationships among adults. She plans to study these groups for periods of 4 to 5 months repeatedly over several years. Dr. Smuts is also investigating infant development and mother-infant relationships among wild bottlenose dolphins in Australia. This work is interdisciplinary, involving collaboration with biologists and psychologists.

Figure 1.3

Barbara Smuts (University of Michigan) sits among the olive baboons she studies in Kenya; Henry McHenry (University of California, Davis) compares archaic and modern African *Homo sapiens* skulls; Carol Worthman (Emory University) analyzes data in the university laboratory. (Courtesy of Barbara Smuts; Henry McHenry, photo by Dr. C. K. Brain; and Carol Worthman)

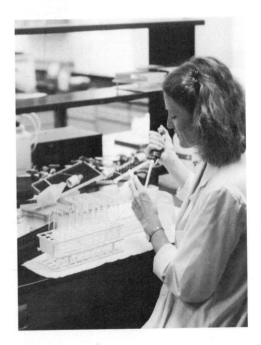

Henry McHenry is a professor of anthropology at the University of California at Davis whose primary research interest is in the field of paleoanthropology. Figure 1.3 shows him measuring and comparing skulls of early *Homo sapiens* from Africa, dated more than 200,000 years ago. Dr. McHenry's research focuses specifically on estimating body size of early humans from their skeletal remains. By comparing these estimates with living humans and other primates, he is able to make inferences on a wide variety of topics, including sex differences in body size, variations in relative brain size, and many other aspects of ecology and social behavior.

An associate professor of anthropology at Emory University in Atlanta, Georgia, Carol Worthman is also director of the Laboratory for Comparative Human Biology at Emory. At present, the laboratory is conducting research on human populations in Papua New Guinea, South America, Tibet, Outer Mongolia, and the United States. Using a variety of hormone measures obtained from blood, urine, and saliva, Dr. Worthman explores a wide range of interrelationships between biology and culture. Her current research includes looking at causes of late maturation in traditional societies, the effects of social practices (such as nursing) on reproductive function and fertility, and reasons for sex differences in rates of depression and conduct disorder.

This book examines the range of fields within modern biological anthropology. It is not, however, organized around these fields but rather around a set of basic questions that biological anthropology seeks to answer. The first question, on which the other questions rest, is: *What is evolution?* How do populations change over time? What is the relationship between genetics and evolution? How does evolution produce variation within species and differences among species? And what is the evidence for evolution? We take up these basic questions later in this chapter and in the following three chapters. Part 1 provides the basic background in genetics and evolutionary theory to understand human biological variation, adaptation, and evolution.

The second question relates to the similarities and differences among living human beings: *How and why do humans vary?* With the exception of identical twins, each of us is biologically unique. We also all have basic similarities, however. Some of our differences are clearly visible; some people are dark and some are light, some are tall and some are short, some have long noses and some have short noses. In spite of these differences, all forms of living humans share a great many traits. We all have the same basic anatomy, the same number of limbs, and so on. Other similarities and differences are less apparent but nonetheless important. Some people have certain blood types, some have resistance to certain diseases, and so on. In looking at human variation, we must focus on how and why we vary. We can answer these questions by examining the ongoing evolution of human populations, discussed in Chapters 5 and 6. Besides providing background in human variation, these chapters expand on the mechanisms of evolution by providing many examples of recent or present-day evolutionary changes in human populations.

The third question is: *What are humans?* Specifically, what is unique about the biology of humans, and what do we share with other animals? That is, what is our place in the natural world? Where do we fit in? Who are our closest living relatives? It is obvious that we share certain traits with many different creatures. Humans and other mammals, along with birds, fish, and reptiles, all have an internal spinal column. Both humans and dogs have four limbs. There are also many differences. Humans have much larger brains than dogs or cats or tropical fish. Humans have small canine teeth. Why do these similarities and differences exist, and what do they mean? These basic questions all make up the scientific study of the larger question, "What are humans?" Chapters 7–9 deal with the classification of living organisms and our relationship to other animals, mammals, and primates.

The fourth question is: *How have humans evolved?* We are interested in determining who our ancestors were, where they came from, and why they evolved. We look at the differences between humans and other creatures to try to determine what has changed. By analyzing the fossil record we attempt to determine how and why these changes have occurred. The study of human evolution seeks to answer questions such as: When and why did humans evolve their large brains? When and why did humans start walking on two legs? When was fire first used to cook food? What did the first stone tools look like, and how were they used? We address these questions in Chapters 10–13.

The fifth question is: *What is the relationship between human biology and culture?* Given that biology affects culture, and vice versa, how does this interrelationship affect the biology of human populations? For example, consider the nature of human growth. The basic process of biological growth from a fertilized egg through adulthood is one that is controlled to a certain extent by genetics. Disease and nutrition, however, also play a major role in affecting the growth process. Both disease and nutrition (and other factors) are affected by culture, including aspects of economics, health care, and such personal habits as smoking or drinking. The study of human growth must take into account both biology and culture. Many other areas in biological anthropology also require this perspective. Three of these are adaptations to the physical environment, human health and disease, and demography. Research in these areas allows us to observe the impact of rapid cultural change in today's world on patterns of biological variation. The study of the interaction of biology and culture will be discussed in Chapters 14–17.

A short epilogue focuses on our future as a species. Will we destroy ourselves and our planet? Will we soon be able to manipulate our genes? Should we? How might we evolve in the future? These and other questions are important to keep in mind throughout the book. Biological anthropology cannot provide all the answers. Indeed, no single field can. The perspective of humans as cultural and biological organisms that vary and evolve, however, is useful in any consideration of our future.

Biological anthropology outside the United States. The four-field approach to anthropology is in many ways unique to the United States. Partly because of the holistic orientation of the first anthropologists in the United States, anthropologists continue to focus on aspects of human culture and biology. In other countries throughout the world, the situation is often different. In some European countries, for example, biological anthropology is a separate discipline from the cultural subfields of archaeology, cultural anthropology, and linguistic anthropology. In many cases, even the names of these fields differ somewhat. In some countries, the term *anthropology* refers exclusively to biological anthropology, and cultural anthropology is often known as ethnology or comparative sociology.

The biocultural nature of American anthropology has had both proponents and opponents. Some argue that excessive training in the social sciences limits specialization in the biological sciences. Indeed, some biological anthropologists complain that their background included too much emphasis on cultural anthropology. To others, the four-field approach is both necessary and beneficial. To understand completely the biocultural nature of human beings, we need a thorough background in both the social and natural sciences. To understand, for example, the genetic effects of marriage systems, we need to understand marriage systems and their relationship to the rest of a culture, as well as human genetics. To understand human evolution, we need to be familiar with the archaeological record of past human behavior. The four-field approach provides a broad background suitable for comprehending the complexities of the human species.

Science and Evolution

Biological anthropology is an evolutionary science. All the major questions just presented may be addressed using modern evolutionary theory. Biological evolution simply refers to change in the genetic makeup of populations over time.

Characteristics of Science

Before we consider how evolution works, it is important to understand exactly what a science is.

Facts. At one time or another, you have probably heard someone make the statement that evolution is a theory, not a fact. Or you might have heard that it is a fact, not a theory. Which is it, theory or fact? The truth of the matter is that someone who makes either of these statements does not understand what a theory or a fact is. Evolution is both fact and theory. A fact is simply a verifiable truth. It is a fact that the earth is round. It is a fact that when you drop something, it falls to the ground (assuming you are in the presence of a gravitational field and you are not dropping something that floats or flies away!). Evolution is a fact. Living organisms have changed in the past and they continue to change today. There are forms of life living today that did not exist millions of years ago. There are also forms of life that did live in the past but are not around today, such as our ancestors (Figure 1.4). Certain organisms have shown definite changes in their biological makeup. Horses, for example, used to have five toes, then three, and today they have one. Human beings have larger brains and smaller teeth today than they did a million years ago. Some changes are even apparent over shorter intervals of time. For example, human teeth are on average smaller today than they were only 10,000 years ago. All of these statements and many others are verifiable truths. They are facts.

Hypotheses. What is a hypothesis? A **hypothesis** is simply an explanation of observed facts. For example, consider gravity. Gravity is a fact. It is observable. Many hypotheses could be generated to explain gravity. You could hypothesize that gravity is caused by a giant living in the core of our planet drawing in air, thus causing a pull on all objects on the earth's surface. Bizarre as it sounds, this is a scientific hypothesis because it can be tested. It is, however, easily shown to be incorrect (air movement can be measured and it does not flow in the postulated direction).

Testability. To be scientific, a hypothesis must be testable. The potential must exist for a hypothesis to be rejected. Just as the presence of the hypothetical giant in the earth can be tested (it doesn't exist!), predictions made about gravitational strength can also be tested. Not all hypotheses can be tested, however, and for this reason they are not scientific hypotheses. That doesn't necessarily mean they are true or false, but only that they cannot be tested. For example, you might come up with a hypothesis that all the fossils we have ever found were put in the ground by God to confuse us. This is not a scientific hypothesis because we have no objective way of testing the statement.

Many evolutionary hypotheses, however, are testable. For example, specific predictions about the fossil record can be made based on our knowledge of evolution. One such prediction is that humans evolved after the extinction of the dinosaurs. The potential exists for this statement to be rejected; all we need is evidence that humans existed before, or at the same time as, the dinosaurs. Since we have found no such evidence, we cannot reject the hypothesis. We can, however, imagine a situation in which the hypothesis could be rejected. If we cannot imagine such a situation, then the hypothesis cannot be tested. For example, imagine that someone tells you that all the people on the earth were created 5 minutes ago, complete with memories! Any evidence you muster against this idea could be explained away. Therefore, this hypothesis is not scientific since there is no possible way to reject it.

Theories. What is the difference between a theory and a hypothesis? In some disciplines the two terms are sometimes used to mean the same

hypothesis An explanation of observed facts.

Figure 1.4

A skull of *Australopithecus africanus,* a hominid that lived two to three million years ago. (© K. Cannon-Bonaventre/Anthro-Photo)

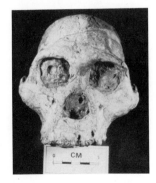

theory A set of hypotheses that have been tested repeatedly and that have not been rejected. This term is sometimes used in a different sense in social science literature.

taxonomy A formal classification of organisms.

species A group of populations whose members can interbreed naturally and produce fertile offspring.

genus Groups of species with similar adaptations.

thing. In the natural and physical sciences, however, theory means something different than hypothesis. A <u>**theory** is a set of hypotheses that have been tested repeatedly and that have not been rejected</u>. Evolution falls into this category. Evidence from many sources has confirmed the basic hypotheses making up evolutionary theory (discussed later in the chapter).

The Development of Evolutionary Theory

As with all general theories, modern evolutionary theory is not static. Scientific research is a dynamic process, with new evidence being used to support, clarify, and, most important, reject previous ideas. There will always be continual refinements in specific aspects of the theory and its applications. Because science is a dynamic process, evolutionary theory did not come about overnight. Charles Darwin (1809–1882) is most often credited as the "father of evolutionary thought" (Figure 1.5). It is true that Darwin provided a powerful idea that forms the center of modern evolutionary thought. He did not work in an intellectual vacuum, however, but rather built on the ideas of earlier scholars. Darwin's model was not the first evolutionary theory; it forms, rather, the basis of the one that has stood the test of time.

Pre-Darwinian thought. To understand Darwin's contribution and evolution in general, it is necessary to take a look at earlier ideas. For many centuries the concept of change, biological or otherwise, was rather unusual in Western thought. Much of Greek philosophy, for example, posits a static, unchanging view of the world. In later Western thought, the universe, earth, and all living creatures were regarded as having been created by God in their present form, showing little if any change over many generations. Many biologists (then called natural historians) shared this view, and their science consisted mainly of description and categorization. A good example is Carolus Linnaeus (1707–1778), a Swedish naturalist who compiled the first formal classification of all known living creatures. A classification is called a **taxonomy** and it serves to help organize information. Linnaeus's taxonomy organized all known living creatures into meaningful groups. For example, humans, dogs, cats, and many other animals are mammals, characterized primarily by the presence of mammary glands to feed offspring. Linnaeus used a variety of traits to place all then known creatures into various categories. Such a taxonomy helps in clarifying relationships between different organisms. For example, bats are classified as mammals because they possess mammary glands, and not as birds simply because they have wings.

Linnaeus also gave organisms a name reflecting their genus and species. A **species** is a group of populations whose members can interbreed and produce fertile offspring. A **genus** is a group of similar species, often sharing certain common forms of adaptation. Modern humans, for example, are known by the name *Homo sapiens*. The first word is the genus

Figure 1.5

Charles Darwin.   (Neg. no. 326697. Courtesy Department of Library Sciences, American Museum of Natural History)

and the second word is the species (more detail on genus and species is given in Chapter 4).

The reason for the relationships among organisms, however, was not often addressed by early natural historians. The living world was felt to be the product of God's work, and the task of the natural historian was description and classification. This static view of the world began to change in the eighteenth and nineteenth centuries. One important reason for this change was that excavations began to produce many fossils that did not fit neatly into the classification system. For example, imagine that you found the remains of a modern horse. This would pose no problem in interpretation; the bones are those of a dead horse, perhaps belonging to a farmer several years ago. Now suppose you found what at first glance appeared to be a horse but was somewhat smaller and had five toes instead of the single hoof of a modern horse. If you found more and more of these five-toed horses, you would ask what creature they belonged to. Because horses do not have five toes today, your only conclusion would be that there once existed horses with five toes and they do not exist any more. This conclusion, though hardly startling now, was a real thunderbolt to those who believed the world was created as it is today, with no change.

Apart from finding fossil remains of creatures that were somewhat similar to modern-day forms, excavations also uncovered fossil remnants of truly unusual creatures, such as the dinosaurs. Discovery of the fossil record began to chip away at the view that the world is as it always had been, and the concept of change began to be incorporated into explanations of the origin of life. Not all scholars, however, came up with the same hypotheses.

One French anatomist, Cuvier (1769–1832), analyzed many of the fossil remains found in quarries. He showed that many of these belonged to animals that no longer existed; that is, they had become extinct. Cuvier used a hypothesis called **catastrophism** to explain these extinctions. The hypothesis posited a series of catastrophes in the planet's past, during which many living creatures were destroyed. Following these catastrophes, organisms from unaffected areas moved in. The changes over time observed in the fossil record could therefore be explained as a continual process of catastrophes followed by repopulation from other regions (Mayr 1982).

Another hypothesis was put forth by the French scientist Lamarck (1744–1829). He believed that evolution occurred through a natural process of organisms adjusting to their environment. One of his ideas was that an organism could change during its lifetime and then pass these changes on to its offspring. According to Lamarck's idea of **acquired characteristics,** a jungle cat that developed stronger leg muscles through constant running and jumping would pass along stronger muscles to its offspring. Of course, it is easy now to reject the concept of acquired characteristics. For example, someone who loses a finger in an accident will still have children with the correct number of fingers. Instead of looking back and

catastrophism The hypothesis that explains evolutionary change in terms of repeated natural catastrophes.

acquired characteristics Lamarck's hypothesis that traits change in response to environmental demands and are passed on to offspring.

Figure 1.6

Darwin's observations of variation in the different regions he visited aboard the H.M.S. *Beagle* shaped his theory of natural selection.

ridiculing Lamarck for his ideas, we must realize that he was actually quite astute in noting the intimate relationship among organisms, their environments, and evolution.

It is interesting to note that a version of Lamarck's ideas was widely accepted in the Soviet Union until the middle of this century. Believing that the work of Darwin did not fit Marxist ideology, the dictator Josef Stalin supported the biologist Lysenko, who had adopted a version of Lamarck's model. Lamarck's notions conformed nicely with Marxist ideology—for example, in the concepts that change in an organism will continue through future generations and that nature, including humans, is capable of being perfected (Futuyma 1983). As an analogy for social change (such analogies can be very tricky!), this model offers reassurance for those seeking permanent social change. In any case, the lesson to be learned here is that even though science seeks to be objective, it is always practiced within a cultural setting. The social and political climate of the

Soviet Union in the 1930s was ready for the rejection of Darwin's ideas and the acceptance of Lysenko's.

Charles Darwin and natural selection. Cuvier and Lamarck are perhaps the best-known examples of what many have called "pre-Darwinian" theorists. Evolution was well accepted, and various models were being developed to explain this fact, before Darwin. Charles Darwin developed the theory of natural selection that has since been supported by testing. His major contribution was to combine information from a variety of different fields, such as geology and economics, to form his theory.

With this background in mind, let us look at Darwin and his accomplishment. Charles Darwin had been interested in biology and geology since he was a small child. Born to well-to-do parents, Darwin attended college and had planned to enter the ministry, although he was not as enthusiastic about this career as he was about his studies of natural history. Because of his scientific and social connections, Darwin was able to accompany the scientific survey ship *Beagle* as an unpaid naturalist. The *Beagle* conducted a five-year journey around the world collecting plant and animal specimens in South America and the Galapagos Islands (in the Pacific Ocean near Ecuador), among other places (Figure 1.6).

During these travels, Darwin came to several basic conclusions about variation in living organisms. First, he found a tremendous amount of observable variation in most living species. Instead of looking at the world in terms of fixed, rigid categories (as did mainstream biology in his time), Darwin saw that individuals within species varied considerably from place to place. With careful attention, you can see the world in much the same way that Darwin did. You will see, for example, that people around you vary to an incredible degree. Some are tall, some are short, some are dark, and some are light. Facial features, musculature, hair color, and many other characteristics come in many different forms even in a single classroom. Remember, too, that what you see are only those visible characteristics. With the right type of equipment, you could look at genetic and biochemical variation within your classroom and find even more evidence of tremendous diversity.

Darwin also noted that the variations he saw made sense in terms of the environment (Figure 1.7). Creatures in cold climates often have fur for protection. Birds in areas where insects live deep inside tree branches have long beaks to allow them to extract these insects and eat them. In other words, organisms appear well adapted to specific environments. Darwin believed that the environment acted to change organisms over time. But how?

To help answer this question, Darwin turned to the writings of the economist Thomas Malthus (1766–1834), who had noted that more individuals are born in most species than can possibly survive. In other words, many organisms die before reaching maturity and reproducing. If it were not for this mortality, populations would grow too large for their

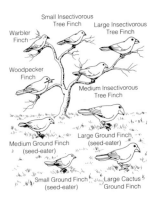

Figure 1.7

The sizes, beak shapes, and diets of this sample of Darwin's finches show differences in adaptation among closely related species.   (From E. Peter Volpe, *Understanding Evolution*, 5th ed. Copyright ©1985 Wm. C. Brown Communication, Inc., Dubuque, Iowa. All Rights Reserved. Reprinted by permission)

natural selection A mechanism for evolutionary change favoring the survival and reproduction of some organisms over others because of their biological characteristics.

environments to support them. Certain fish, for example, can produce as many as 8,000 eggs in a single year (Johanson and Edey 1981). Assume for the moment that half of these eggs are female. Now assume that each of these females then also lays 8,000 eggs in a single year. To make things simple, let us further assume that a female fish breeds only once in her life. If you start with two fish (one male and one female), in the next generation you have 8,000 fish. Half of these are females, and each produces 8,000 more fish, for a total of 32 million fish. If the fish continue reproducing in this way, there will be roughly 2.1×10^{36} fish (that is, 2.1 followed by 36 zeroes) after only 10 generations! Suppose these are relatively small fish, each one weighing only 100 grams (a little less than a quarter of a pound). The total weight of all fish after 10 generations would be roughly 2.1×10^{38} grams (or roughly 2.3×10^{32} tons!).

To give you an idea of exactly how large these numbers are, consider the fact that the total weight of our sun is 1.99×10^{33} grams (Pasachoff 1979). If the cycle begins with two fish, after 10 generations the total weight of the fish will be greater than the weight of the sun! Since we are all not currently smothered in fish, something is wrong with this simple model.

Malthus provided the answer. Most of the fish will die before they reproduce. Some eggs will become diseased and die, and others will be eaten by predators. Only a small number of the eggs will actually survive long enough to reproduce. Malthus is best known for extrapolating the principle of population growth into human terms; his lesson is that unless we control our growth there will soon be too many of us to feed.

To Charles Darwin, the ideas of Malthus provided the needed information to solve the problem of adaptation and evolution. Not all individuals in a species survive and reproduce. Some failure to reproduce may be random, but some is related to specific characteristics of an individual. If there are two birds, one with a short beak and one with a long beak, in an environment that requires reaching inside branches to feed, it stands to reason that the bird with the longer beak is more likely to feed itself, survive, and reproduce. In certain environments, some individuals possess traits that enhance their probability of survival and reproduction. If these traits are due, in part or whole, to inherited characteristics, then they will be passed on to the next generation.

In some ways, Darwin's idea was not new. Animal and plant breeders had used this principle for centuries. Controlled breeding and artificial selection had resulted in many traits in domesticated plants and animals, such as livestock size, milk production in cows, and a variety of other traits. The same principle is used in producing pedigreed dogs and many forms of tropical fish. The difference is that Darwin saw that nature (the environment) could select those individuals that survived and reproduced. Hence, he called his concept **natural selection.**

Although the theory of evolution by natural selection is most often associated with Charles Darwin, another English natural historian, Alfred

Russel Wallace (1823–1913), came up with essentially the same idea. In fact, Darwin and Wallace communicated their ideas to each other and first presented the theory of natural selection in a joint paper in 1858. Many scholars feel that Wallace's independent work urged Darwin finally to put forward the ideas he had developed years earlier but had not published (Gould 1977a). To ensure timely publication, Darwin condensed his many years of work into a 490-page "abstract" entitled *On the Origin of Species by Means of Natural Selection,* published in 1859 (Futuyma 1983).

Examples of natural selection. One excellent example of how natural selection works is the story of populations of the peppered moth in England over the last few centuries (Figure 1.8). These moths come in two distinct colors, dark and light. Early observations found that most of these moths were light-colored, thus allowing them to camouflage themselves on tree trunks. By blending in, they had a better chance of avoiding the birds that tried to eat them. Roughly 1 percent of the moths, however, were dark-colored and thus at an obvious disadvantage. Naturalists noted that the frequency of dark-colored moths increased to almost 90 percent in the century following the beginning of the Industrial Revolution in England (Grant 1985). The reason for this change was the fact that industrialization brought about massive pollution in the surrounding countryside. The trees became darker in color after being covered with soot. The light moths were at a disadvantage, and the dark moths, now better camouflaged, were better-off. Proportionately, more dark moths survived and passed their dark color to the next generation. In evolutionary terminology, the dark moths were *selected for* and the light moths were *selected against*. After antipollution laws were passed and the environment began to recover, the situation reversed: once again light moths survived better, and were selected for, whereas dark moths were selected against.

This well-known study shows us more than just the workings of natural selection. It also illustrates several important principles of evolution. First, we cannot always state with absolute certainty which traits are "good" and which are "bad." It depends on the specific environment. When the trees were light in color, the light-colored moths were at an advantage, but when the situation changed, the dark-colored moths gained the advantage. Second, evolution does not proceed unopposed in one direction. Under certain situations, biological traits can change in a different direction. In the case of the moths, evolution produced a change from light to dark to light again. Third, evolution does not occur in a vacuum. It is affected by changes in the environment and by changes in other species. In this example, changes in the cultural evolution of humans led to a change in the environment, which further affected the evolution of the moths. Finally, the moth study shows us the critical importance of variation to the evolutionary process. If the original population of moths did not possess the dark-colored variation, they might have been wiped

Figure 1.8

Adaptation in the peppered moth. The dark-colored moth is more visible on light-colored tree trunks and therefore at greater risk of being seen and eaten by a bird (*top*). The light-colored moth is at greater risk of being eaten on dark-colored tree trunks (*bottom*). (©Michael Tweedie/ Photo Researchers)

out after the trees turned darker in color. Variation must exist for natural selection to operate effectively.

Another example of natural selection is found in Grant's (1991) continuing work on variation and evolution of Galapagos finches. He found that average beak size changed over time in direct response to changes in the environment. In drought years, the average beak is larger. Why? The simplest explanation is that drought conditions make those finches with larger beaks better able to crack the larger seeds that are more common under drought conditions. In wetter years, seeds are smaller and finches with smaller beaks are favored. Grant has observed these changes over several decades. The changes in beak size over time show that the changing environment affects probability of survival and reproduction.

Both the peppered-moth and finch examples illustrate how patterns of variation in natural populations are related to natural selection. These studies are examples of field observations; organisms and their environment are observed in a natural situation in order to provide clues about variation and evolution. Experimental studies also provide strong evidence for the operation of natural selection. In a recent study, Malhotra and Thorpe (1991) transplanted populations of Dominican lizards into different environments on the island in order to study differences in survival. They found that body size and other biological characteristics changed over time in response to new environmental conditions.

Modern evolutionary thought. Darwin provided part of the answer of how evolution worked, but he did not have all the answers. Many early critics of Darwin's work focused on certain questions that Darwin could not answer. One important question concerns the origins of variation: Given that natural selection operates on existing variation, then where do those variations come from? Why, at the outset, were some moths light and others dark? Natural selection can only act on preexisting variation; it cannot create new variations. Another question is: How are traits inherited? The theory of natural selection states that certain traits are selected for and passed on to future generations. How are these traits passed on? Darwin knew that traits were inherited, but he did not know the mechanism. Still another question involves how new forms and structures come into being.

Darwin is to be remembered and praised for his work in providing the critical base from which evolutionary science developed. He did not, however, have all the answers, as no scientist does. Even today people tend to equate evolutionary science with Darwin to the exclusion of all work since that time. Some critics of evolutionary theory point to a single aspect of Darwin's work, show it to be in error, and then proceed to claim all of evolutionary thought suspect. In reality, a scientific theory will continue to change as new evidence is gathered and as further tests are constructed.

Modern evolutionary theory relies not only on the work of Darwin and Wallace but also on developments in genetics, zoology, embryology, physiology, and mathematics, to name but a few fields. The basic concept of natural selection as stated by Darwin has been tested and found to be valid. Refinements have been added, and some aspects of the original idea have been changed. We now have answers to many of Darwin's questions.

Biological evolution consists of changes in the genetic composition of populations. As shown in Chapter 3, the relative frequencies of genes change over time because of four mechanisms, or evolutionary forces. Natural selection is one of these mechanisms. Those individuals with genetic characteristics that improve their relative survival or reproduction pass their genetic material on to the next generation. In the peppered-moth example discussed earlier, the dark moths were more likely to survive in an environment where pollution made the trunks of trees darker in color. Thus, the relative frequency of genes for dark moth color increased over time (at least until the environment changed again). **?**

Another evolutionary force is **mutation,** a random change in the genetic code that is passed on to offspring. *Random* here means that the mutations do not appear in response to an organism's needs. As the ultimate source of all genetic variation, mutations supply the raw material for natural selection to act on. Our present knowledge of mutations provides answers to many of Darwin's questions regarding the origin of variation.

A third evolutionary force is **genetic drift,** the random fluctuation of gene frequencies from one generation to the next. Reproduction is in many ways a random process. You do not pass on your entire genetic code to your children. Instead, you provide half and your mate provides the other half. Each time you produce a sex cell (sperm or egg, depending on your sex), the same genetic material is not necessarily passed on. What this means is that there may be changes in the relative frequency of genes because of random chance (just as flipping a coin 10 times will not always result in five heads and five tails). As we will see in Chapter 3, genetic drift has the most effect on gene frequency changes when the size of the population is relatively small.

The fourth evolutionary force is **gene flow,** the movement of genes from one population to another. Through this process, genetic material is shared among a set of populations. The greater the rate of sharing, the more likely two populations will be genetically similar (under certain conditions, outlined in Chapter 3).

Evolutionary change from one generation to the next, or over many generations, is the product of the joint effect of the four evolutionary forces. Our discussion here simplifies a complex idea, but it does suggest that evolution is more than simply natural selection. Modern evolutionary theory encompasses all four evolutionary forces and will be discussed in greater detail in the next three chapters.

Evidence for Evolution

Because this book is concerned with human variation and evolution, you will be provided with numerous examples of how evolution works in past and present human populations. It is important to understand from

mutation A mechanism for evolutionary change resulting from a random change in the genetic code and the ultimate source of all genetic variation.

genetic drift A mechanism for evolutionary change resulting from the random fluctuations of gene frequencies from one generation to the next.

gene flow A mechanism for evolutionary change resulting from the movement of genes from one population to another.

the start that biological evolution is a documented fact and that the modern theory of evolution has stood up under many scientific tests.

The fossil record provides evidence of evolution. The story the fossils tell is one of change. Creatures existed in the past that are no longer with us. Sequential changes are found in many fossils showing the change of certain features over time from a common ancestor, as in the case of the horse. Apart from demonstrating that evolution did occur, the fossil record also provides tests of the predictions made from evolutionary theory. For example, the theory predicts that single-celled organisms evolved before multicelled organisms. The fossil record supports this prediction—multicelled organisms are found in layers of earth millions of years after the first appearance of single-celled organisms. Note that the possibility always remains that the opposite could be found! If multicelled organisms were indeed found to have evolved before single-celled organisms, then the theory of evolution would be rejected. A good scientific theory always allows for the possibility that it may be rejected. The fact that we have not found such a case in countless examinations of the fossil record strengthens the case for evolutionary theory. Remember, in science you do not prove a theory; rather, you fail to reject it.

The fossil record is not the only evidence we have that evolution has occurred. Comparison of living organisms provides further confirmation. For example, the African apes are the closest living relatives of humans. We see this in a number of characteristics. African apes and humans share the same type of dental pattern, have a similar shoulder structure, and have DNA (the genetic code) that is over 98 percent identical. Even though any one of these traits, or others, could be explained as coincidental, why do so many independent traits show the same pattern? One possibility, of course, is that they were designed that way by an ultimate Creator. The problem with this idea is that it cannot be tested. It is a matter of faith and not of science. Another problem is that we must then ask ourselves why a Creator would use the same basic pattern for so many traits in different creatures. Evolution, on the other hand, offers an explanation. Apes and humans share many characteristics because they evolved from a common ancestor (Figure 1.9).

Another example of shared characteristics is the python, a large snake. Like many vertebrates, the python has a pelvis, the skeletal structure that connects the lower legs to the upper body (Futuyma 1983). From a structural standpoint, of what possible use is a pelvis to a creature that has no legs? If the python was created, then what purpose would there have been to give it a pelvis? We can of course argue that no one can understand the motivations of a Creator, but that is hardly a scientific explanation. Evolutionary reasoning provides an answer: the python has retained the pelvis from an earlier ancestor that did have legs.

Further, fascinating evidence of shared characteristics is the recent discovery of fossils of early whales with reduced hind limbs (Gingerich et al. 1990). Whales are aquatic mammals that have lost hind limbs and pelvic

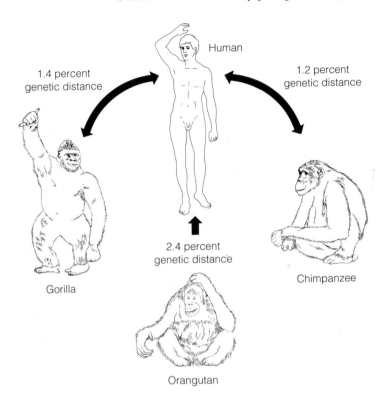

Figure 1.9

The percentage of genetic distance between humans and the great apes (chimpanzee, gorilla, and orangutan). Combined with other biological evidence, genetic data show us how closely related we are to the apes, especially the chimpanzee. (From *Human Evolution: An Illustrated Introduction* by Roger Lewin, © 1984 by Blackwell Scientific Publications. Reprinted with permission by W. H. Freeman and Company)

bones since their evolutionary separation from other mammals over 50 million years ago. The discovery of fossil whales with small, and perhaps somewhat functional, hind limbs provides another example of shared characteristics that can be explained only through evolution. This discovery also provides an excellent illustration of a transitional form—a fossil that links both early and modern forms.

Another line of evidence supporting evolution is the laboratory and field studies of living organisms. Ongoing evolutionary change has been documented in many organisms, including humans. Specific predictions of the effect of evolutionary mechanisms have been tested and verified in controlled experiments and observational studies. The study of moth color is but one of many examples of this kind of analysis.

Science and Religion

The subject of evolution has always been controversial, and the implications of evolution have sometimes frightened people. For example, the fact that humans and apes evolved from a common ancestor has always upset some people who feel that their humanity is somehow degraded by having ancestors supposedly less worthy than ourselves. Another conflict lies in the implications evolution has for religious views. In the United

Figure 1.10

The Scopes Trial. William Jennings Bryan (*right*) represented the state of Tennessee and Clarence Darrow (*left*) represented John Scopes.   (© AP/Wide World Photos)

[handwritten note: In class movie]

States a number of laws have prohibited the teaching of evolution in public schools. Many of these laws stayed on the books until the late 1960s.

Numerous legal battles have been fought over these anti-evolution laws. Perhaps the most famous of these was the "Scopes Monkey Trial" in 1925. John Scopes, a high school teacher in Dayton, Tennessee, was arrested for violating the state law prohibiting the teaching of evolution. The town and trial quickly became the center of national attention, primarily because of the two celebrities in the case—William Jennings Bryan, a former U.S. Secretary of State, who represented the state of Tennessee, and Clarence Darrow, one of the most famous American trial lawyers, who represented Scopes. The battle between these two eloquent speakers captured the attention of the country (Figure 1.10). In the end, Scopes was found guilty of violating the law, and he was fined $100. The fine was later suspended on a legal technicality. The story of this trial, which has been dramatized in play and movie versions as *Inherit the Wind*, is a powerful story portraying the fight of those who feel strongly about academic freedom and freedom of speech against ignorance and oppression. In reality, the original arrest of Scopes appears to have been planned by several local people, including Scopes, to put the town on the map (Gould 1983).

In retrospect, the Scopes trial may seem amusing. We laugh at early attempts to control subject matter in classrooms and often feel that we have gone beyond such battles. Nothing could be further from the truth, however. For many people, evolution represents a threat to their beliefs in the sudden creation of all life by a creator. Attempts to legislate the teaching of the Biblical view of creation in science classes, however, violate the First Amendment of the Constitution as an establishment of religion. To circumvent this problem, opponents of evolution have devised a new strategy by calling their teachings "creation science," supposedly the scientific study of special creation. The word *God* does not always appear in definitions of creation science, but the word *creator* often does.

In March 1981, the Arkansas state legislature passed a law (Act 590) requiring that creation science be taught in public schools for equal amounts of time as evolution. The American Civil Liberties Union challenged this law, and it was overturned in a federal district court in 1982. A similar law passed in Louisiana in 1981 was later overturned. The Louisiana case has since been appealed and brought to the U.S. Supreme Court, which upheld the ruling of the lower court in 1987. Among other legal problems they raise, both the Arkansas and Louisiana laws have been found to be unconstitutional under the First Amendment.

What is "creation science"? Why shouldn't it be taught in science classes? Shouldn't science be open to new ideas? These questions all center on the issue of whether creation science is a science or not. As typically applied, creation science is not a science; at best, it is a grab bag of ideas spruced up with scientific jargon. One of the original definitions is found in Act 590 of the Arkansas law, which defines creation science as the scientific evidence for creation and inferences from these scientific evidences. Creation-science includes the scientific evidences and related inferences that indicate: (1) Sudden creation of the universe, energy, and life from nothing; (2) The insufficiency of mutation and natural selection in bringing about development of all living kinds from a single organism; (3) Changes only within fixed limits of originally created kinds of plants and animals; (4) Separate ancestry for man and apes; (5) Explanation of the earth's geology by catastrophism, including the occurrence of a worldwide flood; and (6) A relatively recent inception of the earth and living kinds. (Montagu 1984:376–377)

None of these statements is supported by scientific evidence, and creationist writers generally use very little actual evidence to support their views. Some have written that the Biblical Flood can be supported by the fossil record. Earth's past is essentially recorded by the order in which different levels of earth and fossils are found. In general, that is, the deeper a fossil is found the older it is. Creationists explain this order as being caused by the flight of animals from the Flood. As the waters rose, they say, birds flew and small mammals ran up mountains to escape drowning; these creatures were therefore drowned at higher elevations.

According to creationists, then, you will find fish at lower levels and birds and mammals at higher levels. The fossil record does show this phenomenon. Isn't this proof for "creation science"? No. Think about the Flood scenario for a moment and you will see that it just doesn't make sense. Why didn't the winged reptiles fly away like the birds did? Why are single-celled organisms found earlier than multicelled organisms of similar size and overall shape? Why did large, heavy creatures such as giant tortoises and hippopotami survive instead of sinking? Why didn't the small, fast dinosaurs survive? Why did certain fish die before others, when they were just as swift and just as good at swimming? Many challenges can be raised to the idea of a single gigantic flood causing the order found in the fossil record (Kitcher 1982; Futuyma 1983). The fossil record, in short, provides ample evidence to reject the Flood hypothesis.

Another example cited by creationists as "proof" of special creation is the "fact" that dinosaur and human footprints have been found at the same geological level along the Paluxy River in Texas. Closer examination has shown that the footprints were not distinguishable and that a number of tracks had been carved to attract tourists and their money (Kitcher 1982).

The main "scientific" work of the creationists consists of attempting to find fault with evolutionary theory. The reasoning is that if evolution can be rejected, then special creation must be true. This strategy actually uses an important feature of scientific research by attempting to reject a given hypothesis. The problem is that none of the creationists' attacks on evolution has been supported by scientific evidence. Certainly some predictions of evolutionary theory have been proven incorrect, but that is to be expected because science is a dynamic process. The basic findings of evolution, however, have been supported time and time again.

Another problem is that this method works only when the hypothesis and its alternative cover all possible cases. Are evolution and special creation by a single creator the only possible explanations? Perhaps the universe was created by several creators. Perhaps the universe and natural law was created by a creator, but life evolved from natural law. You might try to think up other alternatives. Remember, however, that to be scientific a hypothesis must be testable.

On an emotional level, the doctrines of "creation science" attract many people. Given the concept of free speech, why shouldn't creation science be given equal time? The problem with equal time is that it assumes that both ideas have equal merit. Consider that some people still believe the earth is flat. They are certainly entitled to their opinion, but it would be absurd to mandate "equal time" in geography and geology classes for this idea. Also, the concept of equal time is not really that fairminded after all. The specific story many creationists refer to is the Biblical story of Genesis. Many other cultures have their own creation stories. Shouldn't they receive equal time as well? In one sense, they should, though the proper forum for such discussions is probably a course in comparative religions, not a science class.

Perhaps the biggest problem advocates of "creation science" have introduced is that they appear to place religion and science at odds with each other. Religion and science both represent ways of looking at the world and, though they work on different levels, they are not contradictory. You can be religious and believe in God and still accept the fact of evolution and evolutionary theory. Only if you take the story of Genesis as a literal, historical account does a conflict exist. Most major religions in the world accept the findings of evolution. Many people, including some scientists, look to the evolutionary process as evidence of God's work.

Many creationists fear that science has eroded our faith in God and has therefore led to a decline in morals and values. They imply that science (and evolution in particular) makes statements about human morality. It does not. Science has nothing to say about right and wrong; that is the function of social ethics, philosophies, and religion. Religion and science are important to many people. To put them at odds with each other does both a disservice. It is no surprise that many ministers, priests, and rabbis have joined in the fight against the laws of "creation science."

SUMMARY

Anthropology is the study of human biological and cultural variation and evolution. Anthropology asks questions that focus on what humans are and the origins, evolution, and variation of our biology and behaviors, since humans are both biological and cultural organisms. In the United States, anthropology is characterized by four subfields with specific concerns: cultural anthropology (the study of cultural behavior), anthropological archaeology (the study of past cultures), linguistic anthropology (the study of language as a human characteristic), and biological anthropology (the study of human biological evolution and variation).

As a science, anthropology has certain requirements and characteristics. Hypotheses must be testable and verifiable. The main theoretical base of biological anthropology is the theory of evolution. A major feature of evolutionary theory is Darwin's idea of natural selection. In any environment in which resources are necessarily limited, some organisms are more likely to survive and reproduce than others because of their biological characteristics. Those who survive pass these traits on to the next generation.

A current controversy involves the efforts of certain people to pass laws requiring that "creation science" be taught in public schools. Examination of this field shows that it is not a science at all. Apart from these debates, it should be noted that today there is little conflict between religion and science in the United States. Each perspective addresses different questions in different ways.

Supplemental Readings

Edey, M. A., and D. C. Johanson. 1989. *Blueprints: Solving the Mystery of Evolution*. Boston: Little, Brown. A nontechnical, well-written book focusing on the history of evolutionary thought.

Futuyma, D. J. 1983. *Science on Trial: The Case for Evolution*. New York: Pantheon Books. An excellent review of evolution and a detailed critique of "creation science," particularly strong in its discussion of scientific method and evidence for evolution.

Godfrey, L. G., ed. 1983. *Scientists Confront Creationism*. New York: W. W. Norton. A collection of papers discussing the fallacy of "creation science."

Gould, S. J. 1977. *Ever Since Darwin*. New York: W. W. Norton.

———. 1980. *The Panda's Thumb*. New York: W. W. Norton.

———. 1983. *Hen's Teeth and Horse's Toes*. New York: W. W. Norton.

———. 1985. *The Flamingo's Smile*. New York: W. W. Norton.

———. 1991. *Bully for Brontosaurus*. New York: W. W. Norton.

———. 1993. *Eight Little Piggies*. New York: W. W. Norton. Containing articles written by the author for *Natural History* and other popular publications, these six books provide excellent discussions of evolutionary fact and theory as well as the history of evolutionary thought.

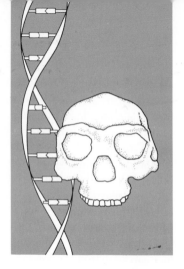

CHAPTER **2**

Human Genetics

Is human behavior the result of biology *or* culture? This question has been asked countless times in human history, often with serious cultural and political consequences. To anthropologists, the question is somewhat meaningless; we recognize *both* biological and cultural factors as important and look at the relative potential contributions of both.

To understand human biological variation and evolution, we must consider the science of genetics. The study of genetics actually encompasses a number of different areas, depending on the level of analysis. Genetics can be studied on the molecular level, with the focus on what genes are and how they act to produce biological structures.

Genetics also involves the process of inheritance. To what extent are we a reflection of our parents? How are traits inherited? This branch of the field is called **Mendelian genetics,** after the scientist Gregor Mendel, who first worked out many of the principles of inheritance.

Finally, genetics can be studied at the level of a population. Here we are interested in describing the patterns of genetic variation within and among different populations. The changes that take place in the frequency of genes within a population constitute the process of **microevolution.** At the level of the population, we seek the reasons for evolutionary change from one generation to the next. Projection of these findings allows us to understand better the long-term pattern of evolution over thousands and millions of years and the origin of new species (**macroevolution**).

Mendelian genetics The branch of genetics concerned with patterns and processes of inheritance. This field was named after Gregor Mendel, the first scientist to work out many of these principles.

microevolution Short-term evolutionary change.

macroevolution Long-term evolutionary change.

Molecular Genetics

DNA: The Genetic Code

The study of genetics at the molecular level concerns the amazing properties of a molecule known as deoxyribonucleic acid, or **DNA** for short. The DNA molecule provides the codes for biological structures and the means to translate this code. It is perhaps best to think of DNA as a set of instructions for determining the makeup of biological organisms. Quite simply, DNA provides information for building, operating, and repairing organisms. In this context, the process of genetic inheritance is seen as the transmission of this information, or the passing on of the instructions needed for biological structures. Evolution can be viewed in this context as the transfer of information from one generation to the next along with the possibility that this information will change.

An understanding of both the structure and function of DNA is necessary to understand the processes of genetic inheritance and evolution. The exact biochemistry of DNA is beyond the scope of this text, but its basic nature can be discussed in the context of information transfer.

The structure of DNA. The physical appearance of the DNA molecule resembles a ladder that has been twisted into the shape of a helix (Figure 2.1). In biochemical terms, the rungs of the ladder are of major importance. These rungs are made up of chemical units called **bases.** There are four possible types of bases, identified by the first letter of their longer chemical names: A (adenine), T (thymine), G (guanine), and C (cytosine). These bases form the "alphabet" used in specifying and carrying out genetic instructions.

All biological structures, from nerve cells to blood cells to bone cells, are made up predominantly of proteins. Proteins in turn are made up of amino acids, whose chemical properties allow them to bond together to form proteins. Each amino acid is coded for by three of the four chemical bases just discussed. For example, the base sequence CGA provides the code for the amino acid alanine, and the base sequence TTT codes for the amino acid lysine. There are 64 possible codes that can be specified, using some combination of three bases. This might not seem like a lot, except for the fact that only 20 amino acids need to be specified by the genetic code. The three-base code provides more than enough possibilities to code for these amino acids. In fact, some amino acids have several different codes, such as alanine, which can be specified by the base sequences CGA, CGG, CGT, and CGC. Some of the base sequences, such as ATT, act to form "punctuation" for the genetic instructions; that is, they provide the code to start or stop "messages." A list of the different DNA sequences is shown in Table 2.1.

The ability of four different bases, taken three at a time, to specify all

DNA The molecule that provides the genetic code for biological structures and the means to translate this code.

base Chemical unit that makes up part of the DNA molecule whose sequence specifies genetic instructions.

Figure 2.1

The structure of the DNA molecule. DNA consists of two strands arranged in a helix joined together by chemical bases (see text).

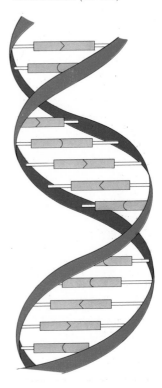

TABLE 2.1
DNA Base Sequences for Amino Acids

First base	Second base							
	A		**T**		**C**		**G**	
A	AAA	Phenylalanine	ATA	Tyrosine	ACA	Cysteine	AGA	Serine
	AAT	Leucine	ATT	Stop	ACT	Stop	AGT	Serine
	AAC	Leucine	ATC	Stop	ACC	Tryptophan	AGC	Serine
	AAG	Phenylalanine	ATG	Tyrosine	ACG	Cysteine	AGG	Serine
T	TAA	Isoleucine	TTA	Asparagine	TCA	Serine	TGA	Threonine
	TAT	Isoleucine	TTT	Lysine	TCT	Arginine	TGT	Threonine
	TAC	Methionine	TTC	Lysine	TCC	Arginine	TGC	Threonine
	TAG	Isoleucine	TTG	Asparagine	TCG	Serine	TGG	Threonine
C	CAA	Valine	CTA	Aspartic acid	CCA	Glycine	CGA	Alanine
	CAT	Valine	CTT	Glutamic acid	CCT	Glycine	CGT	Alanine
	CAC	Valine	CTC	Glutamic acid	CCC	Glycine	CGC	Alanine
	CAG	Valine	CTG	Aspartic acid	CCG	Glycine	CGG	Alanine
G	GAA	Leucine	GTA	Histidine	GCA	Arginine	GGA	Proline
	GAT	Leucine	GTT	Glutamine	GCT	Arginine	GGT	Proline
	GAC	Leucine	GTC	Glutamine	GCC	Arginine	GGC	Proline
	GAG	Leucine	GTG	Histidine	GCG	Arginine	GGG	Proline

Rows refer to the first of the three bases and columns refer to the second of the three bases. These base sequences are for the DNA molecule. The 64 different combinations code for 20 amino acids and one termination sequence ("Stop"). To convert to messenger RNA, substitute U for A, A for T, G for C, and C for G. To convert to transfer RNA, substitute U for A.

the information needed for synthesis of proteins is astounding. It boggles the mind that the diverse structure of complex protein molecules can be specified with only a four-letter "alphabet." As an analogy, consider the way in which computers work. All computer operations, from word processing to complex mathematical simulations, ultimately are translated to a set of computer instructions which use only a simple two-letter alphabet—on or off! These two instructions make up a larger set of codes that provide information on computer operations. These operations are combined to generate computer languages that can be used to write a variety of programs.

The ability of the DNA molecule to make use of the different amino acid codes lies in a simple property of the chemical bases. The base A bonds with the base T, and the base G bonds with the base C. This chemical property allows the DNA molecule to carry out a number of functions, including the ability to make copies of itself and to direct the synthesis of proteins.

Functions of DNA. The DNA molecule can make copies of itself. Remember that the DNA molecule is made up of two strands that form

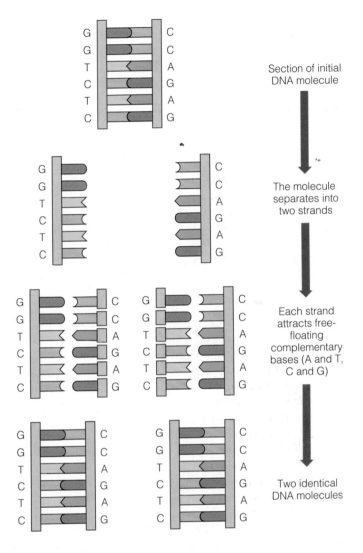

Figure 2.2

Replication of the DNA molecule.

Section of initial DNA molecule

The molecule separates into two strands

Each strand attracts free-floating complementary bases (A and T, C and G)

Two identical DNA molecules

the long arms of the ladder. Each rung of the ladder consists of two bases. If one part of the rung contains the base A, then the other part of the rung will contain the base T, since A and T bond together.

To understand how DNA can make copies of itself, consider the following sequence of bases on one strand of the DNA molecule—GGTCTC. Since A and T bond together and G and C bond together, then the corresponding sequence of bases on the other strand of the DNA molecule is CCAGAG. The DNA molecule can separate into two separate strands. Once separate, each strand will attract free-floating bases. The strand GGTCTC will attract the bases CCAGAG, and the strand CCAGAG will attract the bases GGTCTC. When the new bases have attached themselves to the original strands, the result is two identical DNA molecules. This process is diagrammed in Figure 2.2. Keep in mind that

A — T
G — C

RNA The molecule that functions to carry out the instructions for protein synthesis specified by the DNA molecule.

messenger RNA The form of RNA that transports the genetic instructions from the DNA molecule to the site of protein synthesis.

transfer RNA A free-floating molecule that is attracted to a strand of messenger RNA, resulting in the synthesis of a protein chain.

Exon A section of DNA that codes for the amino acids that make up proteins. It is contrasted with an intron.

Intron A section of DNA that does not code for the amino acids that make up proteins. It is contrasted with an exon.

Figure 2.3

Computer representation of the DNA molecule. (© Will & Demi McIntyre/Photo Researchers, Inc.)

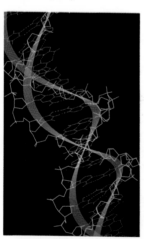

this description is somewhat oversimplified—in reality, the process is biochemically much more complex.

The ability of the DNA molecule to control protein synthesis also involves the attraction of complementary bases, but with the help of another molecule—ribonucleic acid, or **RNA** for short. In simple terms, RNA serves as the messenger for the information coded by the DNA molecule. One major difference between DNA and RNA is that in RNA the base A attracts a base called U (uracil) instead of T.

Consider the DNA base sequence GGT. In protein synthesis, the DNA molecule separates into two strands, and one strand (containing CCA) becomes inactive. The active strand, GGT, attracts free-floating bases to form a strand of **messenger RNA.** Since A bonds with T and G bonds with C, this strand consists of the sequence CCA. This strand then travels to the site of protein synthesis. Once there, the strand of messenger RNA transfers its information by attracting **transfer RNA,** which is a free-floating molecule. The sequence of messenger RNA containing the sequence CCA attracts a transfer RNA molecule with a complementary sequence—GGU. The result is that the amino acid proline (specified by the RNA sequence GGU or the DNA sequence GGT) is included in the chain of amino acids making up a particular protein. To summarize, one strand of the DNA molecule produces the complementary strand of messenger RNA, which then travels to the site of protein synthesis and attracts a complementary strand of transfer RNA, which carries the specified amino acid. This process is illustrated for the DNA sequence GGTCTC in Figure 2.4.

In many organisms (including humans) in which the DNA is contained in a separate part of the cell (the nucleus), the entire process is a bit more complicated. Not all of the DNA sequence is translated into amino acids. During the final stage of messenger RNA creation, sections are "cut out" and are not included in the mature messenger RNA. Thus, a sequence of DNA can contain both sections that code for amino acids that make up proteins (called **exons**) and sections that do not code for amino acids that make up proteins (called **introns**) (Figure 2.5). The evolutionary significance of the noncoding regions is not known at present.

This simplified discussion shows the basic nature of the structure and functions of the DNA molecule. More advanced discussion can be found in most genetics textbooks. For our purposes, however, the broad view will suffice. If we consider DNA as a "code," we can then look at the processes of transmission and change of information without actually having to consider the exact biochemical mechanisms.

Chromosomes and Genes

The DNA is contained within the nucleus of each cell. Another form of DNA, contained in a part of the cell called the mitochondria, is discussed later in Chapter 13. The DNA sequences are bound together by

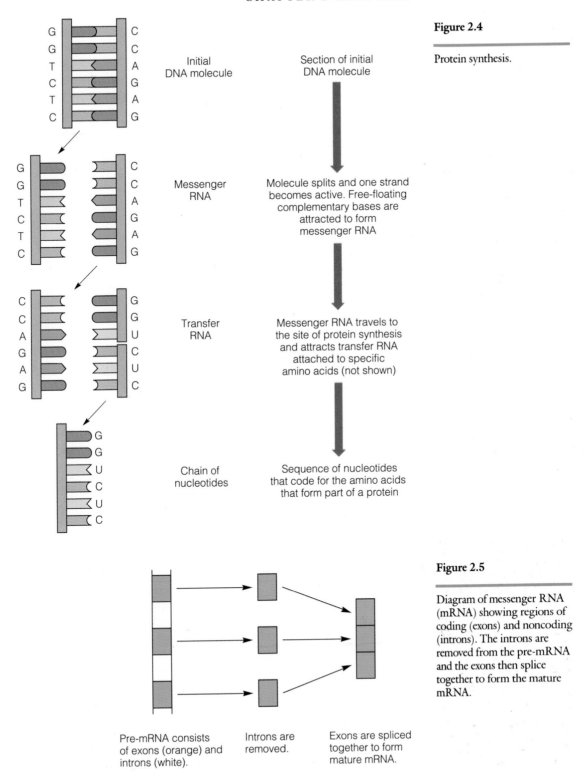

Figure 2.4

Protein synthesis.

Initial
DNA molecule

Section of initial
DNA molecule

Messenger
RNA

Molecule splits and one strand
becomes active. Free-floating
complementary bases are
attracted to form
messenger RNA

Transfer
RNA

Messenger RNA travels to
the site of protein synthesis
and attracts transfer RNA
attached to specific
amino acids (not shown)

Chain of
nucleotides

Sequence of nucleotides
that code for the amino acids
that form part of a protein

Figure 2.5

Diagram of messenger RNA
(mRNA) showing regions of
coding (exons) and noncoding
(introns). The introns are
removed from the pre-mRNA
and the exons then splice
together to form the mature
mRNA.

Pre-mRNA consists
of exons (orange) and
introns (white).

Introns are
removed.

Exons are spliced
together to form
mature mRNA.

chromosome Long strand of DNA sequences.

gene The section of DNA responsible for a given biological function.

hemoglobin The molecule in blood cells that transports oxygen.

structural genes Genes that code for the production of proteins.

regulatory genes Genes that code for the regulation of such biological processes as growth and development.

proteins in long strands called **chromosomes** that are found within the nucleus of each cell. With the exception of those in the sex cells (egg and sperm), chromosomes occur in pairs. Most body cells contain both members of these pairs. Different species have different numbers of chromosomes. For example, humans have 23 pairs, chimpanzees have 24 pairs, fruit flies have 4 pairs, and certain plant species have thousands of pairs. There is no relationship between the number of chromosome pairs a species has and its intelligence or biological complexity.

With certain exceptions, each cell in the human body contains a complete set of chromosomes and DNA. Nerve cells contain the DNA for bone cells and vice versa. Some type of regulation takes place within different cells to ensure that only certain genes are expressed in the right places, but the exact nature of this regulation is not known completely at present.

Structural and regulatory genes. A **gene** is defined as the segment of DNA responsible for a certain function, such as the production of a given protein (Sutton and Wagner 1985). For example, the **hemoglobin** molecule in your blood (which transports oxygen) is made up of four protein chains—two identical alpha chains and two identical beta chains. For each chain, there are sections of the human DNA containing the genetic code for the proteins in that chain. Genes that code for the production of a protein are known as **structural genes.**

Aside from manufacture of proteins, another function of genes is the regulation of biological processes. For example, consider the fact that in many humans the enzyme needed to digest milk sugar stops being produced several years after birth. Or consider the fact that sexual maturation in humans occurs during adolescence and not in infancy. Many biological characteristics are subject to regulation in terms of when they take effect or are expressed. Genes that are responsible for this regulation are known as **regulatory genes,** and they act by turning other genes on or off at the appropriate time.

Regulatory genes may have great evolutionary significance. For example, regulatory genes may help explain the great physical differences between chimpanzees and humans even though over 98 percent of their structural genes are identical. The major genetic difference between humans and chimpanzees may be caused by regulatory genes, which act on timing of growth and development, and could lead to differences in brain size, facial structures, and other physical features.

A possible example of regulatory genes is the absence of teeth in birds. Evolutionary analysis has concluded that modern birds evolved from primitive reptiles. One major change in this evolution is that birds have no teeth (other than the egg tooth they use in hatching). In 1980, however, scientists were able to induce the tissue of a hen to grow teeth! Teeth are produced by certain outer embryonic tissues forming the enamel and other inner tissues forming the dentin underneath. In what appears at first to be a bizarre experiment, Kollar and Fisher (1980) combined the outer tissues of a hen with the inner tissues of a mouse. These grafts produced dentin and teeth. Modern birds lack the necessary type of outer tissue to form dentin but still have the capacity to form it when we combine it in the laboratory with the appropriate tissue from another animal (the mouse, in this case). This experiment shows that the genetic code for teeth still exists in birds, but it is turned off, most likely by some combination of regulatory genes.

Another example suggesting the action of regulatory genes is the lack of five toes in horses. Modern horses have one single toe, although occasionally horses are born with two or three toes (Gould 1983). It appears that horses still have the genetic code for additional toes, but these instructions are turned off.

During the 1980s a group of regulatory genes known as **homeobox genes** was discovered. These genes encode a sequence of 60 amino acids that regulate embryonic development. Specifically, they subdivide a developing embryo into different regions from head to tail that then form limbs and other structures. One fascinating aspect of this discovery is that these genes are similar in many organisms, such as insects, mice, and humans. Preliminary research suggests that the process of embryonic development into head, trunk, and tail may have occurred only once in evolution (De Robertis et al. 1990; Marx 1992).

Mitosis and meiosis. The DNA molecule provides for the transmission of genetic information. Production of proteins and regulation are only two aspects of information transfer. Since organisms start life as a single cell that subsequently multiplies, it is essential that the genetic information within the initial cell is transferred to all future cells. The ability of DNA to replicate itself is involved in the process of cell replication, known as **mitosis** (Figure 2.6). When a cell divides, each chromosome duplicates and then splits. Each chromosome has replicated itself, so that when the cell finishes dividing, the result is two cells with the full set of chromosomes.

The process is different when information is passed on from one generation to the next. The genetic code is passed on from parents to offspring through the sex cells; the sperm in males and the egg in females. The sex cells, however, do not contain the full set of chromosomes but only one chromosome from each pair (i.e., only one-half of the set). If both chromosomes in each pair were passed on, your children would have 23 pairs from both you and your mate, for a total of 46 pairs. Your children's children would receive 46 pairs from each parent, for a total of 92 pairs. If this process continued, there would soon not be enough room in a cell for all of the chromosome pairs!

Sex cells contain only one of each pair of chromosomes. Whereas your other body cells have a total of 46 chromosomes (2 each for 23 pairs), your sex cells contain only 23 chromosomes (1 from each pair). When you have a child, you contribute 23 chromosomes, and your mate contributes

homeobox genes A group of regulatory genes that encode a sequence of 60 amino acids regulating embryonic development.

mitosis The process of replication of chromosomes in body cells.

Figure 2.6

The process of mitosis, the formation of body cells. Each chromosome copies itself, the attached copies line up in the cell, and the original and copy split when the cell divides. The result is two identical cells. (From *Human Antiquity: An Introduction to Physical Anthropology and Archaeology,* 2d ed., by Kenneth Feder and Michael Park, Fig 4.2. Copyright © 1993 by Mayfield Publishing Company)

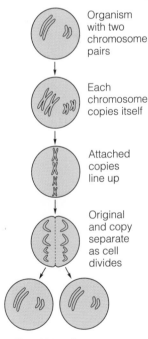

Organism with two chromosome pairs

Each chromosome copies itself

Attached copies line up

Original and copy separate as cell divides

Daughter cells are copies of parent cell

Figure 2.7

The process of meiosis, the formation of sex cells. Meiosis begins in the same way as mitosis: each chromosome makes a copy of itself. The pairs of chromosomes then segregate, forming four sex cells, each with one chromosome rather than a pair of chromosomes. (Adapted from *Human Antiquity: An Introduction to Physical Anthropology and Archaeology*, 2d ed., by Kenneth Feder and Michael Park, Fig. 4.2. Copyright © 1993 by Mayfield Publishing Company)

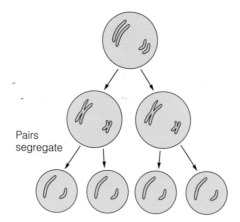

Pairs segregate

Each sex cell has half the normal number of chromosomes

meiosis The creation of sex cells by replication of chromosomes followed by two cell divisions.

Figure 2.8

All 23 pairs of chromosomes typically found in a human being. This set of chromosomes came from a man—note the 23rd pair has an X chromosome and a Y chromosome.   (© CNRI/Science Photo Library/Photo Researchers, Inc.)

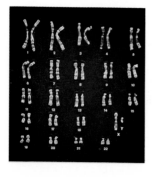

23 chromosomes. Your child then has the normal complement of 46 chromosomes in 23 pairs.

Sex cells are created through the process of **meiosis** (Figure 2.7). Basically, this involves the replication of chromosomes followed by cell division, followed by another cell division without an intervening round of replication. In sperm, the result is that four sex cells are produced from the initial set of 23 pairs of chromosomes. The process is similar in egg cells except that only one of the four progeny cells is functional.

The process of meiosis is extremely important in understanding genetic inheritance. Since only one of each pair of chromosomes is found in a functional sex cell, this means that a person contributes half of his or her offspring's genes. The other half comes from the other parent. Usually, each human child has a full set of 23 chromosome pairs, one of each pair from each parent (Figure 2.8).

Mendelian Genetics

Many of the facts known about genetic inheritance were discovered over a century before the structure of DNA was known. Although people knew where babies came from and noted the close resemblance of parents and children, the mechanisms of inheritance were unknown until the nineteenth century. An Austrian priest, Gregor Mendel (1822–1884), carried out an extensive series of experiments in plant breeding. His carefully tabulated results provided the basis of what we know about the mechanisms of genetic inheritance.

Before Mendel's research, it was commonly assumed that inheritance involved the blending together of genetic information in the egg and sperm. The genetic material was thought to mix together in the same way that different color paints mix together. Mendel's experiments showed a different pattern of inheritance—the genetic information is inherited in discrete units (genes). These genes do not blend together in an offspring.

In one experiment, Mendel crossed pea plants whose seeds were yellow with pea plants whose seeds were green (Figure 2.9). Under the idea of blending, one might expect all offspring to have mustard-colored seeds—a mixture of the yellow and green. In reality, Mendel found that all the offspring plants had yellow seeds. This discovery suggested that somehow one trait (yellow seed color) dominated in its effects.

When Mendel crossed the plants in this new generation together, he found that some of their offspring had yellow seeds and some had green seeds. Somehow the genetic information for green seeds had been hidden for a generation and then appeared again. Mendel counted how many there were of each color. The ratio of plants with yellow seeds to those with green seeds was very close to a 3:1 ratio. This finding suggested to Mendel that a regular process occurred during inheritance that could be explained in terms of simple mathematical principles. With these, and other, results, Mendel formulated several principles of inheritance. Though Mendel's

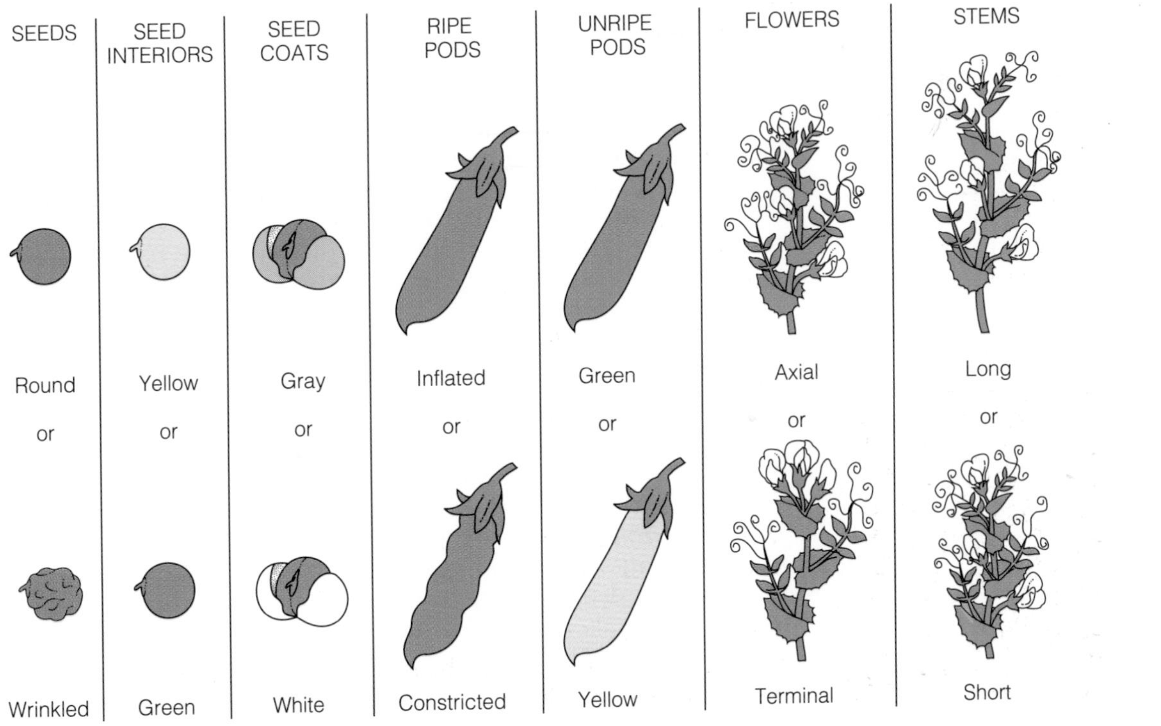

Figure 2.9

The seven phenotypic characteristics investigated by Gregor Mendel in his experiments on breeding in pea plants. Each of the seven traits has two distinct phenotypes.

SEEDS	SEED INTERIORS	SEED COATS	RIPE PODS	UNRIPE PODS	FLOWERS	STEMS
Round	Yellow	Gray	Inflated	Green	Axial	Long
or	or	or	or	or	or	or
Wrinkled	Green	White	Constricted	Yellow	Terminal	Short

locus The specific location of a gene on a chromosome.

allele The alternative form of a gene that occurs at a given locus. Some genes have only one allele, some have two, and some have many alternative forms. Alleles occur in pairs, one on each chromosome.

Mendel's Law of Segregation Sex cells contain one of each pair of alleles.

genotype The genetic endowment of an individual from the two alleles present at a given locus.

homozygous Both alleles at a given locus are identical.

heterozygous The two alleles at a given locus are different.

phenotype The observable appearance of a given genotype in the organism.

dominant allele An allele that masks the effect of the other allele (which is recessive) in a heterozygous genotype.

recessive allele An allele whose effect is masked by the other allele (which is dominant) in a heterozygous genotype.

work remained virtually unknown during his lifetime, his work was rediscovered in 1900. In recognition of his accomplishments, the science of genetic inheritance is called Mendelian genetics.

Genotypes and Phenotypes

The specific position of a gene on a chromosome is called a **locus** (plural **loci**). The alternative forms of a gene at a locus are called **alleles.** For example, a number of different genetic systems control the types of molecules present on the surface of red blood cells. One of these blood groups, known as the MN system, determines whether or not you have M molecules, N molecules, or both on the surface of your red blood cells. The MN system has two forms, or alleles—*M* and *N*. Another blood group system, the ABO system, has three alleles—*A*, *B*, and *O*. Even though three different forms of this gene are found in the human species, each individual only has two genes at the ABO locus. Some genetic loci have only one allele, some have two, and some have three or more.

This is the source of variation

Mendel's Law of Segregation. The genetic basis of any trait is determined by an allele from each parent. At any given locus there are two alleles, one on each member of the chromosome pair. One allele came from the mother and one allele came from the father. Alleles occur in pairs, and when sex cells are formed only one of each pair is passed on (**Mendel's Law of Segregation**).

The two alleles at a locus in an individual specify the **genotype,** the genetic endowment of an individual. The two alleles might be the same form or might be different. If the alleles from both parents are the same, the genotype is **homozygous.** If the alleles from the parents are different, the genotype is **heterozygous.**

The actual observable trait is known as the **phenotype.** The relationship between genotype and phenotype is affected by the relationship between the two alleles present at any locus. If the genotype is homozygous, both alleles contain the same genetic information. What happens in heterozygotes, where the two alleles are different?

Dominant and recessive alleles. In a heterozygote, an allele is **dominant** when it masks the effect of the other allele at a given locus. The opposite of a dominant allele is a **recessive** allele, whose effect may be masked. A simple example helps make these concepts clearer. One genetic trait in human beings is the ability to taste certain substances, including a chemical known as PTC. The ability to taste PTC appears to be controlled by a single locus and is also affected to some extent by environmental factors such as diet. There are two alleles for the PTC-tasting trait: the allele *T,* which is also called the "taster" allele, and the allele *t,* which is also called the "non-taster" allele. Given these two alleles, three combinations of alleles can be present in an individual. A person could have the *T* allele from both parents, which would give the genotype *TT*. A person could have a *t* allele from both parents, giving the genotype *tt*. Both *TT* and *tt* are homozygous genotypes because both alleles are the same. The third possible genotype occurs when the allele from one parent is *T* and the allele from the other parent is *t*. This gives the heterozygous genotype of *Tt*. It does not matter which parent provided the *T* allele and which provided the *t* allele; the genotype is the same in both cases.

What phenotype is associated with each genotype? The phenotype is affected by both the relationship of the two alleles and by the environment. For the moment, let us ignore possible environmental effects. Consider the *T* allele as providing instructions that allow tasting and the *t* allele as providing instructions for nontasting. If the genotype is *TT*, then both alleles code for tasting and the phenotype is obviously "taster." Likewise, if the genotype is *tt*, then both alleles code for nontasting and the phenotype is "nontaster." What of the heterozygote *Tt*? One allele codes for tasting and one codes for nontasting. Does this mean that both will be expressed, and a person will have the tasting ability but not as much as a person with genotype *TT*? Or does it mean that only one of the alleles is expressed? If so, which one?

There is no way you can answer this question using only the data provided so far. You must know if either the *T* or *t* allele is dominant, and this can be determined only through experimentation. For this trait, it turns out that the *T* allele is dominant and the *t* allele is recessive. When both alleles are present in a genotype, the *T* allele masks the effect of the *t* allele. Therefore, a person with the genotype *Tt* has the "taster" phenotype (Table 2.2). The relationship between genotype and phenotype does not take into consideration known environmental effects on PTC tasting. Under certain types of diet, some "tasters" will show less ability to taste weaker concentrations of the PTC chemical.

The action of dominant and recessive alleles explains why Mendel's second-generation pea plants all had yellow seeds. The allele for yellow seed color is dominant, and the allele for green seed color is recessive.

Dominance and recessiveness refers only to the effect an allele has in producing a phenotype. These terms say nothing about the frequency or value of an allele. Dominant alleles can be common or rare, harmful or helpful.

Codominant alleles. Some alleles are **codominant,** meaning that when two different alleles are present in a genotype, then both are expressed. That is, neither allele is dominant or recessive. One example of a codominant genetic system in humans is the MN blood group, mentioned before. There are two alleles—*M*, which codes for the production of M molecules, and *N*, which codes for the production of N molecules. Therefore, there are three possible genotypes: *MM, MN,* and *NN*.

The phenotypes for the homozygous genotypes are easy to determine. Individuals with genotype *MM* have two alleles coding for the production

codominant When both alleles affect the phenotype of a heterozygous genotype and neither is dominant over the other.

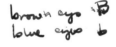
brown eyes *B*
blue eyes *b*

T A B L E 2.2
Genotypes and Phenotypes for PTC Tasting

Genotype	Phenotype
TT	Taster
Tt	Taster
tt	Nontaster

Because *T* is dominant, the genotypes *TT* and *Tt* both produce the taster phenotype. This example is somewhat oversimplified, since in reality the phenotype can also be affected by diet.

TABLE 2.3
Genotypes and Phenotypes of the MN Blood Group System

Genotype	Phenotype
MM	M molecules
MN	M and N molecules
NN	N molecules

The *M* and *N* alleles are codominant, so they are both expressed in the heterozygote.

TABLE 2.4
Genotypes and Phenotypes of the ABO System

The ABO system has three alleles (*A, B, O*) that code for the type of molecule on the surface of the red blood cells (A, B, and O molecules). The *A* and *B* alleles are codominant, and the O allele is recessive to both *A* and *B*.

Genotype	Phenotype
AA	A
AO	A
BB	B
BO	B
AB	AB
OO	O

Note: There are also different forms of the *A* allele not shown here (A_1, A_2, etc.).

of M molecules and will have the M molecule phenotype. Likewise, individuals with the genotype *NN* will have two *N* alleles and will have the N molecule phenotype. But what of the heterozygote genotype *MN*? Again, there is no way to answer this question without knowing the pattern of dominance. Experimentation has shown that the *M* and *N* alleles are codominant. When both are present (genotype *MN*), then both are expressed. Therefore, an individual with genotype *MN* will produce both M and N molecules. Their phenotype is MN, indicating the presence of both molecules (Table 2.3).

In complex genetic systems with more than two alleles some alleles may be dominant and some may be codominant. A good example of dominance and codominance in the same system is the ABO blood group. The alleles, genotypes, and phenotypes of this system are described in Table 2.4.

Predicting Offspring Distributions

When parents each contribute a sex cell, they are passing on only one allele at each locus to their offspring. The possible genotypes and phenotypes of the offspring reflect a 50 percent chance of transmittal for any given allele of a parent. This simple statement of probability allows prediction of the likely distribution of genotypes and phenotypes among the offspring.

Figure 2.10 illustrates this method using the MN blood group system for two hypothetical parents, each with the genotype *MN*. Each parent has a 50 percent chance of passing on an *M* allele and a 50 percent chance of

Figure 2.10

Inheritance of MN blood group phenotypes for two parents both with *MN* genotype.

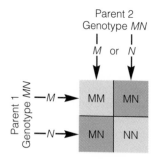

passing on an *N* allele. Given these probabilities, we expect one out of four offspring (25 percent) to have genotype *MM,* and therefore phenotype M. In two out of four cases (50 percent), we expect the offspring to have genotype *MN,* and therefore phenotype MN. Finally, in one out of four cases (25 percent), we expect the offspring to have genotype *NN,* and therefore phenotype N. Of course, different parental genotypes will give a different set of offspring probabilities.

Remember that these distributions give the expected probabilities. The exact distributions will not always occur because each offspring is an independent event. If the hypothetical couple first has a child with the genotype *MN,* this will not influence the genotype of their next child. The distributions give the proportions expected for a very large number of offspring.

To help understand the difference between expected and actual distribution, consider coin flipping. If you flip a coin, you expect to get heads 50 percent of the time and tails 50 percent of the time. If you flip 10 coins one after another, you expect to get five heads and five tails. You may, however, get four heads and six tails.

Analysis of possible offspring shows that recessive alleles can produce an interesting effect; it is possible for children to have a different phenotype than either of the parents. For example, consider two parents both with the genotype *Tt* for the PTC-tasting locus. Both parents have the "taster" phenotype. What genotypes and phenotypes will their children be likely to have? The expected genotype distribution is 25 percent *TT,* 50 percent *Tt,* and 25 percent *tt.*

Given this distribution of genotypes, what is the probable distribution of phenotypes? Genotypes *TT* and *Tt* are both "tasters," and therefore 75 percent of the children are expected to also be "tasters." Twenty-five percent of the children, however, are expected to have the genotype *tt* and will therefore have the "nontaster" phenotype. These children would have a different phenotype than either parent. A recessive trait can therefore remain hidden in one generation. This fact has great implications for genetic disease. For example, the disease cystic fibrosis occurs when a person is homozygous for a recessive allele. Therefore, two parents who have the heterozygous genotype do not manifest the disease but have a 25 percent chance of giving birth to a child who has the recessive homozygous condition, and therefore the disease.

Bb x Bb

↓

bb

Chromosomes and Inheritance

Alleles occur in pairs. Mendel showed that when alleles are passed on from parents to offspring, only one of each pair is contributed by each parent. The specific chromosome at any pair that is passed on is random. There is a 50 percent chance of either chromosome being passed on each time a sex cell is created.

Mendel's Law of Independent Assortment
The segregation of any pair of chromosomes does not affect the probability of segregation for other pairs of chromosomes.

linkage When alleles on the same chromosome are inherited together.

crossing over When segments of DNA switch between pairs of chromosomes.

Mendel's Law of Independent Assortment. Mendel's experiments revealed another aspect of probability in inheritance and the creation of sex cells. **Mendel's Law of Independent Assortment** states that the segregation of any pair of chromosomes does not influence the segregation of any other pair of chromosomes. In other words, chromosomes from separate pairs are inherited independently.

For example, imagine an organism with three chromosome pairs that we will label A, B, and C. To keep the members of each pair straight in our minds, label the chromosome of each pair as 1 or 2. This hypothetical organism has six chromosomes: A1, A2, B1, B2, C1, and C2. During the creation of a sex cell the A1 chromosome has a 50 percent chance of occurring, and so does the A2 chromosome. This same logic extends to the B and C chromosome pairs. Mendel's Law of Independent Assortment states that the segregation of one pair of chromosomes does not affect the segregation of any other pair of chromosomes. It is just as likely to have a sex cell containing A1, B1, and C1 as it is to have a sex cell containing A1, B1, and C2. There are eight possible and equally likely outcomes for the sex cells: A1B1C1, A1B1C2, A1B2C1, A1B2C2, A2B1C1, A2B1C2, A2B2C1, A2B2C2. Given that any individual could have any one of the eight possible sex cells from both parents, the total number of combinations of offspring in this hypothetical organism is $8 \times 8 = 64$.

Independent assortment provides a powerful mechanism for shuffling different combinations of chromosomes and thus introduces great potential for genetic diversity. In humans, who have 23 chromosome pairs, the numbers are even more impressive. From any given individual there are $2^{23} = 8,388,608$ possible combinations of sex cells. This means that two parents could produce a maximum of 70,368,744,177,664 genetically unique offspring!

Linkage. A major implication of Mendel's Law of Independent Assortment is that genes are inherited independently. This is true only to the extent that genes are on different chromosomes. Remember, it is the pairs of chromosomes that separate during meiosis, not each individual pair of alleles. When alleles are on the same chromosome, they are inherited together. This is called **linkage.** Linked alleles are not inherited independently since they are, by definition, on the same chromosome.

Crossing Over. An exception to the rule of linkage is **crossing over,** the switching of segments of DNA between the chromosome pairs during meiosis. Suppose, for example, that there are two genetic loci on the same chromosome, the first having alleles *A* or *a* and the second having alleles *B* or *b*. Suppose that you have the genotypes *Aa* and *Bb* with one chromosome containing the *A* allele and the *B* allele, and the other chromosome having the *a* allele and the *b* allele. Since these two loci are both on the same chromosome, you would expect linkage to cause the two systems to be inherited together. That is, your possible sex cells would have *A* and *B*, or *a* and *b*. Any offspring inheriting the *A* allele would also be expected to

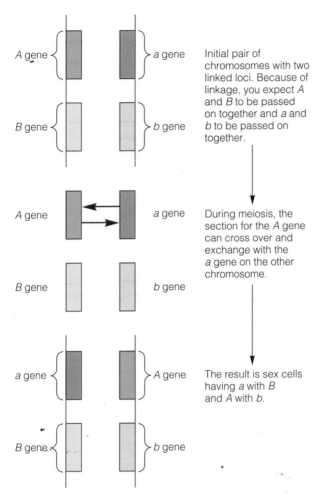

Figure 2.11

Crossing over in chromosomes.

A gene — *a* gene — Initial pair of chromosomes with two linked loci. Because of linkage, you expect *A* and *B* to be passed on together and *a* and *b* to be passed on together.

B gene — *b* gene

A gene — *a* gene — During meiosis, the section for the *A* gene can cross over and exchange with the *a* gene on the other chromosome.

B gene — *b* gene

a gene — *A* gene — The result is sex cells having *a* with *B* and *A* with *b*.

B gene — *b* gene

inherit the *B* allele. Likewise, any offspring inheriting the *a* allele would also inherit the *b* allele. During meiosis, chromosome pairs sometimes exchange pieces, a process known as crossing over. For example, the segment of DNA containing the *a* allele could switch with the segment of DNA containing the *A* allele on the other chromosome. Therefore, you could have a sex cell with *a* and *B,* or a sex cell with *A* and *b* (Figure 2.11). Crossing over does not change the genetic material. The alleles are still the same, but they can occur in different combinations. Crossing over provides yet another mechanism for increasing genetic variation by providing new combinations of alleles.

Sex chromosomes and sex determination. One of the 23 pairs of human chromosomes is called the sex chromosome pair because these chromosomes contain the genetic information determining the individual's sex. There are two forms of sex chromosomes, X and Y. Females have two X chromosomes (XX), and males have one X and one Y chromosome

(XY). Recent research has shown that sex determination is related to a section of the Y chromosome known as the SRY (Sex-determining Region Y) gene that triggers the beginning of male fetal development (Koopman et al. 1991).

The Y chromosome is much smaller than the X chromosome. Almost all genes found on X are therefore not found on Y. This means that males possess only one allele for certain traits because their Y chromosome lacks the corresponding section of DNA. Therefore, males will manifest a trait given only one allele, whereas females require the same allele from both parents to show the trait. An example of this sex difference is hemophilia, a genetic disorder that interferes with the normal process of blood clotting. The allele for hemophilia is recessive and is found on the segment of the X chromosome that has no corresponding portion on the Y chromosome. For females to be hemophiliac, they must inherit two copies of this allele, one from each parent. This is unlikely since the hemophilia allele is rare. Males, on the other hand, need only inherit one copy on the X chromosome from the mother. As a result, hemophilia is more common in males than females.

The Genetics of Complex Physical Traits

The discussion of genetics thus far has focused on simple discrete genetic traits. Traits such as the MN blood group are genetically "simple" because they result from the action of a single locus with a clear-cut mode of inheritance. These traits are also discrete, meaning that they produce a finite number of phenotypes. For example, you either have the M, N, or MN phenotype for the MN blood group system; you cannot have an intermediate phenotype. Your MN phenotype is also produced entirely from genetic factors. It is not influenced by the environment. Except for a complete blood transfusion, your MN blood group phenotype is the same all of your life.

These simple discrete traits are very useful for demonstrating the basic principles of Mendelian inheritance. It is not wise, however, to think of all biological traits as resulting from a single locus, exhibiting a finite number of phenotypes, or not being affected by the environment. Many of the characteristics of interest in human evolution, such as skin color, body size, brain size, and intelligence, do not fall into this simple category. Such traits have a complex mode of inheritance in that one or more genes may contribute to the phenotype and they may be affected by the environment. The combined action of genetics and environment produces traits with a continuous distribution. An example is human height. People do not come in three different heights (short, medium, and tall), nor five, nor twenty. Height can take on an infinite number of phenotypes. People can be 1,700 mm tall, 1,701 mm tall, and any value in between, such as 1,700.3 mm or 1,700.65 mm.

Complex traits tend to produce more individuals with average values than extreme values. It is not uncommon to find human males between

1,676 and 1,981 mm (5.5 and 6.5 feet) tall. It is much rarer to find someone taller than 2,134 mm (7 feet). A typical distribution of a complex trait such as human height is shown in Figure 2.12.

Polygenic traits and pleiotropy. Many complex traits are **polygenic,** the result of two or more loci. When several loci act to control a trait, many different genotypes and phenotypes can result. A number of physical characteristics, such as human skin color and height, may be polygenic. A single allele can also have multiple effects on an organism. When an allele has effects on multiple traits, this is referred to as **pleiotropy.** In chickens, one of the alleles that causes white feather color also acts to slow down overall body growth (Lerner and Libby 1976). In humans, the sickle cell allele affects the structure of the blood's hemoglobin and also leads to changes in overall body growth and health.

The concepts of polygenic traits and pleiotropy are important in considering the interrelated nature of biological systems. Analysis of simple discrete traits on a gene-by-gene basis is useful in understanding genetics, but it should not lead you to think that any organism is simply a collection of single, independent loci.

Figure 2.13 shows several different models of genetic interaction. Figure 2.13a represents the nature of some simple genetic traits, whereby each cause has a single effect. Figure 2.13b represents a polygenic trait, whereby many loci contribute to a single effect. Pleiotropic effects are shown in Figure 2.13c, whereby a single allele has multiple effects. Figure 2.13d is the most realistic model for many complex traits; each allele has multiple effects, and each effect has multiple causes. In this case, the trait is caused by polygenic and pleiotropic effects. To complicate matters, consider variations of this model in which not all alleles have the same

polygenic Refers to a genetic trait affected by two or more loci.

pleiotropy When a single allele can have multiple effects on an organism.

Figure 2.12

The distribution of a continuous trait. Most individuals have a value close to the average for the population. This type of curve is called a normal distribution.

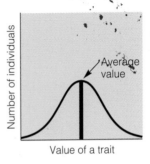

Figure 2.13

The relationship between a gene and a biological effect. (a) Single gene, single effect. (b) Polygenic trait. (c) Pleiotropy. (d) A polygenic trait and pleiotropy.

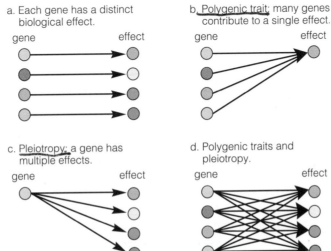

a. Each gene has a distinct biological effect.

b. Polygenic trait; many genes contribute to a single effect.

c. Pleiotropy; a gene has multiple effects.

d. Polygenic traits and pleiotropy.

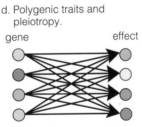

major genes Genes that have the primary effect on the phenotypic distribution of a complex trait.

restriction fragment length polymorphism A genetic trait defined in terms of the length of DNA fragments produced through cutting by certain enzymes.

effect, some alleles are dominant and some are not, and environmental factors act to obscure what we actually observe. It is no wonder that the study of genetics of complex traits is extremely difficult, requiring sophisticated mathematical methods.

Major genes. Recently, more attention has been given to **major genes.** In a major gene model the majority of genetic variation is due to a single locus. The continuous distribution of the trait is the result of environmental effects and can be enhanced by the smaller effect of other loci. In contrast to certain polygenic models whereby all loci contribute equally, a major gene model postulates that a single locus has the greatest effect. A trait controlled by a major gene will often show the same type of distribution as a polygenic trait (see Figure 2.12). Developments in statistical analysis have allowed tests for major genes; in a recent study, Price and colleagues (1990) found that the tendency to be overweight is strongly affected by a major recessive gene.

Recent Developments in Genetics

The science of genetics is growing at a fantastic rate. New laboratory methods, combined with new statistical approaches and computer technology, have enabled great advances in both molecular and Mendelian genetics. Many of these advances are only now becoming part of the tools of biological anthropologists. Continued developments will not only provide greater insight into patterns of human variation and evolution but will also contribute to medical knowledge, such as a greater understanding of the genetic basis of disease.

RFLPs. Some newly discovered forms of genetic variation are known as **restriction fragment length polymorphisms (RFLPs).** Analysis of RFLPs allows detection of differences in DNA sequences among individuals. Certain enzymes produced by different species of bacteria, known as *restriction enzymes,* bind to sections of DNA and cut the DNA sequence at a given point. A difference in a person's DNA sequence will change the specific point at which it is cut. Thus, different DNA sequences will produce different *lengths* of the DNA fragments (White and Lalouel 1988). The ability to directly analyze small sections of DNA has both anthropological and medical implications, particularly the ability to construct a "map" of all human genes.

Geneticists look at combinations of alleles in order to identify sections of DNA associated with various functions. One common application is the attempt to look at the linkage between known genes and genetic diseases. Such linkage provides information on which part of what chromosome the genes affecting the disease are located. The more linkages that can be established, the better the chance of locating a specific region related to the disease of interest. RFLPs aid in this effort by providing a rich source of genetic markers that are likely to vary a lot among individu-

als. The linkage approach works best when any given individual is heterozygous for a given marker. This approach is enhanced by a subset of
RFLPs that are extremely variable, known as the variable number of tan-
dem repeat loci (VNTR). These loci code for sections of DNA that appear
to have no purpose but are repeated numerous times along chromosomes.
The net result of such high variability is an increased ability to find linkages
with other genetic characteristics, especially genes related to disease. Other
applications include mapping of all human genes, paternity testing, and
prenatal diagnosis (Williams 1989; Chakraborty and Daiger 1991).

Polymerase chain reaction. The ongoing attempt to map human
genes (and those of other organisms) has been aided by the development
of a laboratory method known as **polymerase chain reaction (PCR).**
This technique involves the laboratory synthesis of millions of copies of
DNA fragments (Erlich et al. 1991). The methods of PCR are outside the
scope of this text. However, its implications are important. The method
has allowed rapid and relatively easy study of the molecular basis of genetics. Our ability to locate specific genes along chromosomes has been
increased tremendously. For biological anthropologists, PCR methods allow genetic variation to be analyzed from samples that are easy to collect
and transport—such as single plucked hairs!

Genetics and disease. The rapid development of methods of genetic
analysis has led to an increase in the number of loci that have been located
on human chromosomes. By July 1990 the Human Genome Project was
under way, with the purpose of mapping all human genes. At that point in
time, over 6,000 loci had been mapped (Stephens et al. 1990). However,
with an estimated 100,000 loci in humans, there is still a ways to go.

Genetic predisposition to a number of diseases has been mapped to
specific locations on human chromosomes. This information allows us to
identify more accurately an individual's risk for a given disease and can be
used as part of newly developing therapies based on insertion of new
genetic material into affected body cells (Anderson 1992). Diseases that
have been mapped include certain forms of muscular dystrophy (White
and Lalouel 1988), cystic fibrosis (Collins 1992), breast disease (Skolnick
et al. 1990), and breast cancer (Hall et al. 1990). Genetic analysis has also
found mutations affecting various diseases, such as Alzheimer's disease
(Murrell et al. 1991) and a variety of cancers (Malkin et al. 1990). Genetic
mapping does not necessarily mean that these diseases have a solitary
genetic basis—rather, they show genetic predisposition.

Mutations

As shown earlier, the process of genetic inheritance produces new
combinations of genes in offspring. The independent assortment of chro-

polymerase chain reaction A
laboratory method involving
laboratory synthesis of
millions of copies of DNA
fragments.

mosomes during meiosis and the action of crossing over both act to create new genetic combinations. They do not act to create any new genetic material. In order to explain past evolution, we need a mechanism for introducing new alleles and variation. The origin of new genetic variation was a problem to Darwin, but we now know new alleles are brought about through the process of mutation.

Evolutionary Significance of Mutations

A mutation is a change in the genetic code. Mutations are the ultimate source of all genetic variation. Mutations are caused by a number of environmental factors such as background radiation, which includes radiation from the earth's crust and cosmic rays. Such background radiation is all around us, in the air we breathe and the food we eat. Mutations may also be caused by heat and ingested substances such as caffeine.

A growing concern is the effect of environmental changes on mutation rates. Human-made radiation, as from certain industries, not only might be dangerous to exposed individuals but might also affect their future offspring by mutational effects in sex cells. Numerous studies of laboratory animals, such as fruit flies, have shown clearly that the mutation rate increases with exposure to radiation. Less is known about the effect of increased radiation on mutations in humans and other mammals. Studies of the children of survivors of the atomic bomb attacks in Japan at the end of World War II have so far failed to show definite evidence of any increase in the rate of mutations in sex cells (although mutations in body cells in the exposed parents were frequent). Given the definite evidence of radiation effects from experimental animals, this failure may reflect an inadequate sample size or other methodological difficulties in the human studies. Another possibility is that mammalian cells have a high capacity for DNA repair.

Mutations can take place in any cell of the body. To have evolutionary importance, however, the mutation must occur in a sex cell. A mutation in a skin cell on the end of your finger has no evolutionary significance because it will not be passed on to your offspring. Mutations in the body cells rarely have special significance, although some have been implicated in cancer and in the aging process (Lerner and Libby 1976).

Mutations are random. That is, there is no way of predicting when a specific mutation will take place, or what, if any, phenotypic effect it will have. All we can do is estimate the probability of a mutation occurring at a given locus over a given amount of time. The randomness of mutations also means that mutations do not appear when they might be needed. Many mosquitoes have adapted to insecticides because a mutation was present in the population that acted to confer some resistance to the insecticide. If that mutation had not been present, the mosquitoes would have died. The mosquitoes' need for a certain genetic variant had no effect on whether or not the mutation appeared.

Mutations can have different effects depending on the specific type of mutation and the environment. The conventional view of mutations has long been that they are mostly harmful. A classic analogy is the comparison of the genetic code with the engine of an automobile. If an engine part is changed at random, the most likely result is that the car will not operate, or at least not as well, as it did before the change.

Some mutations, however, are advantageous. They lead to change that improves the survival and reproduction of organisms. In recent decades, we have also discovered that some mutations are neutral. That is, the genetic change has no detectable effect on survival or reproduction. There is continued controversy among geneticists about the relative frequency of neutral mutations. Some claim that many mutations are neutral in their effect. Others note the difficulties in detecting the effects of many mutations.

Whether or not a mutation is neutral, advantageous, or disadvantageous depends in large part on the environment. Genetic variants that are harmful in certain environments might actually be helpful in other environments.

point mutation A type of mutation in which the sequence of bases of DNA in a single gene are changed.

chromosomal mutation A type of mutation in which large sections of chromosomes are changed. These changes include rearrangements, deletions, additions, movements, and changes in chromosome numbers.

sickle cell allele An allele of the hemoglobin locus. Individuals homozygous for the sickle cell allele have sickle cell anemia.

Types of Mutations

Mutations fall into two basic groups: point mutations and chromosomal mutations. **Point mutations** are changes in the sequence of bases in the DNA of a single gene. **Chromosomal mutations** are changes in chromosomes and involve large numbers of genes. These include deletions and additions of chromosomal segments, movement of chromosomal segments to new locations, and changes in chromosome number. In recent years, a potentially new type of mutation has been discovered. Some segments of DNA appear to be highly mobile, moving from location to location among the chromosomes. When inserted into different positions, these mobile elements cause changes in the functioning of the genetic code (Drake et al. 1983).

jumping genes. McClintock

Point mutations. When a DNA base is changed, a different amino acid is sometimes specified, which changes the protein structure. Some point mutations are neutral because they do not lead to any change in the specified amino acid. Referring back to Table 2.1, note that many amino acids are specified by different DNA base sequences. For example, the amino acid glycine is specified by the sequence CCA. If a mutation occurs in which the third base changes from an A to a G, the net result is the sequence CCG, which also specifies glycine. This hypothetical mutation leads to no biochemical change and is neutral.

Other changes in base sequences can lead to biochemical changes and affect the survival and reproduction of an individual. One widely studied point mutation is in the allele for the beta chain of the hemoglobin molecule. Here the normal hemoglobin allele has mutated to a form known as the **sickle cell allele.** The red blood cells produced in individuals with two copies of this mutant allele are misshapen and do not transport oxygen efficiently. When two sickle cell alleles are present, the result is a severe

monosymy When only one chromosome rather than a pair is present in body cells.

trisomy When three chromosomes rather than a pair occur in body cells.

form of anemia (sickle cell anemia) that leads to sickness and death. The specific cause of the sickle cell allele is a mutation in the sixth amino acid of the beta chain (out of 146 amino acids). The DNA for the normal beta hemoglobin allele contains instructions for the amino acid glutamic acid at this position (CTC). The point mutation causes the base T to be changed to an A, which specifies the amino acid valine (CAC). This small change affects the entire structure of the red blood cells and in turn the well-being of the individual.

Point mutations can also cause changes by deleting and adding to the sequence of base pairs. If a base is deleted or an extra base added to the sequence of DNA, the entire message will be changed.

Chromosomal mutations. Chromosomal mutations occur when a segment of a chromosome carrying more than one gene is changed. Sometimes the segment will contain thousands of genes. In some cases the entire chromosome is changed. These mutations can occur when an entire section of DNA is deleted or added. Sections of DNA can also change position along the chromosome, thus changing the genetic message. The entire chromosome can also be inverted. An entire chromosome from a pair can be lost (**monosymy** = one chromosome) or can occur in duplicate, giving three chromosomes (**trisomy**).

Several chromosomal mutations in humans are associated with specific mental and physical disorders. Down syndrome is a condition characterized by certain facial features (Figure 2.14), poor physical growth, and mental retardation (usually mild). Down syndrome is most often caused by the duplication of one of the 21st chromosome pair. Affected individuals have a total of 47 chromosomes, one more than the normal 46. Down syndrome can also be caused by mutations of the 21st chromosome. In some individuals the change involves the exchange of parts of the 21st chromosome with other chromosomes.

Several chromosomal mutations involve the sex chromosomes. One, known as Turner's syndrome, occurs when an individual has only one X chromosome instead of two. These individuals thus have only 45 chromosomes and develop as females. Those with Turner's syndrome are generally short, have undeveloped ovaries, and are sterile. Another condition, known as Klinefelter's syndrome, occurs in males with an extra X chromosome. Instead of the normal XY combination, these males have an XXY combination for a total of 47 chromosomes. They are characterized by small testes and reduced fertility.

Rates of Mutations

Specific mutations are relatively rare events, although the *exact* rate of mutations is difficult to determine in many cases. Part of the problem in determining the rate of point mutations is the fact that several different base sequences can specify the same amino acid. If there is no observable change, then the mutation will usually go unnoticed.

trisomy

Figure 2.14

Facial appearance of a child with Down syndrome. (Courtesy March of Dimes Birth Defect Foundation)

A mutation is also more apparent if it involves a dominant allele, since a heterozygote receiving one copy of the mutant allele will show the mutant phenotype. If a mutant allele is recessive, then phenotypic expression will require two copies of the mutant allele, which is a less common event. Recessive mutant alleles go unnoticed under these circumstances.

Another problem in identifying both point mutations and chromosomal mutations is that harmful mutations may result in spontaneous abortion (miscarriage) before pregnancy has been detected. Roughly 15 percent of all recognized conceptions result in spontaneous abortion, of which 50 percent can be traced to specific chromosomal mutations (Sutton and Wagner 1985). For such an event to be recorded, however, requires that a woman be aware that she is pregnant, which will take a month or more after conception. Some researchers feel that a large number of unrecognized conceptions are expelled spontaneously during the first few weeks after conception. If so, a prediction of mutation rates based on recognized conceptions will be an underestimate.

Despite these problems, research has provided estimates of a range in the rates of mutation. For point mutations in humans, this range is from 1 to 100 mutations per million sex cells (Lerner and Libby 1976). This translates to a probability between 0.000001 and 0.0001 of a mutation occurring at a given locus for a given sex cell.

Regardless of the specific mutation rates for a given gene or chromosome, one thing is clear—mutation rates are generally low. Given these low probabilities, it may be tempting to regard mutation as so rare that it has no special evolutionary significance. The problem with this reasoning is that the estimated rates refer to a *single* specific locus. Human chromosomes have many loci. The exact number is not known, but it has been estimated at roughly 100,000 (Woodward 1992). The probability that a specific locus will show a mutation in any individual is low, but the probability of *any* locus showing a mutation is much higher.

As an example, assume a mutation rate of 1 in 100,000 (0.00001) for 100,000 loci. Statistically there is a 63 percent chance of a person having at least 1 mutation. Now assume a small population of 25 people. Given the same mutation rate, the probability of finding at least 1 mutation in this population is over 99.999 percent.

Even though mutation is a rare event for any given locus, there is a high probability of at least one new mutation in each individual. When we consider the genetics of an entire population or species, the net result is that mutation is common within a single generation. In fact, many studies estimate that all of us carry at least one lethal recessive mutant allele.

Genetics and Behavior

Perhaps the most controversial topic in genetics is the question of the extent to which behavior is governed by genetic factors. The controversy arises not so much from academic debate but from the social implications, real and imagined, of this question. Problems arise out of a misunderstanding of the basic concepts of genetics or are produced by those seeking any "scientific" fact, regardless of truth, to support and further their own social or political agenda. Much of this controversy revolves around the concept of race, which is discussed in Chapter 6. The present section focuses on basic strategies involved in relating genes and behavior.

The Nature-Nurture Debate

Is a behavior, such as intelligence or shyness, caused by genes ("nature") or the physical and cultural environment ("nurture")? The debate of nature versus nurture has a long history in Western civilization. The prevalent view among scientists reflects not only current research but also the social and cultural climate of the times. Scientists are people, too, as susceptible to biases and prejudices as everyone else. A major lesson of the history of science is that cultural beliefs influence the methodology and interpretation of scientific results.

At the beginning of the twentieth century, the prevalent view was that "nature" was the more important determinant of many behaviors, particularly intelligence. This emphasis shifted to "nurture" during the period from the 1930s to the 1960s, when environmental factors were seen as being the most, if not the only, important factor.

Much of the debate over nature versus nurture is nonsense, however. Any attempt to relegate human behaviors to either genetics *or* environment is fruitless. Genes and environment are both important. The proper question is not which is more important, but rather how they interact.

For example, consider the nature of maternal behaviors. The studies of primate behavior discussed in Chapters 7 to 9 show clearly that maternal behaviors are in part the result of learning within a social context. Females with good mothers tend to be good mothers themselves. Chimpanzee females learn, and practice, maternal behaviors as part of socialization. Experiments with monkeys have shown that maternally deprived infants tend to grow up to be poor parents. Learning clearly has an effect on maternal behaviors. Does this mean that there is no genetic component?

Consider the differences in parental care between fish and mammals. On average, fish provide much less care to offspring than mammals. The whole structure of mammalian biology is a reflection of the close bonds between mother and infant (see Chapter 7). Regardless of environment, fish cannot provide as much parental care as mammals. A genetic component is at work, if only in terms of the entire group. Regardless of our mammalian heritage of intensive care, however, our own species unfortunately provides many examples of poor parenting. Clearly, both genetic and environmental factors are important in maternal behaviors. It is not "nature" *or* "nurture," but both.

What are the implications of the joint interaction of genetics and environment? If a behavior is affected to some extent by genetics, is there then an innate difference between people with different alleles? In terms of the fish example, this question asks whether or not certain females will automatically be better mothers or not because of genetic differences. Even if genetic differences in a behavior exist, this does not mean that those differences will override environmental factors. We cannot ignore the interaction between genetics and environment. Certain forms of human nearsightedness are due entirely to inheritance, but they can nonetheless be corrected for by glasses (Gould 1987).

Another problem is that the focus is often on extrapolating from large-scale differences (e.g., species) to small-scale differences (e.g., individuals within a species). The fact that, on average, mammals show more parental care than fish does not necessarily mean that some humans will manifest differences in parenting behavior because of genetic factors. It is quite possible that no genetic variation exists within our species for many behaviors. That is, we all have the same alleles (Harpending et al. 1987).

Several different approaches are used today to study the interaction among genetics, environment, and behavior. The field of behavior genetics seeks to determine what, if any, genes have an effect on given behaviors and in what contexts.

Mental Disorders

A major thrust of behavior genetics is the analysis of behavioral diseases. Some mental disorders appear to have a strong genetic basis that can be attributed to the effect of a single allele. Others appear to be affected by both genetics and environment, and still others seem to be purely environmental in nature. Two examples of mental disorders with some degree of genetic control are discussed here—phenylketonuria and schizophrenia.

Case study: Phenylketonuria. Many forms of mental retardation are the result of an inherited condition. One such condition is phenylketonuria (PKU), which is caused by a metabolic defect in which the amino acid phenylalanine cannot be converted into the amino acid tyrosine. In individuals with this defect, an excess of phenylalanine builds up in the body and interferes with the normal development of the nervous system, resulting in severe mental retardation. PKU appears in roughly 1 out of every 10,000 births and is caused by a recessive allele.

PKU provides a good example of some of the complexities involved in genetic analysis. Although the levels of phenylalanine are quite different in those with the recessive homozygous condition and those without it, some variation exists within each group of people. Some people with PKU have slightly higher levels of phenylalanine in their blood than other people with PKU. These variations might reflect a polygenic system, with additional loci contributing minor effects. The variation might also reflect differences in environment, since diet has an effect on phenylalanine levels. In fact, a controlled diet low in phenylalanine from early in infancy can be

dizygotic twins Twins who develop from two separate fertilized eggs (zygotes).

monozygotic twins Identical twins who develop from a single fertilized egg (zygote).

used to moderate the effects of the metabolic defect that produces PKU (Bodmer and Cavalli-Sforza 1976). Thus, even though the condition results from genetic factors, environment can also play a role in determining the behavioral phenotype.

Case study: Schizophrenia. The major mental disorder in the United States today, schizophrenia, encompasses a wide range of behavioral deviations, including a lack of appropriate response to stimuli, a tendency to withdraw from reality, and various delusions and mood switches (Lerner and Libby 1976). The amount of variation in the expression of this condition has led some researchers to suggest that several different mental disorders may be included in the more general term. Others have debated for decades on whether the causes of schizophrenia are genetic or environmental.

The study of schizophrenia illustrates a common method of genetic analysis—the comparison of phenotypes among family members. If a trait has a genetic basis, then greater similarities will be seen in individuals who are more closely related. One commonly used form of analysis is the study of twins. There are two different types of twins: **dizygotic twins,** who grow from two separate zygotes and are no more related than any two siblings, and **monozygotic twins,** who develop from the same zygote and are genetically identical. If a trait is affected by genetic factors, then monozygotic twins will show the greatest similarity, followed by dizygotic twins and other siblings (assuming similar environments). Twin studies also look at the small number of cases where identical twins are separated at birth and raised in different environments after adoption, in order to focus on the potential effects of environmental differences.

It is certain that there is a partial genetic basis to schizophrenia because no cases have been discovered where environmental factors cause schizophrenia in individuals who are not related to a schizophrenic (Nicol and Gottesman 1983). It is also clear, however, that environmental influences are at work. Three studies of twins found that the percentage of twins both having schizophrenia ranged from 27 to 86 percent for monozygotic twins, and between 5 and 22 percent for dizygotic twins (Sutton and Wagner 1985). While there is variation within both groups, the fact that monozygotic twins consistently show a greater proportion of cases where both twins have schizophrenia indicates that genetic factors are at least partially responsible. The range of variation, however, is still substantial, even among the genetically identical twins. *Both* genetic and environmental factors appear to be quite important.

In sum, a number of studies have found strong evidence for a partial genetic basis of schizophrenia and variation caused by environmental factors. The importance of genetics and environment will vary from one study to the next, depending on the specific sample and environmental influences. Some of the variation is also no doubt a product of problems in the definition of schizophrenia. A number of researchers have suggested that the term actually encompasses a number of different mental disorders.

Behavior definition is a major problem in any analysis of genetic influences, and the difficulties increase in trying to analyze behaviors such as intelligence, aggression, and love, all of which are difficult to define.

Intelligence and IQ Test Scores

Perhaps the most widely discussed behavior in the nature-nurture debate has been intelligence. This debate has not been merely academic; it has influenced events and governmental policies throughout human history. In the early twentieth century, prospective immigrants were turned away from the United States and many women underwent involuntary sterilization, both actions based on the then-prevalent views about the genetic basis of intelligence (Gould 1981).

Intelligence is difficult to define. It encompasses a number of separate behavioral capacities such as problem-solving abilities (verbal and mathematical), spatial awareness, memory and accumulated knowledge, and the vaguely defined but important quantity we call "common sense." Some psychologists list up to 120 different components of intelligence (Bodmer and Cavalli-Sforza 1976). In spite of a long history of misguided attempts, intelligence cannot be defined as a single quantity. Nonetheless, most intelligence tests do exactly that—attempt to reduce behaviors taken to demonstrate these abilities to a single, measurable value.

The most commonly used form of intelligence assessment is the IQ test, which provides a single measure called the *intelligence quotient*. This measure was originally derived by dividing a person's "mental age" by his or her chronological age, thus providing a value that takes experience into account. The tests are designed so that the average score is 100. The IQ test was first developed in France by Alfred Binet, who sought a means by which to identify children with learning disabilities. The purpose of the test was not to measure intelligence per se but rather to identify those students who would most likely require special education. The test was designed to provide a rough cutoff point below which a student was felt to be in need of special programs; it was not designed to provide an index for comparing individuals within the "normal" range. That is, someone with an IQ score of 120 should not be considered as inherently "better" or "smarter" than someone with a score of 110.

As used in the United States today, IQ tests serve more as an index of predicted performance in school than as a general measure of intelligence. There are many problems in interpreting IQ scores. Scores vary over a person's lifetime, thus reflecting learning and differences in maturation rather than innate knowledge. The tests have also been found to be culturally biased, and there has been little success in developing a "culture-free" test. Finally, some of the results of early studies of IQ have since been found to contain fabricated data (Dorfman 1978).

Although IQ scores do not provide an accurate reflection of the elusive character of intelligence, they still provide basic information regarding knowledge, learning, and problem solving. What, then, of the issue of

Genetic and nongenetic relationships studied		Genetic correlation	Range of correlations 0.00 0.10 0.20 0.30 0.40 0.50 0.60 0.70 0.80 0.90
Unrelated persons	Reared apart	0.00	
	Reared together	0.00	
Foster parent–child		0.00	
Parent–child		0.50	
Siblings	Reared apart	0.50	
	Reared together	0.50	
Twins — Two-egg	Opposite sex	0.50	
	Like sex	0.50	
Twins — One-egg	Reared apart	1.00	
	Reared together	1.00	

Figure 2.15

Summary of studies reporting on the correlation among individuals' IQ scores. Correlations are measures of similarity; the higher the value, the more similar two individuals' IQ scores. The dots represent the values found in various studies. The genetic correlation is the value expected under a situation of complete inheritance. Even though the correlations increase with genetic relatedness, there is still a great range within any specific class of comparison. For example, monozygotic twins raised together are expected to have a correlation of 1.0, and they have been observed to have correlations ranging from roughly 0.75 to close to 1.0. (Adapted with permission from: S. Singer, *Human Genetics*, 1978, page 79, publisher W. H. Freeman)

genetic versus environmental influences on IQ scores? The bottom line is that both genetics and environment have an influence on the test scores. Many studies have shown that there is a direct relationship between biological relatedness and IQ scores (Figure 2.15). Monozygotic twins show the greatest similarity in test scores, followed by dizygotic twins and other siblings, followed by unrelated individuals. This pattern is expected for a trait that is genetically influenced.

There is also much evidence for environmental influences on IQ test scores. Within each biologically defined category, such as identical twins, correlation in test scores varies from one study to the next. Also, studies comparing environmental factors show that genetic inheritance does not account for all of the variation in IQ scores. The correlation of test scores varies when we compare pairs of individuals raised together with those pairs raised apart. For example, the average correlation between identical twins raised together is higher than the average correlation between identical twins raised apart from each other. If genetics alone were responsible for IQ scores, these correlations would be the same. The fact that they are different, and that the correlation in scores is higher in twins who have been raised together, indicates that a similar environment leads to similar test scores. Findings are similar when comparing similar and different environments of dizygotic twins, siblings, and parents and children (Sutton and Wagner 1985).

A variety of environmental factors have been demonstrated to have an effect on IQ test scores. These include diet, disease, educational quality, and social class, among others (Gould 1981). Intelligence, as reflected by IQ scores, is a highly variable complex trait that reflects the interaction of both genes and environment. The question of which is more important is to a large extent meaningless in considering biocultural organisms such as human beings.

SUMMARY

The DNA molecule specifies the genetic code or set of instructions needed to produce biological structures. DNA acts along with a related molecule, RNA, to translate these instructions into proteins. The DNA is contained along structures called chromosomes within the cell. Chromosomes come in pairs. A segment of DNA that codes for a certain product is called a gene. The different forms of genes present at a locus are called alleles. The DNA molecule has the ability to make copies of itself, allowing transmission of genetic information from cell to cell, and from generation to generation.

Meiosis is the process of sex cell formation that results in one of each chromosome pair being transmitted from parent to offspring. Each individual receives half of his or her alleles from each parent. The two alleles together specify the genetic constitution of an individual—the genotype. The physical manifestation of the genotype is known as the phenotype. The relationship between genotype and phenotype depends on whether an allele is dominant, recessive, or codominant. In complex physical traits, the phenotype is the result of the combined effect of genetics and environment.

The ultimate source of all genetic variation is mutation—a random change in the genetic code. Some mutations are neutral in effect; others are helpful or harmful. The effect of any mutation often depends on the specific environmental conditions. Mutations for any given allele are relatively rare events, but given the large number of loci in many organisms, it is highly probable that each individual has at least one mutant allele.

Genetic factors have been linked to human behaviors. The most clear-cut examples of this relationship are seen in specific biochemical effects associated with certain mental disorders. Other behaviors, such as those measured by intelligence test scores, are more difficult to analyze. Such behaviors appear to be influenced by both genetics and environment. Given the biocultural nature of human beings, it should be no surprise that both genes and environment have an effect on both biology and behavior.

Supplemental Readings

Bodmer, W. F., and L. L. Cavalli-Sforza. 1976. *Genetics, Evolution, and Man.* San Francisco: W. H. Freeman.

Lerner, J. M., and W. J. Libby. 1976. *Heredity, Evolution and Society.* 2d ed. San Francisco: W. H. Freeman. These two texts, though out of date in some areas, contain excellent reviews of the basic principles of molecular and Mendelian genetics, with special attention to human genetics.

Woodward, V. 1992. *Human Heredity and Society.* St. Paul, Minn.: West. A recent and well-written introduction to molecular and Mendelian genetics that focuses on humans.

Cell Biology: A Review

This section, which focuses on the structure of the cell and on the processes of mitosis and meiosis, can be used as a supplement for students wishing to review the basic biology necessary for an understanding of the fundamental principles of Mendelian genetics.

The Cell

All living creatures are made up of cells. Humans, like many organisms, are multicelled. Figure 2.16 shows some of the components of a typical cell. Two major structures are the *nucleus* and the *cytoplasm;* the latter contains a number of other structures. The entire body of the cell is enclosed by a *cell membrane*.

Within the cytoplasm, *mitochondria* convert some cellular material into energy, that is then used for cellular activity (see Chapter 13 for further discussion). *Ribosomes* are small particles that are frequently attached to a larger structure known as the *endoplasmic reticulum*. Composed of RNA and proteins, ribosomes serve as sites for the manufacture of proteins.

As discussed in Chapter 2, the DNA sequences that make up the genetic code are bound together by proteins in long strands known as *chromosomes*. In body cells, chromosomes come in pairs and humans have 23 pairs of chromosomes. The chromosomes within the nucleus of the cell contain all of the DNA, with the exception of something called mitochondrial DNA (see Chapter 13).

Figure 2.16

Schematic diagram of a cell.

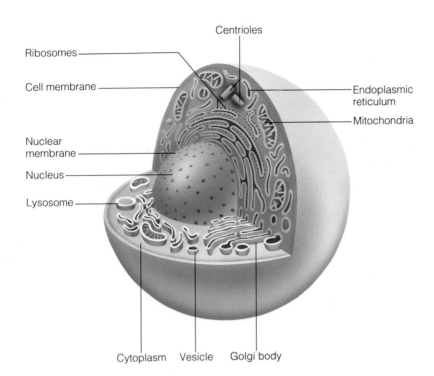

Ribosomes

Cell membrane

Centrioles

Endoplasmic reticulum

Mitochondria

Nuclear membrane

Nucleus

Lysosome

Cytoplasm   Vesicle   Golgi body

Mitosis

DNA has the ability to make copies of itself. This ability is vital for transmitting genetic information from cell to cell and for transmitting genetic information from generation to generation. The replication of DNA is part of the process of cell replication. We will examine two basic processes: mitosis, the replication of body cells, and meiosis, the replication of sex cells.

Mitosis produces two identical body cells from one original. Between cell divisions, each chromosome produces an exact copy of itself, resulting in two pairs with two chromosomes each. When a cell divides, each part contains one of each of the pairs of chromosomes. Thus, two identical body cells, each with the full number of chromosome pairs, is produced. As outlined in Figure 2.17, five stages compose the process of mitosis: interphase, prophase, metaphase, anaphase, and telophase. (Technically speaking, some people do not refer to interphase as a stage.)

During *interphase,* the chromosomes, that are dispersed throughout the nucleus, duplicate. During *prophase,* the chromosomes, each of which is attached to its copy, become tightly coiled and move toward one another

Figure 2.17

The five phases of mitosis. In this example, the original body cell contains two pairs of chromosomes. Mitosis produces two identical body cells, each containing two chromosome pairs (a total of four chromosomes each).

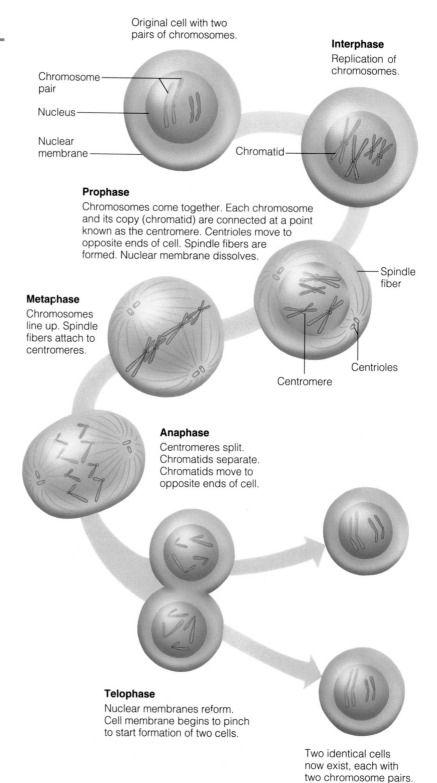

Original cell with two pairs of chromosomes.

Chromosome pair

Nucleus

Nuclear membrane

Interphase
Replication of chromosomes.

Chromatid

Prophase
Chromosomes come together. Each chromosome and its copy (chromatid) are connected at a point known as the centromere. Centrioles move to opposite ends of cell. Spindle fibers are formed. Nuclear membrane dissolves.

Spindle fiber

Centrioles

Centromere

Metaphase
Chromosomes line up. Spindle fibers attach to centromeres.

Anaphase
Centromeres split. Chromatids separate. Chromatids move to opposite ends of cell.

Telophase
Nuclear membranes reform. Cell membrane begins to pinch to start formation of two cells.

Two identical cells now exist, each with two chromosome pairs.

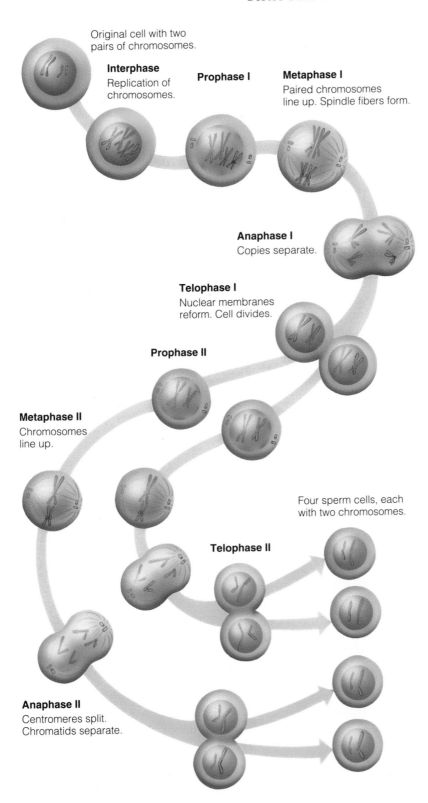

Figure 2.18

The phases of meiosis for a sperm cell. In this example, the original cell contained two chromosome pairs. As a result of meiosis, four sperm cells were produced, each with two chromosomes. The process is similar for egg cells, except that one egg cell and three polar bodies are produced.

Original cell with two pairs of chromosomes.

Interphase
Replication of chromosomes.

Prophase I

Metaphase I
Paired chromosomes line up. Spindle fibers form.

Anaphase I
Copies separate.

Telophase I
Nuclear membranes reform. Cell divides.

Prophase II

Metaphase II
Chromosomes line up.

Telophase II

Four sperm cells, each with two chromosomes.

Anaphase II
Centromeres split. Chromatids separate.

in the nucleus. Each of the two copies is called a *chromatid* and their point of attachment, the *centromere*. Small structures located outside the nuclear membrane, known as *centrioles* (see Figure 2.16), move toward opposite ends of the cell and *spindle fibers* form between the centrioles. The nuclear membrane then dissolves.

During *metaphase*, the duplicated chromosomes line up along the middle of the cell and the spindle fibers attach to the centromeres. During *anaphase*, the centromere divides and the two strands of chromatids (original and duplicate) split and move toward opposite ends of the cell. During *telophase*, new nuclear membranes form around each of the two clusters of chromosomes. Finally, the cell membrane pinches in the middle, creating two identical cells.

Meiosis

Meiosis, the production of sex cells (gametes), differs from mitosis in several ways. The main difference is that sex cells contain only half of an organism's DNA—one chromosome from each pair. Thus, when a new zygote, or fertilized egg, is formed from the joining of egg and sperm, the offspring will have 23 chromosome pairs. One of each pair comes from the mother and one of each pair comes from the father.

Meiosis involves two cycles of cell division. The total sequence of events following the initial duplication of chromosomes (interphase) involves eight stages: prophase I, metaphase I, anaphase I, telophase I, prophase II, metaphase II, anaphase II, and telophase II. Figure 2.18 presents a diagram of this process for the production of sperm cells, for a hypothetical organism with two chromosome pairs. Each of the two pairs of chromosomes has replicated itself by the start of prophase I, leading to eight chromatids: the two chromosomes of each pair duplicate, giving a total of $2 \times 2 \times 2 = 8$ chromatids, each pair of which attaches to one of the centromeres through a process known as *synapsis*. At the end of prophase I the nuclear membrane dissolves. Then, during metaphase I, the paired chromosomes line up and spindle fibers form. The copies separate during anaphase I. During telophase I, the nuclear membranes reform and the cell divides. The realization of two cells, each containing eight chromatids, constitutes prophase II. During metaphase II the chromosomes line up, after which the centromeres split and the chromatids separate, completing anaphase II. The nuclear membranes reform during telophase II, and the cell divides. The net result of this sequence of two cell divisions is four sperm cells, each with two chromosomes—half of the genetic material of the father. The process is similar for the production of egg cells from the female, except that the net result is one egg cell and three structures known as *polar bodies* that do not function as sex cells.

Meiosis thus allows half of a parent's genetic material to be passed on to the next generation. When a sperm cell fertilizes an egg cell, the total number of chromosomes is restored. For humans, the resulting zygote contains $23 + 23 = 46$ chromosomes, or 23 chromosome pairs.

Sex cells may also contain genetic combinations not present in the parent. When synapsis occurs during prophase I, and the chromosomes pair with their copies, becoming attached to one another at several places, the potential exists for genetic material to be exchanged, a process known as *crossing over*. The resulting genetic combinations allow for variation in each sex cell from its source.

Independent assortment also enhances genetic variability. As discussed in Chapter 2, according to this principle, the segregation of any pair of chromosomes does not affect the probability of segregation of any other pair of chromosomes. If you had two chromosome pairs, A and B, with two chromosomes each (A1 and A2, and B1 and B2), only one of each pair will be found in any sex cell. However, you might have one sex cell with A1 and B1 and another sex cell with A1 and B2. Whichever member of the first pair of chromosomes is found in any given sex cell has no bearing on whichever member of the second pair is also found in that sex cell. Independent assortment results from processes occurring during metaphase I. When the paired chromosomes line up, they do so at random and are not influenced by whether they originally came from the person's mother or father. This process allows for tremendous genetic variability in potential offspring.

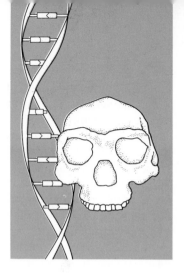

CHAPTER 3

Microevolution

Biological evolution is genetic change through time and can be studied at two different levels. Microevolution consists of changes in the frequency of alleles in a population from one generation to the next. Macroevolution comprises long-term patterns of genetic change over thousands and millions of generations as well as the process of species formation. This chapter deals with the general principles of microevolution. Macroevolution is discussed in Chapter 4. Case studies of human microevolution are given in Chapters 5 and 6.

Population Genetics

Microevolution takes into account changes in the frequency of alleles from one generation to the next. The focus is generally not on the specific genotypes or phenotypes of individuals, but rather on the total pattern of an entire biological population. We are interested in defining the relative frequencies of different alleles, genotypes, and phenotypes for the entire population being studied. We then seek to determine if any apparent change in these frequencies has occurred over time. If changes have occurred, we try to explain them.

Definitions of Population

The term **breeding population** is used frequently in evolutionary theory. In an abstract sense, a breeding population is a group of organisms

breeding population A group of organisms that tend to choose mates from within the group.

that tends to choose mates within the group. This definition is a bit tricky because it is not clear what proportion of mating within a group defines a breeding population.

For example, suppose you travel to a village in a remote mountain region. You find that 99 percent of all the people in the village are married to others who were born in the same village. In this case, the village would appear to fit our ideal definition. But, what if only 80 percent of the people choose their mates from within the village? What if the number were 50 percent? At what point do you stop referring to the population as a "breeding population"? There is no quick and ready answer to this question.

On a practical level, human populations are initially most often defined on the basis of geographic and political boundaries. A small isolated island, for example, easily fits the requirements of a defined population. In most cases, the local geographic unit (such as town or village) is used. Because many human populations have distinct geographic boundaries, this solution often provides the best approach. Care must be taken, however, to ensure that a local geographic unit, such as a town, is not composed of distinct subpopulations, such as groups belonging to different religious sects. A rural Irish village fits this criterion because most of its residents belong to the same religion, social class, and occupational group. New York City, on the other hand, clearly contains a number of subpopulations defined in terms of ethnicity, religion, social class, and other factors. In this case, subpopulations defined on the basis of these factors would serve as our units of analysis.

In many cases, the definition of a population depends on the specific research question asked. For example, if the goal of a study is to look at spatial variation in biological variation, populations defined on the basis of geography are most suitable. If, however, the goal of a study is to look at genetic variation among ethnic groups, then ethnicity should be used to define the populations.

Another potential problem in defining populations is determining the difference between the total census population and the breeding population. Microevolutionary theory specifically concerns those individuals who contribute to the next generation. The total population refers to everybody, whether or not they are likely to breed. The breeding population is smaller than the total population because of a number of factors. First, some individuals in the total population will be too young or too old to mate. Second, cultural factors and geographic distribution may act to limit an individual's choice of mate, and as a consequence some individuals will not breed. If, for example, you live in an isolated area, there may not be enough individuals of the opposite sex from which to choose a mate. Such factors must be taken into consideration in defining a breeding population.

Once a population has been defined, the next step in microevolutionary analysis is to determine the frequencies of genotypes and alleles within the population.

Hardy-Weinberg equilibrium In the absence of evolutionary forces, allele frequencies remain constant from one generation to the next.

Genotype and Allele Frequencies

The genotype frequency is a measure of the relative proportions of different genotypes within a population. Likewise, an allele frequency is simply a measure of the relative proportion of alleles within a population. Genotype frequencies are obtained by dividing the number of individuals with each genotype by the total number of individuals. For example, consider a hypothetical population of 200 people for the MN blood group system where there are 98 people with genotype *MM,* 84 people with genotype *MN,* and 18 people with genotype *NN.* The genotype frequencies are therefore:

Frequency of *MM* = 98/200 = 0.49

Frequency of *MN* = 84/200 = 0.42

Frequency of *NN* = 18/200 = 0.09

Note that the total frequency of all genotypes adds up to 1 (0.49 + 0.42 + 0.09 = 1).

Allele frequencies are computed by counting the number of each allele and dividing that number by the total number of alleles. In the example here, the total number of alleles is 400 because there are 200 people, each with two alleles. To find out the number of *M* alleles for each genotype, count up the number of alleles for each genotype and multiply that number by the number of people with that genotype. Finally, add up the number for all genotypes. In the example, 98 people have the *MM* genotype, and therefore 98 people each have two *M* alleles. The total number of *M* alleles for people with the *MM* genotype is 98 × 2 = 196. For the *MN* genotype, 84 people have one *M* allele, giving a total of 84 × 1 = 84 *M* alleles. For the *NN* genotype, 18 people have no *M* alleles, for a total of 18 × 0 = 0 *M* alleles. Adding the number of *M* alleles for all genotypes gives a total of 196 + 84 + 0 = 280 *M* alleles. The frequency of the *M* allele is therefore 280/400 = 0.7. The frequency of the *N* allele can be computed in the same way, giving an allele frequency of 0.3. Note that the frequencies of all alleles must add up to 1. Another example of allele frequency computation is given in Table 3.1.

The method of counting alleles to determine allele frequencies can only be used when the number of individuals with each genotype can be determined. If one of the alleles is dominant, this may not be possible, and other methods must be used. The computation of allele frequencies when more than two alleles are present at a given locus also may require special methods. Such methods are beyond the scope of this text but may be found in any comprehensive text on population genetics (e.g., Cavalli-Sforza and Bodmer 1971).

Hardy-Weinberg Equilibrium

The mathematical basis of microevolutionary theory rests upon Mendel's principles and the use of a model known as **Hardy-Weinberg equi-**

T A B L E   3.1
Example of Allele Frequency Computation

Imagine you have just collected information on *MN* blood group genotypes for 250 humans in a given population. Your data are:

Number of *MM* genotype = 40

Number of *MN* genotype = 120

Number of *NN* genotype = 90

The allele frequencies are computed as follows:

Genotype	Number of people	Total number of alleles	Number of M alleles	Number of N alleles
MM	40	80	80	0
MN	120	240	120	120
NN	90	180	0	180
Total	250	500	200	300

The relative frequency of the *M* allele is computed as the number of *M* alleles divided by the total number of alleles: 200/500 = 0.4.

The relative frequency of the *N* allele is computed as the number of *N* alleles divided by the total number of alleles: 300/500 = 0.6.

As a check, note that the relative frequencies of the alleles must add up to 1.0 (0.4 + 0.6 = 1.0).

librium. This model, developed independently by G. H. Hardy and W. Weinberg, provides a method of predicting genotype frequencies in future generations under the assumption that mating is at random and that no evolution takes place.

The Hardy-Weinberg equilibrium model is a mathematical statement using symbols to represent allele frequencies. Many microevolutionary models assume a single locus with two alleles (e.g., *A* and *a*). By convention, the symbols p and q are used to represent the frequencies of the *A* allele and the *a* allele, respectively. These symbols are a form of shorthand because it is easier to say p than "the frequency of the *A* allele."

The Hardy-Weinberg equilibrium model states that given allele frequencies of p and q, the expected genotype frequencies are:

Frequency of $AA = p^2$

Frequency of $Aa = 2pq$

Frequency of $aa = q^2$

The mathematical proof of this relationship is given in Appendix 1, which also provides a brief mathematical discussion of population genetics. Assume a population with two alleles (*A* and *a*) with allele frequencies of $p = 0.6$ and $q = 0.4$. Using the Hardy-Weinberg equilibrium model, the predicted genotype frequencies are:

$$AA = (0.6)^2 = (0.6)\,(0.6) = 0.36$$
$$Aa = 2(0.6)\,(0.4) \qquad\quad = 0.48$$
$$aa = (0.4)^2 = (0.4)\,(0.4) = 0.16$$

The Hardy-Weinberg equilibrium model can also be used to show that, given certain assumptions, there will be no change in allele frequency from one generation to the next (see Appendix 1).

The Hardy-Weinberg equilibrium model makes several assumptions. It assumes random mating within the population (with respect to the locus or loci of interest). That is, every individual has an equal chance of mating with any individual of the opposite sex (both sexes are also assumed to have equal allele frequencies). The Hardy-Weinberg equilibrium model also assumes that the population is large enough that there is no variation in allele frequencies caused by sampling (no genetic drift); there is no movement into or out of the population (no gene flow); there are no new alleles (no mutation); and there is no difference in the fertility or mortality of different genotypes (no natural selection). If we compare the expected genotype frequencies with those actually observed and find no difference, then we can conclude that the population is in Hardy-Weinberg equilibrium. If the predicted and observed genotype frequencies are not the same, then the population is not in Hardy-Weinberg equilibrium, and we know that at least one of the assumptions must be incorrect. That is, we know that nonrandom mating, genetic drift, gene flow, mutation, natural selection, or some combination of these factors is present. Further analysis would then be needed to determine which of these assumptions was incorrect.

As an example, consider the following hypothetical case. Imagine a population of 100 people in which 25 people have genotype AA, 60 people have genotype Aa, and 15 people have genotype aa. What are the allele frequencies? Using the method of allele counting described here, your answer should be $p = 0.55$ and $q = 0.45$ (if you did not get this answer, review the material and try again). Using Hardy-Weinberg equilibrium with these allele frequencies results in the following observed and expected genotype frequencies:

Genotype	Observed frequency	Expected frequency
AA	0.2500	0.3025
Aa	0.6000	0.4950
aa	0.1500	0.2025

The observed and expected frequencies are not the same, and so the hypothetical population is not in Hardy-Weinberg equilibrium. Therefore, one or more of the assumptions of the model is incorrect for this case. In actual analyses additional statistical tests must be made to determine how much of a difference between observed and expected genotype frequencies is significant.

Consider another hypothetical example of a population of 100 people. Here the number of people with each genotype is: $AA = 4$, $Aa = 32$, $aa = 64$. The allele frequencies are $p = 0.2$ and $q = 0.8$. The observed and expected genotype frequencies are:

Genotype	Observed frequency	Expected frequency
AA	0.0400	0.0400
Aa	0.3200	0.3200
aa	0.6400	0.6400

Here the hypothetical population is in Hardy-Weinberg equilibrium.

The application of the Hardy-Weinberg equilibrium model in actual studies of human microevolution is somewhat limited because it does not tell us which assumption(s) are invalid. Also, small amounts of evolutionary change may not be detected. In addition, different evolutionary processes may counter one another, giving the impression that none is operating. In spite of these problems, the Hardy-Weinberg equilibrium model is useful in providing a theoretical base for the development of microevolutionary theory (see Appendix 1).

There are two basic reasons a population might not be in a state of Hardy-Weinberg equilibrium. Observed and predicted genotype frequencies may differ because of the effects of evolutionary forces and/or nonrandom mating. **Evolutionary forces** are those mechanisms that actually lead to a change in allele frequency over time. The evolutionary forces are mutation, natural selection, genetic drift, and gene flow. These four forces are the only mechanisms that can cause the frequency of an allele to change over time. For example, if you observe an allele frequency of 0.5 for a population in one generation and then return a generation later to find a frequency of 0.4, then evolution has occurred. This change can only be due to mutation, natural selection, drift, and/or gene flow. Given such a large change, mutation could be ruled out as a major force, for mutation leads to only small changes in any single generation for any given locus. In this case, natural selection, gene flow, and/or genetic drift would be considered more likely forces acting to change allele frequencies. Examination of factors such as migration rates, population size, environmental variation, and differential survival would then be needed to further pinpoint the most likely explanation for the change.

Random mating is one form of mating system. **Nonrandom mating,** however, refers to the patterns of mate choice within a population and its genetic consequences. Nonrandom mating includes **inbreeding,** the mating of biologically related individuals (Figure 3.1), and **assortative mating,** mating on the basis of phenotypic similarity or dissimilarity. Mating

evolutionary forces Four mechanisms that can cause changes in allele frequencies from one generation to the next.

nonrandom mating Patterns of mate choice that influence the distributions of genotype and phenotype frequencies.

inbreeding Mating between biologically related individuals.

assortative mating Mating between phenotypically similar or dissimilar individuals.

Figure 3.1

Inbreeding is used with many domesticated animals to produce certain types of characteristics. (Courtesy of Kenneth Feder, Central Connecticut State University)

polymorphism A discrete
genetic trait in which there are
at least two alleles at a locus
having frequencies greater
than 0.01.

systems do not change allele frequencies, but they do have an effect on the
rate of allele frequency change.

Evolutionary Forces

Mutation

Mutation introduces new alleles into a population. Therefore, the
frequency of different alleles will change over time. For example, consider
a genetic locus with a single allele, *A,* for a population of 100 people (and
200 alleles). Everyone in the population will have genotype *AA,* and the
frequency of the *A* allele is 1.0 (100 percent). Now, assume that one of the
A alleles being passed on to the next generation changes into a new form,
a. Assuming the population stays the same size (to make the mathematics
a bit easier), there will be 199 *A* alleles and 1 *a* allele in the next generation.
The frequency of *A* will have changed from 1.0 to 0.995 (199/200), and
the frequency of *a* will have changed from 0.0 to 0.005 (1/200).

If there is no further evolutionary change, the allele frequencies will
remain the same in future generations. If this mutation continues to recur,
the frequency of the *a* allele will slowly increase, assuming no other evolutionary forces are operating. For typical mutation rates, such a process
would take a very long time.

Mutations can also occur in the reverse direction; that is, an *a* allele
could mutate back to the original form *A.* Not much information is available on back mutation rates in human populations, but they do appear to
be much rarer than the usual mutation rate.

Although mutations are vital to evolution because they provide new
variations, mutation rates are low and do not lead, by themselves, to major
changes in allele frequency. The other evolutionary forces increase or decrease the frequencies of mutant alleles. If you visited a population over
two generations and noted that the frequency of a given allele changed
from 0.30 to 0.40, it would be extremely unlikely that this magnitude of
change would be due solely to mutation. The other evolutionary forces
would be responsible for such large changes.

Many discrete genetic traits are **polymorphisms** (many forms). A
genetic polymorphism is a locus with two or more alleles having frequencies too large to be a result of mutation alone. The usual, somewhat arbitrary, cutoff point for these allele frequencies is 0.01. If an allele has a
frequency greater than 0.01, we can safely assume this relatively high
frequency is caused by factors other than mutation. For example, a locus
with allele frequencies of *A* = 1.0 and *a* = 0.0 would not be polymorphic
because only one allele (*A*) is present in the population. Likewise, a locus
with frequencies of *A* = 0.999 and *a* = 0.001 would also not be a genetic
polymorphism because only one allele has a frequency greater than 0.01.
If the allele frequencies were *A* = 0.2 and *a* = 0.8, this would be evidence

of a genetic polymorphism. Both alleles have frequencies greater than 0.01. Such frequencies are explained by natural selection, genetic drift, and/or gene flow.

fitness An organism's probability of survival and reproduction.

Natural Selection

As discussed in Chapter 1, natural selection filters genetic variation. Individuals with certain biological characteristics that allow them to survive to reproduce, pass on the alleles for such characteristics to the next generation. Natural selection does not create new genetic variation (only mutation can do that), but it does change the relative frequencies of different alleles.

The analysis of natural selection focuses on **fitness,** the probability of survival and reproduction of an organism. For any locus, fitness is measured as the relative genetic contribution of a genotype to the next generation. Imagine a locus with two alleles, *A* and *a,* and the genotypes *AA, Aa,* and *aa.* If all individuals with genotypes *AA* and *Aa* survive and reproduce but only half of those with genotype *aa* survive and reproduce, then the fitness of genotype *aa* is half of that of genotypes *AA* and *Aa.* Fitness refers to the proportion of individuals with a given phenotype who survive and reproduce.

Depending on the fitness of each genotype, natural selection can have different effects. Some of the more common forms of natural selection are discussed here along with a few examples from human populations. Additional examples will be presented in Chapters 5 and 6.

Selection against recessive alleles. Let us assume that the fitness of genotypes *AA* and *Aa* is 100 percent. That is, all individuals with these genotypes survive and reproduce in equal numbers. Further assume that the fitness of individuals with genotype *aa* is 0 percent. That is, no one with genotype *aa* will survive and reproduce. This example corresponds to a situation where a recessive allele (*a*) is fatal for those who have two copies (*aa*). Now, assume a population of 200 people before selection with the following distribution of genotypes: *AA* = 50, *Aa* = 100, *aa* = 50. Using the methods discussed earlier, the allele frequencies can be found: the frequency of *A* is 0.5, and the frequency of *a* is 0.5.

Table 3.2 shows the process of natural selection using these hypothetical numbers. After selection, the number of individuals in each genotype is: *AA* = 50, *Aa* = 100, *aa* = 0. All individuals with genotypes *AA* and *Aa* survive, and none of those with genotype *aa* survive. After selection, there are 150 individuals, and the allele frequencies are *A* = 0.6667 and *a* = 0.3333.

This example shows the effect of selection against a recessive allele. The frequency of the *a* allele drops from 0.5 to 0.3333. Since *a* is a harmful allele, however, you might expect that the *a* allele would be totally eliminated. This does not occur. Since the heterozygote (*Aa*) is not eliminated

TABLE   3.2
Example of Natural Selection against a Recessive Homozygote

This example uses an initial population size before selection of 200 people. The locus has two alleles, *A* and *a*. Initially there are 50 people with genotype *AA*, 100 people with genotype *Aa*, and 50 people with genotype *aa*. The allele frequencies before selection are therefore 0.5 for *A* and 0.5 for *a*. The fitness values have been chosen to illustrate total selection against the recessive homozygote.

	Genotype			
	AA	*Aa*	*aa*	Total
Number of people before selection	50	100	50	200
Fitness (percentage that survives)	100%	100%	0%	
Number of people after selection	50	100	0	150

There are 150 people after selection. Using the method of allele frequency computation shown in Table 3.1 and in the text, the allele frequencies after selection are 200/300 = 0.667 for the *A* allele and 100/300 = 0.333 for the *a* allele.

through selection, these individuals continue to pass the *a* allele on to the next generation. The recessive allele *a* cannot be eliminated in a single generation.

This simple example illustrates another feature of natural selection. Figure 3.2 shows the frequency of the *a* allele for 100 generations of natural selection. The allele frequencies in subsequent generations can be determined by finding out the expected genotype frequencies after selection (using the Hardy-Weinberg model) and examining the expected effects of another generation of selection. Note that the frequency of *a* does not decrease at the same rate over time. The amount of reduction in *a* actually slows down over time. As the frequency of *a* slowly approaches zero, an increasingly lower percentage of the population will be recessive homozygotes; consequently, fewer will be eliminated every generation. Ultimately, a balance will be reached as the reduction in the *a* allele due to selection is offset by new mutations from *A* to *a*. Because mutation rates are very low, this frequency of the *a* allele will be only slightly greater than zero.

Even simple genetic traits with only two alleles have a number of different models of natural selection to investigate. The result of natural

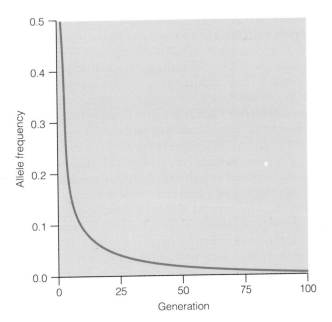

Figure 3.2

Change over time in the frequency of a recessive allele when there is complete selection against the recessive homozygote and the initial allele frequency is 0.5.

selection depends on the initial allele frequencies, whether one allele is dominant or not, and the exact fitness values for each genotype.

A case of selection against recessive homozygotes in humans is Tay-Sachs disease. This affliction is caused by a metabolic disorder that results in blindness, mental retardation, and the destruction of the central nervous system. Children with Tay-Sachs disease generally die within the first few years of life. The disease is caused by a recessive allele and occurs in those individuals who are homozygous. Heterozygotes carry the allele but do not show any major biological impairments.

When deleterious alleles are recessive, such as with Tay-Sachs disease, the frequency is generally not zero, since heterozygotes continue to pass the allele on from generation to generation. Nonetheless, the frequency of a harmful recessive allele will still be very low. This low fequency is maintained by mutation but is kept from increasing by natural selection.

The frequency of Tay-Sachs disease is very low in most human populations, occurring in roughly 10 out of every 1 million births. In some populations of Ashkenazi Jews 1 in every 6,000 children born has Tay-Sachs disease, compared to 1 in every 500,000 births among other groups (Molnar 1992). Some have suggested that the higher frequency might reflect genetic drift (discussed later in this chapter).

Selection against dominant alleles. What if a dominant allele is selected against? As an example, consider the same starting point, as in the previous example: $AA = 50, Aa = 100,$ and $aa = 50$, giving initial allele frequencies of $A = 0.5$ and $a = 0.5$. Complete selection against the dominant allele (A) will mean a fitness of 0 percent for genotypes AA and Aa and a fitness of 100 percent for the genotype aa. After selection, there are no AA individuals, no Aa individuals, and 50 aa individuals (Table 3.3). The allele frequencies after selection are $A = 0.0$ and $a = 1.0$. The dominant allele has been completely eliminated after one generation of selection. There will be no further change unless the allele is reintroduced into the population by mutation or migration from an area where fitness is not zero. If the fitness values of AA and Aa were greater than zero but less than 100 percent, then the A allele would not be eliminated because some individuals with this allele would survive.

An example of a dominant allele in human beings is achondroplastic dwarfism. This type of dwarfism (small body size and abnormal body proportions) is caused by a dominant allele found in very low frequencies in human populations—roughly 0.00005 (Figure 3.3). Because the achondroplastic allele is dominant, individuals with one or two of the alleles will show the disease. Virtually all achondroplastic dwarfs are heterozygotes. The condition is usually caused by a mutation occurring in the sex cells of one parent. We know that a mutation is involved in a majority of these cases because roughly 80 percent of dwarfs have two normal

TABLE 3.3

Example of Natural Selection against the Dominant Allele

This example uses an initial population size before selection of 200 people. The locus has two alleles, A and a. Initially there are 50 people with genotype AA, 100 people with genotype Aa, and 50 people with genotype aa. The allele frequencies before selection are therefore 0.5 for A and 0.5 for a. The fitness values have been chosen to illustrate total selection against the dominant homozygote and the heterozygote.

	Genotype			
	AA	Aa	aa	Total
Number of people before selection	50	100	50	200
Fitness (percentage that survives)	0%	0%	100%	
Number of people after selection	0	0	50	50

There are 50 people after selection. Using the method of allele frequency computation shown in Table 3.1 and in the text, the allele frequencies after selection are $0/100 = 0.0$ for the A allele and $100/100 = 1.0$ for the a allele. The dominant allele A has been eliminated in one generation of natural selection.

parents. Because the condition is caused by a dominant allele, the only way a child could receive the allele would be from a parent or through mutation. If the parent had the allele, he or she would also be a dwarf. Therefore, when both parents of a dwarf are not dwarfs, we know the offspring's dwarfism is the result of a mutation. In cases where two dwarfs mate, the offspring can be homozygous for the disease and such offspring generally die before, or shortly after, birth.

The low frequency of achondroplastic dwarfs is the result of natural selection acting to remove the harmful allele from the population. Although there is no major risk of mortality for a heterozygous achondroplastic dwarf, selection acts on differential reproduction. Given their physical appearance, these dwarfs have few opportunities to mate. The most likely mating is between two dwarfs. In these cases, there is additional selection because they have an increased risk of having children with two copies of the achondroplastic allele; these children generally die early in life. Thus, both differences in mortality and fertility can affect the degree of selection against an allele.

Selection for the heterozygote. The previous examples discussed selection against recessive and dominant homozygotes, which act to increase the frequency of one allele and decrease the frequency of another. Selection could also occur *for* recessive or dominant homozygotes, which would act to increase the frequency of an allele. With time, the allele frequencies will approach 0 or 1, depending on which allele is selected against.

These models might lead us to expect patterns of genetic variation whereby most populations have allele frequencies close to either 0 or 1 and few populations with intermediate values. However, studies of human genetic variation have found that for many loci the allele frequencies are intermediate, with values such as 0.3, 0.5, or 0.8. We could argue that selection is not yet complete and that given enough time all allele frequencies would be close to 0 or 1, but the wealth of information regarding allele frequencies in human groups makes this very unlikely. Why, then, do many loci show intermediate frequencies? Is there a way that natural selection can produce such values?

A classic example of an intermediate allele frequency in human populations is the sickle cell allele, discussed briefly in the last chapter. Since people homozygous for this allele have sickle cell anemia and are likely to die early in life, this appears to be a classic situation of selection against a homozygote. If this were the case, we might expect most human populations to have frequencies of the sickle cell allele close to 0 and, in fact, many do. However, a number of populations in parts of Africa, India, and the Mediterranean show higher frequencies. In some African groups, the frequency of the sickle cell allele is greater than 20 percent (Roychoudhury and Nei 1988). How can a harmful allele exist at such a high frequency?

The answer is a form of selection known as selection for the heterozygote (and therefore against the homozygotes). Consider fitness values of:

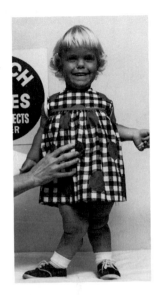

Figure 3.3

Achondroplastic dwarfism is a genetic disorder caused by a dominant allele. This toddler has very short arms and legs. (Courtesy March of Dimes Birth Defect Foundation)

T A B L E   3.4
Example of Natural Selection for the Heterozygote

This example uses an initial population size before selection of 200 people. The locus has two alleles, *A* and *a*. Initially there are 50 people with genotype *AA*, 100 people with genotype *Aa*, and 50 people with genotype *aa*. The allele frequencies before selection are therefore 0.5 for *A* and 0.5 for *a*. The fitness values have been chosen to illustrate selection for the heterozygote and partial selection against both homozygotes.

	Genotype			
	AA	*Aa*	*aa*	Total
Number of people before selection	50	100	50	200
Fitness (percentage that survives)	70%	100%	20%	
Number of people after selection	35	100	10	145

There are 145 people after selection. Using the method of allele frequency computation shown in Table 3.1 and in the text, the allele frequencies after selection are 170/290 = 0.586 for the *A* allele and 120/290 = 0.414 for the *a* allele.

AA = 70 percent, *Aa* = 100 percent, and *aa* = 20 percent. Here, only 70 percent of those with genotype *AA* and 20 percent of those with genotype *aa* survive for every 100 people with genotype *Aa* (the heterozygote). Selection is for the heterozygote and against the homozygotes. Let the frequency of both the *A* and *a* alleles equal 0.5. In a population of 200 people, this means we start with 50 *AA* people, 100 *Aa* people, and 50 *aa* people before selection. Given the fitness values above, there will be 35 people with *AA*, 100 with *Aa*, and 10 with *aa* after selection. The allele frequencies after selection are *A* = 0.586 and *a* = 0.414 (Table 3.4).

Why would the frequency of the *A* allele increase and the frequency of the *a* allele decrease? In selection for the heterozygote, both alleles are being selected for, since every *Aa* person can contribute both alleles to the next generation. Also, both alleles are being selected against. When *AA* persons die or fail to reproduce, then two *A* alleles are lost from the population. When *aa* persons die or fail to reproduce, two *a* alleles are lost from the population. Selection for the heterozygote involves selection for and against both alleles. Because the fitness of *AA* is greater in this example than the fitness of *aa* (70 percent versus 20 percent), proportionately more individuals with genotype *AA* will survive and reproduce. Hence, proportionately more *A* alleles will appear in the next generation.

Figure 3.4 shows the pattern of allele frequency change over 20 generations using the initial values and fitness values in this example. Note that the frequency of *A* continues to increase for the first few generations but soon levels off. There is no change in the allele frequency after approximately eight generations. This is the expected pattern when there is selection for the heterozygote. A balance is reached between selection for and against the two alleles *A* and *a*. The exact value of this balancing point will depend on the fitness values of the homozygous genotypes. Selection for the heterozygote is also called **balancing selection.**

Given this model, the distribution of sickle cell allele frequencies in humans makes sense. In many environments there is selection against the sickle cell homozygote and the frequency is low. In environments where malaria is common, the heterozygotes have an advantage since they are less susceptible to malaria. People homozygous for the sickle cell allele are likely to suffer from sickle cell anemia and die. People homozygous for the normal allele are more likely to suffer from malaria. Thus, there is selection against both homozygotes (although more selection against those with sickle cell anemia) and selection for the heterozygote. A balance of allele frequencies is predicted and has been found in many human populations. A more complete discussion of the sickle cell example is given in Chapter 5.

Selection and complex traits. The previous examples used simple genetic traits to illustrate basic principles of natural selection. Selection also affects complex traits, such as those discussed in Chapter 2. For

balancing selection Selection for the heterozygote and against the homozygotes (the heterozygote is most fit).

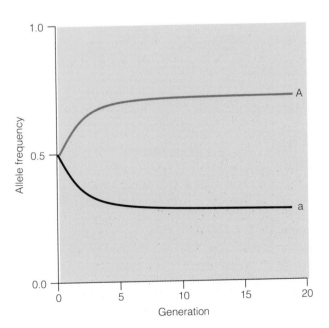

Figure 3.4

Change over time in allele frequencies when there is selection for the heterozygote (*Aa*). The initial allele frequencies are both 0.5. The fitness of each genotype (the relative frequency of survival) is: $AA = 70\%$, $Aa = 100\%$, and $aa = 20\%$.

stabilizing selection
Selection against both extreme values in a continuous trait.

complex traits, we focus on measures of the average value and variation around this average. Because complex traits are continuous, we look at the effects of selection on the average value of a trait and on the lower and higher extremes.

There are several forms of selection on complex traits. **Stabilizing selection** refers to selection against both extremes of a trait's range in values. Individuals with extreme high or low values of a trait are less likely to survive and reproduce, and those with values closer to the average are more likely to survive and reproduce. The effect of stabilizing selection is to maintain the population at the same average value over time. Extreme values are selected against each generation, but the average value in the population does not change.

Human birth weight is a good example of stabilizing selection. The weight of a newborn child is the result of a number of environmental factors, such as mother's age, weight, and history of smoking, among many others. There is also a genetic component to birth weight. Newborns who are very small (less than 2.5 kg) are less likely to survive than newborns who are heavier. Very small babies are more prone to disease and have weaker systems, making their survival more difficult. Newborns who are too large are also likely to be selected against, because a very large child may create complications during childbirth and both mother and child may die. Thus, there is selection against both extremes, small and large.

Stabilizing selection on birth weight has been documented for a number of human populations. These studies show a definite relationship between birth weight and mortality. The results of one study based on 13,730 newborns (Karn and Penrose 1951) are shown in Figure 3.5.

Figure 3.5

Stabilizing selection for human birth weight based on data from Karn and Penrose (1951). Babies born smaller or larger than the optimum birth weight have increased mortality. (From E. Peter Volpe, *Understanding Evolution*, 5th ed. Copyright © 1985 Wm. C. Brown Communication, Inc., Dubuque, Iowa. All Rights Reserved. Reprinted by permission)

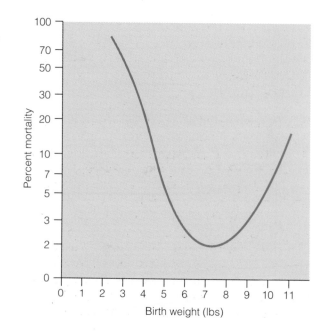

Mortality rates are highest for those newborns with low (less than 2.7 kg) and high (greater than 4.5 kg) birth weights.

Another type of selection for complex traits is known as **directional selection,** selection against one extreme and/or for the other extreme. In other words, a direct relationship exists between survival and reproduction on one hand and the value of a trait on the other. The result is a change over time in one direction. The average value for a trait moves in one direction or the other. Perhaps the most dramatic example of directional selection in human evolution has been the threefold increase in brain size over the last four million years. Another example is the lighter skin that probably evolved in prehistoric humans as they moved north out of Africa (see Chapter 6).

A third type of selection for complex traits is **diversifying selection,** where selection is *for* the extremes and *against* the average value. Although this type of selection is theoretically interesting, there is no evidence of its action at present in human populations (which of course could mean we haven't found it!)

directional selection
Selection against one extreme in a continuous trait and/or selection for the other extreme.

diversifying selection
Selection for the extremes in a continuous trait and against the average value.

Genetic Drift

Genetic drift is the random change in allele frequency from one generation to the next. These random changes are the result of the nature of probability. Think for a moment about flipping a coin in the air. What is the probability of its landing with the head facing up? It is 50 percent. The coin has two possible values, heads and tails, and when you flip it you will get one or the other. Suppose you flip a coin 10 times. How many heads and how many tails do you expect to get? Since the probability of getting a head or a tail is 50 percent, you expect to get five heads and five tails. Try this experiment several times. Did you always get five tails and five heads? Sometimes you will get five heads and five tails, but sometimes you get different numbers. You may get six heads and four tails, or three heads and seven tails, or much less likely, all heads.

The probability for different combinations of heads and tails from flipping a coin 10 times is shown in Table 3.5. The probability of getting all heads (or all tails) is rather low—0.001. Note, however, that the probability of getting four heads and six tails (or six heads and four tails) is much higher—0.205. Also note that the probability of getting exactly five heads and five tails is 0.246. This means that there is roughly a 75 percent chance of *not* getting exactly five heads and five tails.

The probability of 50 percent heads and 50 percent tails is the expected distribution. If you flip 10 coins enough times, you will find that the number of heads and tails grows closer to a 50:50 ratio. Often we hear about the "law of averages." The idea here is that if you flip a coin and get heads several times in a row, then you are very likely to get a tail the next time. This is wrong, and an easy way to lose money if you gamble using this "law." Each time you flip the coin is an independent event. Whatever

**TABLE 3.5
Probability of Getting Different Numbers of Heads and Tails from 10 Coin Flips**

Number of heads	Number of tails	Probability
0	10	0.001
1	9	0.010
2	8	0.044
3	7	0.117
4	6	0.205
5	5	0.246
6	4	0.205
7	3	0.117
8	2	0.044
9	1	0.010
10	0	0.001

These probabilities refer only to the case where 10 coins are flipped. Other numbers of coins will give different probabilities. To see how these probabilities are computed, see Thomas (1986).

happened the time before cannot affect the next flip. *Each* time you flip the coin you have a 50 percent chance of getting a head and a 50 percent chance of getting a tail.

What does this have to do with genetics? The reproductive process in this way is like a coin toss. During the process of sex cell replication (meiosis), only one allele out of two at a given locus is used. The probability of either allele being passed on is 50 percent, just like a coin toss. Imagine a locus with two alleles, *A* and *a*. Now imagine a man and a woman, each with genotype *Aa*, who have a child. The man can pass on either an *A* allele or an *a* allele. Likewise, a woman can pass on either an *A* allele or an *a* allele. As we saw in the last chapter, the probable distribution of genotypes among the children are 25 percent *AA*, 50 percent *Aa*, and 25 percent *aa*. If the couple has four children, you would expect one with *AA*, two with *Aa*, and one with *aa*. Thanks to random chance, however, the couple may get a different distribution of genotypes. You can model such a simple example by flipping a coin to simulate a child receiving an *A* allele or an *a* allele from either parent. Let "heads" represent the *A* allele and "tails" represent the *a* allele.

This author performed the experiment four times to simulate four children born to these parents. Two of the children had genotype *AA* and two had genotype *Aa*. Note that the allele frequencies have changed from the parent's generation to the children's generation. The allele frequencies of the parents were *A* = 0.5 and *a* = 0.5. The four children have a total of 8 alleles, of which 6 are *A* and 2 are *a*. The frequency of *A* in the children is 6/8 = 0.75 and the frequency of *a* is 2/8 = 0.25. You might want to try this experiment several times to see the range of allele frequencies that can result.

When genetic drift occurs in populations, the same principle applies. Allele frequencies can change because of random chance. Sometimes the allele frequency will increase, and sometimes it will decrease. The direction of allele frequency change caused by genetic drift is random. The only time drift will not produce a change in allele frequency is when only one allele is present at a given locus. For example, if each parent passed on an *A* allele to each of the four children, the frequency of the *A* allele would be 1.0 among the children. The *a* allele would have been lost.

Genetic drift occurs in each generation. Such a process is too complicated to simulate using coins, but computers or random number tables can be used to model the effects of drift over time (see Cavalli-Sforza and Bodmer 1971:389). Figure 3.6 shows the results of three computer simulations of drift. In each case, the initial allele frequency was 0.5, and the population size was equal to 10 individuals (20 alleles) in each generation. The simulation was allowed to continue in each case for 20 generations. The graphs show the changes in allele frequency over time. Note that each of the three simulations shows a different pattern. This is expected because genetic drift is a random process. Each simulation is an independent event.

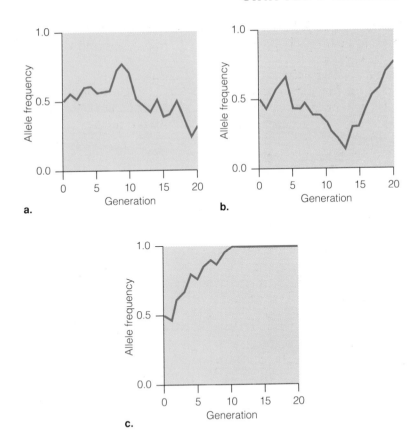

Figure 3.6

Three computer simulations of 20 generations of genetic drift for populations of 10 individuals. Each simulation started with an initial allele frequency of 0.5.

In each of these three graphs, the allele frequency fluctuates up and down. In Figure 3.6a, the allele frequency after 20 generations is 0.3. In Figure 3.6b, the allele frequency after 20 generations is 0.75. In Figure 3.6c, the allele frequency is equal to 1.0 after 10 generations, and it does not change any more. Given enough time, and assuming no other evolutionary forces affect allele frequencies, genetic drift will ultimately lead to an allele's becoming fixed at a value of 0.0 or 1.0. Thus, genetic drift leads to the reduction of variation within a population, given enough time.

The effect of genetic drift depends on the size of the breeding population. The larger the population size, the less change will occur from one generation to the next. Thinking back to the coin toss analogy will show you that this makes sense. If you flip a coin 10 times and get three heads and seven tails, it is not that unusual. If you flip a coin 1 million times, however, it would be much less likely that you would get the same proportions—300,000 heads and 700,000 tails. This is because of a basic principle of probability: the greater the number of events, the fewer deviations from the expected frequencies (50 percent heads and 50 percent tails).

Figure 3.7

Allele frequency distributions for 1,000 computer simulations of 20 generations of genetic drift. The distributions show the number of times a given allele frequency was reached after 20 generations of drift. In all cases, the initial allele frequency was 0.5. Each graph represents a different value of population size: (a) = 10, (b) = 50, (c) = 100, (d) = 1,000.

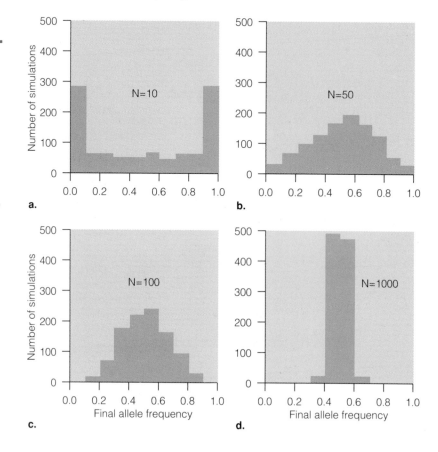

The effect of population size on genetic drift is shown in Figure 3.7. These graphs show the results of 1,000 simulations of genetic drift for four different values of breeding population size: N = 10, 50, 100, 1,000. In each computer run the initial allele frequency was set to 0.5, and the simulation was allowed to continue for 20 generations. The four graphs show the distribution of allele frequency values after 20 generations of genetic drift. Figure 3.7a shows this distribution for a population size of N = 10. Note that the majority of the 1,000 simulations resulted in final allele frequencies of less than 0.1 or greater than 0.9. In small populations, genetic drift more often results in a quick loss of one allele or another. Figure 3.7b shows the distribution of final allele frequencies for a population size of N = 50. Here there are fewer extreme values and more values falling between 0.3 and 0.7. Figures 3.7c and 3.7d show the distributions for population sizes of N = 100 and N = 1,000. It is clear from these graphs that the larger the population size, the fewer deviations in allele frequency caused by genetic drift. The main point here is that genetic drift has the greatest evolutionary effect in relatively small breeding populations.

founder effect A type of genetic drift caused by the formation of a new population by a small number of individuals.

Examples of genetic drift. Genetic drift in human populations is shown in a case study of a group known as the Dunkers, a religious sect that emigrated from Germany to the United States in the early 1700s. Approximately 50 families composed the initial group. Glass (1953) studied the genetic characteristics of the descendants of the original founding group living in Pennsylvania. These populations have never been greater than several hundred people and thus provide a unique opportunity to study genetic drift in a small human group. Glass found that the Dunker population differed in a number of genetic traits from both the modern German and U.S. populations. Furthermore, the allele frequencies of Germany and the United States were almost identical, suggesting that other factors such as natural selection were unlikely. For example, the allele frequencies for the MN blood group were roughly $M = 0.55$ and $N = 0.45$ for both the United States and German samples. In the Dunker population, however, the allele frequencies were $M = 0.655$ and $N = 0.345$. Based on these and additional data, Glass concluded that the genetics of the Dunker population were shaped to a large extent by genetic drift over two centuries. Although 200 years seems like a long time to you and me, it is a fraction of an instant in evolutionary time. Genetic drift can clearly produce rapid changes under the proper circumstances.

Genetic drift in human populations has also been found on Tristan da Cunha, a small island in the south Atlantic Ocean. In 1816, the English established a small garrison on the island. When they left, one man and his wife remained, to be joined later by a handful of other settlers. Given such a small number of original settlers, what do you suppose is the probability that the families represented all the genetic variation present in the population they came from? The probability would be very low. Genetic drift is often caused when a small number of founders form a new population: this type of genetic drift is known as **founder effect.** An analogy would be a barrel containing thousands of red and blue beads, mixed in equal proportions. If you reached into the barrel and randomly pulled out a handful of beads, you might not get 50 percent red and 50 percent blue. Because of random chance, founders are not likely to be an exact genetic representation of the original population. The smaller the number of founders, the greater the deviation will be.

Over time, the population of Tristan da Cunha remained small. The population size was further reduced twice because of emigration and disaster. Given its initial small population, combined with two further reductions and a maximum population size less than 300, the island had the opportunity to experience considerable genetic drift. This effect is seen dramatically through analysis of historical records for the island; for example, two of the original founders contributed genetically to more than 29 percent of the population in 1961 (Roberts 1968; Underwood 1979).

Gene Flow

The fourth evolutionary force is gene flow, the movement of alleles from one population to another. The term *migration* is often used to mean the same thing as gene flow. From a conservative standpoint, this is not completely accurate. Migration refers to the more or less permanent movement of individuals from one place to another. Why the confusion? After all, excepting artificial insemination, your alleles do not move unless you do. You can migrate, however, without passing on any alleles. You can also be involved in gene flow without actually making a permanent move to a new place. In many texts on microevolution the terms *gene flow* and *migration* are used interchangeably. Keep in mind, however, that there are certain distinctions in the real world.

Gene flow involves the movement of alleles between at least two populations. When gene flow occurs, the two populations mix genetically and tend to become more similar. Under most conditions, the more the two populations mix, the more similar they will become genetically (assuming that the two environments are not different enough to produce different effects of natural selection).

Consider a genetic locus with two alleles, A and a. Assume two populations, 1 and 2. Now, assume that all the alleles in population 1 are A and all the alleles in population 2 are a. The allele frequencies of these two imaginary populations are:

Population 1	Population 2
Frequency of A = 1.0	Frequency of A = 0.0
Frequency of a = 0.0	Frequency of a = 1.0

Now imagine a situation where 10 percent of the people in population 1 move to population 2, and vice versa. This movement constitutes gene flow. What effect will the gene flow have? After gene flow has taken place, population 1 is made up of 90 percent A alleles and 10 percent a alleles. Population 2 is made up of 10 percent A alleles and 90 percent a alleles. The allele frequencies of the two populations, though still different, have become more similar as the consequence of gene flow. If the same rate of gene flow (10 percent) continues generation after generation, the two populations will become more and more similar genetically. After 20 generations of gene flow, the two populations will be almost identical. The accumulated effects of gene flow over time are shown for this hypothetical example in Figure 3.8.

Apart from making populations more similar, gene flow can also introduce new variation within a population. In the example, a new allele (*a*) was introduced into population 1 as the result of gene flow. A new mutation arising in one population can be spread throughout the rest of a species by gene flow.

Under certain circumstances, gene flow can work in reverse and act to make populations more different. The standard model of gene flow assumes that the migrants are a random sample of the population. In some cases, such as certain human populations, this is not the case. Migrants will often consist of closely related families. The movement of related individuals, called **kin-structured migration,** can act to offset the usual effects of gene flow (Fix 1978). Though kin-structured migration appears less common than random migration, we cannot ignore its possible genetic consequences.

Cultural influences on migration and gene flow. Compared to many other organisms, humans are relatively mobile creatures. Human populations show a great deal of variation in degree of migration. Even today, many humans live and work within a small area and choose mates from nearby. Some people are more mobile than others, the extent of their mobility depending on a number of factors such as available technology, occupation, income, and other social factors.

In spite of local and regional differences, humans today all belong to the same species. Even though genetic variation exists among populations, they are in fact characterized more by their similarity. A critical factor in

kin-structured migration
The movement of groups of biologically related individuals to another population.

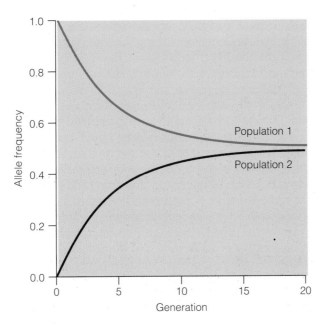

Figure 3.8

Effects of gene flow over time. Population 1 started with an allele frequency of 1.0 and population 2 started with an allele frequency of 0.0. The two populations exchange 10 percent of their genes with each generation. Over time, the continued gene flow acts to make the two populations more similar genetically.

Figure 3.9

Percentage of marriages taking place at various marital distances (the distance between the premarital residences of bride and groom) for the town of Leominster, Massachusetts, 1800–1850. (Source: author's unpublished data)

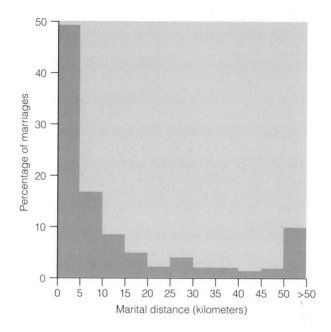

the cohesiveness of the human species, gene flow acts to reduce differences among groups.

The amount of gene flow between human populations depends on a variety of environmental and cultural factors. Geographic distance is a major determinant of migration and gene flow. The further two populations are apart geographically, the less likely they are to exchange mates. Even in today's modern world, with access to jet airplanes and other devices, you are still more likely to choose a spouse from nearby than from across the country. Exceptions to the rule do occur, of course, but the influence of geographic distance is still very strong.

Studies of migration and gene flow often look at distance between birthplaces or premarital residences of married couples. If you had been born in New York City and your spouse had been born in Chicago, the distance between your birthplaces would be approximately 1,300 km (roughly 800 miles). If both you and your spouse had come from the same neighborhood in the same city, your marital distance would be close to zero. The relationship between migration and geographic distance is similar in most human populations (Relethford 1992). Most marriages take place within a few kilometers, and the number of marriages quickly decreases as the distance between populations increases. This indicates that the majority of genes flowing into human populations comes from a local area and a small proportion from farther distances.

The relationship between the frequency of marriages and geographic distance is shown in Figure 3.9. This graph presents the results of a historical study of migration into the town of Leominster, Massachusetts, using marriage records from the year 1800 through 1849. A total of 1,602 marriages took place in the population over the 50-year period. Of these, almost half (49.2 percent) were between a bride and groom who were both native to Leominster. An additional 16.5 percent of the marriages took place between couples whose premarital residences were between 5 and 10 km (roughly 8 to 16 miles). Note that the percentage of marriages diminishes quickly after a distance of 5 km. Also note that almost 10 percent of the couples come from distances greater than 50 km. This type of long-range migration (and gene flow) acts to keep populations from diverging too much from the rest of the species.

Geographic distance is a major determinant of human migration and gene flow, but it is not the only one. Ethnic differences also act to limit them. Most large cities have distinct neighborhoods that correspond to different ethnic communities. A large proportion of marriages take place within these groups because of the common human preference for marrying within one's own social and cultural group. Likewise, religious differences also act as barriers to gene flow because many, though not all, people prefer to marry within the same religion. Further, social class and educational differences can also limit gene flow.

In other parts of the world we see other cultural differences that restrict gene flow. In many Pacific islands, for example, several different language groups coexist within a small geographic area. Differences in language enhance the cultural distances among populations and act to limit the number of marriages across language groups. Friedlaender's (1975) study of migration on Bougainville Island in Melanesia shows the effect of language differences on marriage frequency. He looked at marriages within and among small villages belonging to eight different language groups within roughly a 100-km range. The percentage of marriages within each language group are listed in Table 3.6. For the entire island, 90 percent of all marriages took place within the same language group (the percentage varies from 70 to 98 percent for the eight groups).

Isolation by distance. The level of gene flow among populations influences their genetic similarity. Gene flow acts to reduce differences among groups. Genetic drift, on the other hand, acts to increase differences among groups. The interaction between gene flow and genetic drift has been studied widely among a number of human populations. The balance between gene flow and genetic drift often fits a predicted model of genetic variation known as the **isolation by distance** model. In nonmathematical terms, this model predicts that genetic similarity between populations decreases as geographic distance increases. Considering the decline in gene flow with distance, this makes sense. The less gene flow there is, the more likely it is that populations will differ from one another genetically.

The observed pattern of isolation by distance for three human populations is shown in Figure 3.10. These curves present a highly isolated set

isolation by distance
A model that predicts that genetic similarity between populations decreases as geographic distance increases.

T A B L E   3.6
Rates of Marriage within Language Groups on Bougainville Island

Language group	Percentage of marriages occurring within language group
Aita	95
Eivo	85
Nasioi	95
Rotokas	98
Simeku	90
Siwai	94
Torau	96
Uruava	70

Source: Friedlaender (1975:76).

admixture The interbreeding of individuals from two or more initially distinct gene pools.

of populations (villages on Bougainville Island), a moderately isolated set of populations (Papago Indian villages), and a set of agricultural populations with much less isolation (Ferrara province in Italy). All three studies relied on genetic data collected during the past few decades. In each case, genetic similarity is greatest among individuals with the same population and declines rapidly with geographic distance. The curves also show the relative amount of local isolation. Bougainville villages show the greatest similarity among individuals within the local group, as expected given their relatively small populations and limited gene flow. Papago Indian villages show less local isolation, and the agricultural Italian villages show the least. This makes sense, since agricultural communities, in general, are larger and experience more gene flow (Jorde 1980). These curves provide a graphic summary of differences in the effect of geographic distance on gene flow in human populations.

Admixture. Throughout human history there have been many examples of large-scale migrations from different parts of the world. In many cases, new populations are formed through the process of **admixture,** the mixing of individuals from two or more initially different groups, such as African Americans. Large numbers of Africans were brought against their will to the United States as slaves and, in some cases, the women had children by their masters. Since that time some interbreeding between African Americans and European Americans has continued. Genetically,

Figure 3.10

Isolation by distance in three human populations. The vertical axis represents the degree of genetic similarity between populations; the horizontal axis represents the geographic distance between populations. In all three cases, genetic similarity declines exponentially with geographic distance.   (Source: Bougainville [Relethford 1985], Papago Indians [Workman et al. 1973], Italy [Zanardi et al. 1977])

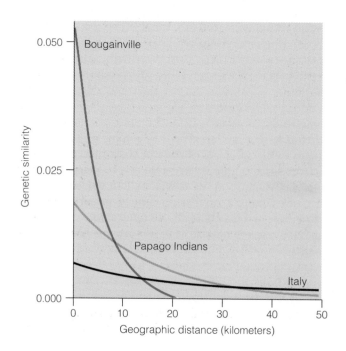

this is a situation of European gene flow into the transplanted African population of the United States.

By analyzing modern allele frequencies, the approximate amount of European admixture can be determined. Though the methods are not exact, they do provide a rough idea of the total amount of gene flow. Most of these studies suggest European admixture in African Americans that ranges from 4 to 31 percent (Chakraborty 1986). The estimate of admixture varies with social and geographic factors; African-American populations in northern states generally have higher proportions of European admixture.

Another example of human admixture is the case of Mexican and Mexican-American populations. The origin of these groups lies in the influx of European genes (mostly Spanish) into the native populations of Central America following European exploration. Differences in the initial degree of contact, along with subsequent differences in admixture, have lead to extensive variation in the European component of these admixed groups (Figure 3.11). Estimates of European admixture vary from 4 to 47 percent (Crawford and Devor 1980) in certain Mexican populations, and are somewhat higher in some Mexican-American groups (Relethford et al. 1983).

Variation in European admixture rates in Mexican-American populations is directly related to a number of social factors, such as ethnic background and social status. In a study of admixture among Mexican Americans living in San Antonio, Texas, Relethford and colleagues (1983) looked at different subgroups defined on the basis of geographic location and socioeconomic standing. One group was an inner-city *barrio*, in a poor area of the city whose residents adhered most strongly to traditional Mexican-American cultural values. The other groups were a middle-class neighborhood and an upper-income suburban neighborhood. The amount of European admixture in the *barrio* was the least of the three groups (54 percent), followed by the middle-class neighborhood (73 percent) and the suburban neighborhood (82 percent). These numbers should not be taken as *exact* measures of gene flow, but they are useful for observing the relative differences in admixture between groups. The relationship between social class and admixture is expected from our knowledge of marriage patterns and other cultural customs. The inner-city *barrio* has traditional beliefs, and marriage outside one's ethnic group is discouraged. With higher socioeconomic status, however, traditional ethnic boundaries seem to be less important, and marriage outside the group is more common. The result is higher levels of European gene flow in higher socioeconomic groups.

Figure 3.11

Mexican Americans in the United States. Mexican-American populations have varying degrees of European and Native-American admixture.   (© Spencer Grant/ Stock, Boston)

Interaction of the Evolutionary Forces

It is convenient to discuss each of the four evolutionary forces separately, but in reality they act together to produce allele frequency change.

Mutation acts to introduce new genetic variants; natural selection, genetic drift, and gene flow act to change the frequency of the mutant allele. Sometimes the evolutionary forces act together, and sometimes they act in opposition. Their exact interaction depends on a wide variety of factors, such as the biochemical and physical effects of different alleles, presence or absence of dominance, population size, population distribution, and the environment, to name but a few. Many biological anthropologists attempt to unravel some of these factors in human population studies.

In general, we look at how natural selection, genetic drift, and gene flow act to increase or decrease genetic variation within and between groups. (Mutation gets less attention because, even though it introduces new genetic variants, the change in allele frequency in one generation is low.) An increase in variation within a population means that individuals within the population will be more genetically different from one another. A decrease in variation within a population means the reverse; individuals will become more similar to one another genetically. An increase in variation among populations means that two or more populations will become more different from one another genetically, and a decrease in variation within populations means the reverse.

Let us first consider the effects of genetic drift, gene flow, and natural selection on allele frequency variation. Genetic drift tends to remove alleles from a population and therefore acts to reduce variation within a population. On the other hand, because genetic drift is a random event and occurs independently in different populations, the pattern of genetic drift will tend to be different on average in different populations. On average, then, genetic drift will act to increase variation among populations. Gene flow acts to introduce new alleles into a population and can have the effect of increasing variation within a population. Gene flow also acts to reduce variation among populations in most cases.

Natural selection can either increase or decrease variation within a population, depending on the specific type of selection and the initial allele frequencies. Selection against recessive homozygotes, for example, will lead to the gradual decrease of one allele and consequently reduce variation. Selection for an advantageous mutation, however, will result in an increase in the frequency of the mutant and act to increase variation within the population. Selection can also either increase or decrease variation among populations, depending on environmental variation. If two populations have similar environments, then natural selection will take place in the same way in both groups and therefore will act to reduce genetic differences between them. On the other hand, if the two populations are in different enough environments that natural selection operates in different ways, then variation between the populations may be increased. Table 3.7 summarizes the effects of different evolutionary forces on variation within and among populations.

Different evolutionary forces can produce the same, or opposite, effects. Different forces can also act in opposition to one another. Genetic

TABLE 3.7
Summary of the Effects of Selection, Drift, and Gene Flow
on Variation within and among Populations

Evolutionary force	Variation within populations	Variation among populations
Selection	Increase or decrease	Increase or decrease
Genetic drift	Decrease	Increase
Gene flow	Increase	Decrease

A decrease in variation within a population makes individuals more similar to
one another, whereas an increase in variation within a population makes
individuals less similar to one another. A decrease in variation among populations makes the populations more similar to one another, whereas an increase
in variation among populations makes the populations less similar to one
another. Note that natural selection can either increase or decrease variation; the
exact effect depends on the type of selection and differences in environment (see
text).

drift and gene flow, for example, have opposite effects on variation within
and among populations. If both of these forces operate at the same time,
they can counteract each other.

   Several examples help illustrate the ways in which different evolutionary forces can interact. Consider the forces of mutation and genetic drift.
How might these two forces interact? Mutation acts to change allele frequency by the introduction of a new allele, whereas genetic drift causes
random fluctuations in allele frequency from one generation to the next. If
both operate at the same time, drift may act to increase or decrease the
frequency of the new mutation. Consider what happens where everyone in
a population has two A alleles and there is then a mutation from A to a in
one individual. The person with the mutation can either pass on the A
allele or the a allele, each with a 50 percent probability. It is possible that
the new mutant allele will be lost from the population because of random
chance. It is also possible that the frequency of the mutant allele will
increase because of random chance. The person with the mutation may
pass the mutant form on to all of his or her children, and each of them
might continue to pass it on to their children.

   To give you an idea of how mutation and genetic drift can interact,
this author performed a simple computer simulation that allowed for a
single mutation followed by genetic drift. In this simulation, a population
size of 10 was used in which all individuals initially had the same allele. A
single mutation event was then allowed, which meant that the frequency
of the mutant allele was $1/20 = 0.05$ (1 mutant allele out of all 20 alleles
in the population). Genetic drift was then simulated for 20 generations.

TABLE   3.8
Results of Computer Simulation of Mutation and Genetic Drift

A total of 1,000 independent computer simulations were performed using a population size of 10 individuals with a single initial mutation (1 mutant allele out of 20 in the population, giving an initial allele frequency of $1/20 = 0.05$). Following mutation, the computer simulated genetic drift for 20 generations. The table below shows the distribution of the frequencies of the mutant allele after 20 generations (see text).

Final frequency of the mutant allele	Number of cases
0.0	889
0.01–0.09	2
0.10–0.19	22
0.20–0.29	11
0.30–0.39	16
0.40–0.49	15
0.50–0.59	9
0.60–0.69	11
0.70–0.79	9
0.80–0.89	9
0.90–0.99	2
1.0	5

This entire simulation experiment was repeated 1,000 times and the results are shown in Table 3.8.

As expected, genetic drift leads to the loss of the mutant allele most of the time (in this case, 889 out of 1,000 times). In most of the remaining cases, however, the frequency of the mutant allele actually increased. In 45 cases, the frequency of the mutant allele was greater than 0.5 after 20 generations. In 5 cases, the mutant allele had become fixed within the population! Such computer simulations are a bit simplistic and somewhat unrealistic, but they do show how two evolutionary forces can interact.

There are many other possibilities for interaction. For example, natural selection reduces the frequency of a harmful recessive mutant allele. Gene flow tends to counter the effects of genetic drift on variation among populations. Genetic drift can increase the frequency of a harmful allele even if it is being selected against.

Much of microevolutionary theory deals with the mathematics describing such interactions. Studies of actual populations must take these interactions into account and try to control for them in analysis. There are some basic rules for interpreting genetic variation. If populations are large, then drift is unlikely to have much of an effect. Gene flow can be measured to some extent by looking at migration rates to determine how powerful an effect it would have. Natural selection can be investigated by looking at patterns of fertility and mortality among different classes of genotypes.

Imagine that you have visited a population over two generations. You note that the frequency of a certain allele has changed from 0.4 to 0.5. Furthermore, assume that the population has been totally isolated during the last generation and that the size of the breeding population has stayed at roughly 50 people. What could have caused the allele frequency change? Because mutation occurs at much lower rates, it could not be responsible. Given that the population was totally isolated, gene flow could not be responsible. Drift may have caused the change in allele frequency, for the size of the breeding population is rather low. Natural selection could also have produced the change. You would have to know more about the specific alleles and genotypes involved, environmental factors, and patterns of mortality and fertility to determine whether selection had an effect. Even given this rather limited information, you can rule out mutation and gene flow and proceed to develop tests to determine the relative influence of drift and selection.

The study of any natural population is much more complex. With laboratory animals, you can control for a variety of factors to help your analysis. In dealing with human populations, however, you must rely on observations as they occur in nature. Case studies showing the effects of different evolutionary forces are given in Chapter 5.

Nonrandom Mating

Recall that one of the assumptions of the Hardy-Weinberg equilibrium model is random mating. Everyone has the same chance of mating with everyone else (with respect to the locus or loci under consideration). In reality, populations often show deviations from random mating. From an evolutionary standpoint, we are interested in nonrandom mating: who mates with whom and the genetic similarities of those who mate. Deviations from random mating do not lead to changes in allele frequencies. Patterns of nonrandom mating, however, can influence the rate of allele frequency change by interacting with the evolutionary forces.

Inbreeding

Inbreeding refers to mating with a close biological relative. Actually, we are all inbred to some extent, but we generally reserve the term for close biological relatedness. Though the definition of "close" is somewhat arbitrary, we are usually interested in matings between first cousins or closer.

Evolutionary significance of inbreeding. Inbreeding is not an evolutionary force because it does not cause any changes in allele frequencies.

inbreeding coefficient The increase in the probability of homozygous offspring because of inbreeding.

What, then, is the genetic effect of inbreeding? Closely related individuals are likely to have similar alleles inherited from a common ancestor, and thus the effect of inbreeding is to make homozygous offspring more likely. For example, brothers and sisters share more alleles than any two unrelated individuals. If brothers and sisters mate, there is an increased probability (25 percent) that their offspring will receive identical alleles. If two first cousins mate, there is also an increased probability (6.25 percent) that their offspring will receive identical alleles.

The increase in the probability of homozygous offspring is also termed the **inbreeding coefficient.** This coefficient can also be interpreted as the proportion of loci that are homozygous because of common ancestry. Computation of inbreeding coefficients is beyond the scope of this text, but Table 3.9 lists these coefficients for several forms of close inbreeding. Note that the increased probability of homozygous offspring in third cousins is relatively low (1.6 percent). Inbreeding coefficients for more distantly related couples, such as fourth cousins, are even lower and have little, if any, genetic impact.

Inbreeding changes the genotype proportions from those expected under Hardy-Weinberg equilibrium. Inbreeding increases the proportion of homozygotes and decreases the proportion of heterozygotes in a population. Allele frequencies are not changed, only the genotype frequencies.

Inbreeding by itself does not lead to changes in allele frequencies. Inbreeding can influence the rate of allele frequency change by interacting with natural selection. For example, if there is selection against recessive homozygotes, then inbreeding leads to a more rapid decline in the frequency of the recessive allele. This occurs because natural selection has more homozygotes to act on as compared to a state of random mating.

The genetic effects of inbreeding are often harmful. Studies have shown that the incidence of congenital birth defects and mortality during the first year of life is higher among inbred offspring than among others (Bittles et al. 1991). The risk of birth defects in offspring of first cousins has been estimated at between 1.3 and 1.8 times that of the offspring of unrelated parents (Bodmer and Cavalli-Sforza 1976). Some studies have suggested that inbreeding can lead to mental retardation, but others have not confirmed this.

T A B L E   3.9
Inbreeding Coefficients for Certain Close Marriages

Marriage	Inbreeding coefficient
Parent–child	$\frac{1}{4}$ = 0.250
Siblings	$\frac{1}{4}$ = 0.250
Uncle–niece Aunt–nephew Half siblings	$\frac{1}{8}$ = 0.125
First cousins	$\frac{1}{16}$ = 0.063
Second cousins	$\frac{1}{32}$ = 0.031
Third cousins	$\frac{1}{64}$ = 0.016

The inbreeding coefficient is an estimate of the increased probability that children of these marriages will have two identical alleles because of descent from a common ancestor.

Rates of human inbreeding. Compared to many other organisms, human populations generally have much lower rates of inbreeding. The inbreeding coefficients for a number of human populations are shown in Table 3.10. Only isolated populations tend to have high inbreeding coefficients (> 0.01), and even here the rates would be less than expected if everyone within the population mated with their first cousins (which would give an inbreeding coefficient of 0.0625). Part of the reason for these low rates is the fact that humans are rather mobile compared to other organisms; there is considerable gene flow. Another factor is the fact that

TABLE 3.10
Average Rates of Inbreeding in Some Human Populations

Average inbreeding coefficient	Population
<0.00001	Netherlands
0.00001–0.0001	United States
0.0001–0.001	Belgium Switzerland Mexico
0.001–0.01	Mormons, United States Ramah Navaho, United States Sardinia Island, Italy
0.01–0.05	Various Indian castes Dunkers, United States Xavante Indian tribes, South America Hutterites, Canada

Source: Reid (1973:98–99).

many societies have cultural rules discouraging, or prohibiting, mating with close relatives.

Inbreeding, however, does take place to some extent in most human populations. Today, inbreeding levels are high in certain societies. In Muslim regions of parts of Africa and Asia between 20 and 55 percent of all marriages are between second cousins or closer. In south India, between 20 and 45 percent of all marriages are between close relatives (Bittles et al. 1991). Higher levels of inbreeding are often found in smaller populations, where there is a lack of suitable unrelated mates. In Ireland, for example, Catholicism prohibits marriage between individuals who are third cousins or closer. Yet in many rural areas dispensations are granted for such marriages because there may be no suitable mates who are not cousins. Some societies even have cultural preferences for certain types of inbreeding. The classic example is inbreeding among ancient Egyptian royalty; Cleopatra herself was the result of 11 generations of inbreeding between half-brothers and half-sisters (Harris 1987). Many societies have a stated preference for males to marry their cross-cousins (marriage with the mother's brother's daughter or the father's sister's daughter) (Underwood 1975).

A variety of social and cultural factors influence levels of human inbreeding. In their study of inbreeding in Finland, Jorde and Pitkänen (1991) found that first-cousin marriages were more common in Swedish-speaking than in Finnish-speaking communities, and more common in upper social classes. In their study of south India, Bittles et al. (1991)

positive assortative mating
Mates chosen on the basis of similar phenotypic characteristics.

negative assortative mating
Mates chosen on the basis of different phenotypic characteristics.

found marriage between relatives more common among Hindu (38 percent) than among Muslim (27 percent) or Christian (22 percent). Their study shows how religious affiliation can affect marriage choice and inbreeding.

Assortative Mating

Another form of nonrandom mating is assortative mating, which describes mating made on the basis of some observable characteristic. One of the most obvious examples of assortative mating in the United States is skin color. The frequency of marriages between European Americans and African Americans is low. Americans tend most often to marry someone with a similar skin color.

It should be no surprise that mating is not random in human populations. If you list the characteristics you prefer in a spouse, you will most often identify social and biological traits. Social characteristics may include economic status, ethnicity, religion, and/or educational level. Phenotypic characteristics are likely to include skin color, height, weight, and hair color.

When mates are chosen on the basis of similar characteristics, it is **positive assortative mating.** If there is a genetic basis for these characteristics, then the genetic effect is the same as that of inbreeding. The frequency of homozygotes is increased relative to random mating. In theory we could also expect the reverse, **negative assortative mating,** whereby mates are chosen on the basis of having different phenotypic characteristics. If it were common, for example, for short males to choose tall females for mates, then that would be a case of negative assortative mating. There is little evidence that negative assortative mating is common in human populations.

The old idea that opposites attract has few data to support it. Studies of marriage choice have shown that people tend to choose spouses with similar social and biological characteristics. In the United States, positive assortative mating has been demonstrated for skin color, height, weight, and eye color, in addition to a variety of social, religious, ethnic, and educational variables (Buss 1985).

SUMMARY

The study of microevolution looks at changes in the frequencies of alleles from one generation to the next. Such analyses allow detailed examination of the factors that can alter allele frequencies in the short term and also provide us with inferences about long-term patterns of evolution. Changes in allele frequencies stem from four evolutionary forces: mutation, natural selection, genetic drift, and gene flow.

Mutation is the ultimate source of all genetic variation but occurs at low enough rates that additional factors are needed to explain polymorphic frequencies (whereby two or more alleles have frequencies greater than 0.01). The other three evolutionary forces are responsible for increasing or decreasing the frequency of a mutant allele. Natural selection changes allele frequencies through the processes of differential survival and reproduction of individuals having certain genotypes. Genetic drift is the random change in allele frequencies from one generation to the next and has the greatest effect in small populations. Gene flow, the movement of alleles between populations, acts to reduce genetic differences between different groups.

The rate of allele frequency change is affected by nonrandom mating patterns, such as inbreeding and assortative mating. The allele frequencies do not change, but the genotype frequencies are affected. More homozygotes occur than expected from random mating, which can result in more rapid change in allele frequencies because of natural selection.

Supplemental Readings

Bodmer, W. F., and L. L. Cavalli-Sforza. 1976. *Genetics, Evolution, and Man.* San Francisco: W. H. Freeman. This text provides a basic, essentially nonmathematical discussion of evolutionary forces.

Cavalli-Sforza, L. L., and W. F. Bodmer. 1971. *The Genetics of Human Populations.* San Francisco: W. H. Freeman. A more detailed version of the above text, with a greater emphasis on mathematics.

Morris, L. N. 1971. *Human Populations, Genetic Variation, and Evolution.* San Francisco: Chandler. This is a collection of somewhat outdated but classic papers on human microevolution. The author also provides succinct and informative summaries before each section of readings.

Underwood, J. H. 1979. *Human Variation and Human Microevolution.* Englewood Cliffs, N. J.: Prentice-Hall. A basic treatment of human microevolution with some, but not extensive, mathematics, clearly written, with many excellent examples of case studies from human populations. This is a recommended starting place for those interested in additional information on human microevolution.

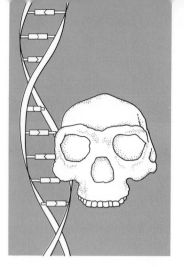

CHAPTER 4

Macroevolution

Chapters 2 and 3 dealt with evolution from the perspectives of molecular, Mendelian, and population genetics. Whereas microevolution is relatively easy to observe and understand in living populations, the long-term nature of evolutionary change is somewhat more difficult to grasp. Part of the problem is that extremely long periods of time, ranging from thousands to millions of years, are involved in macroevolution.

When so-called "creation scientists" dispute evolution, they generally mean macroevolution. Few doubt the existence of short-term, microevolutionary changes when we can see such changes in our daily lives, from changing patterns of disease to the kinds of alterations brought about by animal and plant breeding. The long-term pattern of evolution, however, is generally more difficult to grasp. Creationism argues that we cannot directly observe changes over millions of years and therefore cannot make scientific tests. It is true that we cannot undertake laboratory tests lasting for millions of years, but it is equally not true that we cannot make scientific predictions. Many sciences, including geology and astronomy, are historical in nature. That is, we rely on some record (geologic strata or stellar configurations, for example) to note what has happened. We can establish the facts of change. The same is true of macroevolution. The fossil record provides us with information about what *has* happened. We must then utilize other information available to us to determine *why* such change has occurred. A geologist makes use of the fact that geologic processes occur in a regular manner and therefore occurred in the same way in ancient times. Geologists use available information about current geologic processes to explain patterns of change in the past. In much the same way, evolutionary science takes what we know about microevolution and extends it to explain the long-term pattern of macroevolution.

To many, but not all, evolutionary biologists, macroevolution is merely the net effect of microevolutionary change over long periods of time. Some, however, believe that additional forces must be considered in explaining macroevolution.

Perhaps the single largest task of macroevolutionary theory is to explain the origin of new species. Along with this goes the task of explaining the major changes in the fossil record. For example, what evolutionary factors were responsible for the development of flight in birds? What species lived in the past but are not alive today? Why have some species died out while others continued to the present? Why have some organisms, such as our ancestors, changed so much in relatively short periods of time, whereas other organisms, such as cockroaches, have scarcely changed at all over many millions of years?

The origin of new species has been observed in historical times and in the present. Some new species have been brought about by human intervention and controlled breeding, as with many species of tropical fish. There are also examples of new species having arisen naturally in the recent past, such as certain types of fruit flies. We also have information on populations in the process of forming new species, such as certain groups of snails. Most of what we observe about new species formation comes from analysis of the fossil record.

How do new species come into being? It is ironic that even though the title of Darwin's book was *On the Origin of Species,* it did not deal very much with this question. Instead, Darwin sought to explain the basic nature of evolutionary change, believing that extension of these principles could explain the formation of new species. Indeed, even though there are different models of species formation, all essentially use the processes of microevolution for explanation.

Taxonomy and Evolution

An understanding of the origin of species begins with consideration of the definition of the term *species*. There is considerable controversy regarding its definition and how it relates to models of evolutionary change (Ereshefsky 1992). A discussion of macroevolution and the origin of species must begin with an understanding of certain principles of biological classification.

In Chapter 1, you read about Linnaeus's attempt to construct a system of classification for all living creatures. Instead of simply making up a list of all known organisms, Linnaeus developed a scheme by which creatures could be grouped together according to certain shared characteristics. The system of biological classification is called a taxonomy. Even though we now make use of Linnaeus's scheme to describe patterns of evolution, Linnaeus did not have this objective in mind. Rather, he sought to understand the nature of God's design in living organisms.

We use systems of classification every day, often without being aware that we do so. We all have the tendency to label objects and people according to certain characteristics. We often use terms such as "liberal" and "conservative" to describe people's political views, and terms such as "white" and "black" to describe people's skin color. Movies are classified into different groups by a rating, such as PG, R, and X.

If you think for a moment, you will realize that a great deal of your daily life revolves around your use and understanding of different systems of classification. In biology, a taxonomy is a system of classification that shows relationships between different groups of organisms. This may sound simple enough but can actually be rather difficult. For example, consider the following list of organisms: flounder, bat, shark, canary, lizard, horse, and whale. How would you classify these creatures? One way might be to put certain animals together according to size: the flounder, bat, canary, and lizard in a "small" category, the shark and horse in a "medium" category, and the whale in a "large" category. Another method would be to put the animals in groups according to where they live: the flounder, shark, and whale in the water; the bat and canary in the air; and the lizard and horse on the land. Still another method would be to put the shark in a separate category from all the others because the shark's skeleton is made of cartilage instead of bone.

The problem with this example is that none of these three ways of classification agrees with the other two. There is no consistency. Biologists actually classify these animals into the following groups: fish (flounder and shark), reptiles (lizard), birds (canary), and mammals (bat, horse, whale). These groups reflect certain common characteristics, such as mammary glands for the mammals. But what makes this system of classification any better than those based on size or habitat? For our purposes, we require taxonomies that reflect evolutionary patterns. As we will see, organisms can have similar traits because they inherited these traits from a common ancestor. Thus, the presence of mammary glands in the bat, horse, and whale represents a trait that has been inherited from a common ancestral species.

Taxonomies are useful in trying to understand evolutionary relationships. In order to reflect the evolutionary process, the taxonomy must reflect evolutionary changes. The groups of mammals, birds, reptiles, and fish are based on characteristics that reflect evolutionary relationships. The bat and the whale are placed in the same group because they have a more recent common ancestor than either does with the lizard, as reflected by certain shared characteristics such as mammary glands. Biological classification should reflect evolutionary processes, but only careful analysis of both living and extinct life forms allows us to discover what characteristics reflect evolutionary relationships.

species Includes organisms from separate populations capable of breeding naturally and producing offspring.

Taxonomic Categories

The Linnean taxonomy is a hierarchical classification. That is, each category contains a number of subcategories, which contain further subcategories, and so on. Biological classification uses a number of categories. The more commonly used categories are: kingdom, phylum (plural *phyla*), class, order, family, genus (plural *genera*), and species. In addition, prefixes are often added to distinguish further breakdowns within a particular category, such as subphylum or infraorder. The scientific name given to an organism consists of the genus and species names in Latin. The scientific name for the common house mouse is *Mus musculus.* Modern human beings are known as *Homo sapiens,* translated roughly as "wise humans."

Any given genus may contain a number of different species. The genus *Homo,* for example, contains modern humans (*Homo sapiens*) as well as extinct human species (*Homo erectus* and *Homo habilis*). These three species are placed in the same genus because of certain common characteristics, such as large brain size.

The categories of classification are often vaguely defined. Genus, for example, refers to a group of species that shares similar environments, patterns of adaptation, and physical structures. An example is the horse and the zebra, different species that are placed in the genus *Equus* (there are several species of zebra). These species are four-legged, hoofed grazers. The basis for assigning a given species to one genus or another is often unclear. This uncertainty is even more problematic when fossil remains are assigned to different categories. The only category with a precise meaning is the species, and even that has certain problems in application.

Definitions of Species

The concept of species is a shifting one that can be defined in terms of various contexts.

The biological species concept. Species may be defined on the basis of reproduction. If organisms from two populations are capable of breeding naturally and can produce fertile offspring, then they belong to the same **species.** Note that this definition has several parts. First, organisms from two populations must be capable of interbreeding. Second, these matings must occur in nature. Recent advances in biology have allowed individuals usually considered to be separate species to produce offspring under laboratory conditions. In understanding who we are and how we evolved, we are interested in breeding that takes place naturally. Third and finally, the

Figure 4.1

The horse and donkey can mate and produce offspring (a mule), but two mules cannot produce offspring. Therefore, the horse and donkey belong to two separate species although they are closely related.

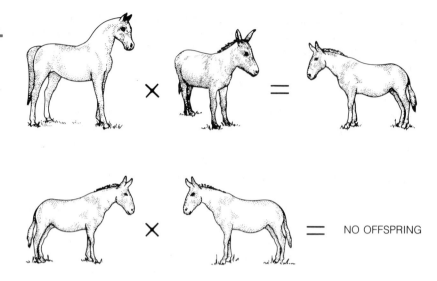

NO OFFSPRING

offspring must be *fertile,* that is, capable of producing further offspring.

Perhaps the best-known example of application of the species concept is the mule. Mules are farm animals produced as the offspring of a horse bred with a donkey. The horse and the donkey interbreed naturally, which satisfies the first and second parts of the species definition. The offspring (mules) are sterile, however, and cannot produce further offspring. The only way to get a mule is to mate a horse and a donkey. Because the offspring are not fertile, the horse and the donkey are considered separate species (see Figure 4.1). On the other hand, all human populations around the world belong to the same species because members can interbreed and produce fertile offspring.

The concept of biological species appears to provide a useful test for the purposes of classification. One of its problems, however, is that it only provides a simple yes or no answer to the question of similarity. It does not reflect any degree of similarity among organisms that belong to different species. For example, horses and donkeys are obviously more similar to each other than either is to an ant. The different species names show only that all are different species, but not which species are more similar to each other. The fact that horses and donkeys can interbreed shows us that they are closely related species.

The idea of species, moreover, flatly assumes that two organisms either belong or do not belong to the same species. It does not allow for any kind of intermediate state. Why should this be a problem? Consider as an example two modern species that had a common ancestor at some point in the past. We usually draw an evolutionary "tree" showing the point at which a new "branch," or species, comes into being. If some populations of species A evolved into species B, then at what point did those populations stop being species A and start being species B? The species concept suggests that this change was instantaneous, because a creature either belongs to one species or the other. Any system of classification tends to ignore variation within groups. In the real world, however, evolution and variation work to break down rigid systems of classification. Organisms become difficult to classify when they are constantly changing.

As an example of this problem, consider the populations of gypsy moths in Asia. When moths from the populations farthest apart are bred, their offspring are sterile. According to the biological species concept, these populations of moths belong to separate species. Populations that are closer together, however, are capable of producing fertile offspring, which suggests that they belong to the same species (Futuyma 1986).

Modes of species change. The biological species concept is useful when comparing two or more populations living at a single point in time. In theory, reproductive isolation can be tested to determine if these populations belong to the same species. How can the biological species concept be applied when comparing groups of organisms over a period of time? This question requires looking at two different modes of the evolutionary change of species.

First, a species can change over time. According to this mode of evolutionary change, a single species exists at any given point in time but evolves over a period of time. An example is the evolution of humans. The most likely scenario of human evolution over the past two million years (see Chapters 12 and 13) is a change from a species known as *Homo habilis* into a species known as *Homo erectus* into our own species *Homo sapiens*. While a single species exists within the genus *Homo* at any point in time, there is continued evolutionary change such that the most recent forms (ourselves) are quite different from the earliest forms. For example, our brains are roughly twice as large. The point here is that a single species evolves over time.

This mode of species change is known as **anagenesis,** or straight-line evolution. It is illustrated as a straight line, as shown in Figure 4.2 where form A evolves into form B and then into form C. Although this mode of evolutionary change is fairly straightforward, complications arise when considering the naming of species. Should form A be called a different species from form B? In the case of human evolution, should *Homo erectus* actually be given a different species name from *Homo sapiens?* The problem is that the traditional biological species concept doesn't really apply. Form A and form B are by necessity isolated from each other reproductively since they lived at different times. There is no way they could interbreed any more than you could mate with an early human that lived 1.5 million years ago (we'll leave out science fiction and time machines here).

Many researchers modify the species concept to deal with this type of situation. Different physical forms along a single lineage (an evolutionary line such as that shown in Figure 4.2) are given different species names out of convenience, and as a label to represent the types of physical change

anagenesis The transformation of a single species over time.

Figure 4.2

Anagenesis, the linear evolution of a species over time. Form A changes over time into form B and then further changes into form C.

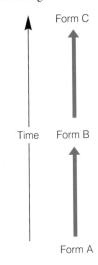

paleospecies Species identified from fossil remains based on their physical similarities and differences to other species.

cladogenesis The formation of one or more new species from another over time.

evolutionary species A definition of species that is based on ancestral and descendant populations that are evolutionarily distinct from other lineages.

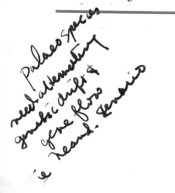

shown over time. Such forms are referred to as **paleospecies** and are used more as labels than as units representing the species concept. In recent years there has been a tendency to move away from the use of paleospecies, at least among some evolutionary biologists.

Anagenesis is not the only mode of species change. If you think about it, anagenesis is not completely sufficient as an explanation of macroevolution. Where do new species come from? The other mode of species change is **cladogenesis,** or branching evolution. Cladogenesis involves the formation of new species (speciation) whereby one or more new species branch off from an original species. In Figure 4.3, a portion of species A first branches off to produce species B (living at the same time), then a portion of species B branches to produce species C. This example starts with one species and ends up with three. The factors responsible for speciation will be discussed later in this chapter.

Evolutionary species. Another approach to species definition is the use of a concept of **evolutionary species.** A species is defined as a linear sequence of ancestral and descendant populations that are evolutionarily distinct from other lineages (Wiley 1978) and any linear sequence of populations is considered to belong to the same species. For example, Figure 4.4 shows four fossil groups connected in evolutionary time. These four groups are physically different enough so that some researchers would opt to label each as a separate species. If forms A and B were sufficiently different biologically, one might be tempted to call them different species

Figure 4.3

Cladogenesis, the origin of new species. Species A splits and forms a new species B, which later splits to form species C. The process begins with a single species (A) and ends with three species (A, B, C).

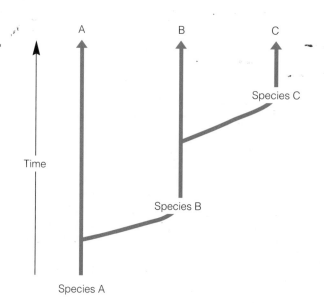

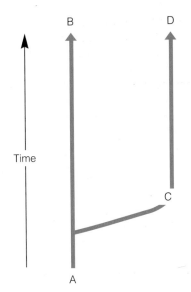

Time

B   D

C

A

Figure 4.4

The evolutionary species concept. If these four fossil forms were all different enough biologically, some researchers would label each form as a different species (a paleospecies). According to the evolutionary species concept, only new branches would count as separate species. Therefore, form A and form B would be considered in the same species, just as form C and form D would be considered in another.

(using the paleospecies approach). Likewise, forms C and D might be considered different species. Again, the biological species concept is problematic here; A and B (or C and D) are by definition reproductively isolated because they exist at different times.

If you followed the evolutionary species concept, your thinking would be different because only branching (cladogenesis) is important in defining a new species. The number of lineages is really the important factor. In this example, forms A and B are considered different stages within the same species, and forms C and D are also considered different stages within a separate species (defined where C branches off from A). This approach seems simple enough, but it is not without problems. Suppose form B was quite different from form A. Maybe form B had one toe, as opposed to three toes in form A. Returning to an example from human evolution, should *Homo erectus* and *Homo sapiens* be placed in the same evolutionary species as some anthropologists suggest (e.g., Wolpoff 1992)?

The problem of species naming is complicated by the fact that evolutionary relationships among fossil forms are not always clear. Some of these problems will be addressed later, in the chapters on primate and human evolution. For now, keep in mind that species names often mean different things to different people. The naming of species might adhere to an evolutionary model or might serve only as convenient labels of physical variation.

reproductive isolation The genetic isolation of populations that may render them incapable of producing offspring.

speciation The origin of a new species.

Patterns of Macroevolution

Evolutionary forces interact to change populations over time (anagenesis) and lead to the formation of new species (cladogenesis). In addition to these processes, the study of macroevolution is concerned with the rate of evolutionary change and the failure of species to adapt over time.

Speciation

The fossil record shows many examples of new species arising. How? You know that genetic differences between populations come about as a result of evolutionary forces. For a population to become a new species, these genetic differences must be great enough to prevent successful interbreeding with the original parent species. For this to occur, the population must become reproductively isolated from the original parent species.

Reproductive isolation. **Reproductive isolation** is genetic change that can lead to an inability to produce fertile offspring. How does this happen? The evolutionary forces can produce such a situation. The first step in **speciation** (the formation of a new species from a parent species) is the elimination or reduction of gene flow between populations. Because gene flow acts to reduce differences between populations, its continued action tends to keep all populations in the same species. Gene flow does not need to be eliminated altogether, but it must be reduced sufficiently to allow the other evolutionary forces to make the populations genetically different. Populations must become genetically isolated from one another for speciation to occur.

The most common form of isolation in animal species is geographic isolation. When two populations are separated by a physical barrier, such as a river or mountain range, or by great distances, gene flow is cut off between the populations. As long as the populations remain isolated, genetic changes occurring in one group will not spread to other groups. As we saw in Chapter 3, geographic distance limits gene flow even in our own highly mobile species. The effects of geographic distance in causing reproductive isolation are even more dramatic in other species.

Geographic separation is the most common means of producing reproductive isolation among animal populations, but other mechanisms may also cause isolation. Some of these can operate within a single geographic region. Populations may be isolated by behavioral differences such as feeding habits. Some groups may eat during the day and others at dusk. Because the groups are not in frequent contact with one another, there is opportunity for isolation to develop. Although geographic isolation is in theory not required, the actual probability of speciation occurring in geographically adjacent groups remains highly controversial. A recent review notes that there is little evidence to date of speciation occurring without geographic isolation (Coyne 1992). ✕

Genetic divergence. Isolation is the first step in the speciation process. By itself, this isolation does not guarantee speciation. Elimination of gene flow provides the opportunity for speciation. Other evolutionary forces must then act upon this isolation to produce a situation in which the isolated groups have changed sufficiently to make fertile interbreeding no longer possible. Isolation, however, does not always lead to speciation.

How can the evolutionary forces lead to speciation? Mutation might act to increase variation among populations because it occurs independently in the genetic composition of separate groups. Without gene flow to spread them, individual mutations will accumulate in each group, making isolated populations genetically divergent. Genetic drift also contributes to differences in allele frequencies among small populations. In addition, if the two populations are in separate environments, then natural selection will lead to genetic differences. Once gene flow has been eliminated, the other evolutionary forces will act to make the populations genetically divergent. When this process continues to the point where the two populations can no longer interbreed and produce fertile offspring, they are separate species.

There is continued debate over the role of the various evolutionary forces in producing genetic divergence. For many years, speciation was felt to be solely the byproduct of natural selection. That is, as two populations came to occupy separate environments, the action of natural selection would cause these groups to become different. Speciation has been viewed as a consequence of this differential adaptation. In recent years, however, more attention has been given to the contributions to speciation of mutation and genetic drift in small populations. In the former view, the old species gradually formed two or more species, with natural selection operating on large populations. The more recent view is that new species often form from small populations and, as such, are affected extensively by mutation and genetic drift.

Shifting Balance Theory

The interaction of the evolutionary forces in speciation is best described by Sewall Wright's (1932, 1982) **shifting balance theory.** Whereas earlier models of macroevolution focused on natural selection operating on the entire species simultaneously, Wright developed a model that dealt with the more realistic situation of a species subdivided into smaller local populations connected by gene flow. Wright envisioned a situation where combinations of alleles produce different overall fitness values. As populations adapt to local environments they move toward a set of allele frequencies with a given overall fitness. However, any given overall fitness may not be the *maximum* possible fitness. Wright suggested that ranges in fitness

shifting balance theory
A model whereby allele frequencies can change to a new set of values providing greater overall fitness through a balance of natural selection and random genetic drift.

nec to eliminate gene flow

Figure 4.5

Peaks and valleys of fitness. Sewall Wright's shifting balance theory deals with the question of how a species can move from a given "peak" (point A) to a higher "peak" representing greater overall fitness (point B).

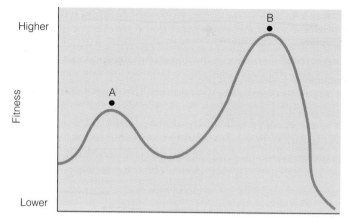

are like a picture of mountain peaks and valleys, with the peaks representing higher overall fitness values, and the valleys representing lower overall fitness values. To Wright, much of macroevolution dealt with the question of how a species could move from one set of allele frequencies (one of many "peaks") to a higher peak (that is, an increase in fitness).

Any set of allele frequencies will resist any decrease in fitness through selection. In Figure 4.5, to get from point A to point B (an increase in fitness), the species must change first to a situation of lower fitness (a valley); this seems counter to the whole notion of natural selection. How then will a species move to a higher "peak"? Wright suggested that random genetic change (drift) combined with fluctuations in selection in local environments will lead different groups within a species to have different peaks of fitness. Random fluctuations would produce some movement away from any given peak (just as genetic drift seems to be responsible for higher frequencies of harmful alleles in some groups, as discussed in the last chapter). As soon as one local group has moved to a higher peak through this process, genetic changes can then spread through an entire species through gene flow. In sum, Wright provided theoretical support for the idea that evolution is quicker and more efficient in species that have been broken down into small, semi-isolated populations. This idea is quite different, and more realistic, than earlier concepts of an entire species as a single breeding population. (After all, a resident of New York is more likely to choose a mate from New York than from Australia; species are not single populations.) Recent experimental evidence confirms many of Wright's predictions (Wade and Goodnight 1991).

Adaptive Radiation

The process of speciation minimally results in two species: the original parent species and the new offspring species. Under certain circumstances, many new species can come into being in a short period of time. This rapid diversification of species is associated with changing environmental conditions. When new environments open up, or when new adaptations to a specific environment develop, many new species can form—a process known as **adaptive radiation.**

New environments often open up following the demise of other species. One example, discussed in greater detail in Chapter 10, is the rise of mammals following the extinction of the dinosaurs. Once the dinosaurs were gone, there were vacant environments for mammals to adapt to. The rise of flowering plants at about the same time also provided many new habitats. The result was an adaptive radiation of mammalian species.

The Tempo and Mode of Macroevolution

During the past two decades, considerable attention has been given to the tempo (how fast?) and mode (the mechanism) of macroevolutionary change. How quickly do new species form? Does speciation occur in large or small populations? What are the effects of natural selection and the other evolutionary forces in producing new species? These are all questions about the tempo and mode of macroevolution.

Gradualism. Charles Darwin saw speciation as a slow and gradual process, taking thousands or millions of years. To Darwin, natural selection acted on populations ultimately to produce new species. The view that macroevolution is a slow and gradual process is called **gradualism.** According to this view, small changes in each generation over time result in major biological changes.

Gradualism, then, regards speciation as a slow process that takes a long time to occur. New species form from large portions of an original species. In such large populations, genetic drift and mutation have little impact in each generation. Natural selection, slowly operating on some initial mutation(s), is primarily responsible for speciation.

The gradualistic model predicts that, given a suitable fossil record, we will see a smooth and gradual transition from one species into another. Although there are examples of such change in the fossil record, it is not always apparent. In some cases we lack transitional forms. Does this lack of evidence indicate problems in the fossil record or in the theory of gradualism itself?

Punctuated equilibrium. An alternative theory has been suggested by Niles Eldredge and Stephen Jay Gould in the form of a model known as **punctuated equilibrium** (Eldredge and Gould 1972; Gould and Eldredge 1977). This theory suggests that the pattern of macroevolution consists of long periods of time when little evolutionary change occurs (stasis) and short periods of time when rapid evolutionary change occurs. To Eldredge and Gould, the tempo of macroevolution is not gradual; rather, it is static at times and rapid at other times. Long periods of stasis

adaptive radiation The formation of many new species following the availability of new environments or the development of a new adaptation.

gradualism A model of macroevolutionary change whereby evolutionary changes occur at a slow steady rate over time.

punctuated equilibrium A model of macroevolutionary change in which long periods of little evolutionary change (stasis) are followed by relatively short periods of rapid evolutionary change.

stasis Little or no evolutionary change occurring over a long period of time.

gradualism

punctuated evolution

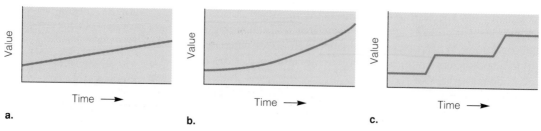

a.   b.   c.

Figure 4.6

The tempo of macro-evolution: gradualism and punctuated equilibrium. Each portion of this figure has a line showing the change in value of a physical trait over time. (a) Gradualism: the change over time is linear and constant. (b) A geometric, gradual pattern. The rate of change increases with time, but the curve is still smooth; there are no discontinuities. (c) Punctuated equilibrium: there are periods of no change (statis) punctuated by periods of rapid change; the net result is a "staircase" pattern.

are punctuated by short periods of rapid evolutionary change. Examples of gradualism and punctuated equilibrium are given in Figure 4.6.

Eldredge and Gould also view speciation as a rapid event occurring within small, isolated populations on the periphery of a species range. Mutations can spread quickly in small populations as a consequence of inbreeding and genetic drift. If such genetic changes are adaptive and if the newly formed species gains access to the parental species' range, it may then spread throughout an area, replacing the original parent species. According to this model, most biological change occurs during speciation. Once a species has been established, it changes little throughout time. Eldredge and Gould argue that stabilizing selection and other factors act to keep a species the same over time. This view contrasts with the gradualistic model, which sees biological change occurring at a slow rate, ultimately leading to separate species.

Punctuated equilibrium makes a prediction about how the fossil record should look. Given stasis, we should see long periods of time when little evolutionary change takes place. Certain organisms, such as the cockroach and coelacanth, seem to follow this pattern—they have not changed much over many millions of years. The punctuated equilibrium model also predicts that new species will appear rather quickly, often without any evidence of a transitional state. Because the model predicts that speciation occurs within small isolated populations, there is little chance that we will have fossil evidence actually documenting the initial stages of the origin of a new species.

The fossil evidence. Gradualism and punctuated equilibrium both make specific predictions of what the fossil record should look like. It should therefore be easy to examine the fossil evidence to determine which model best fits the available data. The fossil record, however, is not always complete enough to allow us to choose between these models. One major problem is that we do not have fossils of every organism that ever lived. Most often, we sample only a small fraction of all these organisms. When we have a "gap" in the fossil record, we cannot always tell whether it is caused by an incomplete record or punctuated equilibrium. It is possible to misinterpret a gradual process as punctuated equilibrium if we do not have a complete sample (Figure 4.7). A gradual change that occurs over 50,000 years could seem "rapid" in the geologic record.

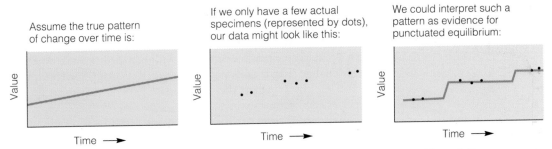

Assume the true pattern of change over time is:

Value / Time →

If we only have a few actual specimens (represented by dots), our data might look like this:

Value / Time →

We could interpret such a pattern as evidence for punctuated equilibrium:

Value / Time →

Figure 4.7

Problems in interpreting the tempo of macroevolutionary change. In this example gradual change could be interpreted as evidence for punctuated equilibrium because of small sample sizes.

Some organisms are preserved better than others, and it is possible in some cases to distinguish between gradualism and punctuated equilibrium. In the case of marine invertebrates, the fossil record is often complete enough to choose between the models. Numerous examples of punctuated equilibrium have been noted using marine invertebrates and other organisms (e.g., Gould and Eldredge 1977; Eldredge 1985).

There is little doubt among evolutionary biologists that stasis and rapid speciation have occurred in some organisms in the fossil record. It is also clear that the fossil record shows many examples of gradualism. Neither model is entirely correct in all cases, nor was it meant to be. Both represent different extremes of thinking about the tempo and mode of evolution. Though there is some debate over the genetic mechanisms of punctuated equilibrium, there is less debate on the facts of stasis and rapid speciation (Futuyma 1988). Whether gradualism or punctuated equilibrium is the dominant mode of macroevolution seems to depend on the specific type of organism and certain environmental conditions. In some cases gradualism is more prevalent, and in other cases punctuated equilibrium is more prevalent. Determining the factors responsible for the tempo and mode of evolution under different conditions is a major research objective of evolutionary biology.

Extinctions and Mass Extinctions

In considering macroevolutionary trends, we must not forget the most common pattern of them all—extinction. It is estimated that over 99 percent of all species that ever existed have become extinct (Futuyma 1986). In historic times, humans have witnessed (and helped cause) the extinction of a number of organisms, such as the passenger pigeon.

What causes extinction? When a species is no longer adapted to a changed environment, it may die. The exact causes of a species' death vary from situation to situation. Rapid ecological change may render an environment hostile to a species. For example, temperatures may change and a species may not be able to adapt. Food resources may be affected by environmental changes, which will then cause problems for a species requiring these resources. Other species may become better adapted to

mass extinction When many
species become extinct at
roughly the same time.

an environment, resulting in competition and ultimately the death of a
species.

Extinction seems, in fact, to be the ultimate fate of all species. Natural
selection is a remarkable mechanism for providing a species with the ability
to adapt to change, but it does not always work. When the environment
changes too rapidly or when the appropriate genetic variations do not
exist, a species can become extinct.

The fossil record shows that extinction has occurred throughout the
history of the planet. Recent analyses have also revealed that on some
occasions a large number of species became extinct at the same time—a
mass extinction. One of the best-known examples of mass extinction
occurred 65 million years ago with the demise of dinosaurs and many
other forms of life. Perhaps the largest mass extinction was the one that
occurred roughly 225 million years ago, when approximately 95 percent
of all species were wiped out (Gould 1991). Mass extinctions can be caused
by a relatively rapid change in the environment, compounded by the close
interrelationship of many species. If, for example, something were to happen to destroy much of the plankton in the oceans, then the oxygen content of our planet would drop, affecting even organisms not living in
the oceans. Such a change would probably lead to a mass extinction of
mammals.

One interesting, and controversial, finding is that extinctions during
the past 250 million years tended to be more intense every 26 million years
(Raup and Sepkoski 1986). This periodic extinction might be due to
intersection of the earth's orbit with a cloud of comets (Gould 1985),
although this notion must be considered speculative until further evidence
is uncovered.

Recent work has suggested that extinctions may often be random in
their effect. That is, certain species may be wiped out and others may
survive for no particular reason. A species' survival may have nothing to
do with its ability or inability to adapt—it may just be unlucky! If so,
some of evolutionary history may reflect a sequence of essentially random
events. Gould (1989) has suggested that evolutionary history is not the
pattern of increasing diversity of species over time traditionally shown in
textbooks, but rather a pattern of decimation of existing species (through extinction) followed by diversification of the surviving species (Figure 4.8).
All future patterns of evolution are constrained by variation present in
survivors. On the basis of his analysis of early invertebrates, Gould suggests that much of later vertebrate evolution (including mammals and
humans) may be contingent on the random survival of a particular lineage.
If we somehow could observe the history of life from the start, Gould
further suggests, random extinction might lead to a totally different pattern of present-day variation. Humans might not have evolved! Although
such speculation is not testable, it is interesting.

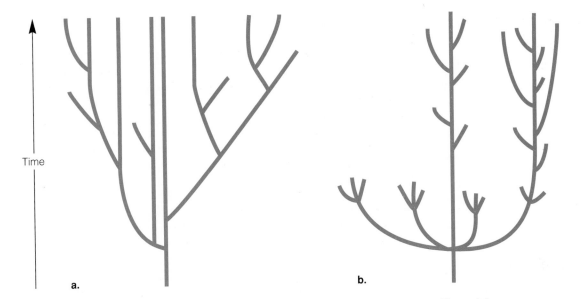

Time

a.

b.

Figure 4.8

Different views of evolutionary history and the role of extinction. (a) Increasing diversity. (b) Decimation followed by diversification of surviving species. (After Gould [1989])

Species Selection

The concept of extinction has been tied to that of natural selection. **Species selection** refers to the differential survival and reproduction of species. Even though natural selection is often discussed at the level of the individual genotype or phenotype, we may also apply the concept to larger groups, such as populations or species. If some species are better able to survive in a given situation, we have a case of differential mortality of species. It also appears that under certain circumstances some species are more likely to give rise to new species—in essence, a form of differential fertility of species (see Stanley 1979, 1981, for an extensive review of species selection).

Species selection has also been tied to the punctuated equilibrium model. According to punctuated equilibrium, the formation of new species is random with respect to specific biological traits. Imagine a species whose average molar length is 20 mm. If a new species forms from this original species through punctuated equilibrium, the length of the molar teeth may be larger, or smaller, than the original parent species. This randomness presents a problem when we look at the fossil record. If a physical trait, such as molar length, changes at random every time a new species forms, then why do we see definite trends in the fossil record? Suppose, for example, that we observe an increase in molar length among different species over time. How can this trend toward larger teeth be explained by the randomness of punctuated equilibrium? Species selection

species selection A process of selection in which some species are favored to survive and/or develop into new species.

early Australopith ↓

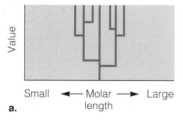
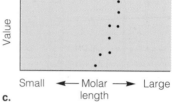

a.   b.   c.

Figure 4.9

Species selection and trends in macroevolution. In each of these graphs, the vertical axis represents time, the top of the graph being the present. The horizontal axis represents a range of values for molar length for a hypothetical organism. (a) In this graph, speciation is random with respect to molar length. Each time a new species evolves, the molar length of the new species is just as likely to be either smaller or larger than the original species. In such a case, modern-day species would show a wide range of molar lengths, and there would be no obvious trend in the evolution of molar teeth over time. (b) In this graph, species selection occurs so that those species with larger average molar lengths are more likely to survive. Species with smaller molar lengths become extinct. The pattern of speciation in this example is that predicted by punctuated equilibrium, but there is an obvious trend in molar length over time. (c) If we had only a few individual specimens from case B for analysis (shown by dots), we could interpret the evolutionary pattern as evidence for gradualism.

provides the answer. In this hypothetical example, all that is required is greater survival of large-toothed species.

This process is illustrated in Figure 4.9, which charts changes in molar length over time for our hypothetical organism. Figure 4.9a shows random change in molar length every time a new species forms. That is, half of the time the resulting species has smaller molar teeth and half of the time it has larger molar teeth. If there is no extinction of species, the end result is a large number of species with different molar lengths. This figure shows no direction in the changes in molar length over time. Figure 4.9b shows species selection whereby species with larger molars are more likely to survive. Species with smaller molars become extinct, and the net result is a definite direction in changes in molar length over time— the teeth become larger. Note, however, that if we did not have extensive fossil evidence to detect the existence of all the short-lived species in Figure 4.9b, the overall trend could also be explained by gradualism (Figure 4.9c).

we are getting to this?

Although species selection may be an additional evolutionary mechanism, not all evolutionary biologists support it (Ruse 1987). In many cases, it is difficult to determine whether species are truly a unit of selection or whether differences in survival are just reflections of the aggregate effects of selection upon individuals within a species.

Sociobiology: The Evolution of Behavior

Thus far, evolution has been discussed primarily in terms of biological characteristics. What about the evolution of behavior? Are behavioral traits subject to the same evolutionary forces? What about behaviors that seem, at first glance, to be nonadaptive? Much of the current discussion of evolution and behavior focuses on the controversial study of **sociobiology.** Some of the initial controversy arose from differences in definition. According to one of its main proponents, sociobiology is defined as "the systematic study of the biological basis of all social behavior" (Wilson 1980:322), including the evolution of social behaviors and their relationship to genetic change. The attempt to link social and cultural variation to genetic differences has been a cause of concern for many critics. That is, can we attribute differences in behavior between human populations to genetic factors?

Other definitions of sociobiology do not focus exclusively on the genetic basis of behavior. For example, Harpending and colleagues define human sociobiology as "the study of human behavior based on a Darwinian paradigm" (1987:127) and examine the evolution of behaviors within the framework of natural selection and adaptation. As they point out, genetic factors may, or may not, be of concern in any given sociobiological study.

In any event, sociobiology is ultimately concerned with the effect of natural selection on behaviors and, conversely, the effect of behaviors on natural selection. In most theoretical discussions of sociobiology, we assume that a given behavior has at least a partial genetic basis. Given a genetic basis, it is relatively easy to see how certain behaviors could be selected for. If they increase an individual's chance of survival and/or reproduction, then the alleles influencing these behaviors will be passed on to the next generation. Behaviors that seem nonadaptive at first may also be explained by sociobiological hypotheses.

Principles of Sociobiology

At the heart of sociobiology lies the premise that behaviors have evolved through natural selection and adaptation to environments. In one sense, there is no argument against this premise. The close bond between mothers and infants in mammals and the large brain size and intellectual capabilities of humans are two examples of biologically based behavioral factors that evolved through natural selection. The controversy surrounding the application of sociobiology involves two areas of analysis: (1) behaviors that do not appear adaptive and (2) behavioral variation within a species.

Central to much sociobiological theory is the concept of maximizing fitness. This refers to behaviors that increase the probability that an individual's alleles will be passed on to the next generation. If such behaviors are determined even partially by genes, then natural selection may cause those behaviors to increase in frequency. A related concept is the idea of **parental investment,** which refers to parental behaviors that increase the probability that the offspring will survive. According to sociobiological theory, mammalian females invest a great deal of time and energy in reproduction and care of offspring (Figure 4.10). Even though this investment reduces the number of offspring a female can have, the benefits outweigh the costs.

Mammalian males, on the other hand, often contribute only sperm. From the male standpoint of increasing fitness, it would seem more advantageous to impregnate many females rather than just one. This argument may explain the large number of mammalian species in which the fathers contribute little care to offspring and are not bonded permanently to any

sociobiology A discipline concerned with evolutionary explanations of social behavior, focusing on the role of natural selection.

parental investment Parental behaviors that increase the probability that offspring will survive.

Figure 4.10

Female chimpanzee and her offspring. The great amount of care and attention given by the mother can be interpreted as maximizing reproductive success by increasing parental investment. (Marine World Africa USA/Darryl W. Bush, Photographer)

kin selection A concept used in sociobiological explanations of altruism. Sacrificial behaviors, for example, can be selected for if they increase the probability of survival of close relatives.

reciprocal altruism Altruistic behaviors directed toward nonrelatives who may reciprocate at some future time.

one female. Although this hypothesis seems reasonable as a first approximation, many primate species show variations from this pattern. In some species, such as gibbons and humans, monogamous pairing does occur, and fathers may be involved directly in care of offspring (see Chapter 9).

Sociobiology is also concerned with behaviors that at first glance do not appear to make sense in terms of natural selection, such as altruism. If you died in an attempt to rescue a child from an oncoming car, then your alleles would not be passed on, including any hypothetical alleles responsible for your altruistic action. Natural selection would be expected to eliminate any such tendencies in future generations.

Still, however, we continue to observe altruistic acts in human and nonhuman societies. Is there any evolutionary benefit in sacrificing oneself? Sociobiology provides an answer in the form of the concept of **kin selection.** Altruistic behaviors are selected for when they are directed toward one's biological relatives. If you die saving your own child, this act will have two genetic consequences. First, because you die, you will no longer pass on your alleles to the next generation. Second, your child will live and have the opportunity to pass on his or her alleles, of which 50 percent came from you. Thus, by saving your child you actually contribute to the survival of some of your own alleles. If your altruistic action was at least partially caused by genetic factors, this behavior will also be passed on through the survival of your child. Sociobiological theory has developed a number of mathematical formulae that deal with the cost and benefit of altruistic actions in terms of the degree of biological relationship between the altruist and the recipient of the action. For example, it is more advantageous for you to save the life of your nephew than your first cousin because you share more alleles with your nephew than with your first cousin.

What of altruistic actions performed for the benefit of nonrelatives? Sociobiological theory has developed the concept of **reciprocal altruism** to explain the evolutionary advantage of such actions. Essentially, the argument states that any altruistic behavior may some day be rewarded. It may be useful to help others because you would be more likely to receive help from them at some future point. Risking your survival to help another may be advantageous at some point in the future (assuming, of course, you don't die in the attempt).

Applications of Sociobiology

From a biological and mathematical standpoint, the ideas of sociobiology are consistent and logical. Does this mean they are correct? Not necessarily. The ultimate utility of any theory lies in the testing and nonrejection of its hypotheses. Even though many scientists have no trouble using sociobiology to explain the behaviors of insects, the application of these concepts to the behaviors of the primates, especially humans, has been the focus of considerable criticism. Is such criticism simply a philosophical reaction to the implied lack of free will, or is it based on solid evidence?

One application of sociobiology is the analysis of the frequent killing of nestling birds by their older siblings (Mock et al. 1990). Is such a behavior pathological, or does it reflect an evolutionary adaptation for the murdering sibling? Mock and colleagues argue that under certain conditions, primarily relating to food resources, the older sibling increases his or her fitness as the result of such an act. It is important to note that sociobiological theory states that such behaviors are adaptive only under certain environmental conditions (not all birds perform such acts; some do only under certain circumstances). Mock and colleagues note that little is known about the exact effects of this behavior on the perpetrator's fitness, data that are necessary to test the implications of the sociobiological model. As with many such studies, more is needed than the demonstration that the model is logically consistent.

The problem with applying sociobiology to human and nonhuman primate behaviors is that the tests are often inconclusive or have alternative explanations. One classic study of primate behavior is Sarah Hrdy's (1977) analysis of infanticide (the killing of infants) among langur monkeys. Langurs typically live in groups with one adult male. There is frequently competition between that male and independent males seeking to displace him. When a new male langur successfully takes over a langur group, he often kills all the infants fathered by the previous male (Figure 4.11). At first, such behavior seems abnormal and contrary to the survival of the species. The sociobiological interpretation, however, is that the new males are increasing their own fitness. First, killing the infants from other males

Figure 4.11

Adult female langurs attempting to rescue an infant from an adult male langur. (Sarah Blaffer Hrdy/Anthro-Photo)

can increase the proportion of one's offspring in the next generation. The competition is eliminated. Second, females who are still nursing infants are not yet able to become pregnant. If the invading male did not kill the other male's children, then he would have to wait until the females were sexually receptive. By killing the infants, the new male ensures that the females are more quickly able to have children by him.

This interpretation poses a number of problems. First, we do not know how widespread this behavior is and whether or not it occurs under different environmental circumstances. Second, we do not know the extent to which such behaviors are affected by genetic factors. If the infanticide hypothesis is verified, then we still need to know to what extent such behaviors are "fixed." Perhaps one of the greatest problems in some applications of sociobiology is that we tend to assume that behaviors under partial genetic control are somehow deterministic—that is, that they occur under all circumstances. There is no reason to make this assumption. After all, we can make a strong case for the closeness of the mother-infant bond in primates as an evolutionary adaptation. The fact that such behavior is in part genetic does not mean that *all* mothers care properly for their infants. Open any newspaper and you will see that child abuse occurs quite frequently.

Another problem with the application of sociobiology to primate behavior is the assumption that any given behavior, if sufficiently widespread, is adaptive. This line of reasoning is often used in evolutionary biology, where every trait is assumed to have, or to have had, some adaptive purpose. If not, then why would the trait exist? Such reasoning ignores other potential evolutionary forces such as genetic drift. It also ignores the fact that many loci have pleiotropic effects. Some traits may be byproducts of another trait that was selected for. The same problem exists when we consider natural selection and behavior. We should not assume beforehand that any given behavior must have an adaptive value.

Finally, the hypothesis that differences in fitness are associated with certain behaviors must be tested. To do this, we need to know something about relative survival and differential reproduction. In other words, we must test the hypothesis that differences in fitness are associated with certain behaviors. To date, this has not often been done. In the case of langur infanticide, data from several generations and additional data on fitness are needed to be able to measure differences in fitness.

The potential problems in applying sociobiological theory to primate behavior are apparent in another example. Packer (1977) studied a group of baboons to determine if reciprocal altruism occurred among the adult males. He found that among unrelated adult males individuals that offered help in dominance disputes were those who most often received help later. The behavior of the baboons followed the predictions of reciprocal altruism. This finding, however, does not support the entire hypothesis of reciprocal altruism. To do this, we would need to know whether or not any differences in fitness were associated with this behavior and the extent to which these altruistic actions were genetically based. It is likely that such behaviors have at least a partial genetic basis. We would not, however, then want to speak of a "reciprocal altruism" allele. The fact that baboons help those who have helped them may instead reflect something about the basic nature of social groups. To some extent social skills may be genetic in nature among baboons, but such skills are part of a larger complex related to the general ability of primates to learn. We would be naive to reduce this complex of traits to a single locus, as popular accounts of sociobiology often do. The relationship between gene product and behavior is not as simple as some commentators might suggest.

Problems of applying sociobiological theory are even more apparent in explaining human behavior. There is no doubt that many human behaviors are partially genetic, although all humans may have the same alleles (Harpending et al. 1987). If so, then variation in behavior among different cultures would not reflect genetic differences.

Conclusions from sociobiology have been somewhat misrepresented and simplified by the media. When we speak of alleles for "shyness," "guilt," and the like, we are reducing complex behaviors to a simplistic model as well as confusing feelings with behaviors. Much of the literature on human sociobiology is flawed by this naive perspective along with a failure to consider methodological problems.

Not all sociobiological research suffers from these problems, however. More recent reviews (e.g., Harpending et al. 1987) suggest new approaches to eliminate these problems. Sociobiology has the potential to become a useful addition to models of human and nonhuman behavior.

Misconceptions about Evolution

Evolution is a frequently misunderstood subject. Many of our basic ideas regarding evolution are misconceptions that have become part of the general culture. The often used phrase "survival of the fittest" conjures up images that are sometimes at odds with the actual findings of evolutionary science. It is common for such misconceptions to continue even after initial exposure to evolutionary theory.

The Nature of Selection

Many people have a basic understanding of the general principles of natural selection. The problem lies in our misinterpretation of the nature of natural selection.

Misconception: Bigger is better. A common misconception is that natural selection will *always* lead to larger structures. According to this idea, the bigger the brain, the better, and the bigger the body, the better.

orthogenesis A discredited idea that evolution would continue in a given direction because of some vaguely defined "force."

At first, this idea seems reasonable. After all, larger individuals may be more likely to survive since they can compete more successfully for food and sexual partners. Therefore, larger individuals are more likely to survive and pass their genes on to the next generation. Natural selection is expected to lead to an increase in the size of the body, brain, and other structures. However, this isn't always true. There are numerous examples of species in which *smaller* body size or structures were more adaptive and selected for. Keep in mind that in evolution nothing is free! A larger body may be more adaptive because of sheer size, but a larger body also has greater energy needs. Any advantage gained by a larger body may be offset by the disadvantage of needing more food. What we have to focus on is a *balance* between the adaptive and nonadaptive aspects of any biological characteristic. By walking upright, humans have their hands free, which is rather advantageous. However, we pay the price with varicose veins, back pain, fallen arches, and other nonadaptive consequences of walking on two legs. Again, we need to focus on the relative costs and benefits of any evolutionary change. Of course, this balance will obviously vary in different environments.

Misconception: Newer is better. There is a tendency to believe that traits more recent in origin are superior because they are newer. Humans walk on two legs, a trait that appeared at least four million years ago. We also have five digits (fingers and toes) that date back many hundreds of millions of years. Is upright walking better because it is newer? Of course not. Both features are essential to our tool-making way of life. The age of a structure has no bearing on its usefulness.

Misconception: Natural selection always works. The idea that natural selection will always provide an opportunity for some members of a species to survive is not accurate. Occasionally this author has heard statements such as "we will evolve to tolerate air pollution." Such statements are absurdities. Natural selection only operates on variations that are present. If no genetic variation occurs to aid in breathing polluted air, natural selection will not help us. Even in cases where genetic variation is present, the environment may change too quickly to respond through natural selection. All we have to do is to examine the fossil record to see how inaccurate this misconception is—that 99 percent of all past species are extinct shows us that natural selection obviously doesn't always work!

Misconception: There is an inevitable direction in evolution. An idea popular in the nineteenth century was **orthogenesis,** the notion that evolution would continue in a given direction because of a vaguely defined nonphysical "force" (Mayr 1982). As an alternative to the theory of natural selection, orthogenesis suggested that evolutionary change would continue in the same direction either until a perfect structure was attained or a species became extinct. Apart from the problems of dealing with metaphysical "forces," orthogenesis has long been rejected by analysis of the fossil record and the triumph of natural selection as an explanatory mechanism for evolutionary change. Some of its basic notions, however, are still perpetuated. A common belief is that humans will evolve larger and larger brains, as a continuation of earlier trends (Figure 4.12). The view of orthogenesis is tied in with notions of "progress" and with the misconception that bigger is better. There are many examples from the fossil record of nonlinear change, and many examples of reversals in sizes of structures. In the case of human evolution, brains actually stopped getting larger 50,000 years ago. In fact, the average brain size of humans since that time has decreased slightly as a consequence of a general decrease in skeletal size and ruggedness (Henneberg 1988).

Is it possible for a trend to continue to change in a given direction under the right circumstances? Of course, but change comes through the action of natural selection, not some mysterious internal force. Continuation of any trend depends on the environment, present genetic variation, and basic biological limits. (A 50-foot spider can't exist because it wouldn't be able to absorb enough oxygen for its volume.) Such change also depends on the relative cost and benefits of change. Suppose that an increase in human brain size was combined somehow with an increase in pelvic size (assuming genetic variation was present for both features). A larger brain *might* confer some advantage, but a larger pelvis would certainly make pregnancy and childbirth more hazardous because of the relatively narrow birth canal in humans. A larger pelvis would also affect walking. Evolution works on the entire organism and not one trait at a time. Any change can have both positive and negative effects, but it is the net balance that is critical to the operation of natural selection.

Structure, Function, and Evolution

A number of misconceptions about evolution focus on the relationship between biological structures and their adaptive (or nonadaptive) functions.

Misconception: Natural selection always produces perfect structures. There is a tendency to view nature as the product of perfect natural engineering. Granted, there are many marvelous and wondrous phenomena in the natural world, but a closer examination shows that biological structures are often far from perfect. Consider human beings. Is the human body perfect? Hardly. Just to note one aspect, consider your skeleton when you stand upright. What is holding in your internal organs? Skin and muscles. Your rib cage provides little support for lower internal organs because it reflects ancestry from a four-legged form. When humans stood up (adaptive), the rib cage offered less support. The result—a variety of complaints and complications, such as hernias. The human skeleton is not perfect, but

Figure 4.12

The theory of orthogenesis predicts continued change in a given direction. The popular but incorrect notion that humans in the future will have progressively larger brains is illustrated.

rather the result of natural selection operating on the variation that was present.

Misconception: All structures are adaptive.   Natural selection is such a powerful model that it is tempting to apply it to all biological structures. Indeed, many anthropologists and biologists have done so. They examine a structure and explain its function in terms of natural selection. Are all structures adaptive? Many structures simply reflect a byproduct of other biological changes and have no adaptive value of their own (Gould and Lewontin 1979). Other structures, such as the human appendix, may have served a function in the past but appear to have no present function.

A classic example of a presumably nonadaptive trait is the chin of modern human beings. The jutting chin is relatively modern (see Chapter 13). Earlier forms of *Homo sapiens* lacked the jutting chin in most cases. According to a strict adaptationist perspective, we would become concerned with the function of the jutting chin and attempt to explain it in terms of natural selection. Actually, the jutting chin is simply a byproduct of different growth patterns in the human face and jaw. When the face receded, the lower jaw, under a different pattern of growth, stayed at its previous size. The result—a jutting chin that has nothing to do with adaptive value, except as a byproduct of adaptive changes in the rest of the face.

Another example deals with an old question: "Why do human men have nipples?" Earlier explanations suggesting that in ancient times men could assist women in breast feeding are ludicrous. The true explanation is simple. Both male and female develop from the same basic body plan during the embryonic stage of prenatal life. Under the influence of sex hormones, various structures develop in different ways (just as the same structure develops into a penis in men and a clitoris in women). The basic body plan for nipples is present in both sexes; for women, these structures develop into breasts capable of lactation. In men, nipples serve no purpose. Thus, male nipples are a byproduct of the fact that males and females share a similar developmental path, and not as the result of some adaptive value (Gould 1991).

Misconception: Current structures always reflect initial adaptations.   The idea here is that any given structure, with an associated function, originally evolved specifically for that function. Human beings, for example, walk on two legs; this allows them to hold tools and other objects that are constructed with the aid of an enlarged brain. Although it is tempting to say that both upright walking and a larger brain evolved at the same time because of the adaptive value of having both structures, this is not what happened. Upright walking evolved at least 1.5 million years before the use of stone tools and the expansion of the brain (Chapter 12).

As another example, consider your fingers. You have five of these digits on each hand, which allow you to perform a variety of manipulative tasks. Humans use their hands to manipulate both natural and human-made objects. Manipulative digits are essential to our nature as tool-using creatures. We might therefore suggest that our grasping hands *first* evolved to meet this need; this is not the case. Grasping hands *first* developed in early primate ancestors to meet the needs of living in the trees (Chapter 11). Even though we don't live in trees, we have retained this trait and use it *for a different purpose*. Natural selection operates on the variation that is present. Structures are frequently modified for different uses.

SUMMARY

Macroevolution, the process of long-term evolution, can occur in two ways: anagenesis, the evolution of a single species over time, or cladogenesis, the splitting off of one or more new species from the original parent species. In cladogenesis, new species form through the process of reproductive isolation followed by genetic divergence. Both steps are understood in terms of evolutionary forces. Reduction or elimination of gene flow provides for the beginning of reproductive isolation. Mutation, genetic drift, and selection can then act on this isolation to produce a new species. The relative importance of the evolutionary forces in speciation is still debated.

Two models of macroevolutionary change can be applied to the fossil record. Gradualism states that most evolutionary change is the result of slow but constant change over many generations. New species are believed to form as a byproduct of natural selection operating over time. Punctuated equilibrium states that there are long periods of time with little evolutionary change (stasis), punctuated by rapid evolutionary events. New species are seen as forming in small, isolated populations. Analysis of the fossil record shows both models apply under certain situations, although it is still not clear which model represents the more common mode of evolution.

The most common evolutionary pattern is extinction. Some scientists have argued that the evolutionary record is best understood as the process of new species forming from old, with many species becoming extinct. The evolutionary trends we observe in the fossil record may reflect the differential survival of species with certain adaptations.

Behavior can also be studied from an evolutionary perspective. The field of sociobiology has recently been developed to generate and test hypotheses of selection and behavior. Sociobiology offers explanations for a variety of behaviors that seem nonadaptive to an individual but are adaptive for the group. Applications of sociobiology to human and nonhuman primate behavior have sometimes been questionable and still suffer from a number of methodological problems.

There are many misconceptions regarding natural selection and evolution. Some of the more common of these are: that bigger is better, that newer is better, that natural selection always works, and that there is an inevitable direction to natural selection. There are also misconceptions regarding the relationship of biological structures, their functions, and their evolutionary origin.

Supplemental Readings

Eldredge, N. 1985. *Time Frames: The Rethinking of Darwinian Evolution and the Theory of Punctuated Equilibria.* New York: Simon & Schuster. Provides a clear review of the punctuated-equilibrium model with many examples, primarily from the author's research on fossil marine invertebrates.

Futuyma, D. J. 1986. *Evolutionary Biology.* 2d ed. Sunderland, Mass.: Sinauer. An excellent text on the evolutionary process with extensive coverage of macroevolution and the fossil record.

In addition, the books by Gould listed at the end of Chapter 1 provide many interesting and relevant essays on macroevolution.

PART TWO

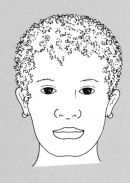

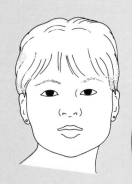

Human Microevolution and Variation

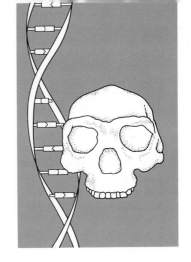

CHAPTER 5

Case Studies of Human Microevolution

The previous four chapters have provided you with an overview of evolutionary theory, including the genetic aspects and concepts of microevolution and macroevolution. This chapter and the next further explore microevolutionary change in human populations.

The focus of this current chapter is how genetic drift, gene flow, and natural selection operate to affect patterns of genetic variation within and between populations. Case studies provide examples of the basic concepts of microevolution, demonstrating how microevolution in humans is similar to and different from that observed in other organisms, while emphasizing the interrelationship between biology and culture.

Studying Human Microevolution

It is important to understand some of the philosophy and methods used in the analysis of human genetic variation. Humans are not easy organisms to work with. Analysis of microevolution is much easier in animals that can be raised in the laboratory than it is in human populations. Animals such as fruit flies and mice can be manipulated, as can the size of the population and the physical environment. In addition, such organisms have short generation lengths, allowing scientists to observe genetic change over several generations in a short period of time. We

129

univariate analysis The analysis of human biological variation focusing on a single trait at a time.

multivariate analysis The analysis of human biological variation that considers the interrelationships of several traits at a time.

cannot control for such variables in human populations. In addition to the moral questions raised by experimentation, we cannot always duplicate the conditions of nature in a laboratory setting.

Much of the study of human variation is observational. We look to see what patterns of genetic variation exist in populations as they occur. By employing a number of methods, we can compare and contrast patterns of variation to find out more about the specific mechanisms of genetic change in human populations from one generation to the next. Although such an approach is often difficult to use, part of the challenge of working with human populations is putting all the pieces together to solve a larger puzzle.

Working with human populations is not without advantages. In studies dealing with genetic drift and gene flow, for example, it is much easier to obtain information regarding movement and population size for humans than for most other organisms. After all, it is relatively easy to find out the birthplace of human beings—you just ask them!

Univariate and Multivariate Approaches

Biological anthropologists rely on a wide variety of traits to analyze human variation. Such traits include single locus traits, such as the MN blood group, as well as complex traits, such as height, head length, skin color, dental measures, and fingerprints. Sometimes we analyze these traits one at a time (**univariate analysis**) and sometimes many at a time (**multivariate analysis**). The difference in these approaches relates to the goals of a study and whether we are focusing on the forces of genetic drift and gene flow on one hand, or natural selection on the other.

The basic starting point is that genetic drift and gene flow are expected to affect *all* loci to the same degree, whereas natural selection is expected to affect each locus differently. For example, if you move from one population to another and have offspring in your new population, all of your genetic material moves with you: gene flow should affect all loci the same. Likewise, the *average* effect of genetic drift is expected to be the same for all loci. Natural selection, however, should affect each locus differently—unless, of course, the loci are both related to the same selective force.

As a result, we tend to study natural selection one locus or trait at a time, unless we are looking at related traits. If we wish to study the effects of genetic drift and gene flow, we try to sample as many loci or traits as possible with the goal of getting the best estimate of overall effect. Of course, any study must consider *all* of the evolutionary forces. The univariate and multivariate approaches together often provide us with information regarding a number of these evolutionary forces.

An example of the multivariate approach is Workman and colleagues' (1963) study of allele frequencies of African Americans in Claxton, Georgia. Table 5.1 lists the frequencies of eight alleles from seven loci for the

T A B L E 5.1

Allele Frequencies of African-American and European-American
Populations in Claxton, Georgia

Locus	Allele	West coast African	Claxton African Americans	Claxton European Americans
Rhesus	d	0.211	0.230	0.358
ABO	A	0.148	0.158	0.246
ABO	B	0.151	0.129	0.050
MN	M	0.476	0.485	0.508
Duffy	Fy^a	0.000	0.046	0.422
P	P	0.780	0.757	0.526
Hemoglobin	S	0.110	0.043	0.000
G6PD	GD^-	0.195	0.118	0.000

Source: Workman et al. (1963:451).

African-American and European-American populations of Claxton and
those of the West Coast of Africa (a presumed source of many ancestors
for the Claxton African Americans). In all cases, the allele frequencies for
the Claxton African Americans lie between those of West Africa and the
Claxton European Americans. In most cases, the allele frequencies of the
Claxton African Americans are more similar to those in West Africa. This
is expected, given the predominately African ancestry of the Claxton
African-American population. European gene flow, however, has caused
the Claxton African-American allele frequencies to move further away
from the West African frequencies. This example shows how admixture of
Europeans has occurred in the African-American population of Claxton.

Is gene flow the only factor operating on the Claxton African-
American allele frequencies? If so, then the relative position of the Claxton
African Americans should be the same for all alleles, because gene flow is
expected to have the same effect on all loci. Figure 5.1 plots their relative
positions for the eight alleles. Most of the Claxton African-American allele
frequencies plot in a similar location, as expected from gene flow. The allele
frequencies for G6PD deficiency and the sickle cell allele (S) are quite
different. They do not fit the pattern of the other alleles, which suggests

West
Africa

P

A, Fy^a

d

B

M

G6PD

S

Claxton
European
Americans

Figure 5.1

The relative genetic position
of the African-American
population in Claxton,
Georgia, as compared to
the European-American
population of Claxton and to
West Coast Africans. Eight
alleles are shown here (see
Table 5.1). Six of the alleles
cluster together, suggesting
the common effect of gene
flow. Two alleles, from the
hemoglobin and G6PD loci,
show a different relative
position, suggesting the effect
of natural selection (see text).

genetic distance An average measure of relatedness between populations based on a number of traits.

genetic distance map A picture showing the genetic relationships between populations, based on genetic distance measures.

that natural selection has been operating on those loci. As shown later in this chapter, this is exactly the case.

The Analysis of Gene Flow and Genetic Drift

A number of methods are used to examine the joint effect of gene flow and genetic drift on patterns of human variation. Two of the more common approaches are discussed here.

Genetic distance analysis. When comparing a number of biological traits across populations, we frequently compute a summary measure known as a **genetic distance.** This is an average measure of relatedness between groups based on a number of traits (i.e., a multivariate approach). Quite simply, the larger the genetic distance, the *less* similar two populations are to each other. For example, imagine that you have investigated a number of traits for three groups, called A, B, and C. You compute one of a number of genetic distance measures and obtain the following distances (don't worry about the units of measure; most distance measures are relative):

Distance between A and B = 9

Distance between A and C = 16

Distance between B and C = 25

Interpretation of these results is fairly straightforward. Populations A and B have the smallest distance, so they are the *most* similar to each other. Population C is the most distant and so is the least similar genetically. Further analysis would require additional data on the history and location of these groups to determine *why* population C is the most different. If, for example, you also knew that population C was on the other side of a mountain from populations A and B, then it would seem reasonable to assume that the mountain acted as a barrier to gene flow and caused population C's genetic dissimilarity.

Interpretation is difficult when there are more than three populations being considered. For that reason, we often take the genetic distance measures and use them to construct what is known as a **genetic distance map,** a picture showing the genetic relationships between groups. These maps are easy to interpret—the closer two populations are on the map, the closer they are genetically. An example of a genetic distance map is shown in Figure 5.2, that shows five hypothetical populations (A, B, C, D, E). It

Figure 5.2

Example of a genetic distance map for five hypothetical populations (A, B, C, D, E). The closer populations are genetically, the closer they plot near each other on the map.

is clear that populations A, B, and C are all similar to one another genetically, as is population D to population E. The most striking feature is that populations D and E are quite distant genetically from the other three populations. Additional data would be needed to determine why. Are D and E separated geographically from the other three populations? This would be easy to check: simply compare the genetic distance map with a geographic distance map. Other hypotheses, such as differences in religion or other cultural variables, could also be tested using a comparative approach. Several examples of genetic distance maps from actual studies will be presented later in the chapter.

Demographic measures. Much information regarding the effect of genetic drift and gene flow can be extracted from analysis of demographic measures, especially population size and migration. These measures can be used to estimate the likely effect of genetic drift and gene flow by means of a variety of complex mathematical methods. If information is available for genetic traits, then these estimates can be compared with observed reality. This type of comparison allows us to test various assumptions of models and to determine the relative effect of gene flow and genetic drift. When genetic traits are not available, the analysis of demographic measures still provides us with an idea of the relative magnitude of genetic change *likely* under certain conditions.

The relationship between demographic measures and microevolution is relatively straightforward. Since the magnitude of genetic drift is related to population size (the smaller the population, the greater the effect of drift), a knowledge of population size can give us an estimate of the effects of genetic drift. Much gene flow is related to migration, so an analysis of marriage records and other vital statistical data can provide us with an idea of the relative magnitude of gene flow. Using appropriate models, scientists can consider the effects of gene flow and genetic drift simultaneously to predict genetic distances and then compare them with actual genetic distances. This approach also gives us an opportunity to study demographic shifts in historical populations—groups for which we have no genetic data but do have demographic information.

The Analysis of Natural Selection

The analysis of natural selection in human populations is complex. Rather than set up laboratory experiments, most of the time we must rely on comparisons of situations existing in nature. Consider the following hypothetical situation. You are interested in testing the hypothesis that mammalian body size is related to temperature. If you were dealing with laboratory animals such as mice, you would set up an experiment in which you would expose different groups of mice to different ambient temperatures and then determine what change, if any, takes place from one generation to the next. But what if you were interested in testing this hypothesis on elephants? It is unlikely that you would be able to overcome the large number of practical difficulties involved in such a project. Where would you get enough space? How many elephants would you need? Could you obtain these elephants? Finally, you would also have to deal with the problem of a long generation length.

If you were interested in humans, the whole laboratory approach would be immoral and illegal in many societies as well as impractical. Does this mean that the hypotheses cannot be tested? No, because you could examine a natural experiment. You would collect data on body size and temperature from human populations across the world to determine if a relationship in fact existed. Your study could be improved by trying to control for other effects. For example, you would not want to select an undernourished population from Africa and a well-nourished population from northern Europe because the differences in body size could be the result of both temperature and nutrition. Careful choice of samples in this type of natural experiment is critical. Though research on human populations is extremely difficult, the challenge is also part of the appeal for many biological anthropologists.

Measuring Natural Selection

There are several approaches to measuring natural selection in human populations. The most direct method involves comparing measures of survival and reproduction (fitness) among individuals with different genotypes. Another method is to look at regional or worldwide variation in a trait to determine if it has any relationship with climate or other environmental factors. A third method is to look at the potential for natural selection by using measures of births and deaths from demographic data.

Individual genetic associations. Because natural selection refers to the process in which individuals with certain genetic characteristics are more likely to survive or reproduce, we want to determine whether individuals with certain genotypes have a greater probability of surviving or reproducing. If you were interested in looking at the potential effects of natural selection on the MN blood group system, you would want to separate your sample into groups of individuals with the same genotype (*MM, MN,* or *NN*). You would then attempt to determine if there were any differences in mortality or fertility among these groups. For instance, do individuals with one genotype live longer than those with other genotypes? Is there any relationship between genotype and the individual's history of disease? Do individuals with certain genotypes have more surviving children than those with other genotypes? Are individuals with one genotype more likely to be sterile than others?

These questions, and others, can be answered in principle by looking at the associations among some measure of health, survival, or fertility and different genotypes. Suppose you were interested in whether or not different *MN* genotypes have different susceptibilities to diseases. You could select a group, determine its *MN* genotypes, and monitor its members for the rest of their lives to track their disease histories. Alternatively, you could select a group of individuals having had a given disease and compare their *MN* genotypes with those of a random sample of people who have not had the disease.

Environmental correspondence. One way of looking for the effects of natural selection is to analyze patterns of variation over a large geographic region. Given that natural selection is related to environmental variation, differences among locations might reflect changes in environment and in genotype. The goal is to determine the level of correspondence between some aspect or aspects of the physical environment and a genotype. To test the idea that climate is related to body size, you would look at the distribution of body size and see how well it matches the distribution of climatic variables. Again, proper selection of your samples is necessary to ensure that you do not measure some other factor affecting biological variation. This method has other potential problems, such as the fact that migration can affect the level of correspondence. For example, if you were looking at the relationship of skin color and latitude, you would not want to include African Americans or European Americans in your analysis because they are relatively recent migrants to the United States.

Demographic measures. Natural selection operates on differences in mortality and fertility, both of which may be measured from demographic records. The death rate of a population is a measure of the proportion of deaths occurring within a given period of time. The birth rate measures fertility within a population. These measures can provide an idea of the overall *potential* for natural selection. They do not tell us what specific effect natural selection will have on a particular set of loci. These measures are also so highly dependent on cultural variation that we cannot always extrapolate to genetic factors. For example, two populations may show different disease rates. Even though it might be tempting to suggest that the difference in disease patterns is due to genetic differences, we must first control for other sources of this variation, cultural and environmental.

Nonetheless, demographic measures do provide us with some information about the potential for natural selection to operate (Crow 1958). With proper controls and research strategies, such measures can even be used to test biological hypotheses in the absence of any direct biological data. A good example of this approach is Meindl and Swedlund's (1977) study of mortality in the populations of Deerfield and Greenfield in historical Massachusetts. Historical data indicated that both populations experienced epidemics of childhood dysentery, a serious disease, between 1802 and 1803. Meindl and Swedlund used death records to determine the effect of these epidemics on the mortality of those who survived the disease. They found that the individuals who survived the disease actually lived longer than those who were not exposed to it. They concluded that the greater longevity of those individuals reflected, in part, genetic differences. One possible interpretation is that those who survived had genetic characteristics that gave them greater resistance to dysentery; this is natural selection in action. Another possibility is that those exposed to the disease developed stronger immune systems as a response. Such augmented resistance is a physiological response, although there is most likely a genetic component involved. Though such demographic analyses cannot provide any definite answers regarding natural selection, they do provide useful supplements to traditional genetic analysis.

Problems in analysis. Some problems are common to any study of natural selection in human populations, regardless of the specific methods of study. The methods described here can demonstrate a relationship between some measure of fitness and some environmental factor. Correlation does not necessarily imply causation, however. We still need to document the link between genetics, environment, and the action of natural selection.

For example, a high degree of association between a specific blood group genotype and a given disease is suggestive, but not conclusive. To complete the analysis, it is necessary to look at the specific biochemical nature of the blood group genotype. What changes in biological structure are related to this genotype, and how do these changes relate to the specific disease? A knowledge of the biochemical nature of the blood groups is required to answer these questions.

Another potential problem is that whatever association we detect may not have been present in the past. It is also possible that natural selection operated on a specific allele in the past but no longer does so. Certain blood group genotypes, for example, are associated with susceptibility to the disease smallpox. Today, smallpox has been eradicated as the result of intensive health care and immunization programs. In the past, however, smallpox was a devastating disease. Thus, smallpox may have been a factor in the natural selection of certain blood types in the past, but it is not at present.

We have an unfortunate tendency to view natural selection in terms of *major* differences between different genotypes. Natural selection is often looked at as an all-or-none phenomenon—one individual survives and another does not. In reality, natural selection often operates on very small differences between different genotypes. One genotype may have only a slight advantage—1 or 2 percent, or even lower—relative to another.

If natural selection works with small differences, then how can substantial change result? The key to understanding this problem is to realize that small changes can have large impacts over a long period of time. Like compound interest in a bank account, the effects of even small levels of natural selection can add up over long periods. Of course, such low amounts of natural selection may be difficult to detect in a single generation. Imagine a population of organisms where the average body weight is

10 kg (22 lbs). Suppose there is a small amount of selection for those individuals with larger body sizes. Each generation, the average body size would increase in the population as a result of natural selection. Suppose the change is only one-tenth of 1 percent. The change in the first generation would be only from 10 kg to 10.001 kg, which is not noticeable. If this selection continues for 1,000 generations, however, the average body size would be over 27 kg (almost 60 lbs). Also, remember that 1,000 generations is a very short time in evolution. Of course, change is not likely to occur in a steady, uniform manner. Even though this hypothetical example is too simple, it does show the cumulative nature of natural selection over long periods of time.

Slight differences in survival and reproduction can add up over time. Slow change over time, however, poses a problem for our analyses of natural selection. If differences are slight, we may not be able to detect them in a short period of time, or we might require extremely large samples. Other evolutionary forces, such as drift and gene flow, would also alter the degree of change from one generation to the next. In many studies of human populations we find that gene flow "swamps" the effect of natural selection. This does not mean that we cannot study natural selection; it merely shows us one of the potential problems we must take into account.

Case Studies of Gene Flow and Genetic Drift

This section provides four brief examples of the effects of gene flow and/or genetic drift in human populations.

Genetic Relationships of Jewish and Non-Jewish Populations

The Jewish Diaspora resulted in Jews spreading throughout much of the world. Given religious and ethnic differences, combined with frequent discrimination in their new lands, many Jewish populations remained culturally isolated. From an understanding of microevolutionary theory, we would expect there to be genetic isolation as well. On the other hand, we know historically that intermarriage between Jews and non-Jews has often occurred, although at different rates in different times and places. What are the present-day genetic relationships between Jewish and non-Jewish populations? How much gene flow has there been between groups in the past? Are Jewish populations throughout the world more similar to each other, or more similar to their non-Jewish neighbors? Has genetic drift further complicated the picture, since many Jewish populations were small in size to begin with?

Many studies have addressed these questions, often with mixed results because of disparate methods and the use of data from different

Figure 5.3

Genetic distance map
showing the relationship
between six Jewish and six
non-Jewish populations.
Circles (●) indicate Jewish
populations and squares (■)
indicate non-Jewish populations. The code letters next
to the circles and squares
represent the geographic area:
CE = Central Europe,
EE = Eastern Europe, SE =
Southern Europe, ME =
Middle East, NA = North
Africa, Y = Yemen.
(Based on data taken from
Kobyliansky et al. [1982])

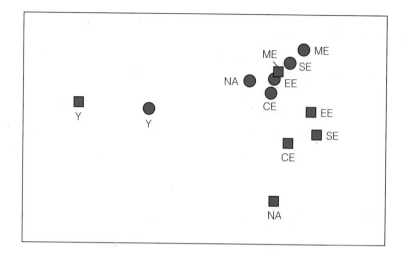

populations. One such study was conducted by Kobyliansky and colleagues at Tel-Aviv University in Israel (Kobyliansky et al. 1982). Pooling
their own data with those from previous studies, they obtained information on seven genetic marker loci for both Jewish and non-Jewish populations in six geographical regions: Eastern Europe, Central Europe,
Southern Europe, the Middle East, North Africa, and Yemen (the latter
being representative of isolated groups). Figure 5.3 presents a genetic
distance map similar to that shown in Figure 5.2, using the method of
Harpending and Jenkins (1973) to compute standard genetic distances
among the 12 populations (6 Jewish and 6 non-Jewish).

The first, most obvious feature of this genetic distance map is that the
two populations from Yemen are relatively close to each other and quite
different from other Jewish and non-Jewish populations in Africa, Asia,
and Europe. This fits in with our knowledge of the isolated nature of the
small Yemenite populations. Second, all of the remaining Jewish populations cluster together and are distinct from most of the non-Jewish populations. This finding suggests that the five remaining Jewish populations
are more similar to each other genetically than any are to their non-Jewish
neighbors. Third, the non-Jewish Middle Eastern population clusters with
the Jewish populations, that suggests Middle Eastern Jews and non-Jews
share common ancestry. All of these findings are consistent with historical
evidence. Except for the isolated Yemenite groups (whose position is most
likely due to low levels of gene flow and increased action of genetic drift),
there seems to have been relatively little gene flow between Jewish and non-
Jewish populations. Of course, this analysis focuses on large geographic
regions. Within these, it is likely there exist populations that differ from
the overall pattern shown here.

Social Organization and Genetics of South American Indians of the Rain Forest

A number of genetic studies have been carried out on the tribal populations living in the rain forests of South America. Studies of these populations have allowed investigation into the ways in which the social structure of small tribes contributes to genetic diversity. Of course, the small size of the populations and their general isolated nature act to increase the likelihood of genetic drift. What makes these studies so fascinating is the specific social and political structures that act in certain ways to increase drift and in other ways to counter it.

Many of these populations have what is known as a **fission-fusion** structure. As populations grow, the limits of the environment are soon reached. Political factions develop, creating unrest within the local villages resulting from too many people in one place. When populations become too large, they will often fission into separate groups. Some of these separate groups will be too small to remain viable villages, and smaller groups may then undergo fusion to form a large group (Figure 5.4).

The formation of new, smaller villages from old (fission) is expected to lead to increased opportunity for genetic drift. The merging of smaller villages to form large ones (fusion) acts to some extent to counter the effects of genetic drift. Adding to this complex situation is the fact that all villages practice **exogamy** (finding a mate in another group) to some extent. Exogamous marriage results in gene flow between villages, which acts to counter the effects of genetic drift.

Village fissioning is a form of the founder effect and is expected to lead to group differences because of genetic drift. The amount of genetic drift can be predicted and then compared to observed allele frequencies to test the hypothesis that genetic variation is being affected by drift. Following up on pioneering work by James Neel, Smouse (1982) and colleagues have performed extensive analyses on a number of genetic systems for several tribal populations, such as the Yanomamo (Figure 5.5), and have found that the observed level of genetic differences between groups exceeds the level expected under random genetic drift. Closer analysis has shown that the village fissions were not random. Rather, many fissions take place along kinship lines. Instead of a random group of individuals forming a new village, often a group of related individuals does so. This nonrandom splitting actually acts to enhance the effects of genetic drift because new villages are less likely to have an equal representation of alleles from the original population. Thus, the individual pattern of village fissioning adds to the effect of genetic drift.

Complicating matters further, mating practices add to the process of genetic drift in these populations. The marriage system in these societies is characterized by multiple wives for each man. Differences in local polit-

fission-fusion A group breaks into smaller populations (fission) and may later combine with other populations to form a larger group (fusion).

exogamy The tendency to choose mates from outside the local population

Figure 5.4

Fission-fusion social structure. Fissioning is the splitting of a population into two or more smaller populations. Fusioning is the merging of two or more populations into a larger population. Circles in this figure indicate the relative sizes of each population: populations A and B both split into two smaller populations; populations A2 and B1 then merge to form a larger population C.

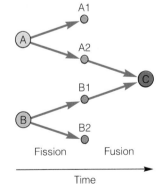

Figure 5.5

The Yanomamo Indians of the South American rain forest. (Courtesy of Napoleon A. Chagnon)

ical power mean that some men have more wives than others and therefore contribute in greater frequencies to the next generation. Though the entire analysis of Smouse and colleagues is too lengthy to discuss here, it should be clear that the complexity of human populations can affect genetic drift in many ways.

Genetic Change in the Åland Islands, Finland

One of the most comprehensive analyses of human microevolution is the Åland Islands study (Jorde et al. 1982; Mielke et al. 1982). The Åland Islands are an archipelago consisting of more than 6,000 islands located between Sweden and Finland (Figure 5.6). Demographic data from the

Figure 5.6

The Åland Islands, Finland.
(From Mielke et al. [1982:259])

middle eighteenth century and genetic data for three generations have been analyzed for 12 to 16 parishes on the islands. The focus of this study was changes in genetic similarity between parishes over space and time. The outer, more isolated, islands were compared to the inner islands, and all parishes were compared over several generations (Figures 5.7 and 5.8).

The outer islands were found to be genetically more different from one another than the inner islands. This difference was due to several factors, including lower levels of gene flow and a greater effect of genetic drift. These findings make sense given the lower observed rates of migra-

Figure 5.7

Three women in the parish of Lemland in the Åland Islands.   (Courtesy of James Mielke, University of Kansas)

Figure 5.8

Man mending a net on the Åland Islands.   (Courtesy of James Mielke, University of Kansas)

tion among the outer islands and their smaller population sizes, which act to increase genetic drift. In addition, migration was high between several outer island parishes and the mainland of Finland, which had the effect of "pulling" these parishes further away genetically from the rest of the Åland Islands.

Over time, genetic differences between all parishes declined, as gene flow became more important and genetic drift less so. The decrease in variation between parishes was related to several factors. First, increased migration occurred because of new and improved transportation technologies (e.g., the addition of steamboats and better-quality roads). Second, changes in farm technology allowed farmers to tend their fields with less help, thus allowing more children to migrate away from the farm. Third, one of the parishes developed into a center for industry, attracting people from throughout the islands and thereby increasing levels of migration and gene flow. The Åland Island study provides an excellent example of how cultural changes can cause rapid fluctuation in patterns of genetic diversity. Similar changes have affected other human populations, such as the Utah Mormons (Jorde 1982) and Massachusetts villages (Relethford 1988b).

English Admixture on the West Coast of Ireland

Historical contacts between groups can have a strong effect on genetic microevolution. A recent study of genetic variation on the west coast of Ireland provides an example (Relethford 1988a, 1991a; Relethford and Blangero 1990). The west coast of Ireland has long been rather isolated. Historically, however, there have been instances of contact, both cultural and genetic, with other populations. For strategic reasons, English soldiers were sent to several islands along the Irish west coast, starting in the

Figure 5.9

Map of the west coast of Ireland. Letters refer to village or island names: A = Aran Islands, B = Ballycroy, C = Carna, E = Erris, G = Garumna, I = Inishbofin. L = Lettermullen. (Source: Relethford [1988a])

sixteenth century and lasting for a few hundred years. Fortification of these islands provided the opportunity to guard the coastline from sea attack. From historical data, we expect that many soldiers remained on the islands and had children with Irish mothers. Gene flow from England thus occurred.

This hypothesis was tested using measurements of the body, head, and face originally collected during the 1890s from seven villages and islands along the Irish west coast. With appropriate methods, genetic distances can be estimated from such complex traits (Williams-Blangero and Blangero 1989; Relethford and Blangero 1990). The location of the seven populations is shown in Figure 5.9. The Aran Islands (*A* on the map) and the island of Inishbofin (*I* on the map) both have histories of fortification by English soldiers.

On the genetic distance map shown in Figure 5.10, both the Aran Islands and Inishbofin are divergent from the remaining coastal populations. This difference is most likely due to English admixture. Comparison

Figure 5.10

Genetic distance map of Irish populations. Letters refer to the same population name abbreviations in Figure 5.9. Note the separation of the Aran Islands (*A*) and Inishbofin (*I*) from the remaining populations. (Source of data: Relethford [1991a])

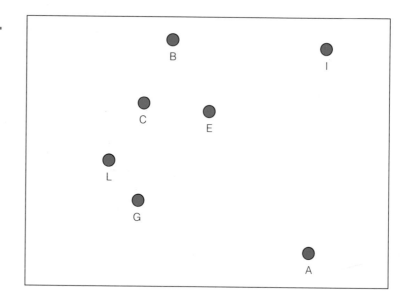

with measurement data from England showed these populations to be roughly intermediate in position between England and the Irish west coast (Relethford 1988a). Further analysis revealed that other factors also operated in the microevolution of these groups. Geographic distance played a secondary role. Once admixture was taken into account, populations geographically closer to another were more genetically similar. Genetic drift also had an effect once admixture was taken into account. Genetic distances were greater between smaller populations, as expected under genetic drift (Relethford 1991a).

Case Studies of Natural Selection

This section provides several examples of natural selection in human populations. Since natural selection operates differently on different loci, the focus will be on individual loci or traits rather than on specific populations.

Hemoglobin, Sickle Cell, and Malaria

Perhaps the best-known example of natural selection operating on a discrete genetic trait is the relationship of hemoglobin variants to malaria. One of the proteins in red blood cells is hemoglobin, which functions to transport oxygen to body tissues (see Chapter 2). The normal structure of the beta chain of hemoglobin is coded for by an allele usually called hemoglobin A. In many human populations, the *A* allele is the only one present, and as a result everyone has the *AA*, or normal adult hemoglobin, genotype.

Hemoglobin variants. Many hemoglobin variants are produced by the mutation of an *A* allele to another form. The most widely studied mutations include hemoglobin S, C, and E. The *S* allele is also known as the sickle cell allele. A person who has two *S* alleles (genotype *SS*) has **sickle cell anemia,** a condition whereby the structure of the red blood cells is altered and oxygen transport is severely impaired (Figure 5.11). Roughly, only 15 percent of those with genotype *SS* survive to adulthood. An estimated 100,000 deaths per year throughout the world are from sickle cell anemia.

If the *S* allele is harmful in homozygotes, we expect natural selection to eliminate *S* alleles from the population in such a way that the frequency of *S* should be relatively low. Mutation introduces the *S* allele, but natural selection eliminates it. Indeed, in many parts of the world the frequency of *S* is extremely low, fitting the model of mutation balanced by selection. In a number of populations, however, the frequency of *S* is much higher—often up to 10 to 20 percent. Such high frequencies seem paradoxical, given the harmful effect of the *S* allele in the homozygous genotype. Why does *S* reach such high frequencies? Genetic drift might seem likely, except for the fact that there is a definite association of geography and higher frequencies of *S*. That is, higher frequencies of *S* occur only in certain environments. Genetic drift is random and influenced by population size, not environment. If genetic drift were responsible for the high frequencies of *S*, we would expect to see high frequencies in isolated groups in many different environments.

Distribution of the sickle cell allele and malaria. The distribution of the sickle cell allele is related to the prevalence of a certain form of malaria. Malaria is an **infectious disease**—that is, caused by the introduction of an organic foreign substance, such as a virus or parasite (a disease that is not caused by an organic foreign substance is a **noninfectious disease**). Malaria is caused by a parasite that enters an organism's body, and four different species of the malarial parasite can affect humans. Ma-

sickle cell anemia A genetic disease occurring in a person homozygous for the sickle cell allele that alters the structure of red blood cells.

infectious disease A disease caused by the introduction of an organic foreign substance into the body.

noninfectious disease A disease caused by factors other than the introduction of an organic foreign substance into the body.

Figure 5.11

Sickle cell anemia. The blood cells on the left are twisted and deformed compared to the shape of normal red blood cells on the right.   (© AP/ Wide World Photos)

laria remains one of the major infectious diseases in the world today. In the late 1970s, as many as 120 million people in the world had some form of malaria (Encyclopaedia Britannica 1988).

The Old World shows a striking correspondence of the higher frequencies of the *S* allele (Figure 5.12) and the prevalence of malaria caused by the parasite *Plasmodium falciparum* (Figure 5.13). This parasite is spread through the bites of certain species of mosquitoes. Except for blood transfusions, humans cannot give malaria to one another directly. The disease is spread by the mosquitoes. Those areas with frequent cases of malaria, such as Central Africa, also have the highest frequencies of the sickle cell allele. The falciparum form of malaria, the most serious of all forms of malaria, is often fatal.

The strong geographic correspondence suggests that sickle cell anemia and malaria are both related to the high frequencies of the *S* allele in parts of the world. Further experimental work has confirmed this hypothesis. Because the *S* allele affects the structure of the red blood cells, it makes the blood an inhospitable place for the malaria parasite.

Figure 5.12

Distribution of the sickle cell allele in the Old World. Compare high-frequency areas with the high-frequency areas of malaria in Figure 5.13.

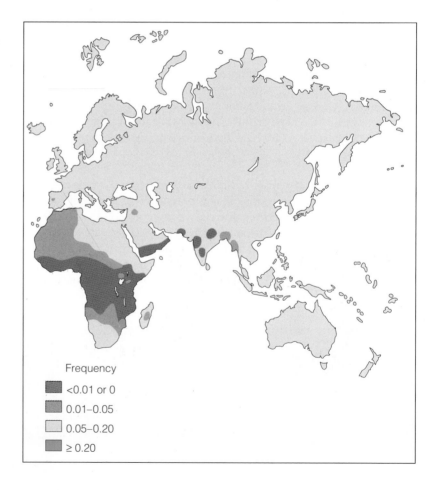

Frequency

- █ <0.01 or 0
- ▓ 0.01–0.05
- ░ 0.05–0.20
- ▒ ≥ 0.20

In a malarial environment people who are heterozygous (genotype *AS*) actually have an advantage. The presence of one *S* allele does not give the person sickle cell anemia, but it does change the blood cells sufficiently so that the malaria parasite does not have as serious an effect. Overall, the heterozygote has the greatest fitness in a malarial environment. As discussed in Chapter 3, this is a case of balancing selection in which selection occurs for the heterozygote (*AS*) and against both homozygotes (*AA* from malaria and *SS* from sickle cell anemia).

In addition to greater survival of the heterozygote in malarial environments, it has also been suggested that women with genotype *AS* have greater fertility. If so, then is selection for the heterozygote in environments with malaria a function of differential mortality, differential fertility, or both? Madrigal (1989) studied this problem by examining the hemoglobin genotype and reproductive histories of women in Limon, Costa Rica. She found that there was no difference between *AA* and *AS* women for a number of measures of differential fertility (family size, number of pregnancies, number of live births, and number of spontaneous abortions).

If the effects of sickle cell anemia and malaria were equal, then we would expect the frequencies of the normal allele (*A*) and the sickle cell

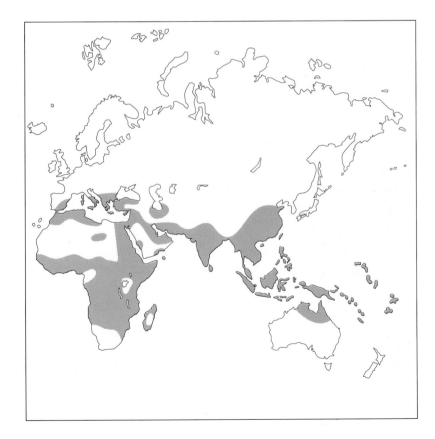

Figure 5.13

Regions where falciparum malaria is common.

Figure 5.14

Reconstruction of past
changes in sickle cell allele
frequency in malarial Africa.
This simulation assumes an
initial allele frequency of
0.00001 caused by mutation.
Relative fitness values are
assumed constant over time:
$AA = 88\%$, $AS = 100\%$,
$SS = 14\%$. The first 40
generations would show little
change since the initial allele
frequency was so low. After
40 generations, the allele frequency would increase rapidly,
reaching an equilibrium after
roughly 100 generations.

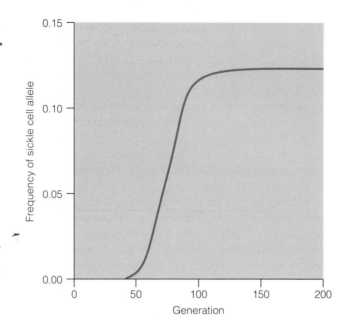

allele (S) ultimately to reach equal frequencies. The two diseases, however,
are not equal in their effects. Sickle cell anemia is much worse. The balance
between these two diseases is such that the maximum fitness of an entire
population occurs when the frequency of S is somewhere between 10 and
20 percent.

An analysis of one African population suggests that for every 100
people with AS who survive to adulthood, 88 people with AA survive and
only 14 of those with SS (Bodmer and Cavalli-Sforza 1976). Clearly, the
relationship between hemoglobin, sickle cell anemia, and malaria represents a very strong case of natural selection. Instead of a difference in
survival between genotypes of only several percent, the differences are
quite striking. Such differences can lead to major changes in allele frequencies in a very short period of time. To illustrate the rapidity of such change,
Figure 5.14 shows a hypothetical example of changes in the frequency of
the sickle cell allele. In this example, the initial frequency of S from mutation was set equal to a reasonable estimate of 0.00001. The fitness values
mentioned earlier were used to examine the kind of change in the frequency of S that could take place. Because the initial allele frequency is
low, there is little change for the first 60 generations or so. (Of course, if
the initial allele frequency were higher, the rate of change would be greater;
a higher initial frequency could occur due to genetic drift or the initial
occurrence of the mutation in a small population.) As the frequency of S
increases, change takes place more rapidly because there are more people
with the AS genotype to be selected for. After 100 generations, there is
little change in the frequency of the S allele because it has reached an
equilibrium based on the balance between the effects of sickle cell anemia
and malaria. In this example, the sickle cell allele would reach an equilib-

rium frequency of 0.122. Of course, this simple illustration does not take other evolutionary forces into account, but it does show how quickly allele frequencies can change under strong natural selection.

The sickle cell example clearly shows the importance of the specific environment on the process of natural selection. In a nonmalarial environment, the *AS* genotype has no advantage, and the *AA* genotype has the greatest evolutionary fitness. In such cases, the frequency of the *S* allele is very low, approaching zero. In a malarial environment, however, the situation is different, and the heterozygote has the advantage. Clearly, we cannot label the *S* allele as intrinsically "good" or "bad"; it depends on circumstances.

The example of sickle cell also shows that evolution has a price. The equilibrium is one in which the fitness for the entire population is at a maximum. The cost of the adaptation, however, is an increased proportion of individuals with sickle cell anemia, because the frequency of *S* has increased. People with the heterozygous genotype *AS* have the greatest fitness, but they also carry the *S* allele. When two people with the *AS* genotype mate, they have a 25 percent chance of having a child with sickle cell anemia (in the previous example, 1.5 percent of all children in a population are expected to have the *SS* genotype). This is not advantageous from the perspective of the individual with the disease. From the perspective of the entire population, however, it is the most adaptive outcome. Every benefit in evolution is likely to carry a price.

Effects of culture change on sickle cell frequency. Sickle cell anemia also provides an excellent example of the interaction of biology and culture. Livingstone (1958) and others have taken information on the distribution and ecology of the malaria parasite and the mosquito that transmits it, along with information on the prehistory and history of certain regions in Africa, and have presented a hypothesis about changes in the frequency of the sickle cell allele. Several thousand years ago, the African environment was not conducive to the spread of malaria. Large areas of the continent consisted of dense forests. The mosquito that spreads malaria thrives best in ample sunlight and pools of stagnant water. Neither condition then existed in the African forests. The extensive foliage prevented much sunlight from reaching the floor of the forest. The forest environment was very absorbent, so that water did not tend to accumulate in pools. In other words, the environment was not conducive to large populations of mosquitoes. Consequently, the malaria parasite did not have a hospitable environment, either.

This situation changed several thousands of years ago when prehistoric African populations brought horticulture into the area. **Horticulture** is a form of farming employing only simple hand tools. As the land was cleared for crops, the entire ecology shifted. Without the many trees, it was easier for sunlight to reach the land surface. Continued use of the land changed the soil chemistry, allowing pools of water to accumulate. Both these changes led to an environment ideal for the growth and spread of mosquito populations, and therefore the spread of the malaria parasite.

horticulture A form of farming in which only simple hand tools are used.

The growth of the human population also provided more hosts for the mosquitoes to feed on, thus increasing the spread of malaria.

Before the development of horticulture in Africa, the frequency of the sickle cell allele was probably low, as it is in nonmalarial environments today. When malaria increased, there was then an evolutionary advantage to those who had the heterozygote *AS* genotype because they would have greater resistance to malaria without suffering the effects of sickle cell anemia. As shown earlier, this change could have taken place in a short period of time, roughly 100 generations, because of the large differences in fitness among hemoglobin genotypes. The initial introduction of the sickle cell allele, through mutation or gene flow, was followed by a rapid change reaching an equilibrium point in which the fitness of the entire human population was at a maximum. Recent research suggests that the sickle cell mutation occurred several times in Africa (Labie et al. 1986), although Livingstone (1989) has argued recently for a single origin.

This scenario shows that human cultural adaptations (horticulture) can affect the ecology of other organisms (the mosquito and malaria parasite), which can then cause genetic change in the human population (an increase in the frequency of the sickle cell allele). This sequence of events is summarized in Figure 5.15.

Figure 5.15

Sequence of cultural and environmental changes leading to changes in the frequency of the sickle cell allele in malarial Africa.

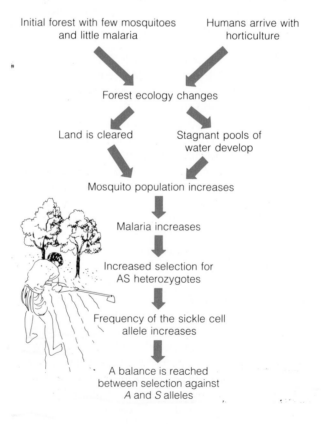

Initial forest with few mosquitoes and little malaria

Humans arrive with horticulture

Forest ecology changes

Land is cleared

Stagnant pools of water develop

Mosquito population increases

Malaria increases

Increased selection for AS heterozygotes

Frequency of the sickle cell allele increases

A balance is reached between selection against *A* and *S* alleles

Of course, we cannot observe these events directly because they occurred in the past. Nonetheless, all available evidence supports this hypothesis. We know the physiological differences between different hemoglobin types. We also know that low frequencies of S occur in nonmalarial environments and higher frequencies occur where there is malaria. Archaeological evidence shows when and where the spread of horticulture took place in Africa. From studies of modern-day agriculture, we also know that malaria spreads quickly following the clearing of land. Taking all this information together, we find the scenario for changes in the frequency of the sickle cell allele in Africa is most reasonable.

The study of human history also provides another example of the evolution of the sickle cell allele. In African American populations, the frequency of S ranges from 0.02 to 0.06, which is higher than the frequency in European Americans (essentially zero), but less than that in malarial regions of Africa (Workman et al. 1963). The biological history of African Americans explains part of this difference; some degree of European admixture has taken place. This admixture would have the effect of reducing the frequency of S in African Americans. Extensive calculations have shown, however, that admixture is not the only factor operating. Researchers found that if admixture alone were operating, then the frequency of S in African Americans should be higher than it actually is. Another reason that the frequencies of the sickle cell allele are lower in African Americans than in West Africans is that natural selection has been operating to remove the S allele from the population. In general, malaria has not been epidemic in the United States. The slaves brought into the United States came from areas in Africa with high frequencies of malaria and the sickle cell allele. When they arrived in the United States, there was no longer the same evolutionary advantage for high frequencies of S because there was less malaria. As a result, the frequency of S has been reduced through natural selection, along with European admixture.

Sickle cell anemia is a health problem among modern African Americans. During the 1960s there was a tendency to label sickle cell anemia as a "black disease." The reason for higher levels of sickle cell anemia among African Americans has nothing to do with skin color but is rather the result of their ancestors coming from a malarial environment with high frequencies of the S allele. Sickle cell anemia is not confined to dark-skinned populations in Africa. High frequencies of S are also found in malarial environments in parts of Europe, India, and South Asia.

Other relationships with malaria. A number of other genetic loci appear to have been affected by natural selection from malaria. Two different alleles of the hemoglobin locus, C and E, appear in high frequencies in certain malarial environments. Several inherited biochemical disorders, collectively known as thalassemia, are also related to malaria. These disorders do not directly affect the structure of the adult hemoglobin molecule but do interfere with its production. Another genetic trait, G6PD defi-

antibody A substance that reacts to other substances invading the body.

antigen A substance invading the body that stimulates the production of antibodies.

Rhesus incompatibility When a pregnant woman and her fetus have incompatible Rhesus blood group phenotypes.

ciency, leads to a deficiency of a certain enzyme and also appears to confer some resistance to malaria. It is not surprising to find a number of loci related to malaria, since it is a severe disease, and any trait that alters the blood sufficiently to confer resistance to the parasite might be selected for over time.

Blood Groups and Natural Selection

The relationship between the sickle cell allele and malaria is the most well-studied example of natural selection for a discrete genetic trait in human populations. It is often frustrating that the situation is not as clear for other traits. The differences in fitness between different genotypes is often much less than that seen for the hemoglobin locus. Also, we often find evidence of multiple relationships between genetic traits and natural selection. It is often difficult to determine which factor is the most important or which was initially responsible for the evolution of a trait.

The human blood groups have been the subject of many investigations of natural selection. There are many different blood groups, defined on the basis of the type of molecules present on the surface of the red blood cells. Some blood groups are associated with different **antibodies** that react to various substances invading the blood stream (foreign **antigens**). Two blood groups—MN and ABO—have already been mentioned in previous chapters. Other red blood cell groups include Rhesus, Diego, Duffy, Lutheran, Lewis, and Xg, to name but a few. Some of these blood groups appear to be neutral in terms of natural selection, or perhaps we just have not been able to detect any effects. Also, some may have been selected for or against in the past, but not at present. Others are definitely related to natural selection, but in ways that are difficult to discern. Three blood groups—Rhesus, ABO, and Duffy—are discussed here in terms of natural selection.

Rhesus blood group. The Rhesus blood group (also called the Rh blood group) has a complicated mode of genetic inheritance involving three linked loci called C, D, and E. One locus—D—is particularly important in terms of natural selection. This locus has two alleles, *D* and *d*, where *D* is dominant. Individuals with genotypes *DD* or *Dd* are called *Rh positive*, and those with genotype *dd* are called *Rh negative*. Those with Rh positive blood have certain antigens in their red blood cells (D), and those with Rh negative blood can produce an opposing antibody (anti-D). In terms of blood chemistry, anti-D antibodies can destroy red blood cells with D molecules on their surface.

Selection occurs for the Rhesus blood group through **Rhesus incompatibility**, a condition in which a pregnant woman and her fetus have incompatible Rhesus blood groups. Rhesus incompatibility occurs when an Rh negative mother has an Rh positive fetus. Normally, the circulatory systems of mother and fetus are separate, but some blood may leak across

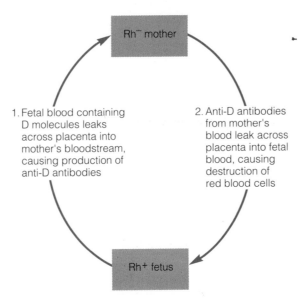

1. Fetal blood containing
   D molecules leaks
   across placenta into
   mother's bloodstream,
   causing production of
   anti-D antibodies

2. Anti-D antibodies
   from mother's
   blood leak across
   placenta into fetal
   blood, causing
   destruction of
   red blood cells

Rh⁻ mother

Rh⁺ fetus

Figure 5.16

Sequence of events in Rhesus incompatibility between an Rh^- mother and an Rh^+ fetus. Since step 1 normally takes time to produce anti-D antibodies, the first Rh^+ fetus is not affected. Subsequent Rh^+ fetuses are affected.

the placenta in both directions or enter the mother's bloodstream at the time of delivery. The fetus's blood carries D molecules. When these molecules enter the mother's blood stream, the mother's immune system produces anti-D antibodies to destroy the red blood cells carrying these "invaders." Once produced, the antibodies can leak back across a placenta to destroy blood cells of a fetus. The destruction of fetal blood cells leads to a form of anemia that can be fatal (Figure 5.16). Interestingly, Rhesus incompatibility is generally not a problem for the first Rh positive fetus born to the mother. The antibodies need time to be produced, and the first Rh positive infant's blood is rarely affected.

Today, Rhesus incompatibility is less of a problem than it once was because we can check blood types and use various techniques to control its effects. In the past, and even in many parts of the world today, this anemia often resulted in death. From an evolutionary standpoint, this is selection against the heterozygote. An Rh negative mother has genotype *dd*, which means that the fetus will receive a *d* allele from her. A fetus with a *d* allele from the mother requires a *D* allele from the father to be Rh positive. The fetus will have the heterozygous genotype *Dd*. We also therefore know that the father is Rh positive because that is the only way he could contribute a *D* allele to the fetus. Table 5.2 lists all possible matings between a man and woman according to their possible genotypes.

Selection against the heterozygote eliminates both alleles from the population in equal amounts. Given enough time, such selection will result in the loss of the initially less common allele (unless the initial allele frequencies were 0.5). For Rhesus incompatibility, there is selection against some heterozygous fetuses, and we should see the total elimination of one

TABLE 5.2
Possible Rhesus-incompatible Matings

Mother		Father		Incompatible mating
Genotype	Phenotype	Genotype	Phenotype	
DD	Rh$^+$	*DD*	Rh$^+$	No
DD	Rh$^+$	*Dd*	Rh$^+$	No
DD	Rh$^+$	*dd*	Rh$^-$	No
Dd	Rh$^+$	*DD*	Rh$^+$	No
Dd	Rh$^+$	*Dd*	Rh$^+$	No
Dd	Rh$^+$	*dd*	Rh$^-$	No
dd	Rh$^-$	*DD*	Rh$^+$	Yes, 100%
dd	Rh$^-$	*Dd*	Rh$^+$	Yes, 50%
dd	Rh$^-$	*dd*	Rh$^-$	No

allele or the other. The *D* allele is more common in human populations today, so we should ultimately see the elimination of the rarer *d* allele if we can assume no other factors are operating on the evolution of this blood group system. A number of human populations, such as Pacific Islanders and Native Americans, appear to have had no *d* alleles before admixture with European groups. The frequency of the *d* allele is higher in other parts of the world.

One possible explanation for high frequencies of the *d* allele is that it is gradually being eliminated and that ultimately it will have a frequency of zero. The fact that different populations have different frequencies of the *d* allele, however, also suggests that factors such as genetic drift and gene flow may also be responsible for the observed pattern of Rhesus blood groups. The possibility also exists that incompatibility is not the only factor involved in natural selection for or against Rhesus genotypes. For example, Gloria-Bottini and colleagues (1992) have found that the infants of diabetic mothers heterozygous at the Rhesus C locus have a lower incidence of hypoglycemia than other infants. This suggests selection *for* a heterozygote. In addition, glucose intolerance was less severe among women that were homozygous for the *e* allele at the E locus (selection against a dominant allele). There is also evidence that selection at the Rhesus loci is affected by the presence or absence of other blood groups, as discussed later in this section.

ABO blood group. The ABO blood group is the most widely studied simple genetic trait in human populations. As shown in Chapter 2, there are three different alleles (*A, B, O*) whereby *A* and *B* are codominant and *O* is recessive. There are four possible phenotypes: type A (genotypes *AA*

T A B L E   5.3
ABO Blood Group Phenotypes and Antibodies

Genotypes	Phenotype	Antigens	Antibodies
AA AO	A	A	anti-B
BB BO	B	B	anti-A
AB	AB	A, B	none
OO	O	none	anti-A, anti-B

and *AO*), type B (genotypes *BB* and *BO*), type O (genotype *OO*), and type AB (genotype *AB*).

Worldwide, the *O* allele is the most common, the *A* allele is next most frequent, and the *B* allele is the least common. The allele frequencies of all human populations fall within certain limits. The frequency of the *O* allele ranges from 0.4 to 1.0, the frequency of the *A* allele ranges from 0 to 0.55, and the frequency of the *B* allele ranges from 0 to 0.3 (Brues 1977). These allele frequencies are too high to be explained by mutation alone (because mutation occurs at low rates). Gene flow, genetic drift, and natural selection must be considered as possible explanations.

If the evolution of the ABO blood group system were totally the result of drift and gene flow, we would expect to see a wider range of allele frequencies. For example, we expect to see populations with frequencies such as *A* = 0.8, *B* = 0.1, and *O* = 0.1. Out of the hundreds of human populations studied for the ABO blood group to date, however, none is in this range. The fact that the allele frequencies fall within a certain range suggests that natural selection has been operating to keep the frequencies for the entire species within certain limits.

One possible clue to the effects of natural selection on the ABO blood groups is that there are certain antibodies associated with different blood groups. There are two antibodies in the ABO system known as anti-A and anti-B. Unlike the Rhesus system, the ABO antibodies are present throughout an individual's life. The anti-A antibody reacts to destroy A-type molecules, and the anti-B antibody reacts to destroy B-type molecules. There is no antibody for O. People with blood type A have the anti-B antibody, people with blood type B have the anti-A antibody, people with blood type O have both, and people with blood type AB have neither (Table 5.3). The fact that individuals with different ABO blood types have different antibodies has important implications for blood transfusions. If you have blood type A, you must not receive a blood transfusion from someone with blood type B. If you do, your anti-B antibodies will attack and destroy the incoming B molecules, with very harmful effects. Of course, any transfusion must also take into account other factors, such as Rhesus blood type.

The fact that different blood types have different antibodies has implications for natural selection and susceptibility to different diseases. If you have blood type A, and hence anti-B antibodies, your immune system will tend to fight off any microorganisms that are biochemically similar to type B molecules. For example, the microorganism that causes venereal syphilis is biochemically similar to A molecules. Therefore, people with blood types B and O will have greater resistance to syphilis because they have the anti-A antibodies. People with blood types A and AB will not have this resistance because they lack the anti-A antibodies. It has been suggested that a link exists between various ABO blood types and a number of infectious diseases, such as smallpox, typhoid, influenza, bubonic plague, and others. Many of these diseases were indeed serious in the past, and differential resistance could be a possible factor in explaining the range of allele frequencies for the ABO system. More work, however, needs to be done to substantiate these claims.

In any case, the action of natural selection is complex because of the wide variety of different disease microorganisms and their relationships to ABO blood types. It has been suggested that each blood type is more susceptible than others to certain diseases. For example, type A seems more susceptible to smallpox, type B seems more susceptible to infantile diarrhea, and type O seems more susceptible to bubonic plague. If these suggestions are verified, it seems that the frequencies of the ABO alleles are subject to a variety of different types of selection. This makes analysis extremely difficult.

The distribution of the ABO alleles is to some extent consistent with selection and infectious disease. India, for example, is a region with a high frequency of the *B* allele (Roychoudhury and Nei 1988). India also has a history of frequent epidemics of both smallpox and bubonic plague. Since blood type O is more susceptible to plague, *O* alleles would be removed from the population. Since type A is more susceptible to smallpox, *A* and *O* alleles would be removed from the population. The net result would be a relatively higher frequency of the *B* alleles—precisely what is found in India.

ABO blood types also appear to be related to noninfectious diseases. Some hospital studies have suggested that people with blood type O have a greater chance of getting duodenal and stomach ulcers. People with blood type A have a greater chance of getting certain forms of cancer. The differences between the phenotypes appear strong, but we do not understand the reasons for these associations. In any case, it is unclear what evolutionary importance these associations have. Most of the noninfectious diseases have severe effects late in life and therefore should not be subject to natural selection because they usually occur after an individual's reproductive life is over. Some people, however, do acquire these diseases early enough in life so that at least the possibility exists that natural selection could be operating through differential survival to noninfectious diseases. We must demonstrate, however, that such selection did (or does) in fact take place, and not merely that it is possible.

Natural selection may also be operating on ABO blood groups as a consequence of incompatibility between mother and fetus. As with the Rhesus blood group, incompatible matings will often lead to the destruction of red blood cells in the fetus. Most often, ABO incompatibility will lead to spontaneous abortion early in prenatal life. Incompatibility occurs when the mother's blood has an antibody corresponding to the type of molecule present in the fetus's blood. An example of incompatibility is a woman with blood type A whose fetus is blood type AB. The woman's blood contains anti-B antibody, which reacts with the B molecules present in the fetus's blood. All possible types of incompatibility between mother and fetus are listed in Table 5.4. Note that in each case the genotype of the fetus is heterozygous. This suggests selection against some heterozygotes.

To make matters more complicated, it turns out that ABO incompatibility affects Rhesus incompatibility. To be incompatible for both is less severe than to be incompatible for either one alone! The reason for this effect is not known, but it appears that ABO incompatibility prevents the build-up of anti-D antibodies when Rhesus incompatibility is present. As the fetal red blood cells enter the mother's bloodstream, the ABO incompatibility destroys them before they can stimulate the production of anti-D. This effect shows how complicated the effects of natural selection can be, and how important it is to look at the entire organism and not just isolated genetic traits.

There seems to be little doubt that natural selection has affected allele frequencies for the ABO blood group system. Studies have shown the relationship among blood type and incompatibility, infectious disease, and noninfectious disease. It does not appear likely that any one of these factors is solely responsible for the observed allele frequency range in human beings. It is also possible that there are other factors of which we are unaware. A further complication is that we generally have data on ABO phenotypes and not on genotypes. Our blood tests can tell us if someone is blood type A, but they cannot tell us if that person has the *AA* or *AO* genotype. Simply because we cannot tell the difference does not mean that natural selection does not affect these genotypes in different ways. As we develop more sophisticated methods of genetic analysis, we may be able to look more closely at the relationship between selection and genotype for the ABO system.

Duffy blood group. The most striking relationship between blood groups and infectious disease is found for the Duffy blood group. There are three alleles for the Duffy blood group: *Fy*[a], *Fy*[b], and *Fy* (the latter is also referred to as the Duffy negative allele). The *Fy* allele is recessive. These alleles code for the production of different molecules on the surface

T A B L E 5.4
ABO Blood Group Maternal-fetal Incompatibilities

Mother's genotype	Incompatible fetal genotypes
AA	*AB*
AO	*AB, BO*
BB	*AB*
BO	*AB, AO*
AB	None
OO	*AO, BO*

of the red blood cells. The fascinating aspect of this blood group is that individuals with the *FyFy* genotype are completely resistant to the form of malaria caused by the parasite *Plasmodium vivax*. Studies have suggested that the vivax parasite can cling to red blood cells containing *Fy*ᵃ or *Fy*ᵇ type molecules, and therefore more easily enter the cell. Individuals with two *Fy* alleles lack both of these molecules and are resistant to the parasite. Though vivax malaria is not as fatal as falciparum malaria, it is still a serious disease that can lead to high rates of mortality. The complete resistance of the *FyFy* genotype to vivax malaria is the clearest example of a relationship between infectious disease and red cell blood groups in human populations.

The worldwide distribution of the Duffy negative allele, however, is somewhat confusing. The highest frequencies of the allele are found in West and Central Africa, reaching 100 percent in pygmies. The frequency is lower in North Africa and in parts of the Middle East. The allele frequency is virtually zero in most of Europe and Asia. This distribution is almost the exact opposite of the distribution of epidemic vivax malaria (Livingstone 1984). In areas where the frequency of the Duffy negative allele is high, vivax malaria is absent. In areas with high levels of vivax malaria, the frequency of the Duffy negative allele is virtually zero. At first glance, the negative correlation between the frequency of the Duffy negative allele and vivax malaria does not appear to make sense. Given that the recessive homozygote provides complete protection against vivax malaria, it would seem logical for high frequencies of the Duffy negative allele to be found in those areas with epidemic vivax malaria. In fact, the opposite occurs. Also, no harmful effects have been detected for those with the Duffy negative allele, thus ruling out a scenario of balanced polymorphism similar to the case of the sickle cell allele.

Livingstone (1984) has presented two hypotheses to explain this seeming paradox. One is that populations first adapted to vivax malaria by showing an increase in the frequency of the Duffy negative allele. When high frequencies were attained, the vivax malaria parasite could no longer maintain itself in these populations. Without a suitable number of hosts, a parasite cannot survive and reproduce. In these populations, vivax malaria disappeared and other forms of malaria parasites (not affected by the Duffy blood group) became more common. In other words, the lack of vivax malaria in populations with high frequencies of Duffy negative reflects past adaptation.

Livingstone (1984) notes that this hypothesis has a problem. Why don't we find increasing frequencies of the Duffy negative allele in those areas of the world today with high rates of vivax malaria? One possibility is that there has been insufficient time for such change to have taken place. Livingstone, however, favors another hypothesis. He concludes that certain populations first developed high frequencies of the Duffy negative allele for some other reason (perhaps some other relationship with natural selection and/or genetic drift in small populations). The preexisting high frequencies of the Duffy negative allele prevented the introduction and spread of vivax malaria in those populations. Livingstone states that the distribution of the Duffy negative allele provides a good example of how "fortuitous genetic variation in human populations may contribute to their differential susceptibility to new infectious diseases" (1984:413).

The HLA System

Blood also contains white cells (leukocytes) that function to provide protection from foreign substances. Our immune systems have the ability to recognize and reject foreign "invaders" in our bodies. The immune system is important in organ and tissue transplants because it determines whether a transplant is accepted or rejected. Part of the immune system's response is determined by the HLA system (human leukocyte antigen). Our white blood cells (and many other body cells) contain certain molecules on their surfaces that affect an individual's ability to recognize and attack foreign substances.

The HLA system has a complicated pattern of inheritance. There are at least seven closely linked loci on the sixth chromosome pair. For each locus there are many possible alleles. Table 5.5 lists the seven HLA loci and the number of alleles known for each at present (a total of 122). Even though we are still discovering new alleles, it appears that the HLA system is the most polymorphic of all human genetic systems.

There is also considerable variation in allele frequencies among human populations. Some alleles are found at polymorphic frequencies throughout the world. For example, the frequency of allele *A2* is 0.270 in Europeans, 0.094 in Africans, and 0.253 in Asians. Other alleles are confined to certain geographic regions, such as the *Bw42* allele, with a frequency of 0.123 in Africans but absent in Europeans and Asians (Harrison et al. 1988). In some cases the distribution of HLA alleles corresponds to patterns we expect from genetic drift and gene flow.

The HLA system is also related to patterns of natural selection. This is not surprising, since the immune system will have a major influence on differences in susceptibility to disease. For example, there is a relationship between those people with the HLA allele *B27* and a condition known as ankylosing spondylitis, a disease that leads to crippling of the spine. Individuals with the *B27* allele are more likely to develop the disease than those who do not have the allele.

Another example of natural selection and the HLA system may be the relationship between the *B8* allele and intolerance of the protein gluten, which is found in wheat and barley. Individuals having this intolerance cannot make efficient use of a diet of wheat or barley. In Europe, groups with the longest history of agriculture appear to have the lowest frequencies of the *B8* allele. Perhaps there has been selection against the allele because of its relationship to gluten intolerance (Harrison et al. 1988).

TABLE 5.5
Number of Loci and Alleles at Each Locus for the HLA System

Locus	Number of alleles
A	23
B	47
C	8
D	19
DR	16
DQ	3
DP	6

The HLA loci are closely linked on the 6th chromosome. The genetics of this system are not fully known, but it is rather complex. See Williams (1985) for further information.

lactase deficiency When an older child or adult lacks the ability to produce the lactase enzyme needed to digest milk sugar.

Lactase Deficiency

As shown in the sickle cell example, cultural variation can affect genetic variation. **Lactase deficiency** is another example of a genetic trait that is influenced by cultural factors. As mammals, human infants receive nourishment from mother's milk. Infants have an enzyme, lactase, that allows milk sugar, lactose, to be digested. In most human populations, the manufacture of the lactase enzyme is "turned off" by four years of age as it is in most mammals after infancy. A person who has a deficiency of this enzyme as a child or adult will not be able to digest milk efficiently and can develop severe cramps, diarrhea, and other intestinal problems if he or she consumes it. The genetics of adult lactase deficiency are not fully understood, but it may be caused by a recessive allele. The environment may also exert some influence because individuals who are lactase-deficient may be able to build up some ability to digest milk over time. Though lactase deficiency is probably not a "simple" discrete trait, the available evidence does suggest a relatively simple mode of inheritance.

Most human populations have high frequencies of lactase deficiency, but some populations do not. The enzyme continues to be produced throughout life, and these people can continue to digest milk sugar. Interestingly, a clear relationship exists between the frequency of lactase deficiency in a population and whether or not the population is involved in dairy farming. Table 5.6 lists the frequency of lactase deficiency in a number of populations of African, Asian, and European ancestry. In general,

T A B L E   5.6

Frequencies of Lactase Deficiency in Some Human Populations

Population		Percentage of lactase deficiency
African ancestry	African Americans	70–77
	Ibos	99
	Bantus	90
	Fulani	22
	Yoruba	99
	Baganda	94
Asian ancestry	Asian Americans	95–100
	Thailand	97–100
	Eskimos	72–88
	Native Americans	58–67
European ancestry	European Americans	2–19
	Finland	18
	Switzerland	12
	Sweden	4

Sources: Lerner and Libby (1976:327); Molnar (1992:124).

the lowest frequency is found in populations of European ancestry with a known history of dairy farming. The highest frequency of lactase deficiency occurs in populations of African and Asian ancestry that did not practice dairy farming. Populations that rely extensively on cheese products generally do not conform to this pattern, probably reflecting the fact that the lactose is broken down in the process of cheese making. The digestion of cheese is not accomplished by the lactase enzyme but by certain intestinal enzymes and bacteria.

The correspondence of low frequencies of lactase deficiency and dairy farming suggests that the ability to digest milk later in life is selected for in environments where milk is a major source of nutrition. This circumstance suggests that humans originally had very high frequencies of lactase deficiency and that as populations grew to rely more and more on milk in their diet after infancy, natural selection acted to decrease the proportion of those with lactase deficiency. After all, we would expect higher survival and reproduction in those individuals best able to utilize available nutrition. An examination of some discrepancies in the usual pattern of frequencies in Table 5.6 supports this hypothesis. Many African populations, such as the Ibos and Bantus, are known horticultural populations that do not practice dairy farming. The Fulani, however, are a group of nomadic cattle herders who rely extensively on milk in their diet. The percentage of lactase deficiency among the Fulani is low (22 percent) and similar to the percentage found in European populations. African Americans have high rates of lactase deficiency, but much lower than those populations found in West Africa from whom they are descended. The reduction in the frequency of lactase deficiency among African Americans may represent European admixture, physiological adaptation to milk diets, and/or some degree of natural selection.

Lactase deficiency provides a good example of rapid natural selection in human populations. Dairy agriculture is less than 12,000 years old and the observed differences among dairy- and nondairy-producing economies must have arisen since then. The study of lactase deficiency also helps us understand something about policy decisions in the modern world. In the United States, which has a large dairy economy, milk is regarded as an essential part of daily nutrition. We think of milk as intrinsically good and in the past have sent milk to peoples in underdeveloped countries in the belief that what is good for us must be good for them. It was soon realized, however, that many of these people were lactase-deficient and the milk was not useful to them. In fact, it was often harmful. We should always consider differences in biology, culture, and environment in formulating policy decisions.

Fertility and Body Size

It has often been suggested that a direct relationship exists between body size and fertility. If so, then body size would be subject to natural selection through differential reproduction of individuals with certain body sizes. Both directional and stabilizing selection could operate on the relationship between fertility and body size. Larger body size of the mother might reflect improved nutrition and general health care, which in turn would improve the chances for successful pregnancies and childbirth. A number of studies, however, have found that there is stabilizing selection in that very small and very large individuals produce fewer offspring.

The relationship between fertility and body size depends on the specific physical and cultural environment. In situations where food resources are limited either through environmental factors or low social class, we might expect smaller body size to be more adaptive, particularly for women. Given the fact that each human possesses a limited amount of energy, smaller women would have less demand for energy for body maintenance and growth and more energy left over for reproduction. It is clear that a number of different relationships may exist between fertility and body size in human populations. Specific environmental and cultural factors must be taken into account, along with information regarding nutrition, disease, and other potential influences on fertility.

One study of fertility and body size was conducted by William Mueller (1979) on a moderately malnourished farming community in Colombia. Mueller also looked at body size in terms of two factors, bone size and fatness. Small-boned and large-boned people had fewer surviving offspring than those with bone size closer to the average. Bone size appears to be subject to stabilizing selection in this population. On the other hand, body fatness appears to be subject to directional selection; people with more fat tended to have more surviving offspring. In the case of fatness, however, Mueller found that the observed relationship was not the result of selection but rather sociocultural factors. In particular, wealthier individuals tended to have more children and were fatter.

Not all studies have found a link between fertility and body size. Little and colleagues (1989) investigated the relationship between parental height and fertility and offspring survival among the Zapotec Indians of southern Mexico. The Zapotec are one of the shortest Central American Indian groups and have poor nutrition and health. Many studies have suggested that in poor environments smaller body size is more adaptive. Little and colleagues found no relationship between fertility and offspring survival and parental height. In this particular case, small body size was related to environmental conditions and not to natural selection. The work illustrates that the action of natural selection is not likely to be the same under all environmental conditions.

SUMMARY

The study of human microevolution focuses on the effects of genetic drift, gene flow, and natural selection on patterns of genetic variation within and between populations. Assessments of genetic drift and gene flow rely on multivariate measures of genetic variation that deal with a number of traits at the same time, because drift and gene flow are expected to have the same effect on all loci. Natural selection is expected to have different effects on different traits, leading researchers to examine one trait at a time.

Genetic drift and gene flow exert critical impact on genetic variation in a wide range of populations. Factors such as geographic distance, cultural change, social organization, culture contact, and religious differences, among others, have all been shown to affect genetic differences between groups.

Studies of natural selection have produced mixed results because of the difficulty in measuring natural selection over short time periods and because selective forces that shaped our past are not always working today. The strong relationship of hemoglobin variants and certain blood groups with the presence of malaria represents the strongest evidence for natural selection on relatively simple genetic traits. Other traits, such as the Rhesus and ABO blood groups, have been linked to a number of selective factors, but it is difficult at present to determine which ones have been most significant. Examination of the relationship between fertility and body size shows us the importance of viewing natural selection in terms of differences in both survival *and* reproduction.

Supplemental Readings

Crawford, M. H., and P. L. Workman, eds. 1973. *Methods and Theories of Anthropological Genetics.* Albuquerque: University of New Mexico Press.

Crawford, M. H., and J. H. Mielke, eds. 1982. *Current Developments in Anthropological Genetics,* Vol. 2, *Ecology and Population Structure.* New York: Plenum Press.

Mielke, J. H., and M. H. Crawford, eds. 1980. *Current Developments in Anthropological Genetics,* Vol. 1, *Theory and Methods.* New York: Plenum Press. These three volumes provide detailed, although somewhat advanced, reviews of theory, methods, and applications in the study of human microevolution.

Harrison, G. A., J. M. Tanner, D. R. Pilbeam, and P. T. Baker. 1988. *Human Biology: An Introduction to Human Evolution, Variation, Growth, and Adaptability.* 3rd ed. Oxford: Oxford University Press.

Molnar, S. 1992. *Human Variation: Races, Types, and Ethnic Groups.* 3rd ed. Englewood Cliffs, N.J.: Prentice-Hall. These two texts provide summaries of the field of human variation and microevolution. Although not as detailed as the first three, they are better designed for new students.

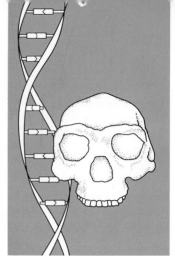

CHAPTER **6**

Approaches to the Study of Human Variation

We each encounter human biological diversity every day of our lives, but we seldom speak of what we see in terms of evolutionary forces. Instead, we use words like "race" without actually defining them. What do phrases like the "white race," the "Japanese race," and the "Jewish race" mean to you? They are extremely confusing because the term "race" is used to stand for a variety of factors such as skin color, national origin, and religion. Sometimes we use the term in a biological sense, sometimes in a social sense.

The definition of race is no mere academic issue. Race is discussed daily in the newspapers and other media. Race has been used to justify discrimination and persecution of people as well as to grant favored status. Statistics on race are gathered by local, state, federal, and international organizations. Economic and political decisions are often based on race.

Race and Racial Classifications

Obviously, race is an important concept in our lives. But what exactly is it? How many races are there? What are the differences between races?

This chapter looks at the biological definition of race and compares the utility of this definition to a microevolutionary approach.

The Biological Concept of Race

From a biological standpoint, a **race** is generally defined as "a division of a species that differs from other divisions by the frequency with which certain hereditary traits appear among its members" (Brues 1977:1). Race in this definition has two characteristics. First, it is a group of populations that share some biological characteristics. Second, these populations differ from other groups of populations according to these characteristics. The concept of race seeks to fill the void between the single "human race" and the thousands of local human populations. Race is meant to provide a classification of biologically similar populations.

The race concept works better biologically with some organisms than with others. For organisms that are isolated from one another in different environments, the race concept often provides a usable, though rough, means of summarizing biological variation. For other organisms, such as humans, the concept has less utility. Humans inhabit a wide number of environments and move between them frequently. The high degree of gene flow among human populations, compared to many other organisms, means that clear-cut boundaries among groups of populations are difficult to establish.

The race concept presents a number of problems that are outlined in the next section. Given these problems, race and racial classifications provide only a crude tool for description, one with little utility for today's biologist or anthropologist, when sophisticated statistical methods and computers allow us to analyze patterns of biological variation more precisely than ever before. Indeed, some authors have suggested that we drop the entire concept, for it has little use biologically (Livingstone 1964; Gould 1977a) and is probably harmful socially.

Problems with the Concept of Race

What is wrong with classifying people into races? After all, we can do it accurately. Or can we?

The number of human races. A major problem with the race concept is that scientists have never agreed on the number of human races. How many can you name, or see? Some have suggested that there are three human races: Europeans, Africans, and Asians (often referred to by the archaic terms "Caucasoid," "Negroid," and "Mongoloid," which are almost never used in scientific research today). But many populations do not fit neatly into these three basic categories. What about native Australians

race A group of populations sharing certain traits that make them distinct from other groups of populations. The concept of race is difficult to apply to patterns of human variation.

Figure 6.1

An Australian aborigine with dark skin and curly hair. (Neg. no. 330831. Photo by A. P. Elkin. Courtesy Department of Library Services, American Museum of Natural History)

(aborigines)? As shown in Figure 6.1, these are dark-skinned people who frequently have curly or wavy hair that is sometimes blond and who have abundant facial hair. On the basis of skin color, we might be tempted to label these people as African, but on the basis of hair and facial shape they might be classified as European. One approach has been to create a fourth category, the "Australoid" race.

As we travel around the world, we find more and more populations that do not fit a three- or four-race system. As a result, some authors added additional races to their list. There has never been clear consensus on the actual number, however. In 1758, for example, Linnaeus described four major human races in his classification of humans. Since that time different authors have suggested four, five, and nine major races, among other numbers. During the twentieth century, hierarchies of races have been suggested. That is, a varying number of major races can be subdivided into minor races, which are further subdivided into even smaller races. Some anthropologists have divided "primary races" into "primary subraces" (Hooten 1946). Others have suggested subdividing major "geographic races" into "local races," which are further subdivided into "microraces" (Garn 1965). Additional populations that are the result of admixture, such as African Americans, are often referred to as "composite races." In each case there has been little agreement on the number of races or subraces.

Two points emerge from a study of the history of attempts to classify and apply the race concept to human populations. First, the lack of agreement among different researchers indicates that the entire concept of race is arbitrary as it applies to humans. If clearly discernible races existed, their number should have long since been determined without argument. How useful is a classification system when there is so much disagreement about the number of units? Second, something is being described here, although in a crude manner. All racial classifications, for example, note the wide range in skin color among human populations and note further an association with geography. The native peoples of Africa tend to have darker skin than those of northern Europe. The geographic distribution of many traits, such as skin color, is well known. Then why doesn't the race concept work well when describing biological variation?

The nature of continuous variation. Biological variation is real; the order we impose on this variation by using the concept of race is not. Race is a product of human minds, not of nature. One reason race fails to describe variation accurately is that much variation is continuous, whereas race is a discrete unit. In other words, we must reduce variation into a few small categories.

Consider human height as an example. Most of us cannot describe a person's height to the nearest centimeter without actually measuring that person. When we look at someone, we are unlikely to know *exactly* how tall that person is. We would not, however, describe everyone as the same height simply because we do not know the exact values. Instead, we use relative terms such as "short," "medium," and "tall." Often our definitions of these categories do not always agree with other people's (many people call anyone shorter than themselves "short" regardless of their actual height). Also, some people might add additional categories, such as "medium tall" or "very short." In any case, these categories have some limited use. When we say that a basketball player is "tall," most people know roughly how tall we mean. But are these categories real? When we forget that these are only convenient crude levels for classification, we can fall into the trap of thinking that they have a reality of their own. Do you actually think all people fall into one of three categories—"short," "medium," or "tall"? Height is a continuous trait that can have an infinite number of values within a certain range.

The same problem applies to races. Many racial classifications in Western societies use skin color as a major distinguishing feature. The races correspond to different measures of skin color—"white," "yellow," "red," "brown," and "black," for example. We know, however, that skin color does not fall into 5, or even 50, different categories. Skin color is a continuous variable. This means that any attempt to divide the continuous range into discrete units (races) is going to be arbitrary.

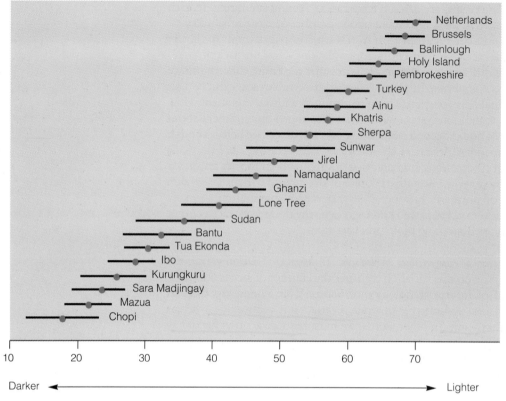

Figure 6.2

Variation in skin color in 22 human populations (males). Dots indicate the mean skin reflectance measured at a wavelength of 685 nanometers; lines indicate 1 standard deviation on each side of the mean.   (All data from published literature)

Early investigations of skin color tended to use a small number of different colors for classification. Since the 1950s, biological anthropologists have used a more objective method of measuring skin color—reflectance spectrophotometry. According to this method, a light source is held up next to a person's skin, and the amount of light reflected back from the skin surface is measured. In most cases, this measurement is taken on the inner surface of the upper arm, since that is a place easy to reach that is not affected greatly by tanning. Skin color is measured as the percentage of light reflected. The higher the percentage of reflectance, the lighter the skin color.

Figure 6.2 shows the average skin reflectance for males in 22 samples. For each sample, the dot represents the average value, and the lines represent 1 standard deviation below and above the average. (A standard deviation is a statistical measure of variation. Roughly 68 percent of the cases in each sample lie between the ends of the lines drawn in Figure 6.2. Each sample contains some individuals who are even lighter or darker than the range shown.) There are no discrete boundaries between different groups. The ranges of skin reflectance overlap one another. In other words, on the basis of skin color it is not possible to tell where one population ends and another starts.

There is also overlap in skin color among traditional racial groupings. Using published data on male skin reflectance, the average skin reflectance for 27 Sub-Saharan African populations is 30 percent. The average skin reflectance for 22 South Asian populations is 49 percent. Generally, Sub-Saharan Africans are darker than South Asians (the lower the percentage reflectance, the darker the skin). However, considerable overlap occurs between these two geographic groups. Individual Sub-Saharan African populations range from 18 to 46 percent reflectance, and individual South Asian populations range from 32 to 56 percent. Some South Asian populations are darker than some Sub-Saharan African populations!

If we look only at the darkest and lightest of these samples, we might be tempted to describe two races, "black" and "white." The range of variation in the entire world, however, shows that we cannot describe different races. Where does one race end and another begin? There are no discrete boundaries, even with a handful of samples. How many races would you use for description? Two? Three? The number is arbitrary. Continuous variables can be broken down into discrete units for convenience, but the boundaries are always arbitrary. Skin color is not a good characteristic for identifying different races, which is ironic when we consider that it is often used as the basis of racial classifications in Western culture.

Despite these arguments, many people are still convinced that human races are easily identifiable. After all, they say, you can walk down any city street in the United States and point out who is "white" and who is "black" (ignoring for the moment those people who are difficult to classify). Under such circumstances, race is easily identifiable (or is it?). This may be true in a limited area, such as a street in a medium-sized American city, but it does not hold true when we look at the world in general. Races seem distinct in certain situations because disproportionate numbers of peoples from different geographic regions are present. We do not find equal representation of all human populations on most U.S. city streets. For example, we tend to see far fewer Australian aborigines than we see people of predominantly European or African ancestry.

In short, the overall composition of the U.S. population tends to give us a distorted view of the total variation in the world. The majority of early settlers in the United States came from Western Europe, one of the regions in the world whose human populations show the lightest skin color. During the next few centuries, many slaves were brought from West Africa, one of the regions where human skin color is darkest. The result has been a disproportionate representation of the range of skin color. More people in the United States have either very light or very dark skin than any shade

Figure 6.3

Original settlement of the United States from the perspective of skin color. From the continuous range of skin color in the human species, the majority of earliest settlers were from the two extreme ends—dark-colored West Coast Africans and light-colored Western Europeans. This differential settlement gives rise to the seeming existence of two distinct races in the United States based on skin color.

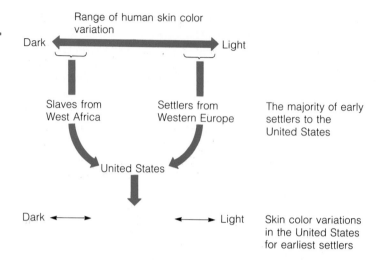

in between (Figure 6.3). On the other hand, a tour through other parts of the world will soon give you a different picture. Many of the people in the world are neither so dark nor so light.

Not all biological traits show continuous variation. Blood group phenotypes, for example, are discrete traits. We do not, however, often find situations in which all members of one race have one phenotype and all members of another race have a different phenotype. Some genetic markers are useful in separating populations in certain geographic areas, but many such traits show patterns of variation that are not well described by racial classification. For example, the frequency of the *a* allele for the Diego blood group is moderately high in native South American populations, ranging up to 0.32. In both Africa and Europe, however, the frequency is 0 (Roychoudhury and Nei 1988). This allele is useful in separating South America from other regions but does not separate Africa and Europe—two regions typically assigned to different races. In addition, there are populations in South America that have a near-zero allele frequency. If we used the Diego blood group, we would have to assign these South American populations to a mixed European/African race!

Another example of a discrete trait is eye form. The so-called "slanted" eyes of Asians are caused in part by a fold of skin at the inner corner of the eye. (This shape is also related to the size and projection of the root of the nose.) This eye shape is found in many Asian populations, and to a lesser extent in other groups as well. At first this trait might seem like a good "racial" trait because its presence allows us to separate populations of Asian ancestry from other groups. It does not, however, separate other groups, such as those of African or European ancestry.

Correspondence of different traits. If race were to be a useful biological concept, the classifications would have to work for a number of independent traits. A classification developed from skin color would also need to show the same racial pattern in other traits, such as head shape, nasal shape, and hair color. If each trait produces a different set of races, then the race concept is not very useful as a description of overall biological similarity. In fact, racial classifications vary according to the biological trait used. This lack of correspondence is expected, given Mendel's work on independent assortment. Several examples of this lack of correspondence were discussed in the last chapter.

High frequencies of the sickle cell allele are found not only in populations belonging to "African races," but also in parts of Europe and India. Any racial classification based on high or low frequencies of the sickle cell allele in a population would not produce the same distribution as skin color. Another example is the frequency of lactase deficiency. Some populations in Africa, because of their dependence on dairy farming, have low frequencies of lactase deficiency similar to rates found in European populations. Still another example comes from the work of Bodmer and Cavalli-Sforza (1976), who looked at the relationships among four "racial groups": Native Americans, Europeans, Australian aborigines, and Africans. Using body and cranial measurements, they found that Native Americans were more similar to Europeans and Australian aborigines were more similar to Africans. When they used a number of genetic marker systems, however, they found a different pattern. Native Americans were more similar to Australian aborigines and Europeans were more similar to Africans.

Using different traits often results in different groupings of populations. For examples such as sickle cell and lactase deficiency we expect this to be the case, because the variation in a trait is related to natural selection, which will operate differently in diverse environments. In using racial classifications, however, we often find that as we add more traits the situation becomes even more complex. The fact that traits show different distributions argues against the utility of the race concept for describing human variation.

With the proper choice of variables, however, we can find combinations that are useful in looking at the relationships between populations on a worldwide basis. By examining a number of traits presumed neutral in terms of natural selection, we try to come up with an average pattern that reflects the tendency of gene flow and genetic drift to affect all loci to the same extent. Often we find clusters of populations that agree in a limited sense with geography. That is, we can identify some separation between Sub-Saharan African populations, European populations, Middle Eastern populations, and so on. This is expected, given the close relationship of geographic distance and gene flow in human populations. Sub-Saharan African populations should be more similar to each other, on average, than

typology A set of discrete groupings in classification that emphasize average tendencies and ignore variation within groups.

to European populations. This does not, however, support the race concept. Genetic distances within regional groups are often greater than those found between regions. Also, it is sometimes still difficult, if not impossible, to draw lines clearly delineating different races. We can identify rough geographic clusters that, in some cases, have a *rough* correspondence with predetermined notions of races. However, because races are often defined in part on the basis of geography, the entire process is somewhat circular.

Variation between and within groups. Racial classifications represent a form of **typology,** a set of discrete groupings. Instead of looking at the continuous range of variation, populations are placed into different races. The problem with typologies and typological thinking is that it tends to ignore the variation and focus exclusively on the "types." An average is considered representative of the entire group. Take, for example, the fact that the average height in Finland is 171 cm (Molnar 1992). Does this mean that *everyone* in Finland is exactly this height? Of course not. There is always variation within the group.

Racial classifications focus on the difference between groups and deemphasize the variation that exists within groups. Lewontin (1972) examined the actual levels of variation between and within seven designated "races": Africans, Europeans, Asians, Native Americans, South Asians, Oceanians, and Australian aborigines. Lewontin took this list of races and then looked at a number of loci for each race. He found that 94 percent of the total variation occurred *within* races and 6 percent of the variation *between* races. His study shows clearly how limited the race concept is for classification.

A related problem is that traits used to distinguish between groups are not useful in classifying individuals. For example, the allele frequency for the *O* allele for the ABO blood group in the San of South Africa is 0.684. The allele frequency for Scotland is 0.716 (Roychoudhury and Nei 1988). These two groups illustrate a common finding: the frequency of the *O* allele in northwest Europe is higher than that found in southern Africa. Suppose you come across an individual with blood type O. Which group does he or she belong to? You can't tell, because both groups have individuals with this blood group. All that differs between groups is the relative *frequency* of the allele.

What use is the race concept? Even if we acknowledge the many problems associated with race as a concept, does it have any use? In the scientific study of human variation, the concept of race has little, if any, use. It is a descriptive tool, not an analytic one. If we examine the biological characteristics of a population and then assign the population to a given race, all we have accomplished is to label some observed phenomenon. We have not explained the causes of variation, nor why some groups are similar to, or different from, others. The name explains nothing.

Until the 1950s, much of biological anthropology was devoted to racial description and classification. Most sciences go through a descriptive phase, followed later by an explanatory phase in which hypotheses are proposed and tested. Indeed, at least until the work of Charles Darwin, much of biology was basically a descriptive science. Today biological anthropologists rarely treat race as a concept. It has no utility for explanation, and its value for description is limited.

In contemporary society, however, race is still a common category. In this context the term has more a social connotation than a biological one. In state and federal government reports, "race" identifies some aspect of geographic origin and ethnic identity. For example, "black" refers to African or African-American descent. "Hispanic" refers to Spanish speakers but actually encompasses a wide variety of peoples from Mexicans to Bolivians. Such classifications have their use, particularly in defining groups of people who have suffered social inequities, but they are not without their own problems. Classification into discrete groups always means that we obscure the subtle gradations of human variation.

Human variation is best analyzed using an approach that focuses on microevolutionary forces and uses individuals or local populations as the unit of analysis. This approach, aided by modern statistical and computer methods, allows better description than the race concept, avoids the problems of classification, and provides a focus for *explanation*.

In any case, we should not confuse social and biological categories, nor draw biological inferences from social identity. Race as a concept has little utility for analyzing human biological variation. Although we still distinguish "social" races, the term tends to generate misunderstanding even when used in this sense.

Skin Color: An Example of Racial versus Microevolutionary Approaches

Skin color has been a widely used characteristic in racial classifications. Typical classifications equate a different skin color with each race, such as "black" (African), "white" (European), "yellow" (Asian), and "red" (Native American). Perhaps the major reason for the popularity of skin color as a racial characteristic is that you can see it: skin color is one of the most noticeable forms of human variation. This was particularly true when the early European explorers first met darker-skinned peoples. You could just as easily attempt to construct a racial classification using frequencies of the ABO blood group system, except that in this case you would not be able to assign people to races just by looking at them.

A common reaction of many people when they look at skin color variation is to see distinct colors. This is particularly true in the United

States, for reasons discussed earlier. Once we identify distinct classes of colors, we label each color as a different race. The problem here is that our observations are not always objective. We often emphasize differences among groups to the exclusion of variation within groups. Do all "white" people have the same skin color? If you look closely, you will see this is not the case. Some are darker or lighter than others. The same applies to "black" people. For example, there is a tendency to think of Africa as a continent originally inhabited by "blacks." Actually, the skin color in native African populations ranges from medium to dark in pigmentation. Figure 6.2 shows that we cannot break up the range of human skin color variation into discrete categories.

Racial approaches to skin color do not take into account the processes behind the variation. The real issues are why people have different skin color. To answer this question, we must abandon typical racial classifications and look more closely at the biological nature of skin color.

The Biology of Skin Color

Human skin color is a complex trait. A number of researchers have suggested that skin color is a polygenic trait, rather than one caused by a major gene, although considerable controversy surrounds the number of loci that might be involved (Byard 1981). Skin color has a strong genetic component (e.g., Williams-Blangero and Blangero 1992) and is affected by the environment, such as the amount of direct sunlight present.

Skin color is caused by three pigments. One pigment, *melanin,* is responsible for the majority of variation in lightness and darkness in skin color. Melanin is a brown pigment secreted by cells in the bottom layer of the skin. All human populations appear to have the same number of melanin-producing cells. Variation in the darkness of the skin depends on how many cells actually produce melanin and how they cluster together (Szabo 1967). The more melanin-producing cells are present or the more they cluster, the darker the skin color.

Another pigment affecting skin color is *hemoglobin,* which gives oxygenated blood cells their red color. Light-skinned peoples have little melanin near the surface of the skin and so the red color shows through. Because of this effect, "white" people are actually "pink." A third pigment is *carotene,* a yellowish pigment obtained from certain foods. A person who eats these foods in sufficient amounts may notice a yellowish tinge to the skin. Carotene, however, is *not* responsible for the yellowish hue of many Asian populations. Their coloring is caused instead by a thickening of the outer layer of the skin.

Skin color is also affected to a certain extent by sex and age. In general, males are darker than females, probably because of differential effects of sex hormones on melanin production. Age also produces variation. The skin darkens somewhat during adolescence, particularly in females.

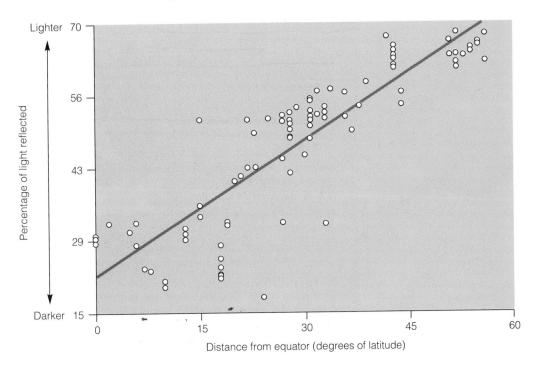

Figure 6.4

Geographic distribution of human skin color for 93 human Old World populations (males). Circles indicate the mean skin reflectance measured at a wavelength of 685 nanometers plotted against the distance, in degrees of latitude, from the equator. The solid line indicates the best-fitting linear curve relating skin reflectance and latitude. (All data from published literature)

Skin Color and Natural Selection

The distribution of skin color. The worldwide distribution of human skin color among native populations shows a striking correspondence with latitude. Figure 6.4 shows the relationship between skin color and distance from the equator for 93 male samples from the Old World. Native populations closer to the equator tend to be the darkest, while those farther from the equator tend to be the lightest. Note that there are no discrete breaks. As in Figure 6.2, skin color shows a continuous distribution, and not separation into "light," "medium," and "dark" races. The distribution of skin color and latitude corresponds to the amount of ultraviolet radiation received at the earth's surface. Because of the way sunlight strikes the earth, ultraviolet radiation is strongest at the equator and diminishes in strength as we move away from the equator. It is even more diminished where cloud cover is extensive.

Skin cancer, sunburn, and ultraviolet radiation. What are the biological effects of ultraviolet radiation? This radiation causes the skin to tan—that is, to produce more melanin. Too much exposure burns the skin, leading to infection. In sufficient amounts, ultraviolet radiation can lead to skin cancer. The greater the intensity of ultraviolet radiation, the greater the risk for skin cancer at a given level of pigmentation. Among the European-American population of the United States, skin cancer rates are much higher in Texas than in Massachusetts (Damon 1977). Dark-skinned individuals have lower rates of skin cancer, since the heavy concentration of melanin near the surface of the skin blocks some of the ultraviolet radiation. Accordingly, the correspondence of latitude and skin color may reflect, in part, the differential effects of skin cancer. Ultraviolet radiation is strongest near the equator, and dark skin is advantageous in such an environment to protect against skin cancer.

Researchers have argued against skin cancer as a selective factor, suggesting that skin cancer, like many cancers, affects mostly older individuals past their reproductive years. If someone dies from skin cancer after reproducing, their death does not affect the process of natural selection. According to this line of reasoning, some researchers have suggested that skin cancer has had a minimal effect, at best, on the evolution of human skin color (e.g., Blum 1961).

The problem with this argument is that the evidence does not support it. Robins (1991) points out that all albinos studied in Nigeria and Tanzania either had skin cancer or precancerous skin lesions by 20 years of age. People are normally dark skinned in these countries, and the albinos, because of a rare genetic condition, would be particularly susceptible to harmful effects of ultraviolet radiation. From an evolutionary standpoint, the important finding is that skin cancers and precancerous conditions occur *early* in life, contrary to the opinion that they are generally found among the elderly. In addition, only 6 percent of Nigerian albinos are in the age range of 31 to 60 years, compared to 20 percent of nonalbinos. This indicates that fewer albinos survive their younger years. Thus, skin cancer could have been a powerful selective agent, particularly among early humans that had limited protection from the sun.

Sunburn could also have been an important factor in natural selection. Severe sunburn can lead to infection and can interfere with the body's ability to sweat efficiently. Dark skin could protect from these effects, and thus be selected for.

Natural selection related to skin cancer and sunburn may be part of the answer to the question of worldwide skin color variation, but it is not the entire answer. Even though there is less ultraviolet radiation farther away from the equator and light-skinned people would have less risk for skin cancer and sunburn, this does not explain *why* light skin evolved in such regions. The model only shows that light skin *could* evolve. Skin cancer and sunburn help explain dark skin near the equator but do not explain light skin farther away from the equator.

The vitamin D hypothesis. A more subtle effect of ultraviolet radiation is the synthesis of vitamin D, a nutrient needed by humans for proper bone growth. Today we may receive vitamin D either through vitamin supplements or through the injection of vitamin D into our milk. Both of these dietary modifications are relatively recent human inventions, however. Formerly, humans had to obtain their vitamin D through diet or from stimulation of the synthesis of certain chemical compounds by ultraviolet radiation. Some foods, such as fish oils, are high in vitamin D but are not found in all environments. For most human populations in the past the major source of vitamin D was the sun.

Because vitamin D synthesis depends on ultraviolet radiation, it seems reasonable to assume that more of it will be produced near the equator, where ultraviolet radiation is strongest. It has been suggested that too much or too little of the vitamin is harmful to the human body. An excess of vitamin D can lead to vitamin poisoning, cause calcification of soft tissues, and interfere with proper kidney functioning while a lack of it can lead to poor bone development and maintenance, including diseases, such as rickets, that lead to deformed bones. Such health hazards can affect fertility as well as mortality. One frequent consequence of childhood rickets is the deformation of a woman's pelvic bones, that can hinder or prevent successful childbirth. In one U.S. study, only 2 percent of European-American women had such pelvic deformities as compared to 15 percent of African-American women (Molnar 1992). This difference presumably relates to skin color; darker women are unable to absorb enough vitamin D for healthy bone growth.

The idea that vitamin D intake must lie in a certain range, without excess or deficit, is at the core of the vitamin D hypothesis of skin color evolution (Loomis 1967). According to this hypothesis, in regions close to the equator, where ultraviolet radiation is the greatest, darker skin serves to block the harmful effects of excessive vitamin D production. In areas farther away, dark skin blocks too much of the sun's rays, which leads to insufficiency of vitamin D. Natural selection thus produced a change toward lighter skin color, that would be adaptive in such environments.

The vitamin D hypothesis thus explains the entire distribution of human skin color, showing the adaptive significance of both dark skin and light skin in different environments. Although logical, some investigations have suggested that this model is *not* correct. Holick and colleagues (1981) have shown that vitamin D synthesis reaches a maximum level during continued exposure to ultraviolet radiation. A light-skinned person's prolonged exposure to ultraviolet radiation will *not* lead to toxic vitamin D levels.

Though the vitamin D hypothesis does not hold up for explaining dark skin near the equator, can it still be used to explain the occurrence of light skin farther away from the equator? Robins (1991) listed a number of reasons why the vitamin D hypothesis fails here as well. First, rickets is a disease associated with recent urbanization. It is essentially absent in rural areas, and there is little evidence of rickets in the fossil record of our ancestors (who lived in rural, not urban, conditions). Second, although dark skin is not as effective as light skin in synthesizing vitamin D, it is still effective enough for production and maintenance of proper vitamin

D levels. Laboratory studies have shown that African Americans can produce their maximum quota of vitamin D in three hours. Though this is not as fast as for European Americans (30 minutes), it is still effective enough for proper health except under conditions of modern urbanization, such as smog and tall buildings that cut down on exposure. Studies have also determined that dark-skinned peoples could produce and maintain sufficient vitamin D in northern climates even with only their heads, necks, and hands exposed to ultraviolet radiation. This is an important point, because in cold climates less of the body would be exposed. In sum, the relationship between rickets and limited vitamin D appears confined to recent urban areas and is also associated with lower social class (the poor have less money for milk). For conditions typical of our ancestors, dark skin would *not* be at a disadvantage in terms of limited vitamin D production.

Skin color and cold injury. The vitamin D hypothesis does not hold true when explaining the distribution of human skin color. One possibility for the occurrence of light skin at distances away from the equator is cold injury. Reviewing a wide range of data, Post and colleagues (1975) noted that, in cold climates, dark-skinned individuals are at greater risk for frostbite than light-skinned individuals. Data reporting this difference are available on soldiers in world wars I and II, the Korean War, and those stationed in Alaska during the late 1950s. For example, during the Korean War, African-American soldiers were over four times more likely to get frostbite than European-American soldiers. Closer analysis of the data from the Korean War shows that this difference persists even after controlling for other sociological and health factors.

These observations suggest that in the colder northern climates darker skin is more prone to cold injury than lighter skin, a hypothesis supported by laboratory experiments on piebald guinea pigs (having both light and dark skin). Cold injury could be induced more frequently and more severely in the darker-skinned animals.

Existing evidence allows a model for the evolution of light skin in northern climates to be developed. Because the fossil record shows the first human ancestors evolved in or near equatorial Africa (see Chapter 12), it seems likely they had darker skin. As human ancestors left the continent (see Chapter 13), they moved into different environments, including colder climates in the north. Once there, selection pressure for dark skin was reduced because there was less ultraviolet radiation and less risk of skin cancer and sunburn. Lighter skin, however, would be advantageous because those individuals would be at less risk for cold injury. Today, many of these problems can be eliminated with cultural adaptations, such as clothing and shelter. In earlier times, however, the direct effect of the physical environment was more intense.

At present, the evidence supports skin cancer and sunburn as selective factors for dark skin in equatorial regions. Farther away from the equator, there is less of an advantage for dark skin, and more of an advantage for light skin, the former being more vulnerable to severe cold injury. Further study will be needed to strengthen support for both of these ideas and to explore the possibility that other factors affect skin color variation. Recent observations that ultraviolet radiation affects functioning of the immune system (Robins 1991) are also worth investigating.

ethnocentrism The belief that one's own culture is superior to other cultures.

The IQ Controversy

The area that generates the most controversy in any discussion of race is behavior, especially aspects of personality and intelligence. Inferences about race and behavior run deep in most cultures. Scientists, though often seeking to be objective, are members of cultures and have often contributed their share of misunderstanding.

Attempts to relate race and behavior are ancient. In his taxonomy, Linnaeus not only divided the human species into four different races but also provided a brief description of typical behavior for each. He pictured Africans as obstinate and regulated by customs, whereas Europeans were gentle and governed by laws. As he was living in a European culture, Linnaeus's descriptions should come as no surprise. Virtually all European scholars consistently ranked their own societies at the top of a behavioral ladder. Such rankings were not objective or even measured; rather they reflected a deep-seated sense of cultural superiority. When European explorers came into contact with different societies, they drew comparisons with their own and consistently found the newly "discovered" races to be inferior. Other cultures have held similar beliefs about their own superiority. Such beliefs are **ethnocentric,** the tendency to view one's own culture as being the "best."

In the United States a continuing source of controversy has been the evaluation of racial differences in intelligence test scores. Part of the confusion in this controversy arises from the designation of groups, identified as European American, African American, and Asian American, as biological races. Given typological thinking, there is a tendency to consider each group as homogeneous, with little variation within the group. In reality, these groups are defined in part on the basis of ancestry and contain a highly varied mixture of genetic and social backgrounds. African-American populations consist of individuals whose ancestors came from a wide geographic region in Africa, not to mention gene flow from European and indigenous American peoples. The European-American populations of the United States are equally diverse, consisting of people whose ancestry ranges from Western Europe through parts of Asia. By now it should be clear that the use of general terms such as *black* and *white* has limited utility if we take these groups as "types" or "races."

Results of IQ Testing

Regardless of how we define "black" and "white," one fact emerges from numerous studies of intelligence testing—the average IQ score for African Americans is 15 points below the average IQ score for European Americans. In general, Asian Americans score higher than European Americans. The controversy comes from interpreting exactly what these differences mean.

As discussed in Chapter 2, IQ scores have been taken as general indices on intelligence even though they were not designed for this specific task. The close association between IQ scores and intelligence in this country has often led to the circular definition that intelligence is what intelligence tests measure. For most psychologists, intelligence includes a variety of different cognitive processes, of which some are crudely measured by IQ tests. Recent developments in the psychological sciences may lead to better definitions and measurements of intelligence (e.g., Hunt 1983), but the bulk of the data, for the moment, relies on IQ test scores.

IQ tests have other problems. There is a certain amount of individual variation, and people may show different scores when tested at different stages of maturation. Physical factors such as stress have been shown to affect individual scores by as much as 15 points. Also, the usual IQ tests are often biased to a specific culture, and there has not been much success in developing a culture-free IQ test. An interesting finding is that African Americans score higher than European Americans on average on IQ tests designed around aspects of African-American language and culture.

Regardless of the exact relationship, or lack of relationship, between intelligence and IQ scores, the fact that African Americans score lower on average than European Americans would seem to indicate a substantial group difference in *some* aspect of learning or problem-solving abilities. In looking at these results, however, remember not to fall into the trap of associating a group's average value with all members of the group. Both groups show appreciable variation in IQ scores. Not all African Americans score lower than all European Americans. In fact, the range of IQ scores within the two groups is very similar.

The nature of variation means that we cannot make any predictions about the IQ scores of an individual based on group averages. Because African Americans and European Americans differ in one obvious biological trait—skin color—it is often tempting to explain differences in average IQ score as also the result of genetic differences between the two groups. It is important to realize that the two groups differ in many environmental factors. On average, African Americans have fewer educational and economic opportunities, less available health care, lower socioeconomic status, and poorer nutrition than European Americans. Do these differences account for the observed difference in IQ test scores? Or are there genetic differences between the two groups? Social ideologies and philosophies often predispose people to answer these questions without any evidence. To someone convinced of racial inequalities, it is a given that IQ tests reveal immutable genetic differences. To someone who is not so convinced, the environment accounts for these differences. In the long run, we need to analyze the data to determine this answer.

Genetic and Environmental Effects on IQ Scores

To date, there is evidence that *both* genetic and environmental factors affect IQ scores. Studies of twins and other relatives reveal strong association between the IQ scores of parents, children, and other relatives. In a recent and comprehensive study of identical twins raised apart, Bouchard and colleagues (1990) found that roughly 70 percent of the variation in observed IQ scores could be related to genetic factors. However, being born to two parents with a high IQ does not guarantee a high IQ; the social and physical environment must also be appropriate. Numerous studies have shown that IQ scores are associated with social class, educational background, nutrition, health status, and other factors.

These studies show us that IQ scores are not a fixed innate trait reflecting a person's genetic code but can be affected by environmental factors. The studies also show us that, all other factors being equal, inherited abilities contribute to performance on these tests.

Faulty reasoning has often been used in evaluating genetic differences between African Americans and European Americans and their effect on IQ test scores. A typical argument runs as follows: if IQ scores have a genetic basis and if two groups are genetically different, then the two groups will have different average IQ scores. The problem with this argument is that it relies on the myth of correspondence. The fact that skin color is different between two groups does not mean that any other trait, such as intelligence, will also be different. Many traits are "fixed" within the human species, such as the number of legs, arms, and eyes. Other traits show great variability, but to the same extent within all groups. Why should intelligence be any different? The story of human evolution, covered in later chapters, argues that intelligence is one of the key factors responsible for our species' survival. Cultural behaviors rely on problem solving, memory, perception, and other psychological factors. Given the primary importance of learned behavior to the human species, it becomes difficult to imagine any scenario that would favor the development of different overall intellectual potential in different populations.

Actually, we need not rely on logical reasoning and consideration of human evolution to look at the issue of genetic differences in IQ scores. The hypothesis that population differences in IQ scores are caused by genetic differences has been repeatedly tested. They are not.

One type of test examines the IQ scores of African Americans according to their amount of European admixture (see Chapter 3). If there are genetic differences between African Americans and European Americans for IQ scores, then African Americans with more European ancestry should have higher IQ scores than those with less European ancestry. Overall, there should be a positive relationship between the extent of

European ancestry and IQ scores. In one test of this hypothesis, hundreds of African Americans from Philadelphia had blood testing to determine their degree of European admixture. The results showed no relationship between admixture and IQ scores (Scarr and Weinberg 1978).

Another type of test looks at differences between European Americans and African Americans in IQ scores after adjusting for variation in the social and physical environment. One well-known study analyzed the massive amounts of data collected on U.S. Army recruits during World War I. The specific tests used were variants of the traditional IQ test that could also be taken by those who could not read. When the total sample of European-American and African-American recruits was tallied, the former had, on average, higher test scores. When comparisons were made between literate European Americans and literate African Americans, however, the difference virtually disappeared. Differences were also found to correlate with the known differences in the quality of education between the northern and southern states at that time: namely, northern African Americans scored higher than southern African Americans.

Another large-scale study of IQ differences was carried out using 650,000 school children. Although the average score for European Americans was higher than for African Americans, there were also strong relationships between test scores and social factors. "Race" was found to be less important in predicting IQ scores than a variety of social factors. When differences in socioeconomic status and other factors were controlled for, the difference between African Americans and European Americans was insignificant (Molnar 1992).

The importance of environmental factors on IQ scores has been demonstrated in numerous studies. This influence is apparent in the IQ scores of individuals taken at different points during their lives. It is common for a person's IQ score to increase as much as 20 to 30 points later in life. This age difference reflects accumulated learning and the fact that we also learn how to take tests. Socioeconomic status and educational levels of parents also have an effect on IQ. Health factors are also important; a poor diet during pregnancy can lead to reduced IQ scores among offspring.

Studies of adopted children also shed light on the relative effects of genetics and environment. One study focused on 130 African-American children that had been adopted by fairly well-off European-American parents. These children had an average IQ of 106, compared to an average of 94 for children that remained in their old neighborhoods. This finding suggests that simply a change in environment resulted in a 12-point increase in IQ. Another study of 63 African-American children adopted into upper-income families showed a difference of 21 points between the children (mean IQ = 106) and their biological mothers (mean IQ = 85) (Woodward 1992).

The available data suggest that differences between African Americans and European Americans reflect environmental differences rather than genetic differences. Based on such studies, the general conclusion is that if the environmental differences are changed, then the differences in

IQ scores will disappear. This is not an easy hypothesis to test for the entire country, since prejudice and differential treatment of European Americans and African Americans are realities that will take a long time to change. Several studies, however, have shown this predicted effect. One of the most famous was conducted in Milwaukee, where efforts were made to improve the environment of African-American children living in the poorest section of the city. A random sample of children received special education, including extensive individual attention for the first six years of life. This group scored much higher on IQ tests than a control group that did not receive such attention (Loehlin et al. 1975).

Not all scientists agree with the conclusion that an improvement in the environment of the lower-scoring group will result in the elimination of racial differences in IQ scores. One controversial study has suggested that differences in environment are not enough to account for differences in IQ scores (Jensen 1969). The social programs of the 1960s, Jensen claims, failed to achieve the desired improvement in IQ. Rather than interpreting this failure as the result of complex social factors and failures in policy implementation, Jensen argues that an inherent genetic difference prevented the overall improvement in African-American IQ scores. Jensen's reasoning has been widely criticized because it relies extensively on the misapplication of genetic theory. Jensen used a genetic measure known as **heritability,** the proportion of total variation attributable to genetic variation. Because the heritability of IQ has often been found to be quite high (he used an estimate of 80 percent), Jensen concluded that only 20 percent of the difference between European Americans and African Americans could be the result of environmental differences, which he felt was an insufficient figure to explain the average 15-point difference in IQ scores.

The major problem with Jensen's hypothesis is that it rests on heritability and an inappropriate interpretation of this concept. Heritability does not measure the genetic control of a trait, but only the *relative* amount of genetic variation in a *specific* environment. If, for example, we decide to look at the heritability of birth weight in mice, we will get different results depending on the genetic and environmental factors in a specific sample. If we choose one sample with genetically related mice, the genetic variation will be, by definition, low. Therefore, whatever variation we see in birth weight among these mice reflects environmental differences. Because the environmental variation is high and the genetic variation low, the heritability is low. If we take another sample with genetically diverse mice but subject them all to the same environment (e.g., diet and temperature), we will have a situation in which environmental differences are low and genetic differences are high. In this group, heritability of birth weight is high. In both cases, genetic and environmental differences are important, but the relative variation caused by each will change. Heritability is not a measure of the extent to which a trait is controlled by genetic factors. Heritability may also vary from one group to the next, as in the hypothetical mouse study.

Because heritability is a measure of the relative contributions of ge-

heritability The proportion of total variance in a trait that is attributable to genetic variation.

netic and environmental variation in a specific population at a specific point in time, it cannot be used to draw any conclusions about differences *between* groups. If a sample of poor, urban African Americans provides an estimate of 70 percent heritability in IQ scores, all this means is that variation in IQ scores *within* this sample reflects genetic variation to a greater extent than environmental variation. If we include affluent African Americans in the sample, the environmental component increases and the estimate of heritability is lower. In any case, this measurement only provides information about variation *within* the sample. The fact that both African-American and European-American samples have high heritability for IQ scores says nothing about the cause of differences *between* the two groups. It only says something about the relative effects of genetic and environmental variation within these groups. Heritability is not a useful measure for determining the causes of differences between groups. This was Jensen's major error, and it discredits his analysis. Further, as discussed earlier, studies examining differences between European Americans and African Americans that control for environmental differences show no significant difference in IQ scores.

Performance on IQ tests clearly reflects an interaction of both genetic *and* environmental factors. Despite many of these findings, people continue to argue about whether IQ is related to genetics *or* to environment. Suggestions that IQ has a strong genetic component have sometimes been considered socially improper and racist. This logic runs as follows: if there is a genetic component to IQ, and because African Americans and European Americans are by definition genetically different, then any difference in average IQ between the races must therefore be genetic. Finally, the argument goes, if the difference is genetic, then the suggestion of a genetic component to IQ implies a "natural" superiority of one race over another, which is a racist attitude. Can you spot the logical problems with this argument? The fact that IQ scores do have a genetic component is *not* justification for assigning labels of inferiority. Just because a trait has a genetic basis does not mean that it will necessarily differ from one group to another. A number of traits do differ between African Americans and European Americans, and a number of traits do *not*. There is no way to determine beforehand whether any particular trait will be different in the two groups. The only way of solving the problem is to test the specific hypothesis. Our findings to date indicate that IQ scores have a strong genetic component, are strongly affected by the environment, and that differences *between* so-called racial groups are environmental in nature.

SUMMARY

The biological concept of race emphasizes differences between groups and deemphasizes variation within groups. In the past, race was moderately useful as a crude means by which to describe patterns of human variation. A major problem in using race as a concept is that distinct "races" take on a reality of their own in people's minds. The race concept has limited use in analyses of biological variation, particularly for widespread species such as human beings. The race concept uses arbitrary classifications of predominantly continuous variation, ignores Mendel's work on independent assortment, does not account for differences in patterns of variation among different traits, and does not account for variation within groups. Apart from these problems, the race concept is further limited because it offers no explanation of variation.

Variation in skin color has often been used as a characteristic for racial classification. Skin color does not come in a handful of shades but rather is a continuous trait. Examination of the distribution of human skin color suggests several environmental factors in its evolution, particularly the relationship of intense ultraviolet radiation with skin cancer and sunburn in equatorial regions, and the greater susceptibility of dark skin to cold injury in northern climates.

The issue of whether populational differences in behavior exist, especially in intelligence, has long been controversial. The most widely studied fact is the 15-point difference in IQ test scores between African Americans and European Americans in the United States. Numerous studies have shown that this difference reflects environmental, not genetic, differences between these groups. Intelligence has a genetic component, but it has not been shown to vary among "races." Prejudice is an unfortunate feature of human nature, but such biases cannot be "supported" by scientific evidence.

Supplemental Readings

Brues, A. M. 1977. *People and Races*. New York: Macmillan. This text, which represents a "traditional" view of human races, contains a great deal of information on variation in human biological traits.

Gould, S. J. 1981. *The Mismeasure of Man*. New York: W. W. Norton. A well-written book tracing the historical development of several methods used to demonstrate racial differences in mental abilities, and their shortcomings.

Molnar, S. 1992. *Human Variation: Race, Types, and Ethnic Groups*. 3rd ed. Englewood Cliffs, N. J.: Prentice-Hall. Provides information on human biological variation as well as a general introduction to the history of racial classification and the controversy on race and behavior.

Montagu, M. F. A., ed. 1964. *The Concept of Race*. New York: Free Press. A collection of articles written by anthropologists and biologists, criticizing the utility of the race concept in biology.

Robins, A. H. 1991. *Biological Perspectives on Human Pigmentation*. Cambridge: Cambridge University Press. An excellent review of the biology, variation, and evolution of human skin color. The final chapter on the evolution of skin color is the best treatment of the subject to date.

PART Three

Our Place in Nature

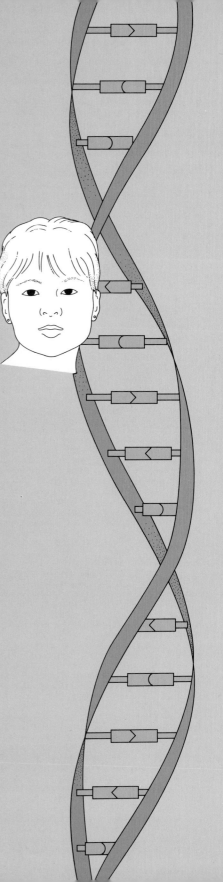

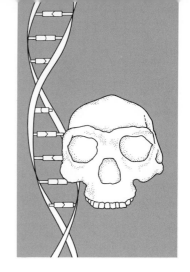

CHAPTER 7

The Mammals

The text has thus far focused on evolutionary theory and its application to biological anthropology (Chapters 1–4) and presented examples of micro-evolution in human populations (Chapters 5–6). We turn now to wider issues of variation and evolution, first considering humans as part of the diversity of mammals and primates (Chapters 7–9) and then the fossil record of primate and human evolution (Chapters 10–13). Chapters 7–9 provide the background on mammalian and primate taxonomy needed to comprehend human macroevolution. To understand the story of human evolution, we must first consider how humans fit into the natural world.

What are humans? This question has been a focus of science, art, and literature. Many different fields, from theology to psychology, have addressed its ultimate significance. Our perspective on ourselves is not abstract; the way we define what we are has great impact on the way we treat each other and the rest of the world.

One of the earliest written definitions of humans is found in the Eighth Psalm of the Bible, where the question is put to God:

> What is man, that thou art mindful of him? and the son of man, that thou visitest him? For thou hath made him a little lower than the angels, and hast crowned him with glory and honor. Thou hast madest him to have dominion over the works of thy hands; thou hast put all things under his feet.

This brief statement reflects a long-standing belief of Western civilization that humans are inherently superior to all other life forms on the planet,

189

parallel evolution Where similar adaptations occur independently in closely related species.

convergent evolution Where similar adaptations occur in rather distinct evolutionary lines.

ranking far above animals yet "lower than the angels." The view that humans are the supreme creatures in the natural world is also apparent in the works of many Greek philosophers, such as Aristotle.

What is the scientific definition of humans? Many sciences attempt to answer this question, zoology, biochemistry, and even computer science among them. In addition, a wide range of disciplines, such as history, geography, economics, political science, sociology, psychology, and anthropology, deal exclusively with human beings and their behaviors. From a scientific viewpoint, we are interested in a definition of humans that incorporates differences and similarities with other living creatures. This is not always as simple as it sounds. For example, are humans the same as fish? Of course not, but can you explain why? Suppose you answer that humans walk on two legs. Certainly that definition separates fish and humans, but it does not separate humans from kangaroos, which also move about on two legs (albeit quite differently).

This chapter is the first of three to examine the place of humans in nature; we will look at the aims and methods of classification and focus on the biological and behavioral characteristics of mammals, the class of vertebrates to which humans belong. The next two chapters examine more closely the specific group of mammals to which we belong—the primates.

Taxonomy

Taxonomy was discussed briefly in Chapters 1 and 4. Here, we turn to a more detailed examination of the philosophies and methods used in constructing biological classifications.

Methods of Classification

Two species may have the same characteristic for several reasons. First, they both may have inherited the trait from a common ancestor. Humans and monkeys, for example, both have five digits on each limb because they both inherited this trait from a distant common ancestor. Second, the two species may have developed the same trait independently in their evolution. The canary and bat are both small animals capable of flight. The shared characteristic of flight is not because they share common ancestry but rather because both species evolved flight independently. The independent evolution of the same trait can be due to **parallel evolution,** whereby similar traits arise independently in closely related species, or to **convergent evolution,** whereby similar traits arise independently in more distantly related species. To reconstruct evolutionary relations, we are more interested in traits that are similar because of common ancestry rather than parallel or convergent evolution.

Homologous and analogous traits. One of our first steps is to look at a biological trait and determine its structure (how it is put together) and its function (how it is used). **Homologous traits** are traits that show similar structure but may or may not show the same function. For example, each of your arms or legs is composed of a single upper bone and two lower bones. These bones are found in many other organisms, including creatures that use their limbs in quite different ways. Figure 7.1 illustrates the arm bones of a human, a bird, and a whale. Note that each of these has an upper arm bone (humerus) and two lower arm bones (radius and ulna). Furthermore, note that the "hand" of each has five digits made up of carpal and metacarpal bones. These three animals use their limbs for different purposes, but the basic structure is the same, with the same bones, but

homologous trait Physical trait in two species that has a similar structure but may or may not show a similar function.

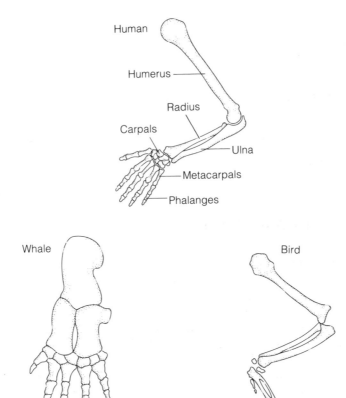

Figure 7.1

Homologous structures: the forelimbs of a human, whale, and bird. Note that the same bones are found in all three vertebrates. Even though the limbs are used differently by all three organisms, the bones show a structural correspondence, reflecting common ancestry.   (Adapted with permission from T. Dobzhansky, F. J. Ayala, G. L. Stebbins, and U. W. Valentine, *Evolution,* 1977, page 264, publisher W. H. Freeman)

analogous trait Physical trait that has a similar function in two species but a different structure.

primitive trait A trait that has not changed from an ancestral state. The five digits of the human hand and foot are primitive traits inherited from earlier vertebrate ancestors.

derived trait A trait that has changed from an ancestral state.

differing in size, shape, and function. The correspondence of the arm and hand bones of the animals in Figure 7.1 indicates these bones are homologous structures. The reason for this correspondence is that these traits have been inherited from a common ancestor.

Traits that have the same function but not the same structure are called **analogous traits.** Figure 7.2 illustrates the wings of a bird and a flying insect. The two structures are quite different, but they serve the same function—flight. In this case, evolution has led to the same function from two different starting points. Because the bird and the insect have different structures that do not reflect evolutionary relationship, they are placed in different taxonomic categories. In this case, the development of wings in both birds and insects reflects a case of convergent evolution.

Primitive and derived traits. Biological traits can also be characterized as primitive or derived. When a trait has been inherited from an earlier form, we refer to that trait as **primitive.** Traits that have changed from an ancestral state are referred to as **derived.** As an example, consider the number of digits in humans and horses. Both humans and horses are mammals. From fossil evidence (see Chapter 10) we know that the first mammals had five digits on each hand and foot (as did other early land vertebrates). Humans have retained this condition, and we refer to the five digits of the human hand and foot as primitive traits. The horse's single digit (a toe), however, is a derived trait relative to the first mammals.

The concept of primitive and derived traits is relative. What is considered primitive at one level of comparison might be considered derived at

Figure 7.2

Analogous structures: the wings of a bird and a fly. Even though both structures provide the same function (flight), they are structurally different, reflecting independent evolutionary origin. (Adapted with permission from T. Dobzhansky, F. J. Ayala, G. L. Stebbins, and U. W. Valentine, *Evolution,* 1977, page 264, publisher W. H. Freeman)

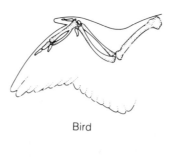

Bird

Fly

another level. For example, neither modern apes or modern humans have a tail. If apes are compared to humans, the absence of a tail is a primitive characteristic—they share this absence because they inherited this characteristic from a common ancestor. Monkeys, however, do have tails. If modern monkeys are compared to modern apes, the lack of a tail in the modern apes is a derived condition—it has changed since the common ancestor of monkeys and apes. The relative nature of primitive and derived traits must always be kept in mind.

To make any comparison, we must have information on modern and fossil forms so that we can determine whether a trait is primitive or derived. We cannot assume that any given organism will be primitive or derived for a given trait without knowing something about the ancestral condition. In other words, we cannot equate the terms *primitive* and *derived* with biased notions of "higher" or "lower" forms. In the past, there was a tendency to regard all traits of modern humans as derived relative to the apes. For some traits, such as increased brain size and upright walking, this holds true. For other traits, such as certain features of the teeth, the opposite is true.

Different approaches to classification. The problem of biological classification may be approached in many different ways. Though most agree that such classification should reflect evolutionary history, opinions differ about how this should be accomplished. Three general schools of thought have developed: phenetics, cladistics, and evolutionary taxonomy.

Phenetics classifies organisms on the basis of overall biological similarity, regardless of whether such similarity is the result of common ancestry or parallel evolution. If parallel evolution is fairly common, phenetic classification may suggest a closer evolutionary relationship than actually exists. As a result, species that do not share a common ancestor may be grouped together in a taxonomic group. For example, a phenetic approach places crocodiles and lizards in the same taxonomic class—Reptilia (reptiles). Birds are usually placed in the Aves class. Although this classification fits traditional views of overall similarity, the problem is that birds and crocodiles are more closely related to each other than either is to lizards (Harvey and Pagel 1991).

An alternative approach, known as **cladistics,** attempts to focus on evolutionary relationships. A cladist would place birds and crocodiles in the same taxonomic group, and lizards in another. The guiding principle of cladistics is that only shared derived traits should be used to construct taxonomies; shared primitive traits should not. The fact that both humans and monkeys have five digits would not be used to judge their relationship, because comparative and fossil data have shown us that five digits are a primitive trait. Nor are all derived traits applicable. The large brain of humans cannot be used to determine an evolutionary relationship with

phenetics A school of thought that stresses the overall physical similarities among organisms in forming biological classifications.

cladistics A school of thought that stresses evolutionary relationships between organisms in forming biological classifications.

evolutionary taxonomy A method of classification that focuses on shared derived traits but gives preference to those traits exhibiting overall biological similarity rather than simply evolutionary relatedness.

monkeys or apes because it is *unique* to humans. In cladistics, only homologous traits that are both shared and derived can be used to evaluate the evolutionary relationship of two species. For example, both humans and apes share certain features of their shoulder anatomy (see Chapter 9) that are not shared with monkeys or other primates. Comparative anatomy and the fossil record show that both humans and apes have these traits in common because they inherited them from a common ancestor that had changed from an ancestral state. That is, humans and apes are similar because of shared derived characteristics.

The relative nature of primitive versus derived must always be kept in mind. There are cladistic methods for determining which traits are primitive and which are derived, usually by comparison with a more distantly related species.

The cladistic school considers parallel evolution to be minimal. However, examples of parallel evolution abound in the fossil record (Cartmill 1982). Another problem with the cladistic method is that it uses traits that occur in one state or the other, primitive or derived. The method fails somewhat when considering continuous traits (Trinkhaus 1990). At what level of measurement do you classify tooth size as "small" or "large"? If we state that large teeth are primitive, we are left with the problem of determining exactly what size should be considered "large." In spite of these, and other, problems, cladistics has become increasingly popular among biological anthropologists. Some of the current debates on classification involving the cladistic approach will be discussed in the next two chapters.

A third approach is known as **evolutionary taxonomy.** This approach is similar to cladistics with its emphasis on shared characteristics but often gives preference to traits that show overall biological similarity rather than traits that show only evolutionary relatedness (Harvey and Pagel 1991). In this sense, evolutionary taxonomy is a mixture of phenetic and cladistic approaches. The evolutionary taxonomist would continue to place lizards and crocodiles in a different taxonomic category than birds, even though crocodiles and birds are more closely related. Much of the conflict around the different schools of thought relates to philosophical differences about the *purpose* of a classification system.

The Vertebrates

As with all living creatures, human beings can be classified according to the different levels of Linnean taxonomy—kingdom, phylum, class, and so on. The complete taxonomic description of modern humans is given in Table 7.1.

The animal kingdom. Kingdom is the most inclusive taxonomic category. All living organisms can be placed into one of five kingdoms: plants, animals, fungi, nucleated single-celled organisms, and bacteria. Major differences between these kingdoms are their source of food and their mobility. Whereas plants produce their own food through photosynthesis, animals must ingest food. Humans belong to the animal kingdom. Given that animals must ingest food, it is no surprise to see that most animals have well-developed nervous, sensory, and movement systems to allow them to sense and acquire food.

Vertebrate characteristics. Humans belong to the phylum **Chordata** (the chordates, animals with a spinal cord). Perhaps the most important characteristic of chordates is that they possess at some point in their life a **notochord,** a flexible internal rod that runs along the back of the animal. This rod acts to strengthen and support the body. In ourselves, it is present early in gestation and is later reabsorbed.

Humans belong to the subphylum **Vertebrata** (the vertebrates, animals with backbones). One characteristic of vertebrates is that they have **bilateral symmetry,** which means that the left and right sides of their bodies are approximately mirror images. Imagine a line running down a human being from the top of the head to a spot between the feet. This line divides the body into two mirror images. The left and right sides of the body are almost the same: there are two eyes, four limbs, and so forth. This pattern contrasts with other phyla of animals such as starfish.

Another characteristic of vertebrates is an internal spinal cord covered by a series of bones known as vertebrae. The nerve tissue is surrounded by

Chordata A vertebrate phylum consisting of organisms that possess a notochord at some period during their life.

notochord A flexible internal rod that runs along the back of an animal.

Vertebrata A subphylum of the phylum Chordata, defined by the presence of an internal, segmented spinal column and bilateral symmetry.

bilateral symmetry When the right and left sides of the body are approximate mirror images.

T A B L E 7.1
Taxonomic Classification of
Human Beings

Taxonomic category	Placement of humans
Kingdom	Animals
Phylum	Chordates
Subphylum	Vertebrates
Class	Mammals
Subclass	Placental mammals
Order	Primates
Suborder	Anthropoids
Superfamily	Hominoids
Family	Hominids
Genus/Species	*Homo sapiens*

these bones and has an enlarged area of nerve tissue at the front end of the cord—the brain.

The general biological structure of human beings can be found in many other vertebrates. Figure 7.1 showed the limb bones of three vertebrates—human, bird, and whale. It is important to note the similarity among these three different organisms. All, like most vertebrates, have the same basic skeletal pattern: a single upper bone and two lower bones in each limb, and five digits. Some vertebrates have changed considerably from this basic pattern. For example, a modern horse has one digit (a toe) on the end of each limb. Humans may seem to be rather specialized and sophisticated creatures, but actually they have retained much of the earliest basic vertebrate skeletal structure.

The subphylum of vertebrates also includes several classes of fish along with the amphibians, reptiles, birds, and mammals. Humans belong to the class of mammals, and much of our biology and behavior can be understood in terms of what it is to be a mammal.

Characteristics of Mammals

The first primitive mammals evolved from early reptiles approximately 200 million years ago. The distinctive features of modern mammals and modern reptiles are the result of that long period of separate evolution in the two classes. It is important to realize that the further back in time we look, the more difficult it is to tell one form from another. Keep in mind that the definition and characteristics of any modern form reflect continued evolution from an earlier ancestor.

Because mammals and reptiles are related through evolution, it is logical and useful to compare these two classes to determine the unique features of each. Modern mammals differ from modern reptiles in reproduction, temperature regulation, diet, skeletal structure, and behavior. As we look at each of these factors separately, do not forget that they are interrelated.

Reproduction

Mammals are often identified as animals that give birth to live offspring, whereas other vertebrates lay eggs. This is not completely accurate. Some fish, such as guppies, give birth to live infants. Also, some mammals, such as the platypus, lay eggs. Others, such as kangaroos, give birth to an extremely immature fetus that completes development inside a pouch in the mother. The most common mammal found today belongs to the subclass of placental mammals, characterized by the development of the fetus inside of the mother's body. Humans are placental mammals.

Placental mammals. The **placenta** is an organ that develops inside the female during pregnancy. It functions as a link between the circulatory system of the mother and child, acting to transport food, oxygen, and antibodies as well as to filter out waste products. The efficiency of the placenta means that the developing offspring of placental mammals have a much greater chance of survival than a reptile developing in an egg or in a nonplacental mammal (both egg layers and marsupials, Figures 7.3 and 7.4). Development inside the mother provides warmth and protection along with proper nutrition. Although placental mammals appear at first

placenta An organ that develops inside a pregnant placental mammal that provides the fetus with oxygen and food and helps filter out harmful substances.

Figure 7.3

The spiny anteater, an egg-laying mammal. (© Zoological Society of San Diego)

Figure 7.4

The wallaby, a marsupial mammal. (© New York Zoological Society)

prenatal The period of life from conception until birth.

postnatal The period of life from birth until death.

r-selection A reproductive pattern characterized by large numbers of offspring and little parental care.

K-selection A reproductive pattern characterized by few offspring but extensive parental care.

glance to be superior to egg-laying reptiles, the presence of a placenta has a cost as well as a benefit. Pregnant mammals consume a great deal of energy, making ample food resources vital to successful birth. Also, the demand on energy sets a limit on the number of offspring any female mammal can have at one time.

A main feature of mammals is that the female has mammary glands that provide food for the newborn infant. Important immunities are also provided in mother's milk. The ready availability of food increases the child's chance of survival. While advantageous, nursing also has a price; energy is expended by the mother during this process, and only a limited number of offspring can be taken care of at one time.

r-selection and K-selection. The **prenatal** (before-birth) and **postnatal** (after-birth) patterns of offspring care in mammals contrast with those of reptiles, which expend less energy during reproduction and care of offspring. Pregnancy and raising offspring take energy; the more offspring an organism has, the less care a parent can give each of them. Some animals produce large numbers of offspring but provide little care to them, a pattern known as **r-selection.** Other animals have few offspring but provide much more care to each of them, a pattern known as **K-selection** (the letters *r* and *K* refer to parameters in mathematical models of population growth. The r-model is based on geometric growth and the K-model is based on growth that stabilizes at a certain point).

These two patterns represent the extremes in reproductive biology. In nature, there is a range of variation in how r-selected or K-selected a given species is. An example of extreme r-selection is the oyster, which produces roughly half a billion eggs a year and provides no parental care. Fish can produce 8,000 eggs a year with a slight amount of parental care. Frogs can lay 200 eggs a year with slightly more parental care, and a lioness can have two offspring a year with a great deal of parental care. The fish is more K-selected than the oyster, and the frog is more K-selected than the fish. The lion is even more K-selected. An example of extreme K-selection is a chimpanzee: a female may have only one offspring every five years but provides extensive care to the offspring during its infancy. Another extreme example is the orangutan: in this species intervals between births are roughly eight years (Galdikas and Wood 1990). In general, mammals are considered K-selected and reptiles are considered r-selected. The development of the placenta and the mammary glands are biological features that maximize the amount of care given to the offspring.

From an evolutionary standpoint, which strategy is better? That is, which provides the maximum probability of survival of a population? In reality, each reproductive strategy has advantages and disadvantages. r-selection has the advantage of producing large numbers of offspring, but because little care is given to them, many, if not most, will die before reaching maturity. Recall from Chapter 1 the example of fish reproduction.

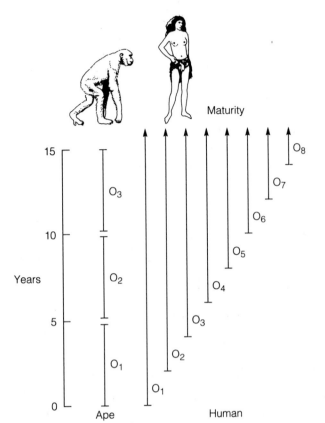

Maturity

15

O_3

10

Years

O_2

5

O_1

0

Ape

O_1

O_2

O_3

O_4

O_5

O_6

O_7

O_8

Human

Figure 7.5

Birth spacing in apes and humans over a 15-year period. The letter O refers to different offspring born during this time period. In apes, the female gives birth to an offspring roughly every five years: the time required for the offspring to reach maturity. Modern humans do not wait for a child to reach maturity (roughly 15 years) before having another child. Instead, births overlap one another (in this example the overlap is two years). This overlap is possibly a consequence of cultural adaptations that allow the care of more than one child at a time. The result is that humans can have more offspring in a given period of time without sacrificing parental care.

Fish are r-selected; many eggs are laid but few hatch and survive to maturity. On the other hand, K-selection has the advantage of extensive child care, but the disadvantage that only a few offspring are produced at any one time. There is no clear-cut answer to which strategy is "better"; it all depends on specific circumstances. In general, r-selected animals are at an advantage in rapidly changing environments and K-selected animals are at an advantage in more stable environments (Pianka 1983).

Human reproduction and child care. As mammals, human beings are relatively K-selected. We are, however, actually less K-selected than many other mammals, including our closest relatives, the apes. In general, the more closely related a mammal is to humans, the more K-selected it is. Humans differ from this pattern. We continue to invest a great amount of parental care in our children, but we are also able to have more children than a typical highly K-selected organism. The difference is that we do not wait until our children are fully mature before having another child. We most often have one child at a time, but their periods of dependency on us overlap (Figure 7.5). For example, a woman may give birth to a child and

homoiotherm Organism capable of maintaining a constant body temperature under most circumstances.

then two years later have another baby, when the first child is not anywhere near maturity. Compared to apes, then, human females can have more children in a given period of time. We do not, however, sacrifice the amount of parental care given to each child by having additional children before previous children have reached maturity.

Cultural adaptations provide numerous ways in which additional babies can be born without seriously affecting the amount of care each child receives. In our own society, such adaptations include labor-saving devices in the home, babysitting, participation in child rearing by the father, the convenience of social networks to help in child care (such as families and friends), improved transportation, easier access to shelter and food, and many others. Our use of language is also critical to our ability to care for several children. Oral commands and requests can be made to older children. Our development of culture has allowed us to break the usual K-selected pattern and have more offspring without sacrificing parental care.

Temperature Regulation

Modern mammals are **homoiotherms;** they are able to maintain a constant body temperature under most circumstances. Modern reptiles are cold-blooded and cannot keep their body temperature constant; they need to use the heat of the sun's rays to keep them warm and their metabolism active. Mammals maintain a constant body temperature in several ways. Mammals are covered with fur or hair that insulates the body, preventing heat loss in cold weather and reducing overheating in hot weather. Temporary changes in the size of blood vessels also aid in temperature regulation. When blood vessels contract (vasoconstriction), blood flow is reduced and less heat is lost from the mammal's extremities. When blood vessels dilate (vasodilation), blood flow is increased to the extremities, thus allowing greater heat loss.

Mammals also maintain a constant body temperature by ingesting large quantities of food and converting the food to energy in the form of heat. When you feel hot, your body is not losing the produced heat quickly enough. When you feel cold, you are losing heat too quickly. The ability to convert food energy to heat allows mammals to live comfortably in many environments where reptiles would slow down or even die.

Mammals are thus able to exploit a large number of environments. Heat production and temperature regulation, however, though obviously useful adaptations in certain environments, are not without a price. To obtain energy, mammals need to consume far greater quantities of food than reptiles. In environments where food resources are limited, mammals may be worse-off than reptiles. Again, the evolutionary benefit of any trait must be looked at in terms of its cost.

Humans, of course, have gone beyond the basic temperature-regulating abilities of other mammals. We have developed a variety of technologies that help keep us warm or cool. Fire and clothes were the earliest inventions of this sort. Today we have all sorts of heating and cooling devices that enable us to live in virtually any environment on the earth, as well as in outer space. Our culture has allowed us to go beyond our biological limits.

Teeth

The saying, "You are what you eat," is not usually made literally, but in fact it embodies an important truth of ecology and evolution. The nutritional requirements of organisms dictate, in part, their environmental needs. Also, diet is reflected in the physical structure of organisms, particularly the teeth and jaws. Because mammals maintain a constant body temperature by converting food energy to heat, they require a considerable amount of food. The physical features of mammalian teeth reflect this need.

The teeth of reptiles (as well as amphibians and fish) are all the same; they all have sharp sides and continue to grow throughout life. The function of reptilian teeth is to hold and kill prey. The food is then most often eaten whole. Mammals, on the other hand, have different types of teeth in their jaws. Mammals only have two sets of teeth during their lives: a set of deciduous ("baby") teeth and a set of permanent teeth. As a mammal grows and matures, the baby teeth fall out and are replaced with the adult teeth. In modern humans this replacement normally starts around age 6 and takes the first 18 or 20 years of life to complete.

Types of teeth. Mammals have four types of teeth: **incisors, canines, premolars,** and **molars.** These teeth are shown for a chimpanzee and a human in Figure 7.6. The incisor teeth are flat and located in the front of the jaw. Both the human and the chimpanzee (and other higher primates) have a total of four incisors in each jaw. These teeth are used for cutting and slicing of food. You use your incisors when you eat an apple or corn on the cob. Behind the incisors are the canine teeth, which are often long and sharp, resembling fangs or tusks. Apes and humans have two canine teeth in each jaw. In many mammals the canine teeth are used as weapons or to kill prey. While the canine teeth of most mammals are rather large and project beyond the level of the rest of the teeth, human canines are

incisor The flat front teeth used for cutting, slicing, and gnawing food.

canine The teeth located in the front of the jaw behind the incisors that are normally used by mammals for puncturing and defense.

premolar One of the types of back teeth used for crushing and grinding food.

molar The teeth furthest back in the jaw used for crushing and grinding food.

Figure 7.6

The lower jaws and teeth of a chimpanzee and a modern human.

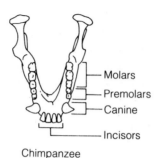

Chimpanzee

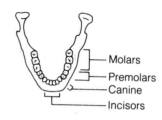

Human

dental formula A shorthand method of describing the number of each type of tooth in one half of one jaw on a mammal.

usually small and nonprojecting. The explanation of small canine teeth in humans has been a major source of controversy among anthropologists and will be discussed in later chapters on human evolution.

The premolar and molar teeth are also known collectively as the back teeth. Both of these types of teeth are often large in surface area and are used for grinding and chewing food. When you chew food between your back teeth, you do not simply move your lower jaw up and down. Instead, your upper and lower back teeth grind together in a circular motion as your jaw moves up and down and sideways as well. The structure of the premolar and molar teeth are different, and in some mammals they have different functions as well.

Dental formulae. Mammals can be characterized by the number of each type of tooth they have. The usual method of counting teeth is to consider the number of each type of tooth in one half of one jaw, upper or lower. Only one half of the jaw is considered because both right and left sides of the jaw contain the same number of teeth. These numbers are expressed using a **dental formula,** which lists the number of incisors, canines, premolars, and molars in one half of a jaw. A dental formula looks like this: I-C-PM-M. Here I = number of incisors, C = number of canines, PM = number of premolars, and M = number of molars. For example, the typical dental formula of humans (as well as apes and some monkeys) is 2-1-2-3. This means that in one half of either jaw there are two incisors, one canine, two premolars, and three molars. Each half of each jaw therefore contains 2 + 1 + 2 + 3 = 8 teeth. The typical number of teeth in humans is therefore 8 × 4 = 32 (two sides of each of two jaws). Some mammals have different numbers of teeth in the top and bottom jaws. In these cases, we use two dental formulae. For example, a dental formula of $\frac{2\text{-}1\text{-}2\text{-}3}{2\text{-}1\text{-}2\text{-}2}$ would indicate two fewer molars in the lower jaw.

Diet and teeth. The basic description of the types of teeth is somewhat simplistic. Many mammals have evolved specialized uses of one or more of these tooth types. As noted earlier, human canines are rather different in form and function than those of many other mammals. The general description is useful, however, in showing the importance of differentiated teeth in mammals. By having different types of teeth capable of slicing, cutting, and grinding, mammals are able to eat a wide variety of different foods in an efficient way. The sharp fanglike teeth of reptiles are good for catching and killing prey, but useless for eating plants, fruits, and nuts. Mammals can eat all these different types of food. In addition, the ability to chew the food rather than swallow it whole allows greater efficiency in eating. By chewing, mammals break down the food into smaller pieces that can be digested more easily and efficiently. Also, saliva released in the mouth during chewing begins the process of digestion.

The nature of mammalian diet and teeth relates to their warm-bloodedness. Mammals need more food than reptiles, and their teeth allow them to utilize a wider range of food and to process it more productively. The benefits of differentiated teeth lie in these abilities. The cost is the fact that the teeth tend to wear out over time. When a mammal's adult teeth are worn down, it may not be able to eat or may develop serious dental problems, which could lead to death. As far as recent humans are concerned, we can circumvent these potential problems to a certain extent with dental technology, hygiene, and processed foods. Even so, dental problems continue to pose serious difficulties to human health.

Skeletal Structure

Both mammals and reptiles share the basic skeletal structure of all vertebrates, but there are some differences, especially in movement. In reptiles the four limbs come out from the side of the body for support and

Figure 7.7

The orientation of the limbs to the body in reptiles and in mammals.

Reptile

Mammal

movement (Figure 7.7). In four-legged mammals, the limbs slope downward from the shoulders and hips. Having the limbs tucked in under the body allows more efficient and quicker movement. The weight of the body is supported better. Humans differ from the pattern of many mammals by using only two limbs for movement. Even so, the configuration of the legs follows the basic pattern; they slope inward from the hips and are not splayed out to the sides.

Behavior

The brains of all vertebrates have similar structures but differ in size, relative proportions, and functions. All vertebrates have a hindbrain, a midbrain, and a forebrain. In most vertebrates, the hindbrain is associated with hearing, balance, reflexive behaviors, and control of the autonomic functions of the body, such as breathing. The midbrain is associated with vision, and the forebrain is associated with chemical sensing such as smelling ability. Compared to fish, reptiles have a relatively larger midbrain and hindbrain because they rely more extensively on vision and hearing. The midbrain of a reptile is particularly enlarged because it functions to coordinate sensory information and body movements.

The brain of a mammal reveals several important shifts in structure and function. The mammalian brain has a greatly enlarged forebrain that is responsible for the processing of sensory information and coordination. In particular, the forebrain contains the **cerebrum,** the outermost layer of brain cells, which is associated with learning, memory, and intelligence. The cerebrum becomes increasingly convoluted, which allows huge numbers of interconnections between brain cells. It accounts for the largest proportion of the mammalian brain.

The overall functions of a brain include basic body maintenance as well as the ability to process information and respond accordingly. Mammals rely more on learning and flexible responses than do reptiles. Behaviors are less instinctual and rigid. Previous experiences (learning) become more important in responding to stimuli. As a consequence, mammals are more capable of developing new responses to different situations and are capable of learning from past mistakes. New behaviors are more likely to develop and can be passed on to offspring through the process of learning. Humans have taken this process even further; our very existence depends on flexible behaviors that must be learned. While our behavior is to a large extent cultural, our ability to transfer information through learning relies on a biological trait: the mammalian brain.

The behavioral flexibility of mammals ties in with their pattern of reproduction. In general, the more K-selected the species, the more intelligent it is and the more it relies on learning rather than instinct. Extensive parental care requires increased intelligence and the ability to learn new behaviors in order to provide maximum care for infants. The increased emphasis on learning requires in turn an extended period of childhood during which to absorb the information needed for the adult life. Furthermore, the extension of childhood requires more extensive child care, so that offspring are protected during the time they need to complete their growth and learning. Thus it is no surprise that the K-selected pattern of reproduction is associated with greater intelligence and flexibility of behaviors.

The major characteristics of mammals are all interrelated. Reproductive behaviors are associated with learning, intelligence, and social behaviors. The ability to maintain body temperature is related to diet and teeth; warm-bloodedness requires vast amounts of energy that in turn is made available from differentiated teeth and a wide dietary base. Also, the reproductive pattern of placental mammals requires great amounts of energy, which in turn relates to diet. In fact, the major characteristics of any group of animals are not merely a list of independent traits; they represent an integrated complex of traits.

Variations on a Theme

Modern reptiles and modern mammals differ markedly in biology and behavior. A major reason for this sharp difference is the fact that

cerebrum The area of the forebrain that consists of the outermost layer of brain cells, associated with memory, learning, and intelligence.

mammals and reptiles have evolved separately for almost 200 million years. Mammals and reptiles have certain features in common that they inherited from a common ancestor. Other features, such as the teeth and the reproductive system, are different because each line has evolved independently from the common ancestor. In the analysis of fossil remains, this means that the older a given form is, the more closely it resembles a common ancestor and the harder it is to classify the fossil as a reptile or a mammal. This difficulty shows a basic problem with taxonomy: evolution leads to change, and a classification system works best when things stay the same.

There is another point to keep in mind when we draw up lists of characteristics that distinguish modern reptiles from modern mammals. The modern forms of these creatures are those that have survived until the present. Modern reptiles include organisms as varied as crocodiles, turtles, and snakes. Many other variations on the basic theme have existed in the past and have become extinct. For example, modern reptiles are often characterized as slow-moving, cold-blooded creatures. This does not mean that all past reptiles had these characteristics. One group, the dinosaurs, became extinct 65 million years ago but were once the dominant form of life on land. Though they are also classified as reptiles, the dinosaurs were nonetheless quite different from modern reptiles. According to some recent interpretations, they moved fast, took care of their young, and were warm-blooded (Bakker 1986). Accordingly, a number of the usual characteristics used to classify reptiles may not be appropriate for dinosaurs. Change over time means that taxonomic classification is often difficult and should best be regarded as a tool to describe general trends.

SUMMARY

Taxonomic classification imposes order on the diversity of living creatures. The biological and behavioral nature of human beings is revealed in the different levels of classification to which humans belong. Humans are animals, chordates, and vertebrates. We share certain characteristics, such as a more developed nervous system, with other creatures in these categories.

Humans are mammals, which means that we rely a great deal on a reproductive strategy of few births and extensive parental care. This reproductive pattern is associated with higher intelligence and a greater capacity for learned behaviors. Other adaptations of mammals include differentiated teeth, a skeletal structure capable of swift movement, and the ability to maintain a constant body temperature.

Supplemental Readings

Passingham, R. 1982. *The Human Primate*. San Francisco: W. H. Freeman. A detailed examination of human biology in comparison to that of other mammals.

Radinsky, L. B. 1987. *The Evolution of Vertebrate Design*. Chicago: University of Chicago Press. An interesting and nontechnical introduction to vertebrate biology and evolution, focusing on anatomical structure.

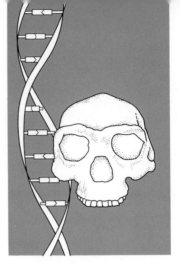

C H A P T E R **8**

The Primates

There are many different forms of mammals, as diverse as mice, whales, giraffes, cats, dogs, and apes. Patterns of biology and behavior vary considerably, although all mammals share to some extent the basic characteristics outlined in the last chapter.

The mammalian class is broken down into a number of orders. Humans are **primates,** as are the apes, such as the chimpanzee and gorilla, which are our closest living relatives. Monkeys are also primates, along with more biologically primitive forms known as prosimians. The basic characteristics of primates are discussed in this chapter, along with a brief survey of the prosimians and monkeys. The next chapter focuses on apes and humans and their relationship to each other.

Primate Characteristics

primates The order of mammals that has a complex of characteristics related to an initial adaptation to life in the trees.

arboreal Living in trees.

terrestrial Living on the ground.

No single characteristic identifies primates; rather, they share a set of features. Many of these features relate to living in the trees. Though it is clear that humans, as well as other modern primates, do not live in the trees, they still retain certain features inherited from ancestors who did.

An **arboreal** (tree-living) environment presents different challenges than a **terrestrial** (ground-living) environment. Living in the trees requires an orientation to a three-dimensional environment. Animals that

208

live on the ground generally contend with only two dimensions: length and width. Arboreal animals must also deal with the third dimension, height. Perception of distance and depth is vital to a tree-living form, which moves quickly from one branch to the next, and from one level of the forest to another. Agility is also important, as is the ability to anchor oneself in space.

Many forms of animals, such as squirrels and birds, have adapted to living in the trees. Primates, however, are capable of extensive rapid movement through the trees and are able to move to all areas of a tree, including small terminal branches. A squirrel can climb up and down the trunk of a tree and even large branches, but primates are better equipped to move out to feed on even the smallest of branches. The two major characteristics of primates that account for their success in the trees are the ability to use hands and feet to grasp branches (rather than digging in with claws), and the ability to perceive distance and depth.

Many primate characteristics relate to living in the trees, but some controversy has arisen over whether the *initial* evolution of these traits was the result of arboreal adaptations. Noting that other mammals, such as squirrels, have adapted to the trees without having grasping hands or depth perception, Cartmill (1974) has suggested an alternative for the origin of primate characteristics. He suggests that grasping hands and depth perception first evolved as adaptations for insect hunting in low branches. Later, these features were adapted for life in the trees. The sections that follow will examine both the arboreal adaptation and insect predation models. The fossil evidence bearing on these models is discussed in Chapter 11.

Not all modern primates have kept the original adaptations of the first primates. For example, humans can still use their hands to grasp objects but cannot do so with their feet. We do not normally use our hands to grasp and hang onto branches. We have taken our inherited ability to grasp and put it to work in another arena: we hold tools, weapons, food, and children. The grasping hands of a human and a tree-living monkey are homologous—that is, they are similar structures because of common descent. The different functions of the hands of humans and tree-living monkeys reflect adaptive changes from the original primate ancestors. Even though humans do things differently, we are still primates and have the basic set of primate characteristics.

The Skeleton

First let us consider some general characteristics in the primate skeletal structure.

Grasping hands. A characteristic of the earliest known mammals (and reptiles) is five digits on each hand or foot. Certain mammals, such

prehensile Capable of grasping.

as the horse, have changed from this ancestral condition and only have a single toe on each limb. Other mammals, such as the primates, have kept the ancestral condition.

Primates, including humans, are primitive in the number of digits on the hands and feet. This statement is confusing because it is hard to reconcile the possession of a primitive trait with the idea that primates, especially humans, represent advanced forms. The problem with such an interpretation is that the term *primitive* is often taken as a sign of being inferior or less "advanced." All it means in a biological sense is that certain traits have not greatly changed since some earlier ancestor. Whether a primitive or derived trait is adaptive or not depends on the specific set of environmental circumstances, not on how old or new a trait is. New is not necessarily better.

In the case of primates, the retention of the primitive characteristic of five digits on the hands and feet turned out to be an important adaptation. The hands and feet of primates are **prehensile,** meaning that they are capable of being used to grasp objects. The ability to grasp involves the movement of the fingers to the palm, thus allowing the fingers to wrap around an object. In many primates, the toes can also wrap around an object. This grasping ability provides a remarkable adaptation to living in the trees. Primates can grab onto branches to move about, to provide support while eating, and in general to allow for a high degree of flexibility in moving about their environment. More specialized structures, such as the horse's single hoof, would be useless in the trees because there would be no way to grasp branches.

Another feature of primate hands and feet is their expanded tactile pads (such as the ball of your thumb) and nails instead of claws. These nails serve to protect the sensitive skin at the ends of the fingers and the toes. The numerous nerve endings in the tips of fingers and toes of primates provide an enhanced sense of touch that is useful in the manipulation of objects.

As mentioned earlier, the characteristics possessed by primates are not the only possible solution to the challenge of living in the trees. Squirrels, for example, use their claws to dig into the bark of limbs and branches when they climb in the trees. The grasping ability of primate hands, however, provides much greater flexibility. Food can be reached at the end of small branches by grasping surrounding branches for support, using a free arm to reach out and grab the food, and then bringing it to the mouth. A small branch might not provide enough surface area for a squirrel to dig its claws into, but a primate could use its grasping hands and feet to hold onto it.

Variations on these themes occur even within primates. Some of the more biologically primitive primates, for example, have a single claw on each hand and foot that they use for specialized purposes. Humans also differ from the general primate condition. We have lost the ability to use our feet for grasping as a result of anatomical changes relating to our ability to walk on two legs. We also have an enhanced ability for fine manipulation of our fingers in addition to the basic grasping ability.

Generalized structure. Biological structures are often classified as specialized or generalized. **Specialized structures** are used in a highly specific way, whereas **generalized structures** can be used in a variety of ways. The hooves of a horse, for example, are a specialization that allows rapid running over land surfaces. The basic skeletal structure of primates is generalized because it allows movement flexibility in a wide variety of circumstances.

The arm and leg bones of primates follow the basic pattern of many vertebrates: each limb consists of an upper bone and two lower bones (refer back to Figure 7.1 in the last chapter). This structure allows limbs to bend at the elbows or knees. In climbing or jumping in a tree, you must have this flexibility or you would not be able to move about (imagine trying to jump from one branch to another with your arms and legs made up of one long bone). That the lower part of the limb is made up of two bones provides even greater flexibility. Hold your arm out straight in front of you with your palm down. Now turn your hand so that the palm side is up. This is easy to do, but only because we have two lower arm bones. When turning the hand over, one lower arm bone crosses over the other. Imagine trying to climb in a tree without the ability to move your hand into different positions. This flexibility is obtained by the retention of a generalized skeletal structure.

Although the grasping hands and generalized skeletons of primates can be interpreted as arboreal adaptations, Cartmill (1974) raises the possibility that they first arose as adaptations to insect predation. Grasping hands and feet would be valuable for running along the ground and on small branches in search of insects. Once these traits evolved, they could then have been valuable for further use of arboreal environments.

Vision

The three-dimensional nature of arboreal life requires keen eyesight, particularly depth perception. This feature has evolved from the need to judge distances successfully. (Jumping through the air from branch to branch demands the ability to judge distances. After all, it is not very adaptive to fall short of your target and plunge to the ground!)

Depth perception involves **binocular stereoscopic vision.** *Binocular* refers to overlapping fields of vision. The eyes of many animals are located at the sides of the skull so that each eye receives a different image with no

---

specialized structure A biological structure adapted to a narrow range of conditions and used in very specific ways.

generalized structure A biological structure adapted to a wide range of conditions and used in very general ways.

binocular stereoscopic vision Overlapping fields of vision with both sides of the brain receiving images from both eyes, thereby providing depth perception.

overlap (Figure 8.1). The eyes of primates are located in the front of the skull so that the fields of vision overlap. Primates see objects in front of them with both eyes. The *stereoscopic* nature of primate vision refers to the way in which the brain processes visual signals. In nonstereoscopic animals, the information from one eye is received in only one hemisphere of the brain. In primates, the visual signals from both eyes are received in both hemispheres of the brain. The result is an image that has depth. Moving quickly and safely in three dimensions makes use of depth perception.

As with skeletal traits, it is possible that binocular stereoscopic vision did not develop initially as an arboreal adaptation. Cartmill's (1974) visual predation model suggests a different initial adaptation. Early insect-eating mammals were able to hunt insects by having depth perception. This adaptation was available to their descendants, who could make use of it in moving about in the trees.

Many primates also have the ability to perceive colors. Color vision is extremely useful in detecting objects in moderate-contrast environments. In fact, color vision is found in other animals for this reason, including whales, fish, bumblebees, and certain birds. Color vision is also important in primate species that use color as a visual signal of various emotional states, such as anger, or receptivity to sexual relations.

Primates are vision-oriented. On average, their sense of smell is less keen. As a result, the areas of the face devoted to smelling are reduced in primates. Compared to other mammals, primates have short snouts.

Figure 8.1

Binocular stereoscopic vision in primates. The fields of vision for each eye overlap, and the optic nerve from each eye is connected to both hemispheres of the brain.   (From *Human Antiquity: An Introduction to Physical Anthropology and Archaeology,* 2d ed., by Kenneth Feder and Michael Park. Fig. 5.1. Copyright © 1993 by Mayfield Publishing Company)

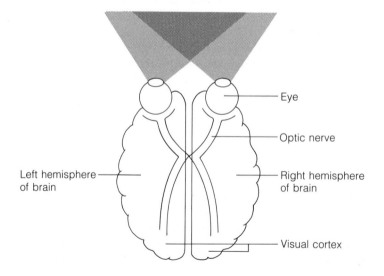

The Brain and Behavior

Primates have expanded on the basic pattern of mammalian brains. Their brains are even larger relative to body size. Primate brains have larger visual areas and smaller areas for smelling, corresponding to their increased emphasis of vision over smell as the main sense. Also, primate brains are even more complex than those of most other mammals. Primates have larger proportions of the brain associated with learning and intelligence. Areas of the brain associated with body control and coordination are also proportionately larger, as expected from the demands of arboreal life. Hand—eye coordination, for example, is crucial for moving about in the trees.

Learning. The greater size and complexity of primate brains are reflected in their behaviors. Primates rely even more extensively than other mammals on learned behaviors. As a result, it is often difficult to assign specific behaviors to a given species of primate because the increased emphasis on learning allows a great deal of flexibility in behavior patterns.

The increased emphasis on learning means that primates spend a greater proportion of their lives growing up, both biologically and socially, than other animals. The more an animal needs to learn, the longer the period of time needed for learning. An increase in the amount of time spent as an infant or child further means that greater amounts of attention and care are required from parents. Again, we see the intimate relationship among reproduction, care of offspring, learning, and intelligence.

The basic pattern of primate learning provides a means by which new behaviors can be passed on from one generation to the next. If we define culture simply as learned behavior, it is obvious that all primates can be said to have culture. Most of the time, however, the distinctive nature of human culture is identified as its reliance on language for transmission. Within this framework, the cultural behaviors and social organization of nonhuman primates are often referred to as *protoculture*. No matter what terms we use, however, or how we define human and nonhuman culture, the fact remains that social learning provides a means by which behaviors are passed on from one generation to the next in all primates (and, indeed, in many other mammals).

An example of learning in primates. Primate studies have provided many good examples of the introduction of new behaviors to a group by one or more individuals, which are then learned by other individuals. Studies of the Japanese macaque monkeys on the island of Koshima during the 1950s revealed a number of cases of cultural transmission of new

Figure 8.2

A macaque washing food in water.   (Steve Gaulin/Anthro-Photo)

behaviors. The Koshima troop has been provisioned (provided with food) since the early 1950s to keep all the monkeys out in the open for observation purposes (Figure 8.2).

In 1953, a young female macaque named Imo began washing sweet potatoes in a stream before eating them. Within three years, this behavior had been learned by almost half of the troop. Two years later, only two adults continued this practice. Of the 19 younger monkeys 15 had adopted this behavior, however, and thereafter almost all newborn infants acquired it by observing their mothers (Bramblett 1976).

Another food-related behavior developed among the troop in 1956 when scientists began feeding the monkeys grains of wheat. The wheat was scattered on a sandy beach to slow down the monkeys' eating so that researchers would have more time to study them. Imo developed a new method of eating the grains of wheat. She took handfuls of sand and wheat down to the water and threw them in. The sand sank while the wheat floated, thus letting her skim the grains off the surface of the water. This new behavior provided a much quicker way of getting the wheat than picking out grains from the sand. The young female's method of wheat washing spread quickly through most of the rest of the troop (Bramblett 1976).

The studies of cultural transmission among the Japanese macaques show the importance of learning in primate societies. The washing of sweet potatoes and the separation of wheat and sand are not innate behaviors in Japanese macaques. These behaviors are transmitted through learning, not genetic inheritance. The studies also show the importance of individual behavior: in both cases, the same monkey introduced the behaviors. If that monkey were not present in that troop, these behaviors might not have developed.

Reproduction and Care of Offspring

As with all mammals, primates are characterized by a small number of offspring and a great deal of parental care. Indeed, primates are the most K-selected mammals of all. Almost all primates have a reproductive pattern of having one offspring at a time. The next offspring is not born until the previous one is mature enough, biologically and socially, to survive on its own. In some primates, such as the apes, there may be as much as five or more years between offspring. As mentioned earlier, humans are an exception to this rule because we can have overlapping births without sacrificing the quality of parental care.

The mother-infant bond. The K-selected nature of primates is seen in the strong and long-lasting bond between mother and infant. Unlike some mammals, infant primates are entirely helpless. They depend on their mothers for food, warmth, protection, affection, and knowledge, and they remain dependent for a long time. Of all the different types of social bonds in primate societies, the mother-infant bond is the strongest. In many primate species this bond continues well past childhood. Chimpanzees, for example, regularly associate with their mothers through their adult lives (Goodall 1986).

The biological importance of the mother-infant bond is easy to see: the infants are dependent on mother's milk for nourishment. Is that all there is to it? Earlier in this century, some researchers suggested that the entire basis of "mother love" seen in primate infants arose from the infant's need for food. Laboratory experiments and field observations soon showed that this is not the case; the social aspects of the mother-infant bond are also crucial for survival.

One of the most famous of these experiments was performed by psychologist Harry Harlow, who isolated infant rhesus monkeys from their mothers. He raised them in cages in which he placed two "surrogate mothers," the first a wire framework in the approximate shape of an adult monkey and the second the same structure covered with terry cloth. He

Figure 8.3

Harlow's maternal deprivation experiment on infant rhesus monkeys. These monkeys preferred to spend almost all of their time clinging to the cloth surrogate mother (*left*), which provided warmth, than to the wire surrogate mother (*right*), which provided food. Even when hungry, the infants would often remain partially attached to the cloth mother. (University of Wisconsin, Primate Laboratory)

then attached a bottle of milk to the "wire mother" (Figure 8.3). Harlow reasoned that if the need for food were stronger than the need for warmth and comfort, the infant monkeys would spend most or all of their time clinging to the "wire mother." If the need for warmth and comfort were more important, the infant would spend most or all of the time clinging to the "cloth mother." The monkeys invariably preferred the warmth and security of the "cloth mothers" to the food provided by the "wire mothers." Even when the infants needed to eat, they often kept part of their body in contact with the "cloth mother." Additional experiments showed that under the stimulus of stress or fear, the monkeys would go to the "cloth mothers" for security (Harlow 1959).

These experiments showed that motherhood was not merely important in terms of nutrition; warmth and comfort were also necessary in an infant's development. But do these experiments mean that natural mothers can be replaced by a bottle and a blanket? Definitely not. As Harlow's monkeys grew up, they showed a wide range of abnormal behaviors. They were often incapable of sexual reproduction, they could not interact normally with other monkeys, and they often were extremely aggressive. The motherless females who later had children did not know how to take care of them and often rejected and mistreated them.

These findings have powerful implications. We often speak of "maternal instincts," suggesting that the behaviors associated with successful mothering are somehow innate. Although the basic bond between mother and infant is part of the biological basis of mammals and maternal feelings are to some extent innate, the specific behaviors that are part of this bond are learned. Mammals, and especially primates, rely extensively on learned behaviors. As a result, variation in behavior is often great and can be influenced by a variety of other factors. Observations of the behavior of primates in their natural environments confirm the fact that maternal behaviors are to a large extent learned. Studies of chimpanzee mothers have shown that young females tend to model their own later parental behaviors after those of their mothers. Similar patterns are seen in humans. For example, the children of abusive parents often tend to be abusive parents themselves. Such research shows us that the study of animal behavior, especially that of other primates, is not an esoteric subject but rather helps us in understanding ourselves.

Paternal care. Maternal care is found throughout the primate order. The mother-infant bond is the strongest social tie within primate groups. Among primates, what role does the father play in child care? Paternal care is highly variable among primate species. In general, primates that are **monogamous** (characterized by a more or less permanent bond forming between a single male and female) are most likely to show high levels of paternal care. For example, gibbons (an Asian ape) and many South American monkey species are monogamous and also show frequent participation of fathers in child care. In fact, in some species the fathers do most of the carrying of infants (Jolly 1985). By contrast, species that are polygamous tend, on average, to show less paternal involvement with offspring. This difference may relate to the fact that in monogamous species it is easy for the male to tell he is the father! In a **polygamous** species, paternal behaviors may be less appropriate from a genetic perspective since a male can never be sure if he is the father.

As with many primate behaviors, there is a great deal of variation from one situation to the next. In a recent study of baboons (an African monkey), Anderson (1992) found regularity in the degree of paternal behaviors. In cases where females mated with a single male more than 70 percent of the time, that male was much more likely to help by carrying the infant. This finding shows that it is often difficult, if not impossible, to

monogamy An exclusive sexual bond between an adult male and an adult female for a long period of time.

polygamy A sexual bond between an adult male and an adult female in which either individual may have more than one mate at the same time.

ascribe a given behavior to an entire species, because there is often a great deal of variation even within single populations. These results also suggest that the adult males are aware of the frequency of mating, thus providing them with some idea of the likely paternity of a child. From a sociobiological perspective, we would expect males to invest time and effort in their own infants, at least infants with a high probability of having been sired by them.

Growing up. The importance of the extended period of infant and child growth in primates cannot be overstated. The long period of growth is necessary for learning motor skills and social behaviors. The close bond between mother and infant provides the first important means by which an infant primate learns. It is not the only important social contact for a growing primate, however. The process of socialization in most primates depends to a large extent on close contact with peers. Interaction with other individuals of the same age provides the opportunity to learn how to interact socially in general, along with specific types of social behaviors.

Experiments by Harlow clearly demonstrate the importance of social contact with peers. Monkeys raised by their mothers but kept apart from other infants often grew up showing a range of abnormal behaviors. They would stare at their cages for long periods of time, were often self-destructive, and did not show normal patterns of sexual behavior (Harlow and Harlow 1962). Although some primate species are basically solitary apart from the mother-infant bond, most belong to larger social groups and require contact with peers during their growth.

Growing up and learning as a primate also requires that infants and children play a great deal of the time. Play behaviors have often been ignored in studies of human and nonhuman behavior because they are regarded as nonproductive behavior. In truth, play behaviors are essential to the proper biological and social development of primates.

Play behaviors can serve several functions. First, physical play allows an infant to develop and practice necessary motor skills. Second, social play provides the opportunity to learn how to behave with others. Needed social skills are learned through play. The importance of play becomes very obvious when we consider what happened to the monkeys that Harlow had separated from their peers. Without normal contact and the opportunity to develop socially, these monkeys became sociopathic.

Social Structure

Primates are essentially social creatures. The close bond between mother and infant, the importance of learning, and the great flexibility in behaviors all point to this fact. Apart from this general need, primates show an amazing amount of variation in the ways in which their societies are structured. The main social group of primates can range in size from two individuals up to several hundred and can have different proportions of males, females, young, and old.

Social groups. A social group is generally defined as a group within which there is frequent communication or interaction among members. This definition is a bit arbitrary but provides us with a starting point for looking at primate societies. **Social structure** consists of the composition of the group and the way in which it is organized. Primates display four basic types of social structure, with many variations on these basic types.

The **mother-infant group,** consisting of the mother and her infant, is the smallest social group. Adult males are solitary and tend to interact with adult females only when mating. The **family group** consists of an adult male, an adult female, and their offspring. Although this is a common pattern among humans in Western nations, it is actually not that common among primates or even among human cultures. In family groups, both adult males and adult females care for their offspring. The **one-male group** consists of a single adult male, several adult females, and their offspring. The **multimale group** is composed of several adult males, several adult females, and offspring. The multimale group is the most common form of social structure found in nonhuman primates, although there are many variations on this basic theme because of factors such as group size and the ratio of adult males to adult females.

Social organization and dominance. Nonhuman primate societies show a ranking of individuals in terms of their relative dominance in the group. A **dominance hierarchy** is the ranking system within the society and reflects which individuals are most and least dominant. Dominance hierarchies are found in most nonhuman primate societies, but they vary widely in their overall importance in everyday life. The dominance hierarchy provides stability in social life. All individuals know their place within the society, eliminating to some extent uncertainty about what to do or who to follow.

The dominance hierarchy in nonhuman primates is usually ruled by those individuals with the greatest access to food or sex or those that control social behaviors to the greatest extent. Societies with strong male dominance hierarchies are likely to show a moderate to large difference in the sizes of adult males and adult females. The **sexual dimorphism** in body size has often been considered the result of competition among males for breeding females. The males who are larger and stronger are considered more likely to gain access to females and hence pass on their genetic potential for larger size and greater strength.

social structure The composition of a social group and the way it is organized, including size, age structure, and number of each sex in the group.

mother-infant group Social structure in which the primary social group consists of mother and her dependent offspring.

family group Social structure in which the primary social group consists of a single adult male, a single adult female, and their offspring.

one-male group Social structure in which the primary social group consists of a single adult male, several adult females, and their offspring.

multimale group A type of social structure in which the primary social group is made up of several adult males, several adult females, and their offspring.

dominance hierarchy The ranking system within a society that indicates which individuals are dominant in social behaviors.

sexual dimorphism The average difference in body size between adult males and adult females.

Figure 8.4

Two adult male baboons engaged in a dominance dispute. Though physical violence does occur in such encounters, much of the display is bluff.   (Irven Devore/Anthro-Photo)

This pattern does not always hold, however. The adult male most likely to attract mates may not be the male most likely to have access to food. Fedigan (1983) has reviewed the literature on the relationship between dominance rank of males and access to breeding females for a number of primate species and has found that this expected relationship is not always present.

An example of a primate species with a strong dominance hierarchy is the savanna baboon, a monkey living on the open grasslands of Africa. Baboons live in large multimale groups. Adult males are dominant over adult females, and there is a constant shift in the relative position of the most dominant males (Figure 8.4). Adult males are larger than adult females, and the largest and strongest adult males have a greater chance of becoming the most dominant.

Size and strength are not the only determinants of a male baboon's dominance status. Coalitions of two or more lower-ranking baboons have often been observed to displace a more dominant male who was actually larger and stronger than either of the lower-ranking males. The ability to enlist aid from others is an important determinant of dominance rank.

In other primate societies we also see that dominance may reflect additional factors. In the Japanese macaque monkeys, for example, the rank of a male's mother has an influence on the male's dominance rank (Eaton 1976). Males born to high-ranking mothers have a greater chance of achieving high dominance themselves, all other factors being equal.

In a number of primate societies, the dominance hierarchy of females is more stable over time than that of the males. Whereas the position of most dominant male can change quickly, the hierarchy among females remains more constant over time. Even in cases where all males are dominant over females, the female dominance hierarchy exerts an effect on social behaviors within the group, such as the case discussed earlier of mother's rank affecting the rank of male offspring.

Environmental factors also affect the pattern of dominance within a social group. For example, Rowell (1966) found that forest-living baboons have less rigid dominance hierarchies than groups living on the savanna. In addition, the daily life of the forest baboons was more relaxed and the level of aggression was lower. In forest environments food is generally more available, and there is less threat from predators. Quite simply, a rigid dominance hierarchy is not needed in this environment.

Primate Suborders

In terms of both biology and behavior, primates are an extremely variable group of mammals. Though the general characteristics discussed earlier are useful in understanding the basic primate adaptations, it becomes difficult to make additional generalizations without considering different subgroups of primates. General primate characteristics may reflect arboreal adaptations, but not all modern primates are arboreal. In addition, not all primates have certain characteristics, such as color vision. To understand what humans are, we must consider biological and behavioral variation within primates.

Given the dynamic nature of evolution, it is hard to draw a line at exactly the place we can distinguish between primates and nonprimates. An example of this difficulty is the tree shrew, an insect-eating mammal. Tree shrews have long snouts, lack stereoscopic vision, and have claws instead of nails on all their digits. Given these characteristics, tree shrews do not fit the definition of primates. They do, however, have some grasping ability, which links them with primates. There was controversy for many decades over whether tree shrews were primitive examples of primates or should be placed within their own taxonomic group. Most anthropologists today exclude them from the primates (Cartmill 1982) but note that they do provide a good example of what an early primatelike mammal may have looked like (see Chapter 11).

The primate order is divided into suborders, which are further divided into other taxonomic categories, such as infraorders, superfamilies, families, and so on. A list of the complete taxonomic designations of many living primates is given in Appendix 2. This chapter covers only the major

Prosimians A suborder of primates that are biologically primitive compared to anthropoids.

Anthropoids The suborder of primates consisting of monkeys, apes, and humans.

categories and a few selected examples from each to give an idea of the relationships between primate groups.

The two major divisions of primates that are traditionally used are the suborder **Prosimians** and the suborder **Anthropoids.** Each of these suborders is broken down into infraorders, and so on. Figure 8.5 shows the traditional primate taxonomy discussed in the next few pages.

Prosimians

The word *prosimian* means literally "before simians" (monkeys and apes). In biological terms, prosimians are more primitive, or more like early primate ancestors, than monkeys and apes.

Figure 8.5

Summary of traditional primate taxonomy. Only the major groups discussed in this chapter are listed. A more complete taxonomy is provided in Appendix 2.

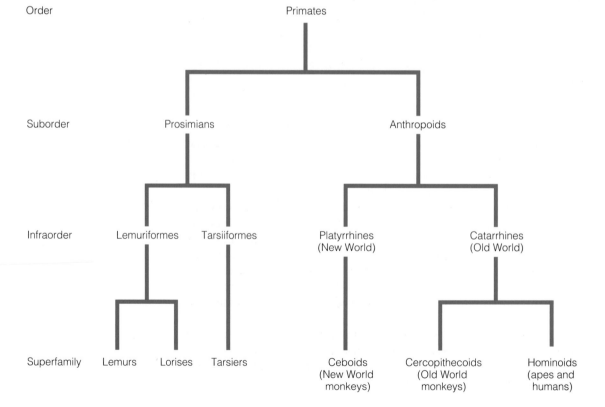

Prosimian characteristics. The prosimians often lack one or more of the general characteristics of primates. For example, some prosimians lack color vision, and some have a single claw on each hand or foot.

Another primitive characteristic of prosimians is that they rely to a much greater extent on the sense of smell than do the anthropoids. Prosimian brains are also generally smaller relative to body size than the brains of anthropoids. Prosimians are usually small in size, tend to be solitary, and are often **nocturnal** (active at night). These characteristics and others point to the basic primitive nature of most prosimians. Many prosimians are vertical clingers and leapers. That is, they cling to tree trunks until they're ready to move and then they propel themselves through the air.

Prosimians themselves show considerable variation. Some prosimians have larger body sizes, some have larger social groups, and some are **diurnal** (active in daylight). This variation makes classification difficult, but it does show us both the general trends of the prosimians as well as specific differences among them.

Types of prosimians. There are three different groups of prosimians in the world today, each with a number of different species. One group, the **lorises,** are small, solitary, nocturnal prosimians found in Asia and Africa (Figure 8.6, page 225). Another group, the **tarsiers,** also small, solitary, and nocturnal, are found in Indonesia. The nocturnal nature of tarsiers is evidenced by their large eyes, the size of which serves to gather available light (Figure 8.7, page 225).

The most biologically diverse group of prosimians are the **lemurs,** which are found only on the island of Madagascar off the southeast coast of Africa (Figure 8.8, page 226). Some species of lemurs are nocturnal and some are diurnal. Social structure is highly variable among the lemurs: some have the family group structure, some have the one-male structure, and some have the multimale structure. Other characteristics, such as body size, diet, and group size, are also variable among lemur species.

The lemurs depart from the typical pattern of prosimians as nocturnal, solitary primates. The wide range of biological and behavioral characteristics of lemurs probably reflects their isolation on the island of Madagascar. Because the island has no competing monkey or ape species, and not many other mammals either, the lemurs have expanded into a variety of ecological niches. Apart from these variations, the lemurs are still definitely prosimians—having, among other primitive features, the characteristic reliance on smell.

Note that in Figure 8.5, lemurs and lorises are placed in the same infraorder (Lemuriformes) and tarsiers are placed in a different one. This placement shows the closer biological relationship between lemurs and lorises than between either of these and tarsiers.

nocturnal Active during the night.

diurnal Active during the day.

loris Nocturnal prosimian found today in Asia and Africa.

tarsier Nocturnal prosimian found today in Indonesia.

lemur A prosimian found today on the island of Madagascar.

Strepsirhine A primate with
a moist nose.

Haplorhine A primate without a moist nose.

Anthropoids

The anthropoids are the higher primates and consist of monkeys and
hominoids (apes and humans). Anthropoids are generally larger in overall
body size, have larger and more complex brains, rely more on visual abilities, and show more complex social structures than other primates. Except
for one monkey species, all anthropoids are diurnal. The anthropoids
include both arboreal and terrestrial species.

All living prosimians are found in the Old World, but anthropoids
are found in both the New World and the Old World. (The Old World
consists of the continents of Africa, Asia, and Europe; the New World is
the Americas.) New World anthropoids are found today in Central and
South America. Old World anthropoids are found today in Africa and Asia
(and one monkey species in Europe). The only New World anthropoids
are monkeys, whereas Old World anthropoids include monkeys, apes, and
humans. Because humans are anthropoids, the rest of this chapter focuses
mainly on the biology and behavior of this group.

Alternative Classifications

The traditional division of primates into Prosimian and Anthropoid
suborders is being challenged by a number of scientists. The problem with
the traditional classification is that tarsiers, usually classified as prosimians,
show several biological characteristics of anthropoids. Lorises and lemurs
have moist noses, a trait related to their keen sense of smell. Tarsiers, like
anthropoids, lack the moist nose. In addition, recent biochemical investigations have supported the idea that tarsiers are more like anthropoids
than prosimians.

Many researchers now advocate placing the lemurs and lorises in one
suborder (**Strepsirhines**), characterized by moist noses, and the tarsiers
and anthropoids in another suborder (**Haplorhines**). This text will continue to use the traditional division between prosimians and anthropoids because it proves to be a useful contrast for discussions of primate
evolution.

The use of the suborders Strepsirhines and Haplorhines is shown in
Figure 8.9 (page 226) and can be contrasted with the traditional scheme
shown in Figure 8.5. The major difference is the placement of the tarsiers.
Are they more similar to lemurs and lorises or to monkeys and apes? Part
of the difference of opinion comes from philosophical differences in classification (phenetics versus cladistics, as discussed in the last chapter).

What is the relevance of alternative classifications? Once again, this
controversy demonstrates the difficulty of taxonomic classification. It is not
always possible to place living creatures unambiguously in certain categories. Such problems actually provide us with strong evidence of the
evolutionary process. The tarsiers, for example, suggest what a transitional
form between prosimians and anthropoids might have looked like.

Figure 8.6

A loris, a prosimian from Southeast Asia.   (Animals Animals © Stouffer Enterprises)

Figure 8.7

A tarsier, a prosimian from Southeast Asia. Unlike other prosimians, the tarsier does not have a moist nose. (© Zoological Society of San Diego)

The Monkeys

Anthropoids include monkeys and hominoids (apes and humans). Monkeys and apes are often confused in the popular imagination. In reality, they are easy to tell apart. Monkeys have tails, apes and humans do not.

Figure 8.8

Ring-tailed lemur from the island of Madagascar. (© Zoological Society of San Diego)

Figure 8.9

An alternative primate taxonomy using the suborders Strepsirhines and Haplorhines. Compare this chart with Figure 8.5, which uses the traditional breakdown into the suborders Prosimians and Anthropoids. The difference is that the present chart groups tarsiers with monkeys and hominoids in the suborder Haplorhines rather than with the lemurs and lorises. There is still considerable controversy about which scheme is more appropriate.

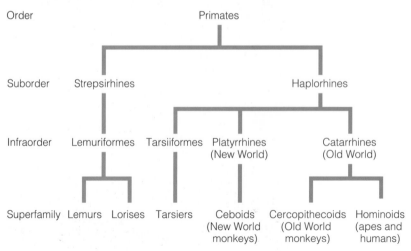

Order — Primates

Suborder — Strepsirhines | Haplorhines

Infraorder — Lemuriformes | Tarsiiformes | Platyrrhines (New World) | Catarrhines (Old World)

Superfamily — Lemurs | Lorises | Tarsiers | Ceboids (New World monkeys) | Cercopithecoids (Old World monkeys) | Hominoids (apes and humans)

Monkeys also have smaller brains relative to body size than apes or humans. The typical pattern of monkey movement is on all fours (**quadrupedal**), and their arms and legs are generally of similar length so that their spines are parallel to the ground. By contrast, apes have longer arms than legs and humans have longer legs than arms.

New World Monkeys

The monkeys of Central and South America are biologically different from the Old World monkeys. Some of these differences are important in reconstructing evolutionary relationships, such as the fact that New World monkeys have four more premolar teeth than Old World monkeys. The dental formulae for many New World monkeys is 2-1-3-3, compared to the 2-1-2-3 dental formula of all Old World monkeys. Other differences relate to the way in which the monkeys live, such as the fact that many New World monkeys have prehensile tails.

Because the tail of many New World monkeys is capable of grasping, it is highly useful in moving about and feeding in the trees (Figures 8.10 and 8.11). Typically, the monkey will use this "fifth limb" to anchor itself while feeding on the ends of small branches. Old World monkeys have tails, but none of them have prehensile tails. Those New World monkeys with prehensile tails are thus more proficient in terms of acrobatic agility. This difference probably relates to the fact that all New World monkeys are arboreal, whereas some Old World monkeys are terrestrial. The prehensile tail of many New World monkeys appears to be a biological specialization that either did not develop in the Old World monkeys or was lost in that line's evolution from some earlier common ancestor of all monkeys. So, we do not yet know if the prehensile tail is a primitive or derived trait.

quadrupedal A form of movement in which all four limbs are of equal size and make contact with the ground and the spine is roughly parallel to the ground.

Figure 8.10

A Bolivian red howler monkey, one of the New World monkeys with a prehensile tail. (© Zoological Society of San Diego)

Figure 8.11

A spider monkey, also capable of using its tail as a "fifth limb." (© Zoological Society of San Diego)

Figure 8.12

Japanese macaques adapted to living in the snow.   (© Steven Kaufman/Peter Arnold, Inc.)

savanna An environment consisting of open grasslands in which food resources tend to be spread out over large areas.

Old World Monkeys

Old World monkeys are biochemically and physically more similar to humans than are New World monkeys. For example, Old World monkeys have the same number of teeth as apes and humans (a dental formula of 2-1-2-3). Old World monkeys inhabit a wide range of environments. Many species live in tropical rain forests, but other species have adapted to the **savanna** (open grasslands). One species has even learned to survive in the snowy environment of the Japanese mountains (Figure 8.12).

The Old World monkeys, like the New World monkeys, are quadrupedal, running on the ground and branches on all fours. Though Old World monkeys are agile in the trees, many species have adapted to spending more time on the ground in search of food. Most Old World species eat a mixed diet of fruits and leaves (Figure 8.13), although some show dental and digestive specializations for leaf eating. Some Old World species occasionally supplement their primarily vegetarian diet with insects or small animals that they hunt.

Social structure is highly variable among Old World monkeys. Most species have the multimale group structure, but several species, such as the hamadryas baboon, have the one-male structure. This social structure appears to be adaptive in environments where food is less abundant. One male seems to be sufficient for protection and reproduction; additional adult males consume food without adding much to group survival.

Although studies of prosimians and monkeys tell us much about primate biology and behavior, the study of the apes provides even more valuable information for understanding the human species. Our close relationship to apes furnishes us with additional information with which to answer the question, "What is human?" The apes and their biological and behavioral similarities to humans are discussed in the next chapter.

Figure 8.13

A mandrill, an Old World monkey.   (© Zoological Society of San Diego)

SUMMARY

Humans belong to a specific order of mammals known as primates. The primates have certain characteristics, such as skeletal flexibility, grasping hands, and keen eyesight, that evolved in order to meet the demands of life in the trees. Though many living primate species, including humans, no longer live in trees, they have retained these basic characteristics and use them in new ways to adapt to the environment. Most humans no longer use their grasping hands to move about in trees but use them instead for tool manufacture and use.

There is a great deal of biological and behavioral variation among the living primates. The order Primates is composed of the more biologically primitive prosimians and the higher primates, the anthropoids. The anthropoids are the monkeys (New World and Old World) and the hominoids (apes and humans). Studies of primate behavior show behavior patterns common to certain species, but also a great deal of variation. The importance of the basic pattern of social learning in primates provides us with the most useful generalization we can extend to the study of human behavior.

Supplemental Readings

Bramblett, C. A. 1976. *Patterns of Primate Behavior*. Mountain View, Calif.: Mayfield. An introductory text in primate biology and behavior that focuses primarily on case studies of 15 different primate species.

Fedigan, L. M. 1982. *Primate Paradigms: Sex Roles and Social Bonds*. Montreal: Eden Press.

Hrdy, S. B. 1981. *The Woman That Never Evolved*. Cambridge: Harvard University Press. These two books provide information on general aspects of primate behavior as well as the often-overlooked nature of sex roles and female primates.

Jolly, A. 1985. *The Evolution of Primate Behavior*, 2d ed. New York: Macmillan.

Richard, A. F. 1985. *Primates in Nature*. New York: W. H. Freeman. These two extensive and comprehensive texts on primate biology and behavior differ from Bramblett's text in focusing on different topics (e.g., dominance systems, ecology) rather than on different species.

Smuts, B. B., D. L. Cheney, R. M. Seyfarth, R. W. Wrangham and T. T. Struhsaker, eds. 1987. *Primate Societies*. Chicago: University of Chicago Press. A collection of 40 review articles focusing on both individual species and selected topics of behavior.

Sussman, R. W., ed. 1979. *Primate Ecology: Problem-Oriented Field Studies*. New York: John Wiley. A collection of research articles dealing with the analysis of primate ecology—specifically, the relationship of group size, structure, and social behaviors to environmental factors. Contains both specific research papers and general theoretical reviews.

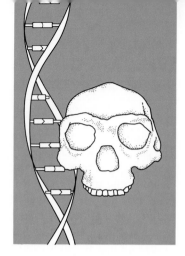

CHAPTER **9**

Apes and Humans

Perhaps one of our most memorable images of apes comes from the 1933 movie *King Kong*. The giant gorilla discovered on "Skull Island" is captured and brought back to New York City for display as the eighth wonder of the world. Ignoring the fantastic nature of some of the plot elements (gorillas could not be that large and still walk), the film draws close comparisons between Kong's behavior and that of the humans in the film. Kong shows love, curiosity, and anger, among other emotions and behaviors. Kong is a mirror for the humans, and the humans a mirror for Kong. We see ourselves in the beast, and the beast in ourselves.

The Hominoids

Whether we choose to look at apes as humanlike or humans as apelike, the fact remains that of all living creatures, the apes are the most similar to humans in both biology and behavior. From a scientific perspective, we acknowledge this similarity by placing apes and humans in a taxonomic category to distinguish them from the other anthropoids. Apes and humans make up the superfamily of **hominoids,** which literally means "humanlike." Hominoids have certain biological and behavioral characteristics that distinguish them from the monkeys.

hominoids A superfamily of anthropoids consisting of apes and humans.

230

Hominoid Characteristics

Unlike monkeys, hominoids do not have tails. Another hominoid characteristic is size: in general, apes and humans are larger than monkeys. Hominoid brains as a rule are larger than monkey brains, both in terms of absolute size and in relationship to body size. Their brains are also more complex, which correlates with the hominoid characteristics of greater intelligence and learning abilities. Hominoids are also the most K-selected of the primates; they invest the most time and effort in raising their young.

Hominoids share with Old World monkeys the 2-1-2-3 dental formula (two incisors, one canine, two premolars, and three molars in each half of the upper and lower jaws). The structure of the molar teeth, however, is different in monkeys and hominoids. The most noticeable difference is that the lower molar teeth of hominoids tend to have five **cusps** (raised areas) as compared to the four cusps in the lower molars of monkeys. The deeper grooves between these five cusps form the shape of the letter Y. As such, this characteristic shape is called the "Y-5" pattern (Figure 9.1). Actually, some humans have only four cusps on their lower molar teeth, but the molar teeth of hominoids and monkeys show other differences as well (see Chapter 11). This difference may seem trivial, but it does help us in identifying fossils because we can often tell whether a form is a monkey or a hominoid on the basis of the molar teeth.

Perhaps one of the most important characteristics of hominoids is their upper body and shoulder anatomy. Hominoids can raise their arms above their heads with little trouble, whereas a monkey would find this difficult. Three basic anatomical features allow hominoids to raise their arms above their heads. First, hominoids have a larger and stronger collarbone than monkeys. Second, the hominoid shoulder joint is very flexible and capable of a wide angle of movement. Third, the hominoid shoulder blades are located more toward their backs. By contrast, monkeys' shoulder blades are located more toward the sides of the chest (Figure 9.2). Homi-

cusp A raised area on the chewing surface of a tooth.

Figure 9.1

The Y-5 lower molar pattern of hominoids. Circles represent cusps. The heavier line resembles the letter Y on its side.

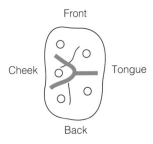

Figure 9.2

Top view of the shoulder complex of a monkey (*left*) and a human (*right*) drawn to the same scale top to bottom. In hominoids (apes and humans), the clavicle is larger and the scapula is located more toward the rear of the body.

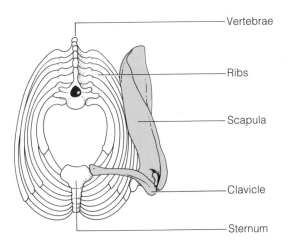

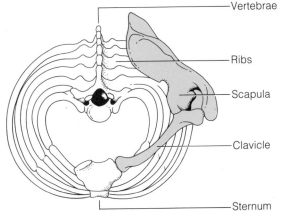

Vertebrae

Ribs

Scapula

Clavicle

Sternum

Vertebrae

Ribs

Scapula

Clavicle

Sternum

suspensory climbing and hanging The ability to raise the arms above the head and hang on branches and to climb in this position.

noid shoulder joints face outward, compared to the downward-facing shoulder joints of monkeys.

Most hominoids have longer front limbs than back limbs. Modern humans are an exception to this rule, with longer legs than arms. This trait facilitates upright walking (discussed later). In apes, the longer front limbs represent an adaptation to hanging from limbs. In addition, hominoids generally have long fingers that help them hang suspended from branches. The wrist joint of hominoids contains a disc of cartilage (called a meniscus) between the lower arm bones and the wrist bones. This disc cuts down on contact between bones. As a result, the wrist joints of hominoids are more flexible than those of monkeys, allowing greater hanging ability.

Hominoid anatomy allows them a different type of movement from that of monkeys. Hominoids are adept at climbing and hanging from branches. They are **suspensory climbers and hangers.** As hominoids, humans have retained this ability, although we seldom use it in our daily lives. One exception is children playing on so-called "monkey bars" at playgrounds (which should more properly be called "hominoid bars"). The ability to suspend by the arms and then swing from one rung of the bars to the next is a basic hominoid trait.

Living hominoids all share this basic ability but vary quite a bit in terms of their normal patterns of movement. Some apes, for example, are proficient arm swingers, whereas others are expert climbers. Humans have evolved a totally different pattern in which the arms are not used for movement, allowing us to carry things while walking on two legs. These differences in locomotion are discussed later in the chapter. In spite of these differences in function, the close relationship between apes and humans is seen in their shared characteristics of the upper body and shoulder.

Classification of the Hominoids

Between 8 and 20 million years ago there were many different types of hominoids. Today we have only the representatives of a few surviving species from this once diverse, widespread group. Living hominoids are divided into three categories: the lesser apes, the great apes, and humans. The lesser apes are the gibbon (eight species) and the siamang (one species), and are the least related to humans. The great apes are the Asian orangutan and the African apes, the gorilla and chimpanzee (two species). A list of the scientific and common names of all living hominoids is given in Table 9.1.

That all of these species have certain shared characteristics allows us to classify them as hominoids and to infer that they are related through evolution. The specific evolutionary relationship of the different hominoids is more difficult to establish. To uncover our own origins, we are interested in determining which apes species is the most similar to us. In this way we are able to compare the anatomy of living and fossil hominoids

T A B L E   9.1

Taxonomy of Living Hominoids

General group	Genus	Species	Common name
Lesser apes	*Hylobates*	*agilis*	Agile gibbon
	Hylobates	*concolor*	Black gibbon
	Hylobates	*hoolock*	Hoolock gibbon
	Hylobates	*klossi*	Kloss's gibbon
	Hylobates	*lar*	White-handed gibbon
	Hylobates	*moloch*	Silvery gibbon
	Hylobates	*muelleri*	Mueller's gibbon
	Hylobates	*pileatus*	Pileated gibbon
	Symphalangus	*syndactylus*	Siamang
Great apes	*Gorilla*	*gorilla*	Gorilla
	Pan	*paniscus*	Pygmy chimpanzee
	Pan	*troglodytes*	Common chimpanzee
	Pongo	*pygmaeus*	Orangutan
Humans	*Homo*	*sapiens*	Human

Source: Jolly (1985:11).

to determine what changed in our line, what changed in the ape line, and what stayed the same.

Methods of analysis. For many years, the standard approach has been to compare the physical structure (**morphology**) of these living forms in order to come up with some measure of relatedness. This approach is essentially the phenetic method described in Chapter 7. Such comparison is not as simple as it seems. Remember that two species may share a trait because of common ancestry or because of parallel evolution. When we try to unravel evolutionary relationships, we are interested in finding traits shared by ancestry. Also, all species tend to show evolution from the common ancestor, which means that sometimes an initially shared trait may be lost through time.

Scientists are now relying on a different type of comparison by looking directly at the biochemistry and genetics of the various hominoid species. Similarities and differences between species are revealed by a number of methods that compare proteins and even the genetic code. Constructing taxonomies from biochemical and genetic data has a definite advantage. If we focus on proteins or sections of DNA not affected by natural selection (or at least those we assume not to be affected), then any degree of similarity should reflect relative evolutionary relationships.

One biochemical method consists of looking at immunological reac-

morphology The physical structure of organisms.

tions. When foreign molecules are introduced into an animal's blood, the animal's immune system provides a defense by producing antibodies to attack the foreign molecules (antigens). If you mix the antibodies from one species with proteins from the blood serum of another species, this reaction will not be as strong. The strength of this reaction relates to the degree of similarity between the two species being compared. Stronger reactions indicate closer molecular similarity. Because molecular structure reflects genetic factors, the stronger the reaction, the more similar genetically the two species being compared.

Comparison of immunological reactions can be used to assess evolutionary relationships and to construct taxonomies. In the case of the hominoids, such research has shown that the orangutan is distinct from the chimpanzee, gorilla, and human. In other words, the African apes and humans resemble each other more than either resembles the orangutan.

The structure of proteins for two or more species can also be compared. As discussed in Chapter 2, the biochemical structure of proteins can be represented by a sequence of smaller biochemical units called amino acids. The amino acid sequence for a given protein is compared between two or more species to determine the minimum number of genetic differences between one form and another. The smaller the number of differences, the more closely related the two species.

When applied to many proteins, this method produces the same result as obtained from looking at immunological reactions. Chimpanzees, gorillas, and humans form a closely related group; orangutans are set apart from this group. Gibbons and siamangs are even less similar to African apes and humans. This finding supports the idea that the African apes and humans shared a more recent common ancestor than any of them shared with the orangutan. In terms of a family tree, orangutans split off the main branch earlier than the African apes and humans. Put another way, the African apes are the closest living relatives of humans.

Comparison of amino acid sequences has also provided information on the relative evolutionary relationships of other primate and nonprimate species. The tree shrew, for example, is more similar to other nonprimate mammals than to any of the primates, supporting the idea that tree shrews are not primates. Tarsiers, traditionally classed as prosimians, actually show greater similarity with the anthropoids. As we saw in the last chapter, such findings suggest revision of the traditional prosimian/anthropoid suborder classification.

The comparison of amino acid sequences makes the assumption that changes in structure reflect evolutionary relationships and not natural selection. In other words, we assume that any similarity in amino acid structure is not the result of parallel evolution. This assumption holds for those proteins that are not affected by natural selection. Of course, determining whether a specific protein is or is not affected by selection is often a difficult task. In any case, repeating the method using a variety of different proteins allows us to detect general patterns. In the case of the hominoids, such research confirms the separateness of orangutans from the African apes and humans.

Another method of molecular comparison is DNA hybridization. **DNA hybridization** involves, first, heating the DNA of a given species until the strands separate. Single strands from another species are combined with those from the first species, causing the two strands partially to reassociate. The degree to which the two strands reassociate depends on their overall similarity in DNA. The more closely related two species are, the greater the extent of this reassociation. Similarity between the DNA of two species is assessed by determining the amount of heat needed to break the associated strands apart—the more heat necessary, the more similar the DNA. Such methods have again shown that humans and the African apes are the most similar to each other, followed by the orangutan and then the gibbon.

In recent years, even more sophisticated methods have been developed to make biochemical and genetic comparisons between living species. For example, newer methods have allowed the comparison of the individual chemical bases that make up DNA. As even more advanced biotechnological methods continue to develop, more and more techniques will become available to provide direct comparisons of the genetic codes of different species.

Models of relationship. What conclusions about hominoid classification can we draw based on these different methods? Anatomical, biochemical, and genetic analyses all support classifications in which the lesser apes (gibbons and siamangs) are distinct from the great apes and humans. In other words, all great apes and humans are more similar to one another than any are to the lesser apes.

The *exact* nature of the relationship among the great apes and humans has long been debated. The oldest of these ideas places all the great apes in a group separate from humans (humans were classified as hominids and all great apes were classified as pongids), implying that all great apes are equally similar to one another and that humans are quite distinct. This model, which had its roots in the then-prevailing concept of human uniqueness, is now rejected. Anatomical and genetic data show that humans and the African apes are more similar to one another than any are to the Asian great ape, the orangutan.

Biochemical and genetic comparisons clearly demonstrate that the African apes and humans are most similar to one another. In a classic study of protein differences and DNA sequences between chimpanzees and humans, King and Wilson (1975) found that the two species are 99 percent identical. Subsequent research confirmed this finding and also found the gorilla to be equally similar. This finding implies that the three species all split from a common ancestor at the same time. (The Asian great ape, the orangutan, is considered separate from these three hominoids.)

DNA hybridization A method of separating and reassociating strands of DNA in different species to assess their genetic similarity.

Figure 9.3

Traditional taxonomic classification of hominoids. To emphasize certain aspects of behavior and physical characteristics, the orangutan, gorilla, and chimpanzee are placed together in a separate category from humans. Although useful, this classification does not reflect that humans and African apes are more similar to each other than either is to the orangutan. Compare this classification with the one shown in Figure 9.4.

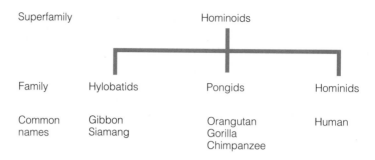

The traditional view of humans as separate from all apes is shown in Figure 9.3, which illustrates the traditional taxonomy of hominoids. This perspective is still widespread, in part because it necessitates a separate family (hominids) for human beings and their immediate ancestors. Although many question humans' uniqueness, it is still useful to separate us from the great apes for certain discussions of anatomy, behavior, and evolution. Figure 9.3 represents a phenetic view, emphasizing overall physical (and behavioral) similarity but does not, however, reflect what we know about overall evolutionary similarity.

A different view, based on the cladistic approach, is shown in Figure 9.4, where hominids are considered a family made up of two subfamilies, the African apes and humans. Despite the accuracy gained in reflecting evolutionary relationships, it becomes confusing for some purposes to classify the African apes with humans and apart from the orangutan. Part of the confusion (especially for introductory students) lies in the practice of using taxonomic names. For instance, Figures 9.3 and 9.4 both use the term *hominid,* but in different ways. In this text, we use the traditional taxonomic scheme presented in Figure 9.3, but remember that a phenetic classification does not always reflect evolutionary relationships.

Another problem in hominoid classification is determining the exact evolutionary relationship between gorillas, chimpanzees, and humans.

Figure 9.4

Revised taxonomic classification of hominoids. To emphasize evolutionary relationships, the African apes are placed in a separate category from the orangutan. Although useful, this classification does not reflect common and unique aspects of behavior or physical appearance. Compare this classification with the one shown in Figure 9.3.

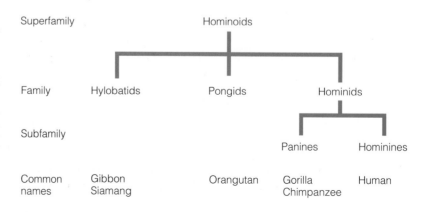

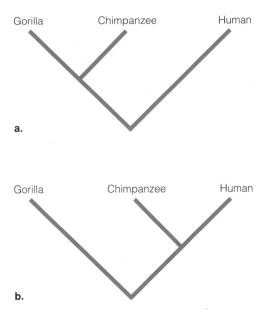

Gorilla   Chimpanzee   Human

a.

Gorilla   Chimpanzee   Human

b.

Figure 9.5

Alternative evolutionary relationships between humans and the African apes. (a) The African apes are more similar to one another than either is to humans. (b) Chimpanzees and humans are more similar to each other than either is to gorillas. To date, evidence exists to support both views to some extent; the final answer awaits further analysis.

Figure 9.5 illustrates the two major schools of thought. The traditional view, shown in Figure 9.5a, states that gorillas and chimpanzees are more similar to each other than either is to humans. An alternative view, shown in Figure 9.5b, states that chimpanzees and humans are more similar to each other than either is to gorillas. There continues to be controversy over which view is correct. Recent genetic analyses have not been able to resolve this conflict; some evidence suggests that Figure 9.5a is correct (e.g., Smouse and Li 1987). Recent studies of mitochondrial DNA suggest that Figure 9.5b is correct, although the data and interpretations are not fully accepted (Gibbons 1990). The close genetic relationship among *all* three hominoids makes precise identification of which two are closer very difficult (Figure 9.6).

Despite the continuing debate over the exact relationships among the great apes, it is clear that the African apes are the closest living relatives of humans. Exact description of the relationships among these three groups awaits further analysis. Enough evidence has accumulated, however, to suggest that regardless of the exact relationship, the common ancestor of all three groups evolved in a relatively short period of time. This subject is considered further in Chapter 11.

The Living Apes

To provide a better comparison of the biology and behavior of the apes and humans, it is necessary to consider briefly the physical character-

Figure 9.6

The genetic structure of apes is very similar to that of humans. In this picture, a small piece of human DNA from a gene called "U2" is fluorescently labeled (greenish-yellow dots) and hybridized to chromosomes from a gorilla (blue). Because of the similarity of base pairs of humans and apes, the human DNA binds to its complementary sequence in the gorilla, revealing the location of the gene in that species.   (© Jon Marks from the *Journal of Human Evolution*, March 1993; with permission of the Academic Press, London)

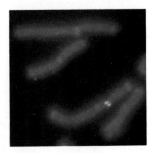

brachiation A method of movement that uses the arms to swing from branch to branch.

istics, distribution, environment, and social structure of all of the hominoids. Although the living hominoids all share a number of features, they also show a great deal of biological and behavioral variation.

Gibbons and Siamangs

Physical characteristics. The gibbon and closely related siamang are the smallest of the living apes. There are eight recognized species of gibbon and one species of siamang. For the purpose of this discussion, the term *gibbon* applies to all these forms.

The physical characteristics of gibbons reflect adaptation to life in the trees. The climbing and hanging adaptations of hominoids have evolved in the gibbon to allow highly agile movement through the trees. The gibbon's usual form of movement, known as **brachiation,** consists of hand-over-hand swinging from branch to branch. Many primates are often portrayed as arm swingers, but only the gibbon can perform this movement quickly and efficiently (Figure 9.7).

A number of anatomical adaptations allow gibbons efficient arm

Figure 9.7

A siamang holding onto a rock with one of its long arms. Siamangs and gibbons are the most acrobatic of the apes and can swing by their arms. (© Zoological Society of San Diego)

swinging. They have small body sizes, weighing 5.5 kg on average (12 lbs) (Richard 1985). Their arms are extremely long relative to their trunks and legs. Gibbon fingers are elongated and their thumbs are relatively short. The long fingers allow gibbons to form a hook with their hands while swinging from branch to branch. The thumb is short enough to prevent its getting in the way while swinging, but still long enough to allow manipulation.

On the ground, gibbons walk on two legs, though their arms are so long they look awkward to us. These long arms they use for balance. Gibbons also walk on two legs when they move along a branch, often using their arms to grab onto overhead branches for support.

Gibbons show almost no sexual dimorphism in body size. Males and females are the same body size, and both have large canine teeth, with male canines slightly larger on average than females. Gibbons are also monogamous (one male pairs for long periods of time with a single female). In primates generally, monogamy and lack of sexual dimorphism in body size tend to go together.

Distribution and environment. Gibbons and siamangs are found in the tropical rain forests of Southeast Asia, specifically Thailand, Vietnam, Burma, and the Malay Peninsula. The rain forest environment is characterized by heavy rainfall that is relatively constant throughout the year. Rain forests have incredibly rich and diverse vegetation. The gibbons' diet consists primarily of fruits supplemented by leaves.

Social structure. The social group of gibbons is a monogamous family structure: an adult male, an adult female, and their offspring. The male and female form a mating pair for their entire lives. For the most part, neither males nor females are dominant over the other. Both exhibit equal levels of aggression.

Gibbons actively defend territories. They do this by making loud vocalizations and putting on aggressive displays to warn off other groups. When groups come into contact in overlapping areas, the males often fight to drive the other group away. Females often aid in these fights.

Though it may be interesting to speculate on the nature of gibbon aggression and territorial behavior as it relates to primate behavior, in reality territorial behavior is rather rare among primates, including the hominoids. Territorial behavior is most often a function of the environment. In tropical rain forests, food is abundant and spread throughout the region. Because food resources are not clumped together, neither are the animal populations. Because food is spread out over a large area, the family groups come into frequent contact with one another, necessitating territorial boundaries to establish group boundaries (Denham 1971). In environments where food resources are clustered, social groups tend to cluster as well and are spaced apart from one another at the outset.

Figure 9.8

Mother and baby orangutans.
(© Zoological Society of San
Diego)

Orangutans

The orangutan is a large ape found only in certain areas of Southeast
Asia. The word *orangutan* translates from Malay as "man of the forest."

Physical characteristics. One of the orangutan's most obvious physical features is its reddish brown hair (Figure 9.8). Males are roughly twice
the size of females; an average adult male weighs between 80 and 90 kg
(roughly 175 to 200 lbs), and an average adult female weighs between
33 and 45 kg (roughly 73 to 99 lbs) (Markham and Groves 1990). Males
also have large pads of fat on their faces. The high degree of sexual dimorphism in orangutans has often been surprising because this trait occurs

Figure 9.9

An orangutan foraging in the trees. (Animals Animals © Mickey Gibson)

most often in terrestrial species. More recent evidence, however, suggests that orangutans spend more time on the ground than we had once thought. The orangutan is responsible, with the gorilla and chimpanzee, for many reports by early explorers of "wild men," "monsters," and "sub-humans."

Orangutans are agile climbers and hangers. In the trees, they use both arms and legs to climb in a slow, cautious manner. They will use one or more limbs to anchor themselves to branches while using the other limbs to feed (Figure 9.9). Younger orangutans occasionally brachiate, but the larger adults generally move through the trees in a different manner. A large orangutan will not swing from one tree to the next; rather, it will

estrus A time during the month when females are sexually receptive.

rock the tree it is on slowly in the direction of the next tree and then move over when the two trees are close together. The orangutan's great agility in climbing is due, in part, to its basic hominoid shoulder structure.

Orangutans are largely arboreal. Males, however, frequently come to the ground and travel along the forest floor for long distances. On the ground, orangutans walk on all fours but with their fists partially closed. Unlike monkeys, who rest their weight on their palms, orangutans rest on their fists: a form of movement often called fist walking.

Recent data suggest that orangutans produce offspring more slowly than the other great apes (Galdikas and Wood 1990). The average birth interval (the time between successive births) for orangutans is 7.7 years, compared to birth intervals of 3.8 years for gorillas and 5.6 years for chimpanzees (human birth intervals are highly variable but, as discussed in Chapter 7, they can be and often are shorter than that of apes).

In some ways orangutans are very similar to humans. Schwartz (1987) has drawn attention to a number of dental and skeletal traits humans and orangutans share that are not found in the African apes. Humans and orangutans also share certain aspects of their reproductive physiology. For example, both humans and orangutans have the same gestation length (270 days), which is longer than that of the African apes. Also, neither humans nor orangutans have a distinct mating cycle. Most primates have a definite time during the month (**estrus**) when the female is in "heat," that is, sexually responsive. Neither humans nor orangutans have an estrus cycle. Orangutans are also genetically very similar to humans; the DNA of humans and orangutans differs by slightly more than 2 percent (Lewin 1984).

Distribution and environment. The orangutan is found today only in Sumatra and Borneo in Southeast Asia. Orangutans are vegetarians, with over 60 percent of their diet consisting of fruit (Jolly 1985). As does the gibbon, the orangutan lives in tropical rain forests.

The natural range of the orangutan was probably greater in the past, judging from the fact that fossil apes similar to orangutans have been found in Asia dating from 12 million years ago (see Chapter 11). Some of the reduced distribution is the result of climatic change in the past. The limited range of orangutans today, as well as that of the other apes, is also due in part to human intervention. As its natural habitats continue to be destroyed, the orangutan is an endangered species and faces extinction (Jolly 1985).

Social structure. The basic social group of orangutans is the mother-infant group. Males are not needed for protection because there is little danger from predators (Horr 1972). Adult males generally live by themselves, interacting only during times of mating. Orangutans are polygamous; they do not form long-term bonds with any one partner. The small group size of orangutans appears to be related to the nature of the environment; when food resources are widely scattered, there is not enough food in any one place for large groups (Denham 1971).

Gorillas

Gorillas, the largest living primates, are found only in equatorial Africa.

Physical characteristics. An adult male gorilla weighs 160 kg (roughly 350 lbs) on average. Adult females weigh less but are still very large for primates (70 kg/155 lbs) (Leutenegger 1982). Besides a much larger body size, the adult males also have larger canine teeth and often large crests of bone on top of their skulls for anchoring their large jaw muscles. Gorillas usually have blackish hair; fully mature adult males have silvery gray hair on their backs. These adult males are called "silverbacks."

Their large size makes gorillas predominantly terrestrial. Their typical means of movement is called **knuckle walking:** they move about on all fours, resting their weight on the knuckles of their front limbs. This form of movement is different from the fist walking of orangutans. Gorilla hands have well-developed muscles and strengthened joints to handle the stress of resting on their knuckles. Because their arms are longer than their legs, gorilla spines are at an angle to the ground. In contrast, the spine of a typical quadrupedal animal, such as a monkey, is roughly parallel to the ground when walking (Figure 9.10).

knuckle walking A form of movement used by chimpanzees and gorillas that is characterized by all four limbs touching the ground, with the weight of the arms resting on the knuckles of the hands.

Figure 9.10

An adult male gorilla knuckle walking. Note the angle of the spine relative to the ground, because of the longer front limbs.   (© Zoological Society of San Diego)

Figure 9.11

A gorilla social group.
(© Michael K. Nichols/Magnum
Photos Inc.)

Distribution and environment. Gorillas are found only in certain forested areas in Africa. Their range is disappearing rapidly, primarily as the result of the replacement of forests by human farming land and human poaching (Fossey 1983). Gorillas live in humid rain forests in both the lowlands and in the mountain regions. Compared to the rain forests of the orangutans, the gorilla's environment is characterized by greater clumping of food resources (Denham 1971).

Many myths have circulated about the gorilla's lust for human and nonhuman flesh, but the truth of the matter is that gorillas are exclusively vegetarian. Over 85 percent of their diet consists of leaves (Jolly 1985). In fact, the intestinal tracts of gorillas are somewhat specialized for the digestion of leaves.

Social structure. Gorillas live in small social groups of about a dozen individuals. The social group consists of an adult male (the silverback), several adult females, and their immature offspring (Figure 9.11). Occasionally one or more younger adult males are part of the group, but they tend not to mate with the females. Though dominance rank varies among the females and subadult males, the adult silverback male is the most dominant individual in the group and is the leader. The silverback sets the pace for the rest of the group, determining when and how far to move in search of food.

A typical day for a gorilla group consists of eating and resting. Given their large body size and the limited nutritional value of leaves, it is no wonder that gorillas spend most of their days eating. Because of their size, gorillas have few problems with predators (except for humans with weapons). The life of a gorilla is for the most part peaceful, a dramatic contrast to their stereotypical image as aggressive, evil creatures.

Because gorillas are rather peaceful and slow-moving, we have a tendency to think they are "slow" in a mental sense as well. This is another myth of gorilla behavior. Laboratory and field studies of gorillas have

Figure 9.12

A pygmy chimpanzee.
(© Frans Lanting/Minden
Pictures)

shown them to be extremely intelligent creatures. As discussed later, they have even learned sign language.

Chimpanzees

The chimpanzee is perhaps the best known of all the nonhuman primates. Most of our experience with chimpanzees, however, is with captive or trained animals. We like to watch chimpanzees perform "just like humans" and delight in a chimpanzee's smile (which actually signals tension, not pleasure).

From a scientific perspective, chimpanzees are equally fascinating. Genetic studies during the last 20 years have shown that humans and chimpanzees are even more similar than they were previously thought to be. Laboratory and field studies have shown that chimpanzees are capable of behaviors we once thought of as unique to humans, such as toolmaking and language acquisition. Any examination of the human condition must take these remarkable creatures's accomplishments into account.

Physical characteristics. There are two living species of chimpanzee, both found in Africa: the common chimpanzee and the lesser-known pygmy chimpanzee (Figure 9.12). Unless otherwise indicated, all infor-

Figure 9.13

Variation in chimpanzee faces.
(© Wrangham/Anthro-Photo)

mation here refers to the common chimpanzee. Chimpanzees are smaller than gorillas and show only slight sexual dimorphism. Adult males weigh about 45 kg (99 lbs) on average and adult females weigh about 37 kg (82 lbs) on average (Leutenegger 1982). Chimpanzees have extremely powerful shoulders and arms. Like humans, chimpanzees show great variation in facial features and overall physical appearance (Figure 9.13).

Chimpanzees, like gorillas, are knuckle walkers with longer arms than legs. Chimpanzees, however, are more active and agile than gorillas. Chimpanzees are both terrestrial and arboreal. They spend considerable time in the trees, either sleeping or looking for food. They often hang by their arms in the trees. On the ground, they sometimes stand on two legs to carry food or sticks.

Distribution and environment. Most chimpanzees are found in the African rain forests, although some groups are also found in the mixed forest–savanna environments on the fringe of the rain forests. The chimpanzee diet consists mainly of fruit (almost 70 percent), although they also eat leaves, seeds, nuts, insects, and meat. Chimpanzees have been observed hunting small animals, such as monkeys, and sharing the meat. Though some of the hunting occurs spontaneously when chimpanzees encounter small animals, other hunting behavior appears to be planned and coordinated.

Figure 9.14

A pygmy chimpanzee mother
and infant. (© Zoological
Society of San Diego)

Social structure. Chimpanzees live in rather large multimale groups
of 50 or more individuals. All chimpanzees in the social group recognize
and interact with others in the group. Chimpanzee groups are less rigid
than other multimale primate societies such as baboons. Although all
members of the group do interact to some extent, it is common for smaller
subgroups to form much of the time. The actual composition of these
subgroups also changes frequently.

Most social behaviors revolve around the bond between mother and
child (Figure 9.14). Chimpanzees tend to associate with their mothers and
other siblings throughout their lives, even after they are fully grown. As

hominid Humans and
humanlike ancestors.

with other primates, young females watch and observe their own mothers taking care of children and learn mothering behaviors. There is no close bond between adult males and infants except for associations through the mother. Overall, chimpanzee society can be seen as a collection of smaller groups, defined in terms of mothers and siblings, forming a larger community. Other associations are also common, such as temporary all-male groups. Some chimpanzees are even solitary for periods of time.

Adult males are generally dominant over adult females, although there is much more overlap than found in baboon societies. Some females, for example, are dominant over the lower-ranking males. As with other primates, dominance is influenced by a variety of factors such as size, strength, and the ability to form alliances. Individual intelligence also appears to affect dominance, as was revealed in Jane Goodall's study of the chimpanzees in the Gombe Stream National Park near Lake Tanganyika. In 1964 the community studied by Goodall had 14 adult males. The lowest-ranking male (Mike) replaced the most dominant male (Goliath) after inventing a particularly innovative display of dominance. There were a number of empty kerosene cans lying around Goodall's camp that the chimpanzees generally ignored. Mike would charge other males while hitting the cans in front of him, creating an unusual and very noisy display. This behavior was so intimidating to other males that Mike rose from the lowest to the highest rank at once (Goodall 1986). This study shows not only the changing nature of dominance heirarchy but also the role of individual intelligence and initiative; all the males had access to the cans, but only Mike used them.

Studies of the Gombe Stream chimpanzee community have also revealed a number of other interesting features of chimpanzee social behaviors and intelligence. The chimpanzees have been observed to make and use tools (discussed at length later in this chapter), hunt in cooperative groups, and sometimes engage in widespread aggression against other groups. We will examine some of these findings when we consider what behaviors may be considered uniquely human.

Modern Humans

Humans are the last of the primates we will study and the most widely distributed in spite of our origin in a specific environment. Humans and humanlike ancestors are also known by the term **hominid.**

Distribution and Environment

As later chapters will outline, humans evolved in a tropical environment. In fact, much of our present-day biology reflects the fact that we are tropical mammals. During the course of human evolution, however, we have expanded into many different environments. Biological adaptations have aided humans in new environments, such as cold weather and high altitude. The cultural adaptations of humans have allowed even greater expansion. Today there is no place on the planet where we cannot live, given the appropriate technology. Humans can live in the frozen wastes of Antarctica, deep beneath the sea, and in the vacuum of outer space. Our cultural adaptations have allowed us to range far beyond our biological limitations. These adaptations have also permitted incredible population growth. In the past, the planet supported no more than roughly 1 to 6 million people at a hunting-and-gathering level of existence (Weiss 1984). Today the population of the world is over five billion and continuing to grow. It is easily argued that the quality of life is still low for much of the world's human population, but there is no doubting that our ability to learn and develop technology has led to immense potential for population expansion.

Brain Size and Structure

One very obvious biological characteristic of the human species is the large brain. Our bulging and rounded skulls and flat faces contrast with these features in other animals, including the rest of the hominoids. Whereas an ape's skull is characterized by a relatively small brain and large face, modern humans have relatively large brains and small faces.

Table 9.2 lists the brain size (in milliliters) for a number of primate species. There is a clear relationship between taxonomic status and brain size: monkeys have the smallest brains, followed by the lesser apes, great

T A B L E   9.2
Brain Volume of Selected Living Primates (in Milliliters)

Primate species	Range	Average
Macaque monkey		100
Baboon		200
White-handed gibbon	82–125	102
Siamang	100–152	124
Orangutan	276–540	404
Gorilla	340–752	495
Common chimpanzee	282–500	385
Modern human	900–2000	1345

Averages for macaque and baboon from Campbell (1985:233).
Hominoid data from Tobias (1971:34–40), where the averages
were taken as the means of males and females.

allometry The change in proportion of various body parts as a consequence of different growth rates.

apes, and humans. Absolute brain size is not as useful a measure of intellectual ability because larger animals tend to have larger brains. Elephants and whales, for example, have brains that are four to five times the size of the average human brain.

An alternative way of looking at brain size is to express the weight of the brain as a ratio of body weight. The larger this ratio, the larger the brain is relative to body size. For humans, this ratio is $1/49 = 0.020$. However, this ratio is not very useful: many other primates have larger ratios, but we tend not to think of them as more intelligent (for example, the ratio for the squirrel monkey is $1/31 = 0.032$) (Passingham 1982).

Among mammals, however, the relationship of brain and body weight is not linear. That is, as the body size increases, the brain size increases—although not at the same rate. Differences in size because of disparate growth rates among various parts of the body (known as **allometry**) are common. Parts of the body grow at different rates. Brain size increases at a nonlinear rate with body size. For example, consider two species of primates in which one species is twice the body weight of the other. If the ratio of brain size to body size were linear, we would expect the brain size of the species with the larger body size to be twice that of the lighter species. Actually, the brain size of the larger-bodied species is on average only 1.6 times as large. Because of this relationship, larger species appear to have smaller brain/body size ratios.

This allometric relationship between brain size and body size is quite regular among almost all primate species. The most notable exception is humans. We have brains that are three times the size we would expect for a primate of our size (Passingham 1982). In addition, our brains have proportionately more cerebral cortex than other primate brains. The cerebral cortex is the part of the brain involved in forming complex associations.

What exactly is the relationship between brain size, relative to body size, and intelligence? This question has been long debated, but with little resolution. Most texts state there is no relationship between relative brain size and intelligence within the human species, although only a few studies were without methodological flaws. It is problematic, however, that the fossil record of human evolution shows an increase in absolute and relative brain size that corresponds to an increase in mental abilities. Could there be a relationship between relative brain size and intelligence between species, but not within species? A recent study by Willerman and colleagues (1991) helps resolve some of the conflict. They measured the brain size of 40 adults using magnetic resonance imaging and compared these values, adjusted for body size, with IQ test scores. Adjusting their results to the general population, they found a correlation of 0.35 between relative brain size and IQ scores (a positive correlation can take on a value from 0 to 1; the higher the value, the closer the correspondence). In statistical terms, this finding means that roughly 12 percent of the observed variation in IQ test scores is related to variation in relative brain size. However, this also indicates that 88 percent of the observed variation in IQ scores is *not* related to such variation. Overall, the results show that relative brain size is a contributing factor, but not the only one. In terms of evolution, the correlation is sufficient to show that natural selection has had an impact over many generations. However, the correlation is also low enough that one could not predict accurately a person's IQ from his or her relative brain size.

Recent studies have also looked at the relationship among brain size, body size, and metabolism. Larger mammals have larger brain sizes and produce greater amounts of metabolic energy. Mammals show a great deal of variation, however, in the amount of energy used by the brain. The brains of many mammals, such as dogs and cats, use 4 to 6 percent of their body metabolism. Primate brains use a considerably greater proportion of energy; the Old World macaque uses 9 percent and modern humans use 20 percent (Armstrong 1983).

What does all this mean? The human brain is not merely large; it also has a different structure than other primates, with the cortex being disproportionately larger. This difference in structure is also probably related to the higher proportion of metabolic energy used by the human brain. The bottom line is that brain size does not tell the whole story. Thus, the human brain is not only larger than the brain of a chimpanzee; it is also structurally different. The increased convolution of the human cerebral cortex (the folding of brain tissue) means that the brain of a human child with the same volume of that of a chimpanzee has more cerebral cortex.

Discussion of brain size and its relationship to intellectual prowess has historically been part of debates about relative differences in the mental abilities of male and female humans. When *absolute* brain size is used to assess these differences, male brains tend on *average* to be larger. This finding has been used in the past to support ill-conceived beliefs in the mental superiority of males. However, as pointed out by Gould (1980), researchers did not take into account the fact that body size is on average larger in human males and that absolute brain size is closely related to body size. That is, men often have larger brains because they tend to be larger overall. This fact, combined with an understanding of some of the methodological problems of earlier studies, has led Gould to conclude there is no gender difference in relative brain size or overall intellectual ability.

Certain studies, however, do indicate that average gender differences may influence *specific* mental abilities. Falk (1992) has reviewed evidence that females tend on average to score higher on tests of verbal ability and males to score higher on tests of spatial and mathematical abilities. Falk suggests that these findings may be due to gender differences in patterns of brain lateralization. Of course, these tests and measures must be replicated cross-culturally to ensure that various forms of bias are not responsible for such observed differences (such as the fact that females in many

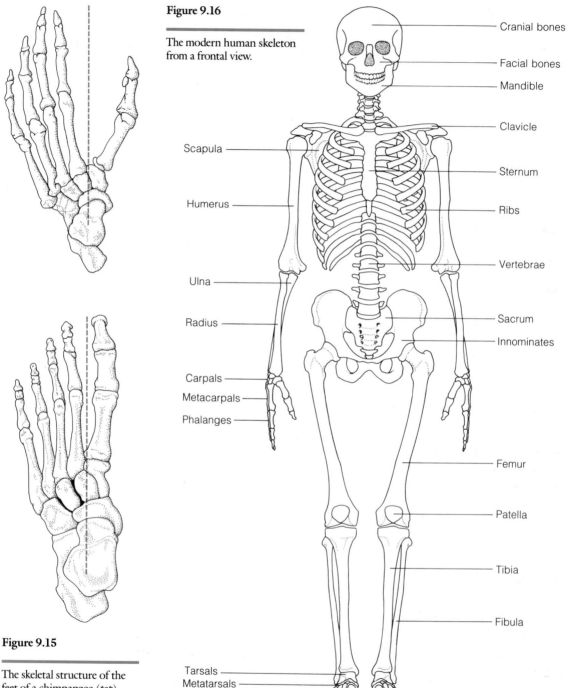

Figure 9.16

The modern human skeleton from a frontal view.

Cranial bones

Facial bones

Mandible

Clavicle

Scapula

Sternum

Humerus

Ribs

Vertebrae

Ulna

Radius

Sacrum

Innominates

Carpals

Metacarpals

Phalanges

Femur

Patella

Tibia

Fibula

Tarsals

Metatarsals

Phalanges

Figure 9.15

The skeletal structure of the feet of a chimpanzee (*top*) and a modern human (*bottom*). Note how the big toe of the human lies parallel to the other toes.

cultures are actively discouraged from mathematics). Also, we must never forget that these results focus on *average* test scores and not on total distribution. Both male and female test score distributions overlap each other. For example, some males score higher in verbal skills than females. As with many comparisons of biology and behavior between the sexes, we do not find exclusively separate distributions, but instead a great deal of overlap.

Bipedalism

Another striking difference between humans and apes is the fact that humans walk on two legs. We are **bipedal** (meaning "two legs"). This does not mean that apes cannot walk on two legs. They can, but not as well and not as often. The physical structure of human beings shows adaptations for upright walking as the normal mode of movement.

Humans are not the only animal that is routinely bipedal. The kangaroo also moves about on two legs, but in a totally different manner than humans. The human form of bipedal movement is best characterized as a "striding gait." Consider walking in slow motion. What happens? First, you stand balanced on two legs. Then you move one leg forward. You shift your body weight so that your weight is transferred to the moving leg. As that leg touches the ground on its heel, all your body weight has been shifted. Your other leg is then free to swing forward. As it does so, you push off with your other foot.

Human walking is more graceful than a slow-motion description sounds. The act of walking consists of alternating legs from swinging free to standing still. We balance on one leg while the other leg moves forward to continue our striding motion. We tend to take these acts for granted, but they are actually quite complicated, requiring both balance and coordination. For example, when you pick one leg up to move it forward, what keeps your body from falling over?

Human bipedalism is made possible by anatomical changes involving the toes, legs, spine, pelvis, and muscles. In terms of actual anatomy, these changes are not major: after all, no bones are added or deleted; the same bones can be found in humans and in apes. The changes involve shape, positioning, and function. The net effect of these changes, however, is dramatic. Humans can move about effectively on two legs, allowing the other limbs to be free for other activities.

The feet of human beings reflect adaptation to bipedalism. The feet of a human and a chimp are shown in Figure 9.15. The big toe of the chimp sticks out in the same way that the thumb of all hominoids sticks out from the other fingers. The divergent big toe allows chimps to grasp with their feet. The big toe of the human is tucked in next to the other toes. When we walk, we use the nondivergent big toe to push off during our strides.

Our balance while we stand and walk is partly the result of changes in our legs. Figure 9.16 shows a human skeleton from the frontal view.

bipedal Moving about on two legs. Unlike the movement of other bipedal animals such as kangaroos, human bipedalism is further characterized by a striding motion.

Figure 9.17

Side view of the skeletons of a chimpanzee (*left*) and a modern human (*right*), illustrating the shape and orientation of the spine.   (Adapted with permission from: Bernard Campbell, *Human Evolution,* Third Edition [New York: Aldine de Gruyter]. Copyright © 1985 Bernard Campbell)

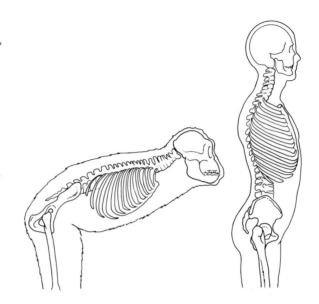

Note that the width of the body at the knees is less than the width of the body at the hips. Humans are literally "knock-kneed." Our upper leg bones (the femurs) slope inward from the hips. When we stand on one leg, the angle of the femur transmits our weight directly underneath us. The result is that we continue to be balanced while one leg is moving. In contrast, the angle of an ape femur is very slight. The legs of an ape are almost parallel from hips to feet. When an ape stands on two legs and moves one of them, the ape is off balance and tends to fall toward one side. When an ape walks on two legs, it must shift its whole body weight over the supporting leg to stay on balance. This shifting explains the characteristic waddling when apes walk on two legs.

The human spine also allows balance when we walk upright (Figure 9.17). The spinal column of humans is vertical, allowing weight to be transmitted down through the center of the body. In knuckle-walking apes, the spine is bent in an arc so that when they stand on two legs the center of gravity is shifted in front of the body. The ape is off balance and must compensate greatly to stay upright. What is difficult for apes is easy for humans. The human spine is vertical but not straight. It curves in several places, allowing it to absorb the shocks occurring while we walk.

The human pelvis is shaped differently than an ape pelvis (Figure 9.18). It is shorter top to bottom, and wider side to side. The sides of the pelvis are broader and flair out more to the sides, providing changes in muscle attachment that permit striding bipedalism. The shortness of the human pelvis allows greater stability when we stand upright.

The changes in the human pelvis also involve changes in the positioning of various muscles. For example, certain leg muscles attach more on

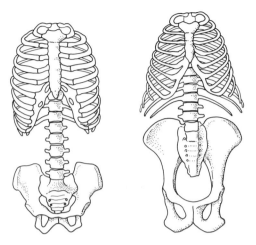

Figure 9.18

The trunk skeletons of a modern human (*left*) and a chimpanzee (*right*) drawn to the same size. Note the proportionately shorter and wider pelvis of the human being, reflecting adaptations to upright walking (see text). (Adapted with permission from: Bernard Campbell, *Human Evolution,* Third Edition [New York: Aldine de Gruyter]. Copyright © 1985 Bernard Campbell)

the sides of the pelvis. This change allows humans to maintain their balance while standing without having to bend their knees. Other muscles, such as the gluteus maximus (the large buttock muscle), are larger in humans than in apes. This muscle helps in standing up and in climbing over uneven terrain. The gluteus minimus and gluteus medius muscles have also shifted position relative to apes, allowing the pelvis to remain stable when one leg is lifted during walking.

Canine Teeth

As we saw in the last chapter, human canine teeth are different from canine teeth in many other mammals. Human canines are small and do not project beyond the level of the other teeth. Human canine teeth serve much the same function as the incisor teeth.

That we have small nonprojecting canines has led to much speculation concerning causes and effects of human evolution. Given that canine teeth serve as weapons in many primate species, the lack of large canine teeth in humans seems to imply that we do not need them for weapons anymore. One scenario is that when human ancestors began using tools, they no longer required large canines. As you will see in later chapters, the uniqueness of human canine teeth is a bit more complex a topic than we once thought.

Sex and Reproduction

We humans consider ourselves the sexiest primates. That is, we are more concerned with sex than is any other primate. The fact that humans do not have the estrus cycle has often been cited as a unique aspect of human sexuality. For the most part, temperate-zone domestic animals breed only during certain seasons and mate around the time of ovulation. Human females, in contrast, cycle throughout the year and often mate at any time during the cycle. This may be a primitive characteristic, however. Some mice and rats cycle continuously. Also, as noted earlier in this chapter, it now appears that orangutans also lack the estrus cycle. In addition, recent field studies on other primates suggest that many individuals mate outside the usual cycle to some extent, such as pygmy chimpanzees (Jolly 1985).

Much has been made of the fact that humans have sexual relations while facing each other (the so-called "missionary position"), whereas other primates typically engage in sex with the male behind the female. One explanation is that there is some social benefit to facing each other during sexual intercourse; it is said to increase emotional bonds between male and female. One problem with this suggestion is that most studies of human sexual behavior have found that humans engage in a wide variety of sexual positions. Though the missionary position has been cited as the most common sexual position for certain societies at certain times, it is not the most common everywhere. Human bipedal anatomy may influence the fact that humans use the missionary position while other primates rarely use it. The changes in the human pelvis have shifted the position of the vagina so that the missionary position is easier to attain. Apes rarely have sex in this manner simply because it is not comfortable for them.

Some authors claim that female orgasm is unique in human beings and have constructed a number of explanations for this fact. There is growing evidence, however, that nonhuman primate females also experience orgasm (Jolly 1985).

Human females have relatively large breasts, whereas other primate females do not. One hypothesis is that large breasts developed to resemble buttocks. Given that face-to-face sex is desirable in reinforcing emotional bonds and that males prefer the buttocks (both questionable assumptions), large breasts would serve to attract human males to the female's front. A 1986 paper suggests instead that large breasts in human females is a by-product of the evolution of fat in human females. Fat reserves are important for females in hunting-and-gathering societies, because fat is stored energy that can be used for reproduction in times of food shortage. It has been hypothesized that hormonal changes accompanying increased fat reserves led to increased breast size in human females (Mascia-Lees et al. 1986). This hypothesis, though interesting, still needs to be tested.

The human pattern of reproduction is basically the same as that of most primates: single births. Unlike apes, humans have additional children before the previous children have grown up socially or physically. Because of cultural adaptations, humans have reduced their amount of K-selection without sacrificing parental care. In fact, a greater proportion of the human life span is taken up in infancy and childhood (Table 9.3). Compared to the other hominoids, we mature more slowly and require a greater amount of our life for learning.

Social Structure

Human social structure is a topic of almost infinite complexity that is thoroughly explored in cultural anthropology textbooks. One observation is obvious—there is extensive variation. Because variation in social structure is great even among the apes, it should come as no surprise that humans, with an even greater emphasis on learned behavior, show greater variation.

A common Western assumption is that the "normal" social structure of human beings is the nuclear monogamous family group: mother, father, and children. Actually, the majority (almost 90 percent) of human societies prefer **polygyny**—a pattern in which one husband has several wives (Harris 1987). In such societies, however, it is still common for many men to have only a single wife. Though multiple wives are permitted, and preferred, many men lack the necessary economic or political status required for many wives. A very few cultures practice **polyandry,** in which one woman has several husbands. The common element in all human social structures is the existence of some mechanism for the care and education of the children.

Humans show a great deal of variation in other aspects of their culture, such as economic systems, political systems, and legal systems. There are also some biological limitations on human cultural behavior, however. Humans are social animals and do not survive well when isolated. Apart

polygyny A form of marriage in which a husband has several wives.

polyandry A form of marriage in which a wife has several husbands.

TABLE 9.3
Relative Lengths of Postnatal Life in Selected Primates

Species	Average length of life in years	Percentage of life spent as		
		Infant	Juvenile	Adult
Lemur	13.5	3.7	14.8	81.5
Macaque	22.5	5.5	21.8	72.7
Chimpanzee	40.0	7.5	17.5	75.0
Human	75.0	8.0	18.7	73.3

As used here, infancy refers to the period of greatest dependency on a mother. Note that not only do chimpanzees and humans live longer than prosimians and monkeys, but a greater proportion of their life is spent as infants. Also note that the average length of life for humans is actually a fairly recent figure. Throughout most of human history and prehistory, the average length of life was between 20 and 40 years. This means that the proportion of the total life spent in the infant and juvenile stages was probably even greater for past human populations.

Source: Jolly (1985:292).

from the occasional hermit, humans thrive best in groups. Humans have biological needs, such as food and sex, that structure our behaviors.

Are Humans Unique?

Humans and apes show a great many similarities as well as a great many differences. When we ask whether humans are unique we do not suggest that we cannot tell an ape and a human apart. Rather, we ask what the extent of these differences is. Are the behaviors of apes and humans completely different, or are differences present only in the expression of specific behaviors? Can we say, for example, that humans make tools and apes do not? Or should we say instead that there are differences in the way in which these two groups make and use tools?

The debate on the uniqueness of human culture was discussed briefly in the last chapter and provides an example of the controversy about differences in behavior. According to the view that apes and humans show distinct and major differences, humans possess culture and apes do not. Any cultural behaviors found in apes are labeled as fundamentally different from human cultural behaviors. According to the view that ape–human differences are variations on something that is fundamentally similar, both humans and apes possess culture—the only difference being that humans rely more on culture or that humans have a more developed culture. This debate is semantic to a large extent. A more worthwhile approach is to examine some of the suggested differences between apes and humans in an effort to determine what is truly different.

Tool Use and Manufacture

Tool use has often been cited as a unique human behavior. As defined here, a tool is an object that is not part of the animal. Human tools include pencils, clothes, eating utensils, books, and houses. All of these are objects that are not part of the biological organism (humans) but are used for a specific purpose. Tool use, however, does not seem to even be a unique primate characteristic. Birds use sticks for nests and beavers use dirt in their dams. Both sticks and dirt could be considered tools by this definition.

A more common definition of modern humans focuses on humans as toolmakers (this definition is complicated by the fact that the earliest hominids may not have made tools—see Chapter 12). The key element of this definition is that some object is taken from the environment and modified to meet a new function. Humans take trees to make lumber to build houses. It can be argued that birds modify sticks and beavers modify dirt, but tool manufacture implies something different. Birds, for example, use sticks for building nests but do not use these sticks for defensive or offensive weapons. Humans, on the other hand, can take sticks and use them to make shelters, defend themselves, hunt, dig up roots, and draw pictures in the sand. When we discuss tool manufacture, we mean the new and different ways to modify an object for a task. Humans can apply the same raw materials to a variety of tasks.

In this sense, tool manufacture has long been considered a unique human activity. But research on apes, particularly Goodall's work on chimpanzees, has since shown that this is not true. Apes make and use tools. Though their tools are extremely simple by modern human standards, it is clear that the difference between apes and humans cannot be reduced to humans making tools and apes not making tools. Differences exist in the method and uses of manufactured tools, but not the presence or absence of toolmaking.

Chimpanzee termite fishing. In the early 1960s, Jane Goodall reported a remarkable finding—chimpanzees were making and using tools! Though chimpanzees are predominantly fruit eaters, they also enjoy a variety of other foods, including termites. One group of chimpanzees demonstrated a method for capturing termites. They took a grass stem or a stick, went up to a termite mound, and uncovered one of the entrance holes left by the termites. They inserted the stick into the hole, twirled the stick a bit to attract termites down in the mound, and then withdrew the stick. Termites attached themselves to the stick, and the chimpanzees ate the termites directly off the stick.

Close analysis of this "termite fishing" behavior shows it to be true tool manufacture along with rather complex tool use. Chimpanzees often spent a great deal of time selecting the appropriate stick. When a suitable stick was not available, they pulled a branch out of the ground or off a bush and stripped away the leaves. This is deliberate manipulation of an object in the environment—toolmaking. The act also reflects a conscious decision-making process.

Termite fishing is not easy. One anthropologist who tried found that it was a difficult process that required a great deal of skill and practice. Even finding the right kind of stick is tricky. If a stick is too flexible or too rigid, it cannot be inserted in the termite tunnel. Taking the stick out without knocking the termites off also calls for careful handling.

Termite fishing is not an innate chimpanzee behavior. It is passed on to others in the group by means of learning. Young chimpanzees watch their elders and imitate them, thus learning the methods and also developing practice. Termite fishing has become part of the local group's culture.

Other examples of toolmaking. Termite fishing is only one of many types of tool manufacture reported among chimpanzees. Sticks are also

Figure 9.19

The chimpanzees have fashioned simple tools to fish for ants. The infant chimpanzee watches and learns this process.   (James Moore/Anthro-Photo)

used to hunt for ants (Figure 9.19). A chimpanzee will dig up an underground nest with its hands and then insert a long stick into the nest. The ants begin swarming up the stick and the chimpanzee withdraws it to eat the ants. Sticks have also been used to probe holes in dead wood and to break into ant and bee nests (Goodall 1986).

Chimpanzees have also been observed to make sponges out of leaves. After a rainfall, a chimpanzee often drinks out of pools of water that collect in the holes of tree branches. Often the holes are too small for the chimp to fit its head into, so the chimp creates a tool to soak up the water: he takes a leaf, puts it in his mouth, and chews it slightly. (Chewing increases the ability of the leaf to absorb water.) The chimp inserts this "sponge" into the hole in the branch to soak up the water.

Other examples of chimpanzee toolmaking and tool use include using leaves as napkins and toilet paper, using sticks as weapons, and using rocks to break open nuts and hard fruits (Goodall 1986).

In recent years, researchers have observed that toolmaking and tool use are not specieswide characteristics among chimpanzees. Not all groups have shown the same behaviors. Some use sticks for ant or termite fishing or sponges for drinking; others do not (McGrew 1992). This variation may reflect the importance of individual discoveries. It might also relate to environmental differences, with tool use being more frequent in areas with less immediately available food. This possibility is still being tested (Gibbons 1992a).

Human and chimpanzee toolmaking. It is obvious that chimpanzees make and use tools in a systematic manner. It is also clear that they use genuine problem-solving abilities in their toolmaking. They see a problem (e.g., termites in the mounds) and create a tool to solve the problem. The implication of these studies is that we can no longer define humans as the only toolmakers. Our definition must be modified, and we must focus on differences in toolmaking between apes and humans.

There are several important differences between chimpanzee and human toolmaking and tool use. First, humans depend on tools; chimpanzees do not. Termite fishing provides a tasty treat for the chimpanzees, but it is not essential for their survival. Chimpanzees survive without tools in many places. Humans, on the other hand, depend on tools for survival. Toolmaking and tool use are not an option for humans; they are an imperative.

A second difference is that humans save their tools. Chimpanzees start over each time they make a tool. Chimpanzees who fish termites do not save the sticks they have made. Humans save their tools, presumably because of the greater importance tools have for human survival.

Third, humans use tools to make other tools. This allows for the construction of a complex technological system. Thus far, no one has seen chimpanzees do this. A further key distinction of modern humans is that we accumulate our knowledge of toolmaking, building on it generation after generation.

In any case, it is clear that we cannot define modern humans solely in terms of having the ability to make tools. The observations made by Goodall and others regarding chimpanzee tool manufacture have caused us to redefine human behavior and to reconsider our relationship with the apes. We now acknowledge much closer similarities than we did several decades ago. The methods, goals, and complexities of human toolmaking are clearly quite different from those of apes. We must also acknowledge, however, that we are not as dissimilar as was once thought.

Language Capabilities

Language has long been considered a unique human property. Language is not merely communication but rather a symbolic form of communication. The nonhuman primates communicate basic emotions in a variety of ways. Chimpanzees, for example, have a large number of vocalizations that they use to convey emotional states such as anger, fear, or stress (Figure 9.20). Many primates also use their sense of touch to communicate some emotions by **grooming,** the handling and cleaning of another individual's fur (Figure 9.21). Grooming helps keep the animals clean and also acts to soothe and reassure tense or frightened individuals. Grooming is a common form of social communication among primates.

What is language? Primate communication through vocalizations, grooming, or other methods does not constitute language. Language, as a symbolic form of communication, has certain characteristics that distin-

grooming The handling and cleaning of another individual's fur or hair. In primates, grooming serves as a form of communication that soothes and provides reassurance.

Figure 9.20

A chimpanzee hooting. (Marine World Africa USA/ Darryl W. Bush, Photographer)

Figure 9.21

Two chimpanzees grooming.
(Marine World Africa USA/
Darryl W. Bush, Photographer)

guish it from simple communication. Language is an *open system;* that is, new ideas can be expressed that have never been expressed before. Chimpanzee vocalizations, on the other hand, form a closed system capable of only conveying a few basic concepts or emotions. Human language can use a finite number of sounds and create an infinite number of words, sentences, and ideas from these sounds.

Another important characteristic of language is *displacement.* Language allows discussion of objects and events that are displaced—that is, not present—in time and/or space. For example, you can say, "Tomorrow I am going to another country." This sentence conveys an idea that is displaced in both time ("tomorrow") and space ("the other country"). We can discuss the past, the future, and faraway places. Displacement is very important for our ability to plan future events—imagine the difficulty in planning a hunt several days from now without the ability to speak of future events!

Language is also arbitrary. The actual sounds we use in our languages need not bear any relationship to reality. Our word for "book" could just as easily be "gurmf" or some other sound. The important point is that we understand the relationship of sounds to objects and ideas. This in turn shows yet another important feature of language—it is learned.

Apes and American Sign Language. Early efforts to teach English to apes were failures. One classic experiment was conducted on a young female chimpanzee named Vicki. After years of extensive work Vicki could only speak four words: "Mama," "Papa," "up," and "cup." Later researchers noted that the failure of this experiment might mean only that apes cannot speak English; it said nothing about their ability to understand.

Figure 9.22

A chimpanzee is using the American Sign Language to convey the message "more eat." (H. S. Terrace/Anthro-Photo)

Looking back at this study, it is no surprise that Vicki could not speak very well, because the vocal anatomy of chimpanzees makes speaking a human language next to impossible.

In the 1960s, two scientists, Allen and Beatrice Gardner, began teaching the American Sign Language to a young female chimpanzee named Washoe. Devised for the deaf, American Sign Language (ASL) is a true symbolic language that does not require vocalization but instead uses hand and finger gestures. Because chimpanzees are capable of making such signs, ASL is the most suitable medium to determine whether or not they are capable of using language (Figure 9.22). Washoe quickly learned many signs and soon developed an extensive vocabulary.

Washoe also demonstrated the ability to generalize: to take a concept learned in one context and apply it to another. For example, she would use the sign meaning *open* to refer to boxes as well as doors. This suggests that Washoe truly understood the general concept of *open* and not just the use of the sign in one specific context. Washoe also invented new signs and "talked" to herself while playing alone, an act human children perform when learning language. Washoe was even observed to swear!

One of the most intriguing findings of the Gardners' research was that Washoe would form simple two- and three-word sentences (for example, "You tickle me"). Early observations suggested that Washoe was not only capable of symbolism but also of grammar and sentence construction.

Washoe was the first ape taught American Sign Language. Since then there have been many experiments into the nature of language capabilities of the apes. Gorillas, as well as chimpanzees, have been taught ASL. Other languages were also invented, including one based on plastic tiles and another using a computer keyboard. Experiments were devised that required two chimpanzees to interact with each other using language. These experiments confirmed the ability to generalize signs and to create new ones. For example, one chimpanzee named Lucy combined the signs *drink* and *fruit* to refer to a watermelon for which she had not been taught a sign. She also invented the phrase "cry hurt food" to refer to radishes, which presumably she found bitter.

Human and ape language abilities. The purpose of the original research with Washoe was to determine what was unique about the way in which a human child learns language. It was suggested that a comparison of human and chimpanzee language acquisition would reveal at what point human abilities surpassed those of the ape. Washoe's abilities exceeded early expectations, and soon the research focus shifted to the language capabilities of the apes themselves. The ability of Washoe and other apes to learn a symbolic language suggested that language acquisition could no longer be regarded as a unique human feature.

There is considerable debate about the meaning of these studies. Some claim that many of the positive results are the result of unconscious cues given to the apes by humans. Also, there is the problem of interpreting the data and seeing what one wants to see. For example, Washoe signed "water bird" the first time she saw a swan. Some researchers have interpreted this as a true invention. Others have suggested that Washoe simply saw the water and then the bird, and responded with the two signs in sequence. Obviously, much of this research is fraught with the danger of speculation and excessive interpretation for the simple reason that we cannot get inside the chimpanzee's mind.

In spite of the debates, there is little doubt that apes can learn and understand the meaning of many signs. Chimpanzees, gorillas, and orangutans have all mastered a certain number. Some chimps have learned over 150 signs by the time they were 7 years old (Snowden 1990). Carefully controlled experiments have shown that the basic vocabulary of apes is not a reflection of unconscious cues given by the scientists. The behavior of signing correctly while playing alone strongly suggests that the apes actually do understand, *in some manner,* the meaning of signs.

Much of the controversy over language acquisition in apes revolves around two different training approaches. Many studies, including the Washoe project, attempted to teach language in an environment similar to that in which human children develop linguistic skills, one offering continued exposure in an unstructured environment with many opportunities for creativity and expression. Other ape studies used controlled, less flexible environments. The controlled experiments were of course designed to minimize cues from humans and to provide more definitive measurements. The problem is that this type of sterile approach is not the most conducive to learning language.

One of the most interesting observations came about by accident during a study conducted by Savage-Rumbaugh, in which researchers were attempting to teach a female pygmy chimpanzee a keyboard-based language. At the time, the chimp was caring for an infant, Kanzi, who frequently interrupted his mother. Later, when the mother was returned to the breeding colony, Kanzi began to use the keyboard to make requests. Over time, he performed well on a variety of measures (Snowden 1990). Significantly, he learned language by observation, and not through direct training. (After all, the experiment was not designed to teach him; he was simply there to be nursed.) In other words, Kanzi learned elements of language in the same way that human children do.

The suggested ability of apes to understand grammar and to construct sentences is also controversial. Though apes do create correct two- and three-word sentences, the few longer sentences they create are often grammatically incorrect. There has also been evidence that the apes respond to unconscious cues in constructing sentences (as opposed to simple vocabulary identification). Though some see definite evidence of grammar (e.g., Linden 1981), others see little evidence (e.g., Terrace 1979). The debate continues.

Regardless of the outcome, it is clear that the difference between human and ape is not as great as we once thought. We can no longer define modern humans in terms of the capability to learn certain aspects of symbolic language. Apes are certainly capable of symbolic behavior, even if we can debate over exactly how much. Both humans and apes can learn symbols, though humans are clearly better at it. Perhaps one of the major differences is the fact that humans rely on language and apes do not. In their natural habitat, apes do not use sign language. The fact that they are capable of learning language to a certain extent should not detract from the point that they do not use language in their natural environment. As with tool manufacture, we see evidence of capabilities in the apes for behaviors that are optional for them but mandatory for modern humans.

The question of human uniqueness becomes more complicated when we consider possible behaviors of our fossil ancestors. Given a common ancestry with the African apes, at what point did our own patterns of toolmaking and language acquisition begin? Studies of modern apes help answer such questions because we can see the *potential* for such behaviors in the modern apes. Using these potentials as a guide to the behavior of the common ancestor of African apes and humans, we can attempt to determine what changes were necessary to arrive at the modern human condition. Chapters 10 through 13 detail this search for our biological and behavioral roots.

SUMMARY

The hominoids (apes and humans) are a group of anthropoids that share certain characteristics, such as the lack of a tail, similar dental features, larger brains, and a shoulder complex suitable for climbing and hanging. The hominoids consist of the lesser apes (gibbon and siamang), the great apes (orangutan, gorilla, and chimpanzee), and humans. Biochemical analyses show that the African apes—the gorilla and chimpanzee—are the most similar to modern humans.

The living apes show a great deal of environmental and anatomical variation. Some are arm swingers (gibbon, siamang), others are knuckle walkers (gorilla, chimpanzee), and one is a climber (orangutan). In spite of the fact that the apes are all similar genetically and have a fairly recent common ancestor (less than 20 million years ago), they show a great deal of social variation. Gibbons and siamangs live in family groups, the orangutan lives in mother-infant groups, the gorilla lives in one-male groups, and chimpanzees live in large multimale communities.

Humans share many features with the other hominoids but also show a number of differences. The main biological characteristics of humans are the large and complex brain, bipedalism, and small canine teeth. All humans live in groups, but a great deal of variation exists from one culture to the next in the exact form of social structure.

Past behavioral definitions of humans have often focused on humans as toolmakers and users of symbolic language. Recent studies of toolmaking and language acquisition in apes show that this definition must be modified. Modern humans remain unique in the specific ways they use tools and language and in their reliance on these behaviors for survival. What is mandatory for modern humans is optional for apes.

Supplemental Readings

Goodall, J. 1986. *The Chimpanzees of Gombe: Patterns of Behavior*. Cambridge: Harvard University Press. A comprehensive review of Jane Goodall's research on chimpanzee behavior since the early 1960s, this is a well-written and superbly illustrated description of all aspects of chimpanzee behavior.

Fossey, D. 1983. *Gorillas in the Mist*. Boston: Houghton Mifflin. A popular and well-written account of the late Dian Fossey's researches on the behavior of the mountain gorilla. Deals specifically with the problem of human intervention and the likely extinction of the mountain gorilla.

Linden, E. 1981. *Apes, Men, and Language*. Middlesex, England: Penguin.

McGrew, W. C. 1992. *Chimpanzee Material Culture: Implications for Human Evolution*. Cambridge: Cambridge University Press. A recent review of the nature of chimpanzee tool use, with an emphasis on variation in behaviors.

Passingham, R. 1982. *The Human Primate*. San Francisco: W. H. Freeman. A detailed examination of the human species from both a biological and behavioral perspective.

Patterson, F., and E. Linden. 1981. *The Education of Koko*. New York: Holt, Rinehart and Winston.

Terrace, H. S. 1979. *Nim: A Chimpanzee Who Learned Sign Language*. New York: Alfred A. Knopf. This book, along with Linden (1981) and Patterson and Linden (1981), presents different views of the research into the abilities of apes to learn American Sign Language.

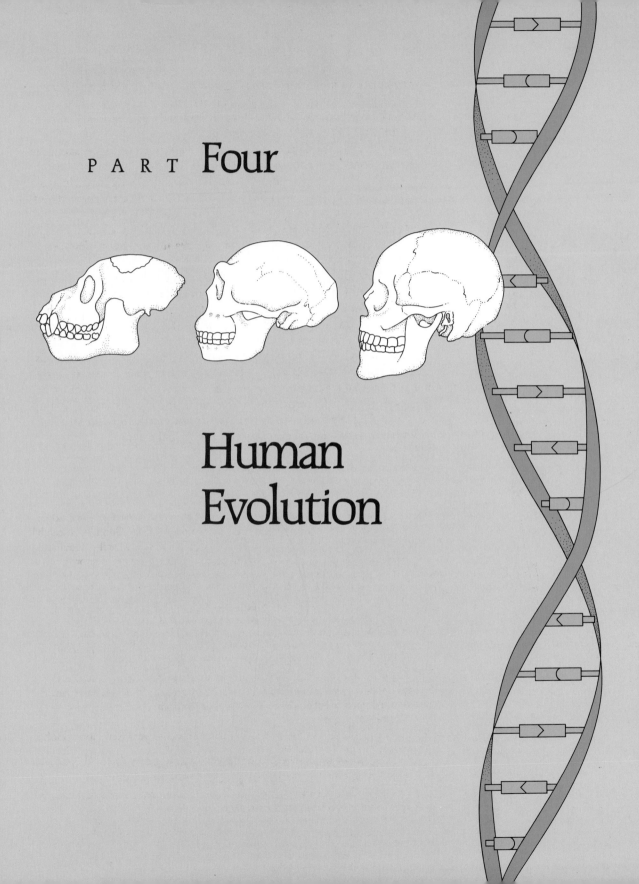

PART Four

Human
Evolution

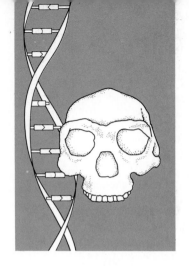

CHAPTER **10**

The Fossil Record

This section of the text (Chapters 10–13) focuses on human evolution, starting with the origin of life and continuing through the origin and evolution of primates to the fossil and archaeological record of human evolution. Previous chapters have dealt with theories of macroevolution (Chapter 4) and our similarities and differences with other mammals (Chapters 7–9). These pieces are pulled together over the next four chapters to provide an understanding of the major patterns (and controversies) in primate and human evolution.

The current chapter deals broadly with the fossil record, first discussing methods of analysis, primarily those used to date fossils. Without dates, sequences in evolution cannot be understood. The second part of this chapter provides background on the evolution of life *before* the first primates or humans appeared. Remember that evolution works on pre-existing variation. Much of what we are today is related to constraints established in even earlier times.

Methods of Analysis

How do we infer macroevolution from the fossil record? The first step in such an analysis is determining the ages of different fossil specimens. At the very least, we must know which fossils are older. Because evolution is

relative dating Estimating the older of two or more fossils or sites but not a specific date.

chronometric dating Estimating the specific date of fossils or sites.

B.P. Before Present (1950), the internationally accepted form of designating past dates.

stratigraphy A relative dating method based on the fact that older remains are found deeper in the earth because of cumulative buildup of the earth's surface over time.

faunal correlation Assigning an approximate age to sites based on the similarity of animal remains with other dated sites.

a process occurring over time, it is essential that we have a way of determining the time sequence of fossils. If we do not know which fossils are older, then we cannot make any inferences about the nature of evolutionary change.

Two basic classes of methods are used to date fossil remains. **Relative dating** determines which fossils are older but not their exact date. **Chronometric dating** determines an "exact" age (subject to some measurement of possible error and statistical fluctuation).

When we refer to exact dates in the fossil record, we conventionally use the term **B.P.**, which means "Before Present." "Present" has been set arbitrarily as the year 1950. Some people use the term B.C., meaning "Before Christ," but since not all peoples share the belief in Christ, the term B.P. is preferable and has been agreed on internationally. A date of 800,000 years B.P. would mean 800,000 years before the year 1950.

Relative Dating Methods

If we have two sites containing fossil material, relative dating methods can tell us which is older, but not by how much. It is preferable to have exact dates, but this is not possible for all sites. Relative dating methods can tell us the basic time sequence of fossil sites.

Stratigraphy. **Stratigraphy** makes use of the geological process of superposition, which refers to the cumulative buildup over time of the earth's surface. When an organism dies or a tool is discarded on the ground, it will ultimately be buried by dirt, sand, mud, and other materials. Winds move sand over the site, and water can deposit mud over the site. In most cases, the older a site is, the deeper it is. If you stand on the ground and dig down through the earth, the deeper you go, the older the deposits. If you find one fossil 3 ft deep and another 6 ft deep, the principle of stratification allows you to infer that the latter fossil is older. You still do not know how old the fossil is or the exact amount of time between the two fossils, but you have established which is older in geologic time.

In some situations stratigraphy is more difficult to use. An example is those sites where the earth's crust has folded and broken through the surface of the ground. In such cases, the usual stratigraphic order is disturbed. This does not invalidate the method, for careful geological analysis can reconstruct the patterns of disturbance and allow relative dates to be determined.

Other relative dating methods. A number of other methods provide relative dates for fossils. One such method is **faunal correlation,** which involves comparison of animal remains found at different sites to determine any similarity in time levels. Imagine that you have discovered a site that contains a certain species of fossil pig. Suppose that you know from previous studies that this species of pig has always been found between 1.5 and 2.0 million years B.P. Logically, this suggests that your newly discovered site is also between 1.5 and 2.0 million years old. The only other possibility would be that patterns of evolution occurred in the same way, but at different rates in different areas—an unlikely proposition. Plant pollens sometimes can be used in a similar manner.

There are chemical methods that also provide relative dates. Fluorine dating, for example, is a method that looks at the accumulation of fluorine in bones. When an organism dies, its bones lose nitrogen and gain fluorine. The rate at which this process occurs varies, so we cannot tell exactly how old a bone is by using the method. The method does, however, allow us to determine if two bones found at the same site are the same age. Other relative dating methods can be applied to human cultural remains. Much like faunal correlation, these methods assign a range of dates based on similar sites with known dates.

Chronometric Dating Methods

Chronometric dating methods provide an "exact" date, subject to statistical variation. Chronometric dating relies on constant physical and chemical processes in the universe. Many of these methods utilize the fact that the average rate of radioactive decay is constant for a given radioactive atom no matter what chemical reaction it might be involved in. If we know that a certain element decays into another at a constant rate, and if we can measure the relative proportions of the original and new elements in some object, then we can mathematically determine the age of the object. Radioactive decay is a probabilistic phenomenon, meaning that we know the average time for decay over many atoms. Such processes allow us to specify an average date within limits of statistical certainty.

Carbon-14 dating. Living organisms take in the element carbon throughout their lives. Ordinary carbon (C^{12}) is absorbed by plants that take in the gas carbon dioxide from the air, and by animals that eat the plants (or animals that eat the animals that ate the plants). Because of cosmic radiation, some of the carbon in the atmosphere is a radioactive isotope known as carbon-14 (C^{14}). An organism takes in both C^{14} and C^{12}, and the proportion of C^{12} to C^{14} is constant during its life, since the proportion is constant in the atmosphere. When an organism dies, no additional C^{14} is ingested, and the accumulated C^{14} begins to decay. The rate at which C^{14} decays is constant—it takes 5,730 years for one half of the C^{14} to decay into N^{14}. Carbon-14 is therefore said to have a **half-life** of 5,730 years. The half-life is the time it takes for half of a radioactive substance to decay.

Carbon-14 dating uses this constant rate of decay to determine the age of materials containing carbon. The process of radioactive decay of C^{14} results in the emission of radioactive particles that can be measured. We

half-life The average length of time it takes for half of a radioactive substance to decay into another form.

carbon-14 dating A chronometric dating method based on the half-life of carbon-14 that can be applied to organic remains such as charcoal over the past 50,000 years.

potassium-argon dating A chronometric dating method based on the half-life of radioactive potassium that can be used to date volcanic rock older than 100,000 years.

look at the rate of radioactive emissions for a sample and compare it to the rate of emissions expected in a living organism (a rate of 15 particles per minute per gram of carbon). For example, suppose a sample is analyzed and is found to emit 3.75 particles per minute per gram of carbon. Compared to a living organism, two half-lives have elapsed (one half-life results in 7.5 particles, and a second half-life results in half of this number = 7.5/2 = 3.75). Because the half-life of C^{14} is 5,730 years, the age of our sample is 5,730 × 2 = 11,460 years ago. If the sample was analyzed in 1993, its date would be 11,417 years B.P. (43 years have passed since 1950, so the date is 11,460 − 43 = 11,417).

In theory, any sample containing carbon can be used. In practice, however, bone tends not to be reliable in all cases because of the chemical changes during fossilization in which carbon is replaced. In most circumstances, charcoal is the best material to use. If we find that a fire occurred at a certain site, either naturally or human-made, we can use the charcoal for carbon-14 dating. Careful attention must be given to possible contaminants at any given site. Another problem is that there has been a certain amount of variability in the proportions of atmospheric carbon over the last few centuries because of industrial pollution. Techniques exist for partial controlling for this factor.

Carbon-14 dating is only useful for sites during the past 50,000 years at most (newer techniques may be able to extend this range, but they are still under development). Any older samples would contain too little C^{14} to be detected. Though carbon-14 dating is extremely valuable in studies of recent hominid evolution, it is not useful for dating the majority of earth's geological history.

Potassium-argon dating.   Another chronometric dating method that utilizes the process of radioactive decay is **potassium-argon dating.** Here, an isotope of potassium (K^{40}) decays into argon gas (Ar^{40}) with a half-life of approximately 1.31 billion years. This rate of radioactive decay means that this method is best used on samples older than 100,000 years (Figure 10.1).

Potassium-argon dating requires rocks that did not possess any argon gas to begin with. The best material for this method is volcanic rock, for the heat generated by volcanic eruptions removes any initial argon gas. Thus, we are sure that any argon gas we find in a sample of volcanic rock is the result of radioactive decay. By looking at the proportions of K^{40} and Ar^{40}, we can determine the number of elapsed half-lives and therefore the age of the volcanic rock (within probabilistic limits).

Though we cannot date a fossil directly with this method, we can assign a date based on the relationship of a fossil find to different levels of volcanic ash. If we find a fossil halfway between two layers of volcanic rock with dates of 4.5 million years B.P. and 4.6 million years B.P., we can then assign the fossil an age of roughly 4.55 million years B.P. Potassium-argon dating is best applied in areas with frequent volcanic eruptions. Fortunately, much of hominid evolution in East Africa took place under such conditions, allowing us to date many fossil sites.

Paleomagnetic reversal. Another method of dating involves paleomagnetism. When we use a compass to find direction, we rely on the fact that the needle points north. During many times in the past, this was not the case. The magnetic pole has at times shifted to the southern end of the planet. These **paleomagnetic reversals** provide a means by which to date certain rocks. When rocks initially form, they retain the magnetic orientation at the time they came into being—either "normal" (north) or "reversed" (south). By using other dating methods, such as potassium-argon, a chart of the reversals over the last eight million years has been developed. Because these reversals last for different amounts of time, they form a varying pattern. A section of rock can then be compared to the chart to determine the age.

Other chronometric dating methods. Many other types of chronometric dating methods can be used in certain circumstances. Some utilize radioactive decay and some use other constant effects for determining age. Archaeologists working in the relatively recent past (within the last 10,000

paleomagnetic reversal
Dating sites based on the fact that the earth's magnetic pole has shifted back and forth from the north to the south in the past at irregular intervals.

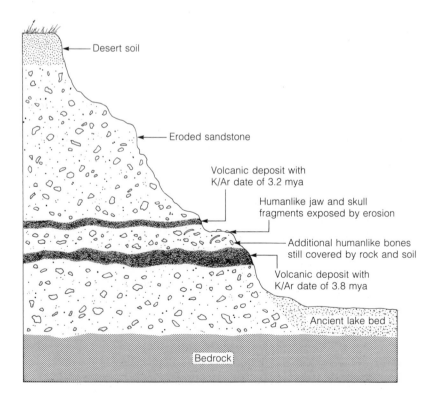

Figure 10.1

Hypothetical example of the use of potassium-argon dating. Hominid remains are found between two layers of volcanic ash, one dating to 3.8 million years B.P. and the other dating to 3.2 million years B.P. The hominid can therefore be dated at between 3.2 and 3.8 million years B.P. (From *Human Antiquity: An Introduction to Physical Anthropology and Archaeology,* 2d ed., by Kenneth Feder and Michael Park, Fig. 7.7. Copyright © 1993 by Mayfield Publishing Company)

Desert soil

Eroded sandstone

Volcanic deposit with K/Ar date of 3.2 mya

Humanlike jaw and skull fragments exposed by erosion

Additional humanlike bones still covered by rock and soil

Volcanic deposit with K/Ar date of 3.8 mya

Ancient lake bed

Bedrock

dendrochronology A chronometric dating method based on the fact that trees in dry climates tend to accumulate one growth ring per year.

fission-track dating A chronometric dating method based on the number of tracks made across volcanic rock as uranium decays into lead.

thermoluminescence A chronometric dating method based on the capacity of certain heated objects to accumulate trapped electrons over time, that allows the date when the object was initially heated to be determined.

electron spin resonance A chronometric dating method that estimates dates from observation of radioactive atoms trapped in calcite crystals present in a number of materials, such as bones and shells.

years) often use a method known as **dendrochronology,** or tree ring counting (Figure 10.2). We know that a tree will accumulate a new ring for every period of growth. The width of each ring depends on available moisture and other factors during that specific period. In dry areas there is usually only one growth period in a year. By looking at the width of tree rings, archaeologists have constructed a master chart of tree ring changes. Any new sample, such as a log from a prehistoric dwelling, can be compared to this chart to determine its age.

In addition to radioactive decay, other physical constants allow an estimate of age to be assigned to a sample. **Fission-track dating** relies on the fact that when uranium decays into lead in volcanic glass (obsidian), it leaves small "tracks" across the surface of the glass. We can count the number of tracks and determine the age of the obsidian from the fact that these tracks occur at a constant rate.

Thermoluminescence is a dating method that relies on the fact that certain heated objects accumulate trapped electrons over time, thus allowing us to determine, in some cases, when the object was initially heated. This method has been applied to pottery, bronze, and burned flints. Thermoluminescence can be used to date objects as far back as one million years.

Electron spin resonance is a fairly new method that provides an estimate of dating from observation of radioactive atoms trapped in calcite crystals present in a number of materials, such as bones and shells. This method is also useful for dating sites back to roughly one million years.

Reconstructing the Past

In addition to dating fossil and archaeological sites, we also need to consider other sources of evidence when putting together a sequence of evolutionary events, and for interpreting them.

Taphonomy. When describing the behavior of early hominids, or other organisms, we rely on a wide variety of data to reconstruct their environment and to provide information on population size, diet, presence or absence of predators, and other ecological aspects. Quite often, we rely on what else is found at a given site other than the fossil. For example, the presence of animal bones, particularly those that are fractured, might indicate hunting. The distribution of animal bones might also give us a clue regarding behavior. The types of animal bones found at human hunting sites are different from those found at carnivore sites. A major problem is figuring out how animal bones and other objects got there and what happened to them. Imagine finding the leg bone of a fossil antelope and the leg bone of a fossil hominid at the same site. How did these bones wind up in the same place? Did the hominid hunt and kill the antelope? Did a predator hunt and kill both the antelope and the hominid? Did both

Figure 10.2

Tree rings can be dated by the method of dendrochronology (see text). (Courtesy of Kenneth Feder and Michael Park, Central Connecticut State University)

bones wash down a river and land at the same place even though they might have originally been separate in time and space?

Some of these questions can be answered by methods developed within the field of **taphonomy,** the study of what happens to plants and animals after they die. This field provides us with valuable information about which bones are more likely to fossilize, which bones are more likely to wash away, the distribution of bones left over by a predator, the likely route of pollen dispersal in the air, and many other similar topics. Taphonomic studies also provide us with ways of finding out whether objects or fossils have been disturbed or whether they have stayed where they were first deposited. Such studies can also help us distinguish between human and natural actions. A fractured leg bone of a deer might result from normal wear and tear on a fossil, or might reflect the action of a prehistoric hunter. By understanding what happens to fossils in general, we are in a better position to infer what happened to *specific* fossils.

Paleoecology. When reconstructing the past, we need to know more than just what early organisms looked like. We also need to know about the environment in which they lived. What did they eat? Were they predators, or prey? What types of vegetation were available? Where were water sources? These questions, and many others, deal with **paleoecology,** the study of ancient environments.

One example of the many methods used in reconstructing ancient environments is **palynology,** the study of fossil pollen. By looking at the types of pollen found at a given site, experts can identify the specific types of plants that existed at that time. They can then make inferences about yearly and seasonal changes in temperature and rainfall based on the relative proportion of plant species. Further information on vegetation can be extracted from analysis of fossil teeth. Microscopic analysis of scratch patterns on teeth can tell us whether an organism relied more heavily on leaves, fruits, or meat. Chemical analysis of teeth can also tell us something about diet. For example, the ratio of the element strontium to the element calcium can reveal whether an organism primarily ate plants or meat. Strontium ratios are higher in plant eaters.

Additional examples of the numerous methods for investigating past environments will be given in the following chapters, where applicable.

Evolutionary trees. Assuming we have good dates for a sample of fossils and we know as much as possible about their biology and environment, what do we do next? One task of evolutionary biology is determining the **phylogeny,** or "family tree," of a group of organisms. How do we know which organisms are related to one another? Which species became extinct and which evolved into other species?

As noted earlier, assignment of fossil specimens into species groups is difficult because we have no direct evidence on which forms were capable of interbreeding. Instead, we have to rely on inferences made from the

taphonomy The study of what happens to plants and animals after they die.

paleoecology The study of ancient environments.

palynology The study of fossil pollen.

phylogeny A family tree or figure showing the evolutionary relationships among species.

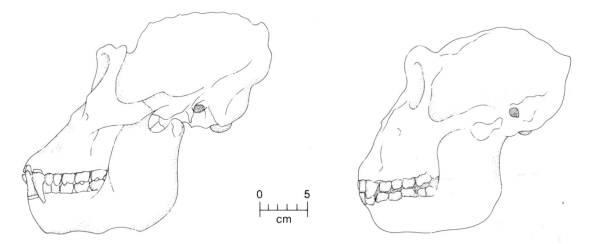

0 | | | | | 5
cm

Figure 10.3

Sexual dimorphism in gorilla skulls. The skull of a male gorilla (*left*) is larger than that of the female gorilla (*right*) and also shows heavy crests of bones on top of the skull and at the rear of the skull for muscle attachment. Such sexual differences must be taken into account in analyzing fossil remains and assigning such remains to paleospecies.

physical appearance, or morphology, of the fossils. Briefly, we examine physical structure and compare it with other fossils and living organisms, keeping in mind the ranges of variation. When we find two specimens that exceed the normal range of variation for similar organisms, we can make a stronger case for assigning the two specimens into different species.

This approach has problems. Individuals within a species can be mistakenly assigned to different species if care is not taken to consider range of variation. For example, the skulls of adult male and female gorillas are quite different in size and other features because of the large amount of sexual dimorphism in this species (Figure 10.3). When we encounter such differences among fossil specimens, we must rely on a knowledge of variation in similar living organisms to determine whether sexual dimorphism is likely to be the cause.

Species identification is further complicated by philosophical differences among scientists. Some feel that the range of variation within species is often rather large and suggest that it is simpler to assign fossils to species already known and described rather than create new categories. A scientist with this view is often called a "lumper" because of the preference for lumping new fossils in preexisting categories. Others take a different approach, seeing the evolutionary record as one of frequent speciation. In this case, they anticipate numerous species and tend to call any new fossil that is somewhat different a new species. Scientists with this view are often referred to as "splitters." Identification of species is also complicated by scientists' view as to whether species should be used as convenient labels or whether species should represent new evolutionary lines. Examples of these different views, and their effect on interpretation, will be discussed in Chapters 12 and 13.

Once species have been identified, evolutionary relationships can be determined from a comparison of primitive and derived homologous traits. As discussed in Chapter 7, most scholars focus on shared derived traits to establish a close evolutionary relationship between two species, but given the problems posed by continuous variation as well as the possibility of parallel evolution, this approach is not always clear-cut.

Evolution before the Primates

Looking at the early beginnings of life also helps us realize the short length of time humans have been in existence. Many anthropologists estimate that our own species, *Homo sapiens*, is between 200,000 and 400,000 years old. The genus *Homo* is over 2 million years old. Hominids are at least 4 million years old. We think of these dates as representing immense periods of time because of our own relatively short lifetimes. In geologic time, however, hominids have only been around a brief instant. Astronomers estimate the age of our universe to be roughly 15 billion years old. Geological evidence shows the earth to be roughly 4.6 billion years old. Compared to these numbers, 4 million years is a short time.

Perspectives on Geologic Time

We lose sight of the immense age of the universe and earth because we are not used to dealing with such large numbers. To many people, the difference between a million and a billion does not seem great, since both numbers are so extremely large. The astronomer Carl Sagan (1977) has used an analogy he calls the "Cosmic Calendar" to help put these dates into perspective. Imagine the entire history of the universe, from its beginning to the present, as taking a single year. That is, the universe came into being at midnight on January 1 of the year, and the present time is midnight on January 1 a year later. Our own galaxy, the Milky Way, comes into being on May 1, the solar system on September 9, and the earth on September 14. Life on earth begins approximately on September 25, and the oldest known fossils (algae) on October 9. It is not until November 12 that photosynthetic plants come into being. Eukaryotes (cells with nuclei) begin on November 15. Almost 11 complete months pass and nothing resembling a human being has yet evolved!

By December 1, a significant oxygen atmosphere has developed on earth. By December 17, the invertebrates have come into being. The first fish and vertebrates appear on December 19, and colonization of land by early insects and amphibians takes place on December 22. Reptiles appear on the 23rd, dinosaurs on the 24th, and the first mammals on the 25th. By December 28, the dinosaurs have become extinct, and the first primates appear on the next day. It is not until the final day of the year, December 31, that apes and humans appear!

The first humans appear at 10:30 P.M. on the final day. Fire is used by 11:00 P.M., and it is not until 11:59:20 that agriculture is invented. The

era The major subdivision of geologic time.

period Subdivision of a geologic era.

epoch Subdivision of a geologic period.

Precambrian The time in earth's history preceding the first major appearance of life.

Figure 10.4

Carl Sagan's "Cosmic Calendar." The history of the universe is compressed into a single year, with the origin of the universe happening on January 1, and the present day occurring at midnight on the following January 1. See the text for additional dates.
(*Source:* Sagan [1977])

Roman Empire occurs around 11:59:56. The European Renaissance takes place at one second before midnight. Everything that has occurred since then takes place in the final second (Figure 10.4).

The first section of this chapter will examine events since the beginning of life on earth. Most of this chapter focuses on the last 65 million years, concentrating on the origin and evolution of primates through the appearance of apes—that is, the last three days of the Cosmic Calendar.

The Origin of Life

Geologists and paleontologists divide the history of the earth into five geological **eras,** known as the Archean, Proterozoic, Paleozoic, Mesozoic, and Cenozoic. Each era is broken down into different geologic **periods,** each of which is further broken down into **epochs.** Table 10.1 presents a list of the eras and periods and the major evolutionary events that occurred during each.

The fossil record shows that the initial radiation of many life forms took place during the Cambrian period of the Paleozoic era. We often refer to the time before this as the **Precambrian,** which includes the Archean and Proterozoic eras. The Precambrian takes up most of the 4.6 billion years of the earth's existence. It dates from the beginning of the planet until 550 million years B.P. During this time, life existed in the form of algae and some early invertebrates. Our oldest fossils preserve some of these organisms, but we lack direct fossil evidence for the first signs of life. We must rely on a knowledge of the early conditions of the planet and combine these observations with laboratory evidence suggesting possible origins of life.

Such evidence indicates that life first began through a process of chemical evolution. Laboratory experiments in the 1950s demonstrated

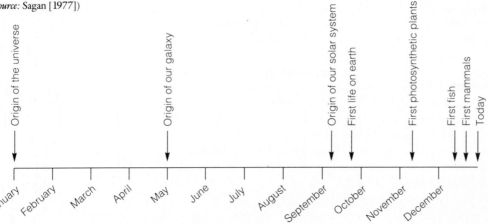

that amino acids could be produced by discharging electrical energy into a mixture of chemicals representing the atmosphere of the ancient earth. Other experiments have produced the same results using somewhat different combinations of gases and forms of energy. Further experiments have shown that certain combinations of chemical molecules, called microspheres, will form. These look and act much like simple cells (Reader 1986). Though they are not life, the laboratory creations show us how a process of chemical evolution could have started. Some scientists believe that a process of chemical selection took place in which certain chemical forms and reactions might have been favored. These models rely on chemical analogies to variation and natural selection in what we might term a "prebiotic" world (Stebbins 1982). For example, a double helix of comple-

TABLE 10.1
Geological Eras and Periods

Era	Period	Millions of years B.P.	Major evolutionary events
Archean		2,500–4,550	The origin of life
Proterozoic		550–2,500	Early invertebrates
Paleozoic	Cambrian	500–550	"Explosion" of life; marine invertebrates
	Ordovician	440–500	Early vertebrates, including jawless fishes; trilobites and many other invertebrates
	Silurian	410–440	First fish with jaws; land plants
	Devonian	360–410	Many fishes; first amphibians; first forests
	Carboniferous	290–360	Radiation of amphibians; first reptiles and insects
	Permian	250–290	Radiation of reptiles; mammallike reptiles
Mesozoic	Triassic	210–250	First dinosaurs; egg-laying mammals
	Jurassic	140–210	Dinosaurs dominate; first birdlike reptiles
	Cretaceous	65–140	Extinction of dinosaurs; first birds and placental mammals
Cenozoic	Tertiary	1.8–65	Origin and evolution of primates; origin of hominids
	Quaternary	0–1.8	Evolution of the genus *Homo*

Note: The Archean and Proterozoic eras are often collectively referred to as the Precambrian eon. *Source for dates:* Schopf (1992).

Paleozoic era The third geologic era, dating roughly between 250 and 550 million years B.P., when the first vertebrates appeared.

mentary bases would provide a stable form capable of surviving rapid changes in the environment, such as alternating cycles of hot and cold. If two strands then separated, the existing chemical bonds might then lead to replication of the original pair. In other words, this would be a self-replicating molecule (Reader 1986).

One objection to models of chemical evolution raises the question of how various chemical reactions could take place in the earth's oceans without their being diluted. Such reactions require close contact between different chemicals, and dilution in water would seem to prevent this. Dickerson (1978) notes several possibilities, including concentration of chemicals following evaporation in a low tidal area and concentration of chemicals on the surface of clay.

Of course, laboratory experiments can only show what might have happened and which chemical reactions are possible, and not what actually did occur. Nonetheless, there is growing evidence that under many environmental conditions normal chemical reactions could lead to the beginnings of life. Creationists like to point out the improbability of such events occurring. Such critics make two errors. First of all, a low probability does not rule out an event when we take into consideration the immense time scale involved. The second error is that such computations deal with the probability of a *specific* set of nucleic acid sequences, whereas many other sequences might also be viable (Futuyma 1983). This is analogous to taking a pack of cards and dealing out a five-card poker hand. Imagine your opponent has a hand containing two aces. The chance of your getting a royal flush (ace, king, queen, jack, and ten, all of the same suit) is low, but the probability of getting a winning hand of *some* sort is much higher.

Though we have no fossil evidence of these very first beginning steps, the evidence we do have is quite old. Fossilized microscopic cells have been found dating back to 3.3 to 3.5 billion years, along with evidence for the origin of photosynthesis (Schopf and Packer 1987). Fossils that indicate cell division have been found in deposits dating back to 850 million years ago, and evidence for multicelled organisms goes back to at least 750 million years ago (Reader 1986).

A complete discussion of the hypotheses and evidence for Precambrian evolution is beyond the scope of this book. The significant events of the Precambrian are the origin of life, the development of a significant oxygen atmosphere, the development of photosynthesis, and the beginnings of multicelled life. The fossil evidence provides us with some of the information about these early stages, and laboratory experiments help us to understand probable causes.

The Paleozoic Era

The **Paleozoic era** lasted from 250 million to 550 million years B.P. The first geological period of the Paleozoic era is the Cambrian, which was a time of rapid evolution of many life forms. In fact, the term *Cambrian explosion* is often used to describe the beginning of this period.

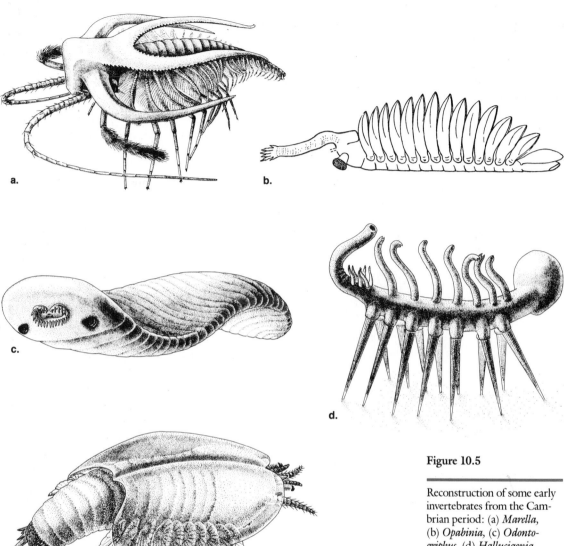

a.

b.

c.

d.

e.

Figure 10.5

Reconstruction of some early
invertebrates from the Cambrian period: (a) *Marella*,
(b) *Opabinia*, (c) *Odonto-
griphus*, (d) *Hallucigenia*,
(e) *Canadaspis*. Recent studies
of *Hallucigenia* have suggested
an alternative reconstruction.
(a, c, d, e: The illustrations by
Marianne Collins from *Wonderful
Life*, The Burgess Shale and the
Nature of History, by Stephen Jay
Gould, are reproduced by
permission of W. W. Norton &
Company, Inc. Copyright © 1989
by Stephen Jay Gould; b:
reprinted with permission from
Cambridge University Press)

Creationists like to suggest that the rapid appearance of life forms is proof
of an instantaneous creation. As you read earlier, this is not correct. Life
forms existed before the Cambrian period and we have fossil evidence of
them. The "explosion" actually took place over millions of years (Gould
1977a).

Early life forms included organisms similar to modern sponges and
jellyfish, and a wide variety of marine invertebrates that have no living
counterpart (Figure 10.5). From a human perspective, the most interesting of the Paleozoic organisms are the first vertebrates—the jawless fishes.

These creatures possessed the internal segmented vertebral column common to all vertebrates but lacked jaws and teeth. The jawless fishes came in many forms and were quite successful from 350 to 410 million years ago. Today only two specialized descendants of this once widespread group survive—the hagfish and the lamprey.

Some of these jawless fishes developed armor plating around their heads from a hard material known as dentin. The first teeth were nothing more than spikes of this material that folded inward. This new feature provided a powerful adaptation for those that had it because it allowed them to eat a greater variety of food. Many scientists believe that the development of teeth meant that the jawed fishes ate the jawless fishes (Reader 1986). Later the teeth developed further and jaws evolved.

If we trace the embryological development of a bird or mammal, we can see how the bones and blood vessels that once served the gill arches of fish have been elaborated to form structures that do other things in higher vertebrates. The first gill arch of jawless fish forms the jaws of the rest of the vertebrates. The bones of mammalian ears come from the second gill arch. Evolution often does not build structures from scratch but rather modifies and revises what already exists.

The next major evolutionary step in the history of life was the invasion of land by early amphibians. Creationists fault the fossil record for not showing intermediate forms. A typical question is: What is intermediate between a creature that lives in the water and one that lives on land? The answer is simple. Amphibians are such an intermediate form for which we have fossil evidence, and many amphibian species are still alive today.

We are used to thinking that fish have gills that allow oxygen to be absorbed from water, and land animals have lungs that allow oxygen to be absorbed from the air. Actually, many fishes, such as the lungfish, have lunglike structures. If you observe tropical fish, you will soon learn that some must periodically swim to the surface of the water to get air. Some examples are the gourami and the Siamese fighting fish.

Looking at tropical fish in a store also can give you clues about the origin of movement on land, another important feature of land colonization. Many fish, such as catfish, are bottom dwellers. They rest on the bottom of the fish tank on strongly developed fins. In the Paleozoic era a group of fish called lobe-fins evolved this ability. Some of these adaptations survive in a fish commonly called the "walking catfish," which often moves on land to get from one stream to another, obtaining oxygen from the air as well.

The movement of lobe-fins is not the most efficient form of locomotion on dry land, but this ability was crucial in the changing environment of the Paleozoic. The lobe-fins could survive when lakes and streams dried up by crawling from pond to pond. An additional bonus of land exploration for these fish was the great availability of new plants that had evolved. Over time these adaptations were selected for, and ultimately amphibians evolved. The fossil evidence shows that these changes took place during the Devonian period of the Paleozoic.

Amphibians represent a transitional form of vertebrate that lives both in water and on land. The early amphibians were successful and many of these forms evolved into modern amphibians. Some early amphibians became highly successful on the land and evolved into early reptiles during the Carboniferous period. This was facilitated by the development of eggs with leathery shells that did not dry out, thus freeing reproduction from the need for a watery environment. The Permian period witnessed an adaptive radiation of reptiles. Reptiles were the dominant form of animal life on the land surface of the planet for more than the next 200 million years.

Mammals and birds eventually evolved from the reptiles. The evolution of mammals from reptiles suggests that an intermediate form of animal intervened. To many, an intermediate form implies some sort of strange-looking creature with a mixture of *modern* reptilian and mammalian features. This is an incorrect view of evolution. Modern reptiles and mammals represent millions of years of evolution from a common ancestor. The first reptiles did not look exactly like modern-day reptiles. In fact, some of the earliest primitive reptiles included a group referred to as the **therapsids,** or mammallike reptiles. The classification of creatures into categories such as mammals or reptiles is a problem when we try to apply these categories to the fossil record. Our definitions of these groups are based on observations of modern-day forms representing millions of years of separate evolution. The farther and farther we go back in time, the more these groups blur together, and the harder it is to absolutely assign a specific form to one category or the other.

The therapsids are classified as reptiles because they have more features that we would call reptilian. They also possessed certain mammalian features, however, such as differentiated teeth. We therefore call them, for lack of a better term, mammallike reptiles. Therapsids underwent an adaptive radiation during the Permian period of the Paleozoic era, with a wide variety of shapes and sizes. If you have ever played with toy dinosaurs as a child, you will recognize a form known as *Dimetrodon* (Figure 10.6), which is not a dinosaur but an ancestor of the mammallike reptiles.

therapsid An early group of reptiles also known as the mammallike reptiles. Therapsids were the ancestors of later mammals.

Figure 10.6

Dimetrodon, a form of reptile ancestral to mammallike reptiles.

Mesozoic era The fourth geologic era, dating roughly between 65 and 250 million years B.P., when the first mammals and birds appeared.

The dental adaptations of the therapsids were well suited to life on land, allowing them to forage plants effectively. Although this group was highly successful, it ultimately declined following an adaptive radiation of what we might term "true reptiles" during the Mesozoic. Although it was once thought that all of the therapsids became extinct following the emergence of "true reptiles," recent fossil evidence shows that some of the mammallike reptiles survived at least until 60 million years ago (Fox et al. 1992).

The Mesozoic Era

The **Mesozoic era,** lasting from 65 million to 250 million years B.P., is often called the "Age of Reptiles" because it was the time when reptiles became the dominant form of life on the earth's surface. One of the most successful groups of reptiles were the dinosaurs (Figure 10.7). The major characteristic of the dinosaurs was the modification of the leg and pelvic structures. Many dinosaurs were bipedal, and some appear to have been extremely quick movers and efficient walkers and runners (Wilford 1985). The therapsids, on the other hand, did not change much beyond the earliest land vertebrates except for modifications in their teeth. Therapsids were not fast movers and had few defensive or offensive abilities. In the Permian period they did not need such adaptations. The world lay open for them to colonize.

Unfortunately for the therapsids, the ancestors of the dinosaurs developed quicker and more efficient locomotion as well as powerful hands and teeth to capture prey. Ultimately, the dinosaurs emerged as the dominant animal life on land and the therapsids declined in numbers. Some of the therapsids, however, evolved into what we call "true mammals."

During the Triassic period the monotremes, or egg-laying mammals, evolved. Some, such as the platypus, have survived until the present day. The first placental mammals evolved during the Jurassic period, which was the heyday of the dinosaurs. Birdlike reptiles also evolved during this time period. At the end of the Cretaceous period the dinosaurs became extinct, and mammals became the dominant animal life.

The paragraph you have just finished reading is a rough summary of many complex events taking place over a long time. It is widely thought that the emergence of mammals led to the disappearance of the dinosaurs. After all, mammals have more efficient systems of reproduction, temperature regulation, and an emphasis on social learning, among other adaptations. The story is not that simple. There is growing evidence that at least some of the dinosaurs possessed a measure of temperature regulation and had a complex form of social organization (Wilford 1985, Bakker 1986). Also, mammals and dinosaurs coexisted for tens of millions of years. Regardless of the adaptations of the earliest mammals, they were limited in their expansion by the success of the dinosaurs. The mammals were confined to a few small environmental niches. Most were small and probably nocturnal, existing on insects and living in the trees. Only when the dino-

Figure 10.7

Two well-known dinosaurs:
Triceratops (*top*) and
Tyrannosaurus (*bottom*).

saurs became extinct and flowering plants evolved did the mammals undergo an adaptive radiation. Until that time they remained in the shadow of the dinosaurs. Evolution requires opportunities.

Why did the dinosaurs (and many other organisms) become extinct? Some of the more fanciful suggestions include excessive constipation because of changes in plant life. Most theories of dinosaur extinction rely on environmental change, such as the cooling of the earth. If the temperature dropped, then the warm-blooded mammals would seem to be better adapted than the cold-blooded reptiles. A problem with this idea is that, as noted earlier, there is evidence that at least some of the dinosaurs were warm-blooded. Recent explanations of dinosaur extinction have relied on the idea that an asteroid or comet hit the earth with tremendous force, kicking up clouds of dust and blocking the sun. Temperatures dropped and many plant forms became extinct. As plants died, so did the plant eaters and those who ate the plant eaters. In other words, the entire ecology

Cenozoic era The fifth, and most recent, geologic era, dating roughly to the last 65 million years, when the first primates appeared during the Cenozoic era.

of the planet was altered. There is growing geologic evidence for such a catastrophic event (e.g., Sheehan et al. 1991), although many researchers suggest other factors may have also played a part.

In any case, the fossil record shows clearly that dinosaurs died out and mammals took their place during the last of the Cretaceous period. New opportunities opened up for the mammals, and they began an adaptive radiation, filling vacant environmental niches. The last 65 million years of the earth's history is the **Cenozoic era,** often called the "Age of Mammals." Some mammals ultimately evolved to exploit the grasslands. Others developed adaptations that allowed them to become sea creatures, such as the whale and dolphin. The important event for our purposes was the continued adaptation to life in the trees. The origin and evolution of the primates is discussed in the next chapter.

SUMMARY

A variety of methods exist for reconstructing past environments and interpreting the fossil record. Dating methods are particularly important, since they allow fossils to be placed in a sequence through time, from which evolutionary trends can be inferred. Collectively, the methods of paleontology allow us to understand the history of life.

Life on earth began following a period of chemical evolution. The earliest life forms evolved in ancient oceans. The first vertebrates were the jawless fishes, which evolved into fish with jaws. One group of jawed fishes, the lobe-fins, were the ancestors of all later land vertebrates. After the amphibians conquered the land, an adaptive radiation of reptiles fully adapted to land conditions began. One of the first sort of reptiles were the therapsids, or mammallike reptiles. These forms possessed certain dental traits that allowed them to exploit new types of food. The later adaptive radiation of the dinosaurs ultimately led to the extinction of the therapsids. Before they disappeared, however, some therapsids evolved into the first true mammals. For millions of years, the dinosaurs were the dominant land animals and the mammals existed in the fringe environmental niche of arboreal nocturnal life. When the dinosaurs disappeared during the mass extinction at the end of the Mesozoic era, the mammals had the opportunity to expand into newly available niches.

Supplemental Readings

Lewin, R. 1982. *Thread of Life: The Smithsonian Looks at Evolution*. New York: W. W. Norton.

Reader, J. 1986. *The Rise of Life: The First 3.5 Billion Years*. New York: Alfred A. Knopf. Well-written, superbly illustrated introductions to evolution from the origin of life to the present.

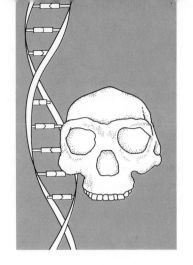

CHAPTER **11**

The Origin and Evolution of the Primates

As discussed in the previous chapter, the dinosaurs became extinct at the end of the Mesozoic era 65 million years ago. Their demise opened up numerous opportunities for other animals, particularly the mammals, to expand into new environments. This adaptive radiation of mammals included the ancestors of modern-day primates.

Modern primates did not appear instantaneously 65 million years ago. There were no monkeys, apes, or humans at that time. Rather, a group of mammals began adapting to life in the trees. This change provided a base for further evolution, leading ultimately to modern-day primates. It is important to realize that the definitions of modern forms discussed in Chapters 8 and 9 do not always apply to early fossil forms. Any classification based on *modern* characteristics reflects many millions of years of evolution. The further back in time we go, the harder it is to distinguish between different forms of primates.

Also, primate and primatelike forms in the past exhibited an amazing diversity. In the past few decades, we have realized it is not a simple matter to draw family trees connecting earlier forms with modern forms. We now know there were many species of prosimians, monkeys, and apes that have no living counterpart.

Early Primate Evolution

Primates evolved during the Cenozoic era, whose epochs are listed in Table 11.1. Each epoch is associated with a major event in primate

Paleocene epoch The first epoch of the Cenozoic era, dating roughly between 55 and 65 million years B.P., when the primatelike mammals appeared.

evolution. Primate evolution should not be thought of as a simple evolutionary "tree" with a few branches. A better analogy would be a series of "bushes" with many different branches at each stage of primate evolution. One or more adaptive radiations of primate forms occurred during each epoch. Many of the new forms became extinct, some evolved to become present-day representatives, and some evolved into the next phase of primate evolution.

Overview of Early Primate Evolution

During the Paleocene epoch an adaptive radiation of primatelike mammals led to the origin of what we would call "true primates." The Paleocene primatelike mammals show evidence of the initial adaptation to life in the trees. Many of these forms died out, but some evolved into primitive prosimians, which were fully adapted to living in the trees. These early prosimians underwent an adaptive radiation during the Eocene epoch. Some of the descendants of this adaptive radiation survive as the modern-day prosimians. Many other prosimian species became extinct. Some of these early prosimians evolved into early anthropoids. A subsequent adaptive radiation of anthropoids during the Oligocene epoch led to separate groups of New World monkeys, Old World monkeys, and apes.

The Paleocene Epoch

The **Paleocene epoch** lasted from 55 to 65 million years B.P. The term *Paleocene* derives from the Greek word meaning "old." A major event

TABLE 11.1
Epochs of the Cenozoic

Epoch	Millions of years B.P.	Major events in primate evolution
Paleocene	55–65	Primatelike mammals
Eocene	38–55	First primates (primitive prosimians); first anthropoids?
Oligocene	22–38	Anthropoid evolution
Miocene	5–22	Radiation of early apes
Pliocene	1.8–5	First hominids and first members of the genus *Homo*
Pleistocene	0.01–1.8	Evolution of the genus *Homo* (*Homo erectus* and *Homo sapiens*)
Holocene	0–0.01	Humans develop agriculture and industry, explore outer space

Source for dates: Conroy (1990).

during the Paleocene was the origin of primates. At the end of the Mesozoic era there were a number of mammals called **insectivores** that were arboreal, were nocturnal, and ate insects. A modern-day representative of this group is the tree shrew (Figure 11.1), that illustrates the probable morphology of the ancestor of primates. Of all living mammals, the insectivores are most similar to the primates, suggesting that they are ancestral to primates. Paleoanthropologists look at the variation in this early group to try to identify forms that show the transition to the order Primates.

One possible early ancestor, known as *Purgatorius,* has been recovered from Cretaceous and Paleocene deposits in Montana. Because the finds consist of only a few teeth, we cannot definitely state that these forms were the ancestor of later primates. The teeth are interesting, however, because of the cusp pattern of the molar teeth. Analysis of cusp patterns can help us identify relationships between groups and also provide information regarding diet. Insectivores typically have rather pointed cusps on their molars. Primates usually have more rounded and bulbous cusps that are effective in eating leaves and fruit. The teeth of the Montana finds have the primate cusp pattern, which suggests an early change in diet and some relationship with later primates.

Continental drift and primate evolution. Most of the fossil evidence on primate origins comes from Paleocene deposits in North America and Europe of a group of insectivores known as the primatelike mammals. This widespread distribution may seem strange, given the fact that North America and Europe are now separated by the Atlantic Ocean. This was not, however, their configuration during the Paleocene. The continents continually move about on large crusted plates on top of a partially molten layer of the earth's mantle—a process known as **continental drift.** This process continues today: North America is slowly drifting away from

insectivore An order of mammals adapted to insect eating.

continental drift The movement of continental land masses on top of a partially molten layer of the earth's mantle that has altered the relative location of the continents over time.

Figure 11.1

A tree shrew, an insectivore similar in certain respects to primates.   (© Zoological Society of San Diego)

postorbital bar The bony ring that separates the eye orbit from the back of the skull in primates.

mosaic evolution The concept that major evolutionary changes tend to take place in stages, not all at once.

Europe, toward Asia. The expansion of the South Atlantic has even been measured from satellites. The placement of the different continents at various times in the past is shown in Figure 11.2.

An understanding of past continental drift is crucial in interpreting the fossil evidence for primate evolution. As continents move, their environments change. When continents separate, populations become isolated; when the continents join, there is an opportunity for large-scale migrations of populations. Roughly 230 million years ago, all the continents were joined together as one large land mass. By 180 million years B.P., this large mass had split in two: one containing North America, Europe, and Asia, and the other containing South America, Africa, Australia, and Antarctica. By the time of the primatelike mammals, South America had split off from Africa, but North America and Europe were still joined. Thus, it is no surprise to find fossils of primatelike mammals on both continents—they represent part of the group's range on a single land mass.

The primatelike mammals. The primatelike mammals were small creatures, usually no larger than a cat and often smaller. They were quadrupedal (four-footed) mammals whose arms and legs were well adapted for climbing. Within this general group there was considerable diversity. Remains have been assigned to 27 different genera (Conroy 1990). Most of this extensive variation was in body size and dental specializations. Some of the primatelike mammals had large incisors for heavy gnawing, others had teeth better adapted for slicing, and still others had teeth adapted for eating nectar and insects. Such variation is expected from an adaptive radiation. These small insectivores had some ability to climb and thus were able to exploit many different types of food.

In spite of their arboreal adaptations, these creatures are not considered true primates. A picture of the skull of one of these creatures (Figure 11.3) shows why. The front teeth are far apart from the rest of the teeth, a feature not found in primates. The eyes are located more toward the sides of the skull, unlike the forward-facing eyes of primates. In addition, the primatelike mammals lack a **postorbital bar,** a bony ring separating the orbit of the eye from the back of the skull. Primates have a postorbital bar. Also, the hands and feet of these animals did not have the grasping ability of primates, and they had claws instead of nails.

If these Paleocene forms are not primates, then how can we say they are related to primates? You should not expect to examine the fossil record and see some point at which modern-day primate structure immediately appears. Evolution is **mosaic,** meaning that not all new structures appear at the same time. Examination of the primatelike mammals shows a number of primate features, such as changes in the teeth and development of climbing abilities. In particular, the molar teeth are primatelike, as are the base of the skull and the structure of the ankle (Gingerich 1986). Not enough changes have occurred that we would call them primates, but

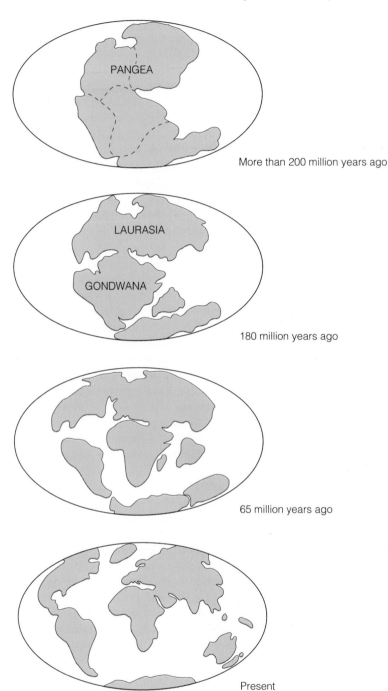

More than 200 million years ago

180 million years ago

65 million years ago

Present

Figure 11.2

Continental drift. Over 200 million years ago all of the continents formed a single land mass (called Pangea). By 180 million years ago, two major land masses had formed (Laurasia and Gondowana). By 65 million years ago (the beginning of primate evolution), South America had split from Africa, but North America and Europe were still joined. (From *Human Antiquity: An Introduction to Physical Anthropology and Archaeology,* 2d ed., by Kenneth Feder and Michael Park. Copyright 1993 by Mayfield Publishing Company)

Figure 11.3

Side view of a skull of a Paleocene primatelike mammal. (Redrawn from Fleagle, *Primate Adaptation and Evolution,* 1988, with permission, Academic Press, Inc.)

enough have taken place that we call them primatelike mammals. They are another example of transitional forms in the fossil record. (Some anthropologists *would* call the Paleocene forms primates but assign them to an extinct suborder. For our purposes we classify them simply as primatelike mammals in order to retain the distinctiveness of modern primates discussed in earlier chapters).

Models of primate origins. The first true primates evolved from a population of primatelike mammals. The general scenario for this change involves continuing adaptation to life in the trees. The primatelike mammals had the beginnings of arboreal adaptations, and many also possessed the more generalized teeth capable of exploiting different types of foods and environments. In an arboreal environment, natural selection would favor those individuals better able to cope with the demands of life in the trees. As discussed in Chapter 8, living in the trees is quite a different experience than living on the ground. First, a three-dimensional orientation is needed. Leaping from branch to branch requires depth perception, which involves forward rotation of the eyes so that the visual fields overlap. Vision, particularly depth perception, becomes a more important sense than smell. The sense of smell is also less important in the trees, where constant breezes and winds act to dissipate any smells.

Second, living in the trees also requires an agile body capable of bending and twisting in midair. The early insectivores retained the early generalized vertebrate skeletal structure, and the first primates made use of this flexibility in the trees. The retention of the primitive trait of five digits was also important because having five digits on hands and feet allows the grasping of limbs and branches. Finally, good hand-eye coordination and a brain capable of rapidly processing a large volume of visual information are essential.

The early primatelike mammals already had traits on which natural selection could act. They had a generalized skeletal structure and five digits. Individuals possessing certain variations such as more forward-facing eyes and grasping abilities would be selected for. Over time, the primatelike mammals adapted to life in the trees and became the first true primates.

The evolutionary path of primates was not the only adaptation to life in the trees. Other mammals, such as squirrels, also adapted to this environment. In considering evolutionary trends, you must remember that there is not necessarily only one set of adaptations to a specific environment. Squirrels use claws to anchor themselves while climbing and do not have the grasping hands and feet of primates. Primates represent only one possible direction, shaped in part by the demands of the environment and the variation present in the original populations. Again, remember that evolution is opportunistic.

Another scenario for the initial origin of the primates has been offered by Matthew Cartmill (1974), who sees the initial changes in grasping ability and vision as adaptations to insect eating. The early insectivores hunted out their prey on the ground and on low-lying slender branches in the forest. The development of grasping hands allowed more successful hunting of prey along small branches. The development of stereoscopic vision made it easier for them to locate prey. In particular, stereoscopic vision allows one to judge the distance to potential prey without moving one's head (which could alert the prey). Cartmill notes that a similar development of stereoscopic vision occurred in cats. According to Cartmill's model, primate adaptations first arose as adaptations to more successful insect predation. Once these traits were established, these adaptations later allowed further exploitation of the trees. As is often the case in evolution, preexisting structures can be used for different purposes. The fossil record is not complete enough to test fully Cartmill's model, but the dental evidence does show that many of the early primatelike mammals were insect eaters. This observation is consistent with the insect predation idea, but it is not conclusive.

Primates became extremely successful in adapting to an arboreal environment because of their biological and behavioral flexibility. This flexibility is even more important when considering the subsequent evolution of the primates.

> **Eocene epoch** The second epoch of the Cenozoic era, dating roughly between 38 and 55 million years B.P., when the first true primates, early prosimians, appeared.

The Eocene Epoch

The **Eocene epoch** lasted from 38 to 55 million years B.P. The word *Eocene* derives from the Greek, meaning "dawn," so named because many modern organisms appeared during this time.

Eocene environments. The climate during the Eocene was warm and humid, and the predominant land environment was tropical and subtropical forests. At the beginning of the Eocene, North America and Europe were still joined, resulting in migration and similarity among the fossils we find in these regions. Many orders of modern-day mammals first appeared during the Eocene, including aquatic mammals (whales, porpoises, and dolphins), rodents, and horses. It was also during this epoch that some surviving primatelike mammals evolved into "true primates." The remainder of the primatelike mammals became extinct, most likely as the result of competition with the new species of rodents.

The Eocene primates. Fossil primates from the Eocene epoch have been found in North America and Europe. During the Eocene there was an adaptive radiation of the first true primates—the early prosimians. This adaptive radiation was part of the general increase in the diversity of mammals associated with the warming of the climate and related environmental changes. Five families of primates containing as many as 67 new genera evolved during the Eocene (Fleagle 1988).

The Eocene forms possessed stereoscopic vision, grasping hands, and other anatomical features characteristic of primates. A picture of the skull

adapids A group of Eocene primates similar in some ways to modern-day lemurs and lorises.

omomyids A group of Eocene primates similar in some ways to modern-day tarsiers.

Algeripithecus The earliest known anthropoid, dated to the Late Eocene.

Oligocene epoch The third epoch of the Cenozoic era, dating roughly between 22 and 38 million years B.P., when the first anthropoids appeared.

Figure 11.4

Side view of a skull of an Eocene primate. (Redrawn from Fleagle, *Primate Adaptation and Evolution*, 1988, with permission, Academic Press, Inc.)

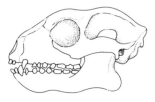

of an Eocene primate (Figure 11.4) shows many of these changes. Compared to the Paleocene primatelike mammals, the snout is reduced and the teeth are closer together. These forms possessed a postorbital bar, had larger brain cases, and had features of cerebral blood supply similar to that of modern primates (Fleagle 1988). The large size of the eyes of some of the Eocene primates suggests they were still nocturnal.

Primitive forms similar in many ways to modern-day prosimians (although only in a general sense—they were not exactly the same), the Eocene primates can be divided generally into two basic groups: the **adapids,** that are similar in certain respects to modern-day lemurs and lorises, and the **omomyids,** that are similar in some ways to modern-day tarsiers. The fossil evidence shows the adapids were primarily diurnal leaf and fruit eaters, and the omomyids were smaller, nocturnal fruit and insect eaters.

What became of the Eocene primates? Many different species ultimately became extinct. Others evolved into the present-day prosimians. We lack sufficient data, however, to identify individual species as the ancestors of present-day prosimians. We can only link, in a general sense, adapids with lemurs and lorises and omomyids with tarsiers.

What of the anthropoids? Were later forms of monkeys descended from adapids, omomyids, or some other (perhaps unknown) group? Most suggest later anthropoids have greater affinities with adapids than with omomyids, although this is far from settled (Conroy 1990). In addition, recent finds in Algeria have further complicated the issue of anthropoid origins. Dental remains of a newly discovered species (***Algeripithecus***) show anthropoid characteristics in certain features of the molar teeth (Godinot and Mahboubi 1992). Dated to the Late Eocene (46–50 million years B.P.), *Algeripithecus* is presently the oldest known anthropoid. This discovery indicates that anthropoids had split off from early primates much earlier than once thought (the date still needs confirmation at the time of this writing). A number of anthropologists now suggest that anthropoids did not evolve from either the Eocene adapids or the omomyids, but rather a third group that gave rise to *Algeripithecus* (Culotta 1992). These alternative "trees" are shown in Figure 11.5. It is too soon to determine which of these models (if any) is correct. We now see that despite the diversity found to date in Eocene primates, we are still likely to have sampled only a fraction of past forms.

The Oligocene Epoch

The **Oligocene epoch** lasted from 22 to 38 million years B.P. The term *Oligocene* translates roughly to the "time of few recent forms," indicating that few modern animals originated during this time.

Oligocene environments. The temperature cooled during the Oligocene and there was an expansion of grasslands and a reduction in forests. North American and European vertebrates were still similar to one an-

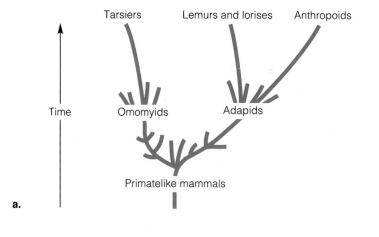

a.

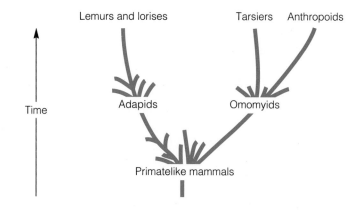

b.

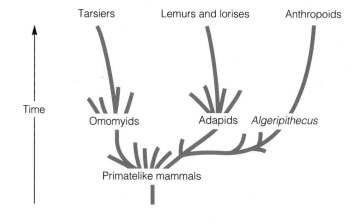

c.

Figure 11.5

Alternative views on anthropoid origins during the late Eocene. (a) The adapids are the common ancestor of lemurs and lorises and of anthropoids. (b) The omomyids are the common ancestors of tarsiers and anthropoids. (c) Anthropoids evolved as a third group earlier in the Eocene than previously thought, where the first anthropoids are represented by the newly discovered species *Algeripithecus*.

Aegyptopithecus A genus of fossil medium-sized, arboreal anthropoids found in Egypt dating to 33 million years B.P., a possible common ancestor of later Old World monkeys and apes.

other as the result of interchange, although this similarity decreases by the end of the Oligocene. Carnivores became widespread during the Oligocene, probably as a result of the change to open grasslands and the resultant increase in herbivores on which they could feed.

Old World anthropoids. At the end of the Eocene epoch, climatic change seems to have resulted in the southward movement of some prosimian populations. After this, we see little further evidence of primate evolution in North America or northern Europe. During the Oligocene epoch we find evidence of further primate evolution in southern climates in Africa and South America.

Most of the Old World evidence comes from an area known as the Fayum beds in Egypt. During the Oligocene the Fayum was a rich tropical forest, in contrast to much of the area today. While limited geographically, the Fayum fossil evidence shows that there was an adaptive radiation of anthropoids, the higher primates. The Fayum had a warm and wet climate, with plants similar to those found today in tropical regions of Southeast Asia. Analysis of Fayum fossils is often complicated by the fact that the region appears to have been somewhat unique. Fossil mammals found there are often different from those found in other Oligocene deposits (Fleagle 1988). New evidence shows that all the Fayum primates lived before 31 million years ago (Fleagle et al. 1986).

The Oligocene primates show the continued radiation of anthropoid forms in both the Old World and the New World. To date, there have been eight genera of Old World anthropoids and three genera of New World anthropoids discovered at Oligocene sites (Conroy 1990). The Oligocene anthropoids show continued reduction of the snout and nasal area, indicating greater reliance on vision than on smell. In addition to the postorbital bar shared with all primates, the Oligocene anthropoids have a fully enclosed eye socket, characteristic of modern anthropoids. All of the Oligocene anthropoids were small and arboreal and were generalized quadrupeds; none show signs of specialized locomotion. Their diet appears to have consisted primarily of fruit supplemented with insects and leaves.

The smaller eye orbits of many Oligocene anthropoids suggest that these forms were diurnal. The transition from a nocturnal lifestyle to a diurnal lifestyle was extremely important in the later evolution of the anthropoids. Given variation in the daily schedule of living creatures, we can imagine a situation in which some ancestral primates began feeding during daylight hours. As this new environmental niche was exploited, natural selection would act to favor individuals that possessed the abilities needed for such a way of life, such as improved vision. Daylight living also offers increased opportunities for social interactions because animals can see one another at greater distances. As a result, we would expect the development of larger social groups and an increase in social behaviors.

One of the most interesting Oligocene anthropoids is the genus *Aegyptopithecus* (Figure 11.6), which has been found in Fayum deposits

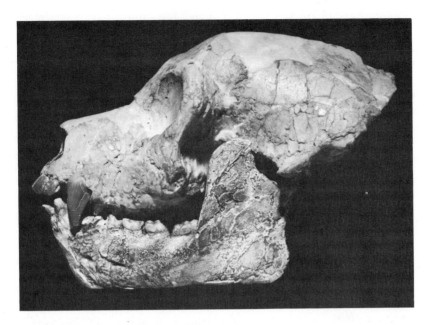

Figure 11.6

Side view of the skull of
Aegyptopithecus. (Peabody
Museum of Natural History, Yale
University)

dating to 33 million years B.P. The genus name translates as "Egyptian ape," named after the location and the early idea that this form was an early ape. In most ways *Aegyptopithecus* represents a typical Oligocene anthropoid. It was monkeylike in general appearance, roughly the size of a cat, a generalized quadruped, and totally at home in the trees. Some scientists have suggested that *Aegyptopithecus* represents the first ape because of its teeth. Teeth are extremely important in evolutionary reconstructions. Teeth and jaws are the hardest parts of the skeleton and are thus more likely to survive millions of years of burial and fossilization; the majority of fossil primate finds consist of jaws and teeth. Comparison of teeth can allow evolutionary relationships to be determined. Close analysis of teeth tells us something about an organism's diet, and hence its basic adaptations.

One important feature of *Aegyptopithecus* teeth is its dental formula. Among modern primates, the prosimians and New World monkeys usually have a 2-1-3-3 dental formula, and the Old World anthropoids (monkeys, apes, and humans) usually have a 2-1-2-3 dental formula. *Aegyptopithecus* had a 2-1-2-3 dental formula that links it with the Old World anthropoids. The teeth and other evidence place *Aegyptopithecus* in the general category of Old World anthropoid, but how can we determine if it is an ape or a monkey form? The skeletal structure, presence of a tail, and the overall appearance suggest that *Aegyptopithecus* was more like a monkey than an ape. Remember, however, that evolution is mosaic and we should not expect the first ape to look exactly like a modern ape. Many

bilophodont The pattern of the molar teeth of monkeys: four cusps, with the front two and back two each connected by a ridge.

scientists suggest that the first changes along the ape lineage were in the teeth.

Although modern Old World monkeys and apes have the same number of teeth and the same dental formula, they have different cusp patterns on their molar teeth. Among modern primates, hominoids have the Y-5 molar pattern on their lower molar teeth (as described in Chapter 9). Modern monkeys have a **bilophodont** pattern in which the molar teeth have four cusps. The front two cusps are connected with a ridge, and the back two cusps are connected with a ridge. The molar teeth of *Aegyptopithecus* resemble those found in modern apes in some respects. To some researchers, this is evidence that *Aegyptopithecus* was the first ape. This conclusion follows if we accept the premise that the molar teeth of hominoids represent the derived condition and the molar teeth of monkeys represent the primitive condition. Recent analyses, however, have shown that the situation is exactly the reverse. The molar teeth of hominoids are primitive; it is the molar teeth of monkeys that have changed more from this ancestral condition. Therefore, the fact that *Aegyptopithecus* has hominoidlike molar teeth cannot be used to call it a hominoid. The same situation applies to another Oligocene genus, *Propliopithecus,* which was also considered a hominoid at one time. Both genera are now seen as primitive Old World anthropoids that lived before the split between monkeys and hominoids (Fleagle and Kay 1983). They are sometimes classified with the hominoids because they share a number of primitive features, but they lived before monkeys and apes separated (Fleagle 1988). The different interpretations of *Aegyptopithecus,* depending on whether bilophodont or Y-5 lower molars are primitive, are illustrated in Figure 11.7.

The *Aegyptopithecus* fossils provide us with interesting suggestions about the behavior of early anthropoids. The variation in size among different specimens suggests that *Aegyptopithecus* was characterized by sex-

Figure 11.7

Different interpretations of the evolutionary status of *Aegyptopithecus.* (a) If bilophodont molars are primitive and Y-5 molars are derived, then *Aegyptopithecus* and later hominoids share a derived trait, and therefore *Aegyptopithecus* is an early hominoid. (b) If Y-5 molars are primitive and bilophodont molars are derived, then *Aegyptopithecus* and later hominoids share a primitive feature. Therefore, *Aegyptopithecus* is more likely to be a common ancestor of all later Old World anthropoids. Figure b is now thought to be correct.

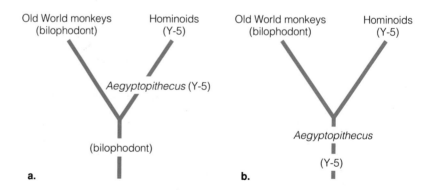

ual dimorphism. Primates that show sexual dimorphism in their teeth generally have multimale social systems, presumably because the larger teeth of males is related to competition for females. Therefore, we have some evidence suggesting the social structure of *Aegyptopithecus* was multimale groups.

Regardless of the specific affinities or behaviors of *Aegyptopithecus*, the Oligocene primate fossils provide us with evidence of the origin and spread of the higher primates. At some point separate lines leading to Old World monkeys and apes developed.

Evolution of the New World monkeys. What about the New World monkeys? The earliest fossil record of New World monkeys dates back roughly 30 million years. Most of this evidence consists of fragmentary dental remains. Many of these fossils resemble living New World monkeys. Other forms have unusual features, such as narrow jaws and protruding incisors, and do not appear to have any living counterparts.

Where did the New World monkeys come from? One suggestion is that some prosimians had moved into South America from North America. If so, then any biological similarities between New World and Old World monkeys represent parallel evolution. This idea had long been popular, and in fact the comparison of New World and Old World monkeys was often used as a classic example of parallel evolution. Recent evidence, however, shows so many similarities between Old World and New World monkeys (living and extinct) that it is very unlikely that monkeys evolved from prosimians twice. It is much more likely that the monkeys evolved once and then spread to different continents.

Two possibilities exist for the initial origin of the New World monkeys. Monkeys either migrated from North America to South America, or from Africa to South America. But by the end of the Eocene these continents had already separated. How, then, did monkeys migrate across the water?

One explanation is that anthropoids reached South America by "rafting." No, this does not mean that these early primates built rafts and sailed to South America! Ocean storms often rip up clumps of land and trees near the shore, which are then pulled out into the ocean. Sometimes these trees contain helpless animals. Often they drown, but occasionally they will be washed up on an island or continent.

Present geological evidence supports the rafting hypothesis. This still leaves the problem of where the anthropoids first came from, however. At present, the available evidence suggests that the Old World is a more likely point of origin than North America. The primary evidence supporting this view is the fact that no fossil evidence for Eocene or Oligocene anthropoids in North America has been found (Fleagle 1988).

Figure 11.8

Simplified "family tree" of
early primate evolution during
the Paleocene, Eocene, and
Oligocene epochs. The top
of the figure represents the
present day. Tentative
evolutionary lines are drawn
indicating the broad relationships of modern primates
with early primates. Question
marks identify particularly
controversial relationships.

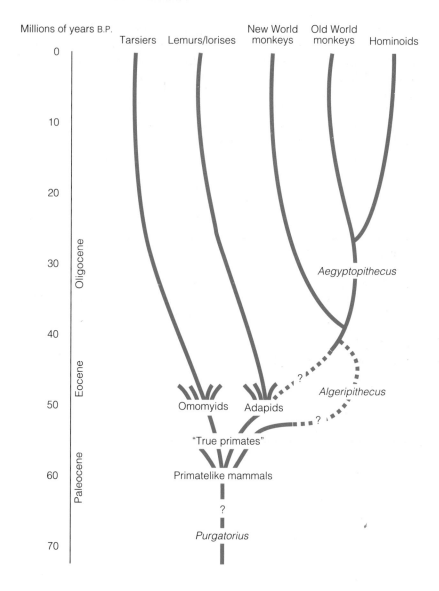

Summary of early primate evolution. For review, Figure 11.8 shows
a suggested picture of early primate evolution from the Paleocene through
the Oligocene. There appear to have been many more "branches" to this
tree, particularly for species that became extinct without issue.

Miocene Apes: The Fossil Evidence

Miocene Evolution

Miocene epoch The fourth
epoch of the Cenozoic era,
dating roughly between 5 and
22 million years B.P., when
the first apes appeared.

The **Miocene epoch** lasted from 5 to 22 million years B.P. Most
Miocene mammals are fairly modern in form, and roughly half of all

modern mammals were present during this time. South America and Australia were isolated by this time because of continental drift. The land mass of **Eurasia** (a term given to the combined land masses of Europe and Asia) and Africa were joined during part of the Miocene (approximately 16–17 million years B.P.).

The early and middle Miocene (before 16 million years B.P.) was a time of heavy tropical forests, particularly in Africa. Subsequently, the climate became cooler and drier, and there was an increase in open grasslands and mixed environments consisting of open woodlands, bushlands, and savannas.

Evidence exists of the adaptive radiation of early hominoids at the beginning of the Miocene, and at the end evidence suggests the first appearance of hominids (i.e., the bipedal primates). We identify many Miocene primates as apes because of their dental characteristics and not their total appearance. For this reason, many researchers call the Miocene hominoids "dental apes."

Table 11.2 lists the genera of Miocene apes known at present according to geographic region and geologic date (this list is likely to have

Eurasia The combined land masses of Europe and Asia, joined during the Miocene epoch.

T A B L E 11.2
Genera of Miocene Apes

| | Date | | |
Region	Early Miocene	Middle Miocene	Late Miocene
Africa			
	Afropithecus		
	Dendropithecus	*Kenyapithecus*	
	Limnopithecus		
	Micropithecus		
	Nyanzapithecus		
	Proconsul	*Otavapithecus*	
	Rangwapithecus		
	Turkanapithecus		
Asia	*Dionysopithecus*		*Gigantopithecus*
			Laccopithecus
			Lufengpithecus
		Sivapithecus	
Europe		*Dryopithecus*	
			Oreopithecus
		Pliopithecus	
		Sivapithecus	

Note that *Sivapithecus* is represented in both Asia and Europe. *Gigantopithecus* is also found in Asia during the Pliocene and Pleistocene epochs.

Source: Conroy (1990) and Conroy et al. (1992), with the exception that *Kenyapithecus* is considered here as a separate genus.

Proconsul A genus of fossil apes that lived in Africa between 17 and 23 million years B.P. that also shows a number of monkey characteristics.

changed by the time you read it; new Miocene hominoids are found almost every year!). Miocene hominoids have been discovered in Africa, Asia, and Europe. The 18 genera listed show how diverse the Miocene apes were relative to modern hominoids (only 6 genera exist today). Of course, different scholars still debate the assignment of specific fossils to different genera and species. Some see evidence for fewer groups and some see evidence for more. In any case, that many genera have been found demonstrates the great diversity in Miocene apes.

In light of this diversity, only a few selected Miocene apes that appear to be related to modern-day apes and humans will be discussed here. Keep in mind that there existed many other forms of Miocene apes that have no living counterpart.

Proconsul

Table 11.2 lists a number of primitive apes that lived during the early and middle Miocene. One of these, the genus **Proconsul,** lived in Africa between 17 and 23 million years B.P. Specimens assigned to this genus show considerable variation, particularly in overall size, making assignment to specific species somewhat difficult. The skeletal structure of *Proconsul* shows a mixture of monkey and ape features (Figure 11.9). Like modern apes, *Proconsul* did not have tails (Ward et al. 1991). The limb proportions, however, are more like that of a monkey than an ape, with limbs of roughly the same size. In a modern ape, the front limbs are generally longer than the rear limbs, reflecting knuckle walking. The arms and hands are monkeylike, but the shoulders and elbows are more like those of apes. The most recent analyses of the limb structure suggest that *Proconsul* was an unspecialized quadruped that lived in the trees and ate fruit (Pilbeam 1984; Walker and Teaford 1989).

Figure 11.9

Reconstructed skeleton of *Proconsul*. (Redrawn from Fleagle, *Primate Adaptation and Evolution,* 1988, with permission, Academic Press, Inc.)

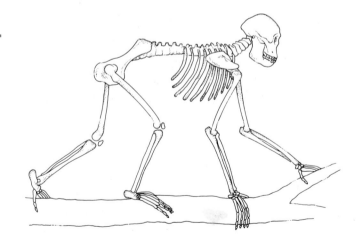

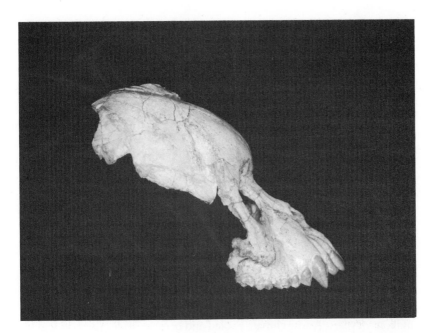

Figure 11.10

Side view of the skull of
Proconsul africanus, the
smaller of several species
of *Proconsul.* (Courtesy of
Milford Wolpoff, University of
Michigan)

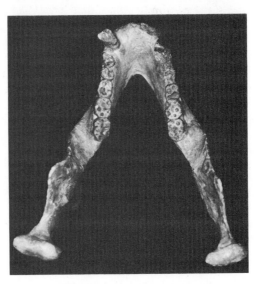

Figure 11.11

The lower jaw of a specimen
of *Proconsul nyanzae,* a
medium-sized species of
Proconsul. Note in particular
the large canine tooth.
(Courtesy of Milford Wolpoff,
University of Michigan)

The skull of a typical *Proconsul* specimen (Figure 11.10) is more like
that of an ape in being large relative to overall body size. The teeth also
demonstrate that these forms were hominoid. They possessed Y-5 molars
and had large protruding canines (Figure 11.11). The shape of the lower
premolar is like that of modern apes, with a single dominant cusp rather

diastema A gap next to the canine teeth that allows space for the canine on the opposing jaw.

Sivapithecus A genus of fossil ape found in Asia and Europe dating between 7 and 14 million years B.P., probably an ancestor of the modern-day orangutans, great apes, and humans.

than two more or less equal-sized cusps as found in humans. In apes, the single large cusp rubs against, and sharpens, the upper canine tooth. Ape jaws also have noticeable gaps (called **diastema**) next to the canine teeth, which allow the jaws to close. Imagine the problem you would have if your canines were long and protruding and you did not have a gap between the teeth in the opposite jaw for them to fit into. You would not be able to close your mouth or chew! *Proconsul* also had a thin layer of enamel on their molar teeth, similar to that found on the teeth of modern African apes. By contrast, humans and orangutans have thick molar enamel.

Overall, the teeth and jaws of *Proconsul* are similar enough to those of modern African apes that they were once thought to be direct ancestors of the chimpanzee and gorilla. Today we realize that the situation is more complex than this. Environmental reconstructions show that *Proconsul* lived in the Miocene forests and primarily ate fruits. The mixture of monkey and ape traits points to them as typical of a transition from early generalized anthropoid to what we think of as an ape. Though definitely not identical to a modern ape, their overall structure is more like that of an ape than a monkey; hence we refer to them as an early form of hominoid.

Proconsul was adapted to forest living and was a successful group for millions of years. As the climate cooled and became drier in certain regions during the Miocene, their habitat shrank. As competition for dwindling resources increased, other apes developed that were more successful in dealing with the new environments.

Sivapithecus

The genus **Sivapithecus** lived in Asia and Europe between 7 and 14 million years ago. The genus name means "Siva's ape," after the Indian deity Siva (pronounced "SHE-va"). Like *Proconsul, Sivapithecus* was a diverse genus ranging in size and geographic distribution. Because of this variation it is not clear exactly how many species actually existed. Current estimates suggest as many as six different species (Kelly 1988; Conroy 1990).

A major distinguishing feature of *Sivapithecus* lies in the jaws and teeth. First, the molars are relatively large, are low-cusped, and have thick enamel. Second, the jaws are relatively massive but do not protrude forward as much as in other apes. Third, in many forms the canines are relatively smaller than in other apes and do not protrude as much. These features are all probably related to a change in diet from soft fruits to foods that are harder to chew, such as nuts, seeds, and hard fruits. This change in diet seems to be associated with the fact that the climate was on average cooler and drier, leading to a change in available foods. It is interesting that, on average, *Sivapithecus* and other apes with thick molar enamel appear in the fossil record after the thin-enameled forms (such as *Procon-*

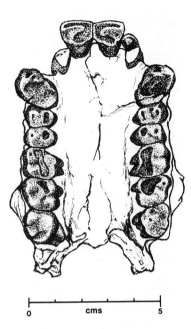

Figure 11.12

Upper and lower jaws of a *Sivapithecus* specimen from Pakistan.   (From Clark Spencer Larsen, Robert M. Matter, and Daniel L. Gebo, *Human Origins: The Fossil Record, Second Edition*, p. 37. Copyright © 1991, 1985 by Waveland Press, Inc., Prospect Heights, Illinois. Reprinted with permission from the publisher)

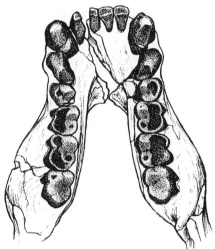

sul) as the climate changed. The upper and lower jaws of a *Sivapithecus* specimen are shown in Figure 11.12.

Thicker enamel represents an adaptation to a diet that is hard to chew. Think about it: What takes more chewing, a piece of orange or a nut? Given the wear on teeth, harder enamel is more adaptive for heavy chewing and grinding between the back teeth. Larger molars would also be adaptive for heavier chewing. The shorter and more massive jaw also relates to

postcranial Referring to that part of the skeleton below the neck.

diet because more power can be applied between the back teeth when the jaw is tucked farther under the face. Smaller canines have also been thought to relate to such a diet. One hypothesis is that large canines hinder certain kinds of chewing. When you chew a hard object such as a nut, your jaw does not simply move up and down. Instead, your lower jaw also moves side to side and your chewing pattern is more circular than up and down. Large canines would make the circular motion more difficult. Therefore, smaller canines are seen as an adaptation to a hard diet because they allow more successful rotary chewing. According to another hypothesis, because larger molars take up more room in the jaw, leaving less room for the canines, the crowding of the teeth leads to dental problems and is therefore selected against.

For a long time all we knew about *Sivapithecus* and other related forms came from remains of teeth and jaws. Based on only this information, many anthropologists felt that some of them were actually hominid. After all, humans have the same basic complex of dental traits: larger molars, thicker molar enamel, less-protruding jaws, and smaller canines. Recent finds, reviewed later, indicate that this idea was not correct. *Sivapithecus* was not a hominid.

In what type of environment did *Sivapithecus* live? Initially it was assumed that the dietary specializations found in their teeth meant that this group lived in open grasslands. Seeds, nuts, and other hard objects associated with thick molar enamel and massive chewing were thought to be found in such terrestrial environments (Jolly 1970). A survey of diets and dental characteristics of living primates has shown that these dental characteristics are found in both terrestrial and tree-living primates (Kay 1981). Environmental data suggest, however, that *Sivapithecus* lived more often in a mosaic of mixed woodland, grassland, and forest regions. Our reconstructions of *Sivapithecus* are hampered by the fact that we know very little about their form of locomotion. Recent reviews of the **postcranial** (the skeleton below the skull) structure of Miocene apes suggest generalized quadrupeds from which modern forms of ape locomotion could have been derived (Fleagle 1983). The few postcranial bones of *Sivapithecus* (Pilbeam et al. 1977; Rose 1986) seem to support this theory. The arm and leg bones are highly mobile, the big toe was capable of grasping in much the same way as does an orangutan, and there is no evidence of bipedalism. To the best of our knowledge, the modern specialized patterns of hominoids, such as knuckle walking, brachiation, and bipedalism, do not appear in these fossil apes.

Recent evidence has changed a lot of our earlier ideas about *Sivapithecus* and hominid origins. In the late 1970s and early 1980s, a number of *Sivapithecus* specimens were found with rather complete skulls, offering us for the first time a glimpse at something other than jaws and teeth. One of these specimens (Figure 11.13) was discovered by David Pilbeam in 1980 during excavations in Miocene deposits in Pakistan (Pilbeam 1982). Its

Figure 11.13

Side view of *Sivapithecus* specimen from Pakistan. (From Clark Spencer Larsen, Robert M. Matter, and Daniel L. Gebo, *Human Origins: The Fossil Record, Second Edition*, p. 36. Copyright © 1991, 1985 by Waveland Press, Inc., Prospect Heights, Illinois. Reprinted with permission from the publisher)

0   cms   5

general appearance is extremely similar to a modern orangutan, as shown in Figure 11.14.

The overall shape and orientation of the two skulls is very similar and quite unlike that of either the chimpanzee or gorilla. The eye orbit of the *Sivapithecus* skull is oval in shape and the two eyes are close together, both features found in the orangutan. The unique triangular appearance of an orangutan's nasal region is also found in *Sivapithecus*. Other similarities also include the shape and size of the incisor teeth. Note the difference in size between the middle two incisor teeth and the outer two in both specimens. In addition, remember that the thick molar enamel found in sivapithecines and in humans is also found in orangutans. Since Pilbeam's discovery, additional *Sivapithecus* skulls showing the same features have been found in various sites in Asia.

Not every species of *Sivapithecus* exhibits all of these features. Specimens in China, for example, share certain features of the incisor teeth and jaw shape with the Pakistani specimen shown in Figures 11.13 and 11.14. However, the shape of the eye orbits and the distance between the eyes is different. This variation suggests that there were a number of Asian species of *Sivapithecus,* one of which appears ancestral to the modern-day orangutan.

Figure 11.14

Side views (*top*) and frontal views (*bottom*) comparing the *Sivapithecus* specimen GSP 15000 (*center*) with a modern chimpanzee (*left*) and a modern orangutan (*right*). (Peabody Museum, Harvard University)

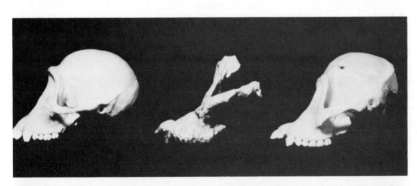

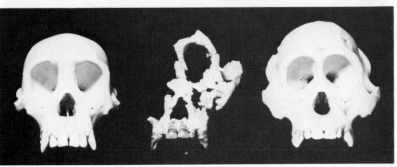

Gigantopithecus A genus of fossil ape found in Asia dating between 0.5 and 9 million years B.P.

Other Miocene Apes

Gigantopithecus. A genus of fossil ape that shows many dental similarities to *Sivapithecus* is **Gigantopithecus,** which means "giant ape." This genus has been found in China, India, and most recently Vietnam (Ciochon 1988). The Indian finds date between 5 and 9 million years B.P., and the Chinese finds may only be 500,000 years old. To date, only lower jaws and isolated teeth have been found. The most striking aspect of the *Gigantopithecus* finds is their size; the teeth, especially the molars, are huge, and the jaws are incredibly thick and massive (see Figure 11.15 for comparisons with teeth and jaws of humans and gorillas). Based on the large size of the jaws and teeth, some have estimated that *Gigantopithecus* was over 6 feet tall. Such estimations are not useful because there are wide differences among species in the relationship of dental size to body size. We need postcranial data to determine the size of *Gigantopithecus*.

The teeth of *Gigantopithecus* show the typical features of all sivapithecines: large molars with thick enamel. They also have relatively small canines whose tips are usually worn down, showing the effects of grinding. Little more is known about this creature other than its diet and dental characteristics. One popular idea is that *Gigantopithecus* is somehow related to the mythical "Abominable Snowman" because of its estimated size and geographic location. No evidence exists to support this idea.

The relatively recent date of some of the Chinese and Vietnamese finds shows that this form was a contemporary of our ancestors. If human ancestors and *Gigantopithecus* lived at the same time, then it is possible that early humans were responsible for its extinction, either through competition or hunting. This hypothesis is purely speculative at this point, and environmental change and/or ecological overspecialization could have also led to the extinction of this giant ape (Ciochon 1988; Ciochon et al. 1990).

Figure 11.15

Comparison of the lower jaws of *Gigantopithecus* (*left*), a modern gorilla (*middle*), and a modern human (*right*). *Gigantopithecus* has the largest overall size, but relatively small canines compared to the gorilla.   (From *Gigantopithecus,* by E. L. Simons and P. C. Ettel. Copyright © 1970 by *Scientific American,* Inc. All rights reserved)

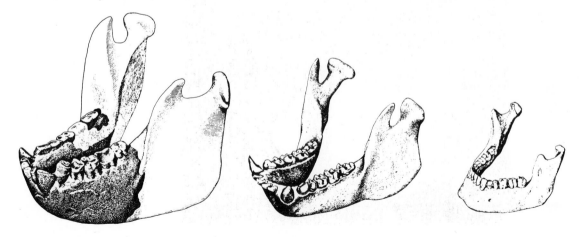

Kenyapithecus. Fossils similar to *Sivapithecus* have been discovered in Africa. One species, named ***Kenyapithecus,*** has been dated to 14 to 17 million years B.P. This species is known only from teeth, jaws, and fragmentary facial remains (Figure 11.16). *Kenyapithecus* shares certain features with *Sivapithecus* (some lump the two in the genus *Sivapithecus*), including thick molar enamel. This species also has relatively small canines. While fragmentary, the fossil evidence for *Kenyapithecus* suggests it might be a common ancestor of later African hominoids (the African apes and humans).

Afropithecus. During the 1980s, Richard Leakey and colleagues discovered dental and cranial fragments of a form closely related to *Sivapithecus* at several sites in Kenya, Africa (Leakey and Walker 1985; Leakey and Leakey 1986a, 1986b). In fact, they first classified it as an African form of *Sivapithecus* and later assigned these fossils to a new genus—*Afropithecus.* The specimens have been dated to 16 to 18 million years B.P. A frontal and

Kenyapithecus An African Miocene ape, similar to *Sivapithecus* in some ways, but with relatively small canines. This genus dates to 14 to 17 million years B.P. It is a possible common ancestor of modern African apes and humans.

Afropithecus An African Miocene ape that lived between 16 and 18 million years ago, and is perhaps a common ancestor of modern great apes and humans. This genus is similar in some ways to *Sivapithecus.*

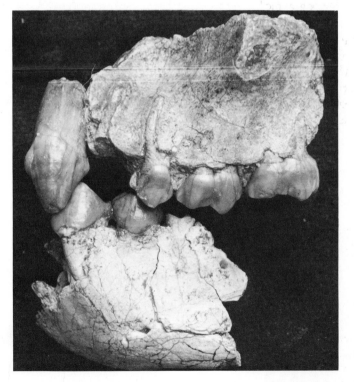

Figure 11.16

Jaw fragments of *Kenyapithecus.* Note the small canine teeth. (Courtesy of Dr. Alan Walker, The Johns Hopkins University School of Medicine)

molecular dating Estimating the sequence and timing of divergent evolutionary lines by applying methods of genetic analysis.

side view of an *Afropithecus* skull is shown in Figure 11.17. Similarities with *Sivapithecus* include large central incisors that project outward and a long upper jaw. The facial profile of *Afropithecus* is different, however, in that it is more linear than the concave shape of *Sivapithecus* (compare facial profile in Figures 11.13 and 11.17). The date and morphology suggest that *Afropithecus* might be a common ancestor for *Sivapithecus* and later Asian and African hominoids.

Miocene Apes: Interpretations

Are the Miocene apes discussed here related to modern apes and humans? If so, then how? Who is the best candidate for the ancestor of the African apes and humans? For the orangutan? Do we have enough data to answer these questions, or are we missing important pieces from fossils not yet discovered? Since discoveries are now happening at a rapid rate, any interpretation of Miocene evolution must be tentative. Don't be surprised if some of this material is out of date by the time you read it!

Molecular Dating

The analysis of Miocene hominoid evolution relies heavily on the fossil evidence, but that is not the only source of information we have. Since the late 1960s, the comparison of the genetics of living organisms using a set of methods known as **molecular dating** has shed new light on hominoid evolution.

In Chapter 9 you read about how scientists use molecular information to judge the relative relationship between living hominoids. These methods provide some idea of which primates are most closely related. If certain

Figure 11.17

Frontal and side views of *Afropithecus*, an African hominoid dated to 16 to 18 million years B.P. that shows certain similarities with *Sivapithecus* and with earlier hominoids.   (From Clark Spencer Larsen, Robert M. Matter, and Daniel L. Gebo, *Human Origins: The Fossil Record, Second Edition*, p. 27. Copyright © 1991, 1985 by Waveland Press, Inc., Prospect Heights, Illinois. Reprinted with permission from the publisher)

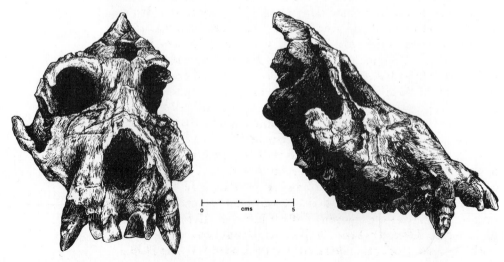

cms
0   5

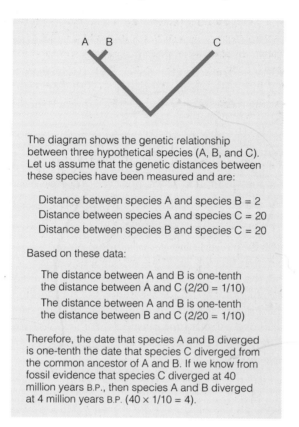

The diagram shows the genetic relationship between three hypothetical species (A, B, and C). Let us assume that the genetic distances between these species have been measured and are:

Distance between species A and species B = 2
Distance between species A and species C = 20
Distance between species B and species C = 20

Based on these data:

The distance between A and B is one-tenth the distance between A and C (2/20 = 1/10)

The distance between A and B is one-tenth the distance between B and C (2/20 = 1/10)

Therefore, the date that species A and B diverged is one-tenth the date that species C diverged from the common ancestor of A and B. If we know from fossil evidence that species C diverged at 40 million years B.P., then species A and B diverged at 4 million years B.P. (40 × 1/10 = 4).

Figure 11.18

Hypothetical example of molecular dating.

assumptions are made, these methods can be used to provide an estimate of the date at which two species split from a common ancestor. When two species separate, mutations occur and neutral mutations accumulate in each line independently. If the rate of accumulation is constant in both lines, then a comparison of molecular differences in living forms would provide us with a relative idea of how long the two species have been separated.

Imagine three species, A, B, and C, where molecular evidence indicates that A and B are more closely related to each other than either is to C. We would hypothesize that initially species C split off from a common ancestor of all three, followed by a split of species A and B later on. Suppose we then determine through molecular comparisons that the difference between A and B is one-tenth of the difference between either A or B and species C. This evidence suggests that the date of divergence of A and B was one-tenth that of the date of divergence between their common ancestor and species C. Now suppose that we know from fossil evidence that species C split off 40 million years ago. We can then infer that species A and B split from a common ancestor at 4 million years ago, since 4 million years is one-tenth of 40 million years. Here we have taken the molecular differences between species and have used it as a "molecular clock," with our clock calibrated using the fossil record (Figure 11.18).

Molecular dating rests on two major assumptions. First, we assume that our calibration date is correct. As more fossil evidence accumulates, we might have to change our estimate of the date at which species C first split off. The second, more critical, assumption is that neutral mutations do accumulate at the same rate in different lines. There are methods for testing this assumption, and it does appear to hold true for some molecular estimates (Cronin 1983).

Constancy in rates of mutation might seem inconceivable, given that mutations occur at random. But remember basic probability. If you flip a coin 10 times, you will not expect to get five heads and five tails. If you flip the coin 10 million times, however, you expect to get results closer to the expected 50:50 ratio. Given millions of generations, the random nature of mutations also seems constant.

The first use of molecular dating was by Sarich and Wilson (1967), who looked at differences in albumin protein and found that the difference between humans and the African apes was one-sixth that found between either and the Old World monkeys. Using the then-established estimate of 30 million years for the separation of Old World monkeys, they computed that humans and the African apes had shared a common ancestor 5 million years ago. At that time most paleoanthropologists thought a date of 15 to 20 million years was more likely and disagreed strongly with Sarich and Wilson's estimate.

Since that time a great deal of research has been done on molecular dating and its assumptions. Some researchers disputed the idea of constancy in mutation fixation rates and proposed nonlinear models in their place. Other proteins have been analyzed. Additional fossil material was found, and new interpretations of older data were made. Most paleoanthropologists accept a much more recent split of humans and apes than was the consensus several decades ago.

Different methods of analysis give different estimates from molecular dating. For example, Cronin (1983) computed a split of human and chimpanzee at roughly 5 million years ago, with the orangutan splitting off at roughly 10 million years ago and the gibbon splitting off at roughly 12 million years ago. Arguing that the data should be interpreted using nonlinear rates of change, Gingerich (1985) computed an average date of 9 million years for the chimpanzee, 16 million years for the orangutan, and 19 million years for the gibbon. The controversy still continues, but the predominant view from molecular dating is that humans and the African apes split sometime between 5 and 10 million years ago.

A Tentative Evolutionary Tree

With accumulation of evidence, a given hypothesis may be viewed as less likely. When a hypothesis is contradicted, it is rejected. The constant feedback between hypothesis generation, data analysis, and testing means that ideas change over time. This process makes many people uncomfortable, but it is in fact the very nature of scientific inquiry.

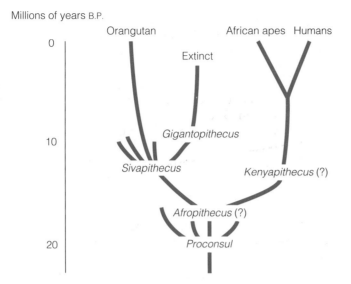

Millions of years B.P.

Orangutan   African apes   Humans

Extinct

Gigantopithecus

Sivapithecus

Kenyapithecus (?)

Afropithecus (?)

Proconsul

0

10

20

Figure 11.19

Tentative evolutionary tree of
Miocene hominoid evolution
based on fossil and molecular
evidence. Question marks
indicate greater uncertainty.

Given the fossil and molecular evidence, what is the most likely scenario for the evolution of the hominoids? The ideas proposed here are hypotheses for further testing, not definitive statements. As new data are discovered, some ideas will be rejected and others will gain support.

During the 1960s and early 1970s, the most accepted model was that *Sivapithecus* represented a hominid and that the split between apes and humans had occurred sometime before 14 million years ago, the oldest date then known for these fossils. This model was based on the close similarity in the teeth of the fossils and known hominids. In particular, the thick molar enamel of *Sivapithecus* was considered a derived trait shared with hominids. Thin molar enamel as found in the African apes was considered the primitive state. Additional research led to the rejection of this hypothesis. Thin enamel represents the derived condition. Thick enamel, shared by orangutans, hominids, and *Sivapithecus,* is the primitive condition. In addition, recent work has shown that the evolution of molar thickness is more complex than once thought. Martin (1985) has performed microscopic analyses of molar enamel and has shown that even though humans and *Sivapithecus* share thick molar enamel, they differ in the mode of enamel formation. Martin's work also shows that *Sivapithecus* was not a hominid.

If *Sivapithecus* was not a hominid, then what was it? One current idea is that *Sivapithecus* is a direct ancestor of the modern-day orangutan and is not ancestral to the African apes or humans (Pilbeam 1984). This hypothesis is based on the strong similarities between *Sivapithecus* and the orangutan. *Gigantopithecus* is felt to have split off later from the *Sivapithecus* line, perhaps 10 million years ago.

Figure 11.19 presents a tentative evolutionary tree, with question marks indicating areas of uncertainty. According to the hypothesis outlined by the tree, some species of *Proconsul* evolved into an early form of thick-enameled ape—*Afropithecus*. The date and primitive features of *Proconsul* make it a reasonable common ancestor of later Miocene apes. *Afropithecus* has been found to have a number of features similar to both earlier and later Miocene apes, suggesting it might be a reasonable candidate for the common ancestor of the great apes and humans. The location and date of *Afropithecus* are also important. Approximately 16 million years ago, the land masses of Eurasia and Africa came into contact through the action of continental drift, when many animal species moved from one continent to the other. It is after this time that we see the first evidence of *Sivapithecus* in Europe and Asia. This, along with the similarity between *Afropithecus* and *Sivapithecus* in a number of features, suggests that *Sivapithecus* evolved from populations of *Afropithecus* expanding out from Africa. Judging from the strong similarity of the Pakistani form of *Sivapithecus* and the orangutan, it appears that the former is an ancestor of the latter. Given geography and dental similarities, *Gigantopithecus* may have evolved from a species of Asian *Sivapithecus*.

Figure 11.19 suggests another evolutionary lineage of thick-enameled apes in Africa. According to this model, a descendant of *Afropithecus* became the common ancestor of the African apes and humans. Although new fossils are being discovered every year, the fossil evidence for this part of African prehistory is still rather sparse. *Kenyapithecus,* which shows similarities with *Afropithecus* and with later hominids, is a possible candidate, particularly since it is in the right place at the right time. This placement is only suggestive, because we lack sufficient information on other species that probably lived at this time. If the late Miocene in Africa is like any other time and place in the Miocene, there is probably considerable diversity we still are unaware of.

New data will most likely modify the specifics of this tentative tree. You may assume the basic pattern, however, to be fairly accurate. We see evidence of primitive early apes with thin enamel giving rise to a number of lines of later apes with thick enamel and relatively larger molars. This change appears related to the changing climate and its effect on food resources. Many of these later apes became extinct, but some became the ancestors of present-day orangutans, gorillas, chimpanzees, and humans. As is often the case in paleoanthropology, we have a good idea of the *general* picture but are still uncertain about all of the *specifics*.

SUMMARY

Following the extinction of the dinosaurs 65 million years ago, early mammal forms spread out into new environments. Some early insectivores began to adapt more and more to life in the trees, developing grasping hands and binocular stereoscopic vision. These changes may have begun in response to the needs of insect predation and were later used to exploit additional food resources in a three-dimensional environment. The origin of primates began with the primatelike mammals of the Paleocene epoch and the ancient prosimians of the Eocene. Primitive anthropoids evolved from a group of Eocene primates. The early Oligocene anthropoids ultimately gave rise to the separate lines of Old World monkeys and hominoids.

The Miocene epoch is characterized by two major adaptive radiations. In the early Miocene, primitive hominoid forms appeared in Africa. These forms, placed in the genus *Proconsul,* were similar in some ways to later apes, but also monkeylike in a number of features. They had jaws and teeth like those of later apes and also lacked a tail. Their postcranial skeleton was generalized and primitive in a number of features. They had thin molar enamel.

During the middle Miocene, several new genera of apes evolved. They had relatively large molars and thick molar enamel. These dental changes correspond to changing climatic patterns and available food resources, specifically the need to process food that was harder to chew. These thick-enameled apes appear to be the ancestor of present-day great apes and humans, although the specific evolutionary relationships between Miocene species and modern species are not clear at present. One species of the genus *Sivapithecus* appears to be the ancestor of the orangutan, based on close similarity of dental and facial traits. An earlier and related form, *Afropithecus,* may be a common ancestor of all later hominoids, or at least similar to whoever was a common ancestor. Some evidence suggests that another related form, *Kenyapithecus,* was a common ancestor of the African apes and humans, although there is not sufficient data to rule this as more than a tentative hypothesis. Regardless of specific evolutionary relationships, the fossil record shows us a picture of extensive variation among Miocene apes.

Supplemental Readings

Conroy, G. C. 1990. *Primate Evolution*. New York: W. W. Norton.

Fleagle, J. G. 1988. *Primate Adaptation and Evolution*. San Diego: Academic Press. These two texts are the best current sources for information on primate evolution.

Lewin, R. 1987. *Bones of Contention: Controversies in the Search for Human Origins*. New York: Simon & Schuster. A lively summary of controversies in human evolution. Chapters 5 and 6 deal with human origins, Miocene hominoids, and molecular dating.

CHAPTER 12

The First
Hominids

How old are human beings? This is one question anthropologists are frequently asked. It seems simple enough, but in fact we have no simple answer. It depends on how we define human beings. If we limit our question to humans who are more or less anatomically similar to modern humans, the answer may be more than 100,000 years old. If we include all the fossils placed in our species, old- and modern-looking, the answer is over 200,000 years old. If we focus on all members of our genus (*Homo*), including forms placed in other species, the answer is over 2 million years old. If we are interested only in hominids, regardless of genus or species, the answer is over 4 million years old.

Past human evolution was not a one-step process. Humans did not emerge instantaneously from an apelike ancestor. What we are, biologically and culturally, is the product of many different evolutionary changes occurring at different times. Here we will focus on the origin of the first hominids and their relationship to later hominid forms, including ourselves.

This chapter examines the fossil record for human evolution from the time of the oldest known hominids through the beginnings of the evolution of the genus *Homo*. The oldest known hominids are classified in the genus *Australopithecus,* characterized primarily by their small brains, large faces and teeth, and bipedal locomotion. The first two sections cover what we presently know about the distribution, anatomy, and behavior of the first hominids. The last two sections discuss past and present evolutionary models and general evolutionary trends.

The Genus *Australopithecus*

All fossil hominids can be placed into two genera: the genus ***Austra-lopithecus*** and the genus ***Homo***. The first hominids belonged to the genus *Australopithecus*. There may have been four or more species of *Australo-pithecus,* one of which evolved into an early form of the genus *Homo*. By 1 million years B.P., all australopithecines became extinct and the genus *Homo* continued to evolve, with an increase in brain size and cultural adaptations.

General Characteristics

Australopithecines (a general term referring to all members of the genus *Australopithecus*) were the first hominids and were basically bipedal apes. They were hominids because they were bipedal, a derived character-istic of hominids not found in any other primate. Australopithecines, however, still retained a number of primitive ape characteristics, and we should not equate them directly with "humans." To do so implies that their behavior and biology were in many ways similar to our own. We do share certain characteristics with the australopithecines, but we are also different in many ways.

The genus named *Australopithecus* translates as "southern ape," so named because the first specimen was found in southern Africa and it was regarded as more apelike than humanlike. Perhaps a better term could be coined now, but scientists have agreed to an international system of nam-ing genera and species. The first name given takes precedence; otherwise, there would be confusion and inconsistency (although some does exist in the naming of fossil species).

Distribution in time and space. Australopithecines have been found dating between 1 and 4 million years B.P. This time period includes por-tions of the **Pliocene epoch** (1.8 to 5 million years B.P.) and the **Pleisto-cene epoch** (0.01 to 1.8 million years B.P.). The time period of the australopithecines is often called the **Plio-Pleistocene.**

An important fact about australopithecines is that they have all been found in Africa. No australopithecines have been discovered outside Af-rica. This fact supports Darwin's early idea that Africa was the birthplace of hominids. It also means that the australopithecines were limited to a specific environment—tropical grasslands. Not until later in the fossil rec-ord do any hominids expand outside Africa, as we will see in the next chapter.

Australopithecines have been discovered in two major areas within

Australopithecus A genus of fossil hominid that lived in Africa between 1 and 4 mil-lion years B.P., characterized by bipedal locomotion, small brain size, large face, and large teeth.

Homo A genus of hominid with three recognized species (*Homo habilis, Homo erectus,* and *Homo sapiens*), dating from over 2 million years ago and characterized by large brain size and dependence on culture as a means of adaptation.

australopithecines All species in the genus *Australopithecus*.

Pliocene epoch The fifth epoch of the Cenozoic era, dating from 1.8 to 5 million years B.P., when hominids appeared.

Pleistocene epoch The sixth epoch of the Cenozoic era, dating from 0.01 to 1.8 mil-lion years B.P., marked by the continued evolution of the genus *Homo*.

Plio-Pleistocene The time frame of the australopithe-cines (from 1 to 4 million years B.P.).

Figure 12.1

Location of the major sites in Africa where *Australopithecus* and *Homo habilis* specimens have been found.

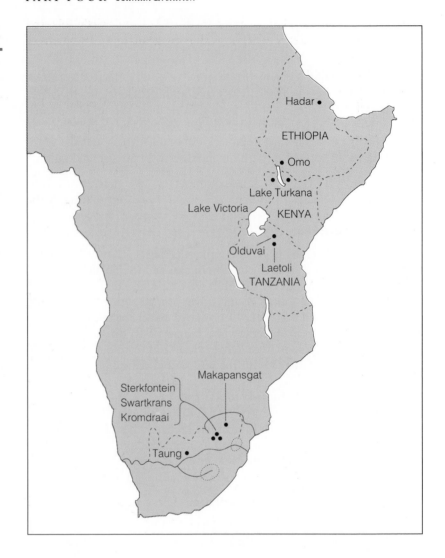

Africa: South Africa and East Africa. Figure 12.1 provides a map of the major australopithecine sites. Historically, the South African sites were discovered first. The geology of South Africa and the nature of fossilization in that area have made absolute dating difficult. As a result, for many years we were not sure exactly how old the australopithecines were. Sites in East Africa have since been discovered and their absolute dates have been determined: extensive volcanic activity in East Africa during the time of the australopithecines allows us to use potassium-argon dating on these sites.

Australopithecine characteristics. Although four species of *Australopithecus* have been identified, a number of physical characteristics are common to all species. These features are discussed here briefly, followed by a more extensive look at variation within the genus and illustrations of their morphology.

The australopithecines were bipedal, as we can tell by their pelvic structure, nondivergent big toe, and angle of the femur. Though they were definitely bipedal, the specific nature of australopithecine bipedalism has been debated. Some scientists believe they were completely adapted to upright walking, and others believe there are indications of considerable climbing ability.

All the australopithecines had relatively small **cranial capacities** (a measurement of the interior volume of the brain case, measured in milliliters). Their cranial capacities ranged from 400 to 530 ml, roughly the size of an ape's. Estimates of body weight vary by species and sex, ranging from 40 to 49 kg (88 to 108 lbs) in males, and from 29 to 34 kg (64 to 75 lbs) in females (McHenry 1992). Body weight is estimated from statistical relationships known to occur between overall body weight and the size of different bones. In any case, the size of their brains relative to body weight makes the australopithecine brain similar to, or even larger than, that of modern apes, but considerably smaller than the brain of modern humans. Studies of casts of the interior portions of the skulls provide estimates of brain size, shape, and surface features. These casts show that the australopithecine brains were most likely apelike in structure (Falk 1992).

The overall appearance of all australopithecine skulls shows a small brain case and a large, protruding face. Though a small brain and a large face are ape features, the australopithecine skulls do not resemble those of modern apes. The jaws and teeth of *Australopithecus* are large compared to those of modern humans. Most australopithecine species have small canine teeth, as do modern humans. The back teeth of all four species are relatively large and have thick molar enamel.

Were the australopithecines toolmakers? It is entirely possible and even likely that the australopithecines used simple wood tools. Most evidence to date suggests that they did not manufacture stone tools. In every case where stone tools have been found, even at the same time level as australopithecines, remains have been found of hominids with larger brains—those in the genus *Homo*. New evidence, however, argues somewhat against this traditional view. Recent analyses of australopithecine hand bones show that they may have had the same degree of manual dexterity (precision grip) associated with toolmakers in the genus *Homo* (Susman 1988). Also, some question the view that tools found at australopithecine sites were always made by *Homo* (e.g., Clark 1988).

What does this all mean? Judging by the face and brain case, we would call the australopithecines apes. In most cases, however, the teeth are hominid in overall structure, although the back teeth are larger than those of modern humans. Finally, they walked upright, which means they should be classified as hominid. These first hominids are not modern humans, but rather the beginnings of later human evolution.

cranial capacity A measurement of the interior volume of the brain case, used as an approximate estimate of brain size.

Australopithecus afarensis
The most primitive of the australopithecines, dating between 3 and 4 million years B.P. and found in East Africa.

Australopithecine Variation

Keeping in mind the general characteristics of *Australopithecus*, we can now turn to a closer investigation of variation within the genus. We will look at three different groups of australopithecines and trace their possible evolutionary relationships. Even though different species names are used, keep in mind that there are unresolved questions about the exact composition of these species. Major differences in opinion on the naming of different fossil species and alternative family trees are discussed at the end of the chapter. For now, the species names serve as convenient labels for describing some of the patterns of variation.

Australopithecus afarensis. The oldest known australopithecines lived in East Africa between 3 and 4 million years B.P. Their discovery is fairly recent; much of our data on these forms comes from Donald Johanson's fieldwork in the early 1970s at the site of Hadar, Ethiopia (see Figure 12.1). The fossils collected by Johanson and colleagues date between 2.9 and 3.5 million years B.P. Additional fossils collected by Mary Leakey at the site of Laetoli, Tanzania, date back to 3.75 million years B.P. Johanson and colleagues (1978) noted the close similarity between the Hadar and Laetoli finds and placed them together in a different species from all other known australopithecines—*Australopithecus afarensis.* The species name, *afarensis,* comes from the Afar region where the Hadar site is located. Recent discoveries in southern Ethiopia may date back as far as 4.3 million years B.P. (Fleagle et al. 1991).

A. afarensis (the *A.* is scientific shorthand for the genus name *Australopithecus*) is the most primitive of the australopithecines. Consequently, *A. afarensis* is more apelike in certain features than the other australopithecine species. Nonetheless, it is definitely hominid, for it possesses the human form of bipedalism. The most dramatic find showing bipedalism is the fossil nicknamed "Lucy," a 40 percent complete skeleton of an adult female (Figure 12.2). We know she was an adult because her third molar teeth had fully erupted, an event that occurs in young adulthood in hominids. We also know she was a female because her pelvis is fairly intact. Determining the sex of a fossil is best done by examination of the pelvis (Figure 12.3). Females have a wider and more rounded pelvic opening. Such comparisons show that Lucy was a female.

Although an adult, Lucy was small. She was a little over a meter tall (about 3 ft 3 in) and weighed roughly 27 kg (60 lbs) (McHenry 1992). Her pelvic bones and femur show bipedal locomotion. In addition to Lucy, other fossils from Hadar show bipedalism, including a knee joint. Also, fossil footprints have been found at the site of Laetoli dating back to 3.75 million years B.P. (Figure 12.4). These prints show the bipedal characteristics of a nondivergent big toe, heel strike, and a well-developed arch.

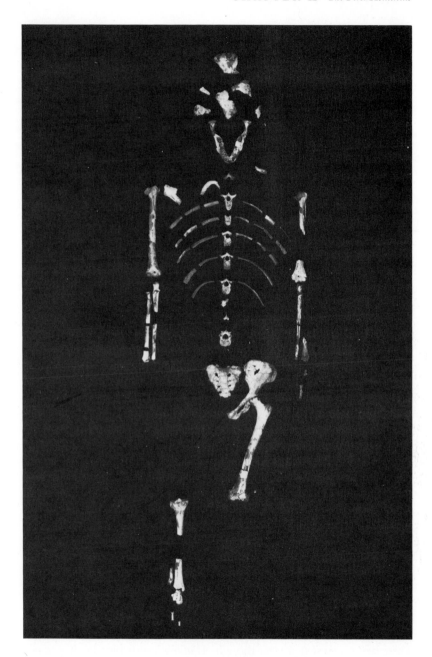

Figure 12.2

The skeletal remains of
"Lucy," a 40 percent complete
specimen of *Australopithecus
afarensis.* (The Cleveland
Museum of Natural History)

Figure 12.3

Comparison of the pelvic anatomy of modern human males and females. (From *Human Antiquity: An Introduction to Physical Anthropology and Archaeology,* 2d ed., by Kenneth Feder and Michael Park, Fig. 7.17. Copyright © 1993 by Mayfield Publishing Company)

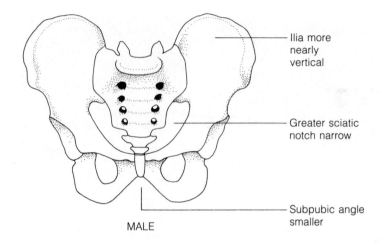

Ilia more nearly vertical

Greater sciatic notch narrow

Subpubic angle smaller

MALE

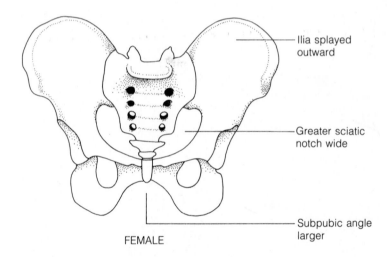

Ilia splayed outward

Greater sciatic notch wide

Subpubic angle larger

FEMALE

All this evidence shows that *A. afarensis* was bipedal. Because bipedal locomotion is unique to humans among living primates, we classify *A. afarensis* as a hominid. Although *A. afarensis* was bipedal, opinion differs on *how* bipedal it was. Some have noted certain ape tendencies in the postcranial material, such as relatively long arms and curved toe bones. These data suggest that even though *A. afarensis* was bipedal, it was not completely modern and did not walk in exactly the same way we do. Also, this evidence suggests that *A. afarensis* had considerable climbing ability (Stern and Susman 1983).

Cranial material for *A. afarensis* is scarce, but enough exists to allow a composite reconstruction (Figure 12.5). Examination of all cranial remains shows that *A. afarensis* had a small brain, ranging in size between

Figure 12.4

Fossil footprints at the Laetoli site. (Photo by Peter Jones, courtesy of Tim White)

Figure 12.5

Reconstruction of the
Australopithecus afarensis skull.
(Institute of Human Origins)

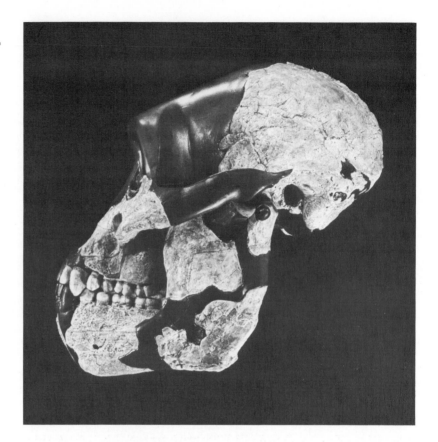

400 and 500 ml (Blumenberg 1985). These remains also show a number
of primitive hominoid features, such as a well-developed crest on the back
of the skull for neck muscle attachment and the shape of the external ear
canal (Johanson and White 1979). Overall, the skull of *A. afarensis* resembles that of a small ape.

The teeth of *A. afarensis* show a number of characteristics intermediate between those of apes and humans. The teeth of modern apes and
humans can be easily distinguished (Figure 12.6). The canines of modern
apes are large and project past the surface of the other teeth, whereas
modern humans have small, nonprojecting canine teeth. The canine teeth
of *A. afarensis* are intermediate; they are larger and more projecting than
modern humans, but smaller than most modern apes. An ape's upper jaw
has a diastema (gap) between the canine and the adjacent incisor. This
space is needed for the large lower canine to fit into when an ape closes its
jaw. Modern humans do not have a diastema. The jaws of *A. afarensis* show
a small diastema, larger than modern humans but smaller than modern
apes. The lower first premolar of a modern ape is pointed with one

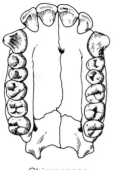
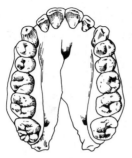
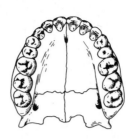

Chimpanzee
upper jaw

Australopithecus afarensis
upper jaw

Modern human
upper jaw

Figure 12.6

Comparison of the teeth and upper jaws of a modern chimpanzee, *Australopithecus afarensis*, and of a modern human. In most features, the teeth and jaws of *Australopithecus afarensis* are intermediate between those of modern apes and modern humans (see text).

cusp, whereas the lower premolar of a modern human has two cusps ("bicuspid"). The lower premolar teeth of *A. afarensis* show two cusps, but one cusp is more developed than the other—an intermediate condition. The orientation of the cusps to the jaw is like that of an ape. Indeed, most features of the jaws and teeth of *A. afarensis* show a state intermediate between that of ape and human.

What can we tell about the behavior of *A. afarensis*? No evidence for stone tool manufacture has been found with *A. afarensis*. As discussed earlier, this does not mean that they may not have been using tools made of perishable materials, such as wooden digging sticks. Analyses of dental remains show a wide range of variation in size, which suggests extensive sexual dimorphism. If our observations on living primates can be applied, such sexual dimorphism suggests a polygynous social structure (one adult male and several adult females). Such inferences, however, may not always be appropriate in dealing with a form unlike any living primate. The discovery of fossils from 13 individuals from one Hadar site representing males and females of all ages has led Johanson to suggest that they were a family group that all perished in a short period of time, perhaps because of a flash flood (Johanson and Edey 1981). Many now think that the fossils of all these individuals were together because of animal scavenging or some other factor that could result in the deposition of bones from different individuals at one site.

In summary, *A. afarensis* shows a number of primitive features in its jaws, teeth, skull, and postcranial skeleton. These features often show an intermediate condition between those found in apes and humans. Because *A. afarensis* was bipedal, it is a hominid, but its primitive features suggest it was not far from the split between ape and hominid evolutionary lines. This hypothesis is supported by molecular evidence (Chapter 11), which suggests a relatively recent ape-human split, roughly five to eight million years ago. In any case, *A. afarensis* seems to have existed almost a million years without any noticeable change, according to Johanson and White's

Australopithecus boisei The most robust of the australopithecines, dating between 1 and 2.5 million years B.P. and found in East Africa.

zygomatic arch The bone on the side of the skull connecting the zygomatic and temporal bones that anchors muscles used in chewing.

sagittal crest A ridge of bone running down the center of the top of the skull that serves to anchor chewing muscles.

Figure 12.7

Lower jaw of *Australopithecus boisei* from the Lake Natron site, Tanzania. Note the small front teeth (incisors and canines) and the massive back teeth (premolars and molars). (From Clark Spencer Larsen, Robert M. Matter, and Daniel L. Gebo, *Human Origins: The Fossil Record, Second Edition*, p. 67 (bottom). Copyright © 1991, 1985 by Waveland Press, Inc., Prospect Heights, Illinois. Reprinted with permission from the publisher)

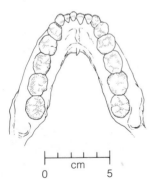

```
    |----|----|----|
    0      cm       5
```

(1979) interpretation of the similarities between the Hadar material and the geologically older Laetoli finds. This lack of change fits with the concept of evolutionary stasis as proposed in the theory of punctuated equilibrium. *A. afarensis* was a successful species for a time, but it ultimately evolved into other australopithecine forms.

Robust australopithecines. Environmental reconstructions show us that climatic factors, such as temperature and rainfall, have varied in the past. In East Africa temperatures dropped roughly 2.5 million years ago, leading to a reduction in woodlands and an increase in open grasslands. Along with this change came an increase in the number of species of certain mammals, such as antelopes, that adapted to this new environment (Vrba 1985). There is also evidence of two or more hominid species appearing at this time, presumably as a consequence of the same set of ecological changes. One was *Australopithecus boisei* (the species name comes from the Boise fund, which sponsored the research leading to the discovery of the first specimen assigned to this species).

A. boisei had very large back teeth and a massive facial structure. This species has been found at the east and west shores of Lake Turkana, Olduvai Gorge, and several other East African locations. Specimens have been found dating from 1 to 2.5 million years B.P. The most recently discovered specimen, found at 2.5 million years B.P. (specimen WT 17000), is more primitive in certain features, and some have suggested it be given a different species name. Here it will be treated as an early example of *A. boisei*. As we will see later, however, this new find has led to considerable rethinking about the nature of australopithecine speciation.

A. boisei was somewhat larger and heavier than *A. afarensis*. It was roughly 1.5 m tall (slightly less than 5 ft). Males weighed roughly 49 kg (108 lbs) and females weighed roughly 32 kg (71 lbs) (McHenry 1992). Like *A. afarensis,* this species had a small brain, ranging from 410 to 530 ml (Blumenberg 1985; Walker et al. 1986). The major differences between this species and other australopithecines are in the skull, jaw, and teeth. By this stage in australopithecine evolution, the overall structure of the teeth has become human. That is, the canines are small and nonprojecting, there is no diastema, and the lower premolar has two cusps. In terms of size, however, the teeth of *A. boisei* are quite different from most modern humans. The front teeth (incisors and canines) are small, both in absolute size and in relationship to the rest of the teeth. The back teeth (premolars and molars) are huge, over four times the size of those of modern humans. Figure 12.7 shows the lower jaw of an *A. boisei* specimen. Note how massive the jaw is and how large the back teeth are, especially in relationship to the front teeth. Also note that the premolars are larger side to side than front to back. These features all show a huge surface area for the back teeth, indicating heavy chewing.

The skulls of *A. boisei* also reflect heavy chewing. A picture of an *A. boisei* skull is shown in Figure 12.8. These skulls show massive dished-in

Figure 12.8

Side, top, and frontal views of an *Australopithecus boisei* skull, specimen KNM-ER 406, from Lake Turkana, Kenya. (© The National Museums of Kenya)

faces, large flaring cheek bones, and a large bony crest running down the top. All these features are related to large jaws and back teeth and powerful chewing muscles (Figure 12.9). Two muscles are responsible for closing the mouth during chewing. One, the masseter, runs from the back portion of the jaw to the forward portion of the **zygomatic arch** (the bone on the side of the skull connecting the zygomatic and temporal bones). The zygomatic arch and facial skeleton anchor this muscle. In hominids with large jaws and masseter muscles, the face and zygomatic arch need to be massive to withstand the force generated during chewing. The other muscle, the temporalis, runs from the jaw up under the zygomatic arch and attaches to the sides and top of the skull. The larger this muscle is, the more the zygomatic arch must flare out from the side of the skull. To anchor the temporalis muscle on the sides and top of the skull, a ridge of bone develops down the center of the skull (called a **sagittal crest**). All these cranial and facial features indicate powerful chewing activity.

A link between *A. afarensis* and *A. boisei* was discovered at West Turkana (Walker et al. 1986). This skull, specimen WT 17000 (also known as the "Black Skull"), dates to 2.5 million years B.P. This date is 500,000

Figure 12.9

Skull of *Australopithecus boisei* with arrows indicating the action of chewing muscles: (*top*) temporalis, (*bottom*) masseter.

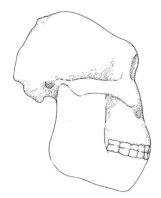

Australopithecus robustus
A robust species of australopithecine, dating between 1
and 2 million years B.P. and
found in South Africa.

years earlier than all previously discovered specimens of *A. boisei.* This
skull shows the characteristic *A. boisei* features such as a large face and
zygomatic arch and a sagittal crest (Figure 12.10). In other points it is
somewhat different, showing primitive hominid features. These include
the angle of the base of the skull and the shape of the jaw joint. This
specimen shares those features with *A. afarensis.* Some have suggested
assigning WT 17000 to a new species, but this classification is probably
not warranted at present. In any case, the skull has the right anatomy and
is the right age to make a link between *A. afarensis* and later *A. boisei.*

Another robust australopithecine species, ***Australopithecus robustus,***
has been identified based on specimens found in South Africa, dated approximately from 1 to 2 million years B.P. The species was so named
because it was the first discovered "robust" species. In cranial and dental
features, *A. robustus* is very similar to *A. boisei* but is generally not as large.
An *A. robustus* skull is shown in Figure 12.11. Like *A. boisei,* it has a large,
flat face and large cheekbones. It also has a sagittal crest. Though not as
massive in size as *A. boisei,* this skull is clearly robust. The lower jaw shown
in Figure 12.12 reveals small front teeth and large back teeth, also similar
to *A. boisei* but not as huge.

The similarities between *A. robustus* and *A. boisei* have led many anthropologists to place them in the same species, suggesting that perhaps
their differences in overall robustness reflect geographic separation. Other

Figure 12.10

The "Black Skull," specimen
KNM-WT 17000, Lake
Turkana, Kenya. This australopithecine shows a mixture
of specialized robust features
(the sagittal crest) and primitive features (the forward
jutting of the jaw). This mix
of features makes it a good
candidate for a transitional
form between *Australopithecus afarensis* and *Australopithecus boisei.*   (A. Walker/©
The National Museums of Kenya)

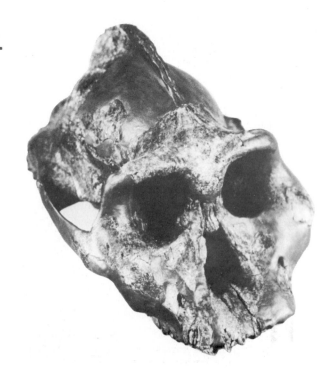

Figure 12.11

Skull of *Australopithecus robustus,* specimen SK 48, Swartkrans, Republic of South Africa. (Transvaal Museum)

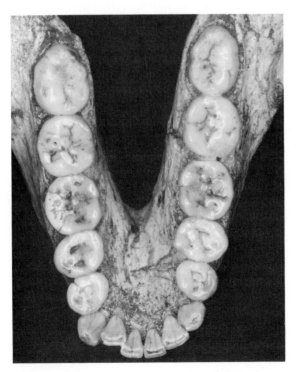

Figure 12.12

Lower jaw of *Australopithecus robustus,* specimen SK 23, Swartkrans, Republic of South Africa. Because of distortion, the rows of the jaw are closer than they should be. Note the small front teeth and the large back teeth. (Transvaal Museum)

Australopithecus africanus
A species of australopithecine dating between 3 and 4 million years B.P. and found in South Africa.

anthropologists have made a case for two different species (e.g., Rak 1983).

What factors led to the changes from early *Australopithecus* to one or both robust australopithecines? Because the major changes are in the teeth, jaws, and chewing characteristics, a different diet seems a likely answer. As the environment became drier, vegetation and fruit would be relatively harder to chew (Vrba 1985). Larger back teeth and more powerful chewing muscles would provide the ability to process this altered food efficiently and would be selected for. Their diet is thought to have consisted of small, hard-to-chew objects, such as seeds, nuts, and hard fruits. Such objects require heavy chewing and large teeth.

Regardless of the specific adaptations of the robust australopithecines, they became extinct by roughly 1 million years B.P. Their extinction could relate to environmental change because another episode of climatic cooling took place during this time. In any case, they are not our ancestors but merely "cousins" who are no longer alive.

Australopithecus africanus. Australopithecine specimens found in South Africa between 2 and 3 million years B.P. have been placed in the species *Australopithecus africanus* (named after Africa). Similar specimens in East Africa dating to roughly 1.5 million years B.P. have also been assigned to this species by some scholars (although there is continuing debate about whether the East African specimens belong to this or another species).

A. africanus had reduced canines, large faces, and an average brain size of 440 ml (Conroy et al. 1990). Compared to the robust australopithecines, *A. africanus* had a smaller face and teeth. For this reason, *A. africanus* has often been called the "gracile" form, indicating its slender appearance relative to the robust forms *A. robustus* and *A. boisei*. The term *gracile* is somewhat misleading, because *A. africanus* was still robust, compared to modern humans, in its face and teeth.

A skull of *A. africanus* is shown in Figure 12.13. Like other australopithecines, it had a small brain and a large face. The face is not as massive as the robust forms, however, and there is no sagittal crest. A lower jaw of *A. africanus* is shown in Figure 12.14. Compared to the robust forms, the front teeth are not as small relative to the back teeth. In overall size, however, the back teeth of *A. africanus* are still larger than those of modern humans.

According to some, the generalized morphology of *A. africanus* makes it a likely candidate for an ancestor to the genus *Homo*. There has been considerable controversy over whether *A. afarensis* or *A. africanus* is the ancestor of the genus *Homo* (this issue is further complicated by a proposal that the two groups should be classified as geographic variants of the same species). In any case, in considering the relationships among the Plio-Pleistocene hominids, we must also take into account a fifth species—

Figure 12.13

Skull of *Australopithecus africanus,* specimen STS 5, Sterkfontein, Republic of South Africa. (Transvaal Museum)

Figure 12.14

Lower jaw of *Australopithecus africanus,* specimen STS 52b, Sterkfontein, Republic of South Africa. The teeth are larger than in modern humans, but the relative proportions of front and back teeth are more similar to those of modern humans than those of the robust australopithecines are. (From Clark Spencer Larsen, Robert M. Matter, and Daniel L. Gebo, *Human Origins: The Fossil Record, Second Edition,* p. 59. Copyright © 1991, 1985 by Waveland Press, Inc., Prospect Heights, Illinois. Reprinted with permission from the publisher)

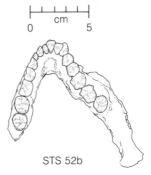

STS 52b

Homo habilis The oldest known species in the genus *Homo,* dating between 1.5 and 2.4 million years B.P. and found in Africa, similar in appearance to australopithecines but with a larger cranial capacity.

Homo habilis. This species differs from the australopithecines in having a larger brain, smaller teeth, and a definite association with stone tools.

Homo Habilis

Starting in the 1930s, Louis and Mary Leakey conducted fieldwork at the site of Olduvai Gorge in Tanzania. Among their early finds were the remains of the then oldest known stone tools, dating back throughout the Pleistocene. For many years the Leakeys searched Olduvai Gorge looking for the maker of these tools. In 1960, they found a jaw, two cranial fragments, and several postcranial remains dating to 1.75 million years B.P. These finds represented a hominid with smaller teeth and a larger brain than that of any of the australopithecines found up to that time. Continued work led to the discovery of several more specimens, and in 1964 Leakey and colleagues proposed a new species based on this material—***Homo habilis*** (Leakey et al. 1964). The species name literally translates as "handy man," named for its association with manufactured stone tools. Since that time, additional fossils attributed to *H. habilis* have been found at East Turkana by the Leakeys' son Richard. *H. habilis* has also been found in South Africa (Clarke 1985). *H. habilis* has been dated to 1.5 to 2.4 million years B.P. Until recently, the oldest specimens of *Homo* were dated to roughly 2 million years ago. After reanalysis, a cranial bone originally found in 1967 has been dated to 2.4 million years (Hill et al. 1992).

coefficient of variation A comparative statistic that measures relative variability within a sample.

General Physical Characteristics

The major distinguishing feature of *Homo habilis,* compared to the australopithecines, is its larger brain size. The teeth and postcranial skeleton also show differences.

Brain size. The most noticeable difference between *H. habilis* and the australopithecines is the larger average brain size of *H. habilis.* The average cranial capacity of *A. africanus* is roughly 440 ml. The average cranial capacity of *H. habilis* is 660 ml, which is 50 percent larger than that of *A. africanus* (Blumenberg 1985). Though some researchers have suggested the larger brain size was the result of larger body size, recent finds suggest that some *H. habilis* specimens were no more than a meter tall; roughly the same size as small *A. africanus* and *A. afarensis* specimens (Johanson et al. 1987). These recent conclusions, however, are preliminary at present.

The cranial capacity of *H. habilis* specimens ranges from 509 to 810 ml, overlapping the range of australopithecines and the later species *Homo erectus.* Some anthropologists have suggested that the large range in cranial capacity is evidence that two different species are being lumped together in the fossils we call *H. habilis* (Stringer 1986; Lieberman et al. 1988). Much of the controversy revolves around a statistical estimate called the **coefficient of variation,** which is a measure of variation adjusting for overall size that can be compared among species of different sizes. Stringer (1986) and others have suggested that the coefficient of variation obtained from lumping all early *Homo* specimens into the single species of *H. habilis* is higher than found among modern apes and humans. In a recent study, however, Miller (1991) has shown that once you adjust for small sample size and other factors, the coefficient of variation for *H. habilis* is what you would expect for a sexually dimorphic primate species. Females, being smaller on average, would have smaller *absolute* cranial capacities. The discovery of a very small *H. habilis* skeleton supports the idea that *H. habilis* was a highly dimorphic species (Lewin 1987b).

A number of anthropologists disagree with this interpretation. Wood (1992), for example, argues that what we call *H. habilis* actually consists of members of at least two species of early *Homo.* His argument is based on the presence or absence of certain anatomical features in addition to consideration of issues of variability.

One of the first skull fragments assigned to the species *H. habilis* is shown in Figure 12.15. This specimen (OH 16), dating to 1.7 million years B.P., was discovered at Olduvai Gorge. The specimen consists of a reconstructed skull cap. Its estimated cranial capacity is 650 ml. Another example of *H. habilis,* ER 1470, is shown in Figure 12.16. This specimen was discovered near Lake Turkana, Kenya, and is dated to 1.8 million years

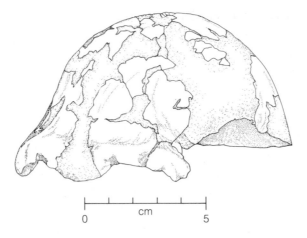

Figure 12.15

Skull of *Homo habilis*, specimen OH 16, Olduvai Gorge, Tanzania. Although this skull is small compared to that of a modern human, its cranial capacity (650 ml) marks it as much larger than the australopithecine skull.   (Figure from *Atlas of Human Evolution*, Second Edition by C. Loring Brace and Harry Nelson, copyright © 1979 by Holt, Rinehart and Winston, Inc., reprinted by permission of the publisher)

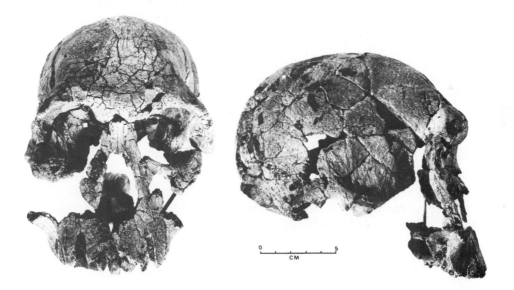

Figure 12.16

Frontal and side views of *Homo habilis*, specimen KNM-ER 1470, Lake Turkana, Kenya.   (© The National Museums of Kenya)

endocast A cast of the interior of the brain case used in analyzing brain size and structure.

B.P. Its cranial capacity is 752 ml (Blumenberg 1985), and it has a rather well-rounded brain case compared to that of the australopithecines.

Figure 12.17 illustrates specimen ER 1813 from the Lake Turkana site in Kenya, dating to 1.8 million years B.P. Whereas some anthropologists classify this specimen as *H. habilis,* others believe it is an East African form of *A. africanus,* and others believe it to be another species of early *Homo.* In facial width and certain features of cranial shape, this specimen resembles others assigned to the species *H. habilis.* It also has the small teeth characteristic of some *H. habilis* specimens. Its cranial capacity, however, is only 509 ml, close to the upper end of the range of variation for *A. africanus.* Is ER 1813 the smallest known specimen of *H. habilis* (in terms of cranial capacity), or is it a large specimen of *A. africanus?* At this point the evidence seems to lean toward the former interpretation, but the question has not been answered completely.

Evidence exists that the brains of *H. habilis* were structurally different than those of the australopithecines in addition to being larger. Falk (1983) investigated an **endocast** (a cast of the interior brain case) of one *H. habilis* specimen and found fissures in the area of the frontal lobes similar to those of modern humans but different from those of apes and australopithecines. This pattern seems to be associated with the development of brain structures linked to language abilities.

Teeth. The teeth of *H. habilis* are in general smaller than those of most australopithecine species, but larger than those of modern humans. In particular, the back teeth are not as large relative to the front teeth as they are in the australopithecines (Figure 12.18). The shape of the pre-

Figure 12.17

Side view of specimen KNM-ER 1813, Lake Turkana, Kenya. This skull is dated to 1.8 million years B.P. The shape and facial and dental measurements suggest to many that this specimen should be placed in the species *Homo habilis.* Its small cranial capacity (509 ml), however, suggests to others that this is an example of an East African form of *Australopithecus africanus* (see text). (From Clark Spencer Larsen, Robert M. Matter, and Daniel L. Gebo, *Human Origins: The Fossil Record, Second Edition,* p. 80 (bottom). Copyright © 1991, 1985 by Waveland Press, Inc., Prospect Heights, Illinois. Reprinted with permission from the publisher)

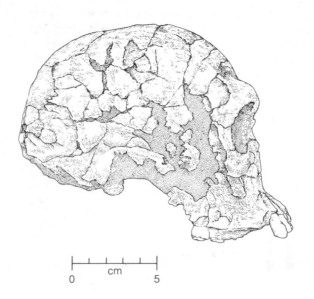

```
|---|---|---|---|---|
0        cm        5
```

molars of *H. habilis* is more similar to that of modern humans; they are more elongated than the premolars of the robust australopithecines.

The skeleton. For many years little was known about the postcranial skeleton of *H. habilis*. The few fossil remains were isolated parts. In 1986, a partial adult skeleton assigned to *H. habilis* was discovered (Johanson et al. 1987). Preliminary analysis suggests this skeleton is similar to that of *A. afarensis* with small size and relatively long arms. Johanson and colleagues assigned this specimen to *H. habilis* on the basis of fragmentary cranial and dental remains; other anthropologists argue that it might be an australopithecine (Falk 1992). Until further discoveries, with more definitive cranial remains, are found, the nature of the postcranial skeleton of *H. habilis* remains unclear.

Behavior

What can we say about the behavior of *H. habilis*? The increase in brain size and changes in brain structure suggest some associated behavioral evolution compared to the australopithecines. When *H. habilis* was first described, there was a tendency to ascribe a variety of modern human behaviors to it, including use of shelter, manufacture of stone tools, and coordinated hunting. Recent work has suggested that the behavior of *H. habilis* was not like that of modern hunting-gathering societies. Certain behaviors, such as stone tool manufacture, did take place.

Stone tool technology. The earliest known stone tools date to 2.5 million years B.P. Many of these stone tools have been found in association with fossil remains of *H. habilis*.

The stone tool culture of *H. habilis*, referred to as the **Oldowan tradition,** consists of relatively simple chopping tools. Several examples of Oldowan tools are shown in Figure 12.19. These tools were made by striking several flakes off a rounded stone to give it a rough cutting edge. They are normally made from materials such as lava and quartz. The stone

Oldowan tradition The stone tool culture of *Homo habilis*.

Figure 12.18

Lower jaw of *Homo habilis*, specimen OH 7, Olduvai Gorge, Tanzania. (Figure from *Atlas of Human Evolution*, Second Edition by C. Loring Brace and Harry Nelson, copyright © 1979 by Holt, Rinehart and Winston, Inc., reprinted by permission of the publisher)

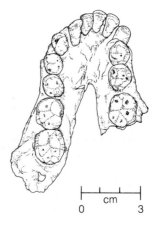

Figure 12.19

Oldowan tools. (From *The Old Stone Age* by F. Bordes, 1968. Reprinted with permission of the publisher, Weidenfeld and Nicolson, Ltd.)

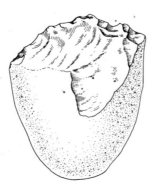

was held steady and was then struck with another stone at the right angle to remove a flake of stone. Several strikes often produced a rough edge capable of cutting through animal flesh or other objects that hominids could not tear themselves. The chipped-off flakes could also be used as small cutting tools. This type of tool manufacture sounds extremely easy but actually involves a great deal of skill, as anthropologists attempting to duplicate these tools have found out. Proper tool manufacture requires skill in finding the right materials and using the right amount of force. Mistakes could ruin a tool and injure a hominid's hand.

These simple chopping tools can be used for a wide variety of purposes. Significantly, they can cut through bone and muscle. Because hominids do not have claws or sharp teeth, these tools would provide the only means to eat an animal. The tools could also be used to sharpen sticks, which then could be used for weapons or digging. Hides could be scraped for a number of uses. These stone tools represent the modification of environmental materials to meet needs that could not otherwise be met. Of course, just finding the tools with *H. habilis* is not enough to demonstrate exactly how they used them.

Until recently, the emphasis on archaeological investigations of *H. habilis* had been on the stone cores produced by flaking. The small flakes, often found in great abundance, were felt to be nothing more than waste material. Analysis of the scratch marks on these flakes, however, shows that they were often used for a variety of tasks, including sawing wood, cutting meat, and cutting grass stems (Klein 1989). Archaeologists analyze these scratches by comparing them to those produced under experimental conditions.

Hunting or scavenging? The older interpretation that *H. habilis* was a hunter has given way to a new interpretation that it was a scavenger. This hypothesis is based on analyses of the stone tools and the distribution of animal bones found alongside these tools. Much of this research is based on *H. habilis* sites at Olduvai Gorge, where both the animal bones and the stone tools had been brought to these sites from further away. To complicate matters, there is extensive evidence of carnivore activity at these sites. One interpretation is that *H. habilis* was responsible for the tools, and the carnivores were responsible for the animal carcasses. In this view, *H. habilis* would bring tools to carnivore dens to scavenge from the remains. It seems unlikely that early hominids would bring stone tools to carnivore dens because of the danger (Potts 1984). Another interpretation is that *H. habilis* was responsible for bringing both carcasses and tools to these sites, and carnivores frequented these sites to scavenge meat.

Electron-scanning microscopes have been used to investigate the cut patterns on stone tools to distinguish marks made by tool use from other factors, such as erosion. These analyses show that the Oldowan tools were used for cutting; many animal bones show the characteristic grooves left by stone tools. Many of these bones, however, also show tooth marks from carnivores. In some cases the tool marks overlap the tooth punctures, showing that stone tools were used on an animal *after* it had been gnawed on by carnivores. Other tools show the opposite pattern. The dead animals were a source of food for both *H. habilis* and carnivores.

But what exactly took place at these sites? One possibility is that *H. habilis* hunted animals and brought the carcasses to sites where they would be disarticulated and the meat would be removed and eaten. Bones would be broken open to get at the nutritious marrow. Carnivores would then scavenge the rest of the meat. Another interpretation is that *H. habilis* was a scavenger, taking the remains of dead animals killed by carnivores or left behind from other nonhuman scavengers, such as hyenas.

The available evidence suggests that *H. habilis* was a scavenger. Over half the cut marks left by stone tools are found on bones with little meat, such as the lower legs. This suggests that *H. habilis* was taking what was left over from carnivores. Also, there is no evidence of complete carcasses of larger animals brought to the Olduvai sites, only portions—and these are most often the bones left over by carnivores (Wolpoff 1980; Potts 1984). In addition, the animal bones are not completely processed and considerable meat and marrow was often left over. This type of behavior is strikingly different from that of modern hunters, who utilize the entire remains of an animal.

Though it is likely that *H. habilis* did hunt occasionally, perhaps in a manner similar to living chimpanzees, the available evidence does not support the idea that it was an organized hunter. Instead, *H. habilis* appears to have been a scavenger of meat from dead and dying animals. Though this might not sound like our idea of a "noble ancestor," the act of scavenging did expand the food resources of early hominids.

Home bases? The association of stone tools with *H. habilis* suggested to many anthropologists a wide variety of cultural behaviors. Given stone tools, these hominids could hunt game and bring portions back to feed others. This interpretation further suggests the presence of social groups with division of labor, in which some individuals brought meat back to others. The stone tools are often found at sites with many animal bones, usually broken into smaller pieces. This association suggests that these sites were **home bases,** camp sites where hunted animals were brought, processed, and distributed to the members of the group. Presumably others would gather fruit and vegetation and bring them back to the home base.

The idea that these sites were home bases for *H. habilis* was widely accepted until recently. Because modern hunters and gatherers have home sites, it seemed reasonable to assume that any collection of stone tools and animal remains in the archaeological record was evidence of home bases. Other interpretations of these sites are possible, however. As discussed, *H. habilis* was most likely a scavenger rather than a hunter. Nevertheless, is it still possible to consider the sites where scavenged carcasses were brought to be home bases?

The evidence of carnivore activity at the Olduvai sites suggests that these were not home bases. Teeth marks left on hominid bones show that

home base Camp site where hunters brought back food for sharing with other members of their group.

H. habilis was often prey to large carnivores. It seems unlikely that early hominids would camp near a carnivore den! Also, much of the scavenging seems to have been done hastily, as though the hominids were trying to finish what they were doing and get away as quickly as possible.

The archaeological evidence shows that *H. habilis* was the first step in future cultural evolution. Though the stone tools were crude and most likely used for scavenging, they marked the beginning of an adaptive pattern that relied more and more on technological advances and increased problem solving. From this point on, the mainstream of human evolution consists of further associated changes in both biology and cultural behaviors. The rest of this story is told in the next chapter. Before ending this discussion of Plio-Pleistocene hominids, though, we must answer one more general question—when and how did *H. habilis* evolve from the australopithecines?

Models of Plio-Pleistocene Hominid Evolution

The study of the historical development of any scientific discipline is important for a number of reasons. Because science is an ongoing, cumulative process, its current state always partially reflects past ideas and hypotheses. Even after hypotheses have been rejected, they may still continue to influence further thinking in a field. Scientists also do not work in a vacuum but are rather part of a larger culture, and current intellectual philosophies can have a major impact on the formulation of hypotheses and interpretation of data. In the case of paleoanthropology, these problems are compounded by the very sequence of fossil discoveries. The following section provides examples of how scientific change occurs by discussing the history of discoveries of the australopithecines and *H. habilis*.

The Discovery of Plio-Pleistocene Hominids: A Historical Perspective

A great many scenarios have been proposed for hominid origins, some logical and some fanciful. Any model must be more than logical. It must also be capable of being tested. The fossil evidence for hominid origins is not as complete as we would like, but it has been useful in testing a number of origin models. Fossil data have been used to test models and also to construct new models based on available evidence.

Early ideas about the first hominids. Since the eighteenth century, many scientists have noted the close relationship of modern humans to modern apes, particularly the chimpanzee. It seemed reasonable for early scholars to suggest that there was some evolutionary relationship between ourselves and the African apes. These similarities led Charles Darwin to suggest that Africa was the birthplace of the hominids, creating popular speculation in turn about the nature of a "missing link" between apes and humans. Although the concept of a "missing link" continues to be exploited by the media, the notion has little scientific value. The "missing link" is supposed to be part modern human and part modern ape. This concept has also led to the popular and incorrect notion that we have evolved from the modern apes. In reality, both modern apes and modern humans have evolved from a common ancestor.

Early theories of hominid origins seldom dealt with the fact that both apes and humans had evolved. Instead, humans were considered to be "more evolved" and evolutionary models were constructed to deal with the nature of the changes in humans. Because few data on fossils were available at the beginning of the twentieth century, the issue of hominid origins had to be addressed through comparisons of modern apes and modern humans. Such comparisons show that four major human features must be explained by any model of hominid origins: (1) large brain, (2) bipedalism, (3) small canine teeth, and (4) a dependence on culture.

At the beginning of the twentieth century a popular model hypothesized that brain size evolved first, followed by bipedalism. Scientists predicted that reduction of the teeth would come later. The hypothetical "missing link" would have the large brain of a modern human and the face and teeth of a modern ape. The fossil evidence then available did not contradict this hypothesis. We now know this is not the way things happened, but at the time fossil evidence uncovered at the site of Piltdown in England seemed to support this view.

Piltdown Man was discovered in 1911 and 1915 alongside remains of prehistoric animals such as mastodons and in association with prehistoric stone tools (Figure 12.20). The specimen consisted of a large skull and an

Piltdown Man Forged fossil specimens found in England and once thought to be a "missing link" between apes and humans.

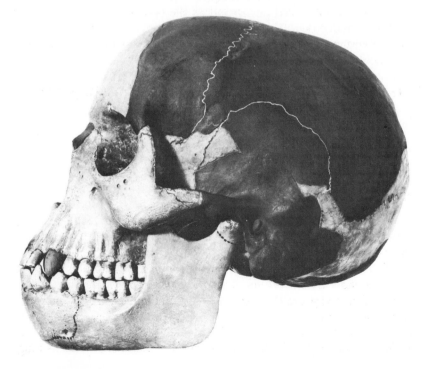

Figure 12.20

Side view of Piltdown Man. The dark-colored areas and the back part of the lower jaw were found; the rest was reconstructed. This find, which confirmed the then-popular notion that early humans had large brains and apelike jaws, was a hoax: the remains of a modern human and an orangutan were placed together at the Piltdown site. (Neg. no. 123869. Courtesy Department of Library Services, American Museum of Natural History)

apelike jaw. The teeth, however, were worn flat, more closely resembling the condition of human teeth. This specimen showed the predicted mix of modern human and modern ape traits. Because of the Piltdown find, other known fossil material now assigned to the genus *Homo* (and discussed in the next chapter) was accordingly judged to be not on the main line of human evolution.

For a time, any other fossil hominid remains were rejected because they did not fit the model supported by Piltdown Man. Indeed, this was *part* of the initial reluctance for scientists to accept *Australopithecus* as a hominid. The first australopithecine was discovered by Raymond Dart in 1924. The specimen consisted of the face, teeth, and cranial fragments (including a cast of the brain case) of a young child. Dart named the specimen *Australopithecus africanus* and concluded that it represented the first hominid. Based on cranial evidence relating to the angle at which the spinal cord enters the skull, he also claimed it was an upright walker. Some scientists claimed (correctly) that such interpretations were hazardous when based on such a young specimen. Others were influenced by the Piltdown evidence, and *A. africanus* did not seem to fit in. The Piltdown specimens fit the then-current idea that brain size evolved first. Dart's find seemed to contradict this idea, and many were therefore disposed to regard *A. africanus* as an unusual ape.

Some scientists were more skeptical about the Piltdown find. Continued investigation showed eventually that the find was a fake. In 1953, fluorine analysis (see Chapter 10) confirmed that the jaw bones and skull bones did not come from the same time period. Close inspection showed the skull was a fossil of a modern human and the jaw was an orangutan's. The teeth had been filed down, and all the bones had been chemically treated to simulate age. The remains of other animals found at the site had been taken from a variety of localities around the world. To this day, no one knows who was responsible for the Piltdown hoax, although several suspects are known to have had both motive and opportunity.

By the 1960s, most anthropologists no longer ranked *Australopithecus* as an unusual ape but as a hominid. As additional adult specimens were discovered, it was found that the dental traits found in *Australopithecus* were hominid, not those of apes. Research in South Africa led to the discovery of enough postcranial data to show conclusively that *Australopithecus* was a biped. The hypothesis that large brains evolved first was rejected. The first hominids were upright walkers with large faces and teeth and small brains. As is common in science, however, the discoveries that led to the rejection of one hypothesis gave rise to additional hypotheses and debates.

The single species and dietary hypotheses. By the late 1950s, many different genus and species names had been given to the australopithecine finds from South Africa. Evolutionary relationships were complicated by the tendency for each new discovery to be given a new name as well as the problem of dating the South African sites. Eventually, most workers resolved the first problem by classifying all the known specimens into two species: *Australopithecus africanus* and *Australopithecus robustus*. Two major evolutionary hypotheses were proposed. The first, known as the **single species hypothesis,** proposed that the two species were actually only a single species—*A. africanus*. The robust specimens were thought to be within the range of variation of that species. In other words, all along there had been only one species showing a certain amount of variation in dental size. Further modifications of the single species hypothesis claimed that only one species of hominid had ever existed at any one point in time—in other words, that all of hominid evolution could be explained by anagenesis.

Another hypothesis was also proposed. In the **dietary hypothesis,** the two forms were considered to be separate species, each with a different form of adaptation. The robust species, with its large teeth and chewing muscles, was a specialized herbivore. *A. africanus* was a more generalized species, eating both meat and plant food and capable of using simple stone tools (which had been found by this time). According to this model, *A. africanus* evolved into the genus *Homo*.

The evidence today clearly rejects the single species hypothesis as it was first formulated. Evidence given in this chapter and the next show that at *least* two species of hominids coexisted for a long time. But even though the multiple species idea is now accepted, we also realize that the situation is not as simple as first formulated in the dietary hypothesis, either. Other specimens ultimately assigned to additional species were discovered in the 1960s and 1970s, complicating the picture of Plio-Pleistocene evolution.

The East African discoveries. Fossil evidence from the Plio-Pleistocene in East Africa has been extremely important in revising our ideas of early hominid evolution. First, the sites in East Africa have often been dated with chronometric methods, thus giving us precise ideas of relationships through time. Second, the variation present in East African hominids has made the simple one-species or two-species models initially derived from the South African data seem overly simplistic. Perhaps much debate could have been eliminated had we had the good fortune to discover some of the East African material first!

The East African evidence has led to the naming of three additional Plio-Pleistocene hominid species: *Australopithecus boisei* in 1959, *Homo habilis* in 1964, and *Australopithecus afarensis* in 1978. In all three cases, the announcement of the new species has met with resistance and the suggestion that the fossils could be placed in other known species. One of these suggestions has been to place *A. boisei* in the species *A. robustus*

single species hypothesis A model of Plio-Pleistocene hominid evolution, no longer accepted, that stated that only one species of hominid was present at any point in time.

dietary hypothesis A model first developed in the 1960s that posits two major evolutionary lines in hominid evolution during the Plio-Pleistocene, one line adapted to a vegetarian diet and the other to an omnivorous diet.

because both are robust australopithecines. Because one species has been found in East Africa and the other in South Africa, they perhaps represent geographic variants of the same species (in which case the species name *A. robustus* would take precedence, because according to international rules the older name supersedes the newer if two species are lumped together).

The naming of *Homo habilis* was also controversial (see Lewin 1987a). Some scientists argued that there were insufficient data to warrant the naming of a new species. The specimens assigned to *H. habilis* might be considered as transitional forms between *A. africanus* and later forms of the genus *Homo*. The discovery of the large-brained specimen ER 1470 seemed to validate the distinctiveness of the species *Homo habilis,* but the situation is still not clear. For one thing, ER 1470 is in some ways different than the first assigned specimens of *H. habilis.* Perhaps another species name is warranted, but is it necessarily the one first proposed for somewhat different fossils? Do all the *H. habilis* specimens belong in a single variable species, or are several species present in the fossil record?

The naming of the most recently discovered species, *Australopithecus afarensis,* has also been the subject of much debate. Some think that these specimens are not sufficiently different from *A. africanus* to warrant a different species name. Others think that there is evidence that what we call *A. afarensis* is in reality two separate species.

New finds have often led to rejection of previous hypotheses. Prior to 1986, many (but not all) anthropologists felt that *A. africanus* was a direct ancestor of the robust australopithecines. The discovery of the "Black Skull" in 1986 rejected this idea, because the find showed a mixture of traits connecting *A. afarensis* with the robust australopithecines.

As additional fossils are discovered, it is possible for us to reject certain hypotheses and to revise others. Given the nature of scientific research, it is best to look at different hypotheses of evolutionary relationship in terms of relative probability. The next section looks at current evolutionary models and some of the answers to the questions posed here.

Alternative Family Trees

Five species of fossil hominid have been discussed in this chapter: four species of *Australopithecus* and one species of *Homo*. The next chapter will examine two additional species, *Homo erectus* and *Homo sapiens,* which show further increases in brain size and technological advances. The most common interpretation is an evolutionary sequence within the genus *Homo* from *H. habilis* to *H. erectus* to *H. sapiens*. But from which species of australopithecine did *H. habilis* evolve?

As a starting point, examine the family tree shown in Figure 12.21. This model, and slight variants of it, are at present the most commonly accepted interpretation of the Plio-Pleistocene hominid evidence (keep in mind that being the most accepted doesn't make a model correct). This model starts with *A. afarensis* as the common ancestor of several later

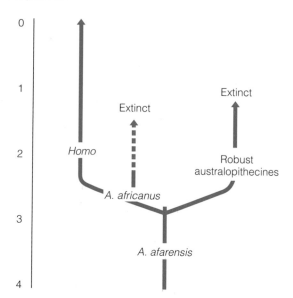

Millions of years B.P.

Figure 12.21

Proposed model of Plio-Pleistocene hominid evolution. *A. afarensis* is seen as the common ancestor of two evolutionary lines. One line shows evolution into *A. africanus* into *Homo*. The other line leads to the robust australopithecines. The dashed lines for *A. africanus* indicate uncertainty regarding the survival of this species in East Africa until 1.5 million years ago.

hominid species, based on its age and primitive characteristics. By 2.5 million years ago, one or more species branched off of this line to become the robust australopithecines, who in turn became extinct by 1 million years ago. There is continuing debate over whether there were actually two different species of robust australopithecine, or whether *A. robustus* and *A. boisei* represent geographic variants of a single species. For this discussion, it hardly matters, since the main point is that the robust forms evolved from *A. afarensis*. The Black Skull, with its mixture of robust and primitive features, provides us with evidence linking *A. afarensis* with the robust forms. By 3 million years ago another species, *A. africanus*, also evolved from a population of *A. afarensis*. By 2.5 million years ago, *A. africanus* gave rise to *Homo*. At this point, *A. africanus* is taken as an intermediate form between *A. afarensis* and *Homo*, based on similarities in facial structure, cranial shape, and other anatomical features. Note that a dotted line extends the time range of *A. africanus* up until 1.5 million years ago, reflecting uncertainty regarding the placement of *some* of the fossils traditionally considered to be small members of *H. habilis*. Several researchers believe that they may instead represent East African forms of *A. africanus* (e.g., Falk 1992).

The family tree shown in Figure 12.21 may not be correct in all details. Further fossil evidence and continued analysis is needed to see if this proposed model can stand the test of time. For this section of the chapter, however, it serves as a useful starting point to introduce a number of current controversies that modify the tree.

Figure 12.22

Alternative model of Plio-Pleistocene hominid. This is the same tree as shown in Figure 12.21 except that *A. afarensis* is the direct ancestor of *Homo*, not *A. africanus*.

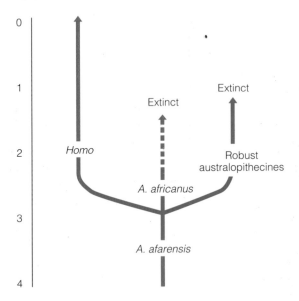

Millions of years B.P.

***Who was the ancestor of* Homo?** A key feature of the suggested model in Figure 12.21 is that *A. africanus* is the direct ancestor of *Homo*. From this perspective, *A. africanus* is our ancestor some 2.5 to 3 million years ago. Not all anthropologists accept this hypothesis, some believing that *A. africanus* was *not* the ancestor of *Homo* but was instead a separate evolutionary line (Kimbel et al. 1988). Based on their interpretations of the fossil evidence, these anthropologists argue instead that there is a direct evolutionary connection between *A. afarensis* and *Homo*. This alternative model is shown in Figure 12.22. Part of the problem in resolving the difference is that there are few complete fossils in East Africa from between 2 and 3 million years ago. Additional data may help us to determine which hypothesis is more likely to be correct.

How many species? Another continuing controversy centers on the assignment of fossil hominids into the species *A. afarensis*. From the initial discoveries at Hadar, the size variation in these hominids has been interpreted in different ways. Johanson and White (1979) proposed that this variation is a product of sexual dimorphism. Others have disagreed, proposing instead that these fossils actually represent two or more separate species (e.g., Olson 1985, Falk 1992). If so, then what would this do to our family tree? One suggestion, shown in Figure 12.23, is to show two separate evolutionary lines present in the fossils usually assigned to the single species of *A. afarensis*. One of these lines leads to the robust australopithecines, the other to the genus *Homo*.

Millions of years B.P.

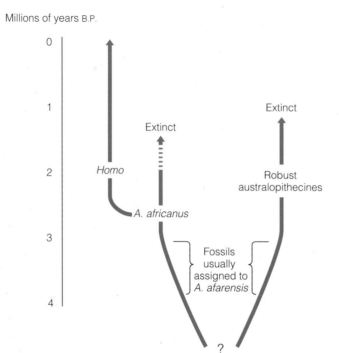

Figure 12.23

Alternative model of Plio-
Pleistocene hominid whereby
the fossils assigned to *A.
afarensis* represent two
separate evolutionary lines.

Consensus? The three models shown here are not the only ones to be
found in the anthropological literature. Many minor variants exist. Some
trees, for example, show the robust australopithecines as two (or more)
different species. Some split the fossils assigned to *H. habilis* into two or
three species. Others lump traditional species together, such as combining
A. afarensis and *A. africanus*. Given this range of ideas regarding the
number of species and their evolutionary relationships, is there *any* agreement at all for this phase of human evolution? Fortunately, yes. All of the
above debates and alternative trees are of course important but focus more
on the *specific* aspects of Plio-Pleistocene hominid evolution. There is considerable consensus on the *general* findings.

Note that all of the trees discussed have several points in common.
First, there is a split at, or prior to, 2.5 to 3.0 million years ago that gives
rise to two different evolutionary paths. One path leads to the robust
australopithecines, characterized by huge molar and premolar teeth and
the cranial anatomy to support large jaws and large chewing muscles. This
line ultimately died out roughly a million years ago. The other path ultimately led to the genus *Homo,* characterized by a large brain, smaller face
and teeth, and an increasing reliance on cultural behaviors for survival.
Regardless of the specific structure of any given family tree, there is much

tool use model A model of hominid origins, no longer accepted, that stated that bipedalism, large brains, and small canines all evolved simultaneously during hominid evolution as a consequence of increased reliance on tool use.

feedback When one factor influences, and is influenced by, other factors in a system.

agreement among anthropologists about the basic general path of early hominid evolution.

Evolutionary Trends

The fossil hominid evidence is clear on *what* happened, at least in general terms. The final question we must address is *why* these patterns evolved. For the Plio-Pleistocene hominids, we must look at three evolutionary trends: (1) the origin of bipedalism; (2) the development of large back teeth, large facial structures, and powerful chewing muscles in the robust australopithecines; and (3) the increase in cranial capacity and the development of a stone tool culture in *H. habilis*.

The Origin of Bipedalism

The australopithecine fossils show us that of all the unique traits used to define hominids (Chapter 9), bipedalism is the oldest. Therefore, any model of hominid origins must consider the origin of bipedalism. Ever since Darwin's time, scientists have proposed hypotheses for the evolutionary advantage of bipedalism. The anatomical changes are known, and it would probably not take major genetic changes to bring about such changes. The critical question is *why* bipedalism would be selected for. Walking on two legs is often less efficient than walking on four legs. Four-legged animals can run faster and maintain their balance more easily than two-legged animals. Why, then, did bipedalism evolve in hominids?

The tool use model. For many decades, the **tool use model,** which postulated that bipedalism, small canines, and large brains were all linked to the use of tools in adapting to the environment, was the accepted explanation for the origin of those characteristics. This idea was first suggested by Charles Darwin and was later expanded by a number of anthropologists such as Washburn (1960). The basis of the model is that **feedback** has occurred among the different hominid adaptations. In other words, one factor influences (and is influenced by) all other factors. This model views hominid characteristics as a complex of interrelated traits that evolved simultaneously.

The use of tools as an adaptive strategy requires learning and intelligence. This is seen in studies of modern chimpanzees who occasionally use tools and pass these skills on to the young. The tool use model of hominid origins states that tool use shifted from being an optional strategy to an essential strategy, presumably as the environment changed. As tool use became more and more important, selection would take place for enhanced learning abilities, intelligence, and relatively larger brains. As

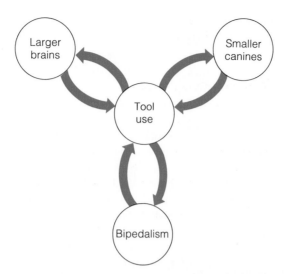

Figure 12.24

The tool use model of hominid origins. According to this model, larger brains, smaller canines, bipedalism, and tool use all developed at the same time. This model is now rejected because we know that bipedalism evolved well before the increase in brain size.

larger brains evolved along with longer periods of infant dependency, tools would become even more important for survival. Thus, tool use affected brain size increase, which in turn affected tool use. This model does not rely on a single cause and single event, but rather on two components (tool use and brain size) that affect each other.

The tool use model also explains the evolution of other hominid characteristics. Upright walking would be advantageous for carrying tools. Freeing the hands would also allow carrying of food, and tools would be useful in obtaining food. Bipedalism would also allow weapons to be carried to fend off predators. Continued bipedalism would lead to even greater reliance on tools. If tools were used for defense (e.g., sticks and stones), then large canines would no longer be necessary for defense and could become smaller (this is a somewhat weak point of the model because it assumes that when a structure is no longer needed it reduces in size). The more tools were used for defense, the more selection for bipedalism and larger brains took place.

The tool use model is a specific hypothesis that was tested using the fossil record (Figure 12.24). If, as the model suggests, the four major hominid characteristics evolved at the same time, then the fossil record should show a gradual change from a form with large canines, small brain, no bipedalism, and no tools to a form with small canines, large brain, bipedalism, and tools. For much of the twentieth century, this model was supported by then-available fossil evidence. During the last two decades, however, newer evidence has led to the rejection of the tool use model as traditionally stated. As we saw earlier in this chapter, bipedalism evolved *before* the increase in brain size. Hominid evolution is mosaic, and we must separate the initial development of bipedalism from its ultimate function in later humans. Bipedalism allows tool use, but it did not evolve because of this characteristic.

Why study the tool use model if it is wrong? First, certain aspects of the model, such as the relationship between brain size and tool use, are still useful. Second, the tool use model provides an excellent example of the ways in which evolutionary models may be tested. Remember that a hypothesis, to be scientific, must be testable.

Many other models have served to explain the origin of bipedalism. Some of the major ideas are outlined below. It is important to stress that perhaps no one single factor was responsible; the origin of bipedalism might have been due to two or more of these factors.

Predator avoidance. Whenever hominids left the woodlands and moved on to the savanna, they were in danger of being hunted by larger carnivores. Four-legged mammals, such as the lion, can move faster than humans over short distances. Walking on two legs would seem to be a disadvantage. In terms of avoiding predators, however, the characteristic shows possible advantages. Some writers have suggested that standing on two legs would allow hominids to see over the savanna and spot potential predators. This is true, but it did not necessarily require the full bipedal adaptations seen in humans. If the only thing needed is the ability to stand up occasionally and scan the surrounding area, any modern ape could do as well. Day (1986) suggests that bipedalism combined with tree-climbing abilities would have been very useful in avoiding predators. It is interesting to note that a number of anthropologists have claimed considerable climbing ability for the earliest hominids.

Reproductive success. Natural selection operates on traits that increase the probability of survival. One way of ensuring increased survival is to increase the number of children or increase the amount of care and protection given to each child. Bipedalism frees the hands, allowing more efficient transportation of babies and greater ease in transporting food.

Owen Lovejoy (1981) has expanded on the idea that bipedalism results in increased reproductive success. His basic premise is that bipedalism evolved as a means of having more offspring and providing better care for them. Lovejoy believes that overlapping births (a characteristic of modern humans) was made possible through bipedalism. When the hands are free to carry food and babies, more than one infant can be cared for at a time (assuming a sedentary population). Overlapping births would therefore result in greater fertility and population growth because a hominid mother would not have to wait until one infant was grown before having another.

Lovejoy argues that caring for infants would reduce the mobility of mothers. How, then, would they obtain food? Lovejoy thinks that monogamous pair bonding developed between males and females so that the more mobile males would bring food back to mothers and infants. In exchange, the males received sex. So that sex would be more frequently available to males, females lost the estrus cycle, becoming continuously sexually receptive. Lovejoy's model therefore also explains the origin of the loss of estrus in hominids.

Though logically consistent, Lovejoy's model has a number of problems. The most serious is that sexual behavior leaves no traces in the fossil record, and even inferences made about social structure are difficult. Some have criticized Lovejoy's model because monogamy is relatively rare among hominoids. When we attempt to infer the behavior of early hominids based on modern apes and humans, however, we are on shaky ground. We have no living primates that approximate the earliest ancestors (essentially bipedal apes). Monogamy *could* have been possible. The real question is: How can we test this hypothesis? If anything, the fossil evidence of the earliest hominids argues against monogamy because the early hominids had considerable sexual dimorphism—a feature most often found in polygynous species.

Lovejoy's model has also been criticized for its basic premise that hominids show greater reproductive success than apes because of overlapping births. Because we cannot obtain measures of fertility from fossil remains, all these arguments have focused on fertility measures from living apes and humans. Some have questioned this assumption (e.g., Allen et al. 1982; Harley 1982), but Lovejoy (1982) has presented countering arguments.

In spite of its problems, Lovejoy's model remains useful in its effort to link bipedalism with increased fertility and/or survival. The monogamy argument and the assumption that females were dependent on males are the additional points many find problematic. Other types of social structure, however, could also account for the basic link between bipedalism and reproductive success. Cann and Wilson (1982) think that the advantages bipedalism provides to mothers is sufficient without invoking the pair-bonding argument. Their idea is attractive because it focuses on the all-important mother-infant bond found in all primate societies. Bipedalism would be useful regardless of the specific type of social structure. Allen and colleagues (1982) note that the most efficient social structure would revolve around a group of related females who could share child care and food procurement. This female kinship group is a social structure found in many primate species, including chimpanzees, and offers an attractive base for the model.

Food acquisition. Along with avoiding predators and reproduction, the other major potential selective factor in survival is obtaining food. Having free hands allows a human to carry more food, which would be particularly advantageous in situations, such as an open woodland or savanna environment, where food was widely distributed. Also, bipedalism is more energy efficient in traveling long distances in search of food. Energy efficiency refers to the amount of energy expended relative to the

TABLE   12.1
Energy Efficiency of Knuckle Walking and Bipedalism

Walking speed	Species	Energy cost	Energy cost compared to normal quadruped (percent)
2.9 km/hr	Chimpanzee	0.522	149
	Human	0.193	86
4.5 km/hr	Chimpanzee	0.426	148
	Human	0.170	94

At both normal walking speeds, bipedal humans are more energy-efficient than knuckle-walking chimpanzees and normal quadrupedal animals of the same size. The normal walking speed of a chimpanzee is 2.9 km/hr; the normal walking speed of a modern human is 4.5 km/hr. Energy cost is measured in milliliters of oxygen per gram per kilometer.

Source: Rodman and McHenry (1980).

task performed. In terms of movement, increased energy efficiency means using less energy to move about looking for and gathering food.

   Though human bipedalism is less efficient than ape locomotion in the act of running, the opposite is true at normal walking speeds. Rodman and McHenry (1980) looked at the energy efficiency of bipedal humans and knuckle-walking chimpanzees at normal walking speeds. The results, shown in Table 12.1, indicate that bipedalism is more energy-efficient at speeds of both 2.9 km per hour (the normal speed of a chimpanzee) and 4.5 km per hour (the normal speed of a human). The results also show that not just walking upright is important but the specific striding bipedal movement of humans as well. Chimpanzees show the same energy efficiency regardless of whether they are knuckle walking or bipedal. Therefore, it is the specific type of bipedalism found in humans that is the most energy-efficient.

   In a changing environment such as that found at the end of the Miocene, food resources would be scattered. The ability to move long distances in search of food would be an advantageous trait, and the shift to a hominid form of bipedalism would provide this ability.

   Temperature regulation. Wheeler (1991b) has suggested recently that bipedalism might be related to temperature regulation among early hominids. Overheating and water loss are considerable threats, particularly to organisms exposed to extensive sunlight on the savanna. Based on laboratory experiments, Wheeler found that standing upright reduces the amount of direct solar radiation that strikes the body. Further, the higher wind speed and lower temperature felt by an animal off the ground would increase the rate of heat dissipation and effective evaporation of sweat. According to Wheeler, bipedalism might have been extremely adaptive for early hominoids venturing into the savannah in search of food.

Of course, it is possible (and perhaps likely) that more than one of the factors listed above played a role in the origin of bipedalism. Many of these are interrelated in an organism's survival. For example, the ability to walk long distances efficiently would enhance food gathering and infant care. As another example, improved temperature regulation would allow a hominid to forage at higher temperatures and to go further distances without having to consume as much water or food (Wheeler 1991a). This increased food gathering ability would also benefit infants.

Given what we know about prehominid locomotion, the shift to bipedalism is reasonable because it involves relatively minor genetic and anatomical changes. Bipedalism is an adaptation that occurred in a changing environment to provide increased survival and reproduction. This change was the first step in human evolution (pun intended).

Dietary Adaptation in the Robust Australopithecines

The large face, cheekbones, and back teeth of the robust australopithecines are all characteristics that support powerful chewing. The increased surface area of the back teeth of the robust australopithecines, especially *A. boisei,* indicates the ability to process large amounts of food. All these features have long been viewed as dietary adaptations. Over time, the robust australopithecines became more specialized to a diet that included a significant amount of hard-to-chew food, such as nuts, seeds, and hard fruits. This specialization allowed the robust australopithecines to make efficient use of environmental resources. As with any specialization, when environmental conditions change, a species may not be able to adjust. Many anthropologists feel this is what ultimately happened to the robust australopithecines, who became extinct roughly a million years ago. If additional data are found confirming the suggestion that the robust forms had tools, this simplified view of dietary adaptations may have to be expanded.

Increased Brain Size in Homo Habilis

The robust australopithecines represent a branch in human evolution, but not our branch. The fossil record shows that *H. habilis* led to the later species *H. erectus* and *H. sapiens.* The major evolutionary changes along our branch of human evolution have been an increase in brain size, a reduction in the size of the face and teeth, and an increase in cultural adaptations. *H. habilis* shows the beginnings of both large brains and stone tool technology. Although it is reasonable to link larger brains with intelligence and cultural adaptations, the origin of larger brains is more difficult

neoteny The retention of juvenile characteristics in adulthood.

Figure 12.25

An infant and adult chimpanzee.   (From *Human Antiquity: An Introduction to Physical Anthropology and Archaeology* 2d ed. by Kenneth Feder and Michael Park, Fig. 8.8. Copyright © 1993 by Mayfield Publishing Company)

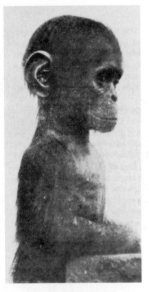

to explain. Any model requires explanation of a genetic mechanism for larger brains as well as the selective advantages of such larger brains.

The genetic basis for larger brains in *H. habilis* and later hominid species most likely lies in the regulation of prenatal and postnatal brain growth. Primates in general show rapid rates of prenatal brain growth. Because primates require larger brains early in life, such rapid rates are necessary. Following birth, the usual primate pattern is for the size of the brain to double during the growth process. Modern humans are different in having more rapid rates of postnatal brain growth, so that our adult brain size is roughly four times that at birth.

Neoteny.   Our large brains can be explained by the process of **neoteny**, which is the retention of juvenile characteristics into adulthood (Gould 1977b). This process is best explained by looking at the difference between an infant chimpanzee and an adult chimpanzee, then comparing this difference to those found between infant and adult humans. Figure 12.25 shows an infant and an adult chimpanzee. With its large rounded skull and relatively small face, the infant looks very similar to an infant human. The adult chimpanzee is different, with a relatively small brain and a large, protruding face. An adult human, however, looks very similar to an infant human. In other words, the shape and relative proportions of brain and face do not change much in humans. Infant apes have relatively large brains because of rapid rates of prenatal brain growth. After birth, however, the rate of brain growth slows down and the face continues to grow. The end result is an adult ape with a relatively small brain. In humans the rapid rate of prenatal brain growth is extended into infancy. Our brains continue to enlarge as our bodies grow. We retain the infant characteristic of a large, well-rounded skull.

Changes in the timing and rates of brain and facial growth can explain the major physical differences between ourselves and apes. Such changes could be the result of a small number of regulatory genes, helping to explain why we look so different from apes but yet have so much of our DNA sequences in common (Gould 1977b). The increase in cranial capacity of *H. habilis* could be a consequence of selection for some initial mutations leading to neoteny. This idea assumes that larger brains and greater intelligence are adaptive. Are they?

Advantages of larger brains.   The benefits of larger brains and greater mental abilities are obvious. They allow greater behavioral flexibility in adaptation through cultural transmission from one generation to the next. Large brains also have a cost. The extension of fetal growth rates into infancy means that offspring will be born even more helpless and require greater parental care, which in turn requires greater reliability of food, more protection, and social structures capable of assisting others. Also, rapid fetal brain growth requires greater maternal energy, which in turn also requires adequate food and environmental stability. Martin (1981) has shown that a lack of adequate maternal energy limits fetal brain growth.

So that new mutations can be selected for, the advantages of larger brains must outweigh the disadvantages. In a population that does not have adequate maternal energy or postnatal parental care, such genes would be selected against. On the other hand, if conditions existed in which adequate maternal energy and postnatal care were available, then more helpless infants with greater rates of brain growth would be selected for. The increase in brain size, intelligence, and cultural adaptations would then provide the basis for additional selection for larger brains. Increased cranial capacity and cultural adaptations are linked in a feedback loop; an increase in cultural adaptations allows further brain growth, which then allows further cultural adaptations.

The radiator theory. If larger brains have an overall advantage, then why didn't they develop among the robust australopithecines? Dean Falk (1990, 1992) has proposed a model of brain evolution in hominids that focuses on heat stress as a constraint on the development of larger brains. Quite simply, large brains in large heads must shed quite a bit of heat. This is particularly a problem if a large-brained hominid is spending a great deal of its time in hot climates such as equatorial Africa. How does the brain cool itself? During heat stress, blood that is cooled by evaporation flows from the skin into the brain case. In modern humans, blood circulates through a network of veins that also allows blood to drain from the brain into the rest of the body. One of Falk's interesting findings was that although some early hominids had this type of drainage system, others had a different one, whereby blood circulated through enlarged sinuses in the occipital and mastoid regions of the skull. Falk suggests that this other drainage system is not as effective in cooling the brain.

It turns out that the robust australopithecines (and the *A. afarensis* fossils from Hadar) had the less efficient system. Skulls of *A. africanus* and *H. habilis* showed a higher frequency of specific foramina (openings in the skull) characteristic of the more effective system. Therefore, it seems that the robust australopithecines did not have a system that would allow a larger brain—they would not have been able to handle the heat stress.

Why didn't the robust australopithecines evolve such a system? Again, evolution works on what variation already exists. For whatever reason (it may have even been random, such as genetic drift), the robust australopithecines had a biological constraint that would have limited any increase in brain size. Their drainage system could only handle the heat stress of a smaller brain. Other hominids, such as *A. africanus,* had a system that *allowed* them to evolve larger brains. Once again, any evolutionary change must be viewed in terms of both costs and benefits. For the robust australopithecines, the costs outweighed the benefits, so they did not evolve larger brains.

SUMMARY

The first hominids belong to the genus *Australopithecus*. The earliest australopithecines, in the species *A. afarensis,* lived between 3 and 4 million years B.P. They were bipedal, but with many primitive features in the teeth, skull, and postcranial skeleton. Between 2.5 and 3 million years B.P., several evolutionary lines developed from *A. afarensis*. One or more lines led to the robust species *A. boisei* and *A. robustus,* and one line led to *Homo habilis*. The robust australopithecines had large back teeth, large faces and cheekbones, and a sagittal crest for anchoring jaw muscles. These characteristics represent specializations for chewing hard foods. The robust australopithecines became extinct by 1 million years B.P.

H. habilis existed in Africa between 1.5 and 2 million years B.P. The main characteristic of this species is its increased cranial capacity, roughly 50 percent larger on average than that of the australopithecines. Remains of *H. habilis* have been found in association with the earliest stone tools. The archaeological evidence suggests that *H. habilis* was a scavenger. The ability to manufacture and use stone tools, along with increased brain size, marks the beginnings of the evolution of the genus *Homo*. The continued evolution of the genus *Homo* is discussed in the next chapter.

Supplemental Readings

Falk, D. 1992. *Braindance*. New York: Henry Holt. This well-written and lively book provides an interesting discussion of several areas of current controversy in the evolution of hominid brains and also gives a general review of the "radiator theory."

Johanson, D., and M. Edey. 1981. *Lucy: The Beginnings of Humankind*. New York: Simon & Schuster. Tells the story of the senior author's discovery and interpretation of *Australopithecus afarensis*. Somewhat out of date but provides a lively historical review of Plio-Pleistocene hominids and is highly recommended.

Lewin, R. 1987. *Bones of Contention: Controversies in the Search for Human Origins*. New York: Simon & Schuster. An excellent account of the history of paleoanthropology. Chapters 3, 4, and 7 to 12 focus on Plio-Pleistocene evolution.

Shipman, P. September 1986. Baffling limb on the family tree. *Discover* 7(9): 87–93. An article for a popular audience that looks at how a new discovery (WT 17000) has led to some reinterpretations of hominid evolution.

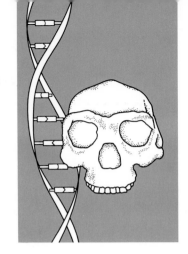

CHAPTER **13**

The Evolution of the Genus *Homo*

Three species are generally recognized in the genus *Homo: Homo habilis, Homo erectus,* and *Homo sapiens.* The evolution of the genus *Homo* involved an increase in brain size, a reduction in the size of the face and teeth, and increased sophistication of stone tool technologies and other cultural adaptations.

Despite this seemingly simple picture, many questions still remain about the specific nature of hominid evolution during the last 1.5 million years. How and why did one species evolve into the next? Were these events true speciations (cladogenesis) or continuations of basic trends over time within a single line (anagenesis)? Has hominid evolution been punctuated or gradual? There are also many questions about behavioral changes. When did hominids first use fire? When did they begin hunting large animals, and why? What types of social organizations existed in the past? What does past evolution tell us about our species today? This chapter looks at the major biological and cultural changes associated with the evolution of *Homo erectus* and *Homo sapiens.*

Homo Erectus

The species name ***Homo erectus*** literally means "upright walking human." This may sound odd, given the fact that five earlier species also walked upright. When the first specimens of *H. erectus* were found in the

Homo erectus A species of genus *homo* that lived between roughly 0.2 to 0.4 and 1.6 million years B.P., first appearing in Africa and later spreading to Asia (and possibly Europe).

355

late nineteenth century, they were thought to represent the oldest evidence of bipedalism. Originally, the species was called "*Pithecanthropus erectus*" (upright walking ape-man). Later the genus name *Homo* was assigned because of the similar adaptations of this early hominid species with our species: larger brains and a reliance on culture.

This section of the chapter reviews the currently known biological and behavioral evidence for *Homo erectus*. We will also look at evolutionary trends within *Homo erectus* and its relationship with earlier (*Homo habilis*) and later (*Homo sapiens*) hominids.

Distribution in Time and Space

The oldest evidence of *H. erectus* comes from Lake Turkana, Kenya, in East Africa. Two skulls and a rather complete skeleton of a third individual have been discovered there dating to 1.6 million years B.P. The most important aspect of the distribution of *H. erectus* is that it is the first hominid species found outside Africa. Asian remains of *H. erectus* have been found in India, China, and Java (Indonesia). Fossils and archaeological sites in Europe possibly provide further evidence of *H. erectus*, although there is a great deal of controversy over whether the European forms should be classified as *H. erectus*, archaic *H. sapiens*, or transitional forms. Figure 13.1 shows the location of all known and possible *H. erectus* sites.

Even if we exclude the European sites from consideration, the Asian material makes it clear that *H. erectus* was the first hominid to expand out from Africa. Because the earliest Asian forms are dated at roughly 1 million years B.P., and because the earliest African forms are older (1.6 million years B.P.), the interpretation that *H. erectus* originated in Africa seems reasonable. The most likely model is that some population(s) of *H. habilis* evolved into *H. erectus* in East Africa in a short period of time. Because of biological and cultural adaptations such as hunting and the use of fire and shelter, *H. erectus* was able to move into new environments, and by 1 million years ago it had reached Southeast Asia.

Our understanding of the geographic expansion of *H. erectus* may soon change as the result of a new fossil discovery in the Georgian republic in the former Soviet Union. A lower jaw appearing to be *H. erectus* has been tentatively dated between 0.9 and 1.6 million years B.P. (Gibbons 1992b). If these dates are confirmed, this find may provide us not only with more definite evidence of *H. erectus* in parts of Europe but also change our ideas regarding the pattern and timing of migration out of Africa.

The origin of *H. erectus* at roughly 1.6 million years B.P. seems reasonable because of the dramatic changes (see later) that took place from *H. habilis* in a relatively short period of time. It is even possible that *H. habilis* populations continued to exist alongside the first populations of *H. erectus* for a short period of time (making the appearance of the species an

Figure 13.1

Location of *Homo erectus* sites. It is still not definite if the sites in Europe represent *Homo erectus* or early *Homo sapiens* (see text).

example of cladogenesis rather than anagenesis). Though the fossil record does suggest this as a likely possibility, more detailed dating needs to be performed to determine the nature and rate of the change from *H. habilis* to *H. erectus*.

Determining the most recent age of *H. erectus* is a more complicated process. The species does not exist today, having evolved into *H. sapiens* at some point in time. It is difficult, however, to establish the time of this change. By 200,000 years B.P., there is definite evidence of early forms of *H. sapiens* (not necessarily completely modern in appearance), and some *H. erectus* fossils may also date to the same time period (some of the dating is uncertain). Before 400,000 years B.P., the fossils are definitely *H. erectus*. In between those time periods, the fossil record is difficult to interpret. Many specimens have been found, but there is disagreement about

postorbital constriction The
narrowness of the skull behind the eye orbits, a characteristic of early hominids.

whether they belong to *H. erectus* or *H. sapiens*. As we will see later in this
chapter, some of these forms are transitional between the two species. We
therefore have an excellent record of evolutionary change but problems in
assigning species names. Given the earlier discussions on taxonomy (Chapter 7), this should come as no surprise. The process of evolution is dynamic, and taxonomies rely on static definitions. It is often hard to
pigeonhole specimens into specific groups. As an approximation, we can
state that the most recent *H. erectus* populations are roughly 200,000 to
400,000 years old.

At the least, *H. erectus* was around for roughly 1.2 million years. This
is a long time for a hominid species. Such longevity suggests that *H. erectus*
was a well-adapted species. Even though *H. erectus* is in many ways intermediate in appearance between *H. habilis* and *H. sapiens,* we should not
regard it as a transitional form. *H. erectus* was not simply a species in the
process of becoming us; rather, it was a long-lived, highly successful life
form. We need to examine the biological and cultural adaptations of
H. erectus to understand its evolutionary success.

General Physical Characteristics

The following section focuses on the physical characteristics of *Homo
erectus,* specifically those of the skull, teeth, and postcranial skeleton.

Cranial and dental characteristics. The most obvious characteristic
of *H. erectus,* compared to early forms such as *H. habilis,* is its larger brain
size. The cranial capacity ranges from 727 to 1225 ml, with an average of
946 ml (Rightmire 1985). On average, the cranial capacity of *H. erectus* is
44 percent larger than *H. habilis* and 115 percent larger than *Australopithecus africanus.* The range in cranial capacity for *H. erectus* overlaps the
high end of the range of *H. habilis* and the low end of the range in modern
H. sapiens.

One of the earliest *H. erectus* skulls from Lake Turkana is shown in
Figure 13.2, and a later skull from China is shown in Figure 13.3. The
brain case is larger than that of *H. habilis,* but it is still smaller than that of
modern *H. sapiens.* The skull is lower and the face still protrudes more
than in modern humans. Neck muscles attach to a ridge of bone along the
back side of the skull. The development of this bony ridge shows that
H. erectus had powerful neck muscles.

Figure 13.4 shows a *H. erectus* skull and a *H. sapiens* skull from a top
view. The frontal region of the skull is still rather narrow (**postorbital
constriction**), suggesting lesser development in the frontal and temporal
lobes of the brain relative to modern humans. This implies that the intellectual abilities of *H. erectus* were not as great as in modern humans. The
best evidence for the mental aptitude of *H. erectus,* however, comes from

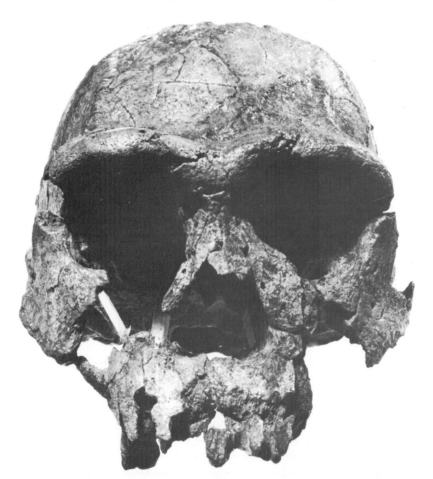

Figure 13.2

Homo erectus skull, specimen KNM-ER 3733, Lake Turkana, Kenya. Dated at 1.6 million years B.P., this is one of the oldest known specimens of *Homo erectus*. (© The National Museums of Kenya)

Figure 13.3

Frontal and side views of *Homo erectus* from the site of Zhoukoudian, China. The specimens from this site are sometimes referred to as "Peking Man" in older literature.   (Neg. No. 315446, 315447. Courtesy Department of Library Ser ices, American Museum of Natural History)

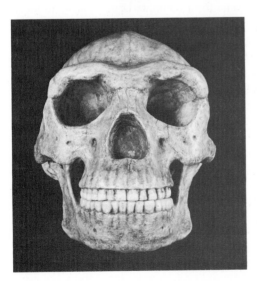

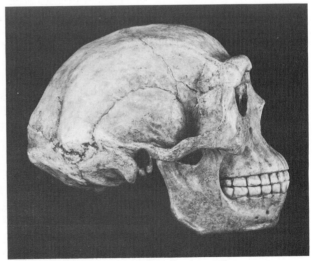

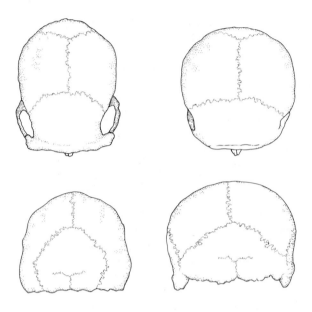

Figure 13.4

Top views of the skulls of *Homo erectus* (*left*) and modern *Homo sapiens* (*right*). Note the greater constriction behind the eyes in *Homo erectus*.

Figure 13.5

Rear views of the skulls of *Homo erectus* (*left*) and modern *Homo sapiens* (*right*). Note the broader brain case of *Homo sapiens*.

Figure 13.6

Lower jaw of *Homo erectus*, specimen Ternifine 3, Ternifine, Algeria, 700,000 years B.P. (From Clark Spencer Larsen, Robert M. Matter, and Daniel L. Gebo, *Human Origins: The Fossil Record, Second Edition*, p. 94 (top). Copyright © 1991, 1985 by Waveland Press, Inc., Prospect Heights, Illinois. Reprinted with permission from the publisher)

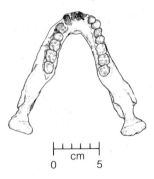

brow ridges The large ridges of bone above the eye orbits, most noticeable in *Homo erectus* and archaic *Homo sapiens*.

the archaeological record, discussed later. Figure 13.5 shows a *H. erectus* skull and a *H. sapiens* skull from the rear view. Note that the brain case of *H. erectus* is much broader toward the bottom of the skull.

The jaws and teeth of *H. erectus* are still large compared to those of modern humans but smaller than those of earlier hominids (Figure 13.6). In particular, the size of the back teeth of *H. erectus* decreased relative to the Plio-Pleistocene hominids. The front teeth are larger than in modern humans, possibly indicating that they were used as tools for holding objects (Wolpoff 1980). Electron scanning microscopic analysis shows that the wear patterns on *H. erectus* teeth are characteristic of extensive meat eating (Lewin 1984).

The face of *H. erectus* protrudes, but not as much as in earlier hominids. One noticeable characteristic of the *H. erectus* face is the development of large ridges of bone above the eye orbits (**brow ridges**). These brow ridges are not apparent in *H. habilis* and are much smaller in archaic and modern *H. sapiens*. The appearance and subsequent loss of large brow ridges in human evolution is an evolutionary reversal that makes sense in terms of the overall pattern of cranial and dental evolution. Changes in diet reduced the amount of force needed for the back teeth, and increased use of the incisors as tools led to an increase in the force exerted at the front of the jaw. Changes in overall brain and face size produced differences in the orientation of neck and chewing muscles. The crest at the back of the skull indicates the attachment of strong neck muscles. On the face the various forces exerted by chewing and neck muscles meet above the eyes.

The brow ridges of *H. erectus* are a structural adaptation to strengthen the face at this critical juncture (Wolpoff 1980).

The postcranial skeleton. The first specimen of *H. erectus* was discovered by Eugene Dubois in Java in 1891. This find consisted of the upper portion of a skull and a femur. Most scientists in the late nineteenth century would have been hesitant to include the skull cap in our genus, for the then-current view was that all human ancestors had large brains. Any fossil with a smaller brain was excluded from our ancestry. The femur that Dubois found, however, was virtually the same as that of a modern human. Because the two bones were found together, Dubois reasoned that upright walking had developed before the completion of a modern human skull. Though this statement now seems perfectly reasonable, it was controversial at the time.

Dubois's find shows again the mosaic nature of human evolution. The femur is similar to that of modern humans, indicating bipedalism. The smaller brain case, however, along with other features of the skull cap, does not resemble modern humans. We now see Dubois's find as a good example of the differences between *H. erectus* and modern humans; the *major* differences are in the skull and not in the postcranial skeleton.

For many years the postcranial evidence for *H. erectus* was limited to portions of individuals—a femur here or a pelvic bone there. In 1984, this situation changed with the discovery of a nearly complete *H. erectus* skeleton at Lake Turkana dating back 1.6 million years (Brown et al. 1985). This skeleton (Figure 13.7) is that of a 12-year-old male; the age of the specimen is fixed by the differential eruption of the teeth. For the first time, the major parts of the postcranial skeleton were found for the same individual. The estimated adult height of this specimen is 160 cm, or roughly 5 ft 3 in (Feldesman and Lundy 1988).

The new *H. erectus* find also provides us with valuable information about the evolution of brain size in early human evolution. Portions of the pelvis are narrow relative to those of modern humans. Because little sexual dimorphism is apparent in *certain* pelvis dimensions, Brown and colleagues (1985) feel that *certain* measurements taken from this specimen can apply to both males and females. Their analysis suggests that *H. erectus* females could not have given birth to very large-brained babies. Reaching these relatively large brain sizes means that fetal brain growth rates must have continued after birth. In other words, neoteny was already a factor in the evolution of brain size. Until many pelvic bones from fully mature adult females are found, this hypothesis must remain tentative.

Cultural Behavior

Given the change in brain size from *H. habilis* to *H. erectus*, it is no surprise that corresponding changes took place in cultural adaptations. The stone tool technology of *H. erectus* was more sophisticated and specialized than that of *H. habilis*. *H. erectus* was a skilled cooperative hunter.

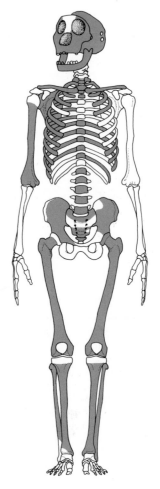

Figure 13.7

Homo erectus skeleton, specimen KNM-WT 15000, Lake Turkana, Kenya. This skeleton of a 12-year-old boy, dated to 1.6 million years B.P., is the most complete specimen of *Homo erectus* yet found. The shaded areas are the bones that were found.

Acheulian tradition The stone tool technology associated with some groups of *Homo erectus*.

biface Stone tool with both sides worked, producing greater symmetry and efficiency.

Figure 13.8

Making an Acheulian tool. Nicholas Toth uses a piece of antler to remove small flakes from both sides of the flint, producing a symmetric hand axe. Shown are flint hand axes and a cleaver.   (Courtesy of Nicholas Toth, Indiana University)

Some populations of *H. erectus* used caves for shelter and others, perhaps, made their own temporary shelters when caves were not available. *H. erectus* also used fire for cooking and warmth, although it is not clear whether they made fire or relied instead on natural fire.

Stone tool technology.   The stone tool technology used by *H. erectus* was more diverse than the simple Oldowan tools used by *H. habilis*. Some *H. erectus* sites contain more sophisticated versions of the Oldowan chopping tools; this variant is called Evolved Oldowan. The most common stone tool technology associated with *H. erectus,* however, is the **Acheulian tradition.** These tools have been found in Africa and Europe. Their first appearance is marked at roughly 1.5 million years ago. In some cases, they were still being used by early *H. sapiens* several hundred thousand years ago.

Acheulian tools are **bifaces;** the stone is worked on both sides. These tools are flatter and have straighter, sharper sides than Oldowan tools. The change in manufacture produced a more efficient tool. In the biface method, smaller flakes must be removed than in an Oldowan chopping tool, a process that requires greater skill. One method of flake removal involves the use of some softer material, such as wood or antler, instead of another stone. Softer materials absorb much of the shock in flake removal, allowing more precise control over flaking.

The basic Acheulian tool is the hand axe (Figure 13.8), which could

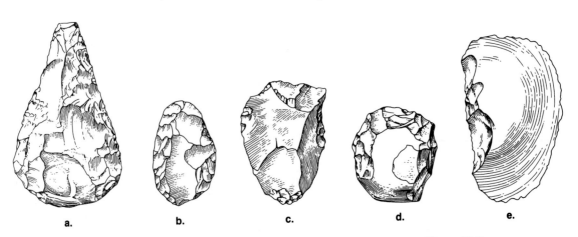

a. b. c. d. e.

Figure 13.9

Examples of Acheulian tools and other tools made by *Homo erectus:* (a) hand axe from Europe, (b) side scraper from Europe, (c) small chopping tool from China, (d) chopper from China, (e) cleaverlike tool from China.   (From *The Old Stone Age* by F. Bordes, 1968. Reprinted with permission of the publisher, Wiedenfeld and Nicolson, Ltd.)

be used for a variety of purposes, including meat preparation. Other tools were also made for different purposes. Scrapers were used for cleaning animal flesh, and cleavers were used for breaking animal bones during butchery (Figure 13.9).

The use of individual tools for different purposes marks an important step in the cultural evolution of hominids. The increased specialization allows more efficient tool use and also requires greater mental sophistication in tool design and manufacture.

Not all *H. erectus* populations made Acheulian tools. At sites in China the tools used by *H. erectus* are somewhat different. The Chinese sites contain many of the smaller tools characteristic of the Acheulian, but not hand axes. Instead, there are large chopping tools that were manufactured differently. Such regional variation in technology is to be expected. Adaptation to specific environments and their related materials requires different methods of manufacture. The variation in *H. erectus* tools is further evidence of cultural adaptations that can be modified to meet different demands.

The regional variation in tool traditions, and the fact that some early *H. sapiens* populations also used Acheulian tools, tells us that cultural and biological variation do not always coincide. Though Acheulian tools are most often associated with *H. erectus*, they are not confined to that species, nor are they universally found within the species. Old tool technologies do not disappear entirely (tools similar to Oldowan choppers are still used today); rather, they are supplemented by newer methods. The increase in *possible* technologies in *H. erectus* is most likely a consequence of biological changes in brain size and structure.

Hunting and gathering. Recent evidence suggests that *H. habilis* was a scavenger instead of a hunter, but the fossil and archaeological records show that *H. erectus* was definitely a hunter of small and large game. The earliest evidence of hunting comes from Olduvai Gorge 1.5 million years ago. The bones of animals found at these sites differ in several ways from those at earlier *H. habilis* sites. All of the bones from larger animals are found, suggesting a single butchering site rather than fragmentary scavenging. The bones are also more fragmented, showing greater use of the animal carcass, including extraction of marrow from bones (Wolpoff 1980). The complete use of animal carcasses matches up with the pattern found in modern hunting and gathering groups and is different from that expected from scavenging. The increased variety of stone tools for butchering also supports the idea that *H. erectus* was a hunter, as does dental evidence, which shows a significant amount of meat in their diet.

One of the best known *H. erectus* sites with evidence of hunting is Zhoukoudian, China. Here *H. erectus* populations lived intermittently in caves between roughly 460,000 and 230,000 years B.P. The caves were used as living sites and are littered with animal bones, remnants of fire, tools and tool scraps, and fossilized hominid feces. In addition, parts of the remains of over 40 *H. erectus* individuals have been found at the Zhoukoudian caves. This site has long been known as the place of "Peking Man," named after the nearby city of Beijing (Peking), China.

The Zhoukoudian caves show evidence of two major cultural adaptations of *H. erectus*—fire and hunting. There are large hearths in the caves, some with ash as deep as 7 ft. Fire was important in the northern environments for warmth, light, and chasing off predators. Fire was also used to cook animal flesh. Charred bones found in the cave represent a number of animal species, such as wild pigs and water buffalo. Deer bones are the most numerous and represent the major prey for *H. erectus* in this region.

Two other significant sites for hunting activity are Torralba and Ambrona in Spain. These neighboring sites date back to roughly 400,000 years B.P. Torralba and Ambrona represent killing and butchering sites. Numerous animal bones, many smashed open, have been found alongside butchering tools. The distribution of bones shows that killing and butchering took place in several stages. Following a kill, the hominids moved portions of the carcasses to another area for additional butchering. No hominid fossils have been found at these sites and it is possible that early *H. sapiens,* rather than *H. erectus,* were the hunters.

The animal bones at Torralba and Ambrona are of large game animals for the most part, including elephants. How did the hominids kill such large creatures? Killing an elephant, even using a modern high-powered rifle, is a difficult task. One possibility is that fires were set and used to drive the animals into nearby bogs, where they would be trapped and could be killed much more easily. There is evidence of fire at these sites, but without the usual hearths, suggesting that fire may indeed have been used as a hunting method. Regardless of the specific method used here, the important point is that hominids had to rely on brains, rather than brawn, in hunting large game. Intelligence, organized hunting, and cooperation are behavioral skills that more than made up for the physical limitations of early hominid hunters.

The bones and stones at different sites show that hunting was an important source of food. Was it the only source? Gathering of vegetables, fruits, nuts, and other foods was surely just as important to the survival of *H. erectus*. In modern hunting-gathering societies, up to 70 percent of the total caloric intake of a group comes from gathering. In the past, anthropologists have tended to focus more on hunting than on gathering. This focus was in part a consequence of the nature of the archaeological record (bones and stones preserve more easily than do vegetables or wooden containers).

Another factor was male bias, unfortunately common in many scientific fields. Modern hunting-gathering societies show a clear division of labor by sex—men are generally the hunters and women the gatherers. The early interpretation of (mostly male) anthropologists focused on what was considered the more "important" and "difficult" task of male hunting. This interpretation influenced other hypotheses on prehistoric human behavior. Males were assumed to be the hunters because they had the necessary strength. Although males are generally stronger than females, this slight difference would not have mattered in hunting. Not even the strongest male today can knock down an elephant by himself! Hunting requires skill and stealth more than strength. The important distinction of hunting versus gathering is that the former activity requires greater mobility. Moving around may not be conducive to successful human pregnancy or nursing. Gathering can be performed in a local area, whereas hunting requires traveling long distances over many days. Also, the crying of infants would be disadvantageous to the hunting process.

Because gathering accounts for the majority of calories, we could also argue for a female-centered view: instead of "man the hunter" we could have "woman the gatherer." Both of these ideas miss the main feature of hunting-and-gathering society—food sharing. Hunting and gathering were equally important activities, and the survival and geographic expansion of *H. erectus* depended on both. The division of labor and food sharing of hunter-gatherers show close and cooperative social structures. We cannot observe *H. erectus* society firsthand, of course. Using what we know from the archaeological record and from modern hunting-gathering societies, however, we can safely infer the existence of small social groups banded together for mutual benefit.

Fire and shelter. The northward movement of *H. erectus* into Asia and (possibly) Europe shows the importance of cultural adaptations. Hominids are tropical primates, and expansion into colder climates required an appropriate level of technology. Fire was an important source of warmth, light, and cooking. In addition, fire can be used for tool manufacture. The tip of a wooden spear can be placed in a fire for a short period to harden the point. We can also speculate that fire allowed social interactions and teaching after dark.

Evidence for controlled fire comes from the cave hearths at Zhoukoudian and other *H. erectus* sites. The earliest known use of controlled fire is dated to almost 1 million years ago (Pfeiffer 1985), although recent evi-

Figure 13.10

Drawing of an early hut, based on the location of support stones and postholes. The opening in the front is an entrance; the opening in the top allows smoke to exit. (Figure from *The Emergence of Humankind,* Fourth Edition, by John E. Pfeiffer. Copyright © 1985 by Harper & Row, Publishers, Inc. Reprinted by permission of HarperCollins Publishers)

dence from South Africa suggests a *possible* earlier date of up to 1.5 million years B.P.). There are older sites with evidence of fire, but it is not clear whether these represent the controlled use of fire. Because fires occur in nature, we cannot merely look for ash and charcoal. We must look for small areas of ash, usually less than a meter in diameter, as evidence of campfires.

Although we know that *H. erectus* used fire, we do not know if they *made* it. The earliest evidence of manufactured fire, only 15,000 years old, consists of a ball of iron pyrites with deep grooves left by repeated striking. It is possible that *H. erectus* could not make fire and had to rely on nature to produce fires. If so, then fires could be kept smoldering for long periods of time at camp sites.

Regardless of how *H. erectus* obtained fire, its use marks an important step in human cultural evolution. Making and using fire represents the controlled exploitation of an energy source. Because we rely on many other sources of controlled energy today, we tend to overlook the vital importance of fire as an energy source.

Another important adaptation for northward expansion was shelter. At Zhoukoudian and other sites in Africa and Europe, early humans used caves for shelter at many times. All early humans were not "cave people," however. Caves were used when they were available. In other areas, shelters were built from wood (Figure 13.10). The best evidence of such shelters comes from the site of Terra Amata in France. Dating back roughly 400,000 years ago, this site provides evidence of manufactured huts. The sticks and leaves used in making such huts have rotted away, but the holes left by the shelters' frameworks remain. At Terra Amata, oval patterns of holes typical of huts have been found. Stones were also arranged around the perimeter of these patterns to anchor the side branches. Hearths, animal bones, and stone tools were found inside these areas. The evidence for shelter shows again the importance of human cultural adaptation. When humans could not locate a resource in the immediate environment, they were able to fashion it themselves.

While suggestive, the evidence from Terra Amata is not conclusive. The problem with the Terra Amata site, as with many archaeological sites, it that our interpretations rest on the assumption that what we find has been undisturbed. Villa (1982) questions this assumption, noting that

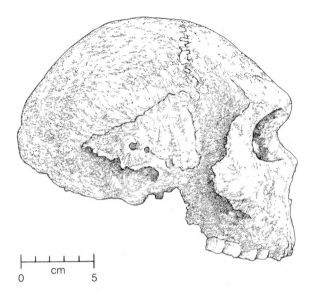

0   cm   5

Figure 13.11

The Petralona skull, Greece. Considered by many to be early *Homo sapiens,* the specimen has a small cranial capacity for that species, a low cranial vault, and thick cranial bones—all features suggestive of *Homo erectus.* This specimen provides a good example of a transitional form. (From Clark Spencer Larsen, Robert M. Matter, and Daniel L. Gebo, *Human Origins: The Fossil Record, Second Edition,* p. 112. Copyright © 1991, 1985 by Waveland Press, Inc., Prospect Heights, Illinois. Reprinted with permission from the publisher)

disturbance of artifacts after burial or deposition is quite common. In the case of Terra Amata, Villa notes that 40 percent of the stone flakes and cores that could be put together from smaller pieces came from different levels, thus throwing into question previous conjectures that different stratigraphic levels represent different time periods. Accordingly, much of our interpretation of Terra Amata as a frequent, seasonal occupation site might also be in error.

The Transition to Homo Sapiens

The oldest known specimens of *H. erectus* date to 1.6 million years ago in East Africa. It seems that *H. erectus* evolved from *H. habilis* quickly in this area, within 200,000 years or less. The archaeological record also implies a quick transition from scavenging to hunting. Evolutionary trends within *H. erectus* have been somewhat controversial. Rightmire (1990) has suggested that *H. erectus* changed little in brain size and other physical features for over a million years. If true, the evolution of *H. erectus* appears to be an example of punctuated equilibrium (see Chapter 4), whereby a new species comes into being quickly and then changes little over its lifetime. Recent analyses suggest that *H. erectus* did change over time. Leigh (1992) has demonstrated that the brain size of *H. erectus* did increase gradually, particularly after 700,000 years B.P. This finding suggests that the punctuated equilibrium model is not an appropriate description of the evolution of *H. erectus.*

The evolution of *H. erectus* into *H. sapiens* is less clear than the initial change from *H. habilis* to *H. erectus.* As mentioned earlier, fossils found between 200,000 and 400,000 years B.P. are often difficult to classify. An example is the skull from Petralona, Greece, shown in Figure 13.11. Dating

Figure 13.12

The Steinheim skull, West Germany. This specimen has a more well-rounded skull and a larger cranial capacity, on average, than *Homo erectus*. The face and brow ridges are still large, however, suggesting a transitional form.   (State Museum for Nature, Stuttgart, Federal Republic of Germany)

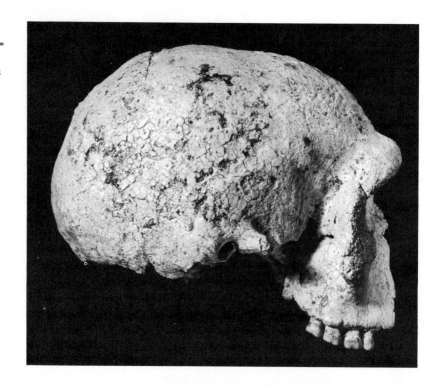

between 200,000 and 300,000 years B.P., this skull has been variously classified as *H. erectus,* as early *H. sapiens,* and as a transitional form between the two species. Its cranial capacity is 1,200 ml, placing it at the upper end of *H. erectus* or the lower end of *H. sapiens*. Its cranial bones are thick, similar to those of *H. erectus,* but the skull is higher and shows the greater expansion more typical of early *H. sapiens.*

Another possible transitional form has been found at Steinheim, Germany (Figure 13.12). It has a small face and the rather well-rounded skull characteristic of *H. sapiens,* but its small cranial capacity (1,000 ml) is more typical of *H. erectus*. Like the Petralona skull, the Steinheim specimen has been classified in different ways. Recently, two skulls found in Yun county, China, dating to 350,000 years B.P., also show a mixture of *H. erectus* and early *H. sapiens* traits (Li and Etler 1992).

The transitional forms show an average increase in cranial capacity and somewhat smaller faces when compared to *H. erectus*. Because of small samples and problems in obtaining more exact dates for these forms, it is difficult to state whether the transition was rapid or gradual. As is often the case in studies of human evolution, we can show general evolutionary trends but not specific rates of change.

The problem of transitional forms also relates to different views of the species concept. If we use species names purely as descriptive labels, then

H. erectus and early *H. sapiens* merely denote different stages along a single evolutionary line. On the other hand, if we use the concept of evolutionary species (Chapter 4), we must consider all populations in a single evolutionary lineage as belonging to the same evolutionary species. That is, all of the *H. erectus* fossils would be placed in the evolutionary species of *H. sapiens* (Wolpoff 1992). Finally, if we consider both *H. erectus* and *H. sapiens* as distinct biological species, we remain with the problem of classifying transitional forms. If *H. sapiens* evolved from *H. erectus* through speciation, then to which species do these transitional forms belong?

In any case, the general trends are apparent. Sometime between 200,000 and 400,000 years ago, some hominid populations began showing further increase in brain size along with a reduction of the face and changes in the shape of the skull. The fossil record shows that by 200,000 years B.P. such changes proceeded to lead to forms that can definitely be assigned to the species *H. sapiens*. The reasons for these changes are not known. One possibility is that changes in climate led to selection for hominids with larger brain size and other features. Another possibility is that the cultural adaptations of *H. erectus* allowed further evolutionary change when the appropriate mutations occurred for such changes (perhaps an increase in neoteny).

archaic *Homo sapiens* An earlier variant of *Homo sapiens*, found at dates ranging from 32,000 to roughly 200,000 years B.P.

anatomically modern *Homo sapiens* Modern *Homo sapiens*, dating to roughly the last 100,000 years.

Archaic *Homo Sapiens*

The oldest specimens that can unambiguously be classified as *H. sapiens* are not identical with modern *H. sapiens*. There is considerable variation within our species past and present. Early twentieth-century scientists tended to assign forms to different species based on these variations, but today most (but not all) anthropologists agree that all hominids within the last 200,000 years or so can be placed within our species. The existing differences do not seem great enough to warrant classification as different species. If we call all these hominids by the same name, however, that implies they are all more similar than is actually the case. How do we name fossils that are not distinct enough to make up a separate species but are still not identical to modern humans? Though some scientists argue for the use of subspecies names, the present convention is to place all these hominids into one of two groups—**archaic *H. sapiens*** and **anatomically modern *H. sapiens***. This section deals with the first group.

Analysis of archaic *H. sapiens* is confusing because of the wide range of variation within this general group in space and time. Some characteristics are found throughout this group, whereas others are specific to certain regions. As with modern humans, archaic *H. sapiens* showed distinct regional differences.

Neandertals A regional population of archaic *Homo sapiens* found in the area around the Mediterranean, dating between roughly 32,000 to 125,000 years B.P.

Distribution in Time and Space

Archaic *H. sapiens* has been found at a number of sites in Africa, Europe, and Asia (Figure 13.13) dating between 32,000 and 200,000 years B.P. Given the large number of sites and specimens, it has become useful to look more closely at patterns of regional variation. Some of the better-known regions include Sub-Saharan Africa, North Asia, South Asia, and Southeast Asia and Australia (often lumped together as "Australasian").

Because of an early interest in European fossils, much emphasis in the past has been placed on a regional population known as the **Neandertals.** The word *Neandertal* is simply the German for "Neander Valley," the site where one of the first specimens was discovered. The Neandertals lived in the regions surrounding the Mediterranean, including Western Europe, Central and Eastern Europe, the Middle East, and North Africa. Neandertal remains have been found dating between roughly 32,000 to 125,000

Figure 13.13

Map of archaic *Homo sapiens* sites.

years B.P. Earlier literature has often used the term *Neandertal* to refer to *all* archaic *H. sapiens* populations, but now we confine the term to a specific region and time period. The popular media have a tendency to portray Neandertals as brutish half-humans, but in truth they were simply a regional population of archaic *H. sapiens* (Trinkaus and Shipman 1992).

Physical Characteristics

Both archaic and anatomically modern *H. sapiens* have large brain sizes and small faces relative to *H. erectus*. The average cranial capacity of modern *H. sapiens* is roughly 1,350 ml (Beals et al. 1984). The transitional forms discussed earlier and the earliest archaic *H. sapiens* have somewhat smaller cranial capacities, showing that an increase in brain size has taken place during the last 200,000 years. In fact, the rate of change between 200,000 years B.P. and 45,000 years B.P. was extremely rapid (Godfrey and Jacobs 1981). There has been no further increase in brain size during the last 45,000 years. In fact, a slight decrease in average brain size has occurred, reflecting a general decrease in skeletal size (Henneberg 1988).

Since both archaic and anatomically modern *H. sapiens* have large brains, brain size cannot be used to distinguish between the two groups. The morphology of the skulls of these two groups, however, is on average different. Archaic *H. sapiens* has a low skull with a sloping forehead, whereas anatomically modern *H. sapiens* has a high skull and a vertical forehead. The face and teeth of archaic *H. sapiens* are larger than those in modern *H. sapiens*. Specimens of archaic *H. sapiens* rarely have a chin, something found in modern *H. sapiens*. The postcranial skeleton of many (not all) archaic *H. sapiens* specimens is very similar to modern forms. In general, the bones of archaic *H. sapiens* are thicker and show greater musculature.

Regional variation. One early archaic *H. sapiens* skull (Figure 13.14) was discovered at the site of Broken Hill, Kabwe, Africa, dating to roughly

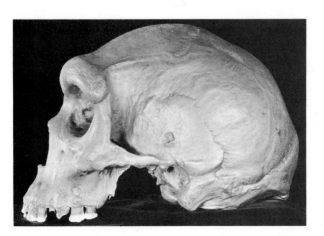

Figure 13.14

The Broken Hill skull, Kabwe, Zambia. An example of early archaic *Homo sapiens* from Africa. (Neg. no. 410816. Courtesy Department of Library Services, American Museum of Natural History)

Würm glaciation One of the times of intense climatic cooling ("ice ages") during the Pleistocene epoch.

125,000 years B.P. The large brain size (1,280 ml) is readily apparent. The face is rather large and so are the brow ridges. The shape of the skull shows typical archaic features: a sloping forehead and a low skull.

Another example of an archaic *H. sapiens* skull (Figure 13.15) is from the site of Dali, China, and dates to between 150,000 and 200,000 years B.P. The cranial capacity is on the low end of the range for *H. sapiens* (1,120 ml) and the brow ridges are large. The skull is also low and has a sloping forehead, both typical archaic features. The Dali skull also illustrates regional variation. As in many archaic North Asian specimens, the face is smaller and flatter than in other regions of the world. These traits, among others, are also found in North Asian specimens earlier and later in time (Thorne and Wolpoff 1992).

The Neandertals. Of all the regional populations of archaic *H. sapiens,* the best known is the Neandertals. Also, some of the Neandertal samples appear to be the most different from other regional populations of archaic *H. sapiens,* although this point is still widely debated.

Many of the Neandertals lived during the time of the **Würm glaciation.** The Pleistocene epoch witnessed alternating periods of glaciation and interglacials as the earth's climate changed. In the Northern Hemisphere large sections of land were covered with advancing ice sheets during glaciations, which receded during interglacial periods. Earlier views on glaciation held that four major glaciations, or "ice ages," took place during the Pleistocene. It is now recognized that the climate changed much more frequently, perhaps as many as seventeen times, in this period. Even during times typically characterized as "ice ages," the temperature and southern advancement of ice varied considerably. In any case, it is clear that the Neandertals lived during times when the climate was cooler in their habitat. The Neandertals did not live right on the ice, but the reduction in average temperature surely had an effect on their environments, especially

Figure 13.15

The Dali skull, Dali County, People's Republic of China. An example of archaic *Homo sapiens* from Asia. (From Clark Spencer Larsen, Robert M. Matter, and Daniel L. Gebo, *Human Origins: The Fossil Record, Second Edition,* p. 119. Copyright © 1991, 1985 by Waveland Press, Inc., Prospect Heights, Illinois. Reprinted with permission from the publisher)

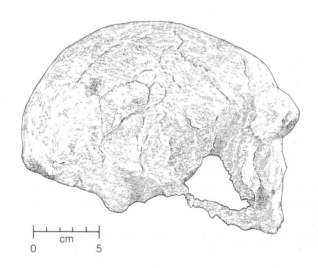

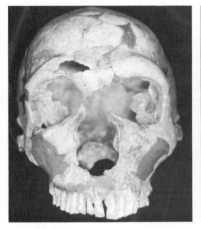
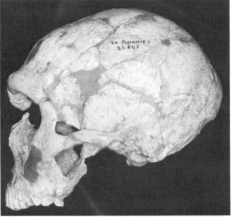

Figure 13.16

Frontal and side view of La
Ferrassie skull, a Neandertal
from France.   (Courtesy of
Milford Wolpoff, University of
Michigan)

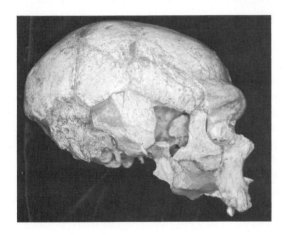
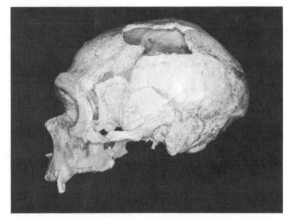

Figure 13.17

Two side views of La Chapelle
skull, a Neandertal from
France.   (Courtesy of Milford
Wolpoff, University of Michigan)

Western Europe. The ability of the Neandertals to survive in these conditions is proof of their cultural adaptations, which included hunting, shelter,
and use of fire.

Neandertals had the typical archaic features of sloping forehead, low
skull, lack of chin, and large brow ridges. They also possessed several
unique characteristics that tend not to be found in other regions (or at a
much lower frequency).

The Neandertals had very large brains, averaging 1,485 ml. The males
had larger average cranial capacities because of their larger body size. It
seems likely that, relative to their body size, the Neandertals may have had
slightly larger brain sizes than many modern human populations. According to a recent review by Holloway (1985), the structural organization of
Neandertal brains, as assessed from endocasts, is no different from that of
modern humans.

Neandertals differ from other archaic *H. sapiens* populations in several
features. Figures 13.16 and 13.17 show two skulls of Western Euro-

occipital bun The protruding of the rear region of the skull, a feature often found in Neandertals.

pean Neandertals, both from sites in France between 40,000 and 55,000 years B.P.

Neandertal faces are generally long and protrude more than in other archaic populations. The nasal region is large, suggesting large noses, and the sinus cavities to the side of the nose expand outward. The large nasal and midfacial areas on Neandertal skulls have often been interpreted as some type of adaptation to cold climate. However, Rak (1986) interprets the large faces of Neandertals in terms of the biomechanics of the skull. He suggests that the Neandertal face acted to withstand stresses brought about by the use of relatively large front teeth. The front teeth of Neandertals are large in relation to their back teeth and often show considerable wear, suggesting their use as tools.

Many Neandertal specimens have a large crest of bone running from behind the ear toward the back of the skull. The back of the skull is rather puffed out (a feature called an **occipital bun**). The occipital bun is caused by relatively late posterior brain growth (Trinkaus and LeMay 1982). Though this feature is most common in Neandertals, it is also found in other archaic and modern *H. sapiens* populations.

There is also variation within Neandertals. Figures 13.18 and 13.19 show the skulls of two Middle Eastern Neandertals. Though they possess the general characteristics of Neandertals, they are not as morphologically extreme. The skulls are a bit more well rounded than most Western European Neandertal skulls. The differences between the two skulls may reflect some aspect of local adaptation to their environment.

Neandertal postcranial remains show essentially modern bipedalism, but also a few differences compared with other *H. sapiens* populations. Neandertals were relatively short and stocky. The limb bone segments farthest from the body (lower arm and lower leg) are relatively short, most likely reflecting cold adaptation (Trinkaus 1981). The limb and shoulder bones are more rugged than those of modern humans. The areas of muscle attachment show that the Neandertals were very strong. It has been sug-

Figure 13.18

Frontal and side view of Neandertal skull from Tabun, Israel.   (Courtesy of Milford Wolpoff, University of Michigan)

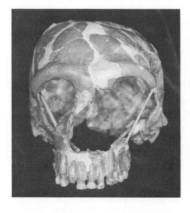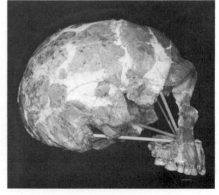

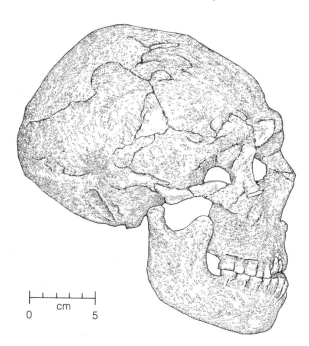

Figure 13.19

Shanidar I skull, Iraq.
(From Clark Spencer Larsen,
Robert M. Matter, and Daniel L.
Gebo, *Human Origins: The Fossil
Record, Second Edition*, p. 128.
Copyright © 1991, 1985 by
Waveland Press, Inc., Prospect
Heights, Illinois. Reprinted with
permission from the publisher)

gested that Neandertal hands were not as capable of fine manipulation as modern human hands are, or had at least different patterns of manipulation (Stoner and Trinkaus 1981).

The pelvic bones are also rather robust compared to those of modern humans, with the exception of the upper portion of the pubis (at the front of the pelvis), which is actually thinner and longer than in modern humans. The uniqueness of the Neandertal pelvis seems to reflect a biomechanical function (Rak and Arensburg 1987). Recent evidence also shows that Neandertals had a smaller pelvic outlet, which may have meant more difficult childbirth than in modern *H. sapiens* (Tague 1992).

Cultural Behavior

Archaic *H. sapiens* were hunters and gatherers, exploiting a wide variety of natural resources. Remains of animal bones at their sites show that they hunted both small game and large, including bears, mammoths, and rhinoceroses. In some areas it appears that archaic *H. sapiens* hunted year round; in others they appeared to have migrated along with animal herds.

Stone tool technology. The stone tools of archaic *H. sapiens* represent an advancement over the Acheulian and chopping tool traditions of *H. erectus*. Much of the evidence for stone tool manufacture comes from

Mousterian tradition The stone tool technology of the Neandertals.

Neandertal sites, where the stone tool tradition is known as the **Mousterian.** Similar tools found in other regions of archaic *H. sapiens* are sometimes referred to as Mousterian or Mousterianlike, as well as by other names (for example, in Africa, the term *Middle Stone Age* is frequently used). In this chapter, the term *Mousterian* is used in a general sense to refer to the basic patterns of tool manufacture among archaic *H. sapiens.* However, as with *H. erectus,* there is often considerable variation from region to region, reflecting availability of local resources and cultural differences in tool making.

The key feature of the Mousterian tradition is the use of a prepared-core technique in tool manufacture. As Figure 13.20 shows, a flint nodule is first chipped around the edges. Small flakes are then removed from the top surface of the core. In the final step, the core is struck precisely at one end.

The use of the prepared-core technique, which produces sharp and symmetric tools (Figure 13.21), tells us two important things about archaic *H. sapiens.* First, they were capable of precise toolmaking, which implies an excellent knowledge of flaking methods and the structural characteristics of stone. Second, they were able to visualize the final tool early in production. Not until the last step does the shape of the finished tool become apparent. Such manufacture is a process quite different from simply chipping away at a stone until a tool is finished.

Archaeological evidence shows considerable variation in the types of Mousterian tools. Archaic *H. sapiens* used different tools for separate purposes to a greater extent than *H. erectus.* Sites also show variation in the frequency of Mousterian tools, once again indicating regional differences.

Figure 13.20

Manufacture of a Mousterian tool, using the prepared-core method. First, the core is shaped by removing small flakes from the sides and top (a–d). Then the finished tool is removed from the core (e). (From *Archaeology: Discovering Our Past,* 2d ed., by Robert Sharer and Wendy Ashmore, Fig. 10.3. Copyright © 1993 by Mayfield Publishing Company)

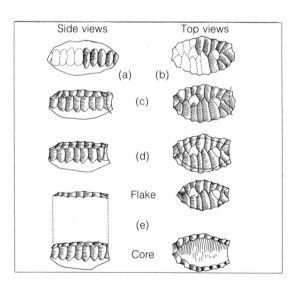

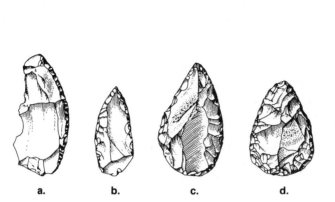

a.   **b.**   **c.**   **d.**   **e.**

Figure 13.21

Examples of Mousterian tools: (a) scraper, (b) point, (c) scraper, (d) point, (e) hand axe.   (From *The Old Stone Age* by F. Bordes, 1968. Reprinted with permission of the publisher, Weidenfeld and Nicolson, Ltd.)

Symbolic behavior. Archaeological evidence suggests that archaic *H. sapiens* may have been capable of symbolic thought, perhaps even holding beliefs in the supernatural. Archaic *H. sapiens* (specifically, some Neandertals) were the first hominid to bury their dead deliberately. Evidence of burial comes from a number of European and Middle Eastern sites, where dead persons' bones have been arranged carefully in graves, often in association with tools, food, and flowers.

The intentional burial of the dead has suggested a ritualistic purpose to some researchers. At a site in Belgium, fires had been lit above two buried bodies. One interpretation is that archaic *H. sapiens* believed the fires would counteract the "coldness" of death. At the Shanidar Cave site in Iraq, flowers had been placed all over the bodies, an event we can reconstruct from the presence of fossil pollen in the graves.

Such evidence suggests the evolution of symbolic expressions and the possibility of supernatural beliefs, because it seems doubtful anyone would go to all that trouble without a reason. This standard interpretation, however, is changing. Klein (1989) notes that burial need not have symbolic purpose; for archaic *H. sapiens* it may have been the easiest way to remove the dead from living space. Also, the flexed positions of many of the dead might not reflect intentional posing but rather a consequence of digging the smallest possible graves. In addition, although the Shanidar burial still stands as one of the best examples of symbolic behavior, it is possible the pollen was introduced by rodents burrowing into the grave *after* burial.

The physical condition of fossil remains offers another window on the behavior of archaic *H. sapiens*. By looking at bone fractures, condition of teeth, and other features, we can get a good idea of the age and health status of early humans. Many archaic *H. sapiens* remains are of elderly individuals with numerous medical problems. Some of the elderly had lost all of their teeth, many had arthritis, and one had lost part of his arm. By looking for signs of healing or infection, we can tell that many of these elderly individuals did not die from these afflictions. How, then, did they survive, in particular, if they had lost all of their teeth? Survival of many of the elderly and impaired archaic *H. sapiens* suggests that others cared for them. This implies not only compassion as a social value but also the existence of a social system that allowed for the sharing of food and of resources.

This perspective may be based more on our interpretive biases, however, than on reality. Dettwyler (1991) questions the traditional view of the elderly and disabled as nonproductive members of a group who must be cared for. Drawing on cross-cultural studies, she notes that physically disabled individuals in many societies still frequently make important contributions.

Language capability. Did archaic *H. sapiens* have language? Lieberman and Crelin (1971), who reconstructed the vocal anatomy of Neandertals, concluded they were incapable of vocalizing certain vowel sounds. The implication was that archaic *H. sapiens* did not possess as wide a range of sounds as modern humans and perhaps had limited language abilities. This hypothesis was criticized, however, because of differences of opinion on vocal anatomy reconstruction. The lack of direct fossil evidence at the heart of the debate was ultimately furnished with the discovery of the first hyoid bone for archaic *H. sapiens,* a bone lying in the neck that can be used to provide information on the structure of the respiratory tract. That this specimen is almost identical in size and shape to the hyoid bone of modern humans indicates that there were no differences in vocal ability between archaics and moderns (Arensberg et al. 1990). Indeed, no evidence from brain anatomy exists to show that archaic *H. sapiens* lacked speech centers (Holloway 1985).

Anatomically Modern *Homo Sapiens*

Human evolution did not end with archaic *H. sapiens.* By 30,000 years B.P., all fossil humans are anatomically modern in form. Though it is clear that archaic *H. sapiens* evolved into anatomically modern *H. sapiens,* the exact nature of this evolution is less certain. This section deals with the biological and cultural characteristics of anatomically modern *H. sapiens,* followed by consideration of the nature of their evolution.

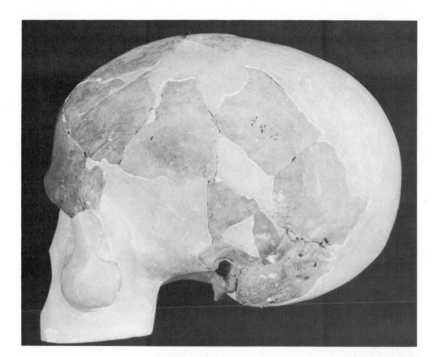

Figure 13.22

The Border Cave skull, South Africa. The fragmentary remains are clearly those of anatomically modern *Homo sapiens* (note the vertical forehead). Dating is not precise, but current estimates suggest an age of more than 100,000 years B.P.   (Photo by Peter Faugust by permission of Phillip V. Tobias)

Distribution in Time and Space

Anatomically modern *H. sapiens* are found in Pleistocene sites in Africa, Europe, and Asia. They are also found in areas previously unoccupied by hominids, such as Australia and the New World. Many anatomically modern *H. sapiens* sites date to the last 30,000 years. Recent evidence suggests that this form is actually much older than once thought. Cranial remains from the Border Cave site in southeast Africa are fragmentary but show typical anatomically modern features (Figure 13.22). The dating for this site is not definite but could range between 90,000 and 115,000 years B.P. Humans may have occupied the Klasies River Mouth, South Africa, at least as early as 90,000 years B.P. (Grün et al. 1990). Other African sites also provide evidence of an early appearance of anatomically modern *H. sapiens*: Omo, Ethiopia (roughly 130,000 years B.P.) and Laetoli (perhaps 120,000 years B.P.). There is also recent, controversial evidence of an early occurrence of anatomically modern *H. sapiens* in the Middle East, with both the Qafzeh and Tabun sites in Israel dating to perhaps 92,000 years B.P. (Grün et al. 1991). These early dates are still somewhat uncertain, and not all researchers accept them or the fossil evidence, but it is becoming increasingly certain that anatomically modern *H. sapiens* existed before the youngest known archaic forms.

Figure 13.23

Frontal and side view of Cro-Magnon skull, France. This specimen is one of the best-known examples of anatomically modern *Homo sapiens*. (Neg. no. 109226, 109227. Courtesy Department of Library Services, American Museum of Natural History)

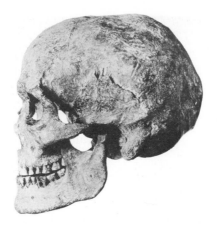
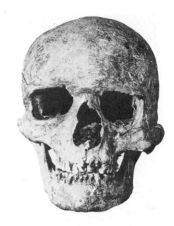

Physical Characteristics

Figure 13.23 shows a skull from one of the more famous anatomically modern sites—Cro-Magnon, France, dating between 23,000 and 27,000 years B.P. This skull shows many of the characteristics of anatomically modern *H. sapiens:* it is high and well rounded. There is no occipital bun; the back of the skull is rounded instead. The forehead rises vertically above the eye orbits and does not slope, as in archaic *H. sapiens*. The brow ridges are small, the face does not protrude very much, and a strong chin is evident.

Another example of anatomically modern *H. sapiens* is shown in Figure 13.24, a skull from the Skhul site at Mt. Carmel, Israel. This skull also has a high, well-rounded skull without an occipital bun and a small chin. Compared to the Cro-Magnon skull, the brow ridges are larger and the face protrudes slightly. The differences between the Skhul and Cro-Magnon skulls are typical of variation within a species, particularly when we consider that they existed at different times in separate places. Other specimens also show similarities and differences when compared to one another. The skull in Figure 13.25 (Combe Capelle, France, 30,000 to 35,000 years B.P.) is high and well rounded, but the face protrudes slightly, and the chin is rather weak. The recent skull from Five Knolls, England (1,500 to 3,500 years B.P.) is high and well rounded, has small brow ridges and face, and a small chin (Figure 13.26). There is clearly variation within both archaic and anatomically modern forms of *H. sapiens*. This variation makes evolutionary relationships difficult to assess.

Cultural Behavior

Discussing the cultural adaptations of anatomically modern *H. sapiens* is difficult because they include prehistoric technologies as well as more recent developments, such as agriculture, generation of electricity, the

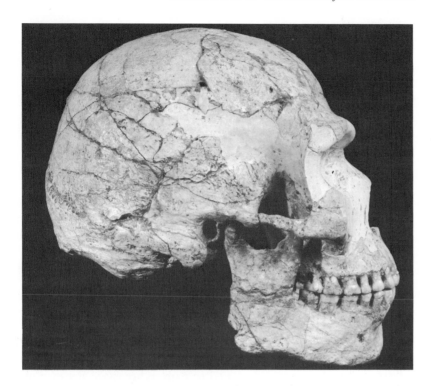

Figure 13.24

An early anatomically modern *Homo sapiens* skull from Skhul, Israel. (Peabody Museum, Harvard University, Photographed by Hillel Burger)

Figure 13.26

Skull of anatomically modern *Homo sapiens,* specimen 18, from the Five Knolls site, England, 1,500–3,500 years B.P. (From Clark Spencer Larsen, Robert M. Matter, and Daniel L. Gebo, *Human Origins: The Fossil Record, Second Edition,* p. 166. Copyright © 1991, 1985 by Waveland Press, Inc., Prospect Heights, Illinois. Reprinted with permission from the publisher)

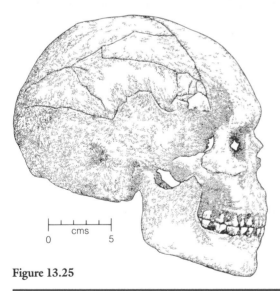

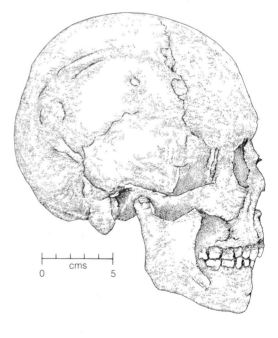

Figure 13.25

The Combe Capelle skull, anatomically modern *Homo sapiens,* France. (From Clark Spencer Larsen, Robert M. Matter, and Daniel L. Gebo, *Human Origins: The Fossil Record,* *Second Edition,* p. 16. Copyright © 1991, 1985 by Waveland Press, Inc., Prospect Heights, Illinois. Reprinted with permission from the publisher)

Upper Paleolithic The Upper Old Stone Age; also refers to the stone tool technologies of anatomically modern *Homo sapiens*.

Lower Paleolithic The Lower Old Stone Age; also refers to the stone tool technologies of *Homo habilis* and *Homo erectus*.

Middle Paleolithic The Middle Old Stone Age; also refers to the stone tool technologies of archaic *Homo sapiens*.

internal combustion engine, and nuclear energy. So that we may provide a comparison with the culture of the archaic forms, this section is limited to prehistory before the development of agriculture (roughly 12,000 years B.P.).

Tool technologies. There is so much variation in the stone tool technologies of anatomically modern *H. sapiens* that it is impossible to define a single tradition. For the sake of discussion, the types of stone tool industries are often lumped together under the term **Upper Paleolithic** (which means "Upper Old Stone Age"). **Lower Paleolithic** consists of the stone tool traditions of *H. habilis* and *H. erectus,* and **Middle Paleolithic** includes the stone tool traditions of archaic *H. sapiens.* Even though we use a single label to describe common features of Upper Paleolithic tool industries, do not be misled into thinking all traditions were the same. Variation, both within and among sites, is even greater in the Upper Paleolithic than in earlier cultures. This variation shows the increasing sophistication and specialization of stone tools.

Figure 13.27 shows some of the tools found at Upper Paleolithic sites. In general, these tools are more precisely made than earlier tools. Many smaller tools appear at this time, possible only through more sophisticated methods of manufacture. Materials other than stone were used, such as bone and antler. Another important feature of Upper Paleolithic culture is that tools were often used to make other tools. For example, small stone tools were made to carve other tools out of bone.

Cave art. Another form of symbolic behavior appears with anatomically modern *H. sapiens*—cave art. Many of these paintings are of large game animals and are anatomically correct and well executed (Figure 13.28). Painting is a form of human activity that is spiritually rewarding but has no apparent function in day-to-day existence. Why, then, did prehistoric humans paint images on the walls of caves? One possible inter-

Figure 13.27

Examples of Upper Paleolithic stone tools: (a) knife, (b) scraper, (c) point, (d) scraper, (e) point. Tools *a, b,* and *c* are from the Perigordian culture; tool *d* is from the Aurignacian culture; tool *e* is from the Solutrean culture. (From *The Old Stone Age* by F. Bordes, 1968. Reprinted with permission of the publisher, Weidenfeld and Nicolson, Ltd.)

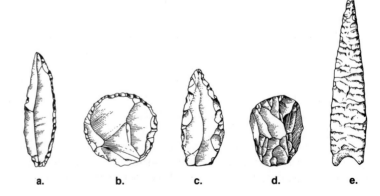

a.　　b.　　c.　　d.　　e.

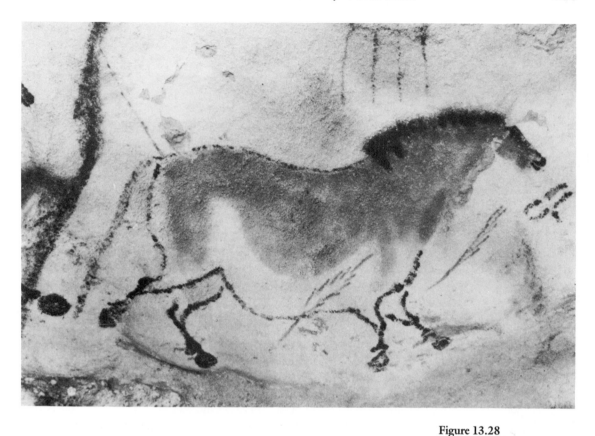

Figure 13.28

Cave painting of a running horse from Lascaux Cave, France. (Museum of Man, Paris; photographer F. Windels)

pretation involves sympathetic magic. By capturing the image of an animal on the wall, humans hoped to improve their chances at hunting.

Dating of cave paintings has usually been based on debris left by human occupation. The problem with this approach is that humans could have been using the caves long after the paintings were done. Recent analyses of the charcoal in the paint pigments using accelerator mass spectrophotometry has given dates of between 12,900 and 14,000 years B.P. for several sites in France and Spain (Valladas et al. 1992).

Geographic expansion. The pace of cultural evolution increased with anatomically modern *H. sapiens*. Methods were developed to start fires. New weapons, such as bows and arrows and fishing implements, were added to our species' accumulated adaptations. Needles and fishing hooks were made from bone. The archaeological evidence shows that humans became more and more successful in adapting to their environments, and consequently populations grew and expanded.

By 50,000 years B.P., populations of anatomically modern *H. sapiens* had reached Australia (Roberts et al. 1990). During times of glaciation the sea levels drop, extending the land mass of the continents. The drop in

Figure 13.29

The Bering Land Bridge. Today the former Soviet Union and Alaska are separated by water. During the "Ice Ages," water was trapped in glaciers, producing a drop in the sea level that exposed the land area known as the Bering Land Bridge. This "bridge" connecting North America and Asia was actually 2,100 km wide!

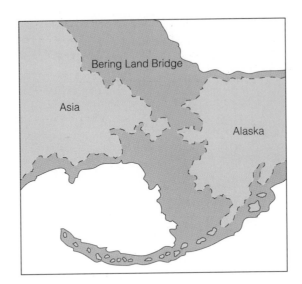

sea level allowed earlier populations of hominids to reach Southeast Asia, but Australia was not then connected to the Asian continent. For humans to reach Australia, they had to cross many kilometers of sea. The only way they could do this was by some sort of raft or boat.

Anatomically modern *H. sapiens* also moved into the New World. The number of such movements, and their dates, are a continuing source of controversy (Rogers et al., 1992). One fact all parties agree on is that humans were living in the New World by 12,000 years B.P. Some argue these dates are the earliest, whereas others cite newer evidence and reanalysis of previous finds indicating a much earlier initial occupation—perhaps 20,000 to 30,000 years ago.

Genetic evidence shows a close relationship between modern Native Americans and modern Northeast Asians. Archaeological evidence also demonstrates an Asian origin for the first migrants to the New World. The most commonly suggested route is across the Bering land bridge. During periods of glaciation the sea levels fell, exposing a stretch of land connecting Asia and North America. This "land bridge" was almost 2,100 kilometers (roughly 1,300 miles) wide (Figure 13.29). It did not appear or disappear suddenly but instead developed over thousands of years as the sea levels dropped. Groups of humans following game herds moved across this region and eventually moved down into North, Central, and South America.

The Origin of Anatomically Modern *Homo Sapiens*

When, where, and how did anatomically modern *H. sapiens* evolve from archaic *H. sapiens*? The general trend indicated by the fossil record is clear; some archaic populations evolved into the more modern forms. The specific questions are harder to answer. Did *all* populations of archaics evolve into modern forms? If so, did this occur at the same time in different places? Or did only a few archaic populations evolve into modern forms and then expand out to replace, or interbreed, with the remaining archaic forms? If so, where and when did the transition to anatomically modern *H. sapiens* first take place? Finally, does our use of such terms as *archaic* and *modern* obscure variation over time and space? We use these categories as a useful sorting device, but we may be in danger of obscuring reality by pigeonholing all human fossil remains into two groups.

Early Models

Many models have been proposed to answer these questions. Past analyses have been complicated by the fact that the best-known samples of archaic *H. sapiens* were the Western European Neandertals, which in many ways are the most unique of all the archaic populations. The distinctiveness of the Neandertals had given rise to various interpretations of the origin of anatomically modern *H. sapiens*. In the early part of this century, it was common to view Neandertals as a side branch of human evolution, perhaps even a different species. At that time the fossil record suggested a 5,000-year "gap" between the last Neandertals and the first modern humans. Such a gap was felt to be too short in duration for the evolutionary changes needed for a transition from Neandertals into modern humans. Another explanation was that the modern forms evolved elsewhere, then invaded and wiped out the Neandertals (see Brace [1964] for a thorough discussion of early views on Neandertal evolution).

This simple model is no longer accepted. For one thing, we now have evidence of overlap in dates for archaic and anatomically modern *H. sapiens*. The major problem with the invasion hypothesis is that it was strongly influenced by previous interpretations of the extent of differences between archaic and modern forms. This early idea emphasized the differences between these forms and tended to ignore their similarities.

An alternative, first proposed by Hrdlicka and later supported by Brace, was the Neandertal phase hypothesis. Here Neandertals represented a stage through which all populations of *H. sapiens* evolved. The problem with this model is that according to the definition of Neandertal given earlier, we find evidence of Neandertals only from regions around the Mediterranean.

Current Models and Debates

Three current models are considered here as hypotheses for the evolution of anatomically modern *H. sapiens*: the **recent African origin model,** the **multiregional evolution model,** and the **assimilation model.**

recent African origin model A model of the evolution of *Homo sapiens* whereby archaic *Homo sapiens* evolved into anatomically modern *Homo sapiens* in Africa and then spread throughout the Old World, replacing archaic populations.

multiregional evolution model A model of the evolution of *Homo sapiens* whereby the change from archaic to modern forms took place in all regions of the Old World.

assimilation model A model of the evolution of modern *Homo sapiens* whereby the transition from archaic to modern *H. sapiens* occurred in a single region such as Africa, followed by assimilation into archaic *H. sapiens* populations elsewhere in the Old World.

Figure 13.30

The recent African origin model of the evolution of anatomically modern *H. sapiens*. Populations of *H. erectus* evolve into archaic *H. sapiens* in different regions of the world. Archaic *H. sapiens* evolves into modern *H. sapiens* only in Africa roughly 200,000 years ago. Populations of modern *H. sapiens* expand out from Africa, replacing archaic populations in other parts of the world. According to this model, other populations of archaics contribute little, if any, to modern *H. sapiens*. (Based on Wilson and Cann [1992])

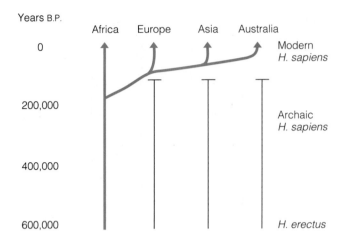

The recent African origin model. According to the recent African origin model, the transition from archaic to anatomically modern *H. sapiens* occurred in Africa roughly 200,000 years ago. The modern forms then expanded out from Africa, replacing earlier archaic populations throughout the Old World (Stringer and Andrews 1988; Wilson and Cann 1992). Little, if any, interbreeding took place with archaic populations outside of Africa. The replacement of archaic with modern forms may have resulted from an evolutionary advantage held by the latter, so that over time, moderns became more and more numerous and the populations of archaics declined and ultimately died out.

If true, the recent African origin model implies that all modern humans share common ancestors in Africa 200,000 years ago. It also implies that no archaic *H. sapiens* populations, other than those in the transitional area within Africa, contributed genetically to modern humans. That is, the ancestors of modern-day Africans were Africans, the ancestors of modern-day Europeans were Africans, and so on. A schematic representation of the recent African origin model is shown in Figure 13.30. In some statements of this model, modern *H. sapiens* is considered a separate species from archaic *H. sapiens*.

The multiregional evolution model. The multiregional evolution model states that archaic *H. sapiens* evolved into modern *H. sapiens* throughout the Old World. By 1 million years ago, *H. erectus* had moved out from Africa into different regions of the Old World. Over time, these populations differed from one another because of genetic drift and adaptation to local environments. Gene flow continued between regions, however, so that all regional populations remained part of a single species. As drift and selection acted to increase differences between regions, gene flow acted to reduce them. Through the *balance* of gene flow, drift, and natural selection, all regional populations changed from archaic to modern forms

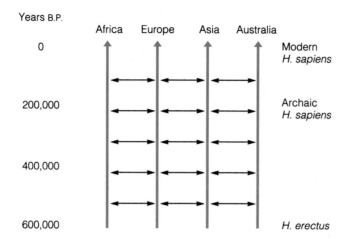

Figure 13.31

The multiregional evolution model of the evolution of anatomically modern *H. sapiens*. Populations of *H. erectus* evolve into archaic *H. sapiens*, that then evolve into anatomically modern *H. sapiens* throughout the Old World. Horizontal lines indicate gene flow, populations thereby remain part of a single evolving species while maintaining regional distinctiveness.

(though not necessarily at the same time), while also maintaining some regional differences (Wolpoff et al. 1984; Thorne and Wolpoff 1992). According to the multiregional evolution model, the ancestors of modern Europeans were archaic Europeans, with a certain amount of gene flow from the rest of the world. Likewise, the ancestors of modern Africans were archaic Africans with some gene flow from the rest of the world. According to strict proponents of the model, the transition from archaic to modern *H. sapiens* did not occur first in any one place, but rather throughout the entire species over time.

Consider the patterns of human biological variation seen among humans today. We are clearly all one species, but it is also obvious that different regions are distinctive from one another. The multiregional evolution model extends this pattern into the past—a single evolving species with local variations. There is a balance between drift and selection on one hand and gene flow on the other, such that just enough gene flow acts to maintain a single species, but not enough occurs so that regional differences are wiped out. A schematic drawing of the multiregional evolution model is shown in Figure 13.31.

The assimilation model. A variant of the multiregional model has been proposed by Fred Smith and colleagues (1989a) that also incorporates a feature of the recent African origin model. According to their model, the transition from archaic to modern *H. sapiens* occurred *first* in a single region such as Africa. Given the interconnections of populations over time, any advantageous genetic change then spread out into other archaic populations through gene flow (assimilation occurred, not replacement or invasion). Because gene flow takes time, moderns appeared first in one region, then later in others as gene flow caught up to them.

This model is analogous to throwing a stone into the middle of a swimming pool. The first change introduced by the stone is a splash in the

Figure 13.32

The assimilation model of the evolution of anatomically modern *H. sapiens*. Populations of *H. erectus* evolve into archaic *H. sapiens*. The initial change from archaic to modern *H. sapiens* occurs in Africa after 200,000 years ago, spreading outward through gene flow. New genes mix with archaic genes in all regions of the Old World.

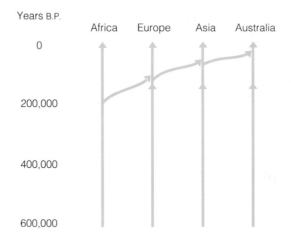

center. Then ripples of change spread out over the rest of the pool's surface. Thus the initial change to modern form occurred in a single region. A schematic diagram of this model is given in Figure 13.32.

Fossil and Genetic Evidence

The three evolutionary models discussed above all make specific predictions that can be tested using the fossil record and evidence from patterns of genetic variation among living human populations.

The fossil evidence. Which model, or models, does the fossil evidence support? It is important to realize that each model makes certain predictions that, in theory, can be tested using the fossil evidence available on archaic and modern *H. sapiens*. Predictions are made regarding the biological relationships between archaic and modern forms within each region, and the relationships between regions. The recent African origin model predicts that anatomically modern fossils in all regions will be more similar to anatomically modern forms in Africa than to archaic forms in these regions. For example, European moderns should be more similar to African moderns than to European archaics. Outside of Africa, there should be more or less abrupt changes over time, corresponding to the influx of African-based populations. A further prediction of the model is that anatomically modern *H. sapiens* will appear first in Africa, and later in other regions.

The multiregional evolution model makes a different set of predictions, proposing that archaic and modern forms within each region are similar, displaying continuity over time. Because of this regional continuity, European archaics should share unique features with European moderns, Asian archaics should share unique features with Asian moderns, and so on. The predictions of the assimilation model about regional similarities are indistinguishable from those of the multiregional model (Kramer

1991). Like the recent African origin model, the assimilation model predicts that modern forms will appear first in one region and then be found at later dates in others, but the fossils will still show regional continuity.

Although the comparison of archaic and modern *H. sapiens* fossils over time and space seems relatively clear-cut, in practice things are often more difficult. Differing interpretations of fossil morphology, disagreement about whether physical features are primitive or derived, and debates over dating of sites all complicate the process. In spite of these problems, there appears to be growing consensus on a number of points (although it is still by no means unanimous). First, modern forms appear to be older in Africa than in other regions (Smith et al. 1989a). While there is continuing debate over dating, this evidence suggests that modern forms arose *initially* in Africa and later in other regions. This finding supports both the recent African origin model and the assimilation model. Of course, another possibility is that because of the sparse nature of the fossil record, we have not yet found early moderns in other regions. This might be so, but it is not a good idea to develop models based on things that have not been found. One is better advised to work with the data at hand, revising hypotheses as new information is obtained.

Second, there is strong evidence for regional continuity in several regions, particularly Asia and Australia (Wolpoff 1989; Kramer 1991), and evidence also exists for continuity in parts of Europe (Smith et al. 1989b; Thorne and Wolpoff 1992). That is, modern forms in a particular region tend to resemble archaics there. This finding supports both the strict multiregional evolution model and the assimilation model, although it is only fair to point out that some paleoanthropologists dispute the fossil evidence for regional continuity (e.g., Stringer and Andrews 1988).

The two lines of evidence together affirm the assimilation model. The evolution of *H. sapiens* appears multiregional, but with initial genetic change occurring in Africa and spreading to other connected populations by gene flow. (This is my interpretation of the current data, and it is by no means agreed on by all anthropologists!)

Indeed the assimilation model need not predict continuity in *every* region. Because of differing amounts of gene flow, certain regions could be more isolated and not necessarily contribute to modern *H. sapiens*. In others, external gene flow might be more important than regional continuity. Believing this to be the case in Western Europe, some researchers minimize the genetic input of the Neandertals to modern European *H. sapiens*. At present, the evidence for regional continuity in Western Europe is not as strong as in Asia and Australia, and it is possible that the Neandertals remained relatively isolated from the rest of the species.

The genetic evidence. Genetic data on modern human populations can also be used to test models of the origin of modern *H. sapiens*. For example, according to the recent African origin model, the genetic diversity of neutral alleles should be greatest within African populations, given the longer time they are expected to accumulate mutations. Also, the great-

mitochondrial DNA (mtDNA) DNA found in the mitochondria of the cells rather than the nucleus and inherited primarily through females.

est genetic distances among modern human groups should be between African and non-African populations (Stringer and Andrews 1988).

Certain genetic data support this view. Studies of blood groups, proteins, and enzymes often show sub-Saharan African populations at the greatest genetic distance from other regions of the world (Cavalli-Sforza 1991). Of course, these results could also be used to support the assimilation model, since it too predicts initial genetic change in Africa. One way of distinguishing between these models is to use the genetic data to estimate the time of separation of groups. Techniques similar to those used in molecular dating (Chapter 11) can determine approximate dates for evolutionary events. For example, using data from 35 protein loci, Nei (1978) estimated the initial split between African and non-African populations occurred roughly 120,000 years ago; that fits the recent African origin model. The basic methodology used here, however, is somewhat flawed (Weiss 1988). Computations of divergence dates from genetic data are based on the assumption that the different groups have been completely isolated since their initial divergence. Because the evidence of regional continuity suggests continued gene flow between regions, these dates may be inaccurate. The molecular clock method works well when looking at differences *between* species but not as well when looking at differences between populations *within* species.

From a genetic standpoint, major support for the recent African origin model came initially from a new method of genetic analysis—the study of **mitochondrial DNA.** Most evolutionary analyses focus on the DNA within the nucleus of each cell. A small amount of DNA also exists within the mitochondria of the cells. Mitochondrial DNA (mtDNA) is different because it is only inherited through the mother. Eggs transmit mtDNA, but sperm usually do not (although recent data have shown that there is some paternal inheritance of mtDNA [Gyllensten et al. 1991]). As a result, there is no shuffling of genes during reproduction as there is with nuclear DNA. If we assume that mtDNA is a neutral genetic trait (some evidence supports this), then the only factor affecting mtDNA evolution over long periods of time is mutation. Because of this characteristic, mtDNA can be used to trace ancestry through females back to an original source. By looking at different types of mtDNA, we can estimate the type and order of different mutations and come up with a genetic profile of a common ancestor.

Rebecca Cann and colleagues (1987) looked at the mtDNA of 147 placentas from women with ancestors from different parts of the world. Based on data suggesting a constant rate of mtDNA mutation, Cann and her colleagues estimated that the mtDNA of *all* modern humans stems from a single woman who lived in Africa between 140,000 and 290,000 years ago. The inference that all of humanity arose from a single female has led some to refer to this hypothetical ancestor as "Eve." Though all of our species' mtDNA came from a single ancestor, this does not mean that all of our species' *nuclear* DNA came from a single woman. Some females may have produced only sons or had no offspring, in which case their particular mtDNA would have been lost.

Not all anthropologists have accepted the "Eve" theory, some have raised questions about methods and interpretations. Collection of additional samples solved a number of methodological problems. For example, Cann used African-American women as representatives of Africans. As discussed in Chapter 5, the European admixture that has entered the African-American gene pool would affect the results of any comparisons. Using further samples collected from sub-Saharan African populations, Vigilant and colleagues (1991) confirmed Cann's earlier results: the estimated common ancestor lived in Africa between 166,000 and 290,000 years ago.

While the mtDNA evidence supports the recent African origin model, it might also be used to support the assimilation model. Stoneking and Cann (1989) feel differently; they note that if there was gene flow between African and non-African populations following the origin of modern *H. sapiens,* then we should see evidence of older, non-African mtDNA in human populations in the rest of the world. Stoneking and Cann argue that for lack of such evidence, no gene flow occurred. However, it is also possible that gene flow did occur but that non-African mtDNA types were lost because of genetic drift. Extinction of mtDNA types can occur rapidly under certain conditions. Take, as an analogy, the transmission of last names. In many Western societies, last names are passed on by only one parent, the father—and through his male offspring. Suppose in such a society a man named Jones has four children. If we assume all other factors are equal, he has a 50:50 chance of having a male or female child. The sons will bear his last name their whole life, whereas the daughters will take on the name of their husband. On average, we can expect that half of his children will pass his last name on to the next generation. However, because of chance, he might have four sons, or three sons and one daughter, or even four daughters. As shown below, 16 permutations of children are possible:

Child 1	Child 2	Child 3	Child 4
Male	Male	Male	Male
Male	Male	Male	Female
Male	Male	Female	Male
Male	Male	Female	Female
Male	Female	Male	Male
Male	Female	Male	Female
Male	Female	Female	Male
Male	Female	Female	Female
Female	Male	Male	Male
Female	Male	Male	Female
Female	Male	Female	Male
Female	Male	Female	Female
Female	Female	Male	Male
Female	Female	Male	Female
Female	Female	Female	Male
Female	Female	Female	Female

Out of these 16 permutations:

The probability of having 4 males is 1 out of 16, or 6.25 percent.
The probability of having 3 males is 4 out of 16, or 25 percent.
The probability of having 2 males is 6 out of 16, or 37.5 percent.
The probability of having 1 male is 4 out of 16, or 25 percent.
The probability of having 0 males is 1 out of 16, or 6.25 percent.

Statistically, the probability of Jones's last name becoming extinct in a single generation is 6.25 percent.

After a number of generations, the probability of a unique last name becoming extinct increases quickly. For example, Relethford (1988a) found that over two-thirds of all surnames on an Irish island in 1821 had become extinct by 1892. Mathematical studies have shown that the extinction of mtDNA types is also likely to be rapid in human populations (Avise et al. 1984).

The mitochondrial DNA evidence suffered greatly in 1992 with the publication of two studies showing that the basic methodology for reconstructing family trees had been incorrectly used in the early studies (Hedges et al. 1992; Templeton 1992). Some newer reanalyses still support an African origin model, but others have suggested that non-Africans had more divergent mtDNA than Africans. These continuing problems, combined with evidence of paternal inheritance suggest that little confidence can be placed in using mtDNA samples to pinpoint the time and place of modern human origins. Of course, these negative results do not rule out the possibility that mtDNA studies may someday be more useful in studying human origins—it is quite common in science for new methods to be revised after their initial application.

Summary. While all three models of the origin of modern humans remain viable to some extent, the combined fossil and genetic evidence to date may best support the assimilation variant of the multiregional model, this explains both the observed regional continuity in the fossil record and the possibility of initial modern origins in Africa. This does not, of course, exclude other alternatives. Rather than dogmatically rejecting these, we should rank the various hypotheses according to relative probability.

Why Did Modern Humans Evolve?

The alternative models for the origin of modern humans are fascinating to debate, but we don't want to lose track of a basic fact that all agree on: only modern humans have been found in the last 30,000 years. In addition to explaining the timing and nature of the transition from archaics to moderns, we must also ask ourselves why this transition occurred in the first place. The available evidence suggests that anatomically modern *H. sapiens* had some evolutionary advantage over archaic *H. sapiens*. But what was this advantage?

Various biological and cultural explanations have been offered to account for this fact. The biological changes from archaic to modern are easy to describe, but they are much more difficult to explain. The change in cranial shape may suggest some associated change in patterns of brain growth and possible behavior. Language, for example, has been claimed as one such ability. According to this view, archaic *H. sapiens* lacked sophisticated speech. Evolutionary changes in anatomically modern *H. sapiens* may have led to advanced speech abilities that would certainly provide an evolutionary advantage. What we know about archaic and modern brain size and structure, however, does not support this model.

Technological changes have also been suggested as mechanisms for the change from archaic to modern forms. This view holds that many of the structural characteristics of archaic *H. sapiens* were the result of stresses generated by the use of their front teeth as tools. The large size and wear patterns of the incisor teeth of archaics (especially Neandertals) support the notion that these teeth were used for a variety of purposes. The stresses generated by heavy use of the front teeth can also be used to explain the large face, large neck muscles, and other features of archaic skulls. Once technological adaptations had developed sufficiently, these physical adaptations were no longer necessary and would not be selected for. Smaller teeth and faces might then be advantageous, because smaller structures require correspondingly less energy for growth and maintenance (Smith et al. 1989a). Similar arguments can be made to explain the reduction in body size and musculature (e.g., Frayer 1984). Once cultural behaviors took the place of larger teeth, faces, and bones, then smaller structures actually became more adaptive. Once again, evolution is best seen in terms of the overall balance between costs and benefits. In the past, as today, human culture can alter the nature of this relationship.

Reduction in the size of the teeth and face might also be due to what Brace (1991) terms the *Probable Mutation Effect*. In the absence of selection, new mutations are likely to lead to the disruption of a biological structure or growth process. In the case of teeth, mutations interfering with the growth process would accumulate in the absence of selection against them. The use of technology to replace larger teeth would result in removal of selection against these mutations. The accumulation of these mutations would therefore lead to a reduction in the size of the teeth. In any case, it is interesting to note that this process still continues. In fact, the rate of dental reduction in humans has increased during the last 10,000 years, most likely reflecting changes in diet and diet related technologies (Brace et al. 1987).

Calcagno and Gibson (1988) have recently presented strong theoretical arguments and empirical evidence refuting the hypothesis that the probable mutation effect was responsible for the reduction in dental and facial size in anatomically modern *H. sapiens*. In particular, they cite clinical evidence from contemporary human populations that show that large teeth can have many disadvantages. Larger teeth are more susceptible to dental decay, problems caused by crowding of teeth, and periodontal disease. In earlier prehistoric times the advantages of larger teeth (e.g., as tools) may have outweighed the disadvantages. When cultural change led to more efficient tools, the advantage for larger teeth diminished, and selection would then be against larger teeth. This is another excellent example of how cultural change can lead to biological change. Calcagno and Gibson's work is also very useful because it shows us how we can apply information obtained from living populations to test hypotheses of past evolution.

The exact reasons for the change from archaic to modern *H. sapiens* are still unknown. All the factors cited may have been important in this transition, as well as others not yet discovered. Further analysis of the biological and cultural adaptations of both archaics and moderns is needed to understand recent human evolution.

SUMMARY

Following the initial emergence of the genus *Homo,* the record of human evolution shows an increase in brain size and complexity, reduction in the face and teeth, and an increasing reliance on cultural adaptations. The basic sequence from *H. habilis* to *H. erectus* to archaic *H. sapiens* to anatomically modern *H. sapiens* is well documented, although the fine detail of this sequence is still under investigation.

The species *H. erectus* appears to have rapidly evolved from some populations of *H. habilis* in East Africa 1.6 million years B.P. *H. erectus* had an increased cranial capacity and exhibited a variety of cultural adaptations, including greater sophistication in stone tool technology, hunting and gathering, the use of fire, and the use and manufacture of shelter. These adaptations allowed hominids to expand out of Africa. By 1 million years ago, *H. erectus* had reached Asia. Later *H. erectus* or early *H. sapiens* populations inhabited the southern range of Europe by roughly 400,000 years B.P. Though the change from *H. habilis* to *H. erectus* was relatively rapid, the change from *H. erectus* to early *H. sapiens* appears to have been more gradual.

By 200,000 to 400,000 years B.P., archaic *H. sapiens* existed in the Old World. The major biological changes reflect a further increase in brain size, which continued until roughly 45,000 years ago. Archaic *H. sapiens* differs from anatomically modern *H. sapiens* in a number of ways, primarily in having a larger face and brow ridges, a sloping forehead, and a less well-rounded skull. Regional differences in archaic *H. sapiens* are apparent from the fossil record. The Neandertals from Western Europe and the Middle East make up the best-known regional population. Contrary to popular thought, the Neandertals were quite intelligent. They had a sophisticated stone tool technology, buried their dead, and adapted to harsh climates.

Anatomically modern *H. sapiens* is best known after 30,000 years B.P. There is growing evidence, however, that the first groups of anatomically modern *H. sapiens* emerged in Africa over 100,000 years ago. The transition from archaic to modern forms can be explained by three models. The recent African origin model states that modern humans arose first in Africa roughly 200,000 years ago and then spread out over the rest of the Old World, replacing archaic populations. According to this model, archaic populations outside of Africa did not contribute genetically to modern humans. The multiregional evolution model states that the transition from *H. erectus* to archaic *H. sapiens* to modern *H. sapiens* occurred throughout the Old World, with biological change reflecting both regional continuity and gene flow between regions that maintained a single species. A variant of this idea, the assimilation model, states that the *initial* change to moderns took place in Africa and then became incorporated into the rest of the species over time through gene flow resulting from migration between neighboring groups. Both fossil and genetic evidence have been used to test these models. While uncertainty and controversy remain, current data best support the assimilation model.

Regardless of which model is correct, the reasons behind the emergence of anatomically modern forms are not known with certainty. Possible factors include biological changes resulting from the increasing impact of cultural adaptations. Human evolution did not end with the emergence of anatomically modern *H. sapiens*. Our species continues to change.

Supplemental Readings

Klein, R. G. 1989. *The Human Career: Human Biological and Cultural Origins*. Chicago: University of Chicago Press. An excellent summary of the fossil and (particularly) archaeological records of human evolution. Considerable attention is given to *H. erectus* and *H. sapiens*.

Smith, F. H., A. B. Falsetti, and S. M. Donnelly. 1989. Modern human origins. *Yearbook of Physical Anthropology* 32:35–68. An excellent review of competing models of the origin of modern *H. sapiens*.

Thorne, A. G., and M. H. Wolpoff. April 1992. The multiregional evolution of humans. *Scientific American* 266(4):76–83. A nontechnical review of the multiregional evolution model and its supporting evidence.

Trinkaus, E., and P. Shipman. 1993. *The Neandertals: Changing the Image of Mankind*. New York: Knopf. An excellent and nontechnical review of the history of Neandertal discoveries and interpretations.

Wilson, A. C., and R. L. Cann. April 1992. The recent African genesis of humans. *Scientific American* 266(4):68–73. Appearing in the same issue as the Thorne and Wolpoff article, this paper provides a nontechnical review of the recent African origin model and its supporting evidence. Reading both papers together is recommended.

Wolpoff, M. H. 1980. *Paleoanthropology*. New York: Knopf. Although now out of date, this remains an excellent source for descriptions and discussions of variations in *H. erectus* and *H. sapiens* fossils.

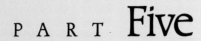

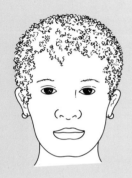  

Human Biology and Culture

CHAPTER **14**

Human Growth

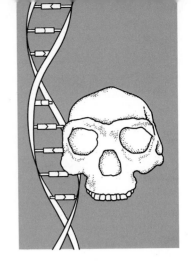

Biological anthropology examines both biological and cultural variation. Patterns of human biological diversity are affected by cultural behaviors. Examples of the interrelationship of human biology and culture have been discussed in earlier chapters. The remaining chapters in this textbook focus on areas of human biological variation that are closely related to cultural behaviors. Given that many biological traits are the joint products of genetic and environmental factors and that cultural behaviors are part of these environmental factors, the close relationship of human biology and culture is to be expected.

These remaining chapters also deal with the areas of biological variation most affected in our rapidly changing world. As human technology continues to develop at a rapid rate, it has many consequent effects on our biology. This chapter focuses on one of these areas—the study of human growth and development, also known as **auxology.**

The growth patterns of any species have both genetic and environmental components. As our environment changes, so do our patterns of physical growth. Some of these effects, such as changes in health care and nutrition, are direct. Other changes, such as the relationship of socioeconomic class and nutrition, are indirect. For example, the poorer a family is, the less likely it is that the children will obtain proper nutrition, which in turn affects their growth. In fact, human growth patterns are so sensitive to environmental changes that they are often used as indices of the well-being of a population. Detrimental effects of toxic waste, for example, may take a generation to show up in the form of increased cancers. The effects

auxology The study of human biological growth and development.

399

growth A change in the size of a living structure, most often because of an increase in cell size or number.

Harris lines Horizontal lines that form on bones because of disruption of the growth process.

Figure 14.1

X-ray of a femur, showing horizontal lines (known as Harris lines) that indicate periods of stress during growth. (Courtesy of Henry McHenry, University of California, Davis)

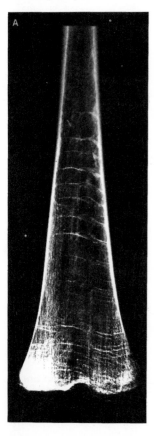

on infant mortality, birth weight, and child growth are more immediate, informing us that biological patterns have been affected.

The study of growth and development is also valuable in understanding evolutionary changes. As previous chapters have outlined, many evolutionary changes do not consist of new structures but rather are modifications of preexisting structures. These modifications reflect changes in the size and shape of a structure, which are in turn affected by genetic regulation of growth and maturation.

The Life Cycle

The life cycle involves changes in physical growth and maturation. These changes can be viewed in terms of various stages of human growth.

The Biology of Growth and Development

The human life cycle includes changes in both physical growth and development. **Growth** refers to the change in size of a living structure. Tissues can become larger through a variety of mechanisms. Many living tissues become larger because of an increase in the number of cells. As cells replicate, there is a geometric increase in the total number of cells: first, one cell, then two, then four, and so on. As the number of cells increases, the size of the biological structure also increases. Growth can also occur through an increase in cell size or an increase in intercellular material.

Not all types of tissue show the same pattern of growth. Some tissues regenerate: they replace themselves over the lifetime of an organism. Skin cells and blood cells are regenerating tissues. Other tissues, such as nerve and muscle tissue, do not regenerate. Once the growth period for nerve and muscle cells is complete, these cells are no longer manufactured. Certain other tissues, such as those found in the liver and kidney, generally do not regenerate but can do so under certain conditions.

Bone tissue grows somewhat differently than other types of tissues. Most bones first form as cartilage or gristle. In limb bones, the cartilage changes into bone tissue in the center and at both ends of the limb. The cartilage continues to grow from these points and turns into bone. When all the cartilage has been converted into bone, the limb bone stops growing. When we examine a bone with X-rays, we can see the bone but not the cartilage. This allows us to assess a person's stage of skeletal growth. We can also detect certain past problems in growth by the presence of **Harris lines,** horizontal lines that form on a bone because of disruption of the growth process (Figure 14.1). Thus, a knowledge of the growth process of bones allows us to estimate age and health status from X-rays, useful in the investigation of children with growth disorders. Such methods also help us investigate the growth and health of prehistoric populations (see Chapter 16 for more information).

Development is the process of differentiation and specialization of cells that produces the tissues and organs. Before the invention of the microscope, many people believed that a miniature human being contained in either the sperm or the egg simply grew larger in the mother. We now know, of course, that we all start life as a single cell. Over time, this cell multiplies (growth), forming new cells. Different cells, however, develop into separate tissues and organs (development). The cell doctrine, first stated by Rudolf Virchow, notes that the cell is the fundamental structure of an organism and that all cells arise from other cells. All body cells, that is, are clones of one another. During development, different cells give rise to different types of tissue. Even though all the body cells (with rare exceptions) carry the same genetic code, different types of cells express these instructions in separate ways.

development The process of differentiation and specialization of cells that produces specific tissues and organs.

zygote A fertilized egg.

embryo The stage of human prenatal life lasting from roughly two to eight weeks following conception, characterized by structural development.

Stages of Growth

The major stages of growth are prenatal (before birth) and postnatal (after birth).

Prenatal life. Prenatal life is the period from fertilization through childbirth. The question of when life begins has ethical as well as biological implications (e.g., the controversy surrounding abortion). To some, life does not begin until birth. Others believe life begins at the moment of conception, and still others mark this point somewhere after the third month of pregnancy. From a biological perspective, we can define the beginnings of prenatal life as the moment of fertilization, because this point marks the origin of a new combination of chromosomes. From an ethical perspective, the definition of life may or may not be the same, since it may be defined in terms of characteristics such as "soul" that are not amenable to scientific evaluation. As is often the case, ethical and moral questions cannot be answered from scientific data but rely more on an individual's world view and beliefs.

After fertilization, the fertilized egg (**zygote**) develops into a cluster of identical cells deriving from the initial fertilized egg. During the first week, the fertilized egg multiplies as it travels into the uterus. By this point, there are roughly 150 cells arranged in a hollow ball that implants itself into the walls of the uterus. Cell differentiation begins. During the second week, the outer layer of this ball forms the beginning of the placenta. Some early differentiation can be seen in the remainder of the ball.

The embryonic stage stretches from roughly two to eight weeks after conception. The **embryo** is very small during this time, reaching an aver-

fetus The stage of prenatal
growth from roughly 8 weeks
following conception until
birth, characterized by further development and rapid
growth.

age length of 25 mm (1 in) by the eighth week. During this time the basic
body structure is complete and many of the different organ systems have
developed; the embryo has a recognizably human appearance, although it
is still not complete (Figure 14.2). The fetal stage lasts from this point
until birth. Development of body parts and organ systems continues,
along with a tremendous amount of body growth and changes in proportions. During the second trimester of pregnancy, the **fetus** shows rapid
growth in overall length. During the third trimester, the fetus shows rapid
growth in body weight, head size, and brain growth.

Postnatal life. The stages of postnatal life are defined somewhat arbitrarily and in different ways for varying purposes. The meaning of the
term *adult,* for example, varies considerably from culture to culture, and
even within some societies, in its biological, social, religious, and legal
dimensions. The same is true of other designated stages of human postnatal growth, such as infancy and childhood.

Figure 14.2

A 2-month-old embryo. The
fingers have developed and the
eye is oval in shape. The total
body length at this stage is
3.18 cm (1.25 in).   (Copyright
Lennart Nilsson, *A Child Is Born,*
Dell Publishing Company)

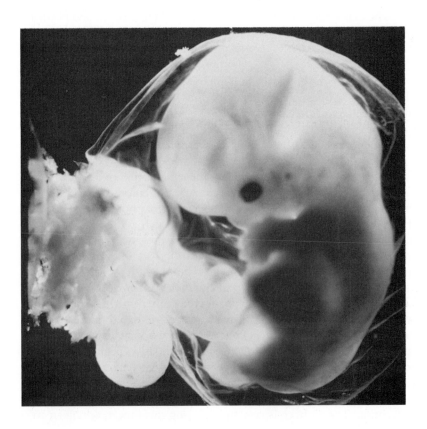

From the perspective of human biological growth, the stages of post-natal growth can be labeled according to basic patterns of physical growth and maturation (the use of these terms in the context of growth and maturation differs somewhat from their use in describing behavior, as in Chapters 7–9). *Infancy* often refers to the first year after birth, a time characterized by rapid growth in overall body size and most biological systems. *Childhood* is the period from infancy through puberty, character-ized mostly by a slow, but constant, rate of growth. The exception to this slow growth rate occurs during midchildhood, when some individuals show a minor increase (**midgrowth spurt**).

Puberty marks the period in which physical and sexual maturity is reached. The term *puberty* is usually used to describe the biological changes taking place at this time, and the term *adolescence* is used to describe psychological changes. The two terms, however, are often inter-changed. Puberty occurs normally somewhere between 8 and 16 years for females and 10 and 22 years for males (Malina 1975). It is characterized by rapid body growth, maturation of the reproductive system, and devel-opment of secondary sexual characteristics. *Adulthood* follows puberty and continues until death.

midgrowth spurt A small increase in the rate of body growth during midchildhood seen in some, but not all, human populations.

puberty The point in the human life cycle when sexual and physical maturity is at-tained.

anthropometry The mea-surement of the human body.

The Pattern of Human Postnatal Growth

The pattern of human postnatal growth is influenced by both genetic and environmental factors. This section focuses on the analysis of postnatal growth, patterns of differential body growth, the growth process, and evolutionary aspects of human growth.

The Analysis of Human Growth

Many different types of measurements can be made on the human body to provide information about the extent and rate of growth.

Measurements. Many measurements can be made of the human body, including measures of length, breadth, body size, and fat composition. The practice of taking measurements on living humans is known as **anthro-pometry**. Anthropometric measurements are taken according to specific methods. Many of these measurements provide data for analyzing human growth and development.

The two anthropometric measurements most often taken on living subjects are stature (height) and weight. Stature provides a composite measure of overall body size, made up of the height of the legs, torso, and

Figure 14.3

The author measures his son's
stature. Stature and weight are
the two most common
measures of human growth.

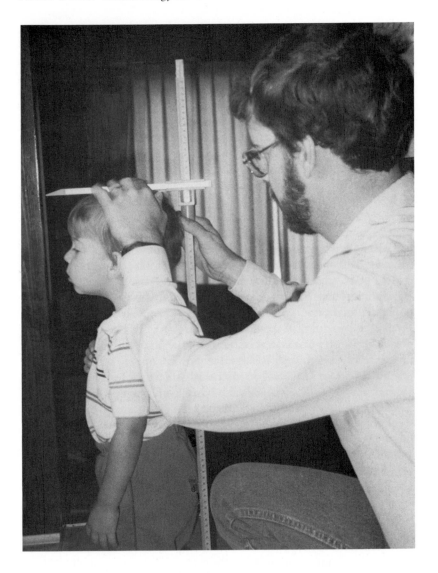

neck and head (Figure 14.3). Weight is also a composite measure, reflecting the overall mass of bone, fat, muscle, and internal organs. Other measurements provide greater detail on the composition of body length.
Sitting height, a common measurement, provides a measurement of upper
body length: roughly speaking, a subject sits on a table and the distance
from the top of the table to the top of the head is measured. The difference
between stature and sitting height provides a measurement of leg length.

Various measurements can also provide a better idea of the composition of total body weight. A device known as a skinfold caliper is used to
measure fat at different parts of the body. One skinfold measurement is
triceps skinfold, whereby the person taking the measurement pinches the
skin and fat lying above the triceps muscle on the back of the subject's arm.

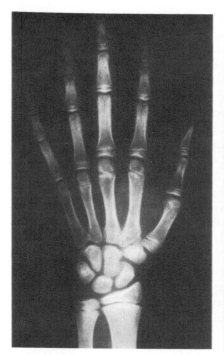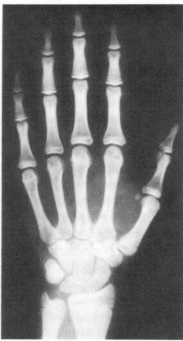

Figure 14.4

Hand-wrist X-rays of two 14-year-old males. The subject on the left has a younger skeletal age (12). The subject on the right has an older skeletal age (16), which can be seen by noting fewer dark areas between the wrist bones. (Reprinted by permission of the publishers from *Fetus into Man* by J. M. Tanner, Cambridge, Mass.: Harvard University Press. Copyright © 1978 by J. M. Tanner)

The thickness of the area pinched is measured with a skinfold caliper (this may sound painful, but it isn't—you can grab the skin and fat on the back of your arm and see for yourself). The overall circumference of your arm, which can be measured with a tape, indicates the total amount of bone, muscle, and fat in your arm. The triceps skinfold measures only the fat. These measures provide a rough idea of body composition (how much is made up of fat, muscle, and bone). Similar measurements can be made on other parts of the body, such as the legs or back. More complex methods, such as underwater weighing and certain biochemical analyses, can provide even more detailed information on body composition.

We can also measure the width of the body. Two common measures are hip and shoulder width. These measures are particularly useful in examining sex differences during puberty, when relative hip growth is pronounced in females and relative shoulder growth is pronounced in males. There are many other anthropometric measurements, including measures of the skull, face, and nose. A useful measure in growth studies is the circumference of the upper skull. This measure can be helpful in comparing the growth of the brain and head during infancy and childhood.

There are also a number of measures of biological maturation. One method determines a person's skeletal age (which may not be the same as chronological age) by analysis of an X-ray of a person's hand and wrist. During growth, the cartilage is still in the process of forming bone. The cartilage is opaque to X-rays and shows up dark on an X-ray picture (Figure 14.4). This picture is then compared to standard reference charts.

cross-sectional study A study of human growth that analyzes samples of children at different ages at one time.

longitudinal study A study of human growth that analyzes a sample of children repeatedly over time (i.e., the same children at different ages).

distance curve A measure of size over time. For example, a distance curve would show how tall someone is at different ages.

velocity curve A measure of the rates of change in growth over time.

acceleration curve A measure of changes in the direction of growth rates over time.

Types of studies. There are two basic types of growth studies. **Cross-sectional studies** measure a sample of people of different age groups at one time. For example, imagine that you go to a local elementary school and measure all the 6-year-old females, all the 7-year-old females, all the 8-year-old females, and so on. This would be a cross-sectional study. The other type of growth study, the **longitudinal study,** measures a group of people at frequent intervals over a designated period of time. Imagine that you go to a local elementary school and measure all 6-year-old males. A year later, you measure the same children, who are now 7 years old. You come back a year later and measure them again when they are 8 years old. This is a longitudinal study.

Each type of growth study has certain advantages and disadvantages. Ideally, longitudinal studies are preferable because they provide exact information on the pattern of growth for individuals over time. Longitudinal studies take a long time, however. If you follow a group of children from birth until adulthood, you must wait 18 years or more until your data are ready to be analyzed. Problems also arise from the fact that certain individuals will drop out, perhaps moving away or dying before you have completed the study. Cross-sectional studies are easier to conduct; you can measure a number of children at different ages in a relatively short period of time.

Growth Curves

Human postnatal growth is not simply a process of the body enlarging over time. For one thing, parts of the body show different patterns of postnatal growth. The growth of fat tissue does not follow the same pattern as body height or reproductive organs. Moreover, growth in any part of the body does not take place at a constant rate. You do not grow taller the same amount per year from birth through adulthood. Finally, some parts of the body actually decrease in size during your life. The total mass of your lymphatic tissues, for example, is almost twice as large during puberty as it is during adulthood. The fat tissue on the back of the arms of males also tends to decrease during puberty.

Human growth is therefore not a process that can be explained by a simple statement such as, "The older you get, the bigger you get." Growth patterns vary according to age and body part. Simple graphs, however, can convey the various patterns of human postnatal growth.

There are several types of growth curves: these include distance curves, velocity curves, and acceleration curves. A **distance curve** simply measures overall size over time. Perhaps somewhere in your parents' house there is a doorpost where your parents have marked your height at different ages in your childhood. This is a distance curve. It provides an indication of how tall you were at different ages. **Velocity curves** measure the rate of change over time—that is, how quickly you are growing. **Acceleration curves** provide information on changes in the direction of growth rates

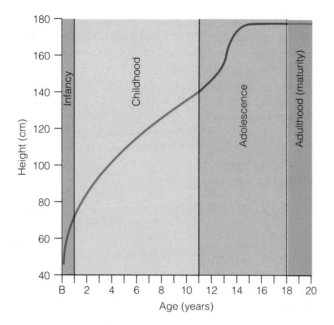

Figure 14.5

Typical distance curve for human height. (From *Growth and Development* by Robert M. Malina © 1975, publisher Burgess Publishing Company, Minneapolis, MN)

and are particularly useful in identifying hormonal changes during growth.

Growth curves can be understood using the simple analogy of driving a car. As you drive down a highway you are going farther in a given direction. A graph of how far you have traveled, plotted against how long you have been traveling, is a distance curve. Velocity refers to how quickly you are moving. If your speed is 50 mph, that is your velocity. If you plot your speed against the time, you get a velocity curve. Sometimes you will be moving at 30 mph, sometimes at 40 mph, and sometimes at 50 mph. Acceleration refers to the rate of change in your velocity. If you are traveling at 30 mph and press down on the gas pedal (the accelerator) to increase to a speed of 35 mph, your acceleration during that time is 5 mph.

Distance curves. Distance curves can be derived for a single individual or for an entire population using average data. Figure 14.5 shows the typical distance curve for postnatal height. The vertical axis of the graph indicates height in centimeters and the horizontal axis indicates age in years. The curve drawn on Figure 14.5 represents a typical average distance curve for many human populations. Note that the curve is not a straight line; humans do not get larger by the same amount every year. The curve shows a rapid increase in total height during infancy. Height continues to increase by a fairly constant amount during childhood and then increases quickly for a short time during puberty. By adulthood, there is little additional growth in height.

adolescent growth spurt
The increase in rate of body growth during the adolescent years because of hormonal changes.

Figure 14.6 shows actual distance curves for height for males and females in the United States. Both sexes follow the basic pattern shown in Figure 14.5. Growth is greatest during infancy and puberty. Taken together, the male and female curves illustrate the value of growth curves in description and comparison. Males and females show little difference in overall height during infancy and childhood. In Western populations, on average, females are taller than males between the ages of 11 and 14. After 14 years of age, males become and remain larger than females on average. Both males and females follow the same basic path but differ in the timing of puberty. The extent of the sex differences, and the age at puberty, vary among populations, but the pattern is normally consistent.

Velocity curves. Whereas distance curves measure the actual amount of growth, velocity curves measure the rate of change in growth. A typical velocity curve for human body height is shown in Figure 14.7. The horizontal axis of the graph indicates age in years. The vertical axis represents the amount of height in centimeters gained per year. How do we compute such rates? Imagine that you were 85 cm tall at age 2 and 95 cm tall at age 3. Your rate of gain in height was 10 cm per year between ages 2 and 3.

The velocity curve for height in Figure 14.7 shows that the greatest rate of change in height occurs immediately after birth. At no other time in your life will you be growing as fast. During infancy, the rate of change decreases quickly. You continue to get taller, but at a slower rate in each succeeding month. During childhood, the rate of change is fairly constant except in individuals who experience a slight midgrowth spurt.

During puberty, the rate of growth in height increases again—a phenomenon known as the **adolescent growth spurt.** This increase in growth

Figure 14.6

Male and female distance curves for height.   (From *Growth and Development* by Robert M. Malina © 1975, publisher Burgess Publishing Company, Minneapolis, MN)

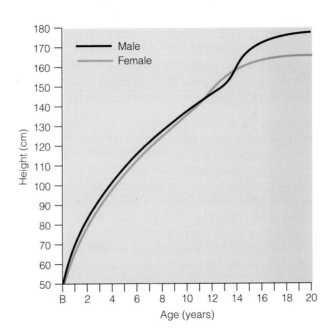

velocity is related to the hormonal changes taking place during puberty. Following puberty, the rate of growth decreases again to reach a level of zero growth by roughly 20 years of age in contemporary Western populations.

Male and female velocity curves for height are compared in Figure 14.8 based on the same data used in Figure 14.6. Both sexes follow the

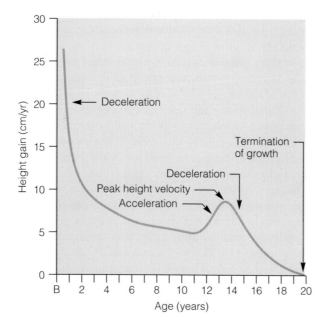

Figure 14.7

Typical velocity curve for human height.   (From *Growth and Development* by Robert M. Malina © 1975, publisher Burgess Publishing Company, Minneapolis, MN)

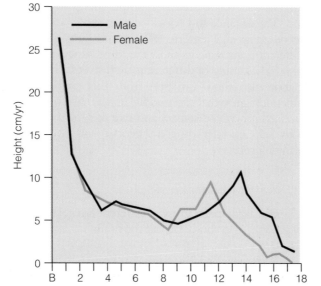

Figure 14.8

Male and female velocity curves for height.   (From *Growth and Development* by Robert M. Malina © 1975, publisher Burgess Publishing Company, Minneapolis, MN)

same basic pattern, but the adolescent growth spurt occurs at different times. Females start to mature biologically roughly two years earlier than males, resulting in an earlier growth spurt. You can see from Figure 14.8 that the greatest rate of growth during puberty occurs at 12 years for females and 14 years for males. This earlier growth spurt explains why females are taller between 11 and 14 years in the distance curve in Figure 14.6. They are growing at a greater rate than males during this time. Males have the growth spurt two years later, on average. This means that males have an average of two years of additional slow but constant growth before their growth spurt. Figure 14.8 shows that females stop height growth by roughly age 16, whereas males continue to grow until age 18. The difference between height in adult males and females is primarily the result of the longer period of growth for males.

The distance and velocity curves presented here provide an explanation of sex differences in body size in terms of growth rates that reflect hormonal differences. But what is the evolutionary explanation for sex differences in timing of growth? Some have suggested that males have delayed growth because they need to be larger and stronger for hunting. This explanation seems unlikely when we consider the vast difference in size and strength between human males and their prey. The more realistic explanation focuses not on why males are larger, but rather on why human females are smaller. Both males and females need energy for growth and maintenance. In addition, females need vast amounts of energy for pregnancy and nursing. Given a finite amount of energy (especially in hunting-gathering societies), larger females might have been at a disadvantage. If too much energy were expended in growth and maintenance of larger bodies, less would be left over for reproductive needs. The earlier spurt in female growth, and consequently smaller adult body size, may be an evolutionary adaptation to divert ample energy to reproduction.

The distance and velocity curves shown in Figures 14.5 through 14.8 represent average patterns for a specific human population. Populations in different environments show the same basic pattern but may vary according to the timing of different growth events. Individuals within any population also show variation from this average pattern. Among other functions, growth curves allow us to make quick comparisons between attained growth (distance) and rate of growth (velocity). Some comparisons help us infer different genetic and environmental effects on the growth process.

Differential Growth

Our body parts grow at different rates. Height has a specific pattern of growth, as do body fat and the brain.

Body size. Human height has been used in this discussion to illustrate the use of distance and velocity curves in analysis. Other measurements of

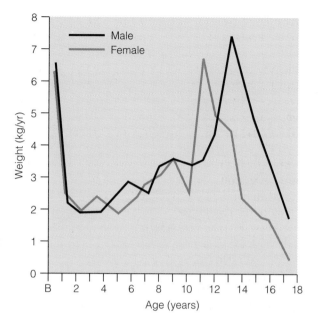

Figure 14.9

Male and female velocity curves for weight. (From *Growth and Development* by Robert M. Malina © 1975, publisher Burgess Publishing Company, Minneapolis, MN)

body size, such as weight and limb bone length, show somewhat similar patterns of growth. For example, Figure 14.9 shows velocity curves for male and female weight. The general picture is similar to that of height, although rate of weight gain in puberty may be equal to that in infancy.

Fat and muscle. Not all body measurements show the same pattern of growth as height and weight do. Body parts grow at different rates. Body fat, in particular, shows patterns of growth quite different from that of the overall body. In both males and females, midarm and midback fat grows most quickly during infancy. During childhood, the rate of increase in fat decreases quickly and actually becomes negative during midchildhood. That is, a reduction in the total amount of fat on the arms and the back takes place during this time.

The amounts of fat and muscle change noticeably during puberty. Figure 14.10 shows distance curves for Johnston and Malina's (1966) study of midarm fat and muscle in children in Philadelphia between 6 and 16 years of age. In both males and females, muscle increases with age, with greater amounts of midarm muscle in males than females at all ages. The distance curve for fat is quite different. Midarm fat tends to increase with age for females. For males, the amount of midarm fat decreases during puberty. Changes in the amount of fat and muscle in males and females reflects changes in hormonal chemistry during puberty. These sex differences may reflect reproductive needs: some evidence links fat stores to successful reproduction in females (Huss-Ashmore 1980).

Figure 14.10

Male and female distance
curves for midchildhood
growth in muscle (*top*) and
fat (*bottom*).   (From *Growth
and Development* by Robert
M. Malina © 1975, publisher
Burgess Publishing Company,
Minneapolis, MN)

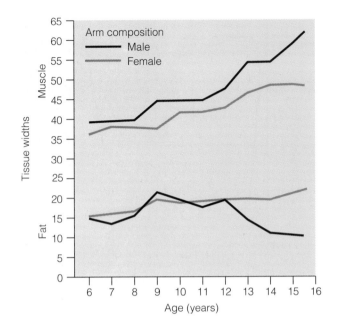

Figure 14.11

Distance curves for (a) body
size and (b) brain growth,
each measured as the percentage of adult size attained at
a given age.   (Adapted from
Growth and Development by
Robert M. Malina © 1975,
publisher Burgess Publishing
Company, Minneapolis, MN)

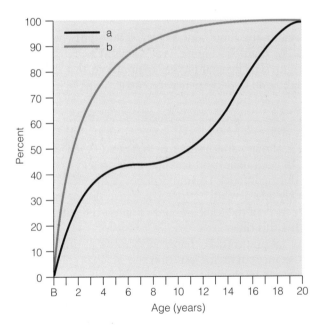

Brain and head growth. The growth of the brain and head dimensions is also quite different from the pattern of height or weight. Figure 14.11 presents distance curves for general body size (curve A) and the
brain and head dimensions (curve B). To compare the two parts of the
body, the vertical axis has been scaled to reflect the percentage of adult size

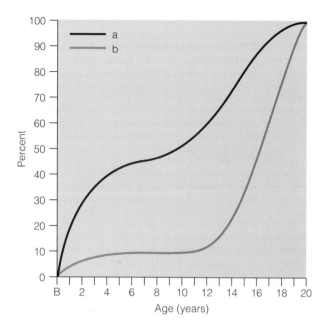

Figure 14.12

Distance curves for (a) body size and (b) reproductive tissues, each measured as the percentage of adult size attained at a given age. (Adapted from *Growth and Development* by Robert M. Malina © 1975, publisher Burgess Publishing Company, Minneapolis, MN)

for both curves. Brain and head growth is rapid during infancy and early childhood and levels off quickly thereafter. Roughly 80 percent of the brain's adult size is reached by 4 years of age, and almost 100 percent by 10 years of age.

As discussed in Chapters 9 and 12, the evolutionary explanation for early rapid brain growth rates is clear. Because humans rely on large brains, intelligence, and learned behavior, it is critical that most brain growth occur early in life. In fact, brain growth is also very rapid during prenatal life. The size of the maternal birth canal, however, limits the size of the brain in a newborn child. If the brain and head are too large, delivery may be impossible and both mother and child may die. For the human to attain a large brain as early in life as possible, the rapid rates of prenatal brain growth are continued into infancy.

Sexual maturation. Figure 14.12 compares the distance curves for body size (curve A) with the distance curve for reproductive tissues such as the gonads (curve B). During infancy and childhood, there is little growth in reproductive organs. During puberty, these organs experience rapid growth, producing the transition to biological maturity. Puberty is also the time of the development of secondary sexual characteristics, such as pubic hair in both sexes and breasts in females. In evolutionary terms, delayed sexual maturation makes sense. If young children were biologically able to have children, they would not yet have had the chance to acquire adequate knowledge to care for them.

catch-up growth An increase in growth that can occur following the removal of a limiting factor to growth.

The Growth Process

The growth curves presented here are descriptions of average patterns of growth. Individuals deviate from these average patterns within any population for a variety of reasons, both genetic and environmental. Extreme deviations from the general path of growth can be fatal. For example, as shown in Chapter 3, babies born too small or too large are less likely to survive than babies of average size.

Catch-up growth. Growth is a flexible process under many conditions. An individual whose growth deviates from his or her own trajectory can sometimes recover under the right circumstances. A classic example is recovery from a condition known as hypothyroidism, a deficiency of thyroid hormone. Without the proper hormone action at the right point in life, growth is reduced in individuals with this deficiency. Compared to other children in the population, the child with hypothyroidism will show slower rates of growth and be smaller at subsequent ages. If thyroid hormone is provided, however, the child may show a subsequent increase in growth rates and "catch up."

This example shows the process known as **catch-up growth.** When a limiting factor is countered, growth can sometimes catch up. Figure 14.13 shows an example of how catch-up growth in height can occur. Curve A represents the expected distance curve for an individual's height. Point B

Figure 14.13

Example of catch-up growth. Curve A represents the expected distance curve of a hypothetical individual's height at various ages. Point B represents the time at which some stress occurred. This stress results in a lowered rate of growth over the next few years (curve C), leading to smaller height than expected at age D. If the stress is removed at this time, the rate of growth in height may increase, leading to accelerated growth (curve E), and attainment of the expected height at age F. Not all deviations from growth can be corrected for, particularly those occurring during sensitive periods of growth (see text).

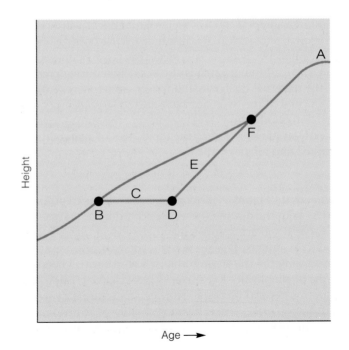

marks the point at which some deviation occurs (because of poor nutrition, disease, or some other factor). This stress results in a decreased rate of growth and smaller height during the next few years (curve C). Point D represents the time at which the stress is removed. Curve E shows catch-up growth occurring because of an increase in the rate of growth in such a way that catch-up growth is complete by point F on the figure. In this hypothetical example, complete catch-up growth was accomplished by an increase in the rate of growth. Catch-up growth can also occur by delaying maturation so that the period of growth is extended (Tanner 1989).

Sensitive periods of growth. The phenomenon of catch-up growth shows us the flexibility and adaptiveness of the growth process. The body can adjust to deviations from the expected path. Any system, however, can be put under too much stress. Catch-up growth will not always take place. In particular, there are times during the growth process in which deviations are more serious and catch-up growth cannot occur. Such times are known as **sensitive periods of growth.** Prenatal life and the first year of postnatal life are particularly sensitive periods. Stresses encountered during these times may not be fully compensated for later, regardless of changes in environmental conditions.

The Evolution of Human Growth

Some patterns of human postnatal growth are quite different from those of other primates. As described in Chapter 12, human postnatal brain growth is characterized by an extension of rapid rates of growth. This rapid postnatal brain and head growth allows adult humans to have brains four times larger than they were at birth, as compared to other primates, whose adult brain size is twice the value at birth. The large human brain is, in part, a function of the growth process.

Comparison of other aspects of growth also reveals interesting evolutionary trends. Postnatal growth in human body size is quite different from that of nonprimate mammals in two ways (Watts 1986; Bogin 1988). First, the entire process of growth is extended. Infancy, childhood, and puberty take up a larger portion of the life span of humans than of other mammals. Second, the adolescent growth spurt has not been found in mammals other than higher primates. Both of these factors are interrelated. The extension of childhood results in the delay of the acceleration of growth that subsequently occurs during puberty. In other mammals, whose childhood is relatively shorter, the rapid growth rates of infancy and puberty follow each other. Thus, there is no detectable adolescent growth spurt.

The delay in puberty, sexual maturation, and the growth spurt produces the extended childhood of humans. The longer childhood reflects in turn the human need for a lengthy period of time during which to learn vital skills. Like brain growth, the pattern of our growth in body size

sensitive period of growth
A time during the life cycle when catch-up growth is not possible.

reflects our continued reliance on learned behaviors. Our postnatal body growth patterns are an extension on the basic pattern of primate growth. Many primate species have been found to have an adolescent growth spurt, though it is not as noticeable as in humans (Watts 1986, but also see Bogin 1988 for a different interpretation).

The evolutionary advantage to delayed maturation is clear—a longer childhood allows more time for learning. But what is the evolutionary advantage, if any, for the adolescent growth spurt? Bogin (1988) states that the increased growth velocity during puberty produces adult body size in a short period of time. Why can't the same result be met by simply extending the period of preadolescent growth? Until recently in human history and prehistory, the average length of life was probably relatively short. Faster growth rates at puberty could allow adult body size to be reached more quickly.

Influences on Human Growth

Human growth is affected by biological factors (genetics and hormones) and by a variety of environmental factors, including nutrition, disease, and the physical environment. Cultural differences also affect growth by causing changes in one or more of these environmental factors. Psychological stress can affect the hormonal chemistry of the body and in turn the growth process.

Biological Influences

The biological influences on human growth are the actions of genetic factors and the endocrine system.

Genetics. Comparisons of growth patterns among related individuals have shown that human growth is partially affected by genetic factors. There is also considerable variation in growth that is not related to genetics but instead to a multitude of environmental factors. In overall size, adult offspring tend to be close to the average of their parents. In somewhat simplistic terms, tall parents generally have tall children under similar environmental conditions.

The adult sizes of parents and children show a close resemblance for height and other linear body measurements. This relationship reflects similarity in patterns of bone growth. The resemblance is less for measures of body width (e.g., shoulder width), and even less for measures of body circumference that show not only bone size but also the amount of fat.

The rates of growth are also related to genetic factors. A number of studies, however, have suggested that the potential for total growth and the rate of growth are inherited independently. Two related individuals may both have the same genetic potential for adult height but may differ in terms of how quickly they reach that height.

Hormones. The body's endocrine glands release chemicals called **hormones** into the blood stream. Hormones act as chemical messengers, stimulating and regulating biological processes in different tissues. The entire growth process is affected by a number of hormones. The patterns of hormone release are, in large part, a function of a person's genotype.

The **hypothalamus** in the brain regulates hormonal secretion. The hypothalamus produces hormone-releasing factors that travel to the **pituitary gland** in the brain, which then secretes hormones into the bloodstream. The pituitary hormones then travel to either specific body tissues or to other **endocrine glands,** which in turn produce other hormones (Figure 14.14). The hypothalamus also regulates the release of hormones. It has the ability to sense hormonal concentrations and turn the secretion of hormones on or off.

One important hormone in growth is the thyroid hormone **thyroxine,** produced by the thyroid gland. Thyroxine acts to increase the consumption of oxygen in different body tissues. This hormone is also important for proper brain growth and the regulation of metabolic rate.

hormone Chemical released by endocrine glands that travels to body tissues and stimulates and regulates biological processes.

hypothalamus A structure of the brain that regulates the secretion of hormones.

pituitary gland A structure in the brain that secretes hormones that either act directly on body tissues or stimulate other endocrine glands to release hormones.

endocrine glands Glands that secrete hormones.

thyroxine Thyroid hormone, secreted by the thyroid gland, that acts to increase oxygen consumption in body tissues.

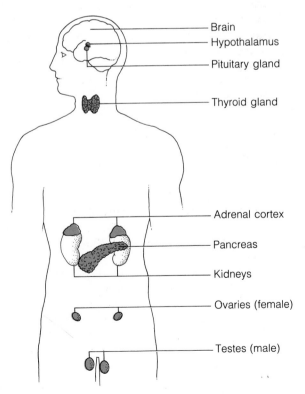

- Brain
- Hypothalamus
- Pituitary gland
- Thyroid gland
- Adrenal cortex
- Pancreas
- Kidneys
- Ovaries (female)
- Testes (male)

Figure 14.14

Location of the major organs and glands of the endocrine system.

growth hormone A hormone secreted by the pituitary gland essential for normal postnatal growth and development.

Another important hormone is **growth hormone,** which is secreted by the pituitary gland. Growth hormone is vital for normal postnatal growth and maturation. This hormone acts to increase protein synthesis and affects the rate of cell multiplication (Figure 14.15). For growth hormone to work properly, however, an individual must be well nourished. This interaction shows how *both* biological and environmental factors af-

Figure 14.15

Extreme effects of growth hormone imbalance. Too little or too much growth hormone can result in extremely small or large body size. The man on the right is 91 cm tall (roughly 3 ft). The man in the center is 295 cm tall (roughly 9 ft 8 in).   (Syndication International)

fect the expression of the individual's genetic potential for growth. In addition, growth hormone requires proper amounts of thyroxine.

The sex hormones (androgens in males and estrogen in females) also affect the timing and pattern of growth. The **androgens,** particularly testosterone, act to stimulate the development of secondary sexual characteristics in males. They also stimulate growth and maturation of bone. The increased muscle growth in adolescent males is also a function of the androgens. The **estrogens** act to stimulate the development of secondary sexual characteristics in females and also to accumulate fat tissues, especially in breasts and buttocks.

The **adrenal gland** produces adrenal hormones, a secondary source of sex hormones. During midchildhood, humans and chimpanzees show an increased secretion of adrenal hormones, known as **adrenarche.** This event occurs at roughly 3 years of age in chimpanzees and at roughly 7 years of age in humans. Adrenarche is responsible for ape-human differences in the ratio of upper to lower body length and is also responsible for midfacial growth. It also appears that adrenarche is related to the midchildhood growth spurt seen in some human populations.

androgens Hormones that stimulate the development of secondary sexual characteristics in males.

estrogens Hormones that act to stimulate the development of secondary sexual characteristics in females.

adrenal gland The gland that produces adrenal hormones, which are a secondary source of sex hormones.

adrenarche The increase in secretion of adrenal hormones during midchildhood (roughly 7 years of age in humans).

Nutrition

Proper nutrition is a critical factor in determining whether or not a person reaches his or her genetic potential for growth. An individual with the genetic potential for an adult height of 2 m must have the adequate quantity and quality of nutrition to attain this height. Ingested nutrients provide the energy for maintenance and growth of the body. During infancy, childhood, and puberty, a greater proportion of this nutrient energy goes into physical growth. Too little nutrient energy can result in a reduction in overall size and delayed maturation. Too much nutrient energy can result in accumulation of fat. Inadequate amounts of certain critical nutrients can also affect basic biological processes.

Basic nutritional needs. Ingested energy (measured in calories) comes from carbohydrates, proteins, and fats. Inadequate caloric energy levels can lead to growth retardation and serious medical problems. The source of calories varies from one environment to the next.

Dietary proteins are also necessary for certain metabolic functions. Proteins provide amino acids, of which 20 are needed by the body for synthesis and repair of body tissues. Adult humans need 8 amino acids that must come from their diet. Children need 9 of these. Without adequate sources of protein in the diet, lack of these amino acids leads to growth retardation, illness, and death. The major sources of proteins in Western human populations are animal products, including meat, eggs, fish, and milk. Plants provide proteins, but they are lacking in one or more amino acids. A vegetarian diet can satisfy all human nutritional needs when a variety of plants are eaten.

TABLE 14.1
Recommended Daily Requirements of
Calories and Proteins for U.S. Children

Age (years)	Calories (kilocalories)	Protein (grams)
1–2	1,100	25
2–3	1,250	25
3–4	1,400	30
4–6	1,600	30
6–8	2,000	35
8–10	2,200	40

Source: Kent-Jones (1988:58).

TABLE 14.2
Recommended Daily Requirements of Calories and Proteins
for U.S. Adolescents and Adults

Age (years)	Calories (kilocalories)		Protein (grams)	
	Males	Females	Males	Females
10–12	2,500	2,250	45	50
12–14	2,700	2,300	50	50
14–18	3,000	2,350	60	55
18–22	2,800	2,000	60	55
22–35	2,800	2,000	65	55
35–55	2,600	1,850	65	55
55–75+	2,400	1,700	65	55

Note: For pregnant women, add 200 kcals to the recommended caloric intake; protein requirement is 65 g. For nursing women add 1,000 kcals to the recommended caloric intake; protein requirement is 75 g. *Source:* Kent-Jones (1988:58).

Our bodies also require other nutrients in varying amounts. We require certain fatty acids, vitamins, and minerals. A diet lacking in one of these nutrients can lead to medical problems. For example, a lack of vitamin C leads to the disease scurvy, and a lack of the mineral iodine leads to thyroid problems. Proper nutrition is not only a matter of how much is eaten but also what is eaten.

Table 14.1 shows the recommended daily allowances for calories and protein for children in the United States from 1 to 10 years of age. Both caloric and protein requirements increase with age, reflecting continued growth and the need to maintain larger bodies. Table 14.2 shows the recommended daily allowances of calories and proteins for adolescent and adult U.S. males and females. At all ages, males require more calories because of their larger average body size. Note also that calorie requirements are greatest at puberty for both sexes (14 to 18 years) and decrease afterward. The figures for females refer to those who are not pregnant or nursing. Pregnancy consumes a great deal of energy, and recommended caloric intake during this time is increased by 200 kcals per day. Nursing requires even greater energy intake; the recommended allowances should be increased by 1,000 kcals for women who are nursing an infant. Protein intake is also higher during pregnancy (recommended intake: 65 g per day) and nursing (recommended intake: 75 g per day).

Effects of nutrition on growth. **Malnutrition** occurs in many human populations and can include problems caused by undernutrition and overnutrition. We tend to equate malnutrition with starvation, but too much food can also lead to problems. If you ingest more calories than needed for growth, maintenance, or physical activity, the excess is deposited as fat in your body. Obesity can lead to medical problems such as hypertension, heart disease, and diabetes. Excessive intake of calories, and resulting obesity, is a major health problem in the United States today that is exacerbated by ingestion of many fatty foods and by insufficient physical exercise.

Throughout much of the world today, however, the major nutritional problem is lack of food, or at least lack of a varied diet. Poor nutrition acts to slow down the growth process, leading to smaller adult body size. Distance curves for weight and height are shown in Figure 14.16 for two

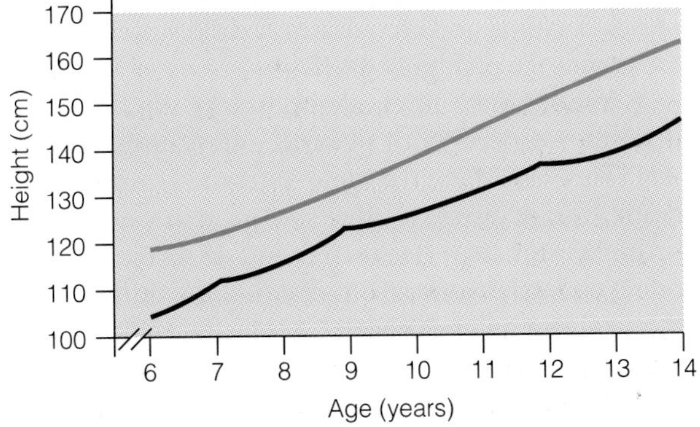

malnutrition Poor nutrition, either from too much or too little food, or the improper balance of nutrients.

Figure 14.16

Distance curves for weight (*top*) and height (*bottom*) for well-nourished and poorly nourished Mexican boys. At all ages, the well-nourished boys are taller and heavier. (From *Growth and Development* by Robert M. Malina © 1975, publisher Burgess Publishing Company, Minneapolis, MN)

protein-calorie malnutrition A group of nutritional diseases resulting from inadequate amounts of protein and/or calories.

kwashiorkor An extreme form of protein-calorie malnutrition, resulting from a severe deficiency in proteins but not calories.

marasmus An extreme form of protein-calorie malnutrition resulting from severe deficiencies in both proteins and calories.

Figure 14.17

A child with kwashiorkor, a severe protein deficiency. (Courtesy of UNICEF/Maggie Murray Lee)

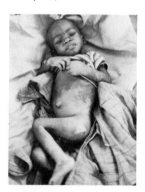

samples of children, well nourished and suboptimally nourished. These curves show clearly that lowered nutritional levels result in smaller body size throughout childhood and puberty.

If nutritional levels do not become so low that they cause medical problems, smaller body size may be a desirable human trait. In fact, reduced growth and smaller body size is an adaptation to a decreased nutritional intake. In environments where the food supply is limited, a smaller person who uses up less energy might be at an advantage.

Severe undernutrition, especially in infancy, can have equally severe effects. Not only is physical growth stunted, but mental retardation may also result. Without an adequate diet, infants and children are more susceptible to infectious diseases. Severe undernutrition is highly prevalent in today's world, particularly in Third World nations, where poor nutrition is associated with overpopulation, poverty, inadequate waste disposal, contaminated water, high rates of infectious disease, and economic and political conflicts. Of course, undernutrition is not limited to the Third World—the problem can also be found in parts of the United States.

A number of nutritional disorders are collectively known as **protein-calorie malnutrition,** an inadequate amount of proteins and/or calories in the diet. Protein-calorie malnutrition is the most serious nutritional problem on the planet. Its various forms have different physical symptoms, but all stem from the basic problems of a poor diet in conditions of poverty and have the same ultimate effects, ranging from growth retardation to death.

The two most severe types of protein-calorie malnutrition are **kwashiorkor** (severe deficiency in proteins but not calories) and **marasmus** (severe deficiencies in both proteins and calories). Kwashiorkor occurs most often in infants and young children who are weaned from their mother's breast into an environment lacking in proteins. Mother's milk generally provides all needed proteins up to about 6 months of age. After this time, additional protein must come from the environment. In populations lacking sufficient proteins, the infant suffers growth retardation, muscle wasting, and lowered resistance to disease. One of the physical symptoms of kwashiorkor is the swelling of the body (Figure 14.17). Marasmus is also most prevalent during infancy and similarly leads to growth retardation, muscle wasting, and even death. A child suffering from marasmus typically looks emaciated (Figure 14.18).

Although the physical appearance of children with kwashiorkor and marasmus differs, both disorders are caused by poverty and inadequate diet. They also share the same outcome—growth retardation and possibly death. The devastating effects of protein-calorie malnutrition should not be underestimated; between 5 and 45 percent of children in some developing countries suffer from one of these nutritional diseases. Solutions to this problem will be complex, requiring economic, educational, and political change in most cases.

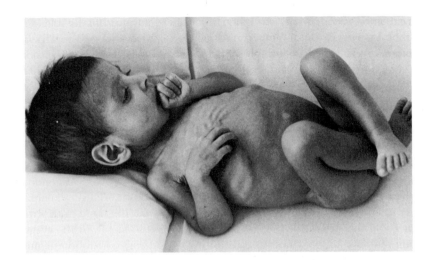

Figure 14.18

A child with marasmus, a severe protein and calorie deficiency. (World Health Organization photo by A. Isaza)

Infectious Disease

Infectious diseases generally do not affect a child's growth if they are treated and if the child is well nourished. In undernourished populations, the situation is different. Here infectious disease and poor nutritional status affect each other cyclically. Undernutrition causes a lowering of the body's resistance to infectious disease. The body cannot produce antibodies if it lacks proteins and calories. Infection can also affect nutritional status by reducing the efficient absorption of nutrients, particularly infections in the gastrointestinal tract. Infectious diseases may also result in a loss of appetite, which further reduces nutritional intake. As nutritional status deteriorates, the body's resistance to infectious disease is lowered further (Martorell 1980).

In some developing countries, high rates of undernutrition and infectious disease go hand in hand, both resulting from the environmental conditions of poverty. Increased population growth can lead to lowered nutrition. It can also lead to an increase in the spread of infectious disease, for the disease microorganisms spread more quickly in large, dense populations. Poverty conditions usually mean poor medical care, furthering the spread and effect of infectious diseases. Sanitation conditions are generally poor, and the water supply is frequently contaminated, both of which contribute to the spread of infectious disease. Poor nutrition and infection amplify each other's effects, resulting in growth retardation and frequently in death.

Cultural Influences

The extent and timing of human growth is also related to a number of cultural and individual behavioral factors.

Social and family structure. Social and demographic factors that affect growth include ethnicity, parent's occupation and socioeconomic status, number of children in the family, and birth order. Close analysis of these relationships shows that such social and demographic measures often reflect differences in the availability of adequate nutrition, prevalence of diseases, and the quality of medical care.

In situations where money is needed for adequate nutrition and health care, we see a relationship between social class and growth. Children belonging to upper-class families are often larger and grow more quickly (Tanner 1989) because of better nutrition and health care. On the other hand, in Western societies obesity is more prevalent in lower social classes because foods high in calories are less costly.

The number of children in a family also has an influence on growth. Children from larger families tend to grow more slowly. Of course, family size and socioeconomic status are interrelated (larger families tend on average to be found in lower social classes), so this is perhaps a consequence of reduced food availability for each child. In many societies, upper-class families tend to have fewer children. Even after controlling for social class differences, however, the relationship between growth and family size persists (Tanner 1989).

Growth patterns have many other social associations. Although the effects of these factors vary somewhat among different groups, studies show that social and family differences can lead to differences in available nutrition, disease prevalence, child care, and other factors, which in turn affect growth.

Personal habits: Smoking and alcohol consumption. The personal habits of parents can also affect the growth of their offspring. Two major habits shown to have strong effects on human growth are smoking and alcohol consumption. When a pregnant woman smokes cigarettes, she affects her child's prenatal development adversely. Numerous studies have shown that mothers who smoke during pregnancy weigh less when they conceive, gain less weight during pregnancy, and have babies that weigh less at birth. Even among women who carry their offspring full term, the birth weight of the children is lower than the birth weight of children born to women who did not smoke during pregnancy (Garn 1985).

The effect of smoking on birth weight is shown clearly in Table 14.3. These data are based on the birth weights of offspring born to 10,435 nonsmokers and 11,200 smokers. At all levels of prepregnancy maternal weight, the average birth weight of children born to women who smoke is less than that of children born to nonsmokers. Smoking during pregnancy causes many biological changes, but the most apparent is the loss of oxygen to the fetus. A lack of sufficient oxygen leads to reduced birth weight and other problems. In addition, smoking introduces into the fetus a number of poisonous substances such as carbon monoxide and nicotine (Montagu 1977).

Lower birth weight can be a problem for newborns. The smaller the baby, the greater the probability for deficits in health, behavior, and later growth. If smoking is accompanied by other detrimental behaviors such as drinking or poor nutrition, the growth and health of the newborn is affected even more.

The observation that a mother's smoking leads to reduced birth weight applies to average tendencies. As with most environmental effects, not all individuals show the same degree of response. Many large and healthy babies have been born to women who smoked during pregnancy. The danger of smoking during pregnancy should not be minimized, however.

Alcohol consumption is also harmful during pregnancy. Numerous studies have shown associations of drinking during pregnancy with an increase in spontaneous abortions, birth defects, and infant mortality. Alcohol consumption also results in physical and mental retardation in the offspring. Alcohol affects prenatal development by introducing toxic substances and by reducing oxygen levels (Abel 1982).

One pattern of observable birth defects caused by major alcohol intake early in pregnancy is referred to as **Fetal Alcohol Syndrome.** These defects include smaller body size, smaller heads, facial deformities, organ disorders, and reduced intelligence, apparently the result of impaired brain

Fetal Alcohol Syndrome A group of birth defects resulting from major alcohol intake by the mother early in pregnancy.

T A B L E   14.3
**Effects of Mother's Smoking
during Pregnancy on Birth Weight
of European-American U.S. Infants**

Mother's prepregnancy weight (in pounds)	Average birth weight of infants (in kilograms)	
	Nonsmokers	Smokers
<100	3.10	2.93
100–119	3.27	3.08
120–139	3.42	3.22
140–159	3.53	3.32
160–179	3.59	3.37
180–199	3.66	3.46
200–219	3.65	3.46
220–239	3.65	3.45

These data represent 10,435 women who did not smoke during pregnancy and 11,200 women who did. This table does not include a few women in the study who weighed more than 240 lbs.

Source: Garn (1985:518).

deprivation dwarfism The reduction in a child's growth because of psychological stress.

differentiation. Though the more extreme problems are associated only with chronic drinkers, serious medical and behavioral problems can also result from even small amounts of alcohol during pregnancy. How much drinking is safe, and when? Most physicians now advise total abstinence during pregnancy, since we do not know exactly how little is safe. As with smoking, alcohol consumption during pregnancy represents increased risk for the growth and health of a child. Some research suggests that Fetal Alcohol Syndrome results from intoxication during the first few weeks after conception. If so, then problems may arise before a woman realizes she is pregnant. The best prevention a woman can practice is moderation or abstinence from alcohol if she is likely to become pregnant.

Psychological stress. Every person, including infants and children, experiences some level of psychological stress during a lifetime. Given that some infants and children live in disruptive home environments, is there a relationship between level of stress and patterns of physical growth? Several studies have shown this to be the case. Infants and children exposed to emotional stress show reduced growth.

One review of this subject (Gardner 1972) noted many cases of what has been called **deprivation dwarfism,** the reduction of physical growth under conditions of emotional stress. Such cases show physical effects caused by stress from the nature of child care (loving versus stern), marital status of parents (married or divorced), amount of interaction with the mother, and similar factors that upset a child's emotional state (Gardner 1972; Pollitt and Leibel 1980). Such stress results in loss of appetite and difficulty in sleeping, which contribute to reduced growth.

One case noted by Gardner (1972) illustrates the close relationship between psychological stress and growth. One young boy's growth was observed over 13 years that included his father's desertion, the divorce of his parents, and his mother's remarriage. The father left the family when the boy was 1 year old and the mother began working full time. At this point, the child's growth in height slowed proportionately to his age. When the mother remarried and spent more time with the child, his growth in height increased. By age 14, the boy's bone growth had caught up to the norm, although his overall height was still slightly less than average for his age.

Gardner (1972) has suggested that a causal relationship exists among emotional stress, sleep loss, and growth retardation. Growth hormone is normally secreted during the first few hours of sleep. When sleep is disrupted, the normal secretion of growth hormone is disturbed, resulting in a reduction in growth. Gardner suggests that emotional stress leads to disruption of sleep patterns and therefore to disruption in growth hormone secretion and physical growth. Other studies (e.g., Pollitt and Leibel 1980) have suggested that growth retardation is not the result of a single cause but rather a variety of interacting biological and social factors.

Pollution. In recent years, many growth studies have focused on the potential effects of a variety of pollutants, particularly those found in urban areas. Several studies have produced results suggesting that frequent exposure to air pollution, from both urbanization and industrial activities, is associated with growth retardation. More research needs to be done in this area, because the studies to date have relied on comparisons of growth across communities (e.g., heavy pollution versus little pollution) and not on individual exposure of children to air pollution (Schell 1991).

Toxic waste is another pollution problem. Perhaps the most well-known example of toxic waste is the case of Love Canal in Niagara Falls, New York, where chemical wastes were dumped between 1940 and 1953. Vianna and Polan (1984) studied birth weights of infants born to mothers who resided near the dump site. They found that the percentage of low-birth-weight infants was higher in the part of the study area that was most contaminated. Paigen and colleagues (1987) looked at the relationship of postnatal growth and exposure to toxic waste. They found that children living in the exposed areas were shorter at all ages than children outside it. Further, they found that decrease in height was associated with length of stay in the Love Canal area. The longer period of time the children lived there, the shorter they were compared to other children.

High noise levels have also been found to affect human growth. Schell (1981) looked at the effect of airport noise on prenatal health in an eastern North American City. When other social and biological factors were corrected for, he found that gestation length was reduced for female babies born to mothers who resided near a major metropolitan airport. In another study, Schell and Ando (1991) found that the growth of 3-year-old boys and girls was related to noise exposure. A higher frequency of very short children was found among samples living closer to an international airport.

Studies of Secular Trends

One type of growth study uses data from several generations to look at changes in growth patterns over time. For example, we could compare the average growth of female children in 1993 with the average growth of female children in 1893 in a given population. Using such a comparison, we could determine whether any basic changes in growth have occurred during the last 100 years. Because a century is usually too short a time for any significant genetic change in growth patterns, any observed changes may be attributed to changes in environmental factors. These comparisons allow us to look at the effects of historical changes in cultural behavior on biological variation.

Such studies attempt to determine if any overall secular trends have

secular trend A change in the average pattern of growth in a population over different generations.

taken place. A **secular trend** in human growth is simply a change in the pattern of growth across generations. Studies have shown a number of secular trends in growth common to many industrial nations during the last century.

Basic Secular Trends

Three basic secular trends have been observed in many Western nations during the past century: (1) an increase in height, (2) an increase in weight, and (3) a decrease in age at menarche.

The secular trend in height and weight. Children in many Westernized nations today are taller and heavier than children of the same age a century or so ago. Figure 14.19 shows the average distance curve for height of European-American North American males in 1880 and 1960. There is no noticeable difference in body length at birth. Note, however, that at all postnatal ages the 1960 males are consistently taller than the 1880 males. This difference is most noticeable during puberty. Comparisons of the distance curve for weight show essentially the same pattern.

Secular differences in height and weight are related to changes in the rate of maturation. The males in 1960 matured more quickly. A consequence of quicker maturation is that children tend to be larger for their age compared to slower-maturing children. This explains why the differences in height and weight between 1880 and 1960 are greatest during puberty. In 1960, biological maturation occurred earlier, resulting in larger body size during the teenage years.

Figure 14.19

Secular trend in European-American males in North America. At all ages the males living in 1960 have greater height than those who lived in 1880. (From *Growth and Development* by Robert M. Malina © 1975, publisher Burgess Publishing Company, Minneapolis, MN)

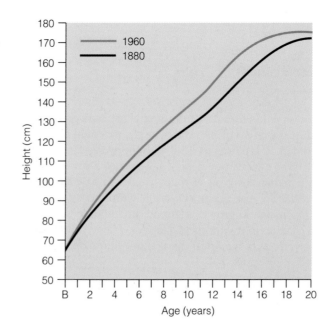

The secular trend in age at menarche. Earlier maturation is also apparent in another measure of human development—the **age at menarche,** the age at which a female experiences her first menstrual period. Figure 14.20 plots the average age at menarche for the United States and several European industrial nations over time. The general trend, as well as the trend within each nation, is one of earlier biological maturation.

Causes of secular trends. The basic secular trends observed in industrial nations during the past century show how environmental change has allowed certain human populations to attain more of their genetic potential for growth. These trends, however, should not be projected indefinitely into the future! Some data suggest that the secular trends in height, weight, and age at menarche have slowed down or stopped (Roche 1979). Future environmental improvements will undoubtedly allow more and more children to attain their genetic potential for growth, but we should not expect average heights of 8 ft or more in another 100 years!

Numerous environmental factors have been suggested as responsible for these past secular trends, including improved nutrition, reduction of childhood infectious disease, improved availability of health care, improved standard of living, and reduction in family size. Many of these factors are interrelated, making precise identification of causes difficult.

Malina (1979) notes that improved nutrition has often been cited as a primary cause of the observed secular trends. Though availability of nutritional intake has improved for many people, especially during infancy, Malina does not think it is solely responsible for the secular trends. Many

age at menarche The age at which a female experiences her first menstrual period.

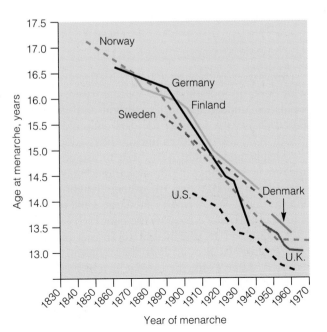

Figure 14.20

Secular trend in age at menarche (the age of the female's first menstrual period) in the United States and several European countries. (From *Growth and Development* by Robert M. Malina © 1975, publisher Burgess Publishing Company, Minneapolis, MN)

Figure 14.21

Secular trend in the height of 10-year-old Japanese males during the twentieth century. Note the decrease in average height during World War II and the rapid increase in average height following the war.   (Source of data: Oiso [1975])

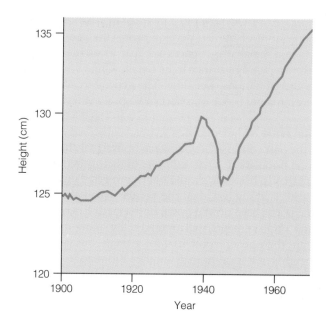

factors have operated together to produce the secular trends. Malina does suggest that one of the most important factors was an improvement in health conditions, resulting in the reduction of childhood infectious diseases. As we will see in Chapter 16, this century has been characterized by a major reduction in such diseases and their harmful effects. Because infectious disease reduces growth rates, their elimination most probably resulted in quicker rates of growth.

Case Study: Japan in the Twentieth Century

Environmental changes and their effects on human growth can often be assessed by looking at the specific nature of secular trends within a population undergoing rapid cultural and environmental change. This section deals with some of the data collected on secular changes in the growth of Japanese children during the twentieth century.

Height and weight have been measured for all school children in Japan every year since 1900, allowing comparison of different ages over time. Figure 14.21 shows the average height of 10-year-old males from 1900 through 1971. Females show the same pattern. The average height of 10-year-old males is roughly the same each year between 1900 and 1920. After 1920, the average height of 10-year-old children increased until 1940. From 1940 through 1946 the average height of 10-year-old children decreased. After 1946, the average height increased rapidly through the 1960s.

The changes in average 10-year-old height are similar for other ages (Oiso 1975). The same trends are also seen in male and female weight for all ages. Discounting the years from 1940 till 1946, there is an overall secular increase in body size over time. This increase is expected, given the changes in health care and nutrition in the twentieth century and the emergence of Japan as an industrial nation with a high standard of living. Indeed, the changes in growth are most dramatic for the last few decades, when many of these environmental changes occurred.

The decrease in average height between 1940 and 1946 coincides with World War II and the immediate postwar period. The entry of Japan into the war resulted in food shortages and near-famine conditions in many parts of the country. It is also interesting that in 1948 school lunch programs were expanded (Oiso 1975; Takahashi 1984). These nutritional changes correspond to the changes in patterns of child growth in Japan.

S U M M A R Y

The study of human growth provides biological anthropologists with a means of investigating the effects of rapid changes in environmental circumstances on biological variation. Human growth is studied by means of distance, velocity, and acceleration curves. Distance curves show the amount of physical growth. Velocity curves show the rate of change. Acceleration curves show changes in velocity rates and reflect hormonal changes. Humans show a characteristic pattern of postnatal growth in body size. The rate of postnatal growth is greatest at birth, declines through early childhood, may increase briefly during midchildhood, and increases again during puberty. The adolescent growth spurt is part of the entire process of biological maturation during puberty. Males and females show the same pattern of growth in body size but differ in the timing of the adolescent growth spurt. Males mature two years later on average, allowing them greater time for continued preadolescent growth.

Body parts show different patterns of growth. The brain and head grow quickly during infancy and childhood—a pattern related to our dependence on learned behavior. Growth in reproductive organs is delayed until puberty. Humans share delayed sexual maturation with other primates, although we show this pattern to a greater extent.

Growth is a flexible or "plastic" process. Genetic and hormonal factors influence growth potential and the timing of growth. Environmental effects can change the path of growth, pushing an individual off one that is genetically determined. When environmental stresses are not serious, catch-up growth can occur if the stress is removed. During certain times of life (sensitive periods of growth) such catch-up growth is not possible, and permanent biological and behavioral changes can result from environmental stresses.

Nutritional quantity and quality are important to human growth. Undernutrition results in growth retardation, increased illness, and even death. The most serious nutritional deprivation occurs today in developing nations, where poverty, disease, and lack of food leads to protein-calorie malnutrition. Infectious disease can also contribute to growth retardation and lead indirectly to death.

Social and cultural factors also play roles in influencing the pattern of human growth. Variation in social class, family size, and other factors can lead to variation in the availability of nutrition and health care. Personal habits, such as cigarette smoking and alcohol consumption, have an adverse effect on human prenatal and postnatal growth. Emotional stress from family conditions can also interfere with the normal process of growth. A variety of stresses in urban environments, including air, noise, and toxic waste pollution, also have detrimental effects on human growth.

Changes in growth patterns over several generations (secular trend) allow us to see the biological effects of rapid environmental change. Industrial nations during the last century have seen an increase in height and weight as well as a reduction in the age at which biological maturation begins. Detailed studies of individual nations, such as Japan, show how specific historical events such as war can lead to short-term changes in the pattern of human growth.

Supplemental Readings

Bogin, B. A. 1988. *Patterns of Human Growth*. Cambridge: Cambridge University Press. Both this and the Tanner text provide good introductions to the study of human growth.

Grabowski, C. T. 1983. *Human Reproduction and Development*. Philadelphia: Saunders College Publishing.

Montagu, A. 1977. *Life Before Birth*. Rev. ed. New York: Signet. Both this and the Grabowski text focus on prenatal growth and development. Montagu's book is especially recommended for its discussion of the effects of drugs, smoking, alcohol, disease, and nutrition during pregnancy.

Tanner, J. M. 1989. *Foetus into Man: Physical Growth from Conception to Maturity*. 2nd ed., rev. and enl. Cambridge, Mass.: Harvard University Press.

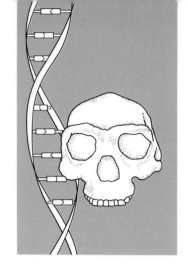

CHAPTER 15

Human Adaptation

As discussed in Chapter 1, adaptation is the successful interaction of a population with its environment. Thus far, adaptation has been discussed in terms of genetic adaptation—that is, natural selection. In this chapter, we examine a broader perspective. Central to the study of adaptation is the concept of **stress,** broadly defined as any factor that interferes with the normal limits of operation of an organism. Organisms maintain these limits through an ability known as **homeostasis.** As ways of dealing with the stresses that alter your body's functioning, adaptations restore homeostasis. For example, within normal limits, your body maintains a relatively constant body temperature. When you stand outside in a cold wind you may shiver. This is your body's way of adapting to cold stress. You might also choose to put on a heavy jacket.

As human beings, we can adapt both biologically and culturally. It is important to note, however, that our biocultural nature can work against us. In adapting to stresses culturally, we can introduce other stresses as a result of our behavior. Pollution, for example, is a consequence of cultural change and has negatively impacted our physical environment in numerous ways.

Key to the interaction between human biology and culture, human adaptation operates on a number of levels—physiologic, developmental, genetic, and cultural—all of which are interrelated, for better or for worse. Thus the countering of a biological stress such as disease by the cultural adaptation of medicine can lower the death rate for human populations but also can increase population size, which in turn can lead to further stresses, such as food shortages and environmental degradation.

In the previous chapter, we saw how an individual's adaptive response

stress Any factor that interferes with the normal limits of an operation of an organism.

homeostasis In a physiologic sense, the maintenance of normal limits of body functioning.

433

acclimatization Changes in organ or body structure that occur within an individual's lifetime in response to one or more stresses.

developmental acclimatization Changes in organ or body structure that occur during the physical growth of any organism.

plasticity The ability of an organism to respond physiologically or developmentally to environmental stress.

to stress may entail modification of the growth process. This chapter examines three specific examples of stress and adaptation, two involving stresses of the physical environment, posed by climate and high altitude, and one dealing with stresses in the cultural environment, due to modernization. Additional examples of human adaptation, such as adaptation to disease, are discussed in Chapters 16 and 17. Throughout this chapter, it is important to remember that not all biological and cultural traits are necessarily adaptive.

Types of Adaptation

How do humans adapt? What are the different ways we have to cope with the stresses of the physical and cultural environment?

Physiologic, Genetic, and Cultural Adaptation

Besides genetic and cultural adaptation, humans are capable of two other forms of adaptation that are physiologic in nature: acclimatization and developmental acclimatization. **Acclimatization** refers to changes in organ or body structure that occur within an individual's lifetime in response to one or more stresses. Examples include shivering when cold and sweating when overheated. Some changes may be temporary; others may be more permanent. When a change occurs during the physical growth of any organism, it is known as **developmental acclimatization.** The ability of organisms to respond physiologically or developmentally to environmental stress is often referred to as **plasticity.**

Adaptation to Ultraviolet Radiation

A focus on ultraviolet radiation is a useful way of coming to grips with some of the basic concepts of adaptation. As mentioned in Chapter 6, excessive ultraviolet radiation can lead to severe sunburn and skin cancer and may even interfere with the proper functioning of the immune system. How have humans adapted, or attempted to adapt, to this stress?

Short-term exposure to ultraviolet radiation in light-skinned peoples results in darkening of the skin, or tanning, which can take two different forms. *Immediate tanning* darkens the skin within 1 to 2 hours, and fades away during the first 24 hours after exposure. *Delayed tanning* is a more gradual process caused by repeated exposure. Delayed tanning begins within 2 to 3 days of initial exposure and reaches a maximum after 19 days. The effects of delayed tanning can last as much as 9.5 months (Robins 1991). From a physiologic perspective, tanning is a response to skin cell damage. Delayed tanning is an adaptive response, whereby darkening of the skin provides some protection against further damage. Immediate tanning does not appear to be very effective in this respect.

Tanning is not the only form of adaptation to ultraviolet radiation. There is strong evidence that in equatorial regions dark skin evolved in response to the stress of excessive levels of ultraviolet radiation (Chapter 6). Individuals with darker skin were more likely to survive and therefore more likely to pass on the genes for darker skin to the next generation. In other words, natural selection occurred as a result of genetic adaptation.

Cultural adaptations can also deal with exposure to ultraviolet radiation. If your occupation or leisure activity increases your risk of exposure, you can wear protective clothing, such as hats or long-sleeved garments, or apply chemical sunscreens. Changes in the hours you work or play outdoors can also help minimize exposure. With the growing concern about skin cancer in the United States, increasing numbers of people are turning to behaviors that provide protection from ultraviolet radiation, or at least minimize exposure.

Climate and Human Adaptation

Though originally tropical primates, we humans have managed to expand into virtually every environment on our planet. Such expansion has been possible largely because of multiple adaptations to the range of temperatures around the world.

Physiologic Responses to Temperature Stress

As warm-blooded creatures, humans have the ability to maintain a constant body temperature. This homeostatic quality works well only under certain limits.

Cold stress. When you are cold, your body is losing heat too rapidly. One response is to increase heat production temporarily through shivering, which also increases your metabolic rate. This response is not very efficient and is costly in terms of energy. A more efficient physiologic response to cold stress is minimization of heat loss through alternate constriction and dilation of blood vessels. **Vasoconstriction,** the narrowing of blood vessels, reduces blood flow and heat loss. **Vasodilation,** the opening of the blood vessels, serves to increase blood flow and heat loss.

When a person is first subjected to cold stress, vasoconstriction acts to minimize the loss of heat from the body to the extremities (i.e., the hands, feet, and face). As a result, skin temperature drops. This response becomes dangerous, however, if it continues too long. Should this start to happen, vasodilation begins, causing blood and heat to flow from the

vasoconstriction The narrowing of blood vessels, which reduces blood flow and heat loss.

vasodilation The opening of the blood vessels, which increases blood flow and heat loss.

Figure 15.1

The Lewis hunting phenomenon. Initial exposure of a finger into ice water produces a decrease in skin temperature, caused by vasoconstriction. After a while, this response gives way to vasodilation, which causes skin temperature to increase. The cycles continue over time but become more frequent and less extreme, thus providing more efficient adaptation.   (Modified after Frisancho [1979:45])

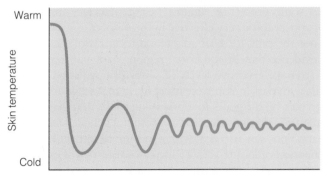

interior of the body to the extremities. The increased blood flow prevents damage to the extremities, but now the body is losing heat again! Neither vasoconstriction nor vasodilation by itself provides an effective physiologic response to cold stress. *Both* must operate, back and forth, to maintain a balance between heat loss and damage to the extremities.

An interesting phenomenon occurs after initial exposure to cold stress. The cycles of alternating vasoconstriction and vasodilation, accompanied by alternating cycles of cold and warm skin temperatures, begin to level out, becoming more frequent and less extreme. Skin temperature changes more quickly, but the increases and decreases are not as great. This pattern, called the *Lewis hunting phenomenon,* demonstrates how effective is the body's ability to adapt. The smaller and more frequent cycles are more efficient (Figure 15.1).

Heat stress. When experiencing heat stress, your body is not removing heat quickly enough. There are four ways in which heat is lost from the body, three of which can also increase heat (Frisancho 1979). *Radiation* is heat flow from objects in the form of electromagnetic radiation. The body removes heat through radiation but also picks up heat radiated by other objects. *Convection* refers to the removal or gain of heat through air molecules. Heat flows from a warm object to a cooler object. *Conduction* is heat exchange through physical contact with another object, such as the ground or clothes. Conduction generally accounts for a very small proportion of heat exchange. *Evaporation* is the loss of heat through the conversion of water to vapor. In the process of sweat evaporation, heat energy is consumed. Evaporation is the only one of these four mechanisms that results in heat loss without heat gain.

The amount of heat loss through these mechanisms varies according to both temperature and humidity. As the temperature increases, the only way your body can cope is to increase the amount of evaporation (your body can't amplify any of the other three mechanisms). As a result, evaporation is the most effective mechanism for heat removal in excessively hot

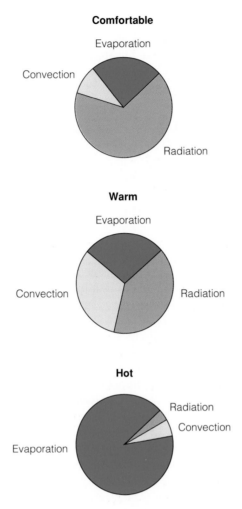

Figure 15.2

Heat loss due to radiation, convection, and evaporation at different temperatures, for a nude human in a room with little air movement. The temperatures are: comfortable = 25° C, or 77° F, warm = 30° C, or 86° F, hot = 35° C, or 95° F. Note that evaporation accounts for 90 percent of heat loss at hot temperatures. (Data from Frisancho [1979:16])

temperatures. Figure 15.2 shows the relative percentage of heat loss due to radiation, convection, and evaporation for a nude human in a room with little air movement. At comfortable temperatures, most heat is lost through radiation, and evaporation accounts for only 23 percent of the total lost. At hot temperatures (35° C = 95° F), evaporation accounts for 90 percent. Vasodilation is also important in heat loss. The opening of the blood vessels helps remove internal heat to the outside skin. The heat can then be transferred to the environment through radiation, convection, and evaporation.

Evaporation has its drawbacks. The removal of water from the body during the process can be harmful or even fatal. The efficiency of evaporation is also affected by humidity. In humid environments, evaporation is less efficient, making heat loss more difficult under hot and humid conditions than under hot and dry conditions.

Bergmann's rule (1) Among mammals of similar shape, the larger mammal loses heat less rapidly than the smaller mammal, and (2) among mammals of similar size, the mammal with a linear shape will lose heat more rapidly than the mammal with a nonlinear shape.

Figure 15.3

Geometric representation of Bergmann's rule relating body size and heat loss. The larger cube has a larger volume (heat production) and a larger surface area (heat loss). The larger cube also has a smaller surface area/volume ratio, however, indicating that it would lose heat less rapidly and therefore be adaptive in colder climates.

Surface area = 24
Volume = 8
Surface area/volume = 3

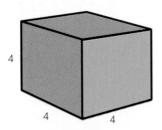

Surface area = 96
Volume = 64
Surface area/volume = 1.5

Climate and Morphological Variation

Differences in physiologic responses and certain morphological variations, most notably the size and shape of the body and head, affect people's ability to handle temperature stress. Nasal size and shape are related to humidity.

The Bergmann and Allen rules. Human populations in colder climates tend to be heavier than those in hotter climates. This does not mean that all people in cold climates are heavy and all people in hot climates are light. Every human group contains a variety of small and large people. Some of this variation is caused by factors such as diet. However, a strong relationship of *average* body size and temperature does exist among indigenous human populations (Roberts 1978).

A nineteenth-century English zoologist, Carl Bergmann, noted the relationship between body size and temperature in a number of mammal species. Bergmann explained his findings in terms of mammalian physiology and principles of heat loss. **Bergmann's rule** states that if two mammals have similar shapes but different sizes, the smaller animal will lose heat more rapidly and will therefore be better adapted to warmer climates, where the ability to lose heat is advantageous. Larger mammals lose heat more slowly and are therefore better adapted to colder climates.

The reason for these relationships is that heat production is a function of the total volume of a mammal, whereas heat loss is a function of total surface area. Consider two hypothetical mammals whose body shape is that of a cube. Imagine that one cube is 2 cm long and the other is 4 cm long in each dimension (Figure 15.3). As a measure of heat production, we can compute the volume of each cube (volume = length × width × height). The volume of the 2-cm cube is 8 cm³; that of the 4-cm cube is 64 cm³. The larger cube can produce more heat because of its greater volume. The greater the volume of a mammal, the greater the heat produced.

As a measure of heat loss, we can compute the surface area of each cube. The surface area of each side is length times width. There are six sides to a cube, so we multiply our result by 6. The surface area of the 2-cm cube is 24 cm²; that of the 4-cm cube is 96 cm². With the greater surface area, the larger cube seems to produce more heat and to lose it at a greater rate. The relevant factor in heat loss in mammals, however, is the ratio of surface area to volume—that is, the rate of heat loss relative to the amount of surface area. The surface area/volume ratio is 24/8 = 3 for the smaller cube, and 96/64 = 1.5 for the larger cube. Therefore, the larger cube loses heat at a slower rate relative to heat production. In cold climates, the larger cube would be at an advantage because it loses heat less quickly. In hot climates, the reverse would be true; they would favor the smaller cube, with its quicker rate of heat loss.

Another aspect of Bergmann's rule involves the shape of an object and its relationship to heat production and loss. Figure 15.4 shows two objects with the same volume but different shapes. The first object is a 4-cm cube with a volume of 64 cm³, a surface area of 96 cm², and a surface area/volume ratio of 1.5. The second object is a rectangular block 2 cm wide, 4 cm deep, and 8 cm high. The volume of this block is also 64 cm³. The surface area is 112 cm² and the surface area/volume ratio is 112/64 = 1.75. Even though both objects produce the same amount of heat as measured by their volumes, the rectangular block loses heat more quickly. Linear objects such as the block would be at an advantage in hot climates, whereas less linear objects, such as the cube, would be at an advantage in cold climates. Accordingly, Bergmann's rule predicts that mammals in hot climates will have linear body shapes and mammals in cold climates will have less linear body shapes. Another zoologist, J. Allen, applied these principles to body limbs and other appendages. **Allen's rule** predicts that mammals in cold climates should have shorter, bulkier limbs, whereas mammals in hot climates should have longer, narrower ones.

Body size and shape. Do the Bergmann and Allen rules hold for human body size and shape? Figure 15.5 shows !Kung men from Africa and an Eskimo. Note the thinness and length of the tribesman's body and limbs. Those of the Eskimo are shorter and bulkier. These physiques do in fact conform to Bergmann and Allen's predictions. Analysis of data from many human populations has found the rules to be accurate in describing the *average* trends among populations. Again, don't forget that extensive variation exists within populations. Also, some populations are exceptions to the general rule. African pygmies, for example, are short and have short limbs, yet they live in a hot climate. The pygmy's short size appears to be due to a hormonal deficiency (Shea and Gomez 1988).

The Bergmann and Allen rules apply to adult human body size and shape. Are these average patterns the result of natural selection (i.e., genetic adaptation) or changes in size and shape during the growth process (i.e., developmental acclimatization)? Do infants born elsewhere who move into an environment attain the same adult size and shape as native-born infants? If so, this suggests a direct influence of the environment on growth. If not, then the growth pattern leading to a certain adult size and shape may be genetic in nature and determined by natural selection. If the growth pattern is entirely genetic, then we may expect to see the same ultimate size and shape regardless of environment. That is, an infant born in a cold climate but raised in a hot climate would still show the characteristic size and shape of humans born in cold climates. Of course, if *both* environmental and genetic factors are responsible for adult size and shape, then the expected pattern is more complex. Unraveling the potential genetic and climatic effects is a difficult process because other contributing influences, such as nutrition, also vary with climate.

The evidence to date suggests that both genetic and environmental factors influence the relationship between climate, growth, body size, and

Allen's rule Mammals in cold climates tend to have short, bulky limbs, allowing less loss of body heat; mammals in hot climates tend to have long, slender limbs, allowing greater loss of body heat.

Figure 15.4

Geometric representation of Bergmann's rule relating body shape and heat loss. The cube has a lower surface area/volume ratio than the rectangular block and would therefore lose heat less rapidly.

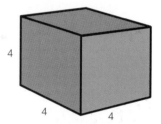

Surface area = 96
Volume = 64
Surface area/volume = 1.5

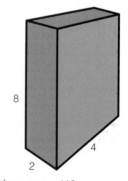

Surface area = 112
Volume = 64
Surface area/volume = 1.75

Figure 15.5

!Kung men (left) and an Eskimo (right) illustrate the relationship among body size, body shape, and climate predicted by the Bergmann and Allen rules. (Richard Lee/Anthro-Photo; Joel Halpern/Anthro-Photo)

cephalic index A measure of cranial shape defined as the maximum width of a skull divided by the total length of the skull.

shape. When children grow up in a climate different from that of their ancestors, they tend to grow in ways the indigenous children do (Malina 1975; Roberts 1978). This finding supports the idea that environment directly influences the growth process. The relationship between growth and climate in such children, however, is not as strong as it is among indigenous children. Therefore, long-term genetic adaptation is also responsible for the association of size, shape, and climate observed in adults. Natural selection leads to changes in growth potential that are further modified by environmental factors. It appears that climate can alter the growth patterns of all children, although those with certain genetic predispositions may show greater response.

Cranial size and shape. The size and shape of the human head has long been of interest to anthropologists. In past times the shape of the head was the focus of studies of racial classification. In the nineteenth century, the Swedish anatomist Anders Retzius developed a measure of cranial shape called the **cephalic index.** This index is derived from two measurements: the total length of the skull and its maximum width. To compute the index, you simply divide the width of the skull by the length

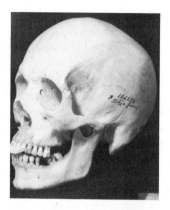
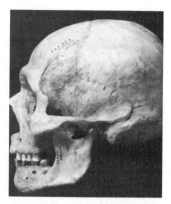

Figure 15.6

Variation in cranial shape: (a) Japanese, (b) North Dakotan Native American, (c) Australian aborigine, (d) Lapp. (Courtesy of Alice Brues, University of Colorado at Boulder)

of the skull and multiply the result by 100. For example, if a person has a head length of 182 mm and a head width of 158 mm, the cephalic index is (158/182) × 100 = 86.8. That is, the person's head width is almost 87 percent of head length. Among human populations today, the cephalic index ranges from roughly 70 to 90 percent.

There is considerable variation in cranial shape among human populations (Figure 15.6). At first, cranial shape was felt to be a measurement capable of determining racial groupings. For example, African skulls were found to have lower cephalic indices than European skulls. Further study showed *rough* agreement but also produced many examples of overlap and similar values in different populations. For example, both Germans and Koreans have average cephalic indices of roughly 83 percent. Likewise, both African pygmies and Greenland Eskimos have average cephalic indices of roughly 77 percent (Harrison et al. 1988). These values do not correspond to any racial classification; they represent *averages* for each population. There is also considerable variation *within* each population.

As more data were obtained and compared geographically, a different

nasal index A measure of the shape of the nasal opening, defined as the width of the nasal opening divided by the height.

pattern emerged—a correspondence was found to exist between cranial shape and climate. Beals (1972) examined the cephalic index and climate for 339 populations from all over the world. He found a direct relationship: populations in colder climates tend to have wider skulls relative to length than those in hot climates. In particular, he found the average cephalic index for populations that experienced winter frost to be higher than for those in tropical environments.

This correspondence makes sense in terms of the Bergmann and Allen rules. The shape of the upper part of the skull is related to heat loss. Rounded heads (those with a high cephalic index) lose heat slowly and therefore are at an advantage in cold climates. Narrow heads lose heat more quickly and are therefore at an advantage in hot climates. It appears that as human populations moved into colder climates, natural selection led to a change in the relative proportions of the skull. Beals and colleagues (1983) have extended this analysis to fossil human crania over the last 1.5 million years and found similar results.

Nasal size and shape. The shape of the nasal opening in the skull is another morphological variation that has a strong relationship to climate. The **nasal index** is the width of the nasal opening divided by the height of the nasal opening, multiplied by 100. Typical values of the nasal index range from roughly 60 to 104 percent (Molnar 1992). Stereotypic racial views associate wide noses (large nasal indices) with African peoples. While it is true that some African populations have very wide noses, others have long, narrow noses.

Numerous studies have found positive associations between the average nasal index of populations and average temperature. Populations in cold climates tend to have narrow noses; those in hot climates tend to have wide noses. Relationships have also been found between average nasal index and average humidity. Populations in dry climates tend to have narrow noses; those in humid climates tend to have wide noses (Franciscus and Long 1991). The mucous membranes of the nose serve to warm and moisten incoming air. High, narrow noses can warm air to a greater extent than low, wide noses and therefore may be more adaptive in cold climates. High, narrow noses also have a greater internal surface area with which to moisten air and are thus more adaptive in dry climates.

Cultural Adaptations

In Western societies we tend to take cultural adaptations to temperature stress for granted. Housing, insulated clothing, heaters, air conditioners, and other technologies are all around us. How do people in other cultures adapt to excessive cold or heat?

Cold stress. The Inuit, or Eskimo people, of the Arctic have realized effective cultural adaptations to cold stress, most notably in their clothing

Figure 15.7

Forms of human shelter such
as this igloo and this Pueblo
house reflect adaptation to
a wide range of climatic
conditions.   (© UPI/The
Bettmann Archive; National
Anthropological Archives, neg.
no. 1846, Smithsonian
Institution)

and shelter. It is not enough just to wear a lot of clothes to stay warm; if
you work hard you tend to overheat. The Inuit wear layered clothing,
trapping air between layers to act as an insulator. Outer layers can be
removed if a person overheats. Also, the Inuit design their clothing with
multiple flaps that can be opened, to prevent build-up of sweat while
working.

While out hunting or fishing, the Inuit frequently construct temporary snow shelters, or igloos, that are quite efficient protection from the
cold. The ice is an excellent insulator, and its reflective surface helps retain
heat (Figure 15.7). More permanent shelters also provide ample protection

from the cold. Inuit houses have an underground entry, which is curved to reduce incoming wind. Inside, the main living area lies at a higher level than the fireplace; this architectural feature serves to increase heat and minimize drafts (Moran 1982).

Not all cold-weather housing is as effective as the types constructed by the Inuit. Among the Quechua Indians of the Peruvian highlands, the temperature inside temporary houses is often not much warmer than it is outside. However, these shelters do provide protection against rain and to some extent the cold. The bedding used by the Quechua is their most effective protection against heat loss (Frisancho 1979).

Heat stress. Human populations live in environments that are dry and hot (i.e., deserts) and that are humid and hot (i.e., tropical rain forests). Moran (1982) has summarized some basic principles of clothing and shelter that are used in desert environments, where the objectives are fourfold: to reduce heat production, to reduce heat gain from radiation, to reduce heat gain from conduction, and to increase evaporation. Clothing is important because it protects from both solar radiation and hot winds. Typical desert clothing is light and loose, thus allowing circulation of air to increase evaporation. The air between the clothing and the body also provides excellent insulation.

Shelters are frequently built compactly to minimize the surface area exposed to the sun. Light colors on the outside help reflect heat. Doors and windows are kept closed during the day to keep the interior cool. Building materials are also adaptive. Adobe, for example, is efficient in absorbing heat during the day and radiating it at night (see Figure 15.7); nighttime temperatures drop precipitously in desert environments.

Heat stress in tropical environments is often a problem because the extreme humidity greatly reduces the efficiency of evaporation through sweating. Cultural adaptations to tropical environments are similar throughout the world. Clothing is minimal, helping increase the potential for evaporation. In some cultures, shelters are built in an open design, without walls, to augment cooling during the day; in others, shelters are built closed to increase warmth at night. The combination of high heat and humidity obviously affects daily routines. Generally people start work early in the day, taking long midday breaks to keep from overheating.

In sum, humans have adapted to a number of environments that produce temperature stress. Humans have managed to adapt to extremes of hot and cold through physiologic changes, long-term genetic adaptations, and adaptive behaviors, particularly those manifested in clothing and shelter technology and in the pace of daily life.

High-Altitude Adaptation

hypoxia Oxygen starvation; occurs frequently at high altitudes.

Some human populations have lived for long periods of time at elevations of over 2,500 m, or roughly 8,200 ft. An estimated 25 million people currently live between 2,500 and 5,000 m (Harrison et al. 1988).

High-Altitude Stresses

High-altitude environments produce several stresses, including oxygen starvation, cold, and sometimes poor nutrition. Studies of high-altitude populations have gained us insight into how humans cope with multiple stresses.

Hypoxia. Oxygen starvation, or **hypoxia,** is more common at high altitudes because of the relationship of barometric pressure and altitude. While the percentage of oxygen in the atmosphere is relatively constant up to almost 70 miles above the earth, barometric pressure decreases quickly with altitude (Figure 15.8). Because air is less compressed at high alti-

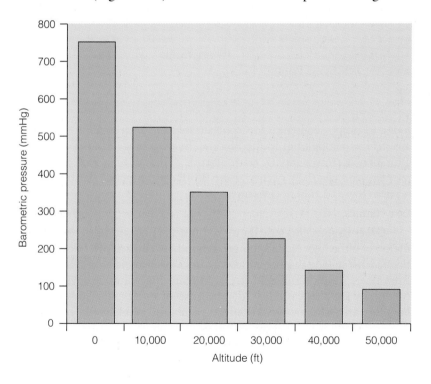

Figure 15.8

The relationship between barometric pressure and altitude. Barometric pressure decreases as altitude increases, causing a decrease in the percentage of arterial oxygen saturation (see Figure 15.10). (Source of data: Frisancho [1979:104])

Figure 15.9

The relationship between arterial oxygen saturation and altitude.   (Source of data: Frisancho [1979:104])

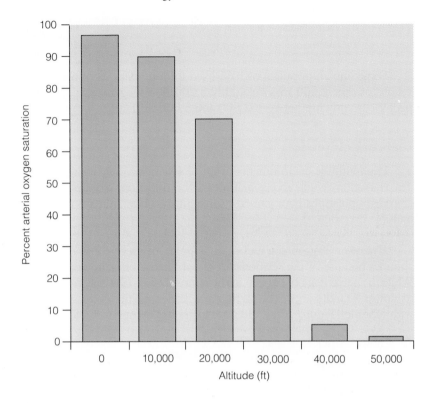

tudes, its oxygen content is less concentrated and less oxygen is thus available to the hemoglobin in the blood. The percentage of arterial oxygen saturation decreases rapidly with altitude (Figure 15.9). For persons at rest, hypoxia generally occurs above 3,000 m; for active persons, it can occur as low as 2,000 m (Frisancho 1979).

Other stresses. Because the air is thinner at high altitudes, the concentration of ultraviolet radiation is greater and the air itself offers less protection against it. The thinner air also causes considerable heat loss from the atmosphere, resulting in cold stress. In many high-altitude environments conditions are also extremely dry because of mountain winds and low humidity. In addition, hypoxia affects plants and animals; for lack of oxygen, trees cannot grow above 4,000 m. The limited availability of plants and animals means that nutritional stress is likely in many high-altitude environments.

Numerous studies have compared the physiology and morphology of high-altitude and low-altitude populations. Early research tended to attribute any differences to the effects of hypoxia on the human body. More recent studies have shown other stresses of high altitude are significant

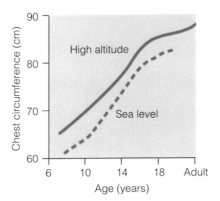

Figure 15.10

Distance curves for chest circumference for high-altitude and low-altitude Peruvian Indian populations. At all ages, the high-altitude population has the greatest chest circumference.
(Courtesy A. R. Frisancho)

factors as well (Frisancho 1990). When dealing with human adaptation, it is best to consider the effect and interaction of *multiple* stresses.

Physiologic Responses to Hypoxia

People who live at low altitudes experience several physiologic changes when they enter a high-altitude environment. Some of these happen immediately; others occur over several months to a year. Such physiologic responses help to maintain sufficient oxygen levels. Respiration increases initially but returns to normal after a few days. Red blood cell production increases for roughly three months. The weight of the right ventricle of the heart is greater than the weight of the left ventricle in individuals that have grown up at high altitudes. Other changes include possible hyperventilation and higher hemoglobin concentration in the blood. In addition to these adaptive responses, loss of appetite and weight loss are common. Memory and sensory abilities may be affected, and hypoxia may influence hormone levels.

The physiologic differences between high-altitude and low-altitude natives are primarily acquired during the growth process. Studies of children who were born at low altitudes but moved into high altitudes during childhood clearly substantiate this phenomenon. In terms of aerobic capacity, for example, the younger the age of migration, the higher the aerobic capacity (Frisancho 1979). In other words, the longer a child lives in a high-altitude environment, the greater the developmental response to that environment. Age at migration has no effect on the aerobic capacity of adults, however, further indicating that most physiologic changes are the result of developmental acclimatization.

Physical Growth in High-Altitude Populations

Studies conducted by Paul Baker and his students of high-altitude and low-altitude Indian populations in Peru found two peculiarities in growth. Chest dimensions and lung volume were greater at all ages in the high-altitude group (Figure 15.10), and high-altitude populations were also

Figure 15.11

Distance curve for stature for
high-altitude and low-altitude
Peruvian Indian populations.
At most ages, the low-altitude
population is taller.   (Courtesy
A. R. Frisancho)

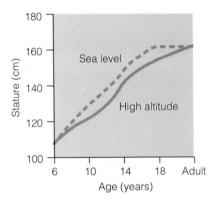

shorter at most ages than low-altitude populations (Figure 15.11) (Frisancho and Baker 1970). The shorter stature is related to delayed maturation,
whereas the increase in chest size is due to growth acceleration during
childhood.

Initially, the researchers interpreted both patterns of physical growth
as direct developmental responses to hypoxia and cold stress at high altitude. Larger chests and larger lung volumes relative to body size would be
better able to provide sufficient oxygen levels. The more energy devoted to
growth of oxygen transport systems, however, would leave less energy
available for growth in other organ systems, especially the skeletal and
muscle systems. Compounded by cold stress at high altitudes, this energy
deficit would lead to an increase in basal metabolic rates and further reduction in energy available for body growth. As discussed below, this view is
now being questioned.

Studies in high-altitude environments around the world show a similar pattern of growth in chest dimensions, although the extent of growth
varies. Migrants to high-altitude populations also show an increase in
chest dimensions, particularly among those that migrate at an early age.
Increased growth of oxygen transport systems appears to be a developmental response to hypoxia.

Are the developmental changes in chest and lung growth in high-
altitude populations genetic in nature? Were they shaped by natural selection? Most research to date assigns a relatively minor role to genetic factors.
A recent study examined high-altitude and low-altitude populations of
European ancestry in Bolivia (Greska 1990). Because these groups do not
have a long history of residence at high altitude, they would not possess
any genetic predisposition for high-altitude adaptations. The study showed
there was an increased capacity of the oxygen transport system in these
populations at high altitude even though they were not of high-altitude
ancestry. The observed changes were instead direct effects of a chronic
hypoxic stress.

The delayed maturation and small stature of the Peruvians have not been found in all studies of growth in high-altitude populations. As a result, some researchers have questioned the initial premise that hypoxia and cold stress have necessarily led to these characteristics, suggesting instead that other causal factors might be at work. A recent study undertaken in Peru has in fact shown that nutrition has had a major influence on stature (Leonard et al. 1990). Though high altitude may play a role in nutritional stress in the Peruvian highlands, income levels and access to land are of greater consequence. Also, other high-altitude populations, such as those found in Ethiopia, have a higher standard of living but do not show the growth deficits observed in Peru. Thus, it appears that although increased chest growth is a functional adaptation to hypoxia, the smaller body size is not necessarily related to high altitude. These results amply illustrate the complexity in assessing the relative value of stresses in any given environment.

Biological Effects of Modernization

The examples of climatic and high-altitude adaptation have shown us how stresses in the physical environment can be met by physiologic, genetic, and/or cultural adaptations. Although, as noted earlier, the biocultural nature of humans offers us increased adaptive flexibility, our cultural adaptations can also introduce new stresses into the environment. This section deals with human adaptation to recent, ongoing cultural change: modernization.

No one can deny the rapid pace of cultural and technological change in today's world. More and more, formerly "traditional" societies have undergone economic and technological development. Compared to rates of change in historic and prehistoric times, modernization in many parts of the world today is occurring almost instantaneously. Such rapid modernization has produced both new adaptations and new stresses. The biological impact is readily apparent. Changes in availability and distribution of food have altered patterns of growth and overall health. Improvements in waste disposal, water supply, and medical technology have reduced the threat of infectious disease and increased the average length of life. At the same time, changes in diet, lifestyle, occupations, and levels of stress have caused health problems. Reduction of death rates without similar reductions in birth rates have led to overpopulation. Industrialization has introduced numerous pollutants and cancer-causing substances. As has been stressed throughout this text, any evolutionary change, biological or cultural, has both costs and benefits.

Figure 15.12

Distance curve for female stature in a traditional Samoan population (Western Samoa) and a modernized Samoan population (American Samoa).   (Source of data: Bindon and Zansky [1986:173]).

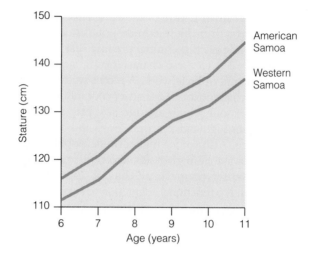

This section will focus on several biological changes that have been observed in modernizing populations. The effect of rapid cultural change on health and demography will be discussed in the next two chapters.

Changes in Height and Weight

The tendency for increased height and weight in developed societies (Chapter 14) has also been observed in populations undergoing modernization in a short period of time. In particular, weight gain has often been quite dramatic, resulting in part from dietary changes and a more sedentary lifestyle. In fact, many modernized groups show high rates of obesity, which in turn predisposes them to serious health problems such as diabetes and cardiovascular disease.

The study of preadolescent growth conducted by Bindon and Zansky (1986) illustrates the effects of modernization on stature in several Samoan populations in Polynesia, in the western Pacific. Among these were Western Samoa, a more traditional group using subsistence agriculture in a rural region, and American Samoa, a modernized group that has become part of a larger wage-earning economy. According to predictions based on the expected effects of modernization, the American Samoan population should show greater height at all ages during growth. The distance curves for females, shown in Figure 15.12, support this hypothesis. At all ages from 6 to 11, females in the modernized group are taller than those in the more traditional group. Males show the same pattern of increase, as does weight for both males and females.

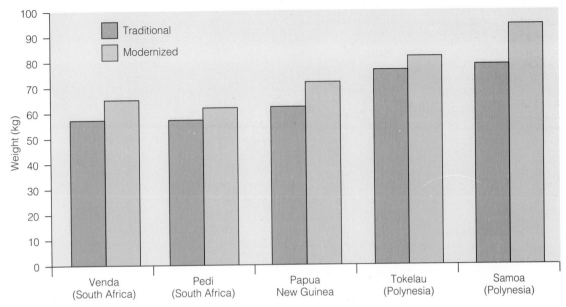

Figure 15.13

Comparison of average weight (in kilograms) for males in traditional and modernized groups within various populations. (Source of data: Harrison et al. [1988:536]).

Studies have commonly found that modernized groups are, on average, heavier than traditional, nonmodernized groups. In Samoa, for example, adults in the modernized groups tend to be more obese (Bindon and Baker 1985). Figure 15.13 shows the average weight of males in traditional and modernized groups within the same population. In each case, males in the modernized groups are heavier.

Changes in Blood Pressure

Blood pressure provides a measure of health. Excessive blood pressure, or hypertension, is a serious condition, both in itself and as a risk factor for other diseases. Blood pressure is based on two readings: *systolic blood pressure* measured during ventricular contraction, and *diastolic blood pressure* measured during ventricular relaxation. Studies of modernized populations show an increase in blood pressure and a tendency for blood pressure to increase with age (Little and Baker 1988). Traditional populations, on the other hand, show lower blood pressure levels and do not show an increase in blood pressure with age. Changes in blood pressure that accompany modernization are due to a number of factors, primarily changes in diet, physical activity and lifestyle, and stress levels.

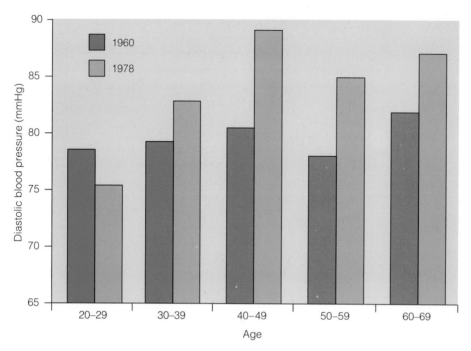

Figure 15.14

Effects of modernization on male diastolic blood pressure (mmHg) in the Gilbert Islands, Republic of Kiribati. From 1960 to 1978 the area underwent modernization. Note that the 1978 blood pressures are higher than in 1960 and that they show an increase with age. These are common findings in studies of modernization and blood pressure.   (Source of data: Lewis [1990:146]).

Figure 15.14 presents a chart of adult male diastolic blood pressure in the Gilbert Islands of the Republic of Kiribati. Two periods are compared: 1960, when the islands were more traditional in economy and lifestyle, and 1978, when the islands had undergone extensive modernization. Figure 15.14 shows clearly the difference in blood pressure levels between these two periods. Blood pressure is higher (in all but one age group) in 1978 than in 1960. Also, there is a noticeable increase in blood pressure with age in the 1978 sample. The 1960 sample exhibits no such trend. These findings are typical of studies of blood pressure in modernizing populations. Obviously, culture change significantly impacts human biology.

Genetics may also play a role in the relationship of blood pressure levels and modernization. In a study of modernization in the Solomon Islands, Melanesia, the *degree* of change in blood pressure levels over time varied across genetically different groups (Zerba et al. 1990). This finding suggests an interaction between genotype and environment, whereby environmental changes can produce different degrees of change depending on the genetics of a group.

Changes in Physical Fitness

Modernization has been observed to affect levels of exercise capacity and overall physical fitness. The change to a more sedentary lifestyle is a primary reason for this shift. A more traditional lifestyle generally involves greater physical activity. Modernization does not, however, have the same effect on everyone. In his study of exercise capacity in the Solomon Islands, Weitz (1990) found variable patterns. Looking at the relationship between degree of modernization and exercise capacity among five populations, he found that females showed the expected pattern: the more modernized a population, the lower the exercise capacity. Among males, however, he found variability, some groups showing greater capacity in modernized populations, and some showing less. Weitz determined that these differences related to occupation. Some males were employed in more sedentary occupations and thus generally received less exercise. For younger males, however, this was not the case. On the Otong Java atoll, which was rapidly modernizing, younger males were often employed to dive for beche-de-mer, a marine animal. This diving generally resulted in higher levels of physical fitness. Weitz also observed a tendency for many young males in modernized groups to increase their physical fitness by spending a great deal of time in strenuous leisure activities. Thus, although modernization tends to have a general effect on average physical fitness, considerable variation may also occur.

SUMMARY

Studies of adaptation focus on the many ways in which organisms respond to environmental stresses. Human adaptation is particularly interesting because humans not only adapt both biologically and culturally but also must deal with stresses from their physical and cultural environments. Biological adaptation includes physiologic responses and genetic adaptation (natural selection). Cultural adaptation includes aspects of technology, economics, and social structure. In any study of human adaptation, we must look at multiple stresses and multiple adaptive (or nonadaptive) mechanisms.

Many studies of human adaptation have focused on cold and heat stress. Though as mammals humans have the capacity for maintenance of body temperature, they must still cope with extremes in temperature. Physiologic responses of the human body to temperature stress include changes in peripheral blood flow and evaporation. Studies have shown that general relationships exist worldwide between body size and shape and temperature. These observed trends agree with the predictions of the Bergmann and Allen rules. In hot climates, small body size and linear body shape maximize heat loss. In cold climates, large body size and less linear body shape minimize heat loss. Cranial studies show that worldwide the shape of the skull also varies predictably, according to the principles of differential heat loss and the Bergmann and Allen rules. Although some of these biological features are the result of genetic adaptation, studies of children have revealed that response to temperature stress can affect growth. Cultural adaptations, especially those involving clothing, shelter, and physical activity, are also important in climatic adaptation.

Over 25 million people around the world live at high altitudes. The major stresses of a high-altitude population are hypoxia (oxygen shortage) and cold stress. Many physiologic changes have been documented in high-altitude peoples, including short-term responses and long-term increases in the size of the lungs and other components of the oxygen transport system. These changes are caused by hypoxic stress during the growth period, and their degree of change is related to the time spent living at high altitudes: the longer one has lived there as a child, the more adapted one is. Early studies of high-altitude populations also noted small body size that, along with delayed maturation, could be due to insufficient energy levels for body growth because of hypoxia and cold stress. More recent studies have shown this is not always the case, because some high-altitude groups do not show this growth deficit. Instead, variation in diet appears to be the key factor.

As the world continues to change at a rapid pace, the biological effects of modernization multiply. Such changes include increases in height, weight, and blood pressure. Although some of these changes reflect improved health, others indicate stressful response to alterations in diet and lifestyle. The next two chapters further explore the impact of modernization on human biology and culture.

Supplemental Readings

Frisancho, A. R. 1979. *Human Adaptation: A Functional Interpretation*. St. Louis, Mo.: C. V. Mosby. This text is a thorough review of adaptation studies through the late 1970s, focusing on biological responses.

Harrison, G. A., J. M. Tanner, D. R. Pilbeam, and P. T. Baker. 1988. *Human Biology: An Introduction to Human Evolution, Variation, Growth, and Adaptability*. 3d ed. Oxford: Oxford University Press. Part 4, written by Paul Baker, provides a thorough review of human adaptation.

Moran, E. F. 1982. *Human Adaptability: An Introduction to Ecological Anthropology*. Boulder, Colo.: Westview Press. This general text provides another review of human adaptation but focuses more on cultural issues.

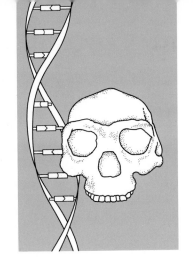

CHAPTER **16**

Human Health
and Disease

One of the most recent and rapid changes in human biology has been in human disease patterns. In the last 100 years, the major causes of death in developed regions of the world have shifted from infectious diseases to noninfectious diseases (remember from Chapter 5 that infectious diseases are those caused primarily by microorganisms). Some infectious diseases, such as smallpox, have been eradicated. Others have been reduced, although certain infectious diseases, such as malaria and schistosomiasis, continue to take their toll in tropical environments. In developed nations, the incidence of noninfectious diseases, such as diabetes, has risen.

These changes are the consequence of cultural innovations. Improvements in public health and sanitation have accounted for the major reduction in the spread of many infectious microorganisms. Advances in medical technology, such as the use of immunizations and antibiotics, have also reduced the risk for many infectious diseases. In addition, changes in health care systems have increased the availability of medical care to a larger proportion of the population.

This chapter focuses on the rapidly growing field of biomedical anthropology. Here we will describe the relationship of this discipline with other health-related fields and present several case studies of biomedical anthropology.

epidemiology The study of patterns of human disease and their causes.

The Study of Biomedical Anthropology

Much scientific research on human health and disease takes place in laboratories. Here scientists work to determine the causes of infectious diseases and to develop cures or preventive measures. A thorough understanding of the spread of infectious disease, however, requires work beyond a laboratory setting. Cultural and ecological factors must be examined in determining the relative risk for different groups of people. Noninfectious diseases also generally reflect a variety of genetic and environmental determinants. Such diseases must be studied in their natural context before we can understand their origin and potential therapy.

Many disciplines study human health and disease. Laboratory studies in biology and chemistry focus on the biological nature of microorganisms and physiological response to disease, among other areas. Geographers study the spread of disease over space. Sociologists are interested in social interactions between patient and physician and the social structure of health care institutions. All these studies can improve health care services by providing basic data on the nature of disease. They represent only a few of the many ways different fields have contributed to an understanding of human health and disease.

Epidemiology

The study of human disease patterns and their causes is known as **epidemiology.** Epidemiology is an interdisciplinary field that focuses on the analysis of rates of diseases in human populations. The study of biomedical anthropology shares many of the goals and methods of epidemiology.

Types of diseases. Diseases can be classified as infectious or noninfectious. Infectious diseases are caused by the introduction of organic matter, such as a virus, bacteria, or a parasite, into the body. Infectious diseases can also be classified as *communicable* or *noncommunicable,* depending on whether the disease can be transmitted directly from one person to another. Malaria, for example, is an infectious disease caused by a parasite. It is not, however, a communicable disease because it cannot be passed from one human to another, except by means of a blood transfusion. Malaria is transmitted instead through the bites of mosquitoes carrying the malarial parasite. Measles, another infectious disease, is communicable because it can be transmitted from one human to another. Diabetes, by contrast, is a noninfectious disease that is caused by a variety of genetic and environmental factors.

The factors responsible for the spread of a disease through a population are different for infectious and noninfectious diseases. Because infectious diseases are spread through microorganisms, we need to look at the evolution and ecology of these microorganisms as well as those of humans. Environmental factors such as temperature, humidity, and sunlight can all affect the size of the microorganism population, which in turn affects disease rates. The type of microorganism and the mode of transmission are also important factors. Viruses, bacteria, and parasites, for example, all act in different ways. Some infectious diseases spread very quickly in human populations because they are transmitted through respiration. Others, including a number of sexually transmitted diseases, are spread only through personal contact.

Noninfectious diseases reflect multiple causes, genetic and environmental. An individual's genotype may give increased resistance or susceptibility to a noninfectious disease, but the phenotype depends on many environmental factors. Noninsulin-dependent diabetes, for example, is affected not only by genetic predisposition but also by sex, age, diet, and lifestyle. Noninfectious diseases are generally more difficult than infectious diseases to analyze because multiple factors affect their occurrence.

incidence rate The rate of new cases of a disease developing in a population in a specified period of time.

prevalence rate The rate of total cases of a disease, old and new, in a population in a specified period of time.

epidemic When new cases of a disease spread rapidly through a population.

endemic When new cases of a disease occur at a relatively constant but low rate over time.

pandemic An epidemic that occurs over a large geographic range.

Rates of diseases. Epidemiological research looks at the rates of incidence and prevalence of both infectious and noninfectious diseases in populations over time and space. Rates are proportions of population size. The **incidence rate** is the rate of new cases of a disease that develop within a given population in a given period of time. Incidence rates are also used to describe the proportion of deaths in a population within a given period. For example, an annual incidence rate for spinal cord injury of 4 per 100,000 means that 4 out of every 100,000 people will have a spinal cord injury each year. The **prevalence rate** is the rate of the total number of cases, old and new, within a given population within a given period. For example, a prevalence rate for spinal cord injury of 90 per 100,000 means that 90 out of 100,000 people now living have a spinal cord injury, regardless of when they had it.

Several terms are used to describe the overall magnitude of disease rates. An **epidemic** pattern is one in which new cases of a disease spread quickly. An **endemic** pattern is a low but constant rate; a few cases are always present, but no major spread occurs. A **pandemic** pattern is an epidemic that takes place over large geographic ranges, such as the major bubonic plague pandemics during the Middle Ages that spread throughout Europe. Another example is the 1918 influenza pandemic. Pandemics are not just something that happened in the past; pandemics occur today as well. Currently, the world has been experiencing a cholera pandemic since 1961, and epidemic spread of the disease has now reached four continents (Table 16.1).

TABLE 16.1

Cholera: An Example of a Current Pandemic

Year	Occurrence of Epidemic
1961	Indonesia (first outbreak)
1963	Bangladesh
1964	India
1965	Former Soviet Union
1970	Africa
1990	Parts of Europe
1991	South America

Source: Dixon and McBride (1992).

Causes of diseases. Incidence and prevalence rates are analyzed to determine their relationship with space and time. Geographic patterns of disease rates can provide clues about factors responsible for the disease. One example of geographic patterning occurs in those areas showing high rates of malaria. As discussed in Chapter 5, the highest rates of malaria are found in environments conducive to the mosquitoes that spread malaria.

Geographic analysis can also help determine which populations are in greatest need of health care services. It can also help in predicting the future spread of a disease. As an example of this approach, let us look at the current geographic range of Lyme disease in the northeastern United States. Lyme disease, which is spread by the deer tick, was first found in parts of Long Island, New York, and Westchester County, New York, and in Connecticut. Analysis of the geographic range of Lyme disease cases shows that the deer tick population is spreading widely into other parts of the United States. Such forecasting allows public health officials to have adequate time for public education and other preventive measures. Careful prediction also allows physicians and other health personnel to become aware of the symptoms and treatments of a spreading disease.

Epidemiology also looks at changing disease rates over time. An increase in disease rates in a population may indicate the start of an epidemic. Changes over time can also be used to evaluate changes in disease prevention or environmental changes. Epidemiologists also investigate short-term changes in disease rates to determine the influence of seasonal change on disease risk. For example, the incidence of mumps cases generally increases during the winter and decreases in the summer. Because mumps is an infectious disease that spreads through personal contact, it seems likely that the close crowding of people in winter months, particularly in schools, increases the probability of contact with an infected person (Lilienfeld and Lilienfeld 1980).

Determining the timing of disease outbreaks can also be useful in assessing potential causes. For example, there has been a rapid increase in cases of a disease known as Rift Valley Fever in towns along the Senegal River in Senegal, West Africa. The outbreak coincides to some extent with the development of a dam downstream from these towns. This suggests a potential connection between dam operations and increased rates of Rift Valley Fever. Perhaps the increased amount of standing water because of the dam has resulted in an increased mosquito population, which in turn has spread the disease (Walsh 1988).

Individual characteristics are also an important focus of epidemiological research. These include age, sex, ethnicity, physiologic state, hygiene, and occupation, among others (Lilienfeld and Lilienfeld 1980). For example, a person's behavior can affect the probability of contact with an infectious microorganism. People with many sexual partners have a higher risk, all other factors being equal, of acquiring a sexually transmitted disease. U.S. military personnel who served in the Vietnam War had a higher risk of contracting malaria than those at home because malaria-carrying mosquitoes were common in Vietnam.

Individual characteristics also play a role in determining the risk of acquiring a noninfectious disease. A diet high in carbohydrates combined with low levels of exercise can increase risk of hypertension, heart disease, and diabetes. Increased exposure to sunlight, either through recreation or occupation, can increase the risk for skin cancer. Working in a chemical plant may also increase the risk for certain types of cancers.

The search for causal factors in disease risk becomes even more complicated when we consider the fact that many factors are interrelated. Suppose, for example, that you find higher rates of skin cancer among male construction workers than among female factory workers. Is this difference the result of biological factors? Or is it caused by the circumstances of occupation? Perhaps comparison of men's and women's rates of skin cancer in outdoor occupations could shed light on this problem. There might be other factors still uncontrolled for, however, such as the fact that in Western societies it is acceptable for men, but not for women, to remove their shirts during work. This is a purely hypothetical example, but it does show potential complications in trying to analyze disease risk. Other real-life examples will be discussed throughout the chapter.

Anthropology and Epidemiology

Epidemiology is not a subfield of anthropology. Rather, anthropology is only one of many disciplines concerned with epidemiological questions. What, then, are the unique characteristics of anthropology in epidemiological research?

Medical anthropology. The study of disease in an anthropological context is often described as the field of *medical anthropology*. In the simplest sense, medical anthropology looks at health and disease as a component of the entire human experience. Using a holistic approach, a medical

Figure 16.1

A !Kung healer transmitting healing power to a woman. Such beliefs can often have therapeutic effects.   (Irven DeVore/Anthro-Photo)

anthropologist is interested in determining the relationship among disease rates, diagnosis, treatment, and other cultural and environmental components in a society. Possible questions include: How do differences in social class affect health care and relative disease risk? How do a culture's religious beliefs influence its health care? What are the differences in diseases between hunting-gathering and agricultural societies? Instead of focusing on the biochemical level, medical anthropologists view health and disease as part of a much larger system.

Medical anthropology also relies on the comparative approach. By looking at cultures in different environments, we may find clues to causes of disease and their prevention. Medical anthropologists are also interested in how cultures diagnose and treat disease (Figure 16.1). This interest is not merely academic; many methods used today in Western medicine have their origins in other cultures. Acupuncture is a good example of this. We also use many drugs developed by other cultures, such as the South American tree extract known as curare, used to relax muscles during anesthesia.

Biomedical anthropology. The field of anthropology includes two distinct approaches to health and disease. Some cultural anthropologists focus more on systems of health care and less on biological factors. These medical anthropologists are interested in the ways in which members of a culture classify diseases and how they attempt cures. Other anthropologists focus on the biological side of health and disease, looking at genetic and environmental factors that affect risk for specific diseases. Though many medical anthropological studies combine both cultural and biological interests, biological anthropologists have shown a growing tendency to pursue what is often called *biomedical anthropology*. The remainder of this chapter focuses on the field of biomedical anthropology. Specific references to cultural anthropological studies of health care and medical belief systems are mentioned where appropriate but are not covered in detail. For further discussion of cultural anthropological studies, you can consult one of many excellent medical anthropology texts, including the books by McElroy and Townsend (1989) and Moore and colleagues (1980) listed under Supplemental Readings at the end of this chapter.

zoonose A disease transmitted directly from animals to humans.

The Evolution of Human Disease

A unique contribution of anthropology to epidemiological research has been its investigation of the evolution of human diseases. A shift began roughly 12,000 years ago from hunting and gathering to agriculture. During the past several centuries, further changes have led to the development and spread of large industrial societies. What effects have these rapid shifts, and related environmental and cultural changes, produced on patterns of human health and disease? Part of this question can be answered by looking at contemporary populations at different levels of subsistence. We can also examine the fossil and archaeological record to infer changes in the patterns of disease. This section focuses on general trends in disease across three different levels of subsistence: hunting-gathering, agriculture, and industrialization.

Disease in Hunting-Gathering Societies

Given that humans have relied exclusively on hunting and gathering until the relatively recent development of agriculture, a large part of our genetic makeup resulted from adaptations to a hunting-gathering way of life. This fact has powerful implications for the analysis of disease. How do these adaptations affect our response to disease under very different environmental circumstances?

Infectious disease. The two most common types of infectious diseases in hunting-gathering populations are caused by parasites and **zoonoses** (diseases transmitted from other animals to humans). Parasitic

Figure 16.2

!Kung women gathering vegetables. The small size and nomadic nature of hunting-gathering populations means that infectious disease is endemic, not epidemic. (M. Shostak/Anthro-Photo)

diseases may reflect the long-term evolutionary adaptation of different parasites to human beings. Among hunting-gathering societies, these parasites include lice and pinworms. The zoonoses are introduced through insect bites, animal wounds, and ingestion of contaminated meat. These diseases include sleeping sickness, tetanus, and schistosomiasis (Armelagos and Dewey 1970). The prevalence of various parasitic and zoonotic diseases varies among different hunting-gathering environments. The disease microorganisms found in arctic or temperate environments are generally not found in tropical environments.

In general, hunting-gathering populations do not experience epidemics of infectious disease. This is because of two ecological factors associated with a hunting-gathering way of life: small population size and nomadism (Figure 16.2). Hunters and gatherers live in small groups of roughly 25 to 50 people that interact occasionally with other small groups in their region. Under such conditions, infectious diseases do not spread. There are not enough people to become infected to keep the disease going at high rates. Without more people to infect, the disease microorganisms die. This does not apply to chronic infectious diseases, whose microorganisms can stay alive long enough to infect people coming into the group. Certain diseases caused by parasitic worms fall into this category. In such cases, the prevalence rate of infectious diseases is low. Most infectious diseases in hunting-gathering societies are endemic rather than epidemic (McElroy and Townsend 1989).

The nomadic lifestyle of hunting-gathering groups also reduces risk to certain infectious diseases. The microorganisms infecting humans may not survive in new environments. Other aspects of the hunting-gathering way of life also reduce the chance of epidemics. Given a small, mobile population, there are few problems with sanitation or contamination of the water supply.

Noninfectious disease. The noninfectious diseases common in industrial societies, such as heart disease, cancer, diabetes, and hypertension, are rare in hunting-gathering societies. Part of the reason for low rates of such noninfectious "Western diseases" may be the diet and lifestyle of hunters and gatherers, but the primary reason may be simply the fact that fewer individuals among hunters and gatherers are likely to live long enough to develop these diseases.

The nutrition of hunting-gathering populations is varied and provides a well-balanced diet. Perhaps this diet, along with greater levels of exercise, accounts for the lack of cardiovascular problems in such societies. The major nutritional problem in hunting-gathering societies is the scarcity of food during hard times, such as drought. To some extent, hunting-gathering populations have adapted to occasional fluctuations in food supply through reduced rates of growth and smaller body sizes. In any case, the rate of malnutrition and starvation in most hunting-gathering groups is usually very low (Dunn 1968).

The reduced rate of noninfectious diseases in hunting-gathering populations, particularly those diseases that occur in old age, reflects the low life expectancy in these groups (**life expectancy** is a measure of the average length of life). Many noninfectious diseases require long periods of time for full development. Life expectancy at birth (the average length of life) is low in hunting-gathering populations: roughly 20 to 30 years (Weiss 1973). These low life expectancies to a large extent reflect high infant mortality. If many people die early in life, the median age at death will be lowered.

Other causes of disease and death. What are the major causes of death in hunting-gathering societies? If many infectious diseases are endemic, what accounts for the low life expectancy in such groups? Injury deaths

life expectancy A measure of the average length of life in a population.

are one factor. In most environments, death could result from burns and hunting injuries. In arctic hunting-gathering populations, death could also result from drowning and exposure to cold. In some hunting-gathering populations, injuries are the major cause of death (Dunn 1968). For females, an additional factor in low life expectancy is death during childbirth.

Dunn (1968) has also listed a number of types of what he calls "social mortality" in hunting-gathering populations. These are deaths related to cultural behaviors such as infanticide (the killing of newborn children), geronticide (the killing of old people), sacrifice, and warfare. Infanticide and geronticide have been recorded for a number of hunting-gathering populations in past times and have often been interpreted as mechanisms of population size regulation.

Agriculture and Disease

The pattern of human disease is quite different in agricultural societies (both slash-and-burn and intensive agriculture). Agriculture allows larger population size and requires a nonnomadic life. The increased population size and lack of mobility has certain implications for the spread of disease.

Infectious disease. Large populations of susceptible individuals allow the spread of short-lived microorganisms. Such conditions in agricultural populations exist because of increased population size and the increased probability of contacting someone with the disease. As a result, agricultural populations often show epidemics of diseases such as smallpox, measles, mumps, and chicken pox (McElroy and Townsend 1989). The size of a population needed for an epidemic varies according to disease. Some infectious diseases require larger population sizes for rapid spread.

Sedentary life increases the spread of infectious disease in other ways. Large populations living continuously in the same area can accumulate garbage. Poor sanitation and contamination of the water supply increases the chance for disease epidemics.

Agricultural practices also cause ecological changes, making certain infectious diseases more likely. The introduction of domesticated animals adds to waste accumulation and provides the opportunity for further exposure to diseases carried by animals. Cultivation of the land can also increase the probability of contact with insects carrying disease microorganisms. Agriculture can also lead to changes that increase or decrease the population of microorganisms or the insects that carry them (Armelagos and Dewey 1970). An example discussed earlier (Chapter 5) is the ecological changes brought about by the introduction of agriculture in Africa, leading to increased rates of malaria.

The use of feces for fertilization can also have an impact on rates of infectious disease. In addition to contamination from handling these waste

Figure 16.3

Chinese farmers planting rice. The larger size and sedentary nature of agricultural populations contributes to epidemics of infectious disease. (Courtesy Kenneth Feder and Michael Park, Central Connecticut State University)

products, the food grown in these fertilizers can become contaminated. This problem was so acute in South Korea that steps had to be taken to reduce the use of feces as fertilizer (Cockburn 1971). Irrigation can also lead to an increase in the spread of infectious disease. One of the major problems today in tropical agricultural societies is the increased snail population that lives in irrigation canals and carries schistosomiasis. Irrigation can also pass infectious microorganisms from one population to the next (Figure 16.3).

Nutritional disease. Although agriculture provides populations with the ability to feed more people, this way of life does not guarantee an improvement in nutrition. Extensive investment in a single food crop, such as rice or corn, may provide too limited a diet for many people, and certain nutritional deficiency diseases can result. For example, populations relying extensively on corn as a major food source may show an increase in pellagra (a disease caused by a deficiency in the vitamin niacin) as well as protein deficiency. Dependency on rice is often associated with protein and vitamin deficiencies (McElroy and Townsend 1989).

An agricultural diet can also lead to dental problems. The increased amount of starches in an agriculturalist's diet, combined with an increase in dirt and grit in the food, can lead to an increase in dental wear and cavities.

Urbanization and Disease

Following the origin and spread of agriculture, a number of human populations became urbanized. An urban area is defined in terms of large population size and density as well as a population with occupational specialization that produces a variety of economic goods and services provided to surrounding areas. During human history and prehistory, we can subdivide cities into preindustrial and industrial. Each type of city has its own associated health problems.

Disease in preindustrial cities. Preindustrial cities date back to several thousand years B.P. Such cities often developed as market or administrative centers for a region, and their increased population size and density provided ample opportunity for epidemics of infectious disease. In addition, a number of early cities had inadequate waste disposal and contaminated water, both factors increasing the spread of epidemics. To feed large numbers of people, food had to be brought in from the surrounding countryside and stored inside the city. In Europe during the Middle Ages, grain was often stored inside the house. Rats and other vermin had easy access to these foods, and their population increased, furthering the spread of disease. In preindustrial cities located in dry parts of the world, grain was stored in ceramic containers, which limited the access of vermin.

Perhaps the best-known example of an epidemic disease in preindustrial cities is the Black Death in Europe during the fourteenth century. The Black Death is another name for the infectious disease bubonic plague. Caused by a bacterium, the disease affects field rodents, among whom it is spread by fleas. With the development of large urban areas and the corresponding large indoor rat populations, the disease spread to rats in the cities. The rats' fleas then infected humans. The spread of bubonic plague during this time was pandemic, affecting populations throughout Europe. It is estimated that up to 20 million Europeans died from bubonic plague between 1346 and 1352 (McEvedy 1988). The ecological changes accompanying the development of urbanization in Europe provided an opportunity for the rapid spread of fleas, rats, and the disease.

Disease in industrial cities. Industrialization, which began several centuries ago, accelerated population growth in urban areas. Technological changes allowed more efficient methods of agriculture and provided the means to support more people than in previous eras. The increased growth of urban areas was accompanied initially by further spread of infectious diseases. As industrialization continued, however, the rate of infectious disease declined and the rate of noninfectious disease increased. This shift in disease patterns was accompanied by a reduction in mortality, especially infant mortality, and an increase in life expectancy.

The Epidemiologic Transition

The shift from infectious diseases to noninfectious diseases as the primary cause of death is a feature of the **epidemiologic transition** model, developed by Omran (1977).

The nature of the epidemiologic transition. According to Omran's model, a pretransition population has high death rates, particularly because of epidemics of childhood infectious diseases. As a culture's medical technologies, public health, and sanitation improve, epidemics become less frequent and less intense. Following the transition, the primary cause of death is not infectious disease but degenerative noninfectious diseases. This shift in disease patterns is also accompanied by an increase in life expectancy at birth.

Figure 16.4 presents death rates per 100,000 people in the United

epidemiologic transition
The change in disease patterns in which there is a decline in infectious diseases and an increase in noninfectious diseases.

Figure 16.4

Death rates for selected diseases in the United States in 1900 and 1975. Note the decrease in infectious disease deaths and the increase in noninfectious disease deaths.   (Source of data: Molnar [1983:219])

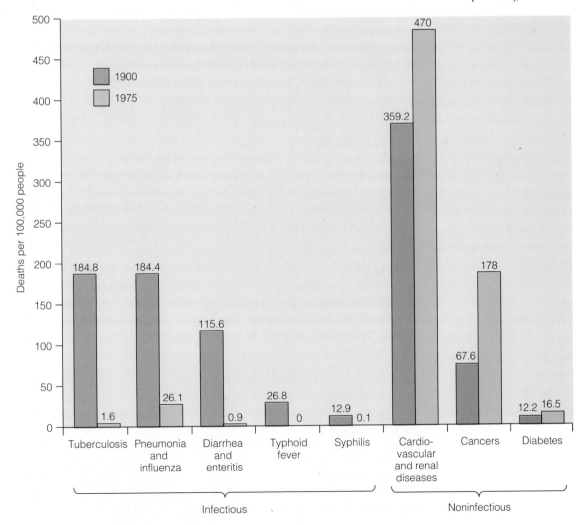

TABLE   16.2
Life Expectancy at Birth in the United States, 1990

Group	Life expectancy at birth (years)
European-American females	79.3
African-American females	74.5
European-American males	72.6
African-American males	66.0
All groups	75.4

Source: Haub (1992).

States in 1900 and 1975 for several selected diseases. Note the tremendous decline in the death rates for infectious diseases such as tuberculosis and pneumonia. On the other hand, there has been an increase in death rates from cardiovascular diseases, cancers, and diabetes. In addition, the total number of deaths per year per 100,000 of the population has decreased from 1622 in 1900 to 890 in 1975. A large proportion of this decrease has been a consequence of the reduction of infant mortality (death during the first year of life). In 1900, the infant mortality rate was 162 deaths per 1,000 live births. By 1975, the infant mortality rate had dropped to 14 deaths per 1,000 live births (Molnar 1983).

The epidemiologic transition has also affected life expectancy in developed societies. In the United States in 1900, life expectancy at birth was 49 years. In 1990, this figure had risen to 75.4 years. It is not the highest in the world; in fact, the United States had the sixteenth-highest life expectancy at birth in 1990 (Haub 1992). Not all people in the United States have the same life expectancy. On average, females have higher life expectancy than males, and European Americans have a higher life expectancy than African Americans (Table 16.2).

The increase in life expectancy is not confined to developed societies. Other groups, undergoing modernization and the epidemiologic transition, have also shown an increase, such as the residents of the modernizing population of American Samoa, discussed in the previous chapter. From 1950 to 1980, life expectancy at birth increased 10 years for males and 18 years for females (Crews 1989).

A controversial topic today is the extent to which life expectancy can be expected to increase in developed societies. Based on statistical analysis of death rates, Olshansky and colleagues (1990) argue that even with major reductions in chronic disease, life expectancy at birth will not increase past 85 years of age.

In the United States, the last century has seen a reduction in infant mortality, a reduction in infectious diseases as the cause of death, an increase in noninfectious diseases as the cause of death, and an overall increase in life expectancy at birth. There appears to have been no overall change in the total life span of humans, however. **Life span** is the measure of maximum longevity. Discounting Biblical accounts of Methuselah and other unsubstantiated claims, there have been no verified claims of humans living past 120 years. Changes in medicine and health care have increased life expectancy, but they have not, as yet, increased the human life span. This means that more and more people are likely to reach the limit of life, a phenomenon with far-reaching implications that will be discussed in the next chapter.

What has caused these rapid changes in disease rates and life expectancy? Cultural changes in industrial societies have often resulted in average improvements in health care, public sanitation, and water quality. These factors aid in reducing the spread and effect of infectious diseases, particularly in infancy. As a result, more people are likely to live to older ages—long enough, therefore, to develop the long-term noninfectious diseases, such as cancer. These diseases often require lengthy periods of time to reach a debilitating stage. A person who dies in early life from an infectious disease will obviously not have had sufficient time to develop noninfectious disorders.

Other contributing factors are changes in the physical environment brought about by urbanization and industrialization. Industrial pollution of the air and water can lead to increased levels of cancer and other noninfectious diseases. Technological and social changes have also led to the increased abundance of drugs such as alcohol and tobacco, which increase disease. Factors such as stress, lifestyle, crowding, and noise levels also appear to play a role in the disease process.

Studies of the epidemiologic transition. The relationship between cultural change and disease rates emerges clearly in specific case studies of the epidemiologic transition. Omran (1977) looked at overall death rates in his study of the epidemiologic transition in New York City. Figure 16.5 shows the changing overall death rate in New York City over time. Before the 1860s, the overall death rate was high and had frequent spikes, primarily because of epidemics of cholera. Following the mid-1860s, both the overall death rate and the intensity of epidemics declined. This decrease corresponds with the establishment of the Health Department. After the 1920s, the spread of better sanitation and water supplies along with an improvement in drugs and health care and the introduction of pasteurized milk caused the death rates to decline even more.

Another study of the epidemiologic transition has been carried out on a smaller scale. Levison and colleagues (1981) analyzed census and burial data from the town of Manti, Utah, from 1849 to 1977. Their study focused on changes in disease patterns as the town changed from a frontier population (1849–1889) to a transitional rural agricultural population (1890–1929) to a modern agricultural community (1930–1977). Census data showed that the life expectancy at birth increased over time,

life span A measure of the maximum length of life recorded for a species.

Figure 16.5

Changes in the death rate in
New York City during the
nineteenth and twentieth
centuries. (Source: Omran
[1977:12]. Courtesy of the
Population Reference Bureau,
Inc., Washington, D.C.)

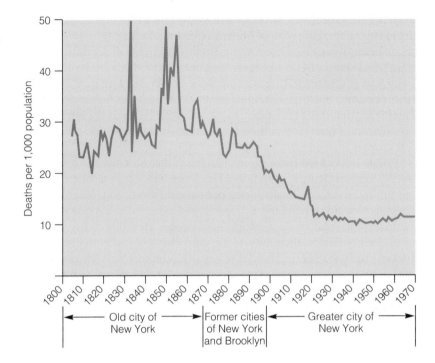

as did the major causes of death. Table 16.3 lists the five leading causes of
death for the three periods. Infectious and parasitic diseases dropped from
the primary cause of death in the initial frontier stage to the third cause of
death during the transitional stage; it was not among the top five causes of
death in the modern stage. Another major shift took place in circulatory
diseases, which were not among the top five causes of death in the frontier
stage but rose to the second place in the transitional stage and the primary
cause of death in the modern stage. By the modern stage cancers had also
risen to become the third cause of death. The changes in disease patterns
were associated with improved sanitation, elimination of dependence on
contaminated water supplies, and the adoption of newer medical techniques. The type of pattern shown in the Manti study parallels those found
in other studies of the epidemiologic transition.

Not all human populations today have experienced the epidemiologic
transition. In many Third World nations death rates, especially among
infants, remain high. Inadequate health care, poor sanitation, contaminated water, poor nutrition, and warfare continue to produce high levels
of mortality. These populational differences show up most clearly in rates
of infant mortality. Worldwide, 8 percent of all children die in the first
year of life. In a few nations, such as Japan, this rate is as low as 1 percent, whereas in some Asian and African nations it is as high as 20 percent
(Teitelbaum 1988).

TABLE 16.3
The Five Leading Causes of Death in Manti, Utah,
from 1849 to 1977

	1849–1889	1890–1929	1930–1977
1.	Infectious and parasitic diseases	Respiratory diseases	Circulatory system diseases
2.	Respiratory diseases	Circulatory system diseases	Injuries
3.	Congenital abnormalities	Infectious and parasitic diseases	Cancers
4.	Digestive system diseases	Congenital abnormalities	Respiratory diseases
5.	Injuries, genitourinary system diseases, and nervous system diseases (tied)	Digestive system diseases	Congenital abnormalities

Source: Levison et al. (1981:90).

Case Studies in Biomedical Anthropology

The previous section looked at human health and disease from a comparative perspective, focusing on the broad relationship between levels of subsistence and disease patterns. This section looks at specific population-disease associations in several case studies of biomedical anthropology. We will investigate two major areas: prehistoric disease and disease in historical and contemporary populations.

Paleopathology

Paleopathology is the study of disease in prehistoric populations. Although studies have been made of prehistoric disease in many animals (including dinosaurs), this section confines itself to disease in prehistoric humans. Paleopathology not only gives us a glimpse into conditions in prehistoric populations, it also provides an evolutionary perspective on disease. By looking at populations in different environments over time, we may be able to gain insights into the long-term relationship of human biology, culture, and disease.

paleopathology The study of disease in prehistoric populations based on analysis of skeletal remains and archaeological evidence.

The goals and methods of paleopathology. The primary source of paleopathological information is skeletal remains. Inspection of bones is augmented with X-rays and other nonintrusive scanning techniques and with chemical analyses. Such studies can tell us something of an individual's history of health and disease, and often even the cause of death. Diseases such as osteoarthritis may affect bones directly. Other diseases, such as syphilis and tuberculosis, may leave indications of their effects on the skeletal system. Physical traumas because of injuries or violence often leave detectable fractures. Signs of healing or infection tell us the long-term effects of such traumas.

The physical evidence, combined with information on sex, age, and other characteristics available from skeletal material, provides us with opportunities to assess the entire life of an individual in terms of health and disease. One of the Neandertals found at Shanidar Cave (Chapter 13) is a good example. This individual had one deformed arm that was later amputated. The signs of healing showed that the loss of the arm was not the cause of death. In addition, the individual was arthritic and had survived facial fractures, the probable loss of one eye, and the decay of most of his teeth. Judging from the skeletal remains, this person lived to be an old man before dying (presumably from the collapse of a cave).

Other information about health and disease can be obtained from the archaeological and fossil records. Works of art often provide indirect information on the diseases found in prehistoric societies. Surgical instruments and splints have also been found. Finally, information about the climate and ecology of a region is vitally necessary in reconstructing disease patterns (Kerley and Bass 1967).

Examples of paleopathology. One of the most common diseases found in the fossil record of humans and nonhumans is *osteoarthritis,* the deterioration of cartilage around a joint, combined with formation of bone tissue at the joint. These effects result in reduction of the joint's mobility along with severe pain. Osteoarthritis has been found in the skeletal remains of humans and in many other organisms, including dinosaurs. It is most frequent among the elderly and is caused by a variety of factors such as joint stress, injury, and improper skeletal development. Figure 16.6 shows the head of a femur (the portion of the upper leg bone that fits into the pelvis) of a prehistoric Indian from Peru. The neck of the femur is swollen, a typical characteristic of osteoarthritis.

Another example of a bone disease is *ankylosing spondylitis,* shown in Figure 16.7. This picture shows a portion of a prehistoric Peruvian's spine. Normally, the vertebrae of the spine are not fused. In this individual abnormal bone growth has fused many of the vertebrae, which would have made it difficult and painful to move.

Some diseases affect the skeletal tissue indirectly. One example is *venereal syphilis,* an infectious disease transmitted through sexual inter-

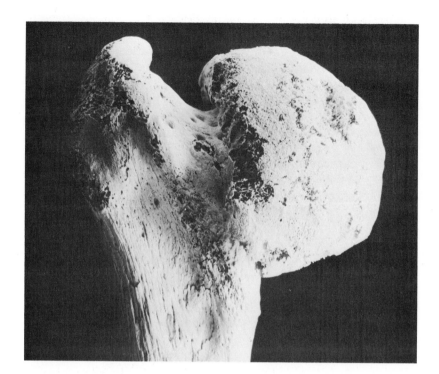

Figure 16.6

Osteoarthritis in a prehistoric Peruvian. The head of the femur is deformed. (Field Museum of Natural History, Chicago, neg. no. 74749B)

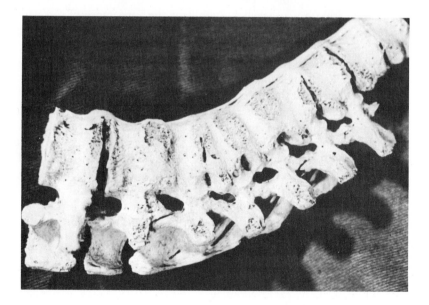

Figure 16.7

Ankylosing spondylitis in a prehistoric Peruvian. The vertebrae have fused together, limiting movement and causing severe pain. (Photo by Mary Edgecomb. Courtesy San Diego Museum of Man)

Figure 16.8

The skull of a prehistoric Eskimo suffering from syphilis. The marks on the top of the skull are typical of a long-term syphilitic infection.   (Photo by Mary Edgecomb, Courtesy San Diego Museum of Man)

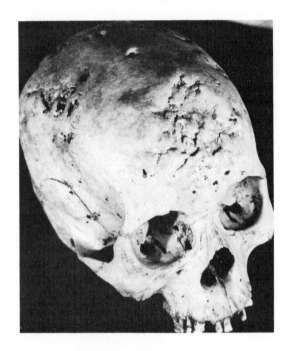

course. Venereal syphilis is one of several related skin diseases. In fact, one of the early signs of venereal syphilis is the appearance of sores and lesions on the skin. When the disease is untreated and advances into its final stages, the entire body is affected and death often results. By this point, venereal syphilis can affect skeletal tissue. Figure 16.8 shows the skull of a prehistoric Eskimo who had venereal syphilis for a long period of time. The lesions at the top of the skull are characteristic of this disease.

Skeletal evidence of venereal syphilis helps us in understanding the origin and spread of this disease. Historical accounts show that venereal syphilis spread rapidly in Europe in the late fifteenth century. This date coincides with the start of European exploration of the New World. Following the settlement of European colonies in the Americas, it was also observed that many Native Americans had syphilis. Did the disease evolve in Europe and spread to the Americas? Did it first appear in the New World and spread to Europe following initial contact with European explorers? Or did it evolve at roughly the same time in several different parts of the world? We do not know the exact answer, but paleopathological research does show that many cases of venereal syphilis occurred in the New World before European contact. This evidence rules out the hypothesis that Europeans brought venereal syphilis to the New World (as they did measles and many other infectious diseases). Venereal syphilis appears to have evolved in the New World prior to European contact (Baker and Armelagos 1988).

The results of unintentional injuries, violence, and surgery are also apparent from paleopathological studies. Figure 16.9 shows the facial remains of a prehistoric Peruvian who suffered a nasal fracture and survived. The region above the nasal opening and between the eye orbits shows the fracture.

The study of paleopathology shows us that prehistoric humans practiced surgery. One of the most common forms of skeletal surgery for which we have paleopathological evidence is **trephination,** the removal of a section of bone from the skull. The reasons for prehistoric trephination are unknown, but they may include relieving cranial pressure following a blow to the head, as a cure for headaches, or to release various "demons" thought to be responsible for a variety of ailments. In any case, trephination was performed extensively in many prehistoric societies, sometimes repeatedly on the same person.

Prehistoric trephinations were performed by using flint tools to scrape or cut through the bone. Sometimes large pieces of bone were removed by making a series of cuts in the skull around a central region and

trephination Surgery involving the removal of a section of bone from the skull.

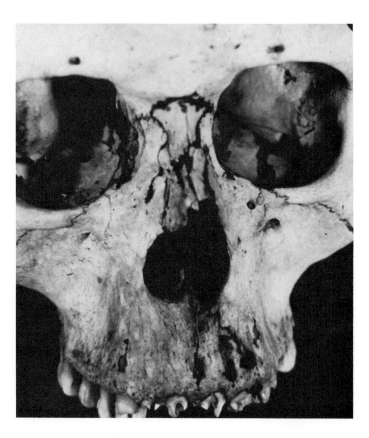

Figure 16.9

Nasal fracture in a prehistoric Peruvian. The affected area shows signs of healing, indicating that this individual survived the initial trauma. (Photo by Mary Edgecomb, Courtesy San Diego Museum of Man)

Figure 16.10

Top view of a prehistoric Mexican who had two trephinations. The hole on the right side healed, but the hole on the left side became infected.

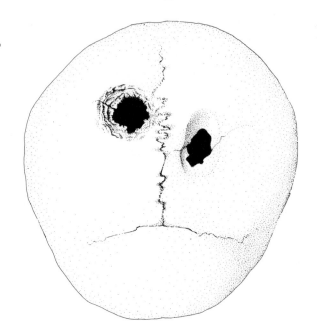

then lifting off that portion (Wilkinson 1975). Figure 16.10 shows the skull of a prehistoric Mexican who had two separate trephinations. The one on the right side of the skull shows signs of healing, but the one on the left shows characteristic signs of infection. It is possible that this second trephination killed the person.

Trephination has been a common practice among many peoples, including Central Americans, South Americans, and Europeans. Despite the obvious dangers of cranial trauma, shock, and postoperative infection, many individuals survived the operation. Some even survived multiple trephinations that removed much of the cranial bone (see Figure 16.11). In one study of trephination in Peru, it is estimated that up to 75 percent of the subjects recovered from the operation (Wood 1979). Given the nature of the tools and techniques involved in trephination, this is an impressive survival rate. Such survival also suggests some knowledge of handling pain and infection.

Case study: The transition to agriculture. Paleopathological research can provide significant information about the health and disease of individuals in prehistoric societies. Such studies also tell us about the evolution of disease in human populations by looking at varying rates of diseases and showing how they relate to known ecological and cultural changes.

The transition from hunting and gathering to agriculture has been studied for a number of prehistoric populations. Paleopathological analyses have been used to determine what changes, if any, have occurred in the health of human populations because of this change in subsistence. As we saw earlier in this chapter, major ecological changes are associated with the transition from hunting and gathering to agriculture. Increased population size and sedentary lifestyle increase the probability of infectious diseases spreading rapidly throughout a population. Agriculture provides more food to support more people, but it also introduces problems of dietary deficiencies.

A number of studies have looked at the effect of agriculture on overall health in prehistoric societies by means of several paleopathological measures. One measure is the frequency of **dental hypoplasias,** defects in the enamel of teeth because of stress. Changes in diet, and other factors that disrupt the growth process, often leave traces by producing dental enamel that is pitted and discolored. In their study of prehistoric North American populations, Goodman and colleagues (1980) found that the frequency of dental hypoplasias increased over time as the population became more dependent on the harvesting of corn. The dental evidence suggests that increased stress accompanied the development of agriculture, presumably because of the increase in infectious diseases and increased reliance on a single food crop.

Some studies have shown similar results to those of Goodman, and others have not. In her study of health in the prehistoric Valley of Oaxaca, Mexico, Hodges (1987) did not find any significant increase in dental hypoplasias as the populations became more dependent on agriculture.

dental hypoplasias Defects in the enamel of teeth, resulting from environmental stress, such as poor nutrition or infectious disease.

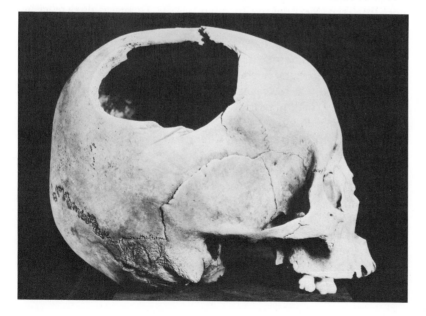

Figure 16.11

A massive trephination in a prehistoric Peruvian. (Field Museum of Natural History, Chicago, neg. no. 74689)

kuru An infectious disease once found in areas of New Guinea that attacked the central nervous system and was spread by coming into contact with the brain tissue of an infected person.

Two factors in Oaxaca, however, may have prevented the expected health decline. First, archaeological evidence shows that the population continued to rely on a diversified diet even after the intensification of agriculture. This may have prevented extensive reliance on a few food items. Second, the maximum possible size of the population was not reached, so the environment was not overly burdened. These two studies, and others, show that changes in disease patterns caused by agriculture may differ according to specific cultures and ecologies.

Studies of Historical and Contemporary Populations

Let us now look at several case studies of disease in historical and contemporary populations. These studies illustrate the interaction between biology and culture in the disease process.

Kuru in New Guinea. **Kuru** is an infectious disease that was once fairly common among the Fore tribe of highland New Guinea. Kuru is caused by a slow virus with a long incubation period. It attacks the nervous system, leading to tremors and convulsions, loss of coordination and movement, and ultimately death (Figure 16.12). The Fore believed that kuru was caused by sorcery (Lindenbaum 1979).

When scientists first encountered kuru, it was a baffling disease that was more frequent among adults (63 percent) than children (37 percent). Among children, roughly the same number of males and females were affected. Among adults, however, women were 25 times more likely to get kuru than men (McElroy and Townsend 1989). There was also a tendency, although not definite, for kuru to run in families.

What could cause a disease to have such a strange pattern of incidence? Before kuru was identified as a slow virus, some believed it was a genetic disease, perhaps partly linked to sex. Further research showed it was an infection that was spread through cannibalism. Among the Fore, to eat the bodies of dead relatives was a sign of respect. The adult women, along with some children, were responsible for the dissection and preparation of the corpse. Thus, they were more likely to come into contact with infected tissues (especially the brain) than adult men. The virus is transmitted by contact with, and inhalation in the vicinity of, the corpse. Adult Fore males had first priority in access to protein from hunts and tended to avoid cannibalism, which they felt was the province of women (Lindenbaum 1979). Thus, cultural beliefs reduced the risk of kuru among adult men. After the early 1960s, the incidence of kuru declined as the New Guinea government took steps to eradicate cannibalism.

The kuru study shows how important an understanding of cultural beliefs and behaviors is in assessing the spread of disease in a population.

Figure 16.12

A victim of kuru bracing herself with both arms to maintain balance.   (Photo by Dr. D. Carleton Gajdusek)

Even though laboratory research was invaluable in showing what caused the disease, cultural studies were needed to understand its complete epidemiology. The study also shows us how sometimes the most bizarre studies may have practical application. Because of his work on kuru, Carleton Gajdusek won a Nobel Prize for the study of slow viruses. This in turn led to more research on viruses with long incubation periods. Today, a rising health threat throughout the world is AIDS, which is linked to a virus that has a relatively long incubation period. Though the diseases are dissimilar in many ways, the study of kuru did contribute to the understanding of viral diseases in human populations.

Smallpox epidemics in the Åland Islands. The exceptionally detailed historical records available from the Åland Islands (see Chapter 5) allow analysis of changing patterns of epidemics over long time periods. The study by Mielke and colleagues (1984) of smallpox epidemics on the Åland Islands provides an interesting view of changing patterns of death over

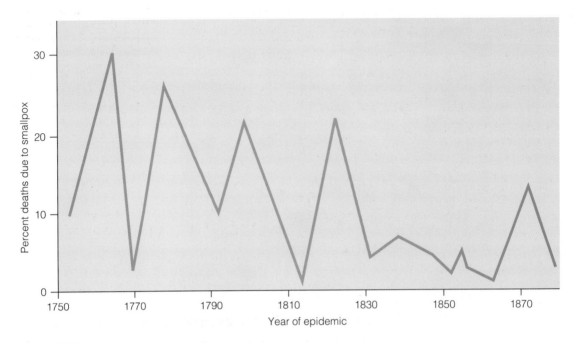

Figure 16.13

Smallpox epidemics in the
Åland Islands, Finland. This
graph shows the percentage
of all deaths due to smallpox
plotted against the midpoints
of the years of epidemics.
Epidemic years are defined as
those during which at least
five people died of smallpox.
(Source of data: Mielke et al.
[1984:281])

time. Figure 16.13 shows the percentage of all deaths due to smallpox over
some 130 years. Only "epidemic" years are shown, defined as those during
which at least 5 people died of smallpox. The actual number of smallpox
deaths varied from 5 to 250 during epidemic years. Figure 16.13 shows a
typical epidemic cycle at the beginning: the percentage of deaths due to
smallpox increase and decrease rapidly. The periods between epidemics
reflect the amount of time needed for a sufficient number of nonimmune
individuals to accumulate so that the epidemic can peak again.

Smallpox vaccinations were introduced into the Åland Islands in 1805
but were not widespread until after the 1820s. Note that in Figure 16.13
the percentage of deaths due to smallpox decreases after 1820. Mielke and
colleagues also found that a greater proportion of adults died from smallpox after vaccinations were introduced. It is likely that many individuals
vaccinated as children lost their immunity in adulthood. Revaccination
was urged, but the effects of this program were not felt until the 1870s and
1880s.

Demographic factors influenced the spread of smallpox epidemics
within the Åland Islands. Populations that were larger and less isolated
had the greatest proportion of epidemics. This finding makes sense in
terms of what we know about how epidemics spread. As noted earlier,
epidemics are more likely in larger populations because of the greater
number of susceptible individuals. Also, populations that experience a
great deal of migration are less isolated and therefore more likely to be
exposed to epidemics. Besides showing how cultural and demographic

factors affect epidemics, the Åland Islands study demonstrates the valuable role death records and other historical data play in epidemiologic studies.

The "New World syndrome." Kenneth Weiss and colleagues (1984) have applied the label **New World syndrome** to a set of noninfectious diseases that appear in elevated frequencies among Native Americans and groups with substantial Native-American admixture. These diseases include noninsulin-dependent diabetes, gallstones, gall bladder cancer, and increased obesity. Rates for these diseases tend to be highest in Native-American populations. Among admixed populations, such as Mexicans and Mexican Americans, the disease rates vary with the amount of Native-American admixture. In other words, the more Native-American ancestry a person has, the greater the risk of developing these diseases, other factors being equal. In addition, all these diseases tend to run in families.

These three characteristics point to genetic susceptibility to the diseases among Native-American peoples. Noninfectious diseases, however, are affected not only by genetic predispositions but also by environmental factors. In the case of the New World syndrome, rates of these diseases have increased dramatically since World War II. To understand this increase, we need to look not only at genetic factors but also at changing environmental conditions.

Weiss and colleagues argue there is strong evidence that genetic susceptibilities to the New World syndrome diseases existed in the earliest inhabitants of the Americas. If such genetic predispositions are unique among New World populations, then there must have been rapid genetic change since the initial occupation of the Americas by migrants from Asia. Weiss and colleagues think that the genes that currently predispose individuals to the New World syndrome were originally advantageous. Today, however, these same genetic factors are generally disadvantageous. Weiss and colleagues therefore ask the question: "What kind of gene has disadvantage now but advantage among northern hunter-gatherers?" (1984:171). They suggest that the relationship of all diseases in the syndrome to nutrient utilization provides a possible answer: these genes conferred changes in metabolism, allowing more efficient use of food resources and fat storage. Given the importance of fat resources in hunting-gathering populations, particularly during pregnancy and nursing, such genes would be advantageous in an environment characterized by frequent food shortages.

Today, however, these same genetic factors are proving disadvantageous to individuals with Native-American ancestry. The reason may lie in the continued "westernization" of these populations and the associated changes in diet. An increase in carbohydrates and fats in the diet will result in greater fat storage, leading to obesity and increased risk for other noninfectious disorders. Populations without Native-American ancestry have also shown increases in certain noninfectious diseases because of changes in culture and lifestyle. Native Americans and related populations, how-

New World syndrome A set of noninfectious diseases that appears in elevated frequencies in persons of Native-American ancestry.

Figure 16.14

Annual age-adjusted male death rate for motor vehicle incidents for New York State outside of New York City, 1978–1982, in five groups of varying population density. The five groups range from rural to urban. Note the death rate is highest in the rural group and decreases in more urban groups.   (Source of data: Relethford and Mahoney [1991:114])

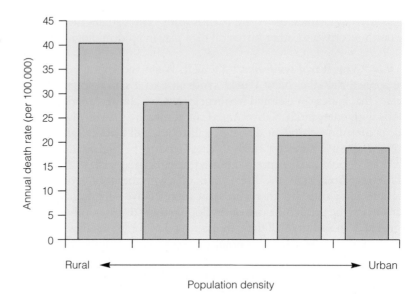

ever, show even greater increases because of their additional genetic susceptibility.

Unintentional-injury deaths in the United States. Unintentional injuries include trauma caused by motor vehicle crashes, pedestrian injury, falls, fire, drowning, and ingestion of poisonous substances, among others. The use of the term *unintentional* distinguishes these traumas from self-inflicted forms, such as suicide, or those inflicted on others, such as assault or homicide. The term *accident* is frequently used to describe unintentional injuries, but it is somewhat misleading. "Accident" implies that such injuries occur at random and can occur with equal probability among all people. This is not the case. Just as infectious and noninfectious diseases have certain risk factors associated with them, so do injuries.

As an example, consider deaths from motor vehicle incidents (including both vehicular crashes and vehicles hitting pedestrians). These deaths are more likely to occur in some groups than others, as Figure 16.14 illustrates. The annual male death rate per 100,000 for motor vehicle incidents in New York State outside of New York City between 1978 and 1982 is shown for five groups of varying population density. These groups range from the most rural communities to the suburbs to large cities. The graph shows clearly that motor vehicle deaths are more likely among rural residents than elsewhere. The higher mortality in rural areas (even after adjustment for miles driven) seems to be related to poorer road conditions, higher driving speeds, dangerous passing, and perhaps slower access to emergency medical services (Relethford and Mahoney 1991).

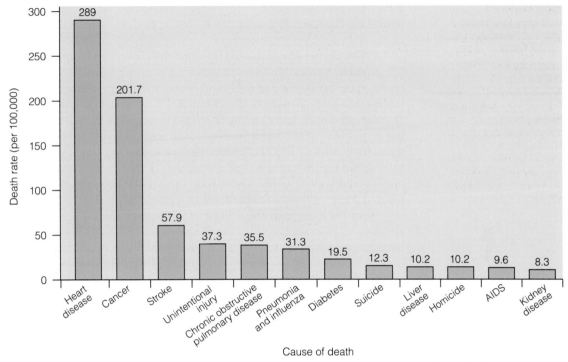

Cause of death

Figure 16.15

The 12 leading causes of death in the United States in 1990. (Source of data: Haub [1992])

Certain factors affect different types of unintentional injury in the same manner. Death rates from motor vehicle incidents, fire, and falling are all high in the elderly. This common pattern may reflect certain physiologic characteristics of the elderly, such as poorer reflexes, eyesight, and physical fitness. One common characteristic across many forms of unintentional injury deaths is the higher rate among males, especially young males. In a study of injury mortality in New York State, Relethford (1991b) found that the greatest sex difference in injury deaths occurred among young adults. Among 15- to 24-year-olds, males are over 3 times more likely to die in a motor vehicle incident, almost 9 times more likely to die from falling, 2 times more likely to die in a fire, and over 10 times more likely to drown than females. Possible reasons include a greater likelihood of engaging in risk-taking behaviors among males, as well as greater use of alcohol and drugs, both of which are frequently implicated in injury deaths.

The study of unintentional injury is relatively new but offers opportunities for anthropological investigation, since injuries relate to social, psychological, and demographic factors. Such study is needed, given that unintentional injury is the fourth leading cause of death in the United States (Figure 16.15). Also, unintentional injury is the *leading* cause of death between the ages of 1 and 44 (Rice and MacKenzie 1989). Finally,

AIDS (Acquired Immune Deficiency Syndrome) A fatal viral disease that results in the breakdown of the body's immune defense system.

it has been estimated that for every injury death, there are 16 nonfatal, but potentially disabling, injuries.

AIDS. At present, **acquired immune deficiency syndrome (AIDS)** is a growing medical problem in many parts of the world. This disease results in the breakdown of the body's immune defense system, ultimately leading to death. Research has linked AIDS to infection from HIV-1 (human immunodeficiency virus type 1). The origin of HIV-1 is unclear, but it may have started as a zoonosis. The virus is transmitted through sexual intercourse, particularly anal intercourse. AIDS is also transmitted by transfusions of contaminated blood and by sharing of contaminated needles among drug users. The disease can also be transmitted from an infected pregnant woman to her fetus.

Since 1981 through the middle of 1991, over 170,000 people had acquired AIDS in the United States (Brookmeyer 1991). AIDS is currently the eleventh leading cause of death in the United States (see Figure 16.15). In the United States, the primary risk groups have been homosexual and bisexual men and intravenous drug users. In addition, individuals who have sexual contact with people in these high risk groups also have elevated risk of acquiring AIDS (Curran et al. 1988). So far, males appear to be at greater risk than females.

In other parts of the world the epidemiologic pattern of AIDS risk is different. In much of Africa, for example, the primary spread of AIDS is through heterosexual contact (McGrath 1990). While some feel that the AIDS epidemic is slowing down in the United States, the epidemic in Africa is still increasing. There are an estimated six million adults and half a million children with AIDS in Africa (Dixon and McBride 1992).

Even though AIDS is a recent disease, it has already had major effects on American culture. The threat of such a deadly disease has led to proposed quarantines, increased discrimination against homosexuals, and the burning of houses of AIDS-infected children. Perhaps the greatest change has been a reduction in sexual activity with multiple partners or with partners whose backgrounds are not known.

In sum, the current spread of AIDS shows us a clear example of how a disease can affect society both biologically and culturally. This is not a new phenomenon. During the Middle Ages, the Black Death continued to have a profound effect on culture long after the epidemics were over. Images of death and despair endured in the arts and in literature.

By studying diseases such as AIDS and the Black Death, medical anthropologists not only contribute to an understanding of the spread of diseases but also show us the relationships between disease and society. We cannot view health and disease as an isolated segment of our total lives. They affect all aspects of living.

Forensic anthropology. Biological anthropologists often provide forensic analysis for police departments and state and federal agencies.

Forensic anthropologists carry out much of their work as consultants to various law enforcement agencies. For example, Dr. Douglas Ubelaker, who works at the National Museum of Natural History at the Smithsonian Institution, is a consultant to the Federal Bureau of Investigation. In his recent book *Bones: A Forensic Detective's Casebook,* co-authored with Henry Scammell, he describes the methods of forensic anthropology, illustrating their use in homicide and missing-persons investigations.

In medical terms, forensics is the identification of dead people. For example, a plane crash or other catastrophe may leave few remains, and forensic analysis can be used to identify the dead. Dental remains can be compared to dental records (teeth and jaws preserve well under such conditions, and most people have unique dental records). Another area is the discovery of skeletal remains. Who was the person whose bones were found? Can these bones be linked to a list of missing persons?

If sufficient remains exist, such as the pelvis, the sex of the individual can be determined. Analyzing the teeth and skeletal bones provides estimates for the age at death. The presence of skeletal fractures or breaks may often provide information on cause of death or may be used in comparison with medical records.

Even when an entire skeleton is not available, clues about sex, age, and physical appearance can be found. If, for example, only a single long bone (such as the femur) is found, an estimate can still be made of a person's height. This is possible because there is a strong relationship between leg length and height, allowing the use of statistical estimation methods.

These are only a few of the examples in which experts in human skeletal anatomy can offer assistance in identifying the dead (Figure 16.16).

Figure 16.16

Anthropologist Michael Park examining a prehistoric human skull. (Courtesy Michael Park, Central Connecticut State University)

SUMMARY

Epidemiology, the study of disease patterns, is an interdisciplinary field that draws on the knowledge of a variety of biological, physical, and social sciences. Anthropology contributes to an understanding of epidemiology by bringing comparative, evolutionary, and holistic perspectives to the study of health and disease. Within biological anthropology, many researchers are interested in the relationship among genetics, environment, culture, and the biological manifestations of a disease.

Anthropology's comparative approach allows us to look at the relationships of health and disease to cultural as well as biological evolution. Hunting-gathering populations have different patterns of disease than agricultural or industrialized populations. Ecological differences account for much of this difference. In hunting-gathering populations, the group size is too small to sustain large epidemics; the major causes of death are from accidents and infections from animals. In agricultural societies, population size is larger, the group is sedentary, and there are often problems in waste disposal and water supply; all these factors result in increased epidemics of infectious disease.

Industrialized nations have gone through an "epidemiologic transition": the primary causes of death have shifted again, from infectious to noninfectious diseases. Life expectancy has also increased, primarily because of the control or elimination of childhood infectious diseases. The reduction in infectious diseases means more of us live to older ages, and as a consequence we are more likely to develop chronic noninfectious diseases. This shift also means that we must expand our views regarding the control of disease. For a century we have thought of solving infectious disease problems by means of an antibiotic or vaccination when in fact improved hygiene is at least as important. The noninfectious diseases, such as diabetes and heart disease, do not have a single cause. As such, we can no longer count on the development of a "magic bullet" (i.e., a single cure) in our search to cure disease. Genetic, environmental, dietary, and other factors affect the relative risk for these diseases. We can modify these factors, but to what extent is still not clear.

Supplemental Readings

Lilienfeld, A., and D. E. Lilienfeld. 1980. *Foundations of Epidemiology.* 2d ed. New York: Oxford University Press. A well-written introduction to the field of epidemiological research, presenting the methods of epidemiology along with numerous examples.

McElroy, A., and P. K. Townsend. 1989. *Medical Anthropology in Ecological Perspective.* 2d ed. Boulder, Colo.: Westview Press.

Moore, L. G., P. W. Van Arsdale, J. E. Glittenberg, and R. A. Aldrich. 1980. *The Biocultural Basis of Health: Expanding Views of Medical Anthropology.* Prospect Heights, Ill.: Waveland Press.

Wood, C. S. 1979. *Human Sickness and Health: A Biocultural View.* Mountain View, Calif.: Mayfield. The final three works in this listing provide a good introduction to the field of medical anthropology both from cultural and biological perspectives.

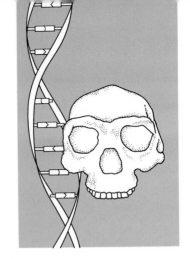

CHAPTER **17**

The Demography
of Human
Populations

The interrelationship of biology and culture in human populations is perhaps most clearly visible in demographic patterns. **Demography** is the study of the size, composition, and distribution of human populations. Like epidemiology, demography is an interdisciplinary subject. Demography is studied by anthropologists, biologists, geographers, historians, economists, sociologists, and others.

As with the study of human health and disease, anthropology brings to demography comparative, evolutionary, and holistic perspectives. Anthropologists do not focus only on demographic processes within a single society, such as the United States. We examine all types of societies, from hunter-gatherers to industrialized nations. We also look at demographic processes in an evolutionary context, seeking to understand demographic shifts in the evolution of our species. Using a holistic perspective, we link demographic processes with patterns of biological and cultural variation.

The Study of Demography

Demographic studies focus on the measurement of three characteristics: fertility, mortality, and migration.

demography The study of the size, composition, and distribution of human populations.

487

fertility Actual reproduction: the number of births per individual.

fecundity Potential reproduction: the number of people capable of having children.

mortality Death.

Demographic Measures

In literate human populations these factors are often revealed in census records and similar data. Birth records, for example, provide data for computing different measures of fertility. Death records also provide information for determining the rate of deaths, the age at death, and the cause of death. In societies where written records are not kept, anthropologists gather demographic data from interviews.

Fertility. The measure of fertility provides us with information on the rate of actual births in a population. When we count birth records or interview people to find out how many children they have had, we are measuring the **fertility** of a population. On the other hand, we are also sometimes interested in measurements of **fecundity,** or the number of individuals capable of having children. Measurements of fertility and fecundity are not always the same; people that are capable of having children do not necessarily have them.

The analysis of fertility is particularly interesting to biological anthropologists because fertility reflects both biological and cultural variation. Some individuals may have more children than others because of biological differences in fertility. One example, discussed in Chapter 5, is incompatibilities in blood types. In addition, some individuals may have more, or fewer, children for cultural reasons. For example, economic factors play a role in determining fertility. Many North American middle- and upper-class couples are deliberately having fewer children today. Part of the reason is that many people postpone having their first child for a number of years to finish an education or become established in a career.

Although fertility is affected by both biological and cultural factors, changes in fertility also affect the biology and culture of a population. For example, an increase in the number of births in a population may lead to an increase in population size. Larger populations require more food, are less affected by genetic drift, and are more likely to experience epidemics of infectious disease. Such changes can, in turn, further affect fertility. The relationship between fertility and biological and cultural variation in populations can best be described in terms of a feedback loop. Fertility is affected by, and causes effects on, biology and culture.

Mortality. The measurement of **mortality** is the measurement of death. Like fertility, mortality can be influenced by biological and cultural factors. The age at death and the cause of death may relate to biological factors, such as susceptibility to certain diseases. Culture can also affect the timing and cause of death. Differences in social class may affect quality of health care. Warfare may increase the probability of early death, as will hazardous employment. A long history of drug use or poor nutrition also affects the probability of death.

As discussed in the last chapter, measures of life expectancy can tell us something about the average age of death and, by extension, about the average health of individuals in a population. Life expectancy is most often determined from a **life table,** a compilation of the number of deaths for different age groups in a population. Both demographers and the life insurance industry use these records, which could more accurately be called "death tables" because they provide a measure of the probability of dying by a given age. The data in life tables can be used to compute the life expectancy of individuals at different ages. One measure, discussed in the last chapter, is life expectancy at birth. This measure provides a good index of overall mortality and health in a population.

A given life expectancy does not mean everyone will live to that age. It is only an average. Many people die before their original life expectancy and many live beyond it. As an average measure, however, life expectancy does tell us something about the net patterns of mortality in a population. If, for example, 40 percent of a population dies in the first year of life, the overall life expectancy for the population will be low. Reduction of the number of infant deaths will lead to an increase in average life expectancy.

Mortality rates are strongly related to age. Plotting death rates against age gives a characteristics curve, as shown in Figure 17.1 for the United States in 1970. Death rates drop quickly after the first year of life, remaining relatively low and constant through midadulthood. Death rates increase rapidly with age among the elderly. The *exact* shape of the curve will vary from one population to another. In underdeveloped nations, for example, infant mortality will be higher. The overall shape of the curve is basically the same in all human populations (Gage 1989).

life table A table that provides an estimate of the probability that an individual will die by a certain age, used to estimate life expectancy.

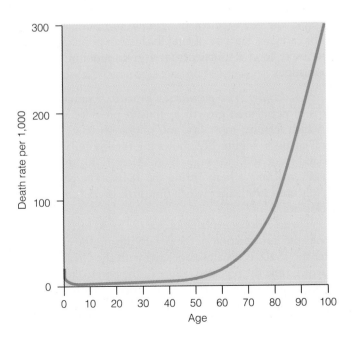

Figure 17.1

Mortality rates in the United States in 1970 as a function of age. This figure shows the typical mortality curve for human populations. Death rates decrease rapidly after the first year of life and increase again among the elderly. (Source of data: Fries and Crapo [1981:146])

migration The movement of individuals from one population to another.

natural increase Number of births minus number of deaths.

carrying capacity The maximum population size capable of being supported in a given environment.

Migration. **Migration** is the movement of people, normally for long periods of time, from one location (village, city, state) to another. As with fertility and mortality, migration is affected by biological and cultural factors and in turn has an effect on biology and culture. Examples of the relationship of migration to biology and culture have been discussed in Chapters 3 and 5 in the context of gene flow.

Population Growth

The overall size of a population results from the net effects of fertility, mortality, and migration.

Components of population growth. Births increase the population size and deaths decrease the population size. Migration can either increase or decrease the population size, depending on whether more people move into a population (increase) or leave the population (decrease). The amount a population can grow, or reduce, is expressed as

Change in population size = births − deaths ± migrants

If we ignore the effect of migration for a moment, the change in population size because of **natural increase** is the number of births minus the number of deaths. If more people are born than die in a certain period of time, then the population grows. If the number of deaths exceeds the number of births, the population size declines.

Under ideal conditions, human populations may grow at an exponential rate. There is a limit, however, to growth in any population, dictated by available land and food resources. This limit, called the **carrying capacity**, can change, given certain ecological or technological changes. For example, the development of agriculture resulted in a dramatic increase in the carrying capacity of land for human populations. The ability to extract more food resources from a given amount of land allowed larger populations.

Case study: Irish population growth. Examination of historical patterns of population growth in Ireland provides an example of the ways in which fertility, mortality, and migration relate to ecological and cultural changes. Figure 17.2 shows the total population of the Republic of Ireland from 1687 through 1966. After 1700, the population increased rapidly, reaching a peak during the 1840s. The population then declined rapidly until 1900, after which time little overall change in population size took place.

The traditional explanation for the rapid increase of Ireland's population is the introduction of the potato during the early 1700s. The decline after the 1840s is usually associated with the Great Famine (1846–1851), at which time the repeated failure of the potato crop led to large numbers of deaths and migrations. The full story of Irish population growth is a bit more complicated, involving agriculture, marriage patterns, and land inheritance.

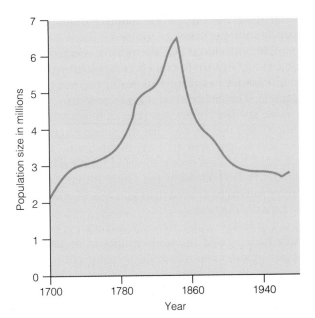

Figure 17.2

Population growth in the Republic of Ireland from 1687 to 1966. (Sources of data: 1687–1791 [Connell 1950], 1821–1966 [Kennedy 1973])

Before the 1700s, agriculture in Ireland had been severely limited because of hilly terrain and large sections of bog. As a result, the carrying capacity of the population was limited. Though fertility among the largely Catholic population of Ireland had been moderately high per married person, many people did not marry, and marriages were usually late. Marriages were most often arranged by the parents of the bride and groom as part of an economic contract. A common prerequisite for marriage in rural areas was for the groom to have land and the bride to have a dowry. Most men acquired land through inheritance, often late in life because of the father's delay in passing the land on to a son. Because the agricultural output of the land was low, in most cases only one son could inherit the land. The other sons tended to leave or had to remain unmarried (Arensberg and Kimball 1968). In either case, overall population growth was kept in check by the fact that few men and women married. Given the religious rules on premarital and extramarital sex, almost all births resulted from marriages. A limit on the number of marriages meant a limit on fertility and population growth.

The introduction of the potato changed these patterns. Potatoes can grow in a wide variety of environments and provide ample nutrition. An increased emphasis on the potato allowed more efficient use of the land. Now fathers could subdivide their land and pass it on to more than one son. Some of the land was also relinquished earlier (Connell 1950). As a result, marriages became more frequent and at an earlier age, which led to many more births and population growth. This situation continued for several generations, and more and more sons required more and more land.

age-sex structure A measure of the composition of a population in terms of the numbers of males and females at different ages.

population pyramid A diagram of the age-sex structure.

Family plots were repeatedly subdivided until families were living on extremely small portions.

The introduction of the potato, combined with cultural views on large family size, led to rapid population growth in Ireland. It also resulted in a precarious ecology. Failures in the potato crop had serious consequences. The potato crop was often destroyed by blight, and the Great Famine saw five continuous years of blight with no relief. Compounding the problem was the fact that the potato crop was used not only for food but also to pay rent to English landlords. During the Great Famine, roughly 1.5 million people died and 1 million left the country (Woodham-Smith 1962). Following the Great Famine, the system returned to an earlier pattern of delayed marriage, less frequent marriage, and fewer subdivisions of the land.

The Irish example shows how changing patterns of fertility and mortality had resulted in rapid changes in population size. Migration also played an important role in the regulation of population size. Even before the Great Famine, large numbers of people left Ireland for economic opportunities in England or the United States. These early migrants were often able to provide aid to families during the Great Famine, thus allowing them to leave the country. Migration out of Ireland became very frequent during the nineteenth and twentieth centuries. In fact, the rate of natural increase (births minus deaths) since the late nineteenth century has been positive. If natural increase is positive, then the population grows. If people had not moved out of the country, then the population would have gotten larger (Aalen 1963).

The Age-Sex Structure of Populations

Demographers also study the composition of populations. Who makes up the population, in terms of sex, age, ethnicity, occupation, and religion, among other characteristics? Most demographic studies focus special attention on the number of males and females per age group in a population, that is, on the **age-sex structure** of a population. A device known as a **population pyramid** is the best way to describe a population's age-sex structure at a particular point in time. The population pyramid is a graph showing the numbers of both sexes at different age groups.

Developing nations. Figure 17.3 shows the age-sex structure of developing regions of the world in 1984 (those where industrial development is fairly recent, such as Mexico, Cuba, and Taiwan). The bottom axis of the graph shows the number of males on the left and the number of females on the right. The vertical axis represents different age groups, from 0 to 4 years of age in the first group, to 80-plus years of age in the top group. The population pyramid allows a succinct display of basic demographic patterns. It is obvious that infants and children greatly outnumber young adults or the elderly.

The age-sex structure of developing nations illustrates the nature of fertility and mortality in these populations. High fertility results in the

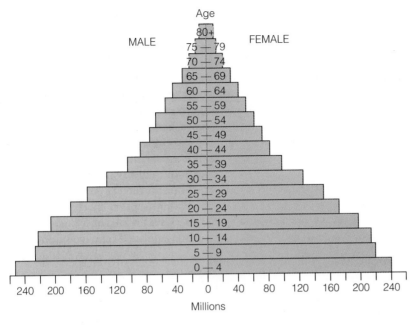

Figure 17.3

The age-sex structure of developing regions of the world in 1984. (Source: Bouvier [1984:12]. Courtesy of the Population Reference Bureau, Inc., Washington, D.C., and United Nations, *Demographic Indicators of Countries: Estimates and Projections as Assessed in 1980* [New York: 1982], pp. 61 and 63, data for 1985)

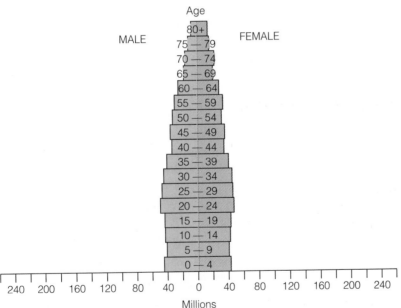

Figure 17.4

The age-sex structure of developed regions of the world in 1984. (Source: Bouvier [1984:12]. Courtesy of the Population Reference Bureau, Inc., Washington, D.C., and United Nations, *Demographic Indicators of Countries: Estimates and Projections as Assessed in 1980* [New York: 1982], pp. 61 and 63, data for 1985)

large numbers of people in young age groups. The pyramid shape results from the fact that fewer people live to the next age group. Developing nations typically have high fertility rates, combined with a reduction in mortality, leading to high rates of population growth.

Developed nations. The age-sex structure of a developed nation, such as the United States or Sweden, is quite different. Figure 17.4 shows the

postpartum taboo Behavior that limits sexual intercourse following the birth of a child.

age-sex structure of the developed regions of the world in 1984. This population pyramid is more rectangular in shape. The largest section of the population is not infants and young children but young adults. This shape results from a reduction in infant mortality combined with lower fertility. Fewer people are born, making the lower age groups smaller. Because more people live longer, the older age groups stay fairly numerous. The many biological and cultural implications of this change in the age-sex structure from developing nations to developed nations will be discussed later in this chapter.

Case Studies of Fertility in Human Populations

Case studies of human mortality have been discussed in earlier chapters, particularly Chapters 5 and 16. Specific studies of migration have also been discussed, especially in Chapter 5. This section focuses on case studies of human fertility.

Birth Spacing among the !Kung

The !Kung San are a group of hunters and gatherers who live in the Kalahari Desert in southern Africa (the "!" preceding their name indicates a clicking sound made in their language). The !Kung have long been of interest to anthropologists. They are one of the groups whose way of life has been used as a model for understanding early human evolution. Although the use of the !Kung as a model has been recently challenged (Lewin 1988), demographic studies of this group are still valuable in understanding fertility control in hunting and gathering populations.

Except for problems caused by occasional droughts, the !Kung are adequately nourished and do not have very high levels of mortality. Because the !Kung do not use any type of modern contraceptive, we would expect fertility to be high, leading to population growth beyond the limits of the environment. What controls on fertility exist in such societies? The !Kung do have some control over fertility, as evidenced by the fact that the average interval between births is 44 months (Potts 1988). This long spacing between births serves to moderate fertility and population growth.

Cultural beliefs can have an effect on fertility by limiting sexual intercourse. A number of societies practice various forms of **postpartum taboos,** prohibitions on sexual activity by women who have recently given birth. Infanticide, the killing of newborns, has also been practiced in a number of human groups.

One major factor in fertility control among the !Kung is breast feeding. When a woman nurses her child, hormonal changes take place that act to prevent ovulation, especially when body fat levels are low. This finding had been previously dismissed by scientists who had noted many cases of women returning to their monthly cycle of ovulation before their child was weaned. As a result, many Western physicians caution women against counting on breast feeding as an effective contraceptive measure.

The case of the !Kung is different because the pattern of nursing is different from that practiced in Western nations and because their body fat levels are lower. In the United States today, nursing tends to occur for long periods of time (10 to 20 minutes) several times a day. Among the !Kung, breast feeding may occur as frequently as every 15 minutes but for only a minute or so. In terms of overall time spent nursing per day, Western women nurse more than !Kung women. The !Kung women, however, nurse much more often. According to Peter Ellison, the frequency of nursing is the important component that acts to prevent ovulation among the !Kung (Ackerman 1987). This effect is compounded by the fact that !Kung women may nurse their children for several years, as opposed to a typical Western pattern of six months to a year.

Cultural variation in breast feeding behaviors has an impact on human fertility. The relationship between frequency of nursing, amount of nursing, and ovulation will depend on other cultural variables. In the United States, the !Kung pattern of nursing is not always possible, particularly when mothers have jobs outside the home. What works for one culture does not necessarily work for another.

The relationship of breast feeding and fertility is also important in understanding some of the population problems experienced by many Third World nations. In societies where modern contraceptives are not always available, breast feeding provides some regulation of fertility. From the 1950s (and even earlier) until recently, women in the United States had generally abandoned breast feeding and adopted bottle feeding. For many, bottle feeding was seen as a more "modern" and "scientific" way to care for children. Bottle feeding also avoided potential embarrassment (usually to men) when women would feed their children in public. After World War II, many women in undeveloped and developing nations quickly adopted this strategy in an attempt to emulate Western ways. As a result, the contraceptive benefits of breast feeding were lost, contributing with other factors to an increase in population growth. In many Third World nations, the shift to bottle feeding has also resulted in major health problems. Quite often, uncontaminated water was not available for making the formula. Economic hardships contributed further, as women would dilute the expensive formula to make it last longer. The result was inadequate nutrition (McElroy and Townsend 1989). The history of the introduction of bottle feeding to these societies has led to more careful consideration of potential effects of importing new products and behaviors into other cultures.

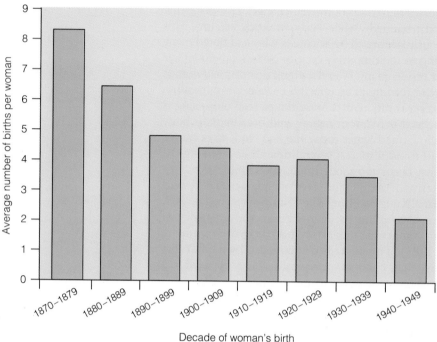

Figure 17.5

Fertility change in the Mennonite population of Goessel, Kansas.   (Source of data: Stevenson et al. [1989:104])

Decreasing Fertility among the Mennonites

The Amish, Hutterites, and Mennonites are Anabaptist groups that were part of a European religious movement in the 1500s advocating the separation of church and state. Frequent persecution for this belief forced many families to move elsewhere, including North America. The cultural isolation of these groups helped maintain a traditional lifestyle. Studies of them show very high fertility levels, in part due to avoidance of contraception. Although the Anabaptist groups have remained isolated on average, some groups have experienced greater amounts of cultural contact and change.

Joan Stevenson and colleagues (1989) conducted a fertility study on three midwestern Mennonite communities. Mennonite groups moved into the American midwest during the 1870s and 1880s. Tracing the reproductive histories of women, Stevenson and her colleagues found that fertility had declined during the twentieth century. The results of their data from the Mennonite community of Goessel, Kansas, are shown in Figure 17.5. The average number of births per woman declined from 8.4 children for women born between 1870 and 1879 to 2.0 children for women born between 1940 and 1949. This decline is related to a drop in the average age of women at the time of their last birth (from 38 years in 1900 to 30 years by 1940). Because there was no change in mother's age at first birth, the decrease in the number of births is a function of a reduction of child-bearing years. That is, the women stopped having babies earlier in life and, as a result, ended up with fewer children.

The drop in fertility is also related to changing beliefs about contraception. Interviews with mothers in Goessel showed that the percentage of women who used birth control pills increased over time. The pills were often used to reduce fertility in later childbearing years. Another interesting finding was that women in the more culturally conservative Mennonite population of Meridian, Kansas, showed less of a decrease in fertility (from 7.9 births in 1870–1879 to 3.8 births in 1940–1949). The results of this study show that cultural change can rapidly change fertility levels. The comparison of Mennonite communities also shows that the effect of cultural change varies quite a bit among populations.

Infertility among the Herero

Not all human populations in the twentieth century show a reduction in fertility. Pennington and Harpending's (1991) study of the Herero, a pastoralist population in Botswana, Africa, shows evidence of an increase in fertility. Figure 17.6 gives the total fertility rate for women during four periods of childbirth (the total fertility rate is an estimate of the number of births per woman after completing childbearing). Since the beginning of the twentieth century, Herero fertility rates have almost tripled.

The Herero study is particularly interesting because many similar groups have shown high fertility over time, whereas the Herero were previously characterized by relative infertility. Fifteen percent of the women interviewed over their years of reproductive age had no children. Pennington and Harpending have shown that the early Herero infertility was most likely due to pelvic inflammatory disease, caused by sexually transmitted

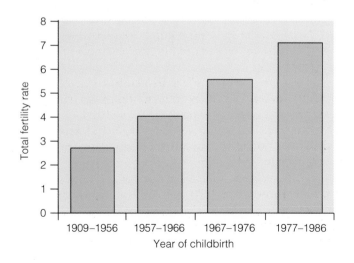

Figure 17.6

Fertility change among the Herero population of Botswana, Africa. The total fertility rate is an estimate of the total number of births after completion of child-bearing.   (Source of data: Pennington and Harpending [1991:139])

Baby Boom The increase in the number of births in the United States between 1946 and 1964.

bacteria. If not treated, this condition can cause infertility. The later increase in fertility rates (see Figure 17.6) corresponds to the wider availability of medical care and treatment. This study shows clearly how disease can affect fertility, perhaps more than once thought.

The Baby Boom in the United States

Following World War II, the population of the United States grew rapidly. Births became more numerous, leading to what demographers call the **Baby Boom,** an increase in the number of births between 1946 and 1964. Several social and economic reasons account for the Baby Boom. It was not simply the fact that men returning from war made up for lost time with their wives. Such an effect usually accompanies the end of a war and lasts for several years, and the Baby Boom was in fact much longer in duration (Figure 17.7).

The economic growth of the United States continued to increase rapidly following the end of World War II. As economic growth increases, so does the demand for labor. This demand is often met by new immigrants into a population. In the United States, however, restrictive laws had reduced the number of immigrants. The pool of available labor was also reduced by the fact that there had been fewer births in the 1920s and 1930s. Thus, fewer young men were available to fill vacancies. Women tended to be locked out of many occupations because of sexual bias. Though it is true that during the war many women took the place of men in the workforce, after the war the preference for women to remain at home raising children prevailed.

Figure 17.7

Changes in the rate of population growth in the United States from 1790 to 1900. The percentage of increase in population size from the previous decade is plotted against year. Note the reversal of the downward trend during the Baby Boom years.   (Source of data: U.S. Department of Commerce [1991])

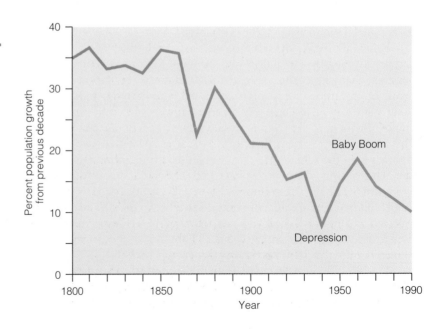

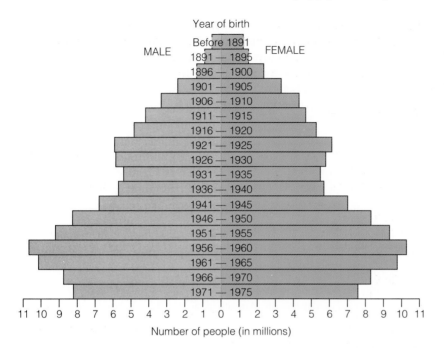

Year of birth

MALE   FEMALE

Before 1891
1891 — 1895
1896 — 1900
1901 — 1905
1906 — 1910
1911 — 1915
1916 — 1920
1921 — 1925
1926 — 1930
1931 — 1935
1936 — 1940
1941 — 1945
1946 — 1950
1951 — 1955
1956 — 1960
1961 — 1965
1966 — 1970
1971 — 1975

11 10 9 8 7 6 5 4 3 2 1 0 1 2 3 4 5 6 7 8 9 10 11

Number of people (in millions)

Figure 17.8

The age-sex structure of the United States in 1975. (From *Population: An Introduction to Concepts and Issues,* Second Edition, by John R. Weeks © 1978 by Wadsworth Publishing Company)

The lack of available labor meant that young men returning from the war had many excellent opportunities for employment. A good income meant that men could afford to marry and raise a family earlier than under lesser conditions. The economic conditions prevailing after World War II meant that a couple could have several children without lowering their standard of living (Weeks 1981). Marriages were earlier and the spacing between births was shorter than in previous times, both of which effects contributed to an increase in the birth rate.

Following 1958, the fertility rates in the United States began to decline. By roughly the mid-1960s, the Baby Boom was over. From this point on, changing economic conditions and greater educational and economic opportunities for women led to delayed marriage and childbirth along with a general desire for smaller families. By 1986, the average number of children per couple was 1.8 (Encyclopaedia Britannica 1988). This number is less than that required for replacement (two), but the population of the United States continued to grow, although at a slower rate. This continued growth results from the fact that so many women were born during the Baby Boom that even if each woman only gave birth to 1.8 children, the population would continue to grow. This growth is expected to continue through the remainder of this century (Weeks 1981). Even today we are experiencing a "mini" Baby Boom because many of the women born in the Baby Boom are now having children.

The Baby Boom affected more than the total size and rate of growth of the United States. It also had an effect on the age structure of the population. Figure 17.8 shows the age-sex structure of the United States

demographic transition theory A model of demographic change that states that as a population becomes economically developed, a reduction in death rates (leading to population growth) will take place first, followed by a reduction in birth rates.

in 1975. Each age group has been labeled according to the year at birth. Note that the number of people who were born between 1966 and 1975 is less than the number born between 1951 and 1965, thus showing the reduction in fertility since the mid-1960s. Also note that the pyramid is narrow for those born between 1931 and 1940. This period corresponds to the Great Depression, a time when the birth rate declined.

Demography and the Modern World

Today's world is constantly changing. Advances in communications technologies bring the peoples of the world in closer contact with one another. The average life expectancy in developed nations continues to increase. More and more, the economic systems of many nations are becoming interconnected. Many demographic changes are taking place as well, acting as both cause and effect of social, political, and economic changes. Several of the major changes in the world's demography are discussed here.

The Demographic Transition

The demographic changes that have taken place in many industrialized nations over the past century have been described by demographic transition theory. Though how applicable this theory is for all populations is still being debated, it does serve as a convenient summary of basic demographic trends that have occurred in a number of societies.

Demographic transition theory states that as a population becomes more economically developed, a reduction in death rates will take place first, followed by a reduction in fertility rates. Three stages are usually identified in this model (Swedlund and Armelagos 1976). Stage 1 populations are those of undeveloped areas with high mortality and high fertility rates. Because the high number of births is balanced by the high number of deaths, the overall population size remains more or less stable. The age-sex structure of a Stage 1 population resembles a true pyramid, with a very wide base and a very narrow apex. The broad base, corresponding to infants and young children, is a product of the high fertility. Because mortality rates are high, however, fewer and fewer people survive to each successive age group—thus the pyramid shape. In a Stage 1 population, the majority of the population consists of very young people, many of whom will not live to grow older.

Stage 2 populations are found in developing regions where demographic and economic factors are changing rapidly. A Stage 2 population is characterized by high fertility and lowered mortality. The transition to lowered mortality, especially in childhood, is a consequence of improvements in health care and medical technologies. Because the fertility rate remains high, there are more births than deaths. As a result, the population grows in size. The age-sex structure still resembles a pyramid, but with the top portion becoming wider as more people survive to older ages (see Figure 17.3). The base of the pyramid is still broad because fertility rates are high.

Stage 3 populations are found in developed regions and are characterized by low rates of fertility and mortality. Because of technological, social, economic, and educational changes, people in developed regions have more of an opportunity to control family size. As is often the case, the fertility rate declines. Because the rates of births and deaths are both low, such populations may show little growth. The age-sex structure becomes more and more rectangular as the base decreases and more people live to older ages (see Figure 17.4). Some nations, such as Sweden, show this pattern clearly. Others, such as the United States, are still in the process of becoming a Stage 3 population.

The demographic transition model has several problems. Mortality and fertility rates represent a continuous range and cannot easily be separated into "low" and "high" phases. Situations unique to certain populations, such as the Baby Boom in the United States, may result in fluctuating rates of fertility. Also, it is not clear to what extent Stage 1 has been characteristic of most of human history (Swedlund and Armelagos 1976). In spite of these problems and others, the model does provide a rough summary of the types of average changes found accompanying economic and industrial development.

World Population Growth

The total human population of the world has increased throughout human evolution, especially during the last several centuries. Estimates of prehistoric population size are crude, but they do provide us with an idea of the extent of population growth. For example, the total world population 50,000 years ago was most likely to be in the neighborhood of 1.3 million people. By 10,000 years ago, the estimated population was 6 million people (Weiss 1984). These low numbers are consistent with what we know about hunting-and-gathering cultures and their carrying capacities.

Following the development and spread of agriculture, the population of the world increased more and more rapidly. The major acceleration came following the Industrial Revolution (roughly 1750). Since this time, the world's population increased at an exponential rate to the present figure

Figure 17.9

World population growth
since the origin of agriculture.
(From *Population: An Introduction
to Concepts and Issues,* Second
Edition, by John R. Weeks ©
1978 by Wadsworth Publishing
Company)

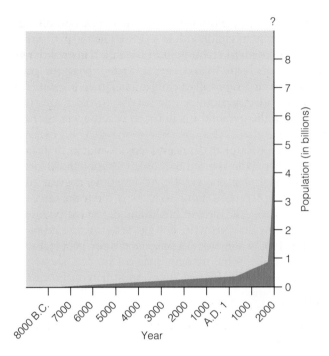

(Figure 17.9). Between 1750 and 1950, the world's population tripled in size. Between 1950 and 1975, the world's population increased almost 63 percent (Weeks 1981). The world population was estimated to be 5,384,000,000 people in mid-1991 and was growing at an annual rate of 1.76 percent. The projected world population in the year 2000 is 6.26 billion, and in the year 2050, 8.50 billion (Haub 1992). Such projections are difficult to compute, relying on extrapolation of current trends. It is possible to be overly optimistic or pessimistic when evaluating trends. Bouvier (1984) believes that by the year 2034 the actual rate of world population growth will begin to diminish. This estimate is based on the continued transition to developed nations, an increase in the efforts to control fertility in developing nations, and a continued increase in life expectancy throughout the world.

Regardless of the specific estimate, the current trend is toward continued population growth. Many people are concerned with a probable lack of resources, such as food and energy. Others feel less concerned and believe new technologies will help bridge the gap between population size and resources. Many developing nations today are making efforts to control fertility, such as providing increased awareness of birth control. The effectiveness of such measures varies depending on the political, economic, social, and religious nature of specific nations.

The overall rate of world population growth masks a number of important trends within specific nations. Today, rapid population growth is most often a problem for the developing nations and less of a problem for developed nations. In fact, the populations in some developed nations may have problems associated with too little growth. Variation in growth rates takes place even within nations. In the United States today, for example, the most rapidly growing segment of the population consists of Mexican Americans and African Americans.

Variation in population growth among nations will most probably lead to major shifts in the world's demographic profile. One way of seeing this effect is to look at the 10 largest urban areas in the world in 1990 along with the projected 10 largest in the future. Table 17.1 lists the 10 largest urban areas of the world in 1990 along with a projection for the year 2034. In 1990, the 3 largest were Tokyo, New York City (metropolitan area), and Seoul. It is estimated that by the year 2034 the 3 largest will be Mexico City, Shanghai, and Beijing. By 2034, the only currently developed nation likely to be in the top 10 is Japan; New York City will not even make this list.

Implications of Changing Age Structure

The transition to developed nations with low rates of fertility and mortality will lead to many changes in culture. The age-sex structure of such nations continues to show a shrinking base and a widening apex. As fewer people are born and as people live longer, the age-sex structure of

T A B L E   17.1
**The 10 Largest Urban Areas in the World:
1990 and Estimated for 2034**

Rank	1990	2034 estimate
1	Tokyo, Japan	Mexico City, Mexico
2	New York City metropolitan area, U.S.A.	Shanghai, China
3	Seoul, South Korea	Beijing, China
4	São Paulo, Brazil	São Paulo, Brazil
5	Osaka, Japan	Bombay, India
6	Mexico City, Mexico	Dacca, Bangladesh
7	Los Angeles, U.S.A.	Calcutta, India
8	Shanghai, China	Jakarta, Indonesia
9	Bombay, India	Madras, India
10	London, U.K.	Tokyo, Japan

Source: Bouvier (1984); Haub (1992).

Figure 17.10

Estimated age-sex structure
of Germany in 2034.
(Projection based on the
former nation of West
Germany prior to German
unification.)   (Source: Bouvier
[1984:26]).

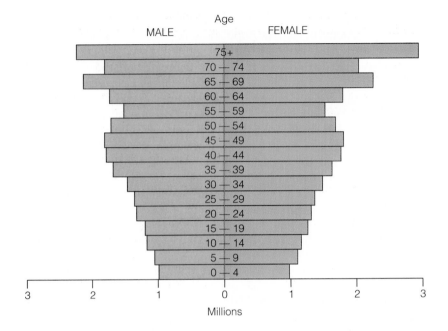

developed nations will continue to resemble a rectangle. Figure 17.10
shows the estimated population pyramid of western Germany in the year
2034, based on current trends and expected economic changes. Bouvier
(1984) presented this figure as typical of a Western European developed
nation that is expected to become more of a service and information-based
economy rather than a manufacturing-based economy. Figure 17.10 shows
that the elderly will make up the majority of such a population.

We can expect many cultural changes to accompany such a shift to
an older population. Many of these shifts are apparent today in North
America. For example, if we assume current average ages for retirement,
it is clear that there will be fewer people of working age in the future.
Such a shift might be seen as having both advantages and disadvantages. A smaller labor pool might mean better economic opportunities for
working-age people. On the other hand, we may also expect greater taxa-
tion to help provide for the well-being of the retired portion of the
population.

Many questions are being asked by those concerned with social and
economic shifts. For example, how well will our Social Security system
function when more people are drawing from it? What changes need to be
made in the insurance industries? How can we provide adequate health
and other care to an aging population?

Economic shifts can also be examined. Perhaps one of the best examples of the effects of changing age structure is in our system of higher
education. During the 1960s and early 1970s, as more and more Baby

Boom children reached college age, the demand for colleges and universities increased. This demand was also accompanied by an increased desire for a college education, in part because of a changing economy and the value of a college degree in earning potential. As college enrollments increased, more schools were built, and more faculty and staff were hired. By the mid-1970s, the effects of the Baby Boom were over, and enrollments began to diminish at many institutions. How, then, can we afford to maintain our colleges? Increases in tuition and taxes are remedies, but they are generally not very popular. Should schools be closed? If so, what happens to the local economies, which are often highly dependent on these schools? What about the future? An increase, although small, is expected in college-age students by the mid-1990s. Also, increasing numbers of older people have been returning to college for more education. If we cut back on programs now, will we need to start them up again in a few years?

Business provides another example of these far-reaching changes. Sound business practice dictates the gearing of products to specific age groups. As the numbers in different age groups change, so does demand for specific products. In the entertainment industry, for example, teenagers have been, and still are, major consumers of tapes and compact discs. As our population ages, however, there will be more demand for tapes and CDs from the growing middle-aged population. Today this is apparent in the Baby Boomers' demand for "oldies," music from the time they were teenagers. What type of changes will occur in this industry and others in the future as a consequence of the changing age structure?

These questions have no easy answers. Awareness of the problems and their connection to a variety of economic, social, and political factors is a start in the right direction. Today's world is marked by an unusually high level of change. A society's successful integration of demographic change requires analysis of current trends and, above all, a basic acknowledgment that, for good or ill, these changes are indeed taking place.

SUMMARY

Demography is the study of the size, composition, and distribution of populations. The focus of demography is on the processes of fertility, mortality, and migration. All these processes are affected by cultural and biological factors and have their own effect in turn on cultural and biological variation. Population growth reflects the balance between fertility, mortality, and migration. In general, a situation of more births than deaths leads to population growth.

Patterns of fertility and mortality also affect the age distribution of a population. Populations with high fertility and mortality rates have more infants and young children than any other age group. As populations undergo economic development, the mortality rates drop, leading to both population growth and an increase in the proportion of older people. Developed nations, where fertility and mortality rates are low, show a reduction in the number of young people and an increase in the number of older people.

Patterns of fertility and mortality are affected extensively by cultural change. In today's world, the total population continues to increase, particularly among the Third World nations. In the United States, population growth continues but at a slower rate than in the recent past. Changes in demographic structure will lead in the near future to strikingly different distributions of the world's population, both by nation and age group.

Supplemental Readings

Scientific American, ed. 1974. *The Human Population*. San Francisco: W. H. Freeman. Both this book, consisting of articles from the magazine, and the Weeks text provide a good introduction to the study of demography.

Swedlund, A. C., and G. J. Armelagos. 1976. *Demographic Anthropology*. Dubuque, Iowa: Wm. C. Brown. This book, unfortunately no longer in print, provides a general review of demography from an anthropological perspective—in particular, the use of paleontological data in reconstructing demographic processes.

Weeks, J. R. 1981. *Population: An Introduction to Concepts and Issues*. 2d ed. Belmont, Calif.: Wadsworth.

Epilogue: The Future of Our Species

This book has focused on human biological variation and evolution, past and present. What about the future? Can biological anthropology, or indeed any science, make predictions about the future of our species? What possible directions will our biological and cultural evolution take?

One thing is for certain—we continue to evolve both biologically and culturally and will do so in the future. Human evolution is increasingly complex because of our biocultural nature. Much of our adaptive nature is culturally based. We can adapt to a situation more quickly through cultural evolution than through biological evolution. Theoretically, we can also direct our cultural evolution. We can focus our efforts on solutions to specific problems, such as finding a vaccine for AIDS or developing ways to further reduce dental decay. Biological evolution, on the other hand, has no inherent direction. Natural selection works on existing variation, not on what we might desire or need.

Our success with cultural adaptations should not lead us to conclude that we do not continue to evolve biologically. Regardless of our triumphs in the field of medicine, many incurable diseases still carry on the process of natural selection. Biological variation still takes place in potential and realized fertility. Perhaps as many as a third to half of all human conceptions fail to produce live births. We still live in a world in which up to 50 percent of the children have an inadequate diet. Even if all inhabitants of the world were raised to an adequate standard of living tomorrow, we would still be subject to natural selection and biological evolution. The fact that we are cultural organisms does not detract from the fact that we

507

are also biological organisms. Scholars in various fields throughout history have argued about whether humans and human behavior should be studied biologically, as products of nature, or culturally, as products of nurture. Both sides were wrong. Humans must be studied as *both* biological and cultural organisms.

Given that we will continue to evolve, how will we evolve? This question cannot be answered. Evolution has many random elements that cannot be predicted. Also, the biocultural nature of humans makes prediction even harder. The incredible rate of cultural and technological change in the past century was not predicted. What kinds of cultural evolution are possible in the next hundred years? We may be able to forecast some short-term changes, but we know nothing about the cultural capabilities of our species hundreds or thousands of years in the future.

Another problem is that our own viewpoint can influence our predictions. An optimistic view might focus on the success of past cultural adaptations and the rate of acquisition of knowledge and then develop a scenario including increased standard of living for all, cheap energy sources, and an elevated life expectancy. A pessimistic view might consider all of the horrors of the past and present, and project a grim future. A pessimist might envisage widespread famine, overcrowding, pollution, disease, and warfare. Most likely, any possible future will be neither pie-in-the-sky nor doom, but a combination of positive and negative changes. If the study of evolution tells us one thing, it is that every change has potential costs and benefits. We need to temper our optimism and pessimism with a sense of balance.

In any consideration of the future, we must acknowledge change as basic to life. Many people find it tempting to suggest we would be better off living a "simpler" life. Others argue that we should stop trying to deal with our problems and let nature take its course or that we should trust in the acts of God. This is unacceptable—indeed our understanding of human evolution argues for the reverse. Our adaptive pattern has been one of learning and problem solving. More than that, these are our primate heritage. Our biology has allowed us to develop the basic mammalian patterns of learned behavior to a high degree. We have the capability for rational thought, for reason, and for learning. Even if many of our cultural inventions have led to suffering and pain, our *potential* for good is immense. In any case, we must continue along the path of learning and intelligence; it is our very nature. Good or bad, the capabilities of the human mind and spirit may be infinite.

Mathematical Population Genetics

Population genetics was discussed in Chapter 3 with a minimum of mathematical formulae. This appendix is intended for those wishing to obtain an elementary understanding of the mathematical basis of population genetics. Additional sources, such as Crow and Kimura (1970), Cavalli-Sforza and Bodmer (1971), Spiess (1977), and Hartl (1988), are recommended for further information.

The formulae presented here are limited to a simple genetic case—a single locus with two possible alleles, A and a. Following convention, the symbol p is used to denote the frequency of the A allele, and the symbol q is used to denote the frequency of the a allele. Because there are only two alleles, $p + q = 1$. For this simple case, there are three genotypes: AA, Aa, and aa.

Hardy-Weinberg Equilibrium

The Hardy-Weinberg equilibrium model, discussed briefly in Chapter 3, states that: (1) under random mating, the expected genotype frequencies are $AA = p^2$, $Aa = 2pq$, and $aa = q^2$, and (2) under certain conditions, the allele frequencies p and q will remain constant from one generation to the next.

There are a number of ways to demonstrate the first conclusion of the Hardy-Weinberg model. Perhaps the simplest proof rests on the fact that

p and q represent probabilities. If the frequency of the A allele is p, then the probability of drawing an A allele from the entire gene pool is equal to p. To obtain the AA genotype in the next generation, it is necessary to have an A allele from both parents. Assuming that the allele frequencies are the same in both sexes, the probability of getting an A allele from one parent is p, and the probability of getting an A allele from the other parent is also p. The probability of *both* these events happening is the product of these probabilities, or $p \times p = p^2$. The same method can be used to determine the probability of getting the aa genotype ($q \times q = q^2$).

Getting an Aa genotype in the next generation requires one parent contributing the A allele (probability $= p$) and the other parent contributing the a allele (probability $= q$). The joint probability is $p \times q = pq$. It is also possible, however, that the order may be reversed. The first parent could contribute the a allele and the second parent could contribute the A allele. The joint probability of this happening is also equal to pq. The overall probability of having the Aa genotype is therefore $pq + pq = 2pq$.

The reasoning behind the Hardy-Weinberg model is summarized as follows:

Genotype of child	Allele from parent 1	2	Probability
AA	A	A	$p \times p = p^2$
Aa	A	a	$p \times q = pq$
		or	
	a	A	$q \times p = pq$
aa	a	a	$q \times q = q^2$

$$pq + pq = 2pq$$

Also note that the sum of genotype frequencies ($p^2 + 2pq + q^2$) is equal to 1.

The second part of the Hardy-Weinberg model states that, in the absence of evolutionary forces, the allele frequencies will remain the same from one generation to the next. This may be easily demonstrated by using the genotype frequencies in a given generation to predict the allele frequencies in the next generations. Allele frequencies are easily derived from genotype frequencies. In the present example, the frequency of allele A is computed as the frequency of genotype AA plus *half* the frequency of genotype Aa (we only wish to count the A alleles that make up half the total number of alleles in heterozygotes). The frequency of the A allele in the next generation, designated p', is therefore equal to

$$p' = \text{frequency of } AA + (\text{frequency of } Aa/2)$$

which is equal to

$$p' = p^2 + \frac{2pq}{2}$$

The 2s cancel out, giving

$$p' = p^2 + pq$$

Factoring p from the equation gives

$$p' = p(p + q)$$

Now, since the quantity $(p + q)$ is equal to 1 by definition, the equation becomes

$$p' = p$$

The fact that the allele frequency in the next generation (p') is equal to the initial allele frequency (p) shows that, given certain assumptions, there will be no change in the allele frequency over time. Therefore, when we *do* see a change in allele frequency over time, we know that one of the assumptions of the Hardy-Weinberg model has been violated. Because the model assumes no evolution has taken place, the fact that the model does not fit means this assumption is incorrect and therefore that a change in allele frequency (evolution) has taken place.

Inbreeding

Inbreeding does not change allele frequencies, but it does change genotype frequencies. The genotype frequencies predicted by Hardy-Weinberg require the assumption that mating is random and that there is no inbreeding. The inbreeding coefficient, F, is a measure of the probability that a homozygous genotype is the result of common ancestry of the parents. For example, the inbreeding coefficient for offspring born to first cousins is $F = 0.0625$. This value indicates the *additional* probability of the child having a homozygous genotype because the parents were first cousins. Inbreeding coefficients are most often computed from genealogical data, although with certain assumptions they may also be estimated from frequencies of last names and from allele frequencies (in certain cases).

At the populational level, there is also a probability of having a homozygous genotype due to random mating (p^2 or q^2, depending on the genotype). Inbreeding increases this probability. Under inbreeding, the genotype frequencies are

AA: $p^2 + pqF$
Aa: $2pq(1 - F)$
aa: $q^2 + pqF$

Thus, inbreeding increases the frequency of homozygotes (AA and aa) and decreases the frequency of heterozygotes. As an example, consider a population where $p = 0.5$ and $q = 0.5$. Under random mating ($F = 0$), the genotype frequencies are: $AA = 0.25$, $Aa = 0.50$, and $aa = 0.25$. If the population had an inbreeding coefficient of $F = 0.05$, these frequencies would be: $AA = 0.2625$, $Aa = 0.4750$, and $aa = 0.2625$.

It is easy to see why inbreeding does not change allele frequencies. Given the genotype frequencies expected under inbreeding, we can compute the frequency of the A allele in the next generation as

$$p' = \text{frequency of } AA + (\text{frequency of } \tfrac{Aa}{2})$$

Substituting the formulae for AA and Aa given earlier, this equation becomes

$$p' = p^2 + pqF + \frac{2pq(1 - F)}{2}$$

The 2s in the equation cancel out. When the remaining terms are multiplied out, the equation becomes

$$p' = p^2 + pqF + pq - pqF$$

After subtracting pqF from pqF, the equation then becomes

$$p' = p^2 + pq$$

Factoring the p in the equation gives

$$p' = p(p + q)$$

Because $p + q = 1$, the allele frequency in the next generation is

$$p' = p$$

Thus, the allele frequency does not change from one generation to the next under inbreeding.

Mutation

Mutation involves the change from one allele into another. For the simple case given here, let us assume that allele a is the mutant form. The mutation rate, usually denoted as u, is the proportion of A alleles that mutates into a alleles in a single generation. The value u therefore represents the probability of any A allele mutating into the a allele. Models also exist to deal with backward mutation (a into A), but these are not presented here because the rate of back mutations is usually very low.

How can mutation change the allele frequency in a population over time? To answer that, assume that mutation is the only force acting to change allele frequencies. The frequency of allele a in the next generation (q') depends on the current frequency of a alleles (q), the frequency of A alleles that have not mutated ($p = 1 - q$), and the rate of mutation (u).

The frequency of the *a* allele in the next generation, q', is therefore equal to

$$q' = q + u(1 - q)$$

The first part of this equation represents the initial frequency of *a* alleles (q), and the second part represents the expected increase in *a* alleles due to mutation of *A* alleles.

As an example, assume that the initial allele frequencies are $p = 1.0$ and $q = 0.0$, and that the mutation rate is $u = 0.0001$. The allele frequencies in the next generation are

$$q' = 0 + 0.0001(1 - 0)$$
$$= 0.0001$$
$$p' = 1 - q' = 0.9999$$

If we carry this to an additional generation, the allele frequencies in the second generation (q'' and p'') are

$$q'' = 0.0001 + 0.0001(1 - 0.0001)$$
$$= 0.0001 + 0.00009999$$
$$= 0.00019999$$
$$p'' = 1 - q'' = 0.9980001$$

Continued mutation, in the absence of any other evolutionary forces, will lead to an increase in q and a decrease in p. For example, after 50 generations of mutation the allele frequencies in the example here are $p = 0.99501223$ and $q = 0.00498777$.

The mutation model presented here is simplified and does not take into consideration back mutation, changes in mutation rates over time, or any of the other evolutionary forces. It does, however, illustrate how mutation will lead to a cumulative increase in the frequency of the mutant allele. These examples also show that such increases are relatively low, even over many generations. Of course, evolution is not caused only by mutation. Other evolutionary forces act to increase, or decrease, the allele frequencies.

Natural Selection

Natural selection is modeled mathematically by assigning a fitness value to each genotype. Fitness is defined as the probability that an individual will survive to reproductive age. The actual proportion of individuals surviving is known as *absolute fitness*. Mathematically, the effects of natural selection are easier to model if relative fitness is used; here the absolute fitness values are converted such that the largest absolute fitness equals 1.

As an example, consider absolute fitness values of $AA = 0.8$, $Aa = 0.8$, and $aa = 0.4$. These numbers mean that 80 percent of those with the AA genotype survived, 80 percent of those with the Aa genotype survived, and 40 percent of those with the aa genotype survived. Because the largest absolute fitness is 0.8, relative fitness values are obtained by dividing each fitness by 0.8. Thus, the relative fitness values are $AA = 1.0$, $Aa = 1.0$, and $aa = 0.5$. The genotype aa has a fitness value of 0.5 relative to the most fit genotypes (AA and Aa). As another example, consider the following absolute fitness values: $AA = 0.7$, $Aa = 0.9$, and $aa = 0.3$. The relative fitness values are $AA = 0.7/0.9 = 0.778$, $Aa = 0.9/0.9 = 1.0$, and $aa = 0.3/0.9 = 0.333$.

The symbol w is used to designate relative fitness. Here w_{AA} is the relative fitness of genotype AA, w_{Aa} is the relative fitness of genotype Aa, and w_{aa} is the relative fitness of genotype aa. The effect of natural selection can now be determined by looking at the genotype frequencies before and after selection. The genotype frequencies before selection are obtained from the Hardy-Weinberg model: $AA = p^2$, $Aa = 2pq$, and $aa = q^2$. The genotype frequencies after selection are obtained by multiplying the genotype frequencies before selection by the respective relative fitness values. After selection, the genotype frequencies are therefore

$$AA = w_{AA}\, p^2$$
$$Aa = 2w_{Aa}\, pq$$
$$aa = w_{aa}\, q^2$$

The frequency of the A allele after selection is then computed by adding the frequency of genotype AA to half the frequency of genotype Aa and dividing this figure by the sum of all genotype frequencies after selection. That is,

$$p' = (w_{AA}\, p^2 + (2w_{Aa}\, pq/2)) / (w_{AA}\, p^2 + 2w_{Aa}\, pq + w_{aa}q^2)$$
$$= (w_{AA}\, p^2 + w_{Aa}\, pq) / (w_{AA}\, p^2 + 2w_{Aa}\, pq + w_{aa}q^2)$$

As an example, consider a population with initial allele frequencies of $p = 0.8$ and $q = 0.2$. Assume relative fitness values for each genotype as $AA = 1.0$, $Aa = 1.0$, and $aa = 0.5$. In this example, there is partial selection against the homozygous genotype aa. Logically, we expect that such selection will lead to a reduction in the frequency of the a allele and an increase in the frequency of the A allele.

Using Hardy-Weinberg, the expected genotype frequencies before selection are

$$AA: p^2 = (0.8)^2 = 0.64$$
$$Aa: 2pq = 2(0.8)(0.2) = 0.32$$
$$aa: q^2 = (0.2)^2 = 0.04$$

Using the relative fitness values, the relative proportion of each genotype after selection is

$$AA: w_{AA}\, p^2 = (1)(0.8)^2 = 0.64$$
$$Aa: 2w_{Aa}\, pq = 2(1)(0.8)(0.2) = 0.32$$
$$aa: w_{aa}\, q^2 = (0.5)(0.2)^2 = 0.02$$

The frequency of the A allele after selection is computed as

$$p' = (0.64 + (0.32/2)) / (0.64 + 0.32 + 0.02)$$
$$= (0.64 + 0.16) / (0.64 + 0.32 + 0.02)$$
$$= 0.8 / 0.98$$
$$= 0.8163$$

Also, the frequency of the a allele after selection is

$$q' = 1 - p' = 0.1837$$

The entire process can be repeated for additional generations. To extend the analysis another generation, use the new values of $p = 0.8163$ and $q = 0.1837$. After an additional generation of selection, the allele frequencies will be $p = 0.8303$ and $q = 0.1697$. If you continue this process, the frequency of A keeps increasing, and the frequency of a keeps decreasing.

Some forms of natural selection can be represented using simplified formulae. For example, complete selection against recessive homozygotes involves relative fitness values of $AA = 1.0$, $Aa = 1.0$, and $aa = 0.0$. Given these values, the frequency of the A allele after one generation of selection is

$$p' = (w_{AA}\, p^2 + w_{Aa}\, pq) /$$
$$(w_{AA}\, p^2 + 2w_{Aa}\, pq + w_{aa}q^2)$$
$$= ((1)p^2 + (1)pq) / ((1)p^2 + 2(1)pq + (0)q^2)$$
$$= (p^2 + pq) / (p^2 + 2pq)$$
$$= (p(p + q)) / (p(p + q + q))$$
$$= (p + q) / (p + q + q)$$
$$= 1 / (1 + q)$$
$$= 1 / (1 + (1 - p))$$
$$= 1 / (2 - p)$$

which is a much easier formula to work with. Other forms of natural selection also have simplified formulae and are listed in the references given at the beginning of this appendix.

As an example, assume initial frequencies of $p = 0.5$ and $q = 0.5$. The frequency of the A allele in the next five generations of natural selection would be 0.6667, 0.7500, 0.8000, 0.8333, and 0.8571.

Genetic Drift

The process of genetic drift is random. As a result, we cannot predict the exact allele frequencies resulting from a generation of genetic drift. We can, however, describe the probability of obtaining a given allele frequency caused by genetic drift. For example, assume a population of 6 people (and hence 12 alleles at each locus) with initial allele frequencies of $p = 0.5$ and $q = 0.5$. A generation of genetic drift could result in the frequency of the A allele ranging from $0/12 = 0.0$ to $12/12 = 1.0$. Other possible allele frequency values are $1/12 = 0.083, 2/12 = 0.167, 3/12 = 0.250, 4/12 = 0.333, 5/12 = 0.417, 6/12 = 0.500, 7/12 = 0.583, 8/12 = 0.667, 9/12 = 0.750, 10/12 = 0.833, 11/12 = 0.917.$

The frequency of the A allele depends on how many A alleles are represented in the next generation (which can range from 0 to 12). Because genetic drift is a random process, we cannot tell how many A alleles will be represented in the next generation. We can, however, compute the probability of each of these events occurring. We would expect, for example, that getting 6 A alleles is more likely than getting 12 A alleles (just as we would expect it to be more likely that we get 6 heads rather than 12 heads or 1 if we flipped a coin 12 times). The exact formula used is a bit complex and is not presented here (see Hartl 1988:70). Using this formula, the probability of getting 6 A alleles in the next generation (and an allele frequency of $6/12 = 0.5$) is 0.223. Therefore, the probability of getting *some* change in allele frequency (some number *other* than 6 A alleles) is $1 - 0.223 = 0.777$. Mathematical investigation also shows that smaller populations are more likely to experience genetic drift than larger populations.

Gene Flow

The process of gene flow is best described mathematically by considering allele frequencies in two populations, 1 and 2. The allele frequencies of population 1 are denoted p_1 and q_1, and the allele frequencies of population 2 are denoted p_2 and q_2. What happens when gene flow takes place between these two populations? Assume that populations 1 and 2 mix together at rate m. The term m is a measure of the proportion of migrants moving from one population into the other. For simplicity, further assume that the rate of migration from population 1 into population 2 is the same as the rate of migration from population 2 into population 1.

The frequency of the A allele in population 1 after one generation of gene flow is then expressed as

$$(1 - m)p_1 + mp_2$$

The first part of the righthand side of the equation shows the contribution to allele frequency from the proportion of individuals who stayed in population 1 $(1 - m)$. The second part of the righthand side of the equation shows the contribution to allele frequency caused by the proportion of individuals migrating from population 2 (m). Likewise, the frequency of allele A in population 2 after one generation of gene flow is

$$mp_1 + (1 - m)p_2$$

As an example, assume initial allele frequencies in population 1 are $p_1 = 0.7$ and $q_1 = 0.3$, and that initial allele frequencies in population 2 are $p_2 = 0.2$ and $q_2 = 0.8$. Further assume a rate of gene flow of $m = 0.3$. After one generation of gene flow, the frequencies of the A allele are

$$(1 - 0.3)(0.7) + (0.3)(0.2)$$
$$= 0.49 + 0.06$$
$$= 0.55$$

for population 1, and

$$(0.3)(0.7) + (1 - 0.3)(0.2)$$
$$= 0.21 + 0.14$$
$$= 0.35$$

for population 2. Thus, the frequency of the A allele has made populations 1 and 2 more similar as a result of gene flow. An additional generation of gene flow at the same rate would result in allele frequencies of

$$(1 - 0.3)(0.55) + (0.3)(0.35)$$
$$= 0.385 + 0.105$$
$$= 0.49$$

for population 1, and

$$(0.3)(0.55) + (1 - 0.3)(0.35)$$
$$= 0.165 + 0.245$$
$$= 0.41$$

for population 2. The two populations continue to become more similar genetically. Another generation of gene flow would result in allele frequencies of 0.466 for population 1 and 0.434 for population 2. After only a few more generations of gene flow, the allele frequencies of the two populations would be essentially equal.

SUMMARY

The formulae presented here represent a simplified view of mathematical population genetics. Each model ignores the effects of other evolutionary forces, although they can easily be extended to consider simultaneous effects. These models also deal only with a simple situation of one locus with two alleles. More complicated analyses require more sophisticated mathematical methods that are best performed on a computer. Nonetheless, these formulae do demonstrate the basic nuts and bolts of population genetic theory.

Taxonomy of Living Primates

The chart that begins on page 520 lists representatives of all living primate groups. As discussed in Chapters 8 and 9, there are alternative classifications, especially the strepsorhine-haplorhine subdivision and the different schemes for classifying hominoids. The taxonomy listed here is a "traditional" one, used more widely than any other. Refer back to Figure 8.9 and Figure 9.5 for alternative classifications.

The Anglicized, rather than Latin, names are used here for the taxonomic categories of suborder, infraorder, superfamily, family, and subfamily.

Individual species were taken from Jolly (1985) but placed in a more traditional taxonomy following Hrdy (1981).

Order: Primates

Suborder: Prosimians

Infraorder	Superfamily	Family	Subfamily
Lemuriformes	Lemuroids	Lemurids	Lemurines
			Lepilemurines
			Cheirogaleines
		Indriids	
		Daubentoniids	
Lorisiformes		Lorisids	Lorisines
			Galagines

Order: Primates

Suborder: Prosimians

Genus	Species	Common name
Lemur	*L. catta*	Ring-tailed lemur
	L. fulvus	Brown lemur
	L. macaco	Black lemur
	L. mongoz	Mongoose lemur
	L. rubriventer	Red-bellied lemur
Hapalemur	*H. griseus*	Gray lemur
	H. simus	Simus lemur
Varecia	*V. variegata*	Ruffed lemur
Lepilemur	*L. dorsalis*	Nosy Be lepilemur
	L. edwardsii	Edward's lepilemur
	L. leucopus	White-footed lepilemur
	L. microdon	Microdon lepilemur
	L. mustelinus	Mustelinus lepilemur
	L. ruficaudatus	Red-tailed lepilemur
	L. septentrionalis	Montagne d'Ambre lepilemur
Microcebus	*M. murinus*	Western mouse lemur
	M. rufus	Eastern mouse lemur
	M. coquereli	Coquerel's mouse lemur
Cheirogaleuse	*C. medius*	Western dwarf lemur
	C. major	Eastern dwarf lemur
Allocebus	*A. trichotis*	Hairy-eared dwarf lemur
Phaner	*P. furcifer*	Forked lemur
Avahi	*A. laniger*	Woolly lemur
Propithecus	*P. diadema*	Diademed sifaka
	P. verreauxi	White sifaka
Indri	*I. indri*	Indri
Daubentonia	*D. madagascariensis*	Aye-aye
Loris	*L. tardigradus*	Slender loris
Nycticebus	*N. coucang*	Common slow loris
	N. pygmaeus	Pygmy slow loris
Arctocebus	*A. calabarensis*	Angwantibo
Perodicticus	*P. potto*	Potto
Galago	*G. alleni*	Allen's galago
	G. crassicaudatus	Thick-tailed galago
	G. demidovii	Demidoff's galago

Order: Primates

Suborder: Prosimians

Infraorder	Superfamily	Family	Subfamily
Tarsiiformes		Tarsiids	

Order: Primates

Suborder: Anthropoids

Infraorder	Superfamily	Family	Subfamily
	Ceboids	Callitrichids	Callitrichines
			Callimiconines
		Cebids	Cebinines
			Aotinines
			Callicebines

Order: Primates

Suborder: Prosimians		
Genus	Species	Common name
	G. elegantulus	Needle-clawed galago
	G. inustus	Inustus galago
	G. senegalensis	Senegal galago
Tarsius	T. bancanus	Borneo tarsier
	T. spectrum	Spectral tarsier
	T. syrichta	Philippine tarsier

Order: Primates

Suborder: Anthropoids		
Genus	Species	Common name
Callithrix	C. argentata	Silvery marmoset
	C. aurita	Buffy tufted-eared marmoset
	C. chrysoleuca	Goldern marmoset
	C. flaviceps	Buffy-headed marmoset
	C. geoffroyi	Geoffroy's marmoset
	C. humeralifer	Santarem marmoset
	C. jacchus	Common marmoset
	C. penecillata	Black tufted-eared marmoset
Cebuella	C. pygmaea	Pygmy marmoset
Saguinus	S. bicolor	Barefaced tamarin
	S. fuscicollis	Saddleback tamarin
	S. imperator	Emperor tamarin
	S. inustus	Inustus tamarin
	S. labiatus	White-lipped tamarin
	S. leucopus	White-footed tamarin
	S. midas	Red-handed tamarin
	S. mystax	Moustached tamarin
	S. nigricollis	Black-and-red tamarin
	S. oedipus	Cotton-top tamarin
Leontopithecus	L. rosalia	Lion tamarin
Callimico	C. goeldii	Goeldi's marmoset
Cebus	C. albifrons	White-fronted cebus
	C. apella	Tufted cebus
	C. capucinus	White-throated cebus
	C. nigrivittatus	Black-capped cebus
Aotus	A. trivirgatus	Night monkey
Callicebus	C. personatus	Masked titi monkey

Order: Primates

Suborder: Anthropoids

Infraorder	Superfamily	Family	Subfamily
			Saimirines
			Pithecines
			Alouattines
			Atelines
Cercopithecoids	Cercopithecids	Cercopithecines	

Order: Primates

Suborder: Anthropoids

Genus	Species	Common name
	C. moloch	Dusky titi monkey
	C. torquatus	Widow titi monkey
Saimiri	S. oerstedi	Red-backed squirrel monkey
	S. sciureus	Common squirrel monkey
Pithecia	P. albicans	White saki
	P. hirsuta	Hairy saki
	P. monachus	Monk saki
	P. pithecia	Pale-headed saki
Cacajao	C. calvus	Bald uakari
	C. melanocephalus	Black-headed uakari
	C. rubicundus	Red uakari
Chiropetes	C. albinasus	White-nosed bearded saki
	C. satanus	Black-bearded saki
Alouatta	A. belzebul	Black-and-red howler
	A. caraya	Black howler
	A. fusca	Brown howler
	A. palliata	Mantled howler
	A. seniculus	Red howler
	A. villosa	Guatemalan howler
Ateles	A. belzebuth	Long-haired spider monkey
	A. fusciceps	Brown-headed spider monkey
	A. geoffroyi	Black-handed spider monkey
	A. paniscus	Black spider monkey
Brachyteles	B. arachnoides	Woolly spider monkey
Lathothrix	L. flavicauda	Hendee's woolly monkey
	L. lagotricha	Humboldt's woolly monkey
Macaca	M. arctoides	Stump-tailed macaque
	M. assamensis	Assamese macaque
	M. cyclopis	Formosan rock macaque
	M. fascicularis	Crab-eating macaque
	M. fuscata	Japanese macaque
	M. maurus	Moor macaque
	M. mulatta	Rhesus macaque
	M. nemestrina	Pig-tailed macaque
	M. nigra	Celebes black macaque
	M. ochreata	Ochre macaque
	M. radiata	Bonnet macaque
	M. silenus	Lion-tailed macaque
	M. sinica	Toque macaque

Order: Primates			
Suborder: Anthropoids			
Infraorder	Superfamily	Family	Subfamily

Colobines

Order: Primates

Suborder: Anthropoids

Genus	Species	Common name
	M. sylvana	Barbary macaque
	M. thibetana	Thibetan macaque
	M. togeana	Togian macaque
Cerocebus	*C. albigena*	Gray-cheeked mangabey
	C. atterimus	Black mangabey
	C. galeritus	Agile mangabey
	C. torquatus	White-collared mangabey
Papio	*P. anubis*	Olive baboon
	P. cynocephalus	Yellow baboon
	P. hamdryas	Hamadryas baboon
	P. papio	Guinea baboon
	P. ursinus	Chacma baboon
Mandrillus	*M. leucophaeus*	Drill
	M. sphinx	Mandrill
Theropithecus	*T. gelada*	Gelada
Cercopithecus	*C. aethiops*	Vervet guenon
	C. ascanius	Red-tailed guenon
	C. cambelli	Campbell's guenon
	C. cephus	Moustached guenon
	C. denti	Dent's guenon
	C. diana	Diana guenon
	C. dryas	Dryas guenon
	C. erythogaster	Red-bellied guenon
	C. erythrotis	Red-eared guenon
	C. hamlyni	Hamlyn's guenon
	C. lhoesti	l'Hoest's guenon
	C. mitis	Blue guenon
	C. mona	Mona guenon
	C. neglectus	De Brazza's guenon
	C. nictitans	Spot-nosed guenon
	C. peraurista	Lesser spot-nosed guenon
	C. pogonias	Crowned guenon
	C. preussi	Preuss's guenon
	C. salongo	Salongo guenon
	C. wolfi	Wolf's guenon
Miopithecus	*M. talapoin*	Talapoin
Allenopithecus	*A. nirgoviridis*	Allen's swamp monkey
Erythrocebus	*E. patas*	Patas monkey
Presbytius	*P. aygula*	Sunda Island langur

Order: Primates

Suborder: Anthropoids

Infraorder	Superfamily	Family	Subfamily
	Hominoids	Hylobatids	
		Pongids	
		Hominids	

Order: Primates

	Suborder: Anthropoids	
Genus	Species	Common name
	P. cristata	Silvered langur
	P. entellus	Hanuman langur
	P. francoisi	Francois's langur
	P. frontata	White-fronted langur
	P. geei	Golden langur
	P. johnii	Nilgiri langur
	P. melalophos	Banded langur
	P. obscura	Dusky langur
	P. phayrei	Phayre's langur
	P. pileata	Capped langur
	P. potenziani	Mentawai langur
	P. rubicunda	Maroon langur
	P. senex	Purple-faced langur
Rhinopithecus	*R. avunculus*	Tonkin snubnosed langur
	R. brelichi	Brelichi snubnosed langur
	R. roxellanae	Golden snubnosed langur
Pygathrix	*P. nemaeus*	Douc langur
Nasalis	*N. larvatus*	Proboscis monkey
Simias	*S. concolor*	Pagai Island langur
Colobus	*C. angolensis*	Angola colobus
	C. badius	Red colobus
	C. guereza	Guereza colobus
	C. kirkii	Kirk's red colobus
	C. polykomos	King colobus
	C. satanas	Black colobus
Procolobus	*P. verus*	Olive colobus
Hylobates	*H. agilis*	Agile gibbon
	H. concolor	Black gibbon
	H. hoolock	Hoolock gibbon
	H. klossi	Kloss's gibbon
	H. lar	White-handed gibbon
	H. moloch	Silvery gibbon
	H. muelleri	Meuller's gibbon
	H. pileatus	Pileated gibbon
Symphalangus	*S. syndactylus*	Siamang
Pongo	*P. pygmaeus*	Orangutan
Pan	*P. troglodytes*	Common chimpanzee
	P. paniscus	Pygmy chimpanzee
Gorilla	*G. gorilla*	Gorilla
Homo	*H. sapiens*	Humans

Glossary

Acceleration curve. A measure of changes in the direction of growth rates over time.

Acclimatization. Changes in organ or body structure that occur within an individual's lifetime in response to one or more stresses.

Acheulian tradition. The stone tool technology associated with some populations of *Homo erectus*. Many of these tools were constructed using a biface method.

Acquired characteristics. Lamarck's hypothesis that traits change in response to environmental demands and are passed on to offspring.

Adapids. A group of Eocene primates similar in some ways to modern-day lemurs and lorises. They were primarily diurnal leaf and fruit eaters.

Adaptation. The process of successful interaction between a population and an environment. Cultural or biological traits that offer an advantage in a given environment are adaptations.

Adaptive radiation. The formation of many new species following the availability of new environments or the development of a new adaptation.

Admixture. The interbreeding of individuals from two or more initially distinct gene pools.

Adolescent growth spurt. The increase in rate of body growth during the adolescent years caused by hormonal changes.

Adrenal gland. The gland that produces adrenal hormones, which are a secondary source of sex hormones.

Adrenarche. The increase in secretion of adrenal hormones during midchildhood (roughly seven years of age in humans).

Aegyptopithecus. A genus of fossil anthropoids found in Egypt dating to 33 million years B.P. It was a medium-sized, arboreal anthropoid, most likely representative of the common ancestor of later Old World monkeys and apes.

Afropithecus. An African Miocene ape that lived between 16 and 18 million years ago, and is perhaps a common ancestor of modern great apes and humans. This genus is similar in some ways to *Sivapithecus*.

Age at menarche. The age at which a human female experiences her first menstrual period.

Age-sex structure. A measure of the composition of a population in terms of the numbers of males and females at different ages.

AIDS (Acquired Immune Deficiency Syndrome). A fatal disease that results in the breakdown of the body's immune defense system.

530

Algeripithecus. At present, the earliest-known anthropoid, dated to the Late Eocene (46 to 50 million years B.P.).

Allele. The alternative forms of a gene that occur at a given locus. Some genes have only one allele, some have two, and some have many alternative forms. Alleles occur in pairs, one on each chromosome.

Allen's rule. States that mammals in cold climates tend to have shorter and bulkier limbs, allowing less loss of body heat, whereas mammals in hot climates tend to have long, slender limbs, allowing greater loss of body heat.

Allometry. The study of the change in proportion of various body parts as a consequence of their growth at different rates.

Anagenesis. The transformation of a single species over time.

Analogous trait. Physical trait that has a similar function in two species but a different structure. The wings of a bird and those of a flying insect are an example of an analogous trait; both perform the same function but have different structures.

Anatomically modern *Homo sapiens*. The modern form of the human species, which dates back 100,000 years or more.

Androgen. Hormone that stimulates the development of secondary sexual characteristics in males.

Anthropoid. Member of the suborder of primates consisting of monkeys, apes, and humans.

Anthropological archaeology. The subfield of anthropology that focuses on cultural variation in prehistoric (and some historic) populations through an analysis of the culture's remains.

Anthropology. The science that investigates human biological and cultural variation and evolution.

Anthropometry. The measurement of the human body.

Antibody. A substance that reacts to other substances invading the body (antigens).

Antigen. A substance invading the body that stimulates the production of antibodies.

Arboreal. Living in trees.

Archaic *Homo sapiens*. An earlier variant of *Homo sapiens,* found at dates ranging from 32,000 to at least 200,000 years B.P. Archaic forms had roughly the same brain size as modern humans but a different-shaped skull, including a sloping forehead and lower cranial height.

Archean era. The first geologic era, dating roughly between 2.5 and 4.6 billion years B.P. Life began during the Archean era.

Assimilation model. A model of the evolution of modern *Homo sapiens* whereby the transition from archaic to modern *H. sapiens* occurred in a single region such as Africa, followed by assimilation into archaic *H. sapiens* populations elsewhere in the Old World. This model is a variant of the multiregional evolution model of modern human origins.

Assortative mating. Mating between phenotypically similar individuals: for example, between two people with the same hair color.

Australopithecine. A general term used to refer to any species in the genus *Australopithecus.*

Australopithecus. A genus of fossil hominid that lived in Africa between 1 and 4 million years B.P., characterized by bipedal locomotion, small brain size, large face, and large teeth.

Australopithecus afarensis. The most primitive of the australopithecines, dating between 3 and 4 million years B.P. and found in East Africa. The teeth and postcranial skeleton show a number of primitive and apelike features.

Australopithecus africanus. A species of australopithecine dating between 2 and 3 million years B.P. and found in South Africa. The teeth and skull of this species are not as large as those of the robust australopithecines.

Australopithecus boisei. The most robust of the australopithecines, dating between 1 and 2.5 million years B.P. and found in East Africa. This species has extremely large back teeth and a large supporting facial and cranial structure, indicating large chewing muscles.

Australopithecus robustus. A robust species of australopithecine, dating between 1 and 2 million years B.P. and found in South Africa. This species has large back teeth, although not as large on average as *Australopithecus boisei.*

Auxology. The study of human biological growth and development.

Baby Boom. The increase in the number of births in the United States between 1946 and 1964.

Balancing selection. Selection for the heterozygote and against the homozygotes (the heterozygote is most fit). Allele frequencies move toward an equilibrium defined by the fitness values of the two homozygotes.

Bases. Chemical units that make up part of the DNA molecule. There are four bases (adenine, thymine, guanine, cytosine). The sequence of bases in the DNA molecule specifies genetic instructions.

Bergmann's rule. States that (1) among mammals of similar shape, the larger mammal loses heat less rapidly than the smaller mammal, and (2) among mammals of similar size, the mammal with a linear shape will lose heat more rapidly than the mammal with a nonlinear shape.

Biface. Stone tool with both sides worked. The result is a more symmetric and efficient tool.

Bilateral symmetry. The right and left sides of the body are approximate mirror images, a characteristic of vertebrates.

Bilophodont. The pattern of the molar teeth of monkeys. The molars have four cusps, with the front two and back two connected by a ridge.

Binocular stereoscopic vision. Overlapping fields of vision (binocular), with both sides of the brain receiving images from both eyes (stereoscopic). Binocular stereoscopic vision provides depth perception.

Biocultural approach. A method of studying humans that looks at the interaction between biology and culture in evolutionary adaptation.

Biological anthropology. The subfield of anthropology formerly referred to as physical anthropology that focuses on the biological evolution of humans and human ancestors, the relationship of humans to other organisms, and patterns of biological variation within and among human populations.

Bipedalism. Moving about on two legs. Unlike the movement of other bipedal animals such as kangaroos, human bipedalism is further characterized by a striding motion.

B.P. Abbreviation for Before Present, the internationally accepted form of designating past dates. The Present has been set arbitrarily at the year 1950. A date of 75,000 years B.P. thus means 75,000 years before the year 1950.

Brachiation. A method of movement that uses the arms to swing from branch to branch. Gibbons and siamangs are true brachiators.

Breeding population. A group of organisms that tend to choose mates from within the group.

Brow ridge. The large ridge of bone above the eye orbit. Brow ridges are most noticeable in *Homo erectus* and archaic *Homo sapiens*.

Canine. One of four types of teeth found in mammals. The canine teeth are located in the front of the jaw behind the incisors. Mammals normally use these teeth for puncturing and defense. Unlike most mammals, humans have small canine teeth that function like incisors.

Carbon-14 dating. A chronometric dating method based on the half-life of carbon-14. This method can be applied to organic remains such as charcoal over the past 50,000 years or so.

Carrying capacity. The maximum population size capable of being supported in a given environment.

Catastrophism. The hypothesis that patterns of evolutionary change observed in the fossil record can be explained by repeated catastrophes followed by repopulation from other areas by different organisms.

Catch-up growth. An increase in growth that can occur following the removal of a limiting factor to growth.

Cenozoic era. The fifth and most recent geologic era, dating roughly to the last 65 million years, also known as the "Age of Mammals." The first primates appeared during the Cenozoic era.

Cephalic index. A measure of cranial shape defined as the total length of a skull divided by the maximum width of the skull.

Cerebrum. The area of the forebrain that consists of the outermost layer of brain cells. The cerebrum is associated with memory, learning, and intelligence.

Chordata. A vertebrate phylum consisting of organisms that possess a notochord at some period during their life.

Chromosomal mutations. A type of mutation in which large sections of chromosomes are changed. These changes include rearrangements, deletions, additions, movements, and changes in chromosome numbers.

Chromosomes. Long strands of DNA sequences.

Chronometric dating. Method of dating fossils or sites that provides an estimate of the specific date (subject to probabilistic limits).

Cladistics. A school of thought that stresses evolutionary relationships between organisms in forming biological classifications. Organisms are grouped together on the basis of the number of derived traits they share.

Cladogenesis. The formation of one or more new species from another over time.

Codominant. When both alleles affect the phenotype of a heterozygous genotype and neither is dominant over the other.

Coefficient of variation. A comparative statistic that measures relative variability within a sample. The coefficient of variations is used frequently to assess species differences, sexual dimorphism, and other aspects of variation.

Comparative approach. A method used by anthropologists that compares populations to determine common and unique behaviors or biological traits.

Continental drift. The movement of continental land masses on top of a partially molten layer of the earth's mantle. Because of continental drift, the relative location of the continents has changed over time.

Convergent evolution. Where similar adaptations occur in rather distinct evolutionary lines. For example, the development of flight in birds and certain insects is an example of convergent evolution.

Cranial capacity. A measurement of the interior volume of the brain case, used as an approximate estimate of brain size.

Crossing over. Occurs when segments of DNA switch between pairs of chromosomes. Crossing over is an exception to linkage.

Cross-sectional studies. Studies of human growth that analyze samples of children at different ages at one time.

Cultural anthropology. The subfield of anthropology that focuses on variations in cultural behaviors among human populations.

Culture. Behavior that is learned and socially transmitted rather than instinctual and genetically transmitted.

Cusp. A raised area on the chewing surface of a tooth.

Demographic transition theory. A model of demographic change that states that as a population becomes economically developed, there will first be a reduction in death rates (leading to population growth), followed by a reduction in birth rates.

Demography. The study of the size, composition, and distribution of populations.

Dendrochronology. A chronometric dating method based on the fact that trees in dry climates tend to accumulate one growth ring per year. The width of the rings varies according to climate, and a sample can be compared with a master chart of tree rings over the past 10,000 years.

Dental formula. A shorthand method of describing the number of each type of tooth in half of one jaw of a mammal. The dental formula consists of four numbers: I-C-PM-M, where I is the number of incisors, C is the number of canines, PM is the number of premolars, and M is the number of molars. When a mammal has a different number of teeth in the upper and lower jaws, two dental formulae are used.

Dental hypoplasias. Defects in the enamel of teeth resulting from environmental stress, such as poor nutrition or infectious disease.

Deprivation dwarfism. The reduction in a child's growth caused by psychological stress.

Derived trait. A trait that has changed from an ancestral state. For example, the large human brain is a derived trait relative to the common ancestor of humans and apes.

Development. The differentiation and specialization of cells making up different tissues and organs.

Developmental acclimatization. Changes in organ or body structure that occur during the physical growth of any organism.

Diastema. A gap next to the canine teeth that allows space for the canine on the opposing jaw.

Dietary hypothesis. A model first developed in the 1960s that states that two major evolutionary lines in hominid evolution took place during the Plio-Pleistocene. One line was characterized by adaptation to a vegetarian diet, the other by adaptations to an omnivorous diet (especially the development of a large brain).

Directional selection. Selection against one extreme in a continuous trait and/or selection for the other extreme.

Distance curve. A measure of size over time—as, for example, a person's height at different ages.

Diurnal. Active during the day.

Diversifying selection. Selection for the extremes in a continuous trait and against the average value.

Dizygotic twins. Twins who develop from two separate fertilized eggs (zygotes). Dizygotic twins are no more genetically similar than any two siblings.

DNA. Deoxyribonucleic acid. The molecule that provides the genetic code for biological structures and the means to translate this code.

DNA hybridization. A method of separating and recombining strands of DNA in different species that allows assessment of their genetic similarity.

Dominance hierarchy. The ranking system within a society that indicates those individuals who are dominant in social behaviors.

Dominant allele. An allele that masks the effect of the other allele (which is recessive) in a heterozygous genotype.

Electron spin resonance. A chronometric dating method that estimates dates from observation of radioactive atoms trapped in calcite crystals present in a number of materials, such as bones and shells. This method is useful for dating sites back to roughly one million years.

Embryo. The stage of prenatal life lasting from roughly two to eight weeks following conception, characterized by structural development.

Endemic. Pertaining to disease, when new cases occur at a relatively constant but low rate over time.

Endocast. A cast of the interior of the brain case, used in the analysis of brain size and structure.

Endocrine glands. Glands that secrete hormones.

Eocene epoch. The second epoch of the Cenozoic era, dating roughly between 38 and 55 million years B.P. The first true primates, early prosimians, appear during this epoch.

Epidemic. Pertaining to disease, when new cases spread rapidly through a population.

Epidemiologic transition. The change in disease patterns, seen in many developed regions of the world, in which there is a decline in infectious diseases and an increase in noninfectious diseases.

Epidemiology. The study of patterns of human disease and their causes.

Epoch. Subdivision of a geologic period.

Era. The major subdivision of geologic time. There are five eras in the earth's history: Archean, Proterozoic, Paleozoic, Mesozoic, and Cenozoic.

Estrogen. Hormone that acts to stimulate the development of secondary sexual characteristics in females.

Estrus. A time during the month when females are sexually receptive (also known as "heat"). Among primates, human and orangutan females lack an estrus period.

Ethnocentrism. The belief that one's own culture is superior to other cultures.

Eurasia. The combined land masses of Europe and Asia.

Evolution. The transformation of species of organic life over long periods of time. Anthropologists study both the cultural and biological evolution of the human species.

Evolutionary forces. The mechanisms that can cause changes in allele frequencies from one generation to the next. The four evolutionary forces are: mutation, natural selection, genetic drift, and gene flow.

Evolutionary species. A definition of species that is based on ancestral and descendant populations that are evolutionarily distinct from other lineages. Any such linear sequence of populations can be considered to belong to the same species.

Evolutionary taxonomy. A method of classification that (like cladistics) focuses on shared derived traits but gives preference to traits that show overall biological similarity rather than traits that just show evolutionary relatedness.

Exogamy. The tendency to choose mates from outside the local population.

Exon. A section of DNA that codes for the amino acids that make up proteins. It is contrasted with an intron, which is a section of DNA that does not code for amino acids making up a protein.

Family group. A type of social structure in which the primary social group is made up of a single adult male, a single adult female, and their offspring.

Faunal correlation. A relative dating method in which sites can be assigned an approximate age based on the similarity of animal remains with other dated sites.

Fecundity. Potential reproduction, often defined as the number of people capable of having children.

Feedback. A situation in which one factor in a system influences, and is influenced by, other factors in the system.

Fertility. Actual reproduction—the number of births per individual.

Fetal Alcohol Syndrome. A group of birth defects resulting from major alcohol intake by the mother early in pregnancy.

Fetus. The stage of prenatal growth from roughly eight weeks following conception until birth, characterized by further development and rapid growth.

Fission-fusion. A form of population structure in which a group breaks into smaller populations (fission) and may then later combine with other populations to form a larger group (fusion).

Fission-track dating. A chronometric dating method based on the number of tracks made across volcanic rock as uranium decays into lead.

Fitness. The probability of survival and reproduction of an organism. Fitness is generally measured in terms of the different genotypes for a given locus.

Founder effect. A type of genetic drift caused by the formation of a new population by a small number of individuals. The small size of the sample can cause marked deviations in allele frequencies from the original population.

Gene. A section of DNA that determines for a given biological function in an organism.

Gene flow. A mechanism for evolutionary change resulting from the movement of genes from one population to another. Gene flow introduces new genes in a population and also acts to make populations more similar genetically to one another.

Generalized structure. A biological structure adapted to a wide range of conditions and used in very general ways. For example, the grasping hands of humans are generalized structures allowing climbing, food gathering, toolmaking, and a variety of other functions.

Genetic distance. An average measure of relatedness between populations based on a number of traits. Genetic distances are used for understanding effects of genetic drift and gene flow, which should affect all loci to the same extent.

Genetic distance map. A picture that shows the genetic relationships between populations, based on genetic distance measures.

Genetic drift. A mechanism for evolutionary change resulting from the random fluctuations of gene frequencies from one generation to the next, or from any form of random sampling of a larger gene pool.

Genotype. For a given locus, the genetic endowment of an individual from the two alleles present.

Genus. A taxonomic category designating groups of species with similar adaptations.

Gigantopithecus. A genus of fossil ape found in Asia, dating between 0.5 and 9 million years B.P. Only teeth and jaw fragments have so far been discovered, but they indicate an ape with a massive jaw and huge back teeth.

Gradualism. A model of macroevolutionary change whereby evolutionary changes occur at a slow steady rate over time.

Grooming. The handling and cleaning of another individual's fur or hair. In primates, grooming serves as a form of communication that soothes and provides reassurance.

Growth. A change in the size of a living structure, most often caused by an increase in cell size or number.

Growth hormone. A hormone secreted by the pituitary gland that is essential for normal postnatal growth and development.

Half-life. The average length of time it takes for half of a radioactive substance to decay into another form.

Haplorhine. A primate without a moist nose (tarsiers, monkeys, apes, and humans).

Hardy-Weinberg equilibrium. A mathematical model demonstrating that, in the absence of evolutionary forces, allele frequencies remain constant from one generation to the next.

Harris lines. Horizontal lines that form on bones because of disruption of the growth process.

Hemoglobin. The molecule in blood cells that transports oxygen.

Heritability. The proportion of total variance in a trait attributable to genetic variation. This measure is not constant; the actual value depends on the degree of environmental variation in any population.

Heterozygous. The two alleles at a given locus are different.

Holistic. Refers to the viewpoint that all aspects of existence are interrelated and important in understanding human variation and evolution.

Home bases. Camp sites where hunters brought back food for sharing with other members of their group.

Homeobox gene. One of a group of regulatory genes that encode a sequence of 60 amino acids that regulate embryonic development. Homeobox genes subdivide from head to tail a developing embryo into different regions, which then form limbs and other structures. These genes are similar in many organisms, such as insects, mice, and humans.

Homeostasis. In a physiologic sense, the maintenance of normal limits of body functioning.

Hominid. Bipedal primates, including modern humans.

Hominoid. A group of anthropoids consisting of apes and humans. Hominoids have a shoulder structure adapted for climbing and hanging, lack a tail, are generally larger than monkeys, and have the largest brain size:body size ratio among primates.

Homo. A genus of hominid with three recognized species (*Homo erectus, Homo habilis,* and *Homo sapiens*), dating from 2.4 million years ago. The major characteristic of *Homo* is large brain size and dependence on culture as a means of adaptation.

Homo erectus. A species of the genus *Homo* that lived between roughly 0.2 to 0.4 and 1.6 million years B.P. *Homo erectus* first appeared in Africa and later spread to Asia (and possibly Europe). *Homo erectus* had a larger brain size than *Homo habilis* but not as large as *Homo sapiens*.

Homo habilis. The oldest known species in the genus *Homo*, dating between 1.5 and 2.4 million years B.P. and found in Africa. In overall appearance, this species is similar to the australopithecines but has a larger cranial capacity (an average of roughly 660 ml, with a range of 509 to 810 ml).

Homoiotherm. Organism capable of maintaining a constant body temperature under most circumstances. Mammals are homoiotherms.

Homologous trait. Physical trait in two species that has a similar structure but may or may not show a similar function. The arm bones in humans and whales are an example of homologous structure; the bones are the same, but they are used for different functions.

Homozygous. Both alleles at a given locus are identical.

Hormones. Chemicals released by endocrine glands that travel to body tissues and stimulate and regulate biological processes.

Horticulture. A form of farming in which only simple hand tools are used.

Hypothalamus. A structure of the brain that regulates the secretion of hormones.

Hypothesis. An explanation of observed facts. To be scientific, a hypothesis must be testable.

Hypoxia. Oxygen starvation. Hypoxia occurs frequently at high altitudes.

Inbreeding. Mating between biologically related individuals.

Inbreeding coefficient. The increase in the probability of homozygous offspring because of inbreeding. Inbreeding coefficients can be computed for individual matings; an average figure can be computed for an entire population.

Incidence rate. The rate of new cases of a disease developing in a population in a specified period of time.

Incisor. One of four types of teeth found in mammals. The incisors are the flat front teeth used for cutting, slicing, and gnawing food.

Infectious disease. A disease caused by the introduction of an organic foreign substance into the body. Such substances include viruses and parasites.

Insectivore. An order of mammals adapted to insect eating.

Intron. A section of DNA that does not code for the amino acids that make up proteins. It is contrasted with an exon, which is a section of DNA that does code for amino acids making up a protein.

Isolation by distance. A population genetics model that predicts that genetic similarity between populations decreases as geographic distance increases. That is, two populations 100 km apart are likely to be less genetically similar than two populations 10 km apart.

Kenyapithecus. An African Miocene ape, similar to *Sivapithecus* in some ways, but with relatively small canines. This genus dates to 14 to 17 million years B.P. It is a possible common ancestor of modern African apes and humans.

Kin selection. A concept used in sociobiological explanations of altruism. Sacrificial behaviors, for example, can be selected for if they increase the probability of survival of close relatives.

Kin-structured migration. The movement of groups of biologically related individuals to another population, which can result in an increase in variation among populations.

Knuckle walking. A form of movement used by chimpanzees and gorillas that is characterized by all four limbs touching the ground, with the weight of the arms resting on the knuckles of the hands.

K-selection. A reproductive pattern characterized by few offspring but extensive parental care.

Kuru. An infectious disease once found in areas of New Guinea that affected the central nervous system and was spread by coming into contact with the brain of an infected person.

Kwashiorkor. An extreme form of protein-calorie malnutrition, resulting from a severe deficiency in proteins but not calories.

Lactase deficiency. A condition in which an older child or adult lacks the ability to produce the lactase enzyme needed to digest milk sugar.

Lemur. A prosimian found today on the island of Madagascar. Lemurs include both nocturnal and diurnal species.

Life expectancy. A measure of the average length of life in a population.

Life span. A measure of the maximum length of life recorded for a species. In humans, this measure is currently 120 years.

Life table. A table that provides an estimate of the probability of an individual dying by a certain age. Life table analysis is used to estimate life expectancy.

Linguistic anthropology. The subfield of anthropology that focuses on the nature of human language, the relationship of language to culture, and the languages of nonliterate peoples.

Linkage. The situation in which alleles on the same chromosome are inherited together.

Locus. The specific location of a gene on a chromosome. (Plural *loci*.)

Longitudinal study. Here, a study of human growth that analyzes a sample of children repeatedly over time (i.e., the same children at different ages).

Loris. Nocturnal prosimian found today in Asia and Africa.

Lower Paleolithic. The Lower Old Stone Age. A general term used to refer collectively to the stone tool technologies of *Homo habilis* and *Homo erectus*.

Macroevolution. Long-term evolutionary change. The study of macroevolution focuses on biological evolution over many generations and on the origin of higher taxonomic categories, such as species.

Major genes. Genes that have the primary effect on the phenotypic distribution of a complex trait. Additional variation can be due to smaller effects from other loci and/or environmental influences.

Malnutrition. Poor nutrition, either from too much or too little nutrition, or the improper balance of nutrients.

Marasmus. An extreme form of protein-calorie malnutrition resulting from severe deficiencies in both proteins and calories.

Mass extinction. When many species become extinct at roughly the same time.

Meiosis. The creation of sex cells by replication of chromosomes followed by cell division. Each sex cell then contains 50 percent of an individual's chromosomes (one from each pair).

Mendelian genetics. The branch of genetics concerned with patterns and processes of inheritance. This field was named after Gregor Mendel, the first scientist to work out many of these principles.

Mendel's Law of Independent Assortment. The segregation of any pair of chromosomes does not affect the probability of segregation for other pairs of chromosomes.

Mendel's Law of Segregation. Sex cells contain one of each pair of alleles.

Mesozoic era. The fourth geologic era, dating roughly between 65 and 250 million years B.P., also known as the "Age of Reptiles." The first mammals and birds also appeared during the Mesozoic era.

Messenger RNA. The form of RNA that transports the genetic instructions from the DNA molecule to the site of protein synthesis.

Microevolution. Short-term evolutionary change. The study of microevolution focuses on changes in allele frequencies from one generation to the next.

Middle Paleolithic. The Middle Old Stone Age. A general term used to refer collectively to the stone tool technologies of archaic *Homo sapiens*.

Midgrowth spurt. A small increase in the rate of body growth during midchildhood seen in some, but not all, populations.

Migration. The movement of individuals from one population to another. Migration may be short-term or long-term, and may or may not have genetic effects.

Miocene epoch. The fourth epoch of the Cenozoic era, dating roughly between 5 and 22 million years B.P. The first apes evolved during the Miocene.

Mitochondrial DNA. DNA that is found in the mitochondria of the cells rather than the nucleus. Mitochondrial DNA (mtDNA) is inherited primarily through females.

Mitosis. The process of replication of chromosomes in body cells. Each cell produces two identical copies.

Molar. One of four types of teeth found in mammals. The molars are back teeth used for crushing and grinding food.

Molecular dating. The application of methods of genetic analysis to estimate the sequence and timing of divergent evolutionary lines.

Monogamy. An exclusive sexual bond between an adult male and an adult female for a long period of time.

Monosymy. A condition in which only one chromosome rather than a pair is present in body cells.

Monozygotic twins. Twins who develop from a single fertilized egg (zygote); these are known as identical twins.

Morphology. The physical structure of organisms.

Mortality. Death. Mortality, fertility, and migration are the three prime measures of population size.

Mosaic evolution. The concept that major evolutionary changes tend to take place in stages, not all at once. Human evolution shows a mosaic pattern in the fact that small canine teeth, large brains, and tool use did not all evolve at the same time.

Mother-infant group. A type of social structure in which the primary social group consists of a mother and her dependent offspring.

Mousterian tradition. The stone tool technology of the Neandertals, characterized by the careful preparation of a stone core from which finished flakes can be removed.

Multimale group. A type of social structure in which the primary social group is made up of several adult males, several adult females, and their offspring. This is the most common form of social structure found in nonhuman primates.

Multiregional evolution model. A model of the evolution of *Homo sapiens* that states that the change from archaic to modern forms took place in all regions of the Old World (although not necessarily at the same time).

Multivariate analysis. The analysis of human biological variation that takes into consideration the interrelationship of several traits at a time.

Mutation. A mechanism for evolutionary change resulting from a random change in the genetic code. Mutation is the ultimate source of all genetic variation. Mutations must occur in sex cells to cause evolutionary change.

Nasal index. A measure of the shape of the nasal opening, defined as the width of the nasal opening divided by the height.

Natural increase. The change in population size expected because of fertility and mortality but not migration. Natural increase is the number of births minus the number of deaths.

Natural selection. A mechanism for evolutionary change resulting from the differential survival and reproduction of organisms because of their biological characteristics.

Neandertal. Member of a regional population of archaic *Homo sapiens* found in the area around the Mediterranean, dating between roughly 32,000 to 125,000 years B.P. The relationship between Neandertals and later *Homo sapiens* populations in these regions is still being debated.

Negative assortative mating. Mates are chosen on the basis of having different phenotypic characteristics.

Neoteny. The retention of juvenile characteristics into adulthood. The rounded skull and large brain of humans are examples of neoteny.

New World Syndrome. A set of noninfectious diseases that appear in elevated frequencies in individuals with Native-American ancestry.

Nocturnal. Active during the night.

Noninfectious disease. A disease caused by factors other than the introduction of an organic foreign substance into the body (e.g., age, nutrition).

Nonrandom mating. Patterns of mate choice, other than total random mating, that influence the distributions of genotype and phenotype frequencies. Nonrandom mating does not lead to changes in allele frequencies.

Notochord. A flexible internal rod that runs along the back of an animal. Animals possessing a notochord at some period in their life are known as chordates.

Occipital bun. A slight protrusion of the rear region of the skull, a feature often found in Neandertals.

Oldowan tradition. The stone tool culture of *Homo habilis*. Oldowan tools are often simple tools made by removing several flakes from a stone. The flakes removed could also be used as cutting tools.

Oligocene epoch. The third epoch of the Cenozoic era, dating roughly between 22 and 38 million years B.P.

Omomyids. A group of Eocene primates similar in some ways to modern-day tarsiers. They were nocturnal fruit and insect eaters.

One-male group. A type of social structure in which

the primary social group is made up of a single adult male, several adult females, and their offspring.

Orthogenesis. A discredited idea that evolution would continue in a given direction because of some vaguely defined nonphysical "force."

Paleocene epoch. The first epoch of the Cenozoic era, dating roughly between 55 and 65 million years B.P. The primatelike mammals lived during the Paleocene.

Paleoecology. The study of ancient environments.

Paleomagnetic reversal. The earth's magnetic pole has shifted back and forth from the north to the south in the past at irregular intervals. Use of this fact allows certain sites to be dated.

Paleopathology. The study of disease in prehistoric populations based on analysis of skeletal remains and archaeological evidence.

Paleospecies. Species identified from fossil remains based on their physical similarities and differences relative to other species.

Paleozoic era. The third geologic era, dating roughly between 250 and 550 million years B.P. The first vertebrates appeared during this era, including the reptiles and mammallike reptiles.

Palynology. The study of fossil pollen. Palynology allows prehistoric plant species to be identified.

Pandemic. An epidemic that occurs over a large geographic range.

Parallel evolution. Where similar evolutionary adaptations occur independently in closely related species.

Parental investment. A concept used in sociobiological models that describes parental behaviors that increase the probability that offspring will survive.

Period. Subdivision of a geologic era.

Phenetics. A school of thought that stresses the overall physical similarities among organisms in forming biological classifications.

Phenotype. The observable appearance of a given genotype in the organism. The phenotype is determined by the relationship of the two alleles at a given locus, the number of loci, and often environmental influences as well.

Phylogeny. A family tree or figure showing the evolutionary relationships among species.

Physical anthropology. See Biological anthropology.

Piltdown Man. Name given to fossil specimens found in England that were once thought to be a "missing link" between apes and humans but were later exposed as a hoax.

Pituitary gland. A structure in the brain that secretes hormones that either act directly on body tissues or stimulate other endocrine glands to release hormones.

Placenta. An organ that develops inside a pregnant placental mammal. It provides the fetus with oxygen and food and helps filter out harmful substances.

Plasticity. The ability of an organism to respond physiologically or developmentally to environmental stress.

Pleiotropy. When a single allele can have multiple effects on an organism.

Pleistocene epoch. The sixth epoch of the Cenozoic era, dating from 0.01 to 1.8 million years B.P. The major event in human evolution was the continued development of the genus *Homo*.

Pliocene epoch. The fifth epoch of the Cenozoic era, dating from 1.8 to 5 million years B.P. The major event in human evolution was the origin of the hominid.

Plio-Pleistocene. A term used to describe the time of the australopithecines (from 1 to 4 million years B.P.).

Point mutation. A type of mutation in which the sequence of bases of DNA in a single gene are changed.

Polyandry. In humans, a form of marriage in which a wife has several husbands. In more general terms, it refers to an adult female having several mates.

Polygamy. In general terms, it refers to having more than one mate.

Polygenic. Refers to a trait that is affected by two or more loci. Complex traits, such as skin color and height, are polygenic.

Polygyny. In humans, a form of marriage in which a husband has several wives. In more general terms, it refers to an adult male having several mates.

Polymerase chain reaction (PCR). A laboratory method that involves the laboratory synthesis of millions of copies of DNA fragments. This technique allows easier study of molecular genetics.

Polymorphism. A discrete genetic trait, such as a blood group, in which there are at least two alleles at a locus having frequencies greater than 0.01.

Population pyramid. A graphic illustration of the age-sex structure of a population.

Positive assortative mating. Mates are chosen on the basis of their having similar phenotypic characteristics. An example is tall people choosing tall mates.

Postcranial. Referring to that part of the skeleton below the neck.

Postnatal. Referring to the period of life from birth until death.

Postorbital bar. The bony ring that separates the eye orbit from the back of the skull. The postorbital bar is a primate characteristic.

Postorbital constriction. The narrowness of the skull behind the eye orbits. Early hominids, such as *Homo habilis* and *Homo erectus,* show considerable postorbital constriction, particularly when compared to modern humans.

Postpartum taboos. Behaviors that limit sexual intercourse following the birth of a child.

Potassium-argon dating. A chronometric dating method based on the half-life of radioactive potassium (which decays into argon gas). This method can be used to date volcanic rock older than 100,000 years.

Precambrian. That time in earth's history preceding the first major appearance of life. Precambrian times encompass the Archean and Proterozoic eras.

Prehensile. Capable of grasping. Primates have prehensile hands and feet, and some primates (certain New World monkeys) have prehensile tails.

Premolar. One of four types of teeth found in mammals. The premolars are back teeth used for crushing and grinding food.

Prenatal. Referring to the period of life from conception until birth.

Prevalence rate. The proportion of total cases of a disease, old and new, in a population during a specified period of time.

Primate. A member of an order of mammals that has a complex of characteristics related to an initial adaptation to life in the trees (even though many modern primates now live on the ground), including binocular stereoscopic vision and grasping hands. The primates are the prosimians, monkeys, apes, and humans.

Primitive trait. In biological terms, a trait that has not changed from an ancestral state. The five digits of the human hand and foot are primitive traits inherited from earlier vertebrate ancestors.

Proconsul. A genus of fossil apes that lived in Africa between 17 and 23 million years B.P. Though classified as apes, this genus also shows a number of monkey characteristics. It most probably represents one of the first forms to evolve following the divergence of the monkey and ape lines.

Prosimian. A suborder of primates. Prosimians are the most biologically primitive of all primates.

Protein-calorie malnutrition. A group of nutritional diseases resulting from inadequate amounts of protein and/or calories. Protein-calorie malnutrition is a severe problem in developing regions today.

Proterozoic era. The second geologic era, dating roughly between 550 million years B.P. and 2.5 billion years B.P. The first invertebrates appeared during the Proterozoic era.

Puberty. The time in the human life cycle when sexual and physical maturity is attained.

Punctuated equilibrium. A model of macroevolutionary change in which long periods of little evolutionary change (stasis) are followed by relatively short periods of rapid evolutionary change.

Quadrupedal. A form of movement in which all four limbs are of equal size and make contact with the ground, and the spine is roughly parallel to the ground. Monkeys are typical quadrupedal primates.

Race. In terms of biological variation, a group of populations sharing certain traits that make them distinct from other groups of populations. In practice, the concept of race is very difficult to apply to patterns of human variation.

Recent African origin model. A model of the evolution of modern *Homo sapiens* whereby archaic *H. sapiens* evolved into modern *H. sapiens* in Africa and then spread out through the rest of the Old World, replacing archaic populations. This model differs from the assimilation model in that it does not propose gene flow with non-African archaic populations.

Recessive allele. An allele whose effect is masked by the other allele (which is dominant) in a heterozygous genotype.

Reciprocal altruism. A concept used in sociobiological explanations of altruism directed toward nonrelatives. Such altruistic behaviors can be selected for, according to this model, if they increase the probability that the target of such actions will reciprocate at some future time.

Regulatory gene. Gene that codes for the regulation of such biological processes as growth and development.

Relative dating. Comparative method of dating fossils and sites that provides an estimate of the older find but not a specific date.

Reproductive isolation. The genetic isolation of populations that can render them incapable of producing fertile offspring.

Restriction Fragment Length Polymorphism (RFLP). A genetic trait defined in terms of the length of DNA fragments produced through cutting by certain enzymes. RFLPs, which are highly variable, are particularly useful in mapping genetic diseases.

Rhesus incompatibility. A condition in which a pregnant woman and her fetus have incompatible Rhesus blood group phenotypes: the woman has the Rhesus negative phenotype and the fetus has the Rhesus positive phenotype.

RNA. Ribonucleic acid. The molecule that functions to carry out the instructions for protein synthesis specified by the DNA molecule.

r-selection. A reproductive pattern characterized by large numbers of offspring and little parental care.

Sagittal crest. A ridge of bone running down the center of the top of the skull that serves to anchor chewing muscles. Sagittal crests are found in some australopithecines.

Savanna. An environment consisting of open grasslands. Food resources tend to be spread out over large areas.

Secular trend. A change in the average pattern of growth in a population over different generations.

Sensitive period of growth. Times during the life cycle when catch-up growth is not possible.

Sexual dimorphism. In terms of body size, the average difference in size between adult males and adult females. Primate species with sexual dimorphism in body size are characterized by adult males being, on average, larger than adult females.

Shifting balance theory. A model whereby allele frequencies can change to a new set of values providing greater overall fitness through a balance of natural selection and random genetic drift.

Sickle cell allele. An allele of the hemoglobin locus. If two such alleles are present, the individual has sickle cell anemia.

Sickle cell anemia. A genetic disease that occurs in a person homozygous for the sickle cell allele; the altered structure of red blood cells leads to greatly reduced fitness.

Single-species hypothesis. A model of Plio-Pleistocene hominid evolution developed in the 1960s that stated that there was only one species of hominid in existence at any point in time. Later fossil discoveries led to the rejection of this model.

Sivapithecus. A genus of fossil ape found in Asia and Europe dating between 7 and 14 million years B.P. On the basis of cranial and dental remains, one of the Asian species of *Sivapithecus* appears to be an ancestor of the modern-day orangutan.

Social structure. The composition of a social group and the way it is organized, including size, age structure, and number of each sex in the group.

Sociobiology. A discipline concerned with evolutionary explanations of social behavior, focusing on the role of natural selection.

Specialized structure. A biological structure adapted to a narrow range of conditions and used in very specific ways. For example, the hooves of horses are specialized structures allowing movement over flat terrain.

Speciation. The origin of a new species.

Species. A taxonomic category designating a group of populations whose members can interbreed naturally and that produce fertile offspring.

Species selection. A process of selection in which some species are more likely to survive and/or develop into new species. Species selection is essentially the differential survival and reproduction of species.

Stabilizing selection. Selection against extreme values, small or large, in a continuous trait.

Stasis. Little or no evolutionary change occurring over a long period of time.

Stratigraphy. A relative dating method based on the fact that older remains are found deeper in the earth (under the right conditions). This method makes use of the fact that a cumulative buildup of the earth's surface takes place over time.

Strepsirhine. A primate with a moist nose (lorises and lemurs).

Stress. Any factor that interferes with the normal limits of operation of an organism.

Structural gene. Gene that codes for the production of proteins.

Suspensory climbing and hanging. The ability to raise the arms above the head and hang on branches and to climb in this position. Hominoids are suspensory climbers and hangers.

Taphonomy. The study of what happens to plants and animals after they die. Taphonomy helps in determining reasons for the distribution and condition of fossils.

Tarsier. Nocturnal prosimian found today in Indonesia. Unlike other prosimians, tarsiers lack a moist nose.

Taxonomy. A formal classification of organisms. The term also applies to the science of classification.

Terrestrial. Living on the ground.

Theory. A set of hypotheses that have been tested repeatedly and that have not been rejected. This term is sometimes used in a different sense in social science literature.

Therapsid. An early group of reptiles also known as the mammallike reptiles. Therapsids were the ancestors of later mammals.

Thermoluminescence. A chronometric dating method that uses the fact that certain heated objects accumulate trapped electrons over time, which allows the date when the object was initially heated to be determined.

Thyroxine. Thyroid hormone, secreted by the thyroid gland, that acts to increase oxygen consumption in body tissues.

Tool use model. A now-rejected model of hominid origins that stated that bipedalism, large brains, and small canines all evolved simultaneously during hominid evolution as a consequence of increased reliance on tool use.

Transfer RNA. A free-floating molecule that is attracted to a strand of messenger RNA, resulting in the synthesis of a protein chain.

Trephination. Surgery involving the removal of a section of bone from the skull.

Trisomy. A condition in which three chromosomes rather than a pair occur. Down syndrome is often caused by trisomy by the addition of an extra chromosome to the 21st chromosome pair.

Typology. A set of discrete groupings in classification. Typologies emphasize average tendencies and ignore variation within groups. Racial classifications are a form of typology.

Univariate analysis. The analysis of human biological variation focusing on a single trait at a time.

Upper Paleolithic. The Upper Old Stone Age. A general term used to collectively refer to the stone tool technologies of anatomically modern *Homo sapiens.*

Variation. The differences that exist among individuals or populations. Anthropologists study both cultural and biological variation.

Vasoconstriction. The narrowing of blood vessels, which reduces blood flow and heat loss.

Vasodilation. The opening of the blood vessels, which increases blood flow and heat loss.

Velocity curves. A measure of the rates of change in growth over time.

Vertebrata. A subphylum of the phylum Chordata, defined by the presence of an internal, segmented spinal column and bilateral symmetry.

Würm glaciation. One of the times of glaciation ("ice ages") during the Pleistocene epoch.

Zoonose. Disease that is transmitted directly from animals to humans.

Zygomatic arch. The bone on the side of the skull which connects the zygomatic and temporal bones. This bone serves to anchor muscles used in chewing.

Zygote. A fertilized egg.

References

Aalen, F. H. A. 1963. A review of recent Irish population trends. *Population Studies* 17:73–78.

Abel, E. L. 1982. Consumption of alcohol during pregnancy: A review of effects on growth and development of offspring. *Human Biology* 54: 421–53.

Ackerman, S. 1987. American Scientist interviews: Peter Ellison. *American Scientist* 75:622–27.

Allen, L. L., P. S. Bridges, D. L. Evon, K. R. Rosenberg, M. D. Russell, L. A. Schepartz, V. J. Vitzthum, and M. H. Wolpoff. 1982. Demography and human origins. *American Anthropologist* 84: 888–96.

Almquist, A. J., and J. E. Cronin. 1988. Fact, fancy, and myth in human evolution. *Current Anthropology* 29:520–22.

Anderson, C. M. 1992. Male investment under changing conditions among Chacma baboons at Suikerbosrand. *American Journal of Physical Anthropology* 87:479–96.

Anderson, W. F. 1992. Human gene therapy. *Science* 256:808–13.

Arensberg, B., L. A. Schepartz, A. M. Tillier, B. Vandermeersch, and Y. Rak. 1990. A reappraisal of the anatomical basis for speech in Middle Paleolithic hominids. *American Journal of Physical Anthropology* 83:137–46.

Arensberg, C. M., and S. T. Kimball. 1968. *Family and Community in Ireland*. 2d ed. Harvard University Press: Cambridge.

Armelagos, G. J., and J. R. Dewey. 1970. Evolutionary response to human infectious diseases. *BioScience* 157:638–44.

Armstrong, E. 1983. Relative brain size and metabolism in mammals. *Science* 220:1302–4.

Avise, J. C., J. E. Neigel, and J. Arnold. 1984. Demographic influences on mitochondrial DNA lineage survivorship in animal populations. *Journal of Molecular Evolution* 20:99–105.

Baker, B. J., and G. J. Armelagos. 1988. The origin and antiquity of syphilis: Paleopathological diagnosis and interpretation. *Current Anthropology* 29: 703–37.

Bakker, R. T. 1986. *The Dinosaur Heresies*. New York: William Morrow.

Beals, K. L. 1972. Head form and climatic stress. *American Journal of Physical Anthropology* 37: 85–92.

Beals, K. L., C. L. Smith, and S. M. Dodd. 1983. Climate and the evolution of brachycephalization.

American Journal of Physical Anthropology 62: 425–37.

Beals, K. L., C. L. Smith, and S. M. Dodd. 1984. Brain size, cranial morphology, climate, and time machines. *Current Anthropology* 25:301–30.

Bindon, J. R., and P. T. Baker. 1985. Modernization, migration, and obesity among Samoan adults. *Annals of Human Biology* 12:67–76.

Bindon, J. R., and S. M. Zansky. 1986. Growth patterns of height and weight among three groups of Samoan preadolescents. *Annals of Human Biology* 13:171–78.

Bittles, A. H., W. M. Mason, J. Greene, and N. A. Rao. 1991. Reproductive behavior and health in consanguineous marriages. *Science* 252:789–94.

Blum, H. F. 1961. Does the melanin pigment of human skin have adaptive value? *Quarterly Review of Biology* 36:50–63.

Blumenberg, B. 1985. Population characteristics of extinct hominid endocranial volume. *American Journal of Physical Anthropology* 68:269–79.

Bodmer, W. F., and L. L. Cavalli-Sforza. 1976. *Genetics, Evolution, and Man.* San Francisco: W. H. Freeman.

Bogin, B. A. 1988. *Patterns of Human Growth.* Cambridge: Cambridge University Press.

Bouchard, T. J., D. T. Lykken, M. McGue, N. L. Segal, and A. Tellegen. 1990. Sources of human psychological differences: The Minnesota study of twins reared apart. *Science* 250:223–28.

Bouvier, L. F. 1984. Planet Earth 1984–2034: A demographic vision. *Population Bulletin* 39(1).

Brace, C. L. 1964. The fate of the "classic" Neandertals: A consideration of hominid catastrophism. *Current Anthropology* 5:3–43.

———. 1991. *The Stages of Human Evolution: Human and Cultural Origins.* 4th ed. Englewood Cliffs, N. J.: Prentice-Hall.

Brace, C. L., K. R. Rosenberg, and K. D. Hunt. 1987. Gradual change in human tooth size in the Late Pleistocene and Post-Pleistocene. *Evolution* 41: 705–20.

Bramblett, C. A. 1976. *Patterns of Primate Behavior.* Palo Alto, Calif.: Mayfield.

Brookmeyer, R. 1991. Reconstruction and future trends of the AIDS epidemic in the United States. *Science* 253:37–42.

Brown, F., J. Harris, R. Leakey, and A. Walker. 1985. Early *Homo erectus* skeleton from west Lake Turkana, Kenya. *Nature* 316:788–92.

Brues, A. M. 1977. *People and Races.* New York: Macmillan.

Buss, D. M. 1985. Human mate selection. *American Scientist* 73:47–51.

Byard, P. J. 1981. Quantitative genetics of human skin color. *Yearbook of Physical Anthropology* 24: 123–37.

Calcagno, J. M., and K. R. Gibson. 1988. Human dental reduction: Natural selection or the probable mutation effect. *American Journal of Physical Anthropology* 77:505–17.

Campbell, B. G. 1985. *Human Evolution.* 3d ed. New York: Aldine.

Cann, R. L., M. Stoneking, and A. C. Wilson. 1987. Mitochondrial DNA and human evolution. *Nature* 325:31–36.

Cann, R. L., and A. C. Wilson. 1982. Models of human evolution. *Science* 217:303–4.

Cartmill, M. 1974. Rethinking primate origins. *Science* 184:436–43.

———. 1982. Basic primatology and prosimian evolution. In *A History of American Physical Anthropology 1930–1980,* ed. F. Spencer, pp. 147–86. New York: Academic Press.

Cavalli-Sforza, L. L. 1991. Genes, people and languages. *Scientific American* 265(5):104–10.

Cavalli-Sforza, L. L., and W. F. Bodmer. 1971. *The Genetics of Human Populations.* San Francisco: W. H. Freeman.

Chakraborty, R. 1986. Gene admixture in human populations: Models and predictions. *Yearbook of Physical Anthropology* 29:1–43.

Chakraborty, R., and S. P. Daiger. 1991. Polymorphisms at VNTR loci suggest homogeneity of the white population of Utah. *Human Biology* 63: 571–87.

Ciochon, R. L. 1988. *Gigantopithecus:* The king of all apes. *Animal Kingdom* 91(2):32–39.

Ciochon, R., J. Olsen, and J. James. 1990. *Other Origins: The Search for the Giant Ape in Human Prehistory.* New York: Bantam Books.

Clark, G. A. 1988. Some thoughts on the Black Skull: An archeologist's assessment of WT-17000 (*A. boisei*) and systematics in human paleontology. *American Anthropologist* 90:357–71.

Clarke, R. J. 1985. *Australopithecus* and early *Homo* in Southern Africa. In *Ancestors: The Hard Evidence,* ed. E. Delson, pp. 171–77. New York: Alan R. Liss.

Cockburn, T. A. 1971. Infectious diseases in ancient populations. *Current Anthropology* 12:45–62.

Collins, F. S. 1992. Cystic fibrosis: Molecular biology and therapeutic implications. *Science* 256:774–79.

Connell, K. H. 1950. *The Population of Ireland 1750–1845*. Oxford: Clarendon Press.

Conroy, G. C. 1990. *Primate Evolution*. New York: W. W. Norton.

Conroy, G. C., M. W. Vannier, and P. V. Tobias. 1990. Endocranial features of *Australopithecus africanus* revealed by 2- and 3-D computed tomography. *Science* 247:838–41.

Conroy, G. C., M. Pickford, B. Senut, J. Van Couvering, and P. Mein. 1992. *Otavipithecus namibiensis*, first Myocene Hominoid from southern Africa. *Nature* 356:144–48.

Coyne, J. A. 1992. Genetics and speciation. *Nature* 355:511–15.

Crawford, M. H., and E. J. Devor. 1980. Population structure and admixture in transplanted Tlaxcaltecan populations. *American Journal of Physical Anthropology* 52:485–90.

Crews, D. E. 1989. Cause-specific mortality, life expectancy, and debilitation in aging Polynesians. *American Journal of Human Biology* 1:347–53.

Cronin, J. E. 1983. Apes, humans and molecular clocks: A reappraisal. In *New Interpretations of Ape and Human Ancestry*, ed. R. L. Ciochon and R. S. Corruccini, pp. 115–36. New York: Plenum Press.

Crow, J. F. 1958. Some possibilities for measuring selection intensities in man. *Human Biology* 30:1–13.

Crow, J. F., and M. Kimura. 1970. *An Introduction to Population Genetics Theory*. Minneapolis, Minn.: Burgess.

Culotta, E. 1992. A new take on anthropoid origins. *Science* 256:1516–17.

Curran, J. W., H. W. Jaffe, A. M. Hardy, W. M. Morgan, R. M. Selik, and T. J. Dondero. 1988. Epidemiology of HIV infection and AIDS in the United States. *Science* 239:610–16.

Damon, A. 1977. *Human Biology and Ecology*. New York: W. W. Norton.

Day, M. H. 1986. Bipedalism: Pressures, origins and modes. In *Major Topics in Primate and Human Evolution*, ed. B. Wood, L. Martin, and P. Andrews, pp. 188–202. Cambridge: Cambridge University Press.

Denham, W. W. 1971. Energy relations and some basic properties of primate social organization. *American Anthropologist* 73:77–95.

De Robertis, E. M., G. Oliver, and C. V. E. Wright. 1990. Homeobox genes and the vertebrate body plan. *Scientific American* 263(1):46–52.

Dettwyler, K. A. 1991. Can paleopathology provide evidence for "compassion"? *American Journal of Physical Anthropology* 84:375–84.

Dickerson, R. E. 1978. Chemical evolution and the origin of life. In *Evolution*, ed. Scientific American, pp. 30–46. San Francisco: W. H. Freeman.

Dixon, B., and G. W. McBride. 1992. Health and disease. *Encyclopaedia Britannica Book of the Year, 1992*, pp. 172–76. Chicago: Encyclopaedia Britannica.

Dorfman, D. D. 1978. The Cyril Burt question: New findings. *Science* 201:1177–86.

Drake, J. W., B. W. Glickman, and L. S. Ripley. 1983. Updating the theory of mutation. *American Scientist* 71:621–30.

Dunn, F. L. 1968. Epidemiological factors: Health and disease among hunter-gatherers. In *Man the Hunter*, ed. R. B. Lee and I. DeVore, pp. 221–28. Chicago: Aldine.

Eaton, G. G. 1976. The social order of Japanese macaques. *Scientific American* 235(4):96–106.

Eldredge, N. 1985. *Time Frames: The Rethinking of Darwinian Evolution and the Theory of Punctuated Equilibria*. New York: Simon & Schuster.

Eldredge, N., and S. J. Gould. 1972. Punctuated equilibria: An alternative to phyletic gradualism. In *Models in Paleobiology*, ed. T. J. M. Schopf, pp. 82–115. San Francisco: Freeman, Cooper.

Encyclopaedia Britannica. 1988. *Encyclopaedia Britannica Book of the Year, 1988*. Encyclopaedia Britannica: Chicago.

Ereshefsky, M., ed. 1992. *The Units of Evolution: Essays on the Nature of Species*. Cambridge: MIT Press.

Erlich, H. A., D. Gelfand, and J. J. Sninsky. 1991. Recent advances in the polymerase chain reaction. *Science* 252:1643–51.

Falk, D. 1983. Cerebral cortices of East African early hominids. *Science* 221:1072–74.

Falk, D. 1990. Brain evolution in *Homo*: The radiator theory. *Behavioral and Brain Sciences* 13:333–81.
———. 1992. *Braindance*. New York: Henry Holt.

Fedigan, L. M. 1983. Dominance and reproductive success in primates. *Yearbook of Physical Anthropology* 26:91–129.

Feldesman, M. R., and J. K. Lundy. 1988. Stature estimates for some African Plio-Pleistocene fossil hominids. *Journal of Human Evolution* 17:583–96.

Fix, A. G. 1978. The role of kin-structured migration in genetic microdifferentiation. *Annals of Human Genetics* 41:329–39.

Fleagle, J. G. 1983. Locomotor adaptations of Oligocene and Miocene hominoids and their phyletic implications. In *New Interpretations of Ape and Human Ancestry*, ed. R. L. Ciochon and R. S. Corruccini, pp. 301–24. New York: Plenum Press.

———. 1988. *Primate Adaptation and Evolution*. San Diego: Academic Press.

Fleagle, J. G., T. M. Brown, J. D. Obradovich, and E. L. Simons. 1986. Age of the earliest African anthropoids. *Science* 234:1247–49.

Fleagle, J. G., and R. F. Kay. 1983. New interpretations of the phyletic position of Oligocene hominoids. In *New Interpretations of Ape and Human Ancestry*, ed. R. L. Ciochon and R. S. Corruccini, pp. 181–210. New York: Plenum Press.

Fleagle, J. G., D. T. Rasmussen, S. Yirga, T. M. Brown, and F. E. Grine. 1991. New hominid fossils from Fejej, Southern Ethiopia. *Journal of Human Evolution* 21:145–52.

Fossey, D. 1983. *Gorillas in the Mist*. Boston: Houghton Mifflin.

Franciscus, R. G., and J. C. Long. 1991. Variation in human nasal height and breadth. *American Journal of Physical Anthropology* 85:419–27.

Frayer, D. W. 1984. Biological and cultural change in the European Late Pleistocene and Early Holocene. In *The Origins of Modern Humans: A World Survey of the Fossil Evidence*, ed. F. H. Smith and F. Spencer, pp. 211–50. New York: Alan R. Liss.

Friedlaender, J. S. 1975. *Patterns of Human Variation*. Cambridge: Harvard University Press.

Fries, J. F., and L. M. Crapo. 1981. *Vitality and Aging*. San Francisco: W. H. Freeman.

Frisancho, A. R. 1979. *Human Adaptation: A Functional Interpretation*. St. Louis: C. V. Mosby.

———. 1990. Introduction: Comparative high-altitude adaptation. *American Journal of Human Biology* 2:599–601.

Frisancho, A. R., and P. T. Baker. 1970. Altitude and growth: A study of the patterns of physical growth of a high altitude Peruvian Quechua population. *American Journal of Physical Anthropology* 32:279–92.

Fox, R. C., G. P. Youzwyshyn, and D. W. Krause. 1992. Post-Jurassic mammal-like reptile from the Paleocene. *Nature* 358:233–35.

Futuyma, D. J. 1983. *Science on Trial: The Case for Evolution*. New York: Pantheon Books.

———. 1986. *Evolutionary Biology*. 2d ed. Sunderland, Mass.: Sinauer.

———. 1988. *Sturm und Drang* and the evolutionary synthesis. *Evolution* 42:217–26.

Gage, T. B. 1989. Bio-mathematical approaches to the study of human variation in mortality. *Yearbook of Physical Anthropology* 32:185–214.

Galdikas, B. M. F., and J. W. Wood. 1990. Birth spacing patterns in humans and apes. *American Journal of Physical Anthropology* 83:185–91.

Gardner, L. I. 1972. Deprivation dwarfism. *Scientific American* 227(1):76–82.

Gardner, L. I., Jr., M. P. Stern, S. M. Haffner, S. P. Gaskill, H. P. Hazuda, J. H. Relethford, and C. W. Eifler. 1984. Prevalence of diabetes in Mexican Americans: Relationship to percent of gene pool derived from Native American sources. *Diabetes* 33:86–92.

Garn, S. M. 1965. *Human Races*. 2d ed. Springfield, Ill.: Charles C. Thomas.

———. 1985. Smoking and human biology. *Human Biology* 57:505–23.

Gibbons, A. 1990. Our chimp cousins get that much closer. *Science* 250:376.

———. 1992a. Chimps: More diverse than a barrel of monkeys. *Science* 255:287–88.

———. 1992b. Jawing with our Georgian ancestors. *Science* 255:401.

Gingerich, P. D. 1985. Nonlinear molecular clocks and ape-human divergence times. In *Hominid Evolution: Past, Present and Future*, ed. P. V. Tobias, pp. 411–16. New York: Alan R. Liss.

———. 1986. *Plesiadapis* and the delineation of the order Primates. In *Major Topics in Primate and Human Evolution*, ed. B. Wood, L. Martin and P. Andrews, pp. 32–46. Cambridge: Cambridge University Press.

Gingerich, P. D., B. H. Smith, and E. L. Simons. 1990. Hind limbs of Eocene *Basilosaurus*: Evidence of feet in whales. *Science* 249:154–57.

Glass, H. B. 1953. The genetics of the Dunkers. *Scientific American* 189(2):76–81.

Gloria-Bottini, F., G. Gerlini, A. Amante, R. Pascone, and E. Bottini. 1992. Diabetic pregnancy: Evidence of selection on the Rh blood group system. *Human Biology* 64:81–87.

Godfrey, L., and K. H. Jacobs. 1981. Gradual, autocatalytic and punctuational models of hominid brain evolution: A cautionary tale. *Journal of Human Evolution* 10:255–72.

Godinot, M., and M. Mahboubi. 1992. Earliest known simian primate found in Algeria. *Nature* 357: 324–26.

Goodall, J. 1986. *The Chimpanzees of Gombe: Patterns of Behavior*. Cambridge: Harvard University Press.

Goodman, A. H., G. J. Armelagos, and J. C. Rose. 1980. Enamel hypoplasias as indicators of stress in three prehistoric populations from Illinois. *Human Biology* 52:515–28.

Gould, S. J. 1977a. *Ever Since Darwin*. New York: W. W. Norton.

———. 1977b. *Ontogeny and Phylogeny*. Cambridge: Harvard University Press.

———. 1981. *The Mismeasure of Man*. New York: W. W. Norton.

———. 1983. *Hen's Teeth and Horse's Toes*. New York: W. W. Norton.

———. 1985. *The Flamingo's Smile*. New York: W. W. Norton.

———. 1987. *An Urchin in the Storm*. New York: W. W. Norton.

———. 1989. *Wonderful Life: The Burgess Shale and the Nature of History*. New York: W. W. Norton.

———. 1991. *Bully for Brontosaurus*. New York: W. W. Norton.

Gould, S. J., and N. Eldredge. 1977. Punctuated equilibria: The tempo and mode of evolution reconsidered. *Paleobiology* 3:115–51.

Gould, S. J., and R. C. Lewontin. 1979. The spandrels of San Marco and the Panglossian paradigm: A critique of the adaptationist programme. *Proceedings of the Royal Society of London* (Series B), 205:581–98.

Grant, P. R. 1991. Natural selection and Darwin's finches. *Scientific American* 265(4):82–87.

Grant, V. 1985. *The Evolutionary Process: A Critical Review of Evolutionary Theory*. New York: Columbia University Press.

Greska, L. P. 1990. Developmental responses to high-altitude hypoxia in Bolivian children of European ancestry: A test of the developmental adaptation hypothesis. *American Journal of Human Biology* 2:603–12.

Grün, R., N. J. Shackleton, and H. J. Deacon. 1990. Electron-Spin-Resonance dating of tooth enamel from Klasies River Mouth Cave. *Current Anthropology* 31:427–32.

Grün, R., C. B. Stringer, and H. P. Schwartz. 1991. ESR dating of teeth from Garood's Tabun cave collection. *Journal of Human Evolution* 20:231–48.

Gyllensten, U., D. Wharton, A. Josefsson, and A. C. Wilson. 1991. Paternal inheritance of mitochondrial DNA in mice. *Nature* 352:255–57.

Hall, J. M., M. K. Lee, B. Newman, J. E. Morros, L. E. Anderson, B. Huey, and M. King. 1990. Linkage of early-onset familial breast cancer to chromosome 17q21. *Science* 250:1684–89.

Harley, D. 1982. Models of human evolution. *Science* 217:296.

Harlow, H. F. 1959. Love in infant monkeys. *Scientific American* 200(6):68–74.

Harlow, H. F., and M. K. Harlow. 1962. Social deprivation in monkeys. *Scientific American* 207(5): 136–46.

Harpending, H., and T. Jenkins. 1973. Genetic distance among southern African populations. In *Methods and Theories of Anthropological Genetics*, ed. M. H. Crawford and P. L. Workman, pp. 177–200. Albuquerque: University of New Mexico Press.

Harpending, H., A. Rogers, and P. Draper. 1987. Human sociobiology. *Yearbook of Physical Anthropology* 30:127–50.

Harris, M. 1987. *Cultural Anthropology*, 2d ed. New York: Harper & Row.

Harrison, G. A., J. M. Tanner, D. R. Pilbeam, and P. T. Baker. 1988. *Human Biology: An Introduction to Human Evolution, Variation, Growth, and Adaptability*. 3d ed. Oxford: Oxford University Press.

Hartl, D. L. 1988. *A Primer of Population Genetics*. 2d ed. Sunderland, Mass.: Sinauer.

Harvey, P. H., and M. D. Pagel. 1991. *The Comparative Method in Evolutionary Biology*. Oxford: Oxford University Press.

Haub, C. V. 1992. Populations and population movements. *Encyclopaedia Britannica Book of the Year 1992*, pp. 250–52. Chicago: Encyclopaedia Britannica.

Hedges, S. B., S. Kumar, K. Tamura and M. Stoneking. 1992. Human origins and analysis of mitochondrial DNA sequences. *Science* 255:737–39.

Henneberg, M. 1988. Decrease of human skull size in the Holocene. *Human Biology* 60:395–405.

Hill, A., S. Ward, A. Deino, G. Curtis, and R. Drake. 1992. Earliest *Homo*. *Nature* 355:719–22.

Hodges, D. C. 1987. Health and agricultural intensification in the prehistoric valley of Oaxaca, Mexico. *American Journal of Physical Anthropology* 73:323–32.

Holick, M. F., J. A. MacLaughlin, and S. H. Doppelt. 1981. Regulation of cutaneous previtamin D₃ photosynthesis in man: Skin pigment is not an essential regulator. *Science* 211:590–93.

Holloway, R. L. 1985. The poor brain of *Homo sapiens neanderthalensis:* See what you please. In *Ancestors: The Hard Evidence*, ed. E. Delson, pp. 319–24. New York: Alan R. Liss.

Hooton, E. A. 1946. *Up from the Ape*. New York: Macmillan.

Horr, D. A. 1972. The Borneo orang-utan. *Borneo Research Bulletin* 4(2):46–50.

Hrdy, S. B. 1977. *The Langurs of Abu*. Cambridge: Harvard University Press.

———. 1981. *The Woman That Never Evolved*. Cambridge: Harvard University Press.

Hunt, E. 1983. On the nature of intelligence. *Science* 219:141–46.

Huss-Ashmore, R. 1980. Fat and fertility: Demographic implications of differential fat storage. *Yearbook of Physical Anthropology* 23:65–91.

Jensen, A. R. 1969. How much can we boost IQ and scholastic achievement? *Harvard Educational Review* 33:1–123.

Johanson, D. C., and M. A. Edey. 1981. *Lucy: The Beginnings of Humankind*. New York: Simon & Schuster.

Johanson, D. C., F. T. Masau, G. G. Eck, T. D. White, R. C. Walter, W. H. Kimbel, B. Asfaw, P. Manega, P. Ndessokia, and G. Suwa. 1987. New partial skeleton of *Homo habilis* from Olduvai Gorge, Tanzania. *Nature* 327:205–9.

Johanson, D. C., and T. D. White. 1979. A systematic assessment of early African hominids. *Science* 203:321–30.

Johanson, D. C., T. D. White, and Y. Coppens. 1978. A new species of the genus *Australopithecus* (Primates: Hominidae) from the Pliocene of Eastern Africa. *Kirtlandia* 28:1–14.

Johnston, F. E., and R. M. Malina. 1966. Age changes in the composition of the upper arm in Philadelphia children. *Human Biology* 38:1–21.

Jolly, A. 1985. *The Evolution of Primate Behavior*. 2d ed. New York: Macmillan.

Jolly, C. J. 1970. The seed eaters: A new model of hominid differentiation based on a baboon analogy. *Man* 5:5–26.

Jorde, L. B. 1980. The genetic structure of subdivided human populations. In *Current Developments in*

Anthropological Genetics. Vol. 1, *Theory and Methods,* ed. J. H. Mielke and M. H. Crawford, pp. 135–208. New York: Plenum Press.

———. 1982. The genetic structure of the Utah Mormons: Migration analysis. *Human Biology* 54: 583–97.

Jorde, L. B., and K. J. Pitkänen. 1991. Inbreeding in Finland. *American Journal of Physical Anthropology* 84:127–39.

Jorde, L. B., P. L. Workman, and A. W. Eriksson. 1982. Genetic microevolution in the Åland Islands, Finland. In *Current Developments in Anthropological Genetics*. Vol. 2, *Ecology and Population Structure,* ed. M. H. Crawford and J. H. Mielke, pp. 333–66. New York: Plenum Press.

Karn, M. N., and L. S. Penrose. 1951. Birth weight and gestation time in relation to maternal age, parity, and infant survival. *Annals of Eugenics* 15:206–33.

Kay, R. F. 1981. The nut-crackers: A new theory of the adaptations of the Ramapithecinae. *American Journal of Physical Anthropology* 55:151–56.

Kelly, J. 1988. A new large species of *Sivapithecus* from the Siwaliks of Pakistan. *Journal of Human Evolution* 17:305–24.

Kennedy, R. E., Jr. 1973. *The Irish: Emigration, Marriage, and Fertility*. Berkeley: University of California Press.

Kent-Jones, J. D. W. 1988. Nutrition. In *The New Encyclopaedia Britannica. Vol. 25,* pp. 55–59. Chicago: Encyclopaedia Britannica.

Kerley, E. R., and W. M. Bass. 1967. Paleopathology: Meeting ground for many disciplines. *Science* 157:638–44.

Kimbel, W. H., T. D. White, and D. C. Johanson. 1988. Implications of KNM-WT 17000 for the evolution of "robust" *Australopithecus*. In *Evolutionary History of the "Robust" Australopithecines*, ed. F. E. Grine, pp. 259–68. New York: Aldine de Gruyter.

King, M. C., and A. C. Wilson. 1975. Evolution at two levels: Molecular similarities and biological differences between humans and chimpanzees. *Science* 188:107–16.

Kitcher, P. 1982. *Abusing Science: The Case Against Creationism*. Cambridge: MIT Press.

Klein, R. G. 1989. *The Human Career: Human Biological and Cultural Origins*. Chicago: University of Chicago Press.

Kobyliansky, E., S. Micle, M. Goldschmidt-Nathan, B. Arensberg, and H. Nathan. 1982. Jewish populations of the world: Genetic likeness and differences. *Annals of Human Biology* 9:1–34.

Kollar, E. J., and C. Fisher. 1980. Tooth induction in chick epithelium: Expression of quiescent genes for enamel synthesis. *Science* 207:993–95.

Koopman, P., J. Gubbay, N. Vivian, P. Goodfellow, and R. Lovell-Badge. 1991. Male development of chromosomally female mice transgenic for Sry. *Nature* 351:117–21.

Kramer, A. 1991. Modern human origins in Australasia: Replacement or evolution? *American Journal of Physical Anthropology* 86:455–73.

Labie, D., J. Pagnier, H. Wajcman, M. E. Fabry, and R. L. Nagel. 1986. The genetic origin of the variability of the phenotypic expression of the Hb S gene. In *Genetic Variation and its Maintenance,* ed. D. F. Roberts and G. F. DeStefano, pp. 149–156. Cambridge: Cambridge University Press.

Leakey, L. S. B., P. V. Tobias, and J. R. Napier. 1964. A new species of the genus *Homo* from Olduvai Gorge. *Nature* 202:7–10.

Leakey, R. E. F., and M. Leakey. 1986a. A new Miocene hominoid from Kenya. *Nature* 324:143–46.

Leakey, R. E. F., and M. Leakey. 1986b. A second new Miocene hominoid from Kenya. *Nature* 324: 146–48.

Leakey, R. E. F., and A. Walker. 1985. New higher primates from the early Miocene of Buluk, Kenya. *Nature* 318:173–75.

Leigh, S. R. 1992. Cranial capacity evolution in *Homo erectus* and early *Homo sapiens. American Journal of Physical Anthropology* 87:1–13.

Leonard, W. H., T. L. Leatherman, J. W. Carey, and R. B. Thomas. 1990. Contributions of nutrition versus hypoxia to growth in rural Andean populations. *American Journal of Human Biology* 2:613–26.

Lerner, I. M., and W. J. Libby. 1976. *Heredity, Evolution, and Society.* San Francisco: W. H. Freeman.

Leutenegger, W. 1982. Sexual dimorphism in nonhuman primates. In *Sexual Dimorphism in Homo sapiens: A Question of Size,* ed. R. L. Hall, pp. 11–36. New York: Praeger.

Levison, C. H., D. W. Hastings, and J. N. Harrison. 1981. Epidemiologic transition in a frontier town —Manti, Utah: 1849–1977. *American Journal of Physical Anthropology* 56:83–93.

Lewin, R. 1983. Is the orangutan a living fossil? *Science* 222:1222–23.

———. 1984. *Human Evolution: An Illustrated Introduction.* New York: W. H. Freeman.

———. 1987a. *Bones of Contention: Controversies in the Search for Human Origins.* New York: Simon & Schuster.

———. 1987b. The earliest "humans" were more like apes. *Science* 236:1061–63.

———. 1988. New views emerge on hunters and gatherers. *Science* 240:1146–48.

Lewis, D. E., Jr. 1990. Stress, migration, and blood pressure in Kiribati. *American Journal of Human Biology* 2:139–51.

Lewontin, R. C. 1972. The apportionment of human diversity. In *Evolutionary Biology.* Vol. 6, ed. T. Dobzhansky, pp. 381–98. New York: Plenum Press.

Li, T., and D. A. Etler. 1992. New Middle Pleistocene hominid crania from Yunxian in China. *Nature* 357:404–7.

Lieberman, D., D. R. Pilbeam, and B. A. Wood. 1988. A probabilistic approach to the problem of sexual dimorphism in *Homo habilis*: A comparison of KNM-ER 1470 and KNM-ER 1813. *Journal of Human Evolution* 17:503–11.

Lieberman, P., and E. S. Crelin. 1971. On the speech of Neanderthal. *Linguistic Inquiry* 2:203–22.

Lilienfeld, A. M., and D. E. Lilienfeld. 1980. *Foundations of Epidemiology.* 2d ed. New York: Oxford University Press.

Linden, E. 1981. *Apes, Men, and Language.* Rev. ed. Middlesex, England: Penguin Books.

Lindenbaum, S. 1979. *Kuru Sorcery: Disease and Danger in the New Guinea Highlands.* Mountain View, Calif.: Mayfield.

Little, B. B., R. M. Malina, P. H. Buschang, and L. R. Little. 1989. Natural selection is not related to reduced body size in a rural subsistence agricultural community in southern Mexico. *Human Biology* 61:287–96.

Little, M. A., and P. T. Baker. 1988. Migration and adaptation. In *Biological Aspects of Human Migration,* ed. C. G. N. Mascie-Taylor and G. W. Lasker, pp. 167–215. Cambridge: Cambridge University Press.

Livingstone, F. B. 1958. Anthropological implications of sickle cell gene distribution in West Africa. *American Anthropologist* 60:533–62.

———. 1964. On the nonexistence of human races. In *The Concept of Race,* ed. A. Montagu, pp. 46–60. New York: Collier.

———. 1984. The Duffy blood groups, vivax malaria, and malaria selection in human populations: A review. *Human Biology* 56:413–25.

———. 1989. Who gave whom hemoglobin S: The use of restriction site haplotype variation for the interpretation of the evolution of the β^s-Globin gene. *American Journal of Human Biology* 1: 289–302.

Loehlin, J. C., G. Lindzey, and J. N. Spuhler. 1975. *Race Differences in Intelligence.* San Francisco: W. H. Freeman.

Loomis, W. F. 1967. Skin-pigment regulation of vitamin-D biosynthesis in man. *Science* 157: 501–6.

Lovejoy, C. O. 1981. The origin of man. *Science* 211:341–50.

———. 1982. Models of human evolution. *Science* 217:304–6.

McElroy, A., and P. K. Townsend. 1989. *Medical Anthropology in Ecological Perspective.* 2d ed. Boulder, Colo.: Westview Press.

McEvedy, C. 1988. The bubonic plague. *Scientific American* 258(2):118–23.

McGrath, J. W. 1990. AIDS in Africa: A bioanthropological perspective. *American Journal of Human Biology* 2:381–96.

McGrew, W. C. 1992. *Chimpanzee Material Culture.* Cambridge: Cambridge University Press.

McHenry, H. M. 1992. How big were the early hominids? *Evolutionary Anthropology* 1:15–20.

Madrigal, L. 1989. Hemoglobin genotype, fertility, and the malaria hypothesis. *Human Biology* 61: 311–25.

Malhotra, A., and R. S. Thorpe. 1991. Experimental detection of rapid evolutionary response in natural lizard populations. *Nature* 353:347–48.

Malina, R. M. 1975. *Growth and Development: The First Twenty Years in Man.* Minneapolis, Minn.: Burgess.

———. 1979. Secular changes in size and maturity: Causes and effects. *Monograph for the Society of Research in Child Development* 44:59–102.

Malkin, D., F. P. Li, L. C. Strong, J. F. Fraumeni, C. E. Nelson, D. H. Kim, J. Kassel, M. A. Gryka, F. Z. Bischoff, M. A. Tainsky, and S. H. Friend. 1990. Germ line p53 mutations in a familial syndrome of breast cancer, sarcomas, and other neoplasms. *Science* 250:1233–38.

Markham, R., and C. P. Groves. 1990. Brief communication: Weights of wild orangutans. *American Journal of Physical Anthropology* 81:1–3.

Martin, L. 1985. Significance of enamel thickness in hominoid evolution. *Nature* 314:260–63.

Martin, R. D. 1981. Relative brain size and basal metabolic rate in terrestrial vertebrates. *Nature* 293: 57–60.

Martorell, R. 1980. Interrelationships between diet, infectious disease, and nutritional status. In *Social and Biological Predictors of Nutritional Status, Physical Growth, and Neurological Development,* ed. L. S. Greene and F. E. Johnston, pp. 81–106. New York: Academic Press.

Marx, J. 1992. Homeobox genes go evolutionary. *Science* 255:399–401.

Mascia-Lees, F. E., J. H. Relethford, and T. Sorger. 1986. Evolutionary perspectives on permanent breast enlargement in human females. *American Anthropologist* 88:423–28.

Mayr, E. 1982. *The Growth of Biological Thought.* Cambridge: Harvard University Press.

Meindl, R. S., and A. C. Swedlund. 1977. Secular trends in mortality in the Connecticut River Valley, 1700–1850. *Human Biology* 49:389–414.

Mielke, J. H., E. J. Devor, P. L. Kramer, P. L. Workman, and A. W. Eriksson. 1982. Historical population structure of the Åland Islands, Finland. In *Current Developments in Anthropological Genetics.* Vol. 2, *Ecology and Population Structure,* ed. M. H. Crawford and J. H. Mielke, pp. 255–332. New York: Plenum Press.

Mielke, J. H., L. B. Jorde, P. G. Trapp, D. L. Anderton, K. Pitkänen, and A. W. Eriksson. 1984. Historical epidemiology of smallpox in Åland, Finland: 1751–1890. *Demography* 21:271–95.

Miller, J. A. 1991. Does brain size variability provide evidence of multiple species in *Homo habilis*? *American Journal of Physical Anthropology* 84:385–98.

Mock, D. W., H. Drummond, and C. H. Stinson. 1990. Avian siblicide. *American Scientist* 78: 438–49.

Molnar, S. 1983. *Human Variation: Races, Types and Ethnic Groups.* 2d ed. Englewood Cliffs, N.J.: Prentice-Hall.

———. 1992. *Human Variation: Races, Types, and Ethnic Groups.* 3d ed. Englewood Cliffs, N.J.: Prentice-Hall.

Montagu, A. 1977. *Life Before Birth.* New York: Signet.

Montagu, A., ed. 1984. *Science and Creationism.* Oxford: Oxford University Press.

Moore, L. G., P. W. Van Arsdale, J. E. Glittenberg, and R. A. Aldrich. 1980. *The Biocultural Basis of Health: Expanding Views of Medical Anthropology.* Prospect Heights, Ill.: Waveland Press.

Moran, E. F. 1982. *Human Adaptability: An Introduc-*

tion to Ecological Anthropology. Boulder, Colo.: Westview Press.

Mueller, W. H. 1979. Fertility and physique in a malnourished population. *Human Biology* 51: 153–66.

Murrell, J., M. Farlow, B. Ghetti, and M. D. Benson. 1991. A mutation in the amyloid precursor protein associated with hereditary Alzheimer's disease. *Science* 254:97–99.

Nei, M. 1978. The theory of genetic distance and evolution of human races. *Japanese Journal of Human Genetics* 23:341–69.

Nicol, S. E., and I. I. Gottesman. 1983. Clues to the genetics and neurobiology of schizophrenia. *American Scientist* 71:398–404.

Oiso, T. 1975. A historical review of nutritional improvement in Japan after World War II. In *Physiological Adaptability and Nutritional Status of the Japanese. B. Growth, Work Capacity and Nutrition of Japanese,* ed. K. Agahina and R. Shigiya, pp. 171–91. Tokyo: University of Tokyo Press.

Olshansky, S. J., B. A. Carnes, and C. Cassel. 1990. In search of Methuselah: Estimating the upper limit to human longevity. *Science* 250:634–40.

Olson, T. R. 1985. Cranial morphology and systematics of the Hadar formation hominids and "*Australopithecus*" *africanus.* In *Ancestors: The Hard Evidence,* ed. E. Delson, pp. 102–19. New York: Alan R. Liss.

Omran, A. R. 1977. Epidemiologic transition in the United States: The health factor in population change. *Population Bulletin* 32:3–42.

Packer, C. 1977. Recriprocal altruism in olive baboons. *Nature* 265:441–43.

Paigen, B., L. R. Goldman, M. M. Magnant, J. H. Highland, and A. T. Steegman, Jr. 1987. Growth of children living near the hazardous waste site, Love Canal. *Human Biology* 59:489–508.

Pasachoff, J. M. 1979. *Astronomy: From the Earth to the Universe.* Philadelphia: W. B. Saunders.

Passingham, R. 1982. *The Human Primate.* San Francisco: W. H. Freeman.

Pennington, R., and H. Harpending. 1991. Infertility in Herero pastoralists of southern Africa. *American Journal of Human Biology* 3:135–53.

Pfeiffer, J. E. 1985. *The Emergence of Humankind.* 4th ed. New York: Harper & Row.

Pianka, E. R. 1983. *Evolutionary Ecology.* 3d ed. New York: Harper & Row.

Pilbeam, D. 1982. New hominoid skull material from the Miocene of Pakistan. *Nature* 295:232–34.

———. 1984. The descent of hominoids and hominids. *Scientific American* 250(3):84–96.

Pilbeam, D., G. E. Meyer, C. Badgley, M. D. Rose, M. H. L. Pickford, A. K. Behrensmeyer, and S. M. Ibrahim Shah. 1977. New hominoid primates from the Siwaliks of Pakistan and their bearing on hominoid evolution. *Nature* 270:689–95.

Pollitt, E., and R. Leibel. 1980. Biological and social correlates of failure to thrive. In *Social and Biological Predictors of Nutritional Status, Physical Growth, and Neurological Development,* ed. L. S. Greene and F. E. Johnston, pp. 173–200. New York: Academic Press.

Post, P. W., F. Daniels, Jr., and R. T. Binford, Jr. 1975. Cold injury and the evolution of "white" skin. *Human Biology* 47:65–80.

Potts, M. 1988. Birth control. In *The New Encyclopaedia Britannica.* Vol. 15, pp. 113–20. Encyclopaedia Britannica: Chicago.

Potts, R. 1984. Home bases and early hominids. *American Scientist* 72:338–47.

Price, R. A., R. Ness, and P. Laskarewski. 1990. Common major gene inheritance of extreme overweight. *Human Biology* 62:747–65.

Rak, Y. 1983. *The Australopithecine Face.* New York: Academic Press.

———. 1986. The Neanderthal: A new look at an old face. *Journal of Human Evolution* 15:151–64.

Rak, Y., and B. Arensburg. 1987. Kebara 2 Neanderthal pelvis: First look at a complete inlet. *American Journal of Physical Anthropology* 73:227–31.

Raup, D. M., and J. J. Sepkoski. 1986. Periodic extinction of families and genera. *Science* 231:833–36.

Reader, J. 1986. *The Rise of Life: The First 3.5 Billion Years.* New York: Knopf.

Reid, R. M. 1973. Inbreeding in human populations. In *Methods and Theories of Anthropological Genetics,* ed. M. H. Crawford and P. L. Workman, pp. 83–116. Albuquerque: University of New Mexico Press.

Relethford, J. H. 1985. Isolation by distance, linguistic similarity, and the genetic structure on Bougainville Island. *American Journal of Physical Anthropology* 66:317–26.

———. 1988a. Effects of English admixture and geographic distance on anthropometric variation and genetic structure in 19th-century Ireland. *American Journal of Physical Anthropology* 76:111–24.

———. 1988b. Estimation of kinship and genetic distance from surnames. *Human Biology* 60:475–92.

———. 1991a. Genetic drift and anthropometric variation in Ireland. *Human Biology* 63:155–65.

———. 1991b. Sex differentials in unintentional injury mortality in relation to age at death. *American Journal of Human Biology* 3:369–75.

———. 1992. Cross-cultural analysis of migration rates: Effects of geographic distance and population size. *American Journal of Physical Anthropology* 89:459–66.

Relethford, J. H., and J. Blangero. 1990. Detection of differential gene flow from patterns of quantitative variation. *Human Biology* 62:5–25.

Relethford, J. H., and M. C. Mahoney. 1991. Relationship between population density and rates of injury mortality in New York State (exclusive of New York City), 1978–1982. *American Journal of Human Biology* 3:111–18.

Relethford, J. H., M. P. Stern, S. P. Gaskill, and H. P. Hazuda. 1983. Social class, admixture, and skin color variation in Mexican-Americans and Anglo-Americans living in San Antonio, Texas. *American Journal of Physical Anthropology* 61:97–102.

Rice, D. P., E. J. MacKenzie, and associates. 1989. *Cost of Injury in the United States: A Report to Congress 1989.* San Francisco: Institute for Health and Aging, University of California and Baltimore: Injury Prevention Center, The Johns Hopkins University.

Richard, A. F. 1985. *Primates in Nature.* New York: W. H. Freeman.

Rightmire, G. P. 1985. The tempo of change in the evolution of Mid-Pleistocene *Homo.* In *Ancestors: The Hard Evidence,* ed. E. Delson, pp. 255–64. New York: Alan R. Liss.

———. 1990. *The Evolution of Homo erectus.* Cambridge: Cambridge University Press.

Roberts, D. F. 1968. Genetic effects of population size reduction. *Nature* 220:1084–88.

———. 1978. *Climate and Human Variability.* 2d ed. Menlo Park, Calif.: Benjamin Cummings.

Roberts, R. G., R. Jones, and M. A. Smith. 1990. Thermoluminescence dating of a 50,000-year-old human occupation site in northern Australia. *Nature* 345:153–56.

Robins, A. H. 1991. *Biological Perspectives on Human Pigmentation.* Cambridge: Cambridge University Press.

Roche, A. 1979. Secular trends in stature, weight, and maturation. *Monograph for the Society of Research in Child Development* 44:3–27.

Rodman, P. S., and H. M. McHenry. 1980. Bioenergetics and the origin of human bipedalism. *American Journal of Physical Anthropology* 52:103–6.

Rogers, R. A., L. A. Rogers, and L. D. Martin. 1992. How the door opened: The peopling of the New World. *Human Biology* 64:281–302.

Rose, M. D. 1986. Further hominoid postcranial specimens from the Late Miocene Nagri formations of Pakistan. *Journal of Human Evolution* 15:333–67.

Rowell, T. E. 1966. Forest-living baboons in Uganda. *Journal of Zoology, London* 149:344–64.

Roychoudhury, A. K., and M. Nei. 1988. *Human Polymorphic Genes: World Distribution.* Oxford: Oxford University Press.

Ruse, M. 1987. Biological species: Natural kinds, individuals, or what? *British Journal for the Philosophy of Science* 38:225–42.

Sagan, C. 1977. *The Dragons of Eden: Speculations of the Evolution of Human Intelligence.* New York: Ballantine Books.

Sarich, V. M., and A. C. Wilson. 1967. Immunological time scale for hominoid evolution. *Science* 158:1200–1203.

Scarr, S., and A. Weinberg. 1978. Attitudes, interests, and IQ. *Human Nature* 1(4):29–36.

Schell, L. M. 1981. Environmental noise and prenatal growth. *American Journal of Physical Anthropology* 56:63–70.

———. 1991. Effects of pollutants on human prenatal and postnatal growth: Noise, lead, polychlorobiphenyl compounds, and toxic wastes. *Yearbook of Physical Anthropology* 34:157–88.

Schell, L. M., and Y. Ando. 1991. Postnatal growth of children in relation to noise from Osaka International Airport. *Journal of Sound and Vibration* 151:371–82.

Schopf, J. W., ed. 1992. *Major Events in the History of Life.* Boston: Jones and Bartlett.

Schopf, J. W., and B. M. Packer. 1987. Early Archean (3.3-billion to 3.5-billion-year-old) microfossils from Warrawoona Group, Australia. *Science* 237:70–73.

Schwartz, J. H. 1987. *The Red Ape: Orang-utans and Human Origins.* Boston: Houghton Mifflin.

Shea, B. T., and A. M. Gomez. 1988. Tooth scaling and evolutionary dwarfism: An investigation of allometry in human pygmies. *American Journal of Physical Anthropology* 77:117–32.

Sheehan, P. M., D. E. Fastovsky, R. G. Hoffman, C. B.

Berghaus, and D. L. Gabriel. 1991. Sudden extinction of the dinosaurs: Latest Cretaceous, Upper Great Plains, U.S.A. *Science* 254:835–39.

Skolnick, M. H., L. A. Cannon-Albright, D. E. Goldgar, J. H. Ward, C. J. Marshall, G. B. Schumann, H. Hogle, W. P. McWhorter, E. C. Wright, T. D. Tran, T. Bishop, J. P. Kushner, and H. J. Eyre. 1990. Inheritance of proliferative breast disease in breast cancer kindreds. *Science* 250:1715–20.

Smith, F. H., A. B. Falsetti, and S. M. Donnelly. 1989a. Modern human origins. *Yearbook of Physical Anthropology* 32:35–68.

Smith, F. H., J. F. Simek, and M. S. Harrill. 1989b. Geographic variation in supraorbital torus reduction during the later Pleistocene (c. 80,000–15,000 B.P.). In *The Human Revolution,* ed. P. Mellars and C. Stringer, pp. 172–93. Princeton: Princeton University Press.

Smouse, P. E. 1982. Genetic architecture of swidden agricultural tribes from the lowland rain forests of South America. In *Current Developments in Anthropological Genetics.* Vol. 2, *Ecology and Population Structure,* ed. M. H. Crawford and J. H. Mielke, pp. 139–78. New York: Plenum Press.

Smouse, P. E., and W. Li. 1987. Likelihood analysis of mitochondrial restriction-cleavage patterns for the human-chimpanzee-gorilla trichotomy. *Evolution* 41:1162–76.

Snowden, C. T. 1990. Language capacities of non-human animals. *Yearbook of Physical Anthropology* 33:215–43.

Spiess, E. B. 1977. *Genes in Populations.* New York: John Wiley.

Stanley, S. M. 1979. *Macroevolution: Pattern and Process.* San Francisco: W. H. Freeman.

Stanley, S. M. 1981. *The New Evolutionary Timetable: Fossils, Genes, and the Origin of Species.* New York: Basic Books.

Stebbins, G. L. 1982. *Darwin to DNA, Molecules to Humanity.* San Francisco: W. H. Freeman.

Stephens, J. C., M. L. Cavanaugh, M. I. Gradie, M. L. Mador, and K. K. Kidd. 1990. Mapping the human genome: Current status. *Science* 250:237–44.

Stern, J. T., Jr., and R. L. Susman. 1983. The locomotor anatomy of *Australopithecus afarensis. American Journal of Physical Anthropology* 60:279–317.

Stevenson, J. C., P. M. Everson, and M. H. Crawford. 1989. Changes in completed family size and reproductive span in Anabaptist populations. *Human Biology* 61:99–115.

Stoneking, M., and R. L. Cann. 1989. African origin of human mitochondrial DNA. In *The Human Revolution,* ed. P. Mellars and C. Stringer, pp. 17–30. Princeton: Princeton University Press.

Stoner, B. P., and E. Trinkaus. 1981. Getting a grip on the Neandertals: Were they all thumbs? *American Journal of Physical Anthropology* 54:281–82.

Stringer, C. B. 1986. The credibility of *Homo habilis.* In *Major Topics in Primate and Human Evolution,* ed. B. Wood, L. Martin and P. Andrews, pp. 266–94. Cambridge: Cambridge University Press.

Stringer, C. B., and P. Andrews. 1988. Genetic and fossil evidence for the origin of modern humans. *Science* 239:1263–68.

Susman, R. L. 1988. Hand of *Paranthropus robustus* from Member I, Swartkrans: Fossil evidence for tool behavior. *Science* 240:781–84.

Sutton, H. E., and R. P. Wagner. 1985. *Genetics: A Human Concern.* New York: Macmillan.

Swedlund, A. C., and G. J. Armelagos. 1976. *Demographic Anthropology.* Dubuque, Iowa: Wm. C. Brown.

Szabo, G. 1967. The regional anatomy of the human integument with special reference to the distribution of hair follicles, sweat glands and melanocytes. *Philosophical Transactions of the Royal Society of London* 252B:447–85.

Tague, R. G. 1992. Sexual dimorphism in the human bony pelvis, with a consideration of the Neandertal pelvis from Kebara Cave, Israel. *American Journal of Physical Anthropology* 88:1–21.

Takahashi, E. 1984. Secular trend in milk consumption and growth in Japan. *Human Biology* 56:427–37.

Tanner, J. M. 1989. *Foetus into Man: Physical Growth from Conception to Maturity.* 2d ed., rev. and enl. Cambridge: Harvard University Press.

Teitelbaum, M. S. 1988. Population. In *The New Encyclopaedia Britannica.* Vol. 25, pp. 1038–47. Encyclopaedia Britannica: Chicago.

Templeton, A. R. 1992. Human origins and analysis of mitochondrial DNA sequences. *Science* 255:737.

Terrace, H. S. 1979. *Nim: A Chimpanzee Who Learned Sign Language.* New York: Knopf.

Thomas, D. H. 1986. *Refiguring Anthropology: First Principles of Probability and Statistics.* Prospect Heights, Ill.: Waveland Press.

Thorne, A. G., and M. H. Wolpoff. 1992. The multiregional evolution of humans. *Scientific American* 266(4):76–83.

Tobias, P. V. 1971. *The Brain in Hominid Evolution.* New York: Columbia University Press.

Trinkaus, E. 1981. Neanderthal limb proportions and cold adaptation. In *Aspects of Human Evolution,* ed. C. B. Stringer, pp. 187–224. London: Taylor and Francis.

———. 1990. Cladistics and the hominid fossil record. *American Journal of Physical Anthropology* 83:1–11.

Trinkaus, E., and M. LeMay. 1982. Occipital bunning among later Pleistocene hominids. *American Journal of Physical Anthropology* 57:27–35.

Trinkaus, E., and P. Shipman. 1992. *The Neandertals: Changing the Image of Mankind.* New York: Knopf.

Ubelaker, D., and H. Scammell. 1992. *Bones: A Forensic Detective's Casebook.* New York: HarperCollins.

Underwood, J. H. 1975. *Bicultural Interactions and Human Variation.* Dubuque, Iowa: Wm. C. Brown.

———. 1979. *Human Variation and Human Microevolution.* Englewood Cliffs, N.J.: Prentice-Hall.

United States Department of Commerce. 1991. *1990 Census Profile, March 1991.* Washington: U.S. Department of Commerce, Economics and Statistics Administration, Bureau of the Census.

Valladas, H., H. Cachier, P. Maurice, F. B. de Quiros, J. Clottes, V. C. Valdes, P. Uzquiano, and M. Arnold. 1992. Direct radiocarbon dates for prehistoric paintings at the Altamira, El Castillo and Niaux caves. *Nature* 357:68–70.

Vianna, N. J., and A. K. Polan. 1984. Incidence of low birth weight among Love Canal residents. *Science* 226:1217–19.

Vigilant, L., M. Stoneking, H. Harpending, K. Hawkes, and A. C. Wilson. 1991. African populations and the evolution of human mitochondrial DNA. *Science* 253:1503–7.

Villa, P. 1982. Conjoinable pieces and site formation processes. *American Antiquity* 47:276–90.

Vrba, E. S. 1985. Ecological and adaptive changes associated with early hominid evolution. In *Ancestors: The Hard Evidence,* ed. E. Delson, pp. 63–71. New York: Alan R. Liss.

Wade, M. J., and C. J. Goodnight. 1991. Wright's shifting balance theory: An experimental study. *Science* 253:1015–18.

Walker, A., R. E. Leakey, J. M. Harris, and F. H. Brown. 1986. 2.5 Myr *Australopithecus boisei*

from west of Lake Turkana, Kenya. *Nature* 322:517–22.

Walker, A., and M. Teaford. 1989. The hunt for *Proconsul. Scientific American* 260(1):76–82.

Walsh, J. 1988. Rift Valley Fever rears its head. *Science* 240:1397–99.

Ward, C. V., A. Walker, and M. F. Teaford. 1991. *Proconsul* did not have a tail. *Journal of Human Evolution* 21:215–20.

Washburn, S. L. 1960. Tools and human evolution. *Scientific American* 203:62–75.

Watts, E. S. 1986. Evolution of the human growth curve. In *Human Growth: A Comprehensive Treatise.* Vol. 1, *Developmental Biology, Prenatal Growth,* ed. F. Falkner and J. M. Tanner, pp. 153–66. New York: Plenum Press.

Weeks, J. R. 1981. *Population: An Introduction to Concepts and Issues.* 2d ed. Belmont, Calif.: Wadsworth.

Weiss, K. M. 1973. *Demographic Models for Anthropology.* Memoirs of the Society for American Archaeology, no. 27. Washington, D.C.: Society for American Archaeology.

———. 1984. On the number of members of the genus *Homo* who have ever lived, and some evolutionary implications. *Human Biology* 56:637–49.

———. 1988. In search of times past: Gene flow and invasion in the generation of human diversity. In *Biological Aspects of Human Migration,* ed. C. G. N. Mascie-Taylor and G. W. Lasker, pp. 130–66. Cambridge: Cambridge University Press.

Weiss, K. M., R. E. Ferrell, and C. L. Hanis. 1984. A New World syndrome of metabolic diseases with a genetic and evolutionary basis. *Yearbook of Physical Anthropology* 27:153–78.

Weitz, C. A. 1990. Effects of acculturation and age on the exercise capacities of Solomon Islanders. *American Journal of Physical Anthropology* 81:513–25.

Wheeler, P. E. 1991a. The influence of bipedalism on the energy and water budgets of early hominids. *Journal of Human Evolution* 21:117–36.

———. 1991b. The thermoregulatory advantage of hominid bipedalism in open equatorial environments: The contribution of increased convective heat loss and cutaneous evaporative cooling. *Journal of Human Evolution* 21:107–15.

White, R., and J. M. Lalouel. 1988. Chromosome mapping with DNA markers. *Scientific American* 258:40–48.

Wijsman, E. M., and L. L. Cavalli-Sforza. 1984. Migration and genetic population structure with special reference to humans. *Annual Review of Ecology and Systematics* 15:279–301.

Wiley, E. O. 1978. The evolutionary species concept reconsidered. *Systematic Zoology* 27:17–26.

Wilford, J. N. 1985. *The Riddle of the Dinosaur*. New York: Knopf.

Wilkinson, R. G. 1975. Trephination by drilling in ancient Mexico. *Bulletin of the New York Academy of Medicine* 51(7):838–50.

Willerman, L., R. Schultz, J. N. Rutledge, and E. D. Bigler. 1991. *In vivo* brain size and intelligence. *Intelligence* 15:223–28.

Williams, R. C. 1985. HLA II: The emergence of the molecular model for the human major histocompatibility complex. *Yearbook of Physical Anthropology* 28:79–95.

———. 1989. Restriction fragment length polymorphism (RFLP). *Yearbook of Physical Anthropology* 32:159–84.

Williams-Blangero, S., and J. Blangero. 1989. Anthropometric variation and the genetic structure of the Jirels of Nepal. *Human Biology* 61:1–12.

———. 1992. Quantitative genetic analysis of skin reflectance: A multivariate approach. *Human Biology* 64:35–49.

Wilson, A. C., and R. L. Cann. 1992. The recent African genesis of humans. *Scientific American* 266(4): 68–73.

Wilson, E. O. 1980. *Sociobiology: The Abridged Edition*. Cambridge: Harvard University Press.

Wolpoff, M. H. 1980. *Paleoanthropology*. New York: Knopf.

———. 1985. Human evolution at the peripheries: The pattern at the eastern edge. In *Hominid Evolution: Past, Present and Future*, ed. P. V. Tobias, pp. 355–65. New York: Alan R. Liss.

———. 1989. Multiregional evolution: The fossil alternative to Eden. In *The Human Revolution*, ed. P. Mellars and C. Stringer, pp. 62–108. Princeton: Princeton University Press.

———. 1992. One hundred years of *Pithecanthropus* is enough. *American Journal of Physical Anthropology*, supplement 14:175–76 (abstract).

Wolpoff, M. H., J. N. Spuhler, F. H. Smith, J. Radovcic, G. Pope, D. W. Frayer, R. Eckhardt, and G. Clark. 1988. Modern human origins. *Science* 241:772–73.

Wolpoff, M. H., W. X. Zhi, and A. G. Thorne. 1984. Modern *Homo sapiens* origins: A general theory of hominid evolution involving the fossil evidence from East Asia. In *The Origins of Modern Humans: A World Survey of the Fossil Evidence*, ed. F. H. Smith and F. Spencer, pp. 411–83. New York: Alan R. Liss.

Wood, B. 1992. Origin and evolution of the genus *Homo*. *Nature* 355:783–90.

Wood, C. S. 1979. *Human Sickness and Health: A Biocultural View*. Mountain View, Calif.: Mayfield.

Woodham-Smith, C. 1962. *The Great Hunger: Ireland 1845–1849*. New York: Harper & Row.

Woodward, V. 1992. *Human Heredity and Society*. St. Paul, Minn.: West.

Workman, P. L., B. S. Blumberg, and A. J. Cooper. 1963. Selection, gene migration and polymorphic stability in a U.S. White and Negro population. *American Journal of Human Genetics* 15:71–84.

Workman, P. L., H. Harpending, J. M. Lalouel, C. Lynch, J. D. Niswander, and R. Singleton. 1973. Population studies on southwestern Indian tribes. VI. Papago population structure: A comparison of genetic and migration analyses. In *Genetic Structure of Populations*, ed. N. E. Morton, pp. 166–94. Honolulu: University Press of Hawaii.

Wright, S. 1932. The roles of mutation, inbreeding, crossbreeding and selection in evolution. *Proceedings of the Sixth International Congress of Genetics* 1:356–66.

———. 1982. The shifting balance theory and macroevolution. *Annual Review of Genetics* 16:1–19.

Zanardi, P., G. Dell'Acqua, C. Menini, and I. Barrai. 1977. Population genetics in the province of Ferrara. I. Genetic distances and geographic distances. *American Journal of Human Genetics* 29:169–77.

Zerba, K. E., J. S. Friedlaender, and C. F. Sing. 1990. Heterogeneity of the blood pressure distribution among Solomon Island societies with increasing acculturation. *American Journal of Physical Anthropology* 81:493–511.

Index